Title 37 - Code of Federal Regulations
Patents, Trademarks, and Copyrights

CHAPTER I — UNITED STATES PATENT AND TRADEMARK OFFICE, DEPARTMENT OF COMMERCE

SUBCHAPTER A - GENERAL

PATENTS

Part

1   Rules of practice in patent cases

3   Assignment, recording and rights of assignee

4   Complaints regarding invention promoters

5   Secrecy of certain inventions and licenses to export and file applications in foreign countries

Index I - Rules pertaining to patents

PRACTICE BEFORE THE PATENT AND TRADEMARK OFFICE

10   Representation of others before the Patent and Trademark Office

11   Representation of others before the United States Patent and Trademark Office

Index II - Rules relating to practice before the United States Patent and Trademark Office

15 [Reserved]

15a [Reserved]

41   Practice before the Board of Patent Appeals and Interferences

SUBCHAPTER B — ADMINISTRATION

100 [Reserved]

101 [Reserved]

102 Disclosure of government information

104 Legal processes

SUBCHAPTER C—PROTECTION OF FOREIGN MASK WORKS

150 Requests for Presidential proclamations pursuant to 17 U.S.C. 902(a)(2)

SUBCHAPTER A - GENERAL

PART 1 - RULES OF PRACTICE IN PATENT CASES

Subpart A - General Provisions

GENERAL INFORMATION AND CORRESPONDENCE

Sec.

1.1   Addresses for non-trademark correspondence with the United States Patent and Trademark Office.

1.2   Business to be transacted in writing.

1.3   Business to be conducted with decorum and courtesy.

1.4   Nature of correspondence and signature requirements.

1.5   Identification of patent, patent application, or patent-related proceeding.

1.6   Receipt of correspondence.

1.7   Times for taking action; Expiration on Saturday, Sunday, or Federal holiday.

1.8   Certificate of mailing or transmission.

1.9   Definitions.

1.10   Filing of papers and fees by "Express Mail."

RECORDS AND FILES OF THE PATENT AND TRADEMARK OFFICE

1.11   Files open to the public.

1.12   Assignment records open to public inspection.

1.13   Copies and certified copies.

1.14   Patent applications preserved in confidence.

1.15   [Reserved]

Rev. 8, July 2010

FEES AND PAYMENT OF MONEY

1.16 National application filing, search, and examination fees.

1.17 Patent application and reexamination processing fees.

1.18 Patent post allowance (including issue) fees.

1.19 Document supply fees.

1.20 Post issuance fees.

1.21 Miscellaneous fees and charges.

1.22 Fees payable in advance.

1.23 Method of payment.

1.24 [Reserved]

1.25 Deposit accounts.

1.26 Refunds.

1.27 Definition of small entities and establishing status as a small entity to permit payment of small entity fees; when a determination of entitlement to small entity status and notification of loss of entitlement to small entity status are required; fraud on the Office.

1.28 Refunds when small entity status is later established; how errors in small entity status are excused.

Subpart B - National Processing Provision

PROSECUTION OF APPLICATION AND APPOINTMENT OF ATTORNEY OR AGENT

1.31 Applicant may be represented by one or more patent practitioners or joint inventors.

1.32 Power of attorney.

1.33 Correspondence respecting patent applications, reexamination proceedings, and other proceedings.

1.34 Acting in a representative capacity.

1.36 Revocation of power of attorney; withdrawal of patent attorney or agent.

WHO MAY APPLY FOR A PATENT

1.41 Applicant for patent.

1.42 When the inventor is dead.

1.43 When the inventor is insane or legally incapacitated.

1.44 [Reserved]

1.45 Joint inventors.

1.46 Assigned inventions and patents.

1.47 Filing when an inventor refuses to sign or cannot be reached.

1.48 Correction of inventorship in a patent application, other than a reissue application, pursuant to 35 U.S.C. 116.

THE APPLICATION

1.51 General requisites of an application.

1.52 Language, paper, writing, margins, compact disc specifications.

1.53 Application number, filing date, and completion of application.

1.54 Parts of application to be filed together; filing receipt.

1.55 Claim for foreign priority.

1.56 Duty to disclose information material to patentability.

1.57 Incorporation by reference.

1.58 Chemical and mathematical formulae and tables.

1.59 Expungement of information or copy of papers in application file.

1.60 [Reserved]

1.61 [Reserved]

1.62 [Reserved]

OATH OR DECLARATION

1.63 Oath or declaration.

1.64 Person making oath or declaration.

1.66 Officers authorized to administer oaths.

1.67 Supplemental oath or declaration.

1.68 Declaration in lieu of oath.

1.69 Foreign language oaths and declarations.

1.70 [Reserved]

SPECIFICATION

1.71 Detailed description and specification of the invention.

1.72 Title and abstract.

1.73 Summary of the invention.

1.74 Reference to drawings.

1.75 Claim(s).

1.76 Application data sheet.

1.77 Arrangement of application elements.
1.78 Claiming benefit of earlier filing date and cross-references to other applications.
1.79 Reservation clauses not permitted.

THE DRAWINGS

1.81 Drawings required in patent application.
1.83 Content of drawing.
1.84 Standards for drawings.
1.85 Corrections to drawings.
1.88 [Reserved]

MODELS, EXHIBITS, SPECIMENS

1.91 Models or exhibits not generally admitted as part of application or patent.
1.92 [Reserved]
1.93 Specimens.
1.94 Return of models, exhibits or specimens.
1.95 Copies of exhibits.
1.96 Submission of computer program listings.

INFORMATION DISCLOSURE STATEMENT

1.97 Filing of information disclosure statement.
1.98 Content of information disclosure statement.
1.99 Third-party submission in published application.

EXAMINATION OF APPLICATIONS

1.101 [Reserved]
1.102 Advancement of examination.
1.103 Suspension of action by the Office.
1.104 Nature of examination.
1.105 Requirements for information.
1.106 [Reserved]
1.107 [Reserved]
1.108 [Reserved]
1.109 [Reserved]
1.110 Inventorship and date of invention of the subject matter of individual claims.

ACTION BY APPLICANT AND FURTHER CONSIDERATION

1.111 Reply by applicant or patent owner to a non-final Office action.
1.112 Reconsideration before final action.
1.113 Final rejection or action.
1.114 Request for continued examination.

AMENDMENTS

1.115 Preliminary amendments.
1.116 Amendments and affidavits or other evidence after final action and prior to appeal.
1.117 [Reserved]
1.118 [Reserved]
1.119 [Reserved]
1.121 Manner of making amendments in applications.
1.122 [Reserved]
1.123 [Reserved]
1.124 [Reserved]
1.125 Substitute specification.
1.126 Numbering of claims.
1.127 Petition from refusal to admit amendment.

TRANSITIONAL PROVISIONS

1.129 Transitional procedures for limited examination after final rejection and restriction practice.

AFFIDAVITS OVERCOMING REJECTIONS

1.130 Affidavit or declaration to disqualify commonly owned patent or published application as prior art.
1.131 Affidavit or declaration of prior invention.
1.132 Affidavits or declarations traversing rejections or objections.

INTERVIEWS

1.133 Interviews.

Rev. 8, July 2010

TIME FOR REPLY BY APPLICANT; ABANDONMENT OF APPLICATION

1.134 Time period for reply to an Office action.
1.135 Abandonment for failure to reply within time period.
1.136 Extensions of time.
1.137 Revival of abandoned application, terminated reexamination proceeding, or lapsed patent.
1.138 Express abandonment.
1.139 [Reserved]

JOINDER OF INVENTIONS IN ONE APPLICATION; RESTRICTION

1.141 Different inventions in one national application.
1.142 Requirement for restriction.
1.143 Reconsideration of requirement.
1.144 Petition from requirement for restriction.
1.145 Subsequent presentation of claims for different invention.
1.146 Election of species.

DESIGN PATENTS

1.151 Rules applicable.
1.152 Design drawings.
1.153 Title, description and claim, oath or declaration.
1.154 Arrangement of application elements in a design application.
1.155 Expedited examination of design applications.

PLANT PATENTS

1.161 Rules applicable.
1.162 Applicant, oath or declaration.
1.163 Specification and arrangement of application elements in a plant application.
1.164 Claim.
1.165 Plant Drawings.
1.166 Specimens.
1.167 Examination.

REISSUES

1.171 Application for reissue.
1.172 Applicants, assignees.
1.173 Reissue specification, drawings, and amendments.
1.174 [Reserved]
1.175 Reissue oath or declaration.
1.176 Examination of reissue.
1.177 Issuance of multiple reissue patents.
1.178 Original patent; continuing duty of applicant.
1.179 [Reserved]

PETITIONS AND ACTION BY THE DIRECTOR

1.181 Petition to the Director.
1.182 Questions not specifically provided for.
1.183 Suspension of rules.
1.184 [Reserved]

APPEAL TO THE BOARD OF PATENT APPEALS AND INTERFERENCES

1.191 Appeal to Board of Patent Appeals and Interferences.
1.192 [Reserved]
1.193 [Reserved]
1.194 [Reserved]
1.195 [Reserved]
1.196 [Reserved]
1.197 Return of jurisdiction from the Board of Patent Appeals and Interferences; termination of proceedings.
1.198 Reopening after a final decision of the Board of Patent Appeals and Interferences.

PUBLICATION OF APPLICATIONS

1.211 Publication of applications.
1.213 Nonpublication request.
1.215 Patent application publication.
1.217 Publication of a redacted copy of an application.
1.219 Early publication.
1.221 Voluntary publication or republication of patent application publication.

MISCELLANEOUS PROVISIONS

1.248 Service of papers; manner of service; proof of service in cases other than interferences.
1.251 Unlocatable file.

PROTESTS AND PUBLIC USE PROCEEDINGS

1.291 Protests by the public against pending applications.
1.292 Public use proceedings.
1.293 Statutory invention registration.
1.294 Examination of request for publication of a statutory invention registration and patent application to which the request is directed.
1.295 Review of decision finally refusing to publish a statutory invention registration.
1.296 Withdrawal of request for publication of statutory invention registration.
1.297 Publication of statutory invention registration.

REVIEW OF PATENT AND TRADEMARK OFFICE DECISIONS BY COURT

1.301 Appeal to U.S. Court of Appeals for the Federal Circuit.
1.302 Notice of appeal.
1.303 Civil action under 35 U.S.C. 145, 146, 306.
1.304 Time for appeal or civil action.

ALLOWANCE AND ISSUE OF PATENT

1.311 Notice of Allowance.
1.312 Amendments after allowance.
1.313 Withdrawal from issue.
1.314 Issuance of patent.
1.315 Delivery of patent.
1.316 Application abandoned for failure to pay issue fee.
1.317 Lapsed patents; delayed payment of balance of issue fee.
1.318 [Reserved]

DISCLAIMER

1.321 Statutory disclaimers, including terminal disclaimers.

CORRECTION OF ERRORS IN PATENT

1.322 Certificate of correction of Office mistake.
1.323 Certificate of correction of applicant's mistake.
1.324 Correction of inventorship in patent, pursuant to 35 U.S.C. 256.
1.325 Other mistakes not corrected.

ARBITRATION AWARDS

1.331 [Reserved]
1.332 [Reserved]
1.333 [Reserved]
1.334 [Reserved]
1.335 Filing of notice of arbitration awards

AMENDMENT OF RULES

1.351 Amendments to rules will be published.
1.352 [Reserved]

MAINTENANCE FEES

1.362 Time for payment of maintenance fees.
1.363 Fee address for maintenance fee purposes.
1.366 Submission of maintenance fees.
1.377 Review of decision refusing to accept and record payment of a maintenance fee filed prior to expiration of patent.
1.378 Acceptance of delayed payment of maintenance fee in expired patent to reinstate patent.

Subpart C - International Processing Provisions

GENERAL INFORMATION

1.401 Definitions of terms under the Patent Cooperation Treaty.
1.412 The United States Receiving Office.
1.413 The United States International Searching Authority.

Rev. 8, July 2010

1.414 The United States Patent and Trademark Office as a Designated Office or Elected Office.

1.415 The International Bureau.

1.416 The United States International Preliminary Examining Authority.

1.417 Submission of translation of international publication.

1.419 Display of currently valid control number under the Paperwork Reduction Act.

WHO MAY FILE AN INTERNATIONAL APPLICATION

1.421 Applicant for international application.

1.422 When the inventor is dead.

1.423 When the inventor is insane or legally incapacitated.

1.424 [Reserved]

1.425 [Reserved]

THE INTERNATIONAL APPLICATION

1.431 International application requirements.

1.432 Designation of States by filing an international application.

1.433 Physical requirements of international application.

1.434 The request.

1.435 The description.

1.436 The claims.

1.437 The drawings.

1.438 The abstract.

FEES

1.445 International application filing, processing and search fees.

1.446 Refund of international application filing and processing fees.

PRIORITY

1.451 The priority claim and priority document in an international application.

1.452 Restoration of right of priority.

REPRESENTATION

1.455 Representation in international applications.

TRANSMITTAL OF RECORD COPY

1.461 Procedures for transmittal of record copy to the International Bureau.

TIMING

1.465 Timing of application processing based on the priority date.

1.468 Delays in meeting time limits.

AMENDMENTS

1.471 Corrections and amendments during international processing.

1.472 Changes in person, name, or address of applicants and inventors.

UNITY OF INVENTION

1.475 Unity of invention before the International Searching Authority, the International Preliminary Examining Authority and during the national stage.

1.476 Determination of unity of invention before the International Searching Authority.

1.477 Protest to lack of unity of invention before the International Searching Authority.

INTERNATIONAL PRELIMINARY EXAMINATION

1.480 Demand for international preliminary examination.

1.481 Payment of international preliminary examination fees.

1.482 International preliminary examination fees.

1.484 Conduct of international preliminary examination.

1.485 Amendments by applicant during international preliminary examination.

1.488 Determination of unity of invention before the International Preliminary Examining Authority.

1.489 Protest to lack of unity of invention before the International Preliminary Examining Authority.

NATIONAL STAGE

1.491 National stage commencement and entry.
1.492 National stage fees.
1.494 [Reserved]
1.495 Entering the national stage in the United States of America.
1.496 Examination of international applications in the national stage.
1.497 Oath or declaration under 35 U.S.C. 371(c)(4).
1.499 Unity of invention during the national stage.

Subpart D - *Ex Parte* Reexamination of Patents

CITATION OF PRIOR ART

1.501 Citation of prior art in patent files.
1.502 Processing of prior art citations during an *ex parte* reexamination proceeding.

REQUEST FOR REEXAMINATION

1.510 Request for *ex parte* reexamination.
1.515 Determination of the request for *ex parte* reexamination.
1.520 *Ex parte* reexamination at the initiative of the Director.
1.525 Order for *ex parte* reexamination.
1.530 Statement by patent owner in *ex parte* reexamination; amendment by patent owner in *ex parte* or *inter partes* reexamination; inventorship change in *ex parte* or *inter partes* reexamination.
1.535 Reply by third party requester in *ex parte* reexamination.
1.540 Consideration of responses in *ex parte* reexamination.
1.550 Conduct of *ex parte* reexamination proceedings.
1.552 Scope of reexamination in *ex parte* reexamination proceedings.
1.555 Information material to patentability in *ex parte* reexamination and *inter partes* reexamination proceedings.
1.560 Interviews in *ex parte* reexamination proceedings.

1.565 Concurrent office proceedings which include an *ex parte* reexamination proceeding.
1.570 Issuance of *ex parte* reexamination certificate after *ex parte* reexamination proceedings.

Subpart E - [Reserved]

Subpart F - Adjustment and Extension of Patent Term

ADJUSTMENT OF PATENT TERM DUE TO EXAMINATION DELAY

1.701 Extension of patent term due to examination delay under the Uruguay Round Agreements Act (original applications, other than designs, filed on or after June 8, 1995, and before May 29, 2000).
1.702 Grounds for adjustment of patent term due to examination delay under the Patent Term Guarantee Act of 1999 (original applications, other than designs, filed on or after May 29, 2000).
1.703 Period of adjustment of patent term due to examination delay.
1.704 Reduction of period of adjustment of patent term.
1.705 Patent term adjustment determination.

EXTENSION OF PATENT TERM DUE TO REGULATORY REVIEW

1.710 Patents subject to extension of the patent term.
1.720 Conditions for extension of patent term.
1.730 Applicant for extension of patent term; signature requirements.
1.740 Formal requirements for application for extension of patent term; correction of informalities.
1.741 Complete application given a filing date; petition procedure.
1.750 Determination of eligibility for extension of patent term.
1.760 Interim extension of patent term under 35 U.S.C. 156(e)(2).
1.765 Duty of disclosure in patent term extension proceedings.
1.770 Express withdrawal of application for extension of patent term.
1.775 Calculation of patent term extension for a human drug, antibiotic drug, or human biological product.

1.776 Calculation of patent term extension for a food additive or color additive.

1.777 Calculation of patent term extension for a medical device.

1.778 Calculation of patent term extension for an animal drug product.

1.779 Calculation of patent term extension for a veterinary biological product.

1.780 Certificate or order of extension of patent term.

1.785 Multiple applications for extension of term of the same patent or of different patents for the same regulatory review period for a product.

1.790 Interim extension of patent term under 35 U.S.C. 156(d)(5)

1.791 Termination of interim extension granted prior to regulatory approval of a product for commercial marketing or use.

Subpart G - Biotechnology Invention Disclosures

DEPOSIT OF BIOLOGICAL MATERIAL

1.801 Biological material.

1.802 Need or opportunity to make a deposit.

1.803 Acceptable depository.

1.804 Time of making an original deposit.

1.805 Replacement or supplement of deposit.

1.806 Term of deposit.

1.807 Viability of deposit.

1.808 Furnishing of samples.

1.809 Examination procedures.

APPLICATION DISCLOSURES CONTAINING NUCLEOTIDE AND/OR AMINO ACID SEQUENCES

1.821 Nucleotide and/or amino acid sequence disclosures in patent applications.

1.822 Symbols and format to be used for nucleotide and/or amino acid sequence data.

1.823 Requirements for nucleotide and/or amino acid sequences as part of the application.

1.824 Form and format for nucleotide and/or amino acid sequence submissions in computer readable form.

1.825 Amendments to or replacement of sequence listing and computer readable copy thereof.

Appendix A - Sample Sequence Listing

Subpart H - *Inter Partes* Reexamination of Patents that Issued From an Original Application Filed in the United States on or After November 29, 1999

PRIOR ART CITATIONS

1.902 Processing of prior art citations during an *inter partes* reexamination proceeding.

REQUIREMENTS FOR *INTER PARTES* REEXAMINATION PROCEEDINGS

1.903 Service of papers on parties in *inter partes* reexamination.

1.904 Notice of *inter partes* reexamination in *Official Gazette*.

1.905 Submission of papers by the public in *inter partes* reexamination.

1.906 Scope of reexamination in *inter partes* reexamination proceeding.

1.907 *Inter partes* reexamination prohibited.

1.913 Persons eligible to file request for *inter partes* reexamination.

1.915 Content of request for *inter partes* reexamination.

1.919 Filing date of request for *inter partes* reexamination.

1.923 Examiner's determination on the request for *inter partes* reexamination.

1.925 Partial refund if request for *inter partes* reexamination is not ordered.

1.927 Petition to review refusal to order *inter partes* reexamination.

INTER PARTES REEXAMINATION OF PATENTS

1.931 Order for *inter partes* reexamination.

INFORMATION DISCLOSURE IN *INTER PARTES* REEXAMINATION

1.933 Patent owner duty of disclosure in *inter partes* reexamination proceedings.

OFFICE ACTIONS AND RESPONSES (BEFORE THE EXAMINER) IN *INTER PARTES* REEXAMINATION

1.935 Initial Office action usually accompanies order for *inter partes* reexamination.

1.937 Conduct of *inter partes* reexamination.

1.939 Unauthorized papers in *inter partes* reexamination.

1.941 Amendments by patent owner in *inter partes* reexamination.

1.943 Requirements of responses, written comments, and briefs in *inter partes* reexamination.

1.945 Response to Office action by patent owner in *inter partes* reexamination.

1.947 Comments by third party requester to patent owner's response in *inter partes* reexamination.

1.948 Limitations on submission of prior art by third party requester following the order for *inter partes* reexamination.

1.949 Examiner's Office action closing prosecution in *inter partes* reexamination.

1.951 Options after Office action closing prosecution in *inter partes* reexamination.

1.953 Examiner's Right of Appeal Notice in *inter partes* reexamination.

INTERVIEWS PROHIBITED IN *INTER PARTES* REEXAMINATION

1.955 Interviews prohibited in *inter partes* reexamination proceedings.

EXTENSIONS OF TIME, TERMINATION OF PROCEEDINGS, AND PETITIONS TO REVIVE IN *INTER PARTES* REEXAMINATION

1.956 Patent owner extensions of time in *inter partes* reexamination.

1.957 Failure to file a timely, appropriate or complete response or comment in *inter partes* reexamination.

1.958 Petition to revive terminated *inter partes* reexamination or claims terminated for lack of patent owner response.

APPEAL TO THE BOARD OF PATENT APPEALS AND INTERFERENCES IN *INTER PARTES* REEXAMINATION

1.959 Appeal in *inter partes* reexamination.

1.961 [Reserved]

1.962 [Reserved]

1.963 [Reserved]

1.965 [Reserved]

1.967 [Reserved]

1.969 [Reserved]

1.971 [Reserved]

1.973 [Reserved]

1.975 [Reserved]

1.977 [Reserved]

1.979 Return of Jurisdiction from the Board of Patent Appeals and Interferences; termination of proceedings.

1.981 Reopening after a final decision of the Board of Patent Appeals and Interferences.

APPEAL TO THE UNITED STATES COURT OF APPEALS FOR THE FEDERAL CIRCUIT IN *INTER PARTES* REEXAMINATION

1.983 Appeal to the United States Court of Appeals for the Federal Circuit in *inter partes* reexamination.

CONCURRENT PROCEEDINGS INVOLVING SAME PATENT IN *INTER PARTES* REEXAMINATION

1.985 Notification of prior or concurrent proceedings in *inter partes* reexamination.

1.987 Suspension of *inter partes* reexamination proceeding due to litigation.

1.989 Merger of concurrent reexamination proceedings.

1.991 Merger of concurrent reissue application and *inter partes* reexamination proceeding.

1.993 Suspension of concurrent interference and *inter partes* reexamination proceeding.

1.995 Third party requester's participation rights preserved in merged proceeding.

Rev. 8, July 2010

REEXAMINATION CERTIFICATE IN *INTER PARTES* REEXAMINATION

1.997 Issuance and publication of *inter partes* reexamination certificate concludes *inter partes* rexamination proceeding.

SUBCHAPTER A – GENERAL

PART 1 — RULES OF PRACTICE IN PATENT CASES

Subpart A — General Provisions

GENERAL INFORMATION AND CORRESPONDENCE

§ 1.1   Addresses for non-trademark correspondence with the United States Patent and Trademark Office.

(a) *In general.* Except as provided in paragraphs (a)(3)(i), (a)(3)(ii) and (d)(1) of this section, all correspondence intended for the United States Patent and Trademark Office must be addressed to either "Director of the United States Patent and Trademark Office, P.O. Box 1450, Alexandria, Virginia 22313-1450" or to specific areas within the Office as set out in paragraphs (a)(1), and (a)(3)(iii) of this section. When appropriate, correspondence should also be marked for the attention of a particular office or individual.

(1) *Patent correspondence.*

(i) *In general.* All correspondence concerning patent matters processed by organizations reporting to the Commissioner for Patents should be addressed to: Commissioner for Patents, PO Box 1450, Alexandria, Virginia 22313-1450.

(ii) *Board of Patent Appeals and Interferences.* See § 41.10 of this title. Notices of appeal, appeal briefs, reply briefs, requests for oral hearing, as well as all other correspondence in an application or a patent involved in an appeal to the Board for which an address is not otherwise specified, should be addressed as set out in paragraph (a)(1)(i) of this section.

(2) [Reserved]

(3) *Office of General Counsel correspondence.—*

(i) *Litigation and service.* Correspondence relating to pending litigation or otherwise within the scope of part 104 of this title shall be addressed as provided in § 104.2.

(ii) *Disciplinary proceedings.* Correspondence to counsel for the Director of the Office of Enrollment and Discipline relating to disciplinary proceedings pending before a Hearing Officer or the Director shall be mailed to: Mail Stop 8, Office of the Solicitor, United States Patent and Trademark Office, P.O. Box 1450, Alexandria, Virginia 22313-1450.

(iii) *Solicitor, in general.* Correspondence to the Office of the Solicitor not otherwise provided for shall be addressed to: Mail Stop 8, Office of the Solicitor, United States Patent and Trademark Office, P.O. Box 1450, Alexandria, Virginia 22313-1450.

(iv) *General Counsel.* Correspondence to the Office of the General Counsel not otherwise provided for, including correspondence to the General Counsel relating to disciplinary proceedings, shall be addressed to: General Counsel, United States Patent and Trademark Office, PO Box 1450, Alexandria, Virginia 22313-1450.

(v) *Improper correspondence.* Correspondence improperly addressed to a Post Office Box specified in paragraphs (a)(3)(i) and (a)(3)(ii) of this section will not be filed elsewhere in the United States Patent and Trademark Office, and may be returned.

(4) *Office of Public Records correspondence.*

(i) *Assignments.* All patent-related documents submitted by mail to be recorded by Assignment Services Division, except for documents filed together with a new application, should be addressed to: Mail Stop Assignment Recordation Services, Director of the United States Patent and Trademark Office, P.O. Box 1450, Alexandria, Virginia 22313-1450. *See* § 3.27.

(ii) *Documents.* All requests for certified or uncertified copies of patent documents should be addressed to: Mail Stop Document Services, Director of the United States Patent and Trademark Office, P.O. Box 1450, Alexandria, Virginia 22313-1450.

(5) *Office of Enrollment and Discipline correspondence.* All correspondence directed to the Office of Enrollment and Discipline concerning enrollment, registration, and investigation matters

should be addressed to Mail Stop OED, Director of the United States Patent and Trademark Office, P.O. Box 1450, Alexandria, Virginia 22313-1450.

(b) *Patent Cooperation Treaty.* Letters and other communications relating to international applications during the international stage and prior to the assignment of a national serial number should be additionally marked "Mail Stop PCT."

(c) *For reexamination proceedings.*

(1) Requests for *ex parte* reexamination (original request papers) and all subsequent *ex parte* reexamination correspondence filed in the Office, other than correspondence to the Office of the General Counsel pursuant to § 1.1(a)(3) and § 1.302(c), should be additionally marked "Mail Stop *Ex Parte* Reexam."

(2) Requests for *inter partes* reexamination (original request papers) and all subsequent *inter partes* reexamination correspondence filed in the Office, other than correspondence to the Office of the General Counsel pursuant to § 1.1(a)(3) and § 1.302(c), should be additionally marked "Mail Stop *Inter partes* Reexam."

(d) Payments of maintenance fees in patents not submitted electronically over the Internet, and correspondence related to maintenance fees may be addressed to: Director of the United States Patent and Trademark Office, Attn: Maintenance Fee, 2051 Jamieson Avenue, Suite 300, Alexandria, Virginia 22314.

(e) *Patent term extension.* All applications for extension of patent term under 35 U.S.C. 156 and any communications relating thereto intended for the United States Patent and Trademark Office should be additionally marked "Mail Stop Patent Ext." When appropriate, the communication should also be marked to the attention of a particular individual, as where a decision has been rendered.

(f) [Reserved]

[46 FR 29181, May 29, 1981; para. (d) added, 49 FR 34724, Aug. 31, 1984, effective Nov. 1, 1984; para. (e), 49 FR 48416, Dec. 12, 1984, effective Feb. 11, 1985; para. (f) added, 52 FR 9394, Mar. 24, 1987; para. (g) added, 53 FR 16413, May 9,1988; para. (h) added, 54 FR 37588, Sept. 11, 1989, effective Nov. 16, 1989; para. (i) added, 60 FR 20195, Apr. 25, 1995, effective June 8, 1995; para. (a) revised and para. (g) removed and reserved, 61 FR 56439, Nov. 1, 1996, effective Dec. 2, 1996; para. (b)

revised, 64 FR 48900, Sept. 8, 1999, effective Oct. 30, 1999; paras. (a) and (d) revised, 66 FR 39447, July 31, 2001, effective Oct. 1, 2001; revised, 68 FR 14332, Mar. 25, 2003, effective May 1, 2003; para (a)(2) corrected, 68 FR 19371, Apr. 21, 2003, effective May 1, 2003; section heading, para. (a) introductory text and para. (a)(4) revised, para. (a)(2) removed and reserved, and note following para. (f) removed, 68 FR 48286, Aug. 13, 2003, effective Sept. 12, 2003; para. (c) revised, 68 FR 70996, Dec. 22, 2003, effective Jan. 21, 2004; para. (a)(4)(i) revised and para. (f) removed and reserved, 69 FR 29865, May 26, 2004, effective June 25, 2004; para. (a) introductory text revised and para. (a)(5) added, 69 FR 35427, June 24, 2004, effective July 26, 2004; para. (a)(1)(ii) revised and para. (a)(1)(iii) removed, 69 FR 49959, Aug. 12, 2004, effective Sept. 13, 2004; para. (c)(1) revised, 72 FR 18892, Apr. 16, 2007, effective May 16, 2007; para. (d) revised, 73 FR 47534, Aug. 14, 2008, effective Oct. 2, 2008; paras. (a)(3)(ii) and (a)(3)(iii) revised, 75 FR 36294, June 25, 2010, effective June 25, 2010]

§ 1.2 Business to be transacted in writing.

All business with the Patent and Trademark Office should be transacted in writing. The personal attendance of applicants or their attorneys or agents at the Patent and Trademark Office is unnecessary. The action of the Patent and Trademark Office will be based exclusively on the written record in the Office. No attention will be paid to any alleged oral promise, stipulation, or understanding in relation to which there is disagreement or doubt.

§ 1.3 Business to be conducted with decorum and courtesy.

Applicants and their attorneys or agents are required to conduct their business with the United States Patent and Trademark Office with decorum and courtesy. Papers presented in violation of this requirement will be submitted to the Director and will not be entered. A notice of the non-entry of the paper will be provided. Complaints against examiners and other employees must be made in correspondence separate from other papers.

[Amended, 61 FR 56439, Nov. 1, 1996, effective Dec. 2, 1996; revised, 68 FR 14332, Mar. 25, 2003, effective May 1, 2003; revised, 68 FR 38611, June 30, 2003, effective July 30, 2003]

§ 1.4   Nature of correspondence and signature requirements.

(a)   Correspondence with the Patent and Trademark Office comprises:

(1)   Correspondence relating to services and facilities of the Office, such as general inquiries, requests for publications supplied by the Office, orders for printed copies of patents, orders for copies of records, transmission of assignments for recording, and the like, and

(2)   Correspondence in and relating to a particular application or other proceeding in the Office. See particularly the rules relating to the filing, processing, or other proceedings of national applications in subpart B, §§ 1.31 to 1.378; of international applications in subpart C, §§ 1.401 to 1.499; of *ex parte* reexaminations of patents in subpart D, §§ 1.501 to 1.570; of extension of patent term in subpart F, §§ 1.710 to 1.785; of inter partes reexaminations of patents in subpart H, §§ 1.902 to 1.997; and of the Board of Patent Appeals and Interferences in part 41 of this title.

(b)   Since each file must be complete in itself, a separate copy of every paper to be filed in a patent, patent file, or other proceeding must be furnished for each file to which the paper pertains, even though the contents of the papers filed in two or more files may be identical. The filing of duplicate copies of correspondence in the file of an application, patent, or other proceeding should be avoided, except in situations in which the Office requires the filing of duplicate copies. The Office may dispose of duplicate copies of correspondence in the file of an application, patent, or other proceeding.

(c)   Since different matters may be considered by different branches or sections of the United States Patent and Trademark Office, each distinct subject, inquiry or order must be contained in a separate paper to avoid confusion and delay in answering papers dealing with different subjects.

(d)(1)   *Handwritten signature.* Each piece of correspondence, except as provided in paragraphs (d)(2), (d)(3), (e) and (f) of this section, filed in an application, patent file, or other proceeding in the Office which requires a person's signature, must:

(i)   Be an original, that is, have an original handwritten signature personally signed, in permanent dark ink or its equivalent, by that person; or

(ii)   Be a direct or indirect copy, such as a photocopy or facsimile transmission (§ 1.6(d)), of an original. In the event that a copy of the original is filed, the original should be retained as evidence of authenticity. If a question of authenticity arises, the Office may require submission of the original.

(2)   *S-signature.* An S-signature is a signature inserted between forward slash marks, but not a handwritten signature as defined by § 1.4(d)(1). An S-signature includes any signature made by electronic or mechanical means, and any other mode of making or applying a signature not covered by a handwritten signature of § 1.4(d)(1). Correspondence being filed in the Office in paper, by facsimile transmission as provided in § 1.6(d), or via the Office electronic filing system as an attachment as provided in § 1.6(a)(4), for a patent application, patent, or a reexamination proceeding may be S-signature signed instead of being personally signed (*i.e.*, with a handwritten signature) as provided for in paragraph (d)(1) of this section. The requirements for an S-signature under this paragraph (d)(2) of this section are as follows.

(i)   The S-signature must consist only of letters, or Arabic numerals, or both, with appropriate spaces and commas, periods, apostrophes, or hyphens for punctuation, and the person signing the correspondence must insert his or her own S-signature with a first single forward slash mark before, and a second single forward slash mark after, the S-signature (e.g., /Dr. James T. Jones, Jr./); and

(ii)   A patent practitioner (§ 1.32(a)(1)), signing pursuant to §§ 1.33(b)(1) or 1.33(b)(2), must supply his/her registration number either as part of the S-signature, or immediately below or adjacent to the S-signature. The number (#) character may be used only as part of the S-signature when appearing before a practitioner's registration number; otherwise the number character may not be used in an S-signature.

(iii)   The signer's name must be:

(A)   Presented in printed or typed form preferably immediately below or adjacent the S-signature, and

(B)   Reasonably specific enough so that the identity of the signer can be readily recognized.

(3)   *Forms.* The Office provides forms to the public to use in certain situations to assist in the filing of correspondence for a certain purpose and to meet certain requirements for patent applications and pro-

ceedings. Use of the forms for purposes for which they were not designed is prohibited. No changes to certification statements on the Office forms (*e.g.*, oath or declaration forms, terminal disclaimer forms, petition forms, and nonpublication request forms) may be made. The existing text of a form, other than a certification statement, may be modified, deleted, or added to, if all text identifying the form as an Office form is removed. The presentation to the Office (whether by signing, filing, submitting, or later advocating) of any Office form with text identifying the form as an Office form by a party, whether a practitioner or non-practitioner, constitutes a certification under § 11.18(b) of this chapter that the existing text and any certification statements on the form have not been altered other than permitted by EFS-Web customization.

(4) *Certifications*. (i) *Section 11.18 certifications*: The presentation to the Office (whether by signing, filing, submitting, or later advocating) of any paper by a party, whether a practitioner or non-practitioner, constitutes a certification under § 11.18(b) of this subchapter. Violations of § 11.18(b)(2) of this subchapter by a party, whether a practitioner or non-practitioner, may result in the imposition of sanctions under § 11.18(c) of this subchapter. Any practitioner violating § 11.18(b) of this subchapter may also be subject to disciplinary action. *See* §§ 11.18(d) and 11.804(b)(9) of this subchapter.

(ii) *Certifications as to the signature*:

(A) *Of another*: A person submitting a document signed by another under paragraph (d)(2) of this section is obligated to have a reasonable basis to believe that the person whose signature is present on the document was actually inserted by that person, and should retain evidence of authenticity of the signature.

(B) *Self certification*: The person inserting a signature under paragraph (d)(2) of this section in a document submitted to the Office certifies that the inserted signature appearing in the document is his or her own signature.

(C) *Sanctions*: Violations of the certifications as to the signature of another or a person's own signature, set forth in paragraphs (d)(4)(ii)(A) and (B) of this section, may result in the imposition of sanctions under § 11.18(c) and (d) of this chapter.

(e) Correspondence requiring a person's signature and relating to registration practice before the Patent and Trademark Office in patent cases, enrollment and disciplinary investigations, or disciplinary proceedings must be submitted with an original hand written signature personally signed in permanent dark ink or its equivalent by that person.

(f) When a document that is required by statute to be certified must be filed, a copy, including a photocopy or facsimile transmission, of the certification is not acceptable.

(g) An applicant who has not made of record a registered attorney or agent may be required to state whether assistance was received in the preparation or prosecution of the patent application, for which any compensation or consideration was given or charged, and if so, to disclose the name or names of the person or persons providing such assistance. Assistance includes the preparation for the applicant of the specification and amendments or other papers to be filed in the Patent and Trademark Office, as well as other assistance in such matters, but does not include merely making drawings by draftsmen or stenographic services in typing papers.

(h) *Ratification/confirmation/evidence of authenticity*: The Office may require ratification, confirmation (which includes submission of a duplicate document but with a proper signature), or evidence of authenticity of a signature, such as when the Office has reasonable doubt as to the authenticity (veracity) of the signature, *e.g.*, where there are variations of a signature, or where the signature and the typed or printed name, do not clearly identify the person signing.

[24 FR 10332, Dec. 22, 1959; 43 FR 20461, May 11, 1978; para. (a), 48 FR 2707, Jan. 20, 1983, effective Feb. 27, 1983; para. (a), 49 FR 48416, Dec. 12, 1984, effective Feb. 11, 1985; para. (a)(2), 53 FR 47807, Nov. 28, 1988, effective Jan. 1, 1989; paras. (d)-(f) added, 58 FR 54494, Oct. 22, 1993, effective Nov. 22, 1993; para. (d) revised & para. (g) added, 62 FR 53131, Oct. 10, 1997, effective Dec. 1, 1997; paras. (a)(2) and (d)(1) revised, 64 FR 48900, Sept. 8, 1999, effective Oct. 30, 1999; paras. (b) and (c) revised, 65 FR 54604, Sept. 8, 2000, effective Nov. 7, 2000; para. (a)(2) revised, 65 FR 76756, Dec. 7, 2000, effective Feb. 5, 2001; para. (d)(1)(iii)(A) amended, 67 FR 79520, Dec. 30, 2002, effective Dec. 30, 2002; para. (d)(1)(iii)(B) revised, 68 FR 14332, Mar. 25, 2003, effective May 1, 2003; para. (d)(1)(iii) removed and reserved, paras. (a)(1), (a)(2), (b), (d)(1), introductory text, and (d)(1)(ii) revised, 68 FR 48286, Aug. 13, 2003, effective Sept. 12, 2003; para. (a)(2) revised, 69 FR 49959, Aug. 12, 2004, effective Sept. 13, 2004; paras. (d) and (e) revised and para. (h) added, 69 FR 56481, Sept. 21, 2004, effective Sept. 21, 2004; para. (d)(2) introductory text and paragraph (d)(2)(ii) revised, 70 FR 56119, Sept. 26, 2005, effective Nov. 25, 2005; paras. (d)(2) introductory text, (d)(3), and (d)(4)(ii) revised, 72 FR 2770, Jan. 23, 2007, effective Jan. 23, 2007; paras. (d)(3) and (d)(4)(i) revised, para. (d)(4)(ii)(C) added, 73 FR 47650, Aug. 14, 2008, effective Sept. 15, 2008]

§ 1.5   Identification of patent, patent application, or patent-related proceeding.

(a)   No correspondence relating to an application should be filed prior to receipt of the application number from the Patent and Trademark Office. When a letter directed to the Patent and Trademark Office concerns a previously filed application for a patent, it must identify on the top page in a conspicuous location, the application number (consisting of the series code and the serial number; e.g., 07/123,456), or the serial number and filing date assigned to that application by the Patent and Trademark Office, or the international application number of the international application. Any correspondence not containing such identification will be returned to the sender where a return address is available. The returned correspondence will be accompanied with a cover letter which will indicate to the sender that if the returned correspondence is resubmitted to the Patent and Trademark Office within two weeks of the mail date on the cover letter, the original date of receipt of the correspondence will be considered by the Patent and Trademark Office as the date of receipt of the correspondence. Applicants may use either the Certificate of Mailing or Transmission procedure under § 1.8 or the Express Mail procedure under § 1.10 for resubmissions of returned correspondence if they desire to have the benefit of the date of deposit in the United States Postal Service. If the returned correspondence is not resubmitted within the two-week period, the date of receipt of the resubmission will be considered to be the date of receipt of the correspondence. The two-week period to resubmit the returned correspondence will not be extended. In addition to the application number, all letters directed to the Patent and Trademark Office concerning applications for patent should also state the name of the applicant, the title of the invention, the date of filing the same, and, if known, the group art unit or other unit within the Patent and Trademark Office responsible for considering the letter and the name of the examiner or other person to which it has been assigned.

(b)   When the letter concerns a patent other than for purposes of paying a maintenance fee, it should state the number and date of issue of the patent, the name of the patentee, and the title of the invention. For letters concerning payment of a maintenance fee in a patent, see the provisions of § 1.366(c).

(c)   [Reserved]

(d)   A letter relating to a reexamination proceeding should identify it as such by the number of the patent undergoing reexamination, the reexamination request control number assigned to such proceeding, and, if known, the group art unit and name of the examiner to which it been assigned.

(e)   [Reserved]

(f)   When a paper concerns a provisional application, it should identify the application as such and include the application number.

[24 FR 10332, Dec. 22, 1959; 46 FR 29181, May 29, 1981; para. (a), 49 FR 552, Jan. 4, 1984, effective Apr. 1, 1984; para. (a), 49 FR 48416, Dec. 12, 1984, effective Feb. 11, 1985; paras. (a) & (b), 53 FR 47807, Nov. 28, 1988, effective Jan. 1, 1989; para. (a) revised, 58 FR 54494, Oct. 22, 1993, effective Nov. 22, 1993; para. (f) added, 61 FR 42790, Aug. 19, 1996, effective Sept. 23, 1996; para. (a) amended, 61 FR 56439, Nov. 1, 1996, effective Dec. 2, 1996; para. (c) revised, 64 FR 48900, Sept. 8, 1999, effective Oct. 30, 1999; section heading revised, para. (c) removed and reserved, 68 FR 48286, Aug. 13, 2003, effective Sept. 12, 2003; para. (e) removed and reserved, 69 FR 49959, Aug. 12, 2004, effective Sept. 13, 2004]

§ 1.6   Receipt of correspondence.

(a)   *Date of receipt and Express Mail date of deposit.* Correspondence received in the Patent and Trademark Office is stamped with the date of receipt except as follows:

(1)   The Patent and Trademark Office is not open for the filing of correspondence on any day that is a Saturday, Sunday, or Federal holiday within the District of Columbia. Except for correspondence transmitted by facsimile under paragraph (a)(3) of this section, or filed electronically under paragraph (a)(4)

of this section, no correspondence is received in the Office on Saturdays, Sundays, or Federal holidays within the District of Columbia.

(2) Correspondence filed in accordance with § 1.10 will be stamped with the date of deposit as "Express Mail" with the United States Postal Service.

(3) Correspondence transmitted by facsimile to the Patent and Trademark Office will be stamped with the date on which the complete transmission is received in the Patent and Trademark Office unless that date is a Saturday, Sunday, or Federal holiday within the District of Columbia, in which case the date stamped will be the next succeeding day which is not a Saturday, Sunday, or Federal holiday within the District of Columbia.

(4) Correspondence may be submitted using the Office electronic filing system only in accordance with the Office electronic filing system requirements. Correspondence submitted to the Office by way of the Office electronic filing system will be accorded a receipt date, which is the date the correspondence is received at the correspondence address for the Office set forth in § 1.1 when it was officially submitted.

(b) [Reserved]

(c) *Correspondence delivered by hand.* In addition to being mailed, correspondence may be delivered by hand during hours the Office is open to receive correspondence.

(d) *Facsimile transmission.* Except in the cases enumerated below, correspondence, including authorizations to charge a deposit account, may be transmitted by facsimile. The receipt date accorded to the correspondence will be the date on which the complete transmission is received in the United States Patent and Trademark Office, unless that date is a Saturday, Sunday, or Federal holiday within the District of Columbia. See § 1.6(a)(3). To facilitate proper processing, each transmission session should be limited to correspondence to be filed in a single application or other proceeding before the United States Patent and Trademark Office. The application number of a patent application, the control number of a reexamination proceeding, the interference number of an interference proceeding, or the patent number of a patent should be entered as a part of the sender's identification on a facsimile cover sheet. Facsimile transmissions are not permitted and, if submitted, will not be accorded a date of receipt in the following situations:

(1) Correspondence as specified in § 1.4(e), requiring an original signature;

(2) Certified documents as specified in § 1.4(f);

(3) Correspondence which cannot receive the benefit of the certificate of mailing or transmission as specified in § 1.8(a)(2)(i)(A) through (D) and (F), and § 1.8(a)(2)(iii)(A), except that a continued prosecution application under § 1.53(d) may be transmitted to the Office by facsimile;

(4) Color drawings submitted under §§ 1.81, 1.83 through 1.85, 1.152, 1.165, 1.173, or 1.437;

(5) A request for reexamination under § 1.510 or § 1.913;

(6) Correspondence to be filed in a patent application subject to a secrecy order under §§ 5.1 through 5.5 of this chapter and directly related to the secrecy order content of the application;

(7) [Reserved]

(8) [Reserved]

(9) In contested cases before the Board of Patent Appeals and Interferences except as the Board may expressly authorize.

(e) [Reserved]

(f) *Facsimile transmission of a patent application under § 1.53(d).* In the event that the Office has no evidence of receipt of an application under § 1.53(d) (a continued prosecution application) transmitted to the Office by facsimile transmission, the party who transmitted the application under § 1.53(d) may petition the Director to accord the application under § 1.53(d) a filing date as of the date the application under § 1.53(d) is shown to have been transmitted to and received in the Office,

(1) Provided that the party who transmitted such application under § 1.53(d):

(i) Informs the Office of the previous transmission of the application under § 1.53(d) promptly after becoming aware that the Office has no evidence of receipt of the application under § 1.53(d);

(ii) Supplies an additional copy of the previously transmitted application under § 1.53(d); and

(iii) Includes a statement which attests on a personal knowledge basis or to the satisfaction of the Director to the previous transmission of the application under § 1.53(d) and is accompanied by a copy of the sending unit's report confirming transmission of the application under § 1.53(d) or evidence that came into being after the complete transmission and within one business day of the complete transmission of the application under § 1.53(d).

(2) The Office may require additional evidence to determine if the application under § 1.53(d) was transmitted to and received in the Office on the date in question.

(g) *Submission of the national stage correspondence required by § 1.495 via the Office electronic filing system.* In the event that the Office has no evidence of receipt of the national stage correspondence required by § 1.495, which was submitted to the Office by the Office electronic filing system, the party who submitted the correspondence may petition the Director to accord the national stage correspondence a receipt date as of the date the correspondence is shown to have been officially submitted to the Office.

(1) The petition of this paragraph (g) requires that the party who submitted such national stage correspondence:

(i) Informs the Office of the previous submission of the correspondence promptly after becoming aware that the Office has no evidence of receipt of the correspondence under § 1.495;

(ii) Supplies an additional copy of the previously submitted correspondence;

(iii) Includes a statement that attests on a personal knowledge basis, or to the satisfaction of the Director, that the correspondence was previously officially submitted; and

(iv) Supplies a copy of an acknowledgment receipt generated by the Office electronic filing system, or equivalent evidence, confirming the submission to support the statement of paragraph (g)(1)(iii) of this section.

(2) The Office may require additional evidence to determine if the national stage correspondence was submitted to the Office on the date in question.

[48 FR 2707, Jan. 20, 1983, effective Feb. 27, 1983; 48 FR 4285, Jan. 31, 1983; para. (a), 49 FR 552, Jan. 4, 1984, effective Apr. 1, 1984; revised, 58 FR 54494, Oct. 22, 1993, effective Nov. 22, 1993; para. (a) amended, 61 FR 56439, Nov. 1, 1996, effective Dec. 2, 1996; paras. (d)(3), (d)(6) & (e) amended, para. (f) added, 62 FR 53131, Oct. 10, 1997, effective Dec. 1, 1997; para (a)(1) revised and para. (a)(4) added, 64 FR 48900, Sept. 8, 1999, effec-

tive Oct. 30, 1999; para.(d)(9) revised, 65 FR 54604, Sept. 8, 2000, effective Nov. 7, 2000; para. (d)(5) revised, 65 FR 76756, Dec. 7, 2000, effective Feb. 5, 2001; para. (b) removed and reserved and paras. (e), (f) & (f)(1)(iii) revised, 68 FR 14332, Mar. 25, 2003, effective May 1, 2003; paras. (a)(4), (d)(7) and (d)(8) removed and reserved, and paras. (d), introductory text, (d)(3), and (d)(4) revised, 68 FR 48286, Aug. 13, 2003, effective Sept. 12, 2003; para. (d)(9) revised, 69 FR 49959, Aug. 12, 2004, effective Sept. 13, 2004; para. (d)(4) revised and para. (e) removed and reserved, 69 FR 56481, Sept. 21, 2004, effective Sept. 21, 2004; paras. (a)(4) & (g) added, 72 FR 2770, Jan. 23, 2007, effective Jan. 23, 2007]

§ 1.7   Times for taking action; Expiration on Saturday, Sunday or Federal holiday.

(a) Whenever periods of time are specified in this part in days, calendar days are intended. When the day, or the last day fixed by statute or by or under this part for taking any action or paying any fee in the United States Patent and Trademark Office falls on Saturday, Sunday, or on a Federal holiday within the District of Columbia, the action may be taken, or the fee paid, on the next succeeding business day which is not a Saturday, Sunday, or a Federal holiday. See § 1.304 for time for appeal or for commencing civil action.

(b) If the day that is twelve months after the filing date of a provisional application under 35 U.S.C. 111(b) and § 1.53(c) falls on Saturday, Sunday, or on a Federal holiday within the District of Columbia, the period of pendency shall be extended to the next succeeding secular or business day which is not a Saturday, Sunday, or a Federal holiday.

[48 FR 2707, Jan. 20, 1983, effective Feb. 27, 1983; corrected 48 FR 4285, Jan. 31, 1983; revised, 65 FR 14865, Mar. 20, 2000, effective May 29, 2000 (adopted as final, 65 FR 50092, Aug. 16, 2000)]

§ 1.8   Certificate of mailing or transmission.

(a) Except in the situations enumerated in paragraph (a)(2) of this section or as otherwise expressly excluded in this chapter, correspondence required to be filed in the U.S. Patent and Trademark Office within a set period of time will be considered as being timely filed if the procedure described in this section is followed. The actual date of receipt will be used for all other purposes.

(1) Correspondence will be considered as being timely filed if:

(i) The correspondence is mailed or transmitted prior to expiration of the set period of time by being:

(A) Addressed as set out in § 1.1(a) and deposited with the U.S. Postal Service with sufficient postage as first class mail;

(B) Transmitted by facsimile to the Patent and Trademark Office in accordance with § 1.6 (d); or

(C) Transmitted via the Office electronic filing system in accordance with § 1.6(a)(4); and

(ii) The correspondence includes a certificate for each piece of correspondence stating the date of deposit or transmission. The person signing the certificate should have reasonable basis to expect that the correspondence would be mailed or transmitted on or before the date indicated.

(2) The procedure described in paragraph (a)(1) of this section does not apply to, and no benefit will be given to a Certificate of Mailing or Transmission on, the following:

(i) *Relative to Patents and Patent Applications—*

(A) The filing of a national patent application specification and drawing or other correspondence for the purpose of obtaining an application filing date, including a request for a continued prosecution application under § 1.53(d);

(B) [Reserved]

(C) Papers filed in contested cases before the Board of Patent Appeals and Interferences, which are governed by § 41.106 (f) of this title;

(D) The filing of an international application for patent;

(E) The filing of correspondence in an international application before the U.S. Receiving Office, the U.S. International Searching Authority, or the U.S. International Preliminary Examining Authority;

(F) The filing of a copy of the international application and the basic national fee necessary to enter the national stage, as specified in § 1.495(b).

(ii) [Reserved]

(iii) *Relative to Disciplinary Proceedings—*

(A) Correspondence filed in connection with a disciplinary proceeding under part 11 of this chapter.

(B) [Reserved]

(b) In the event that correspondence is considered timely filed by being mailed or transmitted in accordance with paragraph (a) of this section, but not received in the U.S. Patent and Trademark Office after a reasonable amount of time has elapsed from the time of mailing or transmitting of the correspondence, or after the application is held to be abandoned, or after the proceeding is dismissed or decided with prejudice, or the prosecution of a reexamination proceeding is terminated pursuant to § 1.550(d) or § 1.957(b) or limited pursuant to § 1.957(c), or a requester paper is refused consideration pursuant to § 1.957(a), the correspondence will be considered timely if the party who forwarded such correspondence:

(1) Informs the Office of the previous mailing or transmission of the correspondence promptly after becoming aware that the Office has no evidence of receipt of the correspondence;

(2) Supplies an additional copy of the previously mailed or transmitted correspondence and certificate; and

(3) Includes a statement that attests on a personal knowledge basis or to the satisfaction of the Director to the previous timely mailing, transmission or submission. If the correspondence was sent by facsimile transmission, a copy of the sending unit's report confirming transmission may be used to support this statement. If the correspondence was transmitted via the Office electronic filing system, a copy of an acknowledgment receipt generated by the Office electronic filing system confirming submission may be used to support this statement.

(c) The Office may require additional evidence to determine if the correspondence was timely filed.

[41 FR 43721, Oct. 4, 1976; 43 FR 20461, May 11, 1978; para. (a). 47 FR 47381, Oct. 26, 1982, effective Oct. 26, 1982; para. (a),48 FR 2708, Jan. 20, 1983; para. (a) 49 FR 48416, Dec. 12, 1984, effective Feb. 11, 1985; para. (a), 49 FR 5171, Feb. 6, 1985, effective Mar. 8, 1985; 52 FR 20046, May 28, 1987; subparas. (a)(2)(xiv)-(xvi), 54 FR 37588, Sept. 11, 1989, effective Nov. 16, 1989; revised, 58 FR 54494, Oct. 22, 1993, effective Nov. 22, 1993; para. (a) revised, 61 FR 56439, Nov. 1, 1996, effective Dec. 2, 1996; paras. (a)(2)(i)(A) & (b) revised; 62 FR 53131, Oct. 10, 1997, effective Dec. 1, 1997; para. (a)(2)(i)(F) revised, 67 FR 520, Jan. 4, 2002, effective Apr. 1, 2002; para. (b)(3) revised, 68 FR 14332, Mar. 25, 2003, effective May 1, 2003; para. (a)(2)(ii) removed and reserved, 68 FR 48286, Aug. 13, 2003, effective Sept. 12, 2003; para. (a)(2)(i)(B) removed and reserved and para. (a)(2)(i)(C) revised, 69 FR 49959, Aug. 12, 2004, effective Sept. 13, 2004; paras. (a) and (b) revised, 69 FR 56481, Sept. 21, 2004, effective Oct. 21, 2004; paras. (a)(1)(i) & (b)(3) revised, 72 FR 2770, Jan. 23, 2007, effective Jan. 23, 2007; para. (b) introductory text revised, 72 FR 18892, Apr. 16, 2007, effective May 16, 2007; para. (a)(2)(iii)(A) revised, 73 FR 47650, Aug. 14, 2008, effective Sept. 15, 2008]

§ 1.9　　Definitions.

(a)(1)　A national application as used in this chapter means a U.S. application for patent which was either filed in the Office under 35 U.S.C. 111, or which entered the national stage from an international application after compliance with 35 U.S.C. 371.

(2)　A provisional application as used in this chapter means a U.S. national application for patent filed in the Office under 35 U.S.C. 111(b).

(3)　A nonprovisional application as used in this chapter means a U.S. national application for patent which was either filed in the Office under 35 U.S.C. 111(a), or which entered the national stage from an international application after compliance with 35 U.S.C. 371.

(b)　An international application as used in this chapter means an international application for patent filed under the Patent Cooperation Treaty prior to entering national processing at the Designated Office stage.

(c)　A published application as used in this chapter means an application for patent which has been published under 35 U.S.C. 122(b).

(d)　[Reserved]

(e)　[Reserved]

(f)　[Reserved]

(g)　For definitions in Board of Patent Appeals and Interferences proceedings, see part 41 of this title.

(h)　A Federal holiday within the District of Columbia as used in this chapter means any day, except Saturdays and Sundays, when the Patent and Trademark Office is officially closed for business for the entire day.

(i)　National security classified as used in this chapter means specifically authorized under criteria established by an Act of Congress or Executive Order to be kept secret in the interest of national defense or foreign policy and, in fact, properly classified pursuant to such Act of Congress or Executive Order.

(j)　Director as used in this chapter, except for part 11 of this chapter, means the Under Secretary of Commerce for Intellectual Property and Director of the United States Patent and Trademark Office.

(k)　Paper as used in this chapter means a document that may exist in electronic form, or in physical form, and therefore does not necessarily imply physical sheets of paper.

[43 FR 20461, May 11, 1978; 47 FR 40139, Sept. 10, 1982, effective Oct. 1, 1982; 47 FR 43275, Sept. 30, 1982, effective Oct. 1, 1982; para. (d), 49 FR 34724, Aug. 31, 1984, effective Nov. 1, 1984; para. (g), 49 FR 48416, Dec. 12, 1984, effective Feb. 11, 1985; para. (d) revised, 58 FR 54504, Oct. 22, 1993, effective Jan. 3, 1994; para. (a) amended, 60 FR 20195, Apr. 25, 1995, effective June 8, 1995; para. (h) added, 61 FR 56439, Nov. 1, 1996, effective Dec. 2, 1996; paras. (d) & (f) revised, 62 FR 53131, Oct. 10, 1997, effective Dec. 1, 1997; paras. (c)-(f) removed and reserved and para. (i) added, 65 FR 54604, Sept. 8, 2000, effective Nov. 7, 2000; para. (c) revised, 65 FR 57024, Sept. 20, 2000, effective Nov. 29, 2000; para. (j) added, 68 FR 14332, Mar. 25, 2003, effective May 1, 2003; para. (k) added, 68 FR 38611, June 30, 2003, effective July 30, 2003; para. (g) revised, 69 FR 49959, Aug. 12, 2004, effective Sept. 13, 2004; para. (j) revised, 73 FR 47650, Aug. 14, 2008, effective Sept. 15, 2008]

§ 1.10　　Filing of correspondence by "Express Mail."

(a)(1)Any correspondence received by the U.S. Patent and Trademark Office (USPTO) that was delivered by the "Express Mail Post Office to Addressee" service of the United States Postal Service (USPS) will be considered filed with the USPTO on the date of deposit with the USPS.

(2)　The date of deposit with USPS is shown by the "date in" on the "Express Mail" label or other official USPS notation. If the USPS deposit date cannot be determined, the correspondence will be accorded the USPTO receipt date as the filing date. See § 1.6(a).

(b)　Correspondence should be deposited directly with an employee of the USPS to ensure that the person depositing the correspondence receives a legible copy of the "Express Mail" mailing label with the "date-in" clearly marked. Persons dealing indirectly with the employees of the USPS (such as by deposit in an "Express Mail" drop box) do so at the risk of not receiving a copy of the "Express Mail" mailing label with the desired "date-in" clearly marked. The paper(s) or fee(s) that constitute the correspondence should also include the "Express Mail" mailing label number thereon. See paragraphs (c), (d) and (e) of this section.

(c)   Any person filing correspondence under this section that was received by the Office and delivered by the "Express Mail Post Office to Addressee" service of the USPS, who can show that there is a discrepancy between the filing date accorded by the Office to the correspondence and the date of deposit as shown by the "date-in" on the "Express Mail" mailing label or other official USPS notation, may petition the Director to accord the correspondence a filing date as of the "date-in" on the "Express Mail" mailing label or other official USPS notation, provided that:

(1)   The petition is filed promptly after the person becomes aware that the Office has accorded, or will accord, a filing date other than the USPS deposit date;

(2)   The number of the "Express Mail" mailing label was placed on the paper(s) or fee(s) that constitute the correspondence prior to the original mailing by "Express Mail;" and

(3)   The petition includes a true copy of the "Express Mail" mailing label showing the "date-in," and of any other official notation by the USPS relied upon to show the date of deposit.

(d)   Any person filing correspondence under this section that was received by the Office and delivered by the "Express Mail Post Office to Addressee" service of the USPS, who can show that the "date-in" on the "Express Mail" mailing label or other official notation entered by the USPS was incorrectly entered or omitted by the USPS, may petition the Director to accord the correspondence a filing date as of the date the correspondence is shown to have been deposited with the USPS, provided that:

(1)   The petition is filed promptly after the person becomes aware that the Office has accorded,

or will accord, a filing date based upon an incorrect entry by the USPS;

(2)   The number of the "Express Mail" mailing label was placed on the paper(s) or fee(s) that constitute the correspondence prior to the original mailing by "Express Mail"; and

(3)   The petition includes a showing which establishes, to the satisfaction of the Director, that the requested filing date was the date the correspondence was deposited in the "Express Mail Post Office to Addressee" service prior to the last scheduled pickup for that day. Any showing pursuant to this paragraph must be corroborated by evidence from the USPS or that came into being after deposit and within one business day of the deposit of the correspondence in the "Express Mail Post Office to Addressee" service of the USPS.

(e)   Any person mailing correspondence addressed as set out in § 1.1(a) to the Office with sufficient postage utilizing the "Express Mail Post Office to Addressee" service of the USPS but not received by the Office, may petition the Director to consider such correspondence filed in the Office on the USPS deposit date, provided that:

(1)   The petition is filed promptly after the person becomes aware that the Office has no evidence of receipt of the correspondence;

(2)   The number of the "Express Mail" mailing label was placed on the paper(s) or fee(s) that constitute the correspondence prior to the original mailing by "Express Mail";

(3)   The petition includes a copy of the originally deposited paper(s) or fee(s) that constitute the correspondence showing the number of the "Express Mail" mailing label thereon, a copy of any returned postcard receipt, a copy of the "Express Mail" mailing label showing the "date-in," a copy of any other official notation by the USPS relied upon to show the date of deposit, and, if the requested filing date is a date other than the "date-in" on the "Express Mail" mailing label or other official notation entered by the USPS, a showing pursuant to paragraph (d)(3) of this section that the requested filing date was the date the correspondence was deposited in the "Express Mail Post Office to Addressee" service prior to the last scheduled pickup for that day; and

(4)   The petition includes a statement which establishes, to the satisfaction of the Director, the

original deposit of the correspondence and that the copies of the correspondence, the copy of the "Express Mail" mailing label, the copy of any returned postcard receipt, and any official notation entered by the USPS are true copies of the originally mailed correspondence, original "Express Mail" mailing label, returned postcard receipt, and official notation entered by the USPS.

(f) The Office may require additional evidence to determine if the correspondence was deposited as "Express Mail" with the USPS on the date in question.

(g) Any person who mails correspondence addressed as set out in § 1.1 (a) to the Office with sufficient postage utilizing the "Express Mail Post Office to Addressee" service of the USPS, but has the correspondence returned by the USPS due to an interruption or emergency in "Express Mail" service, may petition the Director to consider such correspondence as filed on a particular date in the Office, provided that:

(1) The petition is filed promptly after the person becomes aware of the return of the correspondence;

(2) The number of the "Express Mail" mailing label was placed on the paper(s) or fee(s) that constitute the correspondence prior to the original mailing by "Express Mail";

(3) The petition includes the original correspondence or a copy of the original correspondence showing the number of the "Express Mail" mailing label thereon and a copy of the "Express Mail" mailing label showing the "date-in"; and

(4) The petition includes a statement which establishes, to the satisfaction of the Director, the original deposit of the correspondence and that the correspondence or copy of the correspondence is the original correspondence or a true copy of the correspondence originally deposited with the USPS on the requested filing date. The Office may require additional evidence to determine if the correspondence was returned by the USPS due to an interruption or emergency in "Express Mail" service.

(h) Any person who attempts to mail correspondence addressed as set out in § 1.1 (a) to the Office with sufficient postage utilizing the "Express Mail Post Office to Addressee" service of the USPS, but has the correspondence refused by an employee of the

USPS due to an interruption or emergency in "Express Mail" service, may petition the Director to consider such correspondence as filed on a particular date in the Office, provided that:

(1) The petition is filed promptly after the person becomes aware of the refusal of the correspondence;

(2) The number of the "Express Mail" mailing label was placed on the paper(s) or fee(s) that constitute the correspondence prior to the attempted mailing by "Express Mail";

(3) The petition includes the original correspondence or a copy of the original correspondence showing the number of the "Express Mail" mailing label thereon; and

(4) The petition includes a statement by the person who originally attempted to deposit the correspondence with the USPS which establishes, to the satisfaction of the Director, the original attempt to deposit the correspondence and that the correspondence or copy of the correspondence is the original correspondence or a true copy of the correspondence originally attempted to be deposited with the USPS on the requested filing date. The Office may require additional evidence to determine if the correspondence was refused by an employee of the USPS due to an interruption or emergency in "Express Mail" service.

(i) Any person attempting to file correspondence under this section that was unable to be deposited with the USPS due to an interruption or emergency in "Express Mail" service which has been so designated by the Director, may petition the Director to consider such correspondence as filed on a particular date in the Office, provided that:

(1) The petition is filed in a manner designated by the Director promptly after the person becomes aware of the designated interruption or emergency in "Express Mail" service;

(2) The petition includes the original correspondence or a copy of the original correspondence; and

(3) The petition includes a statement which establishes, to the satisfaction of the Director, that the correspondence would have been deposited with the USPS but for the designated interruption or emergency in "Express Mail" service, and that the correspondence or copy of the correspondence is the

original correspondence or a true copy of the correspondence originally attempted to be deposited with the USPS on the requested filing date.

[48 FR 2708, Jan. 20, 1983, added effective Feb. 27, 1983; 48 FR 4285, Jan. 31, 1983, paras. (a) & (c), 49 FR 552, Jan. 4, 1984, effective Apr. 1, 1984; paras. (a)-(c) revised and paras. (d) - (f) added, 61 FR 56439, Nov. 1, 1996, effective Dec. 2, 1996; paras. (d) & (e) revised, 62 FR 53131, Oct. 10, 1997, effective Dec. 1, 1997; para. (a) revised, 67 FR 36099, May 23, 2002, effective June 24, 2002; paras. (c), (d), (d)(3), (e) & (e)(4) revised, 68 FR 14332, Mar. 25, 2003, effective May 1, 2003; para. (a)(1) revised, 68 FR 48286, Aug. 13, 2003, effective Sept. 12, 2003; paras. (g) through (i) added, 69 FR 56481, Sept. 21, 2004, effective Sept. 21, 2004]

RECORDS AND FILES OF THE PATENT AND TRADEMARK OFFICE

§ 1.11 Files open to the public.

(a) The specification, drawings, and all papers relating to the file of: A published application; a patent; or a statutory invention registration are open to inspection by the public, and copies may be obtained upon the payment of the fee set forth in § 1.19(b)(2). If an application was published in redacted form pursuant to § 1.217, the complete file wrapper and contents of the patent application will not be available if: The requirements of paragraphs (d)(1), (d)(2), and (d)(3) of § 1.217 have been met in the application; and the application is still pending. See § 2.27 of this title for trademark files.

(b) All reissue applications, all applications in which the Office has accepted a request to open the complete application to inspection by the public, and related papers in the application file, are open to inspection by the public, and copies may be furnished upon paying the fee therefor. The filing of reissue applications, other than continued prosecution applications under § 1.53(d) of reissue applications, will be announced in the *Official Gazette*. The announcement shall include at least the filing date, reissue application and original patent numbers, title, class and subclass, name of the inventor, name of the owner of record, name of the attorney or agent of record, and examining group to which the reissue application is assigned.

(c) All requests for reexamination for which all the requirements of § 1.510 or § 1.915 have been satisfied will be announced in the *Official Gazette*. Any reexaminations at the initiative of the Director pursuant to § 1.520 will also be announced in the *Official Gazette*. The announcement shall include at least the date of the request, if any, the reexamination request control number or the Director initiated order control number, patent number, title, class and subclass, name of the inventor, name of the patent owner of record, and the examining group to which the reexamination is assigned.

(d) All papers or copies thereof relating to a reexamination proceeding which have been entered of record in the patent or reexamination file are open to inspection by the general public, and copies may be furnished upon paying the fee therefor.

(e) Except as prohibited in § 41.6 (b), the file of any interference is open to public inspection and copies of the file may be obtained upon payment of the fee therefor.

[42 FR 5593, Jan. 28, 1977; 43 FR 28477, June 30, 1978; 46 FR 29181, May 29, 1981, para. (c), 47 FR 41272, Sept. 17, 1982, effective Oct. 1, 1982; para. (a), 49 FR 48416, Dec. 12, 1984, effective Feb. 11, 1985; paras. (a), (b) and (e), 50 FR 9278, Mar. 7, 1985, effective May 8, 1985; para. (e) revised, 60 FR 14488, Mar. 17, 1995, effective Mar. 17, 1995; para. (b) revised, 62 FR 53131, Oct. 10, 1997, effective Dec. 1, 1997; para. (a) revised, 65 FR 57024, Sept. 20, 2000, effective Nov. 29, 2000; para. (c) revised, 68 FR 14332, Mar. 25, 2003, effective May 1, 2003; para. (e) revised, 69 FR 49959, Aug. 12, 2004, effective Sept. 13, 2004; para. (a) revised, 70 FR 56119, Sept. 26, 2005, effective Nov. 25, 2005; para. (c) revised, 71 FR 44219, Aug. 4, 2006, effective Aug. 4, 2006]

§ 1.12 Assignment records open to public inspection.

(a)(1) Separate assignment records are maintained in the United States Patent and Trademark Office for patents and trademarks. The assignment records, relating to original or reissue patents, including digests and indexes (for assignments recorded on or after May 1, 1957), and published patent applications are open to public inspection at the United States Patent and Trademark Office, and copies of patent assignment records may be obtained upon request and payment of the fee set forth in § 1.19 of this chapter.

See § 2.200 of this chapter regarding trademark assignment records.

(2) All records of assignments of patents recorded before May 1, 1957, are maintained by the National Archives and Records Administration (NARA). The records are open to public inspection. Certified and uncertified copies of those assignment records are provided by NARA upon request and payment of the fees required by NARA.

(b) Assignment records, digests, and indexes relating to any pending or abandoned patent application, which is open to the public pursuant to § 1.11 or for which copies or access may be supplied pursuant to § 1.14, are available to the public. Copies of any assignment records, digests, and indexes that are not available to the public shall be obtainable only upon written authority of the applicant or applicant's assignee or patent attorney or patent agent or upon a showing that the person seeking such information is a bona fide prospective or actual purchaser, mortgagee, or licensee of such application, unless it shall be necessary to the proper conduct of business before the Office or as provided in this part.

(c) Any request by a member of the public seeking copies of any assignment records of any pending or abandoned patent application preserved in confidence under § 1.14, or any information with respect thereto, must:

(1) Be in the form of a petition including the fee set forth in § 1.17(g); or

(2) Include written authority granting access to the member of the public to the particular assignment records from the applicant or applicant's assignee or attorney or agent of record.

(d) An order for a copy of an assignment or other document should identify the reel and frame number where the assignment or document is recorded. If a document is identified without specifying its correct reel and frame, an extra charge as set forth in § 1.21(j) will be made for the time consumed in making a search for such assignment.

[47 FR 41272, Sept. 17, 1982, effective Oct. 1, 1982; paras. (a) and (c), 54 FR 6893, Feb. 15, 1989, effective April 17, 1989; paras. (a) and (d), 56 FR 65142, Dec. 13, 1991, effective Dec. 16, 1991; paras. (a)(1) and (d), 57 FR 29641, July 6, 1992, effective Sept. 4, 1992; para. (a)(2) added, 57 FR 29641, July 6, 1992, effective Sept. 4, 1992; para. (c) amended, 60 FR 20195, Apr. 25, 1995, effective

June 8, 1995; para. (c) amended, 61 FR 42790, Aug. 19, 1996, effective Sept. 23, 1996; para. (c)(1) amended, 65 FR 54604, Sept. 8, 2000, effective Nov. 7, 2000; paras. (a)(1) and (b) revised, 65 FR 57024, Sept. 20, 2000, effective Nov. 29, 2000; paras. (a)(1) and (a)(2) revised, 68 FR 48286, Aug. 13, 2003, effective Sept. 12, 2003; para. (b) revised, 69 FR 29865, May 26, 2004, effective June 25, 2004; para. (c)(1) revised, 69 FR 56481, Sept. 21, 2004, effective Nov. 22, 2004]

§ 1.13　　Copies and certified copies.

(a) Non-certified copies of patents, patent application publications, and of any records, books, papers, or drawings within the jurisdiction of the United States Patent and Trademark Office and open to the public, will be furnished by the United States Patent and Trademark Office to any person, and copies of other records or papers will be furnished to persons entitled thereto, upon payment of the appropriate fee. See § 2.201 of this chapter regarding copies of trademark records.

(b) Certified copies of patents, patent application publications, and trademark registrations and of any records, books, papers, or drawings within the jurisdiction of the United States Patent and Trademark Office and open to the public or persons entitled thereto will be authenticated by the seal of the United States Patent and Trademark Office and certified by the Director, or in his or her name, upon payment of the fee for the certified copy.

[Revised, 58 FR 54504, Oct. 22, 1993, effective Jan. 3, 1994; revised, 65 FR 57024, Sept. 20, 2000, effective Nov. 29, 2000; para. (b) revised, 68 FR 14332, Mar. 25, 2003, effective May 1, 2003; revised, 68 FR 48286, Aug. 13, 2003, effective Sept. 12, 2003; para. (b) revised, 68 FR 70996, Dec. 22, 2003, effective Jan. 21, 2004]

§ 1.14　　Patent applications preserved in confidence.

(a) *Confidentiality of patent application information.* Patent applications that have not been published under 35 U.S.C. 122(b) are generally preserved in confidence pursuant to 35 U.S.C. 122(a). Information concerning the filing, pendency, or subject matter of an application for patent, including status information, and access to the application, will only be given to the public as set forth in § 1.11 or in this section.

(1) Records associated with patent applications (see paragraph (g) for international applications) may be available in the following situations:

(i) *Patented applications and statutory invention registrations.* The file of an application that has issued as a patent or published as a statutory invention registration is available to the public as set forth in §1.11(a). A copy of the patent application-as-filed, the file contents of the application, or a specific document in the file of such an application may be provided upon request and payment of the appropriate fee set forth in § 1.19(b).

(ii) *Published abandoned applications.* The file of an abandoned application that has been published as a patent application publication is available to the public as set forth in § 1.11(a). A copy of the application-as-filed, the file contents of the published application, or a specific document in the file of the published application may be provided to any person upon request, and payment of the appropriate fee set forth in § 1.19(b).

(iii) *Published pending applications.* A copy of the application-as-filed, the file contents of the application, or a specific document in the file of a pending application that has been published as a patent application publication may be provided to any person upon request, and payment of the appropriate fee set forth in § 1.19(b). If a redacted copy of the application was used for the patent application publication, the copy of the specification, drawings, and papers may be limited to a redacted copy. The Office will not provide access to the paper file of a pending application that has been published, except as provided in paragraph (c) or (i) of this section.

(iv) *Unpublished abandoned applications (including provisional applications) that are identified or relied upon.* The file contents of an unpublished, abandoned application may be made available to the public if the application is identified in a U.S. patent, a statutory invention registration, a U.S. patent application publication, or an international patent application publication of an international application that was published in accordance with PCT Article 21(2). An application is considered to have been identified in a document, such as a patent, when the application number or serial number and filing date, first named inventor, title and filing date or other application specific information are provided in the text of the patent, but not when the same identification is made in a paper in the file contents of the patent and is not included in the printed patent. Also, the file contents may be made available to the public, upon a written request, if benefit of the abandoned application is claimed under 35 U.S.C. 119(e), 120, 121, or 365 in an application that has issued as a U.S. patent, or has published as a statutory invention registration, a U.S. patent application publication, or an international patent application that was published in accordance with PCT Article 21(2). A copy of the application-as-filed, the file contents of the application, or a specific document in the file of the application may be provided to any person upon written request, and payment of the appropriate fee (§ 1.19(b)).

(v) *Unpublished pending applications (including provisional applications) whose benefit is claimed.* A copy of the file contents of an unpublished pending application may be provided to any person, upon written request and payment of the appropriate fee (§ 1.19(b)), if the benefit of the application is claimed under 35 U.S.C. 119(e), 120, 121, or 365 in an application that has issued as a U.S. patent, an application that has published as a statutory invention registration, a U.S. patent application publication, or an international patent application publication that was published in accordance with PCT Article 21(2). A copy of the application-as-filed, or a specific document in the file of the pending application may also be provided to any person upon written request, and payment of the appropriate fee (§ 1.19(b)). The Office will not provide access to the paper file of a pending application, except as provided in paragraph (c) or (i) of this section.

(vi) *Unpublished pending applications (including provisional applications) that are incorporated by reference or otherwise identified.* A copy of the application as originally filed of an unpublished pending application may be provided to any person, upon written request and payment of the appropriate fee (§ 1.19(b)), if the application is incorporated by reference or otherwise identified in a U.S. patent, a statutory invention registration, a U.S. patent application publication, or an international patent application publication that was published in accordance with PCT Article 21(2). The Office will not provide access to the paper file of a pending application, except as provided in paragraph (c) or (i) of this section.

(vii) *When a petition for access or a power to inspect is required.* Applications that were not published or patented, that are not the subject of a benefit claim under 35 U.S.C. 119(e), 120, 121, or 365 in an application that has issued as a U.S. patent, an application that has published as a statutory invention registration, a U.S. patent application publication, or an international patent application publication that was published in accordance with PCT Article 21(2), or are not identified in a U.S. patent, a statutory invention registration, a U.S. patent application publication, or an international patent application that was published in accordance with PCT Article 21(2), are not available to the public. If an application is identified in the file contents of another application, but not the published patent application or patent itself, a granted petition for access (see paragraph (i)) or a power to inspect (see paragraph (c)) is necessary to obtain the application, or a copy of the application.

(2) Information concerning a patent application may be communicated to the public if the patent application is identified in a published patent document or in an application as set forth in paragraphs (a)(1)(i) through (a)(1)(vi) of this section. The information that may be communicated to the public (*i.e.,* status information) includes:

(i) Whether the application is pending, abandoned, or patented;

(ii) Whether the application has been published under 35 U.S.C. 122(b);

(iii) The application "numerical identifier" which may be:

(A) The eight-digit application number (the two-digit series code plus the six-digit serial number); or

(B) The six-digit serial number plus any one of the filing date of the national application, the international filing date, or date of entry into the national stage; and

(iv) Whether another application claims the benefit of the application (*i.e.,* whether there are any applications that claim the benefit of the filing date under 35 U.S.C. 119(e), 120, 121 or 365 of the application), and if there are any such applications, the numerical identifier of the application, the specified relationship between the applications (*e.g.,* continua-

tion), whether the application is pending, abandoned or patented, and whether the application has been published under 35 U.S.C. 122(b).

(b) *Electronic access to an application.* Where a copy of the application file or access to the application may be made available pursuant to this section, the Office may at its discretion provide access to only an electronic copy of the specification, drawings, and file contents of the application.

(c) *Power to inspect a pending or abandoned application.* Access to an application may be provided to any person if the application file is available, and the application contains written authority (*e.g.,* a power to inspect) granting access to such person. The written authority must be signed by:

(1) An applicant;

(2) An attorney or agent of record;

(3) An authorized official of an assignee of record (made of record pursuant to § 3.71 of this chapter); or

(4) A registered attorney or agent named in the papers accompanying the application papers filed under § 1.53 or the national stage documents filed under § 1.495, if an executed oath or declaration pursuant to § 1.63 or § 1.497 has not been filed.

(d) *Applications reported to Department of Energy.* Applications for patents which appear to disclose, purport to disclose or do disclose inventions or discoveries relating to atomic energy are reported to the Department of Energy, which Department will be given access to the applications. Such reporting does not constitute a determination that the subject matter of each application so reported is in fact useful or is an invention or discovery, or that such application in fact discloses subject matter in categories specified by 42 U.S.C. 2181(c) and (d).

(e) *Decisions by the Director.* Any decision by the Director that would not otherwise be open to public inspection may be published or made available for public inspection if:

(1) The Director believes the decision involves an interpretation of patent laws or regulations that would be of precedential value; and

(2) The applicant is given notice and an opportunity to object in writing within two months on the ground that the decision discloses a trade secret or other confidential information. Any objection must identify the deletions in the text of the decision con-

sidered necessary to protect the information, or explain why the entire decision must be withheld from the public to protect such information. An applicant or party will be given time, not less than twenty days, to request reconsideration and seek court review before any portions of a decision are made public under this paragraph over his or her objection.

(f) *Publication pursuant to § 1.47.* Information as to the filing of an application will be published in the *Official Gazette* in accordance with § 1.47(c).

(g) *International applications.* (1) Copies of international application files for international applications which designate the U.S. and which have been published in accordance with PCT Article 21(2), or copies of a document in such application files, will be furnished in accordance with PCT Articles 30 and 38 and PCT Rules 94.2 and 94.3, upon written request including a showing that the publication of the application has occurred and that the U.S. was designated, and upon payment of the appropriate fee (see § 1.19(b)), if:

(i) With respect to the Home Copy (the copy of the international application kept by the Office in its capacity as the Receiving Office, see PCT Article 12(1)), the international application was filed with the U.S. Receiving Office;

(ii) With respect to the Search Copy (the copy of an international application kept by the Office in its capacity as the International Searching Authority, see PCT Article 12(1)), the U.S. acted as the International Searching Authority, except for the written opinion of the International Searching Authority which shall not be available until the expiration of thirty months from the priority date; or

(iii) With respect to the Examination Copy (the copy of an international application kept by the Office in its capacity as the International Preliminary Examining Authority), the United States acted as the International Preliminary Examining Authority, an International Preliminary Examination Report has issued, and the United States was elected.

(2) A copy of an English language translation of a publication of an international application which has been filed in the United States Patent and Trademark Office pursuant to 35 U.S.C. 154(d)(4) will be furnished upon written request including a showing that the publication of the application in accordance with PCT Article 21(2) has occurred and that the U.S.

was designated, and upon payment of the appropriate fee (§ 1.19(b)(4)).

(3) Access to international application files for international applications which designate the U.S. and which have been published in accordance with PCT Article 21(2), or copies of a document in such application files, will be permitted in accordance with PCT Articles 30 and 38 and PCT Rules 44*ter.*1, 94.2 and 94.3, upon written request including a showing that the publication of the application has occurred and that the U.S. was designated.

(4) In accordance with PCT Article 30, copies of an international application-as-filed under paragraph (a) of this section will not be provided prior to the international publication of the application pursuant to PCT Article 21(2).

(5) Access to international application files under paragraphs (a)(1)(i) through (a)(1)(vi) and (g)(3) of this section will not be permitted with respect to the Examination Copy in accordance with PCT Article 38.

(h) *Access by a Foreign Intellectual Property Office.*

(1) Access to the application-as-filed may be provided to any foreign intellectual property office participating with the Office in a bilateral or multilateral priority document exchange agreement (participating foreign intellectual property office), if the application contains written authority granting such access. Written authority under this paragraph should be submitted prior to filing a subsequent foreign application with a participating intellectual property office in which priority is claimed to the patent application.

(2) Written authority provided under paragraph (h)(1) of this section must include the title of the invention (§ 1.71(a)), comply with the requirements of paragraph (c) of this section, and be submitted on a separate document (§ 1.4(c)).

(3) Written authority provided under paragraph (h)(1) of this section will be treated as authorizing the Office to provide to all participating foreign intellectual property offices indicated in the written authority in accordance with their respective agreements with the Office:

(i) A copy of the application-as-filed; and

(ii) A copy of the application-as-filed with respect to any application the filing date of which is claimed by the application in which written authority under paragraph (h)(1) of this section is filed.

(i) *Access or copies in other circumstances.* The Office, either *sua sponte* or on petition, may also provide access or copies of all or part of an application if necessary to carry out an Act of Congress or if warranted by other special circumstances. Any petition by a member of the public seeking access to, or copies of, all or part of any pending or abandoned application preserved in confidence pursuant to paragraph (a) of this section, or any related papers, must include:

(1) The fee set forth in § 1.17(g); and

(2) A showing that access to the application is necessary to carry out an Act of Congress or that special circumstances exist which warrant petitioner being granted access to all or part of the application.

[42 FR 5593, Jan. 28, 1977; 43 FR 20462, May 11, 1978; para. (e) added, 47 FR 41273, Sept. 17, 1982, effective Oct. 1, 1982; para. (b), 49 FR 552, Jan. 4, 1984, effective Apr. 1, 1984; para. (d), 49 FR 48416, Dec. 12, 1984, effective Feb. 11, 1985; para. (b), 50 FR 9378, Mar. 7, 1985, effective May 8, 1985; 53 FR 23733, June 23, 1988; para. (e), 54 FR 6893, Feb. 15, 1989, effective April 17, 1989; para. (b) revised, 58 FR 54504, Oct. 22, 1993, effective Jan. 3, 1994; para. (e) amended, 60 FR 20195, Apr. 25, 1995, effective June 8, 1995; paras. (a), (b) and (e) amended, 61 FR 42790, Aug. 19, 1996, effective Sept. 23, 1996; para. (a) revised & para. (f) added, 62 FR 53131, Oct. 10, 1997, effective Dec. 1, 1997; para. (g) added, 63 FR 29614, June 1, 1998, effective July 1, 1998, (adopted as final, 63 FR 66040, Dec. 1, 1998); revised, 65 FR 54604, Sept. 8, 2000, effective Nov. 7, 2000; paras. (a), (b), (c), (e), (i) and (j) revised, 65 FR 57024, Sept. 20, 2000, effective Nov. 29, 2000; para (h) corrected, 65 FR 78958, Dec. 18, 2000; para.(i)(2) revised, 66 FR 67087, Dec. 28, 2001, effective Dec. 28, 2001; para. (d)(4) revised, 67 FR 520, Jan. 4, 2002, effective Apr. 1, 2002; paras. (g) & (g)(1) revised, 68 FR 14332, Mar. 25, 2003, effective May 1, 2003; revised, 68 FR 38611, June 30, 2003, effective July 30, 2003; paras. (g)(1)(ii) & (g)(3) revised, 68 FR 59881, Oct. 20, 2003, effective Jan. 1, 2004; para. (g)(1)(ii) corrected, 68 FR 67805, Dec., 4, 2003; para. (g)(5) revised, 68 FR 67805, Dec. 4, 2003, effective Jan. 1, 2004; para. (g)(2) revised, 68 FR 70996, Dec. 22, 2003, effective Jan. 21, 2004; para. (e) revised, 69 FR 49959, Aug. 12, 2004, effective Sept. 13, 2004; para. (h)(1) revised, 69 FR 56481, Sept.

21, 2004, effective Nov. 22, 2004; paras. (a)(1)(iii), (a)(1)(v), (a)(1)(vi), (a)(1)(vii), (a)(2) introductory text, & (b) revised, para. (h) redesignated as para. (i) and para. (h) added, 72 FR 1664, Jan. 16, 2007, effective Jan. 16, 2007]

§ 1.15   **[Reserved]**
(Editor's note: substance supplanted by Part 102)

[32 FR 13812, Oct. 4, 1967; 34 FR 18857, Nov. 26, 1969; amended 53 FR 47685, Nov. 25, 1988, effective Dec. 30, 1988; removed and reserved, 68 FR 14332, Mar. 25, 2003, effective May 1, 2003]

FEES AND PAYMENT OF MONEY

§ 1.16   National application filing, search, and examination fees.

(a) Basic fee for filing each application under 35 U.S.C. 111 for an original patent, except design, plant, or provisional applications:

(1) For an application filed on or after December 8, 2004:

By a small entity (§ 1.27(a)) if the application is submitted in compliance with the Office electronic filing system

(§ 1.27(b)(2)) $82.00
By a small entity (§ 1.27(a)). . . . $165.00
By other than a small entity $330.00

(2) For an application filed before December 8, 2004:

By a small entity (§ 1.27(a)). . . . $425.00
By other than a small entity $850.00

(b) Basic fee for filing each application for an original design patent:

(1) For an application filed on or after December 8, 2004:

By a small entity (§ 1.27(a)). . . . $110.00
By other than a small entity $220.00

(2) For an application filed before December 8, 2004:

By a small entity (§ 1.27(a)). . . . $190.00
By other than a small entity $380.00

(c) Basic fee for filing each application for an original plant patent:

(1) For an application filed on or after December 8, 2004:

By a small entity (§ 1.27(a)). . . . $110.00
By other than a small entity $220.00

(2) For an application filed before December 8, 2004:

By a small entity (§ 1.27(a)) . . . $300.00
By other than a small entity $600.00

(d) Basic fee for filing each provisional application:

By a small entity (§ 1.27(a)) $110.00
By other than a small entity $220.00

(e) Basic fee for filing each application for the reissue of a patent:

(1) For an application filed on or after December 8, 2004:

By a small entity (§ 1.27(a)) . . . $165.00
By other than a small entity $330.00

(2) For an application filed before December 8, 2004:

By a small entity (§ 1.27(a)) . . . $425.00
By other than a small entity $850.00

(f) Surcharge for filing any of the basic filing fee, the search fee, the examination fee, or the oath or declaration on a date later than the filing date of the application, except provisional applications:

By a small entity (§ 1.27(a)) $65.00
By other than a small entity $130.00

(g) Surcharge for filing the basic filing fee or cover sheet (§ 1.51(c)(1)) on a date later than the filing date of the provisional application::

By a small entity (§ 1.27(a)) $25.00
By other than a small entity $50.00

(h) In addition to the basic filing fee in an application, other than a provisional application, for filing or later presentation at any other time of each claim in independent form in excess of 3:

By a small entity (§ 1.27(a)) $110.00
By other than a small entity $220.00

(i) In addition to the basic filing fee in an application, other than a provisional application, for filing or later presentation at any other time of each claim (whether dependent or independent) in excess of 20 (note that § 1.75(c) indicates how multiple dependent claims are considered for fee calculation purposes):

By a small entity (§ 1.27(a)) $26.00
By other than a small entity $52.00

(j) In addition to the basic filing fee in an application, other than a provisional application, that contains, or is amended to contain, a multiple dependent claim, per application:

By a small entity (§ 1.27(a)) . . . $195.00

By other than a small entity $390.00

(k) Search fee for each application filed under 35 U.S.C. 111 on or after December 8, 2004, for an original patent, except design, plant, or provisional applications:

By a small entity (§ 1.27(a)) . . . $270.00
By other than a small entity $540.00

(l) Search fee for each application filed on or after December 8, 2004, for an original design patent:

By a small entity (§ 1.27(a)) $50.00
By other than a small entity $100.00

(m) Search fee for each application filed on or after December 8, 2004, for an original plant patent:

By a small entity (§ 1.27(a)) . . . $165.00
By other than a small entity $330.00

(n) Search fee for each application filed on or after December 8, 2004, for the reissue of a patent:

By a small entity (§ 1.27(a)) . . . $270.00
By other than a small entity $540.00

(o) Examination fee for each application filed under 35 U.S.C. 111 on or after December 8, 2004, for an original patent, except design, plant, or provisional applications:

By a small entity (§ 1.27(a)) . . . $110.00
By other than a small entity $220.00

(p) Examination fee for each application filed on or after December 8, 2004, for an original design patent:

By a small entity (§ 1.27(a)) $70.00
By other than a small entity $140.00

(q) Examination fee for each application filed on or after December 8, 2004, for an original plant patent:

By a small entity (§ 1.27(a)) $85.00
By other than a small entity $170.00

(r) Examination fee for each application filed on or after December 8, 2004, for the reissue of a patent:

By a small entity (§ 1.27(a)) . . . $325.00
By other than a small entity $650.00

(s) Application size fee for any application under 35 U.S.C. 111 filed on or after December 8, 2004, the specification and drawings of which exceed 100 sheets of paper, for each additional 50 sheets or fraction thereof:

By a small entity (§ 1.27(a)) . . . $135.00
By other than a small entity $270.00

[Added, 47 FR 41273, Sept. 17, 1982, effective date Oct. 1, 1982; 50 FR 31824, Aug. 6, 1985, effective date Oct. 5, 1985; paras. (a), (b), (d) - (i), 54 FR 6893, Feb. 15, 1989, effective Apr. 17, 1989; paras. (a)-(j), 56 FR 65142, Dec. 13, 1991, effective Dec. 16, 1991; paras. (a)-(d) and (f)-(j), 57 FR 38190, Aug. 21, 1992, effective Oct. 1, 1992; paras. (a), (b), (d) and (f)-(i), 59 FR 43736, Aug. 25, 1994, effective Oct. 1, 1994; paras. (a)-(g) amended and paras. (k) and (l) added, 60 FR 20195, Apr. 25, 1995, effective June 8, 1995; paras. (a), (b), (d), & (f)-(i) amended, 60 FR 41018, Aug. 11, 1995, effective Oct. 1, 1995; paras. (a), (b), (d), and (f)-(i) amended and para. (m) added, 61 FR 39585, July 30, 1996, effective Oct. 1, 1996; paras. (a), (b), (d), and (f) - (i) amended, 62 FR 40450, July 29, 1997, effective Oct. 1, 1997; paras. (d) & (l) amended, 62 FR 53131, Oct. 10, 1997, effective Dec. 1, 1997; paras. (a)-(d) and (f)-(j) revised, 63 FR 6758, Dec. 8, 1998, effective Nov. 10, 1998; paras. (a) and (b) revised, 64 FR 67774, Dec. 3, 1999, effective Dec. 29, 1999; paras. (a), (b), (d), and (f)-(i) revised, 65 FR 49193, Aug. 11, 2000, effective Oct. 1, 2000; paras. (a)-(l) revised, 65 FR 78958, Dec. 18, 2000; paras. (a), (b), (d), (f)-(i) and (k) revised, 66 FR 39447, July 31, 2001, effective Oct. 1, 2001; paras. (a), (g), and (h) revised, 67 FR 70847, Nov. 27, 2002, effective Jan. 1, 2003; paras. (a), (b), (d), and (f) through (i) revised, 68 FR 41532, July 14, 2003, effective Oct. 1, 2003; paras. (a), (b), (d), and (f) through (i) revised, 69 FR 52604, Aug. 27, 2004, effective Oct. 1, 2004; revised, 70 FR 3880, Jan. 27, 2005, effective Dec. 8, 2004; paras. (f) and (s) revised, 70 FR 30360, May 26, 2005, effective July 1, 2005; paras. (a) through (e) and (h) through (s) revised, 72 FR 46899, Aug. 22, 2007, effective Sept. 30, 2007; paras. (a) through (e), (h) through (k), and (m) through (s) revised, 73 FR 47534, Aug. 14, 2008, effective Oct. 2, 2008]

§ 1.17   Patent application and reexamination processing fees.

(a)   Extension fees pursuant to § 1.136(a):

  (1)   For reply within first month:

    By a small entity (§ 1.27(a)) $65.00

    By other than a small entity $130.00

  (2)   For reply within second month:

    By a small entity (§ 1.27(a)) . . . $245.00

    By other than a small entity $490.00

  (3)   For reply within third month:

    By a small entity (§ 1.27(a)) . . . $555.00

    By other than a small entity . . . $1,110.00

  (4)   For reply within fourth month:

    By a small entity (§ 1.27(a)) . . . $865.00

    By other than a small entity . . . $1,730.00

  (5)   For reply within fifth month:

    By a small entity (§ 1.27(a)). . .$1,175.00

    By other than a small entity . . .$2,350.00

(b)   For fees in proceedings before the Board of Patent Appeals and Interferences, see § 41.20 of this title.

(c)   [Reserved]

(d)   [Reserved]

(e)   To request continued examination pursuant to § 1.114:

    By a small entity (§1.27(a)) $405.00

    By other than a small entity $810.00

(f)   For filing a petition under one of the following sections which refers to this paragraph: . . . . . . $400.00.

   § 1.36(a)—for revocation of a power of attorney by fewer than all of the applicants.

   § 1.53(e)—to accord a filing date.

   § 1.57(a)—to accord a filing date.

   § 1.182—for decision on a question not specifically provided for.

   § 1.183—to suspend the rules.

   § 1.378(e)—for reconsideration of decision on petition refusing to accept delayed payment of maintenance fee in an expired patent.

   § 1.741(b)—to accord a filing date to an application under § 1.740 for extension of a patent term.

(g)   For filing a petition under one of the following sections which refers to this paragraph: . . . $200.00

   § 1.12—for access to an assignment record.

   § 1.14—for access to an application.

   § 1.47—for filing by other than all the inventors or a person not the inventor.

   § 1.59—for expungement of information.

   § 1.103(a)—to suspend action in an application.

   § 1.136(b)—for review of a request for extension for extension of time when the provisions of § 1.136 (a) are not available.

   § 1.295—for review of refusal to publish a statutory invention registration.

   § 1.296—to withdraw a request for publication of a statutory invention registration filed on or after the date the notice of intent to publish issued.

   § 1.377—for review of decision refusing to accept and record payment of a maintenance fee filed prior to expiration of a patent.

   § 1.550(c)—for patent owner requests for extension of time in *ex parte* reexamination proceedings.

§ 1.956—for patent owner requests for extension of time in *inter partes* reexamination proceedings.

§ 5.12—for expedited handling of a foreign filing license.

§ 5.15—for changing the scope of a license.

§ 5.25—for retroactive license.

(h)   For filing a petition under one of the following sections which refers to this paragraph . . $130.00

§ 1.19(g)—to request documents in a form other than provided in this part.

§ 1.84—for accepting color drawings or photographs.

§ 1.91—for entry of a model or exhibit.

§ 1.102(d)—to make an application special.

§ 1.138(c)—to expressly abandon an application to avoid publication.

§ 1.313—to withdraw an application from issue.

§ 1.314—to defer issuance of a patent.

(i)   Processing fee for taking action under one of the following sections which refers to this paragraph: $130.00

§ 1.28(c)(3)—for processing a non-itemized fee deficiency based on an error in small entity status.

§ 1.41—for supplying the name or names of the inventor or inventors after the filing date without an oath or declaration as prescribed by § 1.63, except in provisional applications.

§ 1.48—for correcting inventorship, except in provisional applications.

§ 1.52(d)—for processing a nonprovisional application filed with a specification in a language other than English.

§ 1.53(b)(3)—to convert a provisional application filed under § 1.53(c) into a nonprovisional application under § 1.53(b).

§ 1.55—for entry of late priority papers.

§1.71(g)(2)—for processing a belated amendment under § 1.71(g).

§ 1.99(e)—for processing a belated submission under § 1.99.

§ 1.103(b)—for requesting limited suspension of action, continued prosecution application for a design patent (§ 1.53(d)).

§ 1.103(c)—for requesting limited suspension of action, request for continued examination (§ 1.114).

§ 1.103(d)—for requesting deferred examination of an application.

§ 1.217—for processing a redacted copy of a paper submitted in the file of an application in which a redacted copy was submitted for the patent application publication.

§ 1.221—for requesting voluntary publication or republication of an application.

§ 1.291(c)(5)—for processing a second or subsequent protest by the same real party in interest.

§ 1.497(d)—for filing an oath or declaration pursuant to 35 U.S.C. 371(c)(4) naming an inventive entity different from the inventive entity set forth in the international stage.

§ 3.81—for a patent to issue to assignee, assignment submitted after payment of the issue fee.

(j)   For filing a petition to institute a public use proceeding under § 1.292. . . . . $1,510.00

(k)   For filing a request for expedited examination under § 1.155(a) $900.00

(l)   For filing a petition for the revival of an unavoidably abandoned application under 35 U.S.C. 111, 133, 364, or 371, for the unavoidably delayed payment of the issue fee under 35 U.S.C. 151, or for the revival of an unavoidably terminated reexamination proceeding under 35 U.S.C. 133 (§ 1.137(a)):

By a small entity (§ 1.27(a)) . . . $270.00

By other than a small entity $540.00

(m)   For filing a petition for the revival of an unintentionally abandoned application, for the unintentionally delayed payment of the fee for issuing a patent, or for the revival of an unintentionally terminated reexamination proceeding under 35 U.S.C. 41(a)(7) (§ 1.137 (b)):

By a small entity (§ 1.27(a)) . . . $810.00

By other than a small entity . . $1,620.00.

(n)   For requesting publication of a statutory invention registration prior to the mailing of the first examiner's action pursuant to § 1.104 . . . . . . $920.00 reduced by the amount of the application basic filing fee paid.

(o)   For requesting publication of a statutory invention registration after the mailing of the first examiner's action pursuant to § 1.104 . . . . . $1,840.00 reduced by the amount of the application basic filing fee paid.

(p) For an information disclosure statement under § 1.97(c) or (d) or a submission under § 1.99 .... $180.00

(q) Processing fee for taking action under one of the following sections which refers to this paragraph $50.00

§ 1.41—to supply the name or names of the inventor or inventors after the filing date without a cover sheet as prescribed by § 1.51(c)(1) in a provisional application

§ 1.48—for correction of inventorship in a provisional application.

§ 1.53(c)(2) —to convert a nonprovisional application filed under § 1.53(b) to a provisional application under § 1.53(c).

(r) For entry of a submission after final rejection under § 1.129(a):

By a small entity (§ 1.27(a)) ... $405.00
By other than a small entity $810.00

(s) For each additional invention requested to be examined under § 1.129(b):

By a small entity (§ 1.27(a)) ... $405.00
By other than a small entity $810.00

(t) For the acceptance of an unintentionally delayed claim for priority under 35 U.S.C. 119, 120, 121, or 365(a) or (c) (§§ 1.55 and 1.78) or for filing a request for the restoration of the right of priority under § 1.452........................ $1,410.00

[Added 47 FR 41273, Sept. 17, 1982, effective Oct. 1, 1982; para. (h), 48 FR 2708, Jan. 20, 1983, effective Feb. 27, 1983; para. (h), 49 FR 13461, Apr. 4, 1984, effective June 4, 1984; para. (h), 49 FR 34724, Aug. 31, 1984, effective Nov. 1, 1984; paras. (e), (g), (h) and (i), 49 FR 48416, Dec. 12, 1984, effective Feb. 11, 1985; paras. (h), (n) and (c), 50 FR 9379, Mar. 7, 1985, effective May 8, 1985; 50 FR 31824, Aug. 6, 1985, effective Oct. 5, 1985; paras. (a)-(m), 54 FR 6893, Feb. 15, 1989, 54 FR 9431, March 7, 1989, effective Apr. 17, 1989; para. (i)(1), 54 FR 47518, Nov. 15, 1989, effective Jan. 16, 1990; paras. (a)-(o), 56 FR 65142, Dec. 13, 1991, effective Dec. 16, 1991; para. (i)(1), 57 FR 2021, Jan. 17, 1992, effective March 16, 1992; para. (p) added, 57 FR 2021, Jan. 17, 1992, effective March 16, 1992; para. (i)(1), 57 FR 29642, July 6, 1992, effective Sept. 4, 1992; corrected 57 FR 32439, July 22, 1992; paras. (b)-(g), (j), and (m)-(o), 57 FR 38190, Aug. 21, 1992, effective Oct. 1, 1992; para. (h), 58 FR 38719, July 20, 1993, effective Oct. 1, 1993; paras. (b)-(g), (j) and (m)-(p), 59 FR 43736, Aug. 25, 1994, effective Oct. 1, 1994; paras. (h) & (i) amended and paras. (q)-(s) added, 67 FR 20195, Apr. 25, 1995, effective June 8, 1995; paras. (b)-(g), (j), (m)-(p),

(r) & (s) amended, 60 FR 41018, Aug. 11, 1995, effective Oct. 1, 1995; paras. (b)-(g), (j), (m)-(p), (r) and (s) amended, 61 FR 39585, July 30, 1996, effective Oct. 1, 1996; paras. (b)-(g), (j), (m)-(p), (r) & (s) amended, 62 FR 40450, July 29, 1997, effective Oct. 1, 1997; paras. (a) -(d), (h), (i) & (q) revised, paras. (e)-(g) reserved, 62 FR 53131, Oct. 10, 1997, effective Dec. 1, 1997; para. (q) corrected, 62 FR 61235, Nov. 17, 1997, effective Dec. 1, 1997; paras. (a)-(d), (l) and (m) revised, 63 FR 67578, Dec. 8, 1998, effective Nov. 10, 1998; paras. (r) and (s) revised, 63 FR 67578, Dec. 8, 1998, effective Dec. 8, 1998; paras. (r) and (s) revised, 64 FR 67774, Dec. 3, 1999, effective Jan. 10, 2000; para. (e) added and para. (i) revised, 65 FR 14865, Mar. 20, 2000, effective May 29, 2000 (adopted as final, 65 FR 50092, Aug. 16, 2000); paras. (a)-(e), (m), (r) and (s) revised, 65 FR 49193, August 11, 2000, effective October 1, 2000; paras. (h), (i), (k), (l), (m), (p), and (q) revised, 65 FR 54604, Sept. 8, 2000, effective Nov. 7, 2000; heading and paras. (h), (i), (l), (m) and (p) revised, 65 FR 57024, Sept. 20, 2000, effective Nov. 29, 2000; para. (t) added, 65 FR 57024, Sept. 20, 2000, effective Nov. 29, 2000; paras. (a)-(e), (r) and (s) revised, 65 FR 78958, Dec. 18, 2000; heading and para. (h) revised, 66 FR 47387, Sept. 12, 2001, effective Sept. 12, 2001; paras. (a)(2)-(a)(5), (b)-(e), (m) and (r)-(t) revised, 66 FR 39447, July 31, 2001, effective Oct. 1, 2001; paras. (a)(2) through (a)(5), (e), (m), and (r) through (t) revised, 67 FR 70847, Nov. 27, 2002, effective Jan. 1, 2003; para. (h) revised, 68 FR 38611, June 30, 2003, effective July 30, 2003; paras. (a)(2) through (a)(5), (b) through (e), (m), and (r) through (t) revised, 68 FR 41532, July 14, 2003, effective Oct. 1, 2003; paras. (c) and (d) removed and reserved and paras. (b) and (h) revised, 69 FR 49959, Aug. 12, 2004, effective Sept. 13, 2004; paras. (a)(2) through (a)(5), (e), (m), and (r) through (t) revised, 69 FR 52604, Aug. 27, 2004, effective Oct. 1, 2004; paras. (f) and (g) added and paras. (h) and (i) revised, 69 FR 56481, Sept. 21, 2004, effective Nov. 22, 2004; paras. (a), (l) and (m) revised, 70 FR 3880, Jan. 27, 2005, effective Dec. 8, 2004; para. (i) revised, 70 FR 54259, Sept. 14, 2005, effective Sept. 14, 2005; para. (f) revised, 70 FR 56119, Sept. 26, 2005, effective Nov. 25, 2005; paras. (l) & (m) revised, 72 FR 18892, Apr. 16, 2007, effective May 16, 2007; paras. (a)(2) through (a)(5), (e), (l), (m), and (r) through (t) revised, 72 FR 46899, Aug. 22, 2007, effective Sept. 30, 2007; paras. (a)(4) and (a)(5) corrected, 72 FR 55055, Sept. 28, 2007, effective Sept. 30, 2007; para. (f) revised, 72 FR 46716, Aug. 21, 2007 (implementation enjoined and never became effective); para. (t) revised, 72 FR 51559, Sept. 10, 2007, and corrected 72 FR 57864, Oct. 11, 2007, effective Nov. 9, 2007; paras. (a), (l), and (m) revised, 73 FR 47534, Aug. 14, 2008, effective Oct. 2, 2008; para. (f) revised, 74 FR 52686, Oct. 14, 2009, effective Oct. 14, 2009 (to remove changes made by the final rules in 72 FR 46716 from the CFR)]

§ 1.18 Patent post allowance (including issue) fees.

(a) Issue fee for issuing each original patent, except a design or plant patent, or for issuing each reissue patent:

By a small entity (§ 1.27(a)) . . . $755.00
By other than a small entity . . . $1,510.00

(b) Issue fee for issuing an original design patent:

By a small entity (§ 1.27(a)) . . . $430.00
By other than a small entity. . . . $860.00

(c) Issue fee for issuing an original plant patent:
By a small entity (§ 1.27(a)) . . . $595.00
By other than a small entity . . . $1,190.00

(d) Publication fee $300.00

(e) For filing an application for patent term adjustment under § 1.705 . . . . $200.00

(f) For filing a request for reinstatement of all or part of the term reduced pursuant to § 1.704(b) in an application for patent term adjustment under § 1.705 . . . . $400.00

[Added, 47 FR 41273, Sept. 17, 1982, effective Oct. 1, 1982; 50 FR 31824, Aug. 6, 1985, effective Oct. 5, 1985; revised, 54 FR 6893, Feb. 15, 1989, effective Apr. 17, 1989; revised, 56 FR 65142, Dec. 13, 1991, effective Dec. 16, 1991; paras. (a)-(c), 57 FR 38190, Aug. 21, 1992, effective Oct. 1, 1992; revised, 59 FR 43736, Aug. 25, 1994, effective Oct. 1, 1994; amended, 60 FR 41018, Aug. 11, 1995, effective Oct. 1, 1995; amended, 61 FR 39585, July 30, 1996, effective Oct. 1, 1996; amended, 62 FR 40450, July 29, 1997, effective Oct. 1, 1997; amended, 63 FR 67578, Dec. 8, 1998, effective Nov. 10, 1998; revised, 65 FR 49193, Aug. 11, 2000, effective Oct. 1, 2000; heading revised and paras. (d)-(f) added, 65 FR 56366, Sept. 18, 2000, effective Nov. 17, 2000; para. (d) revised, 65 FR 57024, Sept. 20, 2000, effective Nov. 29, 2000; paras. (a)-(c) revised, 65 FR 78958, Dec. 18, 2000; paras. (a)-(c) revised, 66 FR 39447, July 31, 2001, effective Oct. 1, 2001; paras. (a) through (c) revised, 67 FR 70847, Nov. 27, 2002, effective Jan. 1, 2003; paras. (a) through (c) revised, 68 FR 41532, July 14, 2003, effective Oct. 1, 2003; paras. (a) through (c) revised, 69 FR 52604, Aug. 27, 2004, effective Oct. 1, 2004; paras. (a)-(c) revised, 70 FR 3880, Jan. 27, 2005, effective Dec. 8, 2004; paras. (a) through (c) revised, 72 FR 46899, Aug. 22, 2007, effective Sept. 30, 2007; paras. (a) through (c) revised, 73 FR 47534, Aug. 14, 2008, effective Oct. 2, 2008]

§ 1.19 Document supply fees.

The United States Patent and Trademark Office will supply copies of the following patent-related documents upon payment of the fees indicated. Paper copies will be in black and white unless the original document is in color, a color copy is requested and the fee for a color copy is paid.

(a) Uncertified copies of patent application publications and patents:

(1) Printed copy of the paper portion of a patent application publication or patent, including a design patent, statutory invention registration, or defensive publication document. Service includes preparation of copies by the Office within two to three business days and delivery by United States Postal Service; and preparation of copies by the Office within one business day of receipt and delivery to an Office Box or by electronic means (*e.g.*, facsimile, electronic mail) $3.00

(2) Printed copy of a plant patent in color $15.00

(3) Color copy of a patent (other than a plant patent) or statutory invention registration containing a color drawing $25.00

(b) Copies of Office documents to be provided in paper, or in electronic form, as determined by the Director (for other patent-related materials see § 1.21(k)):

(1) Copy of a patent application as filed, or a patent-related file wrapper and contents, stored in paper in a paper file wrapper, in an image format in an image file wrapper, or if color documents, stored in paper in an Artifact Folder:

(i) If provided on paper:

(A) Application as filed . . . . $20.00.

(B) File wrapper and contents of 400 or fewer pages . . . . $200.00.

(C) Additional fee for each additional 100 pages or portion thereof of file wrapper and contents . . . . $40.00.

(D) Individual application documents, other than application as filed, per document . $25.00.

(ii) If provided on compact disc or other physical electronic medium in single order:

(A) Application as filed . . . . $20.00.

(B) File wrapper and contents, first physical electronic medium: . . . . $55.00.

(C) Additional fee for each continuing physical electronic medium in the single order of paragraph (b)(1)(ii)(B) of this section: ...... $15.00.

(iii) If provided electronically (*e.g.*, by electronic transmission) other than on a physical electronic medium as specified in paragraph (b)(1)(ii) of this section:

(A) Application as filed: .... $20.00.

(B) File wrapper and contents: .. $55.00.

(iv) If provided to a foreign intellectual property office pursuant to a priority document exchange agreement (see § 1.14 (h)(1)) 0.00

(2) Copy of patent-related file wrapper contents that were submitted and are stored on compact disc or other electronic form (*e.g.*, compact discs stored in an Artifact Folder), other than as available in paragraph (b)(1) of this section:

(i) If provided on compact disc or other physical electronic medium in a single order:

(A) First physical electronic medium in a single order: .... $55.00.

(B) Additional fee for each continuing physical electronic medium in the single order of paragraph (b)(2)(i) of this section: .... $15.00.

(ii) If provided electronically other than on a physical electronic medium per order: ..... $55.00.

(3) Copy of Office records, except copies available under paragraph (b)(1) or (2) of this section: .... $25.00.

(4) For assignment records, abstract of title and certification, per patent: .... $25.00.

(c) Library service (35 U.S.C. 13): For providing to libraries copies of all patents issued annually, per annum $50.00

(d) For list of all United States patents and statutory invention registrations in a subclass..... $3.00

(e) Uncertified statement as to status of the payment of maintenance fees due on a patent or expiration of a patent........................ $10.00

(f) Uncertified copy of a non-United States patent document, per document........... $25.00

(g) Petitions for documents in a form other than that provided by this part, or in a form other than that generally provided by the Director, will be decided in accordance with the merits of each situation. Any petition seeking a decision under this section must be accompanied by the petition fee set forth in § 1.17 (h)

and, if the petition is granted, the documents will be provided at cost.

(h) [Reserved]

[Added 47 FR 41273, Sept. 17, 1982, effective date Oct. 1, 1982; para. (b), 49 FR 552, Jan. 4, 1984, effective date Apr. 1, 1984; paras. (f) and (g) added, 49 FR 34724, Aug. 31, 1984, effective date Nov. 1, 1984; paras. (a) and (c), 50 FR 9379, Mar. 7, 1985, effective date May 8,1985; 50 FR 31825, Aug. 6, 1985, effective date Oct. 5, 1985; revised, 54 FR 6893, Feb. 15, 1989; 54 FR 9432, March 7, 1989, effective Apr. 17, 1989, revised 56 FR 65142, Dec. 13, 1991, effective Dec. 16, 1991; paras. (b)(4), (f) and (h),57 FR 38190, Aug. 21, 1992, effective Oct.1, 1992; para. (a)(3), 58 FR 38719, July 20, 1993, effective Oct. 1, 1993; paras. (a)(1)(ii), (a)(1)(iii), (b)(1)(i), & (b)(1)(ii) amended, 60 FR 41018, Aug. 11, 1995, effective Oct. 1, 1995; paras. (a)(2) and (a)(3) amended, 62 FR 40450, July 29, 1997, effective Oct. 1, 1997; paras. (a)(1)(i) through (a)(1)(iii) revised, 64 FR 67486, Dec. 2, 1999, effective Dec. 2, 1999; introductory text and paras. (a) and (b) revised, 65 FR 54604, Sept. 8, 2000, effective Nov. 7, 2000; paras. (g) and (h) removed and reserved, 65 FR 54604, Sept. 8, 2000, effective Nov. 7, 2000; para. (a) revised, 65 FR 57024, Sept. 20, 2000, effective Nov. 29, 2000; paras. (a)(1) and (b)(1) revised, 67 FR 70847, Nov. 27, 2002, effective Jan. 1, 2003; introductory text and para. (b) revised and para. (g) added, 69 FR 56481, Sept. 21, 2004, effective Nov. 22, 2004; para. (b)(1)(iv) added, 72 FR 1664, Jan. 16, 2007, effective Jan. 16, 2007]

§ 1.20   Post issuance fees.

(a) For providing a certificate of correction for applicant's mistake (§ 1.323)............. $100.00

(b) Processing fee for correcting inventorship in a patent (§ 1.324)...................... $130.00

(c) In reexamination proceedings

(1) For filing a request for *ex parte* reexamination (§ 1.510(a))..................... $2,520.00

(2) For filing a request for *inter partes* reexamination (§ 1.915(a))................. $8,800.00

(3) For filing with a request for reexamination or later presentation at any other time of each claim in independent form in excess of 3 and also in excess of the number of claims in independent form in the patent under reexamination:

By a small entity (§ 1.27(a)).. $110.00

By other than a small entity .. $220.00

(4) For filing with a request for reexamination or later presentation at any other time of each

claim (whether dependent or independent) in excess of 20 and also in excess of the number of claims in the patent under reexamination (note that § 1.75(c) indicates how multiple dependent claims are considered for fee calculation purposes):

By a small entity (§ 1.27 (a)). . $26.00

By other than a small entity . . . $52.00

(5) If the excess claims fees required by paragraphs (c)(3) and (c)(4) are not paid with the request for reexamination or on later presentation of the claims for which the excess claims fees are due, the fees required by paragraphs (c)(3) and (c)(4) must be paid or the claims canceled by amendment prior to the expiration of the time period set for reply by the Office in any notice of fee deficiency in order to avoid abandonment.

(d) For filing each statutory disclaimer (§ 1.321):

By a small entity (§ 1.27(a)) $70.00

By other than a small entity $140.00

(e) For maintaining an original or reissue patent, except a design or plant patent, based on an application filed on or after December 12, 1980, in force beyond four years, the fee being due by three years and six months after the original grant:

By a small entity (§ 1.27(a)) . . . $490.00

By other than a small entity $980.00

(f) For maintaining an original or reissue patent, except a design or plant patent, based on an application filed on or after December 12, 1980, in force beyond eight years, the fee being due by seven years and six months after the original grant:

By a small entity (§ 1.27(a)) . . $1,240.00

By other than a small entity . . . $2,480.00

(g) For maintaining an original or reissue patent, except a design or plant patent, based on an application filed on or after December 12, 1980, in force beyond twelve years, the fee being due by eleven years and six months after the original grant:

By a small entity (§ 1.27(a)) . . $2,055.00

By other than a small entity . . . $4,110.00

(h) Surcharge for paying a maintenance fee during the six-month grace period following the expiration of three years and six months, seven years and six months, and eleven years and six months after the date of the original grant of a patent based on an application filed on or after December 12, 1980:

By a small entity (§ 1.27(a)) $65.00

By other than a small entity $130.00

(i) Surcharge for accepting a maintenance fee after expiration of a patent for non-timely payment of a maintenance fee where the delay in payment is shown to the satisfaction of the Director to have been —

(1) Unavoidable $700.00

(2) Unintentional $1,640.00

(j) For filing an application for extension of the term of a patent

(1) Application for extension under § 1.740 . . . . $1,120.00

(2) Initial application for interim extension under § 1.790 . . . . $420.00

(3) Subsequent application for interim extension under § 1.790 . . . . $220.00

[Added 47 FR 41273, Sept. 17, 1982, effective date Oct. 1, 1982; paras. (k), (l) and (m) added, 49 FR 34724, Aug. 31, 1984, effective date Nov. 1, 1984; paras. (c), (f), (g) and (m), 50 FR 9379, Mar. 7, 1985, effective date May 8, 1985; 50 FR 31825, Aug. 6, 1985, effective date Oct. 5, 1985; 51 FR 28057, Aug. 4, 1986; 52 FR 9394, Mar. 24, 1987; paras. (a)-(n), 54 FR 6893, Feb. 15, 1989, 54 FR 8053, Feb. 24, 1989, effective Apr. 17, 1989; revised 56 FR 65142, Dec. 13, 1991, effective Dec. 16, 1991; paras. (a), (c), (e)-(g) and (i), 57 FR 38190, Aug. 21, 1992, effective Oct. 1, 1992; para. (i), 58 FR 44277, Aug. 20, 1993, effective Sept. 20, 1993; paras. (c), (e)-(g), (i)(1) and (j), 59 FR 43736, Aug. 25, 1994, effective Oct. 1, 1994; para. (j) revised, 60 FR 25615, May 12, 1995, effective July 11, 1995; paras. (c), (e)-(g), (i)(2), & (j)(1) amended, 60 FR 41018, Aug. 11, 1995, effective Oct. 1, 1995; paras. (a), (e) - (g), (i)(1), (i)(2), and (j)(1) -(j)(3) amended, 61 FR 39585, July 30, 1996, effective Oct. 1, 1996; paras. (c), (e) - (g), (i)(1), (i)(2), and (j)(1) - (j)(3) amended, 62 FR 40450, July 29, 1997, effective Oct. 1, 1997; paras. (d)-(g) revised, 63 FR 67578, Dec. 8, 1998, effective Nov. 10, 1998; para. (e) revised, 64 FR 67774, Dec. 3, 1999, effective Dec. 29, 1999; paras. (e)-(g) revised, 65 FR 49193, Aug. 11, 2000, effective Oct. 1, 2000; paras. (b) and (d)-(h) revised, 65 FR 78958, Dec. 18, 2000; para. (b) corrected, 65 FR 80755, Dec. 22, 2000; para. (c) revised, 65 FR 76756, Dec. 7, 2000, effective Feb. 5, 2001; paras. (e)-(g) revised, 66 FR 39447, July 31, 2001, effective Oct. 1, 2001; paras. (e) through (g) revised, 67 FR 70847, Nov. 27, 2002, effective Jan. 1, 2003; para. (i) revised, 68 FR 14332, Mar. 25, 2003, effective May 1, 2003; paras. (e) through (g) revised, 68 FR 41532, July 14, 2003, effective Oct. 1, 2003; paras. (e) through (g) revised, 69 FR 52604, Aug. 27, 2004, effective Oct. 1, 2004; paras. (c)-(g) revised, 70 FR 3880, Jan. 27, 2005, effective Dec. 8, 2004; paras. (c)(3), (c)(4), and (e) through (g) revised, 72 FR 46899, Aug. 22, 2007, effective

Sept. 30, 2007; paras. (c)(3),(c)(4), and (d) through (g) revised, 73 FR 47534, Aug. 14, 2008, effective Oct. 2, 2008]

§ 1.21   Miscellaneous fees and charges.

The Patent and Trademark Office has established the following fees for the services indicated:

(a)   Registration of attorneys and agents:

(1)   For admission to examination for registration to practice:

(i)   Application Fee (non-refundable) $40.00

(ii)   Registration examination fee

(A)   For test administration by commercial entity $200.00

(B)   For test administration by the USPTO $450.00

(2)   On registration to practice or grant of limited recognition under § 11.9(b) or (c)...... $100.00

(3)   [Reserved]

(4)   For certificate of good standing as an attorney or agent $10.00

(i)   Suitable for framing........ $20.00

(ii)   [Reserved]

(5)   For review of decision:

(i)   By the Director of Enrollment and Discipline under § 11.2(c) $130.00

(ii)   Of the Director of Enrollment and Discipline under § 11.2(d)................. $130.00

(6)   [Reserved]

(7)   Annual practitioner maintenance fee for registered attorney or agent.

(i)   Active Status $118.00

(ii)   Voluntary Inactive Status $25.00

(iii)   Fee for requesting restoration to active status from voluntary inactive status........ $50.00

(iv)   Balance due upon restoration to active status from voluntary inactive status........ $93.00

(8)   Annual practitioner maintenance fee for individual granted limited recognition $118.00

(9)(i)   Delinquency fee............ $50.00

(ii)   Administrative reinstatement fee $100.00

(10)   On application by a person for recognition or registration after disbarment or suspension on ethical grounds, or resignation pending disciplinary proceedings in any other jurisdiction; on application by a person for recognition or registration who is asserting rehabilitation from prior conduct that resulted in an adverse decision in the Office regarding the person's moral character; and on application by a person for recognition or registration after being convicted of a felony or crime involving moral turpitude or breach of fiduciary duty; on petition for reinstatement by a person excluded or suspended on ethical grounds, or excluded on consent from practice before the Office $1,600.00

(b)   Deposit accounts:

(1)   For establishing a deposit account $10.00

(2)   Service charge for each month when the balance at the end of the month is below $1,000   .... $25.00

(3)   Service charge for each month when the balance at the end of the month is below $300 for restricted subscription deposit accounts used exclusively for subscription order of patent copies as issued $25.00

(c)   [Reserved]

(d)   Delivery box: Local delivery box rental, per annum $50.00

(e)   International type search reports: For preparing an international type search report of an international type search made at the time of the first action on the merits in a national patent application $40.00

(f)   [Reserved]

(g)   Self-service copy charge, per page... $0.25

(h)   For recording each assignment, agreement, or other paper relating to the property in a patent or application, per property $40.00

(i)   Publication in *Official Gazette*: For publication in the *Official Gazette* of a notice of the availability of an application or a patent for licensing or sale:

Each application or patent $25.00

(j)   Labor charges for services, per hour or fraction thereof $40.00

(k)   For items and services that the Director finds may be supplied, for which fees are not specified by statute or by this part, such charges as may be determined by the Director with respect to each such item or service .... Actual cost

(l)   [Reserved]

(m)   For processing each payment refused (including a check returned "unpaid") or charged back by a financial institution $50.00

(n) For handling an application in which proceedings are terminated pursuant to § 1.53(e) $130.00

(o) [Reserved]

[Added 47 FR 41274, Sept. 17, 1982, effective date Oct. 1, 1982; paras. (b) and (l), 49 FR 553, Jan. 4, 1984, effective date Apr. 1, 1984; paras. (a)(5) and (6) added, 50 FR 5171, Feb. 6, 1985, effective date Apr. 8, 1985; 50 FR 31825, Aug. 6, 1985, effective date Oct. 5, 1985; paras. (a), (b)(1), (d)-(j), (l)-(m), 54 FR 6893, Feb. 15, 1989; 54 FR 8053, Feb. 24, 1989; 54 FR 9432, March 7, 1989, effective Apr. 17, 1989; para. (n) added 54 FR 47518, Nov. 15, 1989, effective Jan. 16, 1990; paras. (o)-(q) added 54 FR 50942, Dec. 11, 1989, effective Feb. 12, 1990; paras. (a)-(c), (e)-(h), (j)-(l) & (n) amended, 56 FR 65142, Dec. 13, 1991, effective Dec. 16, 1991; paras. (p) and (q) deleted, 56 FR 65142, Dec. 13, 1991, effective Dec. 16, 1991; paras. (a)(1), (a)(5), (a)(6), (b)(2), (b)(3), (e) and (i), 57 FR 38190, Aug. 21, 1992, effective Oct. 1, 1992; para. (p) added, 57 FR 38190, Aug. 21, 1992, effective Oct. 1, 1992; para. (p) deleted, 59 FR 43736, Aug. 25, 1994, effective Oct. 1, 1994; para. (l) amended, 60 FR 20195, Apr. 25, 1995, effective June 8, 1995; para. (a)(1) amended, 60 FR 41018, Aug. 11, 1995, effective Oct. 1, 1995; paras. (a)(1), (a)(3) and (a)(6) revised, 61 FR 39585, July 30, 1996, effective Oct. 1, 1996; paras. (a)(1)(ii), (a)(6), and (j) amended, 62 FR 40450, July 29, 1997, effective Oct. 1, 1997; paras. (l) & (n) revised, 62 FR 53131, Oct. 10, 1997, effective Dec. 1, 1997; para. (a)(6)(ii) revised, 63 FR 67578, Dec. 8, 1998, effective Dec. 8, 1998; para (m) revised, 65 FR 33452, May 24, 2000, effective July 24, 2000; para. (a)(6) revised, 65 FR 49193, Aug. 11, 2000, effective Oct. 1, 2000; para. (o) removed and reserved, 66 FR 39447, July 31, 2001, effective Oct. 1, 2001; para. (k) revised, 68 FR 14332, Mar. 25, 2003, effective May 1, 2003; para. (a) revised, 69 FR 35427, June 24, 2004, effective July 26, 2004; para. (l) removed and reserved, 70 FR 30360, May 26, 2005, effective July 1, 2005; para. (c) removed and reserved, 71 FR 64636, Nov. 3, 2006, effective Feb. 1, 2007; para. (a)(3) removed and reserved and paras. (a)(7), (a)(8) and (a)(9) added, 73 FR 67750, Nov. 17, 2008, effective Dec. 17, 2008]

§ 1.22 Fees payable in advance.

(a) Patent fees and charges payable to the United States Patent and Trademark Office are required to be paid in advance; that is, at the time of requesting any action by the Office for which a fee or charge is payable with the exception that under § 1.53 applications for patent may be assigned a filing date without payment of the basic filing fee.

(b) All fees paid to the United States Patent and Trademark Office must be itemized in each individual application, patent, or other proceeding in such a manner that it is clear for which purpose the fees are paid. The Office may return fees that are not itemized as required by this paragraph. The provisions of § 1.5(a) do not apply to the resubmission of fees returned pursuant to this paragraph.

[48 FR 2708, Jan. 20, 1983, effective Feb. 27, 1983; para. (b) revised, 65 FR 54604, Sept. 8, 2000, effective Nov. 7, 2000; revised, 68 FR 48286, Aug. 13, 2003, effective Sept. 12, 2003]

§ 1.23 Methods of payment.

(a) All payments of money required for United States Patent and Trademark Office fees, including fees for the processing of international applications (§ 1.445), shall be made in U.S. dollars and in the form of a cashier's or certified check, Treasury note, national bank notes, or United States Postal Service money order. If sent in any other form, the Office may delay or cancel the credit until collection is made. Checks and money orders must be made payable to the Director of the United States Patent and Trademark Office. (Checks made payable to the Commissioner of Patents and Trademarks will continue to be accepted.) Payments from foreign countries must be payable and immediately negotiable in the United States for the full amount of the fee required. Money sent to the Office by mail will be at the risk of the sender, and letters containing money should be registered with the United States Postal Service.

(b) Payments of money required for United States Patent and Trademark Office fees may also be made by credit card, except for replenishing a deposit account. Payment of a fee by credit card must specify the amount to be charged to the credit card and such other information as is necessary to process the charge, and is subject to collection of the fee. The Office will not accept a general authorization to charge fees to a credit card. If credit card information is provided on a form or document other than a form provided by the Office for the payment of fees by credit card, the Office will not be liable if the credit card number becomes public knowledge.

[43 FR 20462, May 11, 1978; revised, 64 FR 48900, Sept. 8, 1999, effective Oct. 30, 1999; revised, 65 FR 33452, May 24, 2000, effective June 5, 2000; para. (b) revised, 69 FR 43751, July 22, 2004, effective Aug. 23, 2004]

§ 1.24 [Reserved]

[47 FR 41274, Sept. 17, 1982, effective Oct. 1, 1982; 48 FR 2708, Jan. 20, 1983, effective date Feb. 27, 1983; 50 FR 31825, Aug. 6, 1985, effective Oct. 5, 1985; 51 FR 28057, Aug. 4, 1986; 56 FR 65142, Dec. 13, 1991, effective Dec. 16, 1991; para. (b) revised, 65 FR 54604, Sept. 8, 2000, effective Nov. 7, 2000; removed and reserved, 65 FR 57024, Sept. 20, 2000, effective Nov. 29, 2000]

§ 1.25 Deposit accounts.

(a) For the convenience of attorneys, and the general public in paying any fees due, in ordering services offered by the Office, copies of records, etc., deposit accounts may be established in the Patent and Trademark Office upon payment of the fee for establishing a deposit account § 1.21(b)(1)). A minimum deposit of $1,000 is required for paying any fee due or in ordering any services offered by the Office. However, a minimum deposit of $300 may be paid to establish a restricted subscription deposit account used exclusively for subscription order of patent copies as issued. At the end of each month, a deposit account statement will be rendered. A remittance must be made promptly upon receipt of the statement to cover the value of items or services charged to the account and thus restore the account to its established normal deposit value. An amount sufficient to cover all fees, services, copies, etc., requested must always be on deposit. Charges to accounts with insufficient funds will not be accepted. A service charge (§ 1.21(b)(2)) will be assessed for each month that the balance at the end of the month is below $1,000. For restricted subscription deposit accounts, a service charge (§ 1.21(b)(3)) will be assessed for each month that the balance at the end of the month is below $300.

(b) Filing, issue, appeal, international-type search report, international application processing, petition, and post-issuance fees may be charged against these accounts if sufficient funds are on deposit to cover such fees. A general authorization to charge all fees, or only certain fees, set forth in §§ 1.16 to 1.18 to a deposit account containing sufficient funds may be filed in an individual application, either for the entire pendency of the application or with a particular paper filed. An authorization to charge fees under § 1.16 in an international application entering the national stage under 35 U.S.C. 371 will be treated as an authorization to charge fees under § 1.492. An authorization to charge fees set forth in § 1.18 to a deposit account is subject to the provisions of § 1.311(b). An authorization to charge to a deposit account the fee for a request for reexamination pursuant to § 1.510 or § 1.913 and any other fees required in a reexamination proceeding in a patent may also be filed with the request for reexamination. An authorization to charge a fee to a deposit account will not be considered payment of the fee on the date the authorization to charge the fee is effective as to the particular fee to be charged unless sufficient funds are present in the account to cover the fee.

(c) A deposit account holder may replenish the deposit account by submitting a payment to the United States Patent and Trademark Office. A payment to replenish a deposit account must be submitted by one of the methods set forth in paragraphs (c)(1), (c)(2), (c)(3), or (c)(4) of this section.

(1) A payment to replenish a deposit account may be submitted by electronic funds transfer through the Federal Reserve Fedwire System, which requires that the following information be provided to the deposit account holder's bank or financial institution:

(i) Name of the Bank, which is Treas NYC (Treasury New York City);

(ii) Bank Routing Code, which is 021030004;

(iii) United States Patent and Trademark Office account number with the Department of the Treasury, which is 13100001; and

(iv) The deposit account holder's company name and deposit account number.

(2) A payment to replenish a deposit account may be submitted by electronic funds transfer over the Office's Internet Web site *(www.uspto.gov)*.

(3) A payment to replenish a deposit account may be addressed to: Director of the United States Patent and Trademark Office, Attn: Deposit Accounts, 2051 Jamieson Avenue, Suite 300, Alexandria, Virginia 22314.

[49 FR 553, Jan. 4, 1984, effective Apr. 1, 1984; 47 FR 41274, Sept. 17, 1982, effective Oct. 1,1982; 50 FR 31826,

Aug. 6, 1985, effective Oct. 5, 1985; para. (b) revised, 65 FR 54604, Sept. 8, 2000, effective Nov. 7, 2000; para (b) revised, 65 FR 76756, Dec. 7, 2000, effective Feb. 5, 2001; para. (b) revised, 67 FR 520, Jan. 4, 2002, effective Apr. 1, 2002; para. (c) added, 68 FR 14332, Mar. 25, 2003, effective May 1, 2003; para. (c)(2) revised, 69 FR 43751, July 22, 2004, effective Aug. 23, 2004; para. (c)(4) revised, 70 FR 56119, Sept. 26, 2005, effective Nov. 25, 2005; para. (c)(3) revised, para. (c)(4) removed, 73 FR 47534, Aug. 14, 2008, effective Oct. 2, 2008]

§ 1.26   Refunds.

(a)   The Director may refund any fee paid by mistake or in excess of that required. A change of purpose after the payment of a fee, such as when a party desires to withdraw a patent filing for which the fee was paid, including an application, an appeal, or a request for an oral hearing, will not entitle a party to a refund of such fee. The Office will not refund amounts of twenty-five dollars or less unless a refund is specifically requested, and will not notify the payor of such amounts. If a party paying a fee or requesting a refund does not provide the banking information necessary for making refunds by electronic funds transfer (31 U.S.C. 3332 and 31 CFR part 208), or instruct the Office that refunds are to be credited to a deposit account, the Director may require such information, or use the banking information on the payment instrument to make a refund. Any refund of a fee paid by credit card will be by a credit to the credit card account to which the fee was charged.

(b)   Any request for refund must be filed within two years from the date the fee was paid, except as otherwise provided in this paragraph or in § 1.28(a). If the Office charges a deposit account by an amount other than an amount specifically indicated in an authorization (§ 1.25(b)), any request for refund based upon such charge must be filed within two years from the date of the deposit account statement indicating such charge, and include a copy of that deposit account statement. The time periods set forth in this paragraph are not extendable.

(c)   If the Director decides not to institute a reexamination proceeding, for *ex parte* reexaminations filed under § 1.510, a refund of $1,690 will be made to the reexamination requester. For *inter partes* reexaminations filed under § 1.913, a refund of $7,970 will be made to the reexamination requester. The reexamination requester should indicate the form in which any refund should be made (*e.g.*, by check, electronic funds transfer, credit to a deposit account, etc.). Generally, reexamination refunds will be issued in the form that the original payment was provided.

[47 FR 41274, Sept. 17, 1982, effective Oct. 1, 1982; 50 FR 31826 Aug. 6, 1985, effective Oct. 5, 1985; para. (c), 54 FR 6893, Feb. 15, 1989, effective Apr. 17, 1989; para. (c), 56 FR 65142, Dec. 13, 1991, effective Dec. 16, 1991; paras. (a) and (c), 57 FR 38190, Aug. 21, 1992, effective Oct. 1,1992; para. (a) revised, 62 FR 53131, Oct. 10, 1997, effective Dec. 1, 1997; para. (a) revised and para. (b) added, 65 FR 54604, Sept. 8, 2000, effective Nov. 7, 2000; para. (c) revised, 65 FR 76756, Dec. 7, 2000, effective Feb. 5, 2001; paras. (a) & (c) revised, 68 FR 14332, Mar. 25, 2003, effective May 1, 2003; para. (a) revised, 68 FR 48286, Aug. 13, 2003, effective Sept. 12, 2003: paras. (a) and (b) revised, 72 FR 46716, Aug. 21, 2007 (implementation enjoined and never became effective); paras. (a) and (b) revised, 74 FR 52686, Oct. 14, 2009, effective Oct. 14, 2009 (to remove changes made by the final rules in 72 FR 46716 from the CFR)]

§ 1.27   Definition of small entities and establishing status as a small entity to permit payment of small entity fees; when a determination of entitlement to small entity status and notification of loss of entitlement to small entity status are required; fraud on the Office.

(a)   *Definition of small entities.* A small entity as used in this chapter means any party (person, small business concern, or nonprofit organization) under paragraphs (a)(1) through (a)(3) of this section.

(1)   *Person.* A person, as used in paragraph (c) of this section, means any inventor or other individual (*e.g.*, an individual to whom an inventor has transferred some rights in the invention) who has not assigned, granted, conveyed, or licensed, and is under no obligation under contract or law to assign, grant, convey, or license, any rights in the invention. An inventor or other individual who has transferred some rights in the invention to one or more parties, or is under an obligation to transfer some rights in the invention to one or more parties, can also qualify for small entity status if all the parties who have had rights in the invention transferred to them also qualify for small entity status either as a person, small business concern, or nonprofit organization under this section.

(2) *Small business concern.* A small business concern, as used in paragraph (c) of this section, means any business concern that:

(i) Has not assigned, granted, conveyed, or licensed, and is under no obligation under contract or law to assign, grant, convey, or license, any rights in the invention to any person, concern, or organization which would not qualify for small entity status as a person, small business concern, or nonprofit organization; and

(ii) Meets the size standards set forth in 13 CFR 121.801 through 121.805 to be eligible for reduced patent fees. Questions related to standards for a small business concern may be directed to: Small Business Administration, Size Standards Staff, 409 Third Street, SW., Washington, DC 20416.

(3) *Nonprofit Organization.* A nonprofit organization, as used in paragraph (c) of this section, means any nonprofit organization that:

(i) Has not assigned, granted, conveyed, or licensed, and is under no obligation under contract or law to assign, grant, convey, or license, any rights in the invention to any person, concern, or organization which would not qualify as a person, small business concern, or a nonprofit organization; and

(ii) Is either:

(A) A university or other institution of higher education located in any country;

(B) An organization of the type described in section 501(c)(3) of the Internal Revenue Code of 19 86 (26 U.S.C. 501(c)(3)) and exempt from taxation under section 501(a) of the Internal Revenue Code (26 U.S.C. 501(a));

(C) Any nonprofit scientific or educational organization qualified under a nonprofit organization statute of a state of this country (35 U.S.C. 201 (i)); or

(D) Any nonprofit organization located in a foreign country which would qualify as a nonprofit organization under paragraphs (a)(3)(ii)(B) of this section or (a)(3)(ii)(C) of this section if it were located in this country.

(4) *License to a Federal agency.* (i) For persons under paragraph (a)(1) of this section, a license to the Government resulting from a rights determination under Executive Order 10096 does not constitute a license so as to prohibit claiming small entity status.

(ii) For small business concerns and nonprofit organizations under paragraphs (a)(2) and (a)(3) of this section, a license to a Federal agency resulting from a funding agreement with that agency pursuant to 35 U.S.C. 202 (c)(4) does not constitute a license for the purposes of paragraphs (a)(2)(i) and (a)(3)(i) of this section.

(5) *Security Interest.* A security interest does not involve an obligation to transfer rights in the invention for the purposes of paragraphs (a)(1) through (a)(3) of this section unless the security interest is defaulted upon.

(b) *Establishment of small entity status permits payment of reduced fees.*

(1) A small entity, as defined in paragraph (a) of this section, who has properly asserted entitlement to small entity status pursuant to paragraph (c) of this section will be accorded small entity status by the Office in the particular application or patent in which entitlement to small entity status was asserted. Establishment of small entity status allows the payment of certain reduced patent fees pursuant to 35 U.S.C. 41(h)(1).

(2) Submission of an original utility application in compliance with the Office electronic filing system by an applicant who has properly asserted entitlement to small entity status pursuant to paragraph (c) of this section in that application allows the payment of a reduced filing fee pursuant to 35 U.S.C. 41(h)(3).

(c) *Assertion of small entity status.* Any party (person, small business concern or nonprofit organization) should make a determination, pursuant to paragraph (f) of this section, of entitlement to be accorded small entity status based on the definitions set forth in paragraph (a) of this section, and must, in order to establish small entity status for the purpose of paying small entity fees, actually make an assertion of entitlement to small entity status, in the manner set forth in paragraphs (c)(1) or (c)(3) of this section, in the application or patent in which such small entity fees are to be paid.

(1) *Assertion by writing.* Small entity status may be established by a written assertion of entitlement to small entity status. A written assertion must:

(i) Be clearly identifiable;

(ii) Be signed (see paragraph (c)(2) of this section); and

(iii) Convey the concept of entitlement to small entity status, such as by stating that applicant is a small entity, or that small entity status is entitled to be asserted for the application or patent. While no specific words or wording are required to assert small entity status, the intent to assert small entity status must be clearly indicated in order to comply with the assertion requirement.

(2) *Parties who can sign and file the written assertion.* The written assertion can be signed by:

(i) One of the parties identified in § 1.33(b) (*e.g.*, an attorney or agent registered with the Office), § 3.73(b) of this chapter notwithstanding, who can also file the written assertion;

(ii) At least one of the individuals identified as an inventor (even though a § 1.63 executed oath or declaration has not been submitted), notwithstanding § 1.33(b)(4), who can also file the written assertion pursuant to the exception under § 1.33(b) of this part; or

(iii) An assignee of an undivided part interest, notwithstanding §§ 1.33(b)(3) and 3.73(b) of this chapter, but the partial assignee cannot file the assertion without resort to a party identified under § 1.33(b) of this part.

(3) *Assertion by payment of the small entity basic filing or basic national fee.* The payment, by any party, of the exact amount of one of the small entity basic filing fees set forth in §§ 1.16(a), 1.16(b), 1.16(c), 1.16(d), 1.16(e), or the small entity basic national fee set forth in § 1.492(a), will be treated as a written assertion of entitlement to small entity status even if the type of basic filing or basic national fee is inadvertently selected in error.

(i) If the Office accords small entity status based on payment of a small entity basic filing or basic national fee under paragraph (c)(3) of this section that is not applicable to that application, any balance of the small entity fee that is applicable to that application will be due along with the appropriate surcharge set forth in § 1.16(f), or § 1.16(g).

(ii) The payment of any small entity fee other than those set forth in paragraph (c)(3) of this section (whether in the exact fee amount or not) will not be treated as a written assertion of entitlement to small entity status and will not be sufficient to establish small entity status in an application or a patent.

(4) *Assertion required in related, continuing, and reissue applications.* Status as a small entity must be specifically established by an assertion in each related, continuing and reissue application in which status is appropriate and desired. Status as a small entity in one application or patent does not affect the status of any other application or patent, regardless of the relationship of the applications or patents. The refiling of an application under § 1.53 as a continuation, divisional, or continuation-in-part application (including a continued prosecution application under § 1.53(d)), or the filing of a reissue application, requires a new assertion as to continued entitlement to small entity status for the continuing or reissue application.

(d) *When small entity fees can be paid.* Any fee, other than the small entity basic filing fees and the small entity national fees of paragraph (c)(3) of this section, can be paid in the small entity amount only if it is submitted with, or subsequent to, the submission of a written assertion of entitlement to small entity status, except when refunds are permitted by § 1.28(a).

(e) *Only one assertion required.*

(1) An assertion of small entity status need only be filed once in an application or patent. Small entity status, once established, remains in effect until changed pursuant to paragraph (g)(1) of this section. Where an assignment of rights or an obligation to assign rights to other parties who are small entities occurs subsequent to an assertion of small entity status, a second assertion is not required.

(2) Once small entity status is withdrawn pursuant to paragraph (g)(2) of this section, a new written assertion is required to again obtain small entity status.

(f) *Assertion requires a determination of entitlement to pay small entity fees.* Prior to submitting an assertion of entitlement to small entity status in an application, including a related, continuing, or reissue application, a determination of such entitlement should be made pursuant to the requirements of paragraph (a) of this section. It should be determined that all parties holding rights in the invention qualify for small entity status. The Office will generally not question any assertion of small entity status that is made in accordance with the requirements of this section, but note paragraph (h) of this section.

(g)(1) *New determination of entitlement to small entity status is needed when issue and maintenance fees are due.* Once status as a small entity has been established in an application or patent, fees as a small entity may thereafter be paid in that application or patent without regard to a change in status until the issue fee is due or any maintenance fee is due.

(2) *Notification of loss of entitlement to small entity status is required when issue and maintenance fees are due.* Notification of a loss of entitlement to small entity status must be filed in the application or patent prior to paying, or at the time of paying, the earliest of the issue fee or any maintenance fee due after the date on which status as a small entity as defined in paragraph (a) of this section is no longer appropriate. The notification that small entity status is no longer appropriate must be signed by a party identified in § 1.33(b). Payment of a fee in other than the small entity amount is not sufficient notification that small entity status is no longer appropriate.

(h) *Fraud attempted or practiced on the Office.*

(1) Any attempt to fraudulently establish status as a small entity, or pay fees as a small entity, shall be considered as a fraud practiced or attempted on the Office.

(2) Improperly, and with intent to deceive, establishing status as a small entity, or paying fees as a small entity, shall be considered as a fraud practiced or attempted on the Office.

[47 FR 40139, Sept. 10, 1982, added effective Oct. 1, 1982; para. (c) added, 47 FR 43276, Sept. 30, 1982; paras. (b), (c), and (d), 49 FR 553, Jan. 4, 1984, effective Apr. 1, 1984; revised, 62 FR 53131, Oct. 10, 1997, effective Dec.1, 1997; revised, 65 FR 54604, Sept. 8, 2000, effective Sept. 8, 2000; para. (a) revised, 69 FR 56481, Sept. 21, 2004, effective Sept. 21, 2004; paras. (b) and (c)(3) revised, 70 FR 3880, Jan. 27, 2005, effective Dec. 8, 2004]

§ 1.28 Refunds when small entity status is later established; how errors in small entity status are excused.

(a) *Refunds based on later establishment of small entity status.* A refund pursuant to § 1.26, based on establishment of small entity status, of a portion of fees timely paid in full prior to establishing status as a small entity may only be obtained if an assertion under § 1.27(c) and a request for a refund of the excess amount are filed within three months of the

date of the timely payment of the full fee. The three-month time period is not extendable under § 1.136. Status as a small entity is waived for any fee by the failure to establish the status prior to paying, at the time of paying, or within three months of the date of payment of, the full fee.

(b) *Date of payment.*

(1) The three-month period for requesting a refund, pursuant to paragraph (a) of this section, starts on the date that a full fee has been paid;

(2) The date when a deficiency payment is paid in full determines the amount of deficiency that is due, pursuant to paragraph (c) of this section.

(c) *How errors in small entity status are excused.* If status as a small entity is established in good faith, and fees as a small entity are paid in good faith, in any application or patent, and it is later discovered that such status as a small entity was established in error, or that through error the Office was not notified of a loss of entitlement to small entity status as required by § 1.27(g)(2), the error will be excused upon: compliance with the separate submission and itemization requirements of paragraphs (c)(1) and (c)(2) of this section, and the deficiency payment requirement of paragraph (c)(2) of this section:

(1) *Separate submission required for each application or patent.* Any paper submitted under this paragraph must be limited to the deficiency payment (all fees paid in error), required by paragraph (c)(2) of this section, for one application or one patent. Where more than one application or patent is involved, separate submissions of deficiency payments (*e.g.*, checks) and itemizations are required for each application or patent. See § 1.4(b).

(2) *Payment of deficiency owed.* The deficiency owed, resulting from the previous erroneous payment of small entity fees, must be paid.

(i) *Calculation of the deficiency owed.* The deficiency owed for each previous fee erroneously paid as a small entity is the difference between the current fee amount (for other than a small entity) on the date the deficiency is paid in full and the amount of the previous erroneous (small entity) fee payment. The total deficiency payment owed is the sum of the individual deficiency owed amounts for each fee amount previously erroneously paid as a small entity. Where a fee paid in error as a small entity was subject to a fee decrease between the time the fee was paid in error and the time the deficiency is paid in full, the deficiency owed is equal to the amount (previously) paid in error;

(ii) *Itemization of the deficiency payment.* An itemization of the total deficiency payment is required. The itemization must include the following information:

(A) Each particular type of fee that was erroneously paid as a small entity, (*e.g.*, basic statutory filing fee, two-month extension of time fee) along with the current fee amount for a non-small entity;

(B) The small entity fee actually paid, and when. This will permit the Office to differentiate, for example, between two one-month extension of time fees erroneously paid as a small entity but on different dates;

(C) The deficiency owed amount (for each fee erroneously paid); and

(D) The total deficiency payment owed, which is the sum or total of the individual deficiency owed amounts set forth in paragraph (c)(2)(ii)(C) of this section.

(3) *Failure to comply with requirements.* If the requirements of paragraphs (c)(1) and (c)(2) of this section are not complied with, such failure will either: be treated as an authorization for the Office to process the deficiency payment and charge the processing fee set forth in § 1.17(i), or result in a requirement for compliance within a one-month non-extendable time period under § 1.136(a) to avoid the return of the fee deficiency paper, at the option of the Office.

(d) *Payment of deficiency operates as notification of loss of status.* Any deficiency payment (based on a previous erroneous payment of a small entity fee) submitted under paragraph (c) of this section will be treated under § 1.27(g)(2) as a notification of a loss of entitlement to small entity status.

[47 FR 40140, Sept. 10, 1982, added effective Oct. 1, 1982; para. (a), 49 FR 553, Jan. 4, 1984, effective Apr. 1, 1984; para. (d)(2), 57 FR 2021, Jan. 17, 1992, effective Mar. 16, 1992; para. (c) revised, 58 FR 54504, Oct. 22, 1993, effective Jan. 3, 1994; para. (a) revised, 60 FR 20195, Apr. 25, 1995, effective June 8, 1995; paras. (a) & (c) revised, 62 FR 53131, Oct. 10 1997, effective Dec. 1, 1997; revised, 65 FR 54604, Sept. 8, 2000, effective Nov. 7, 2000]

Subpart B — National Processing Provisions

PROSECUTION OF APPLICATION AND APPOINTMENT OF ATTORNEY OR AGENT

§ 1.31 Applicant may be represented by one or more patent practitioners or joint inventors.

An applicant for patent may file and prosecute his or her own case, or he or she may give a power of attorney so as to be represented by one or more patent practitioners or joint inventors. The United States Patent and Trademark Office cannot aid in the selection of a patent practitioner.

[50 FR 5171, Feb. 6, 1985, effective Mar. 8, 1985; revised, 69 FR 29865, May 26, 2004, effective June 25, 2004; revised 69 FR 35427, June 24, 2004, effective July 26, 2004; revised, 70 FR 56119, Sept. 26, 2005, effective Nov. 25, 2005]

§ 1.32 Power of attorney.

(a) *Definitions.*

(1) *Patent practitioner* means a registered patent attorney or registered patent agent under § 11.6.

(2) *Power of attorney* means a written document by which a principal authorizes one or more patent practitioners or joint inventors to act on his or her behalf.

(3) *Principal* means either an applicant for patent (§ 1.41(b)) or an assignee of entire interest of the applicant for patent or in a reexamination proceeding, the assignee of the entirety of ownership of a patent. The principal executes a power of attorney designating one or more patent practitioners or joint inventors to act on his or her behalf.

(4) *Revocation* means the cancellation by the principal of the authority previously given to a patent practitioner or joint inventor to act on his or her behalf.

(5) *Customer Number* means a number that may be used to:

(i) Designate the correspondence address of a patent application or patent such that the correspondence address for the patent application, patent or other patent proceeding would be the address associated with the Customer Number;

(ii) Designate the fee address (§ 1.363) of a patent such that the fee address for the patent would be the address associated with the Customer Number; and

(iii) Submit a list of patent practitioners such that those patent practitioners associated with the Customer Number would have power of attorney.

(b) A power of attorney must:

(1) Be in writing;

(2) Name one or more representatives in compliance with (c) of this section;

(3) Give the representative power to act on behalf of the principal; and

(4) Be signed by the applicant for patent (§ 1.41(b)) or the assignee of the entire interest of the applicant.

(c) A power of attorney may only name as representative:

(1) One or more joint inventors (§ 1.45);

(2) Those registered patent practitioners associated with a Customer Number;

(3) Ten or fewer patent practitioners, stating the name and registration number of each patent practitioner. Except as provided in paragraph (c)(1) or (c)(2) of this section, the Office will not recognize more than ten patent practitioners as being of record in an application or patent. If a power of attorney names more than ten patent practitioners, such power of attorney must be accompanied by a separate paper indicating which ten patent practitioners named in the power of attorney are to be recognized by the Office as being of record in the application or patent to which the power of attorney is directed.

[Added, 69 FR 29865, May 26, 2004, effective June 25, 2004; paras. (a) and (c)(3) revised, 70 FR 56119, Sept. 26, 2005, effective Nov. 25, 2005]

§ 1.33   Correspondence respecting patent applications, reexamination proceedings, and other proceedings.

(a) *Correspondence address and daytime telephone number.* When filing an application, a correspondence address must be set forth in either an application data sheet (§ 1.76), or elsewhere, in a clearly identifiable manner, in any paper submitted with an application filing. If no correspondence address is specified, the Office may treat the mailing address of the first named inventor (if provided, see

§§ 1.76 (b)(1) and 1.63 (c)(2)) as the correspondence address. The Office will direct, or otherwise make available, all notices, official letters, and other communications relating to the application to the person associated with the correspondence address. For correspondence submitted via the Office's electronic filing system, however, an electronic acknowledgment receipt will be sent to the submitter. The Office will generally not engage in double correspondence with an applicant and a patent practitioner, or with more than one patent practitioner except as deemed necessary by the Director. If more than one correspondence address is specified in a single document, the Office will select one of the specified addresses for use as the correspondence address and, if given, will select the address associated with a Customer Number over a typed correspondence address. For the party to whom correspondence is to be addressed, a daytime telephone number should be supplied in a clearly identifiable manner and may be changed by any party who may change the correspondence address. The correspondence address may be changed as follows:

(1) Prior to filing of § 1.63 oath or declaration by any of the inventors. If a § 1.63 oath or declaration has not been filed by any of the inventors, the correspondence address may be changed by the party who filed the application. If the application was filed by a patent practitioner, any other patent practitioner named in the transmittal papers may also change the correspondence address. Thus, the inventor(s), any patent practitioner named in the transmittal papers accompanying the original application, or a party that will be the assignee who filed the application, may change the correspondence address in that application under this paragraph.

(2) *Where a § 1.63 oath or declaration has been filed by any of the inventors.* If a § 1.63 oath or declaration has been filed, or is filed concurrent with the filing of an application, by any of the inventors, the correspondence address may be changed by the parties set forth in paragraph (b) of this section, except for paragraph (b)(2).

(b) *Amendments and other papers.* Amendments and other papers, except for written assertions pursuant to § 1.27(c)(2)(ii) of this part, filed in the application must be signed by:

(1) A patent practitioner of record appointed in compliance with § 1.32(b);

(2) A patent practitioner not of record who acts in a representative capacity under the provisions of § 1.34;

(3) An assignee as provided for under § 3.71(b) of this chapter; or

(4) All of the applicants (§ 1.41(b)) for patent, unless there is an assignee of the entire interest and such assignee has taken action in the application in accordance with § 3.71 of this chapter.

(c) All notices, official letters, and other communications for the patent owner or owners in a reexamination proceeding will be directed to the correspondence address. Amendments and other papers filed in a reexamination proceeding on behalf of the patent owner must be signed by the patent owner, or if there is more than one owner by all the owners, or by an attorney or agent of record in the patent file, or by a registered attorney or agent not of record who acts in a representative capacity under the provisions of § 1.34. Double correspondence with the patent owner or owners and the patent owner's attorney or agent, or with more than one attorney or agent, will not be undertaken.

(d) A "correspondence address" or change thereto may be filed with the Patent and Trademark Office during the enforceable life of the patent. The "correspondence address" will be used in any correspondence relating to maintenance fees unless a separate "fee address" has been specified. See § 1.363 for "fee address" used solely for maintenance fee purposes.

(e) A change of address filed in a patent application or patent does not change the address for a patent practitioner in the roster of patent attorneys and agents. See § 11.11 of this title.

[36 FR 12617, July 2, 1971; 46 FR 29181, May 29, 1981; para. (d) added, 49 FR 34724, Aug. 31, 1984, effective Nov. 1, 1984; para. (c), 50 FR 5171, Feb. 6, 1985, effective Mar. 8, 1985; paras. (a) & (b) revised, 62 FR 53131, Oct. 10 1997, effective Dec. 1, 1997; paras. (a) and (b) revised, 65 FR 54604, Sept. 8, 2000, effective Nov. 7, 2000; para. (a) revised, 68 FR 14332, Mar. 25, 2003, effective May 1, 2003; (a) introductory text, (b) introductory text, and paras. (b)(1), (b)(2) and (c) revised, 69 FR 29865, May 26, 2004, effective June 25, 2004; para. (c) revised, 69 FR 35427, June 24, 2004, effective July 26, 2004; para. (c) revised, 70 FR 3880, Jan. 27, 2005, effective Dec. 8, 2004; para. (a) introductory text revised, paras. (a)(1), (b)(1), and (b)(2) revised, and para. (e) added, 70 FR 56119, Sept. 26, 2005, effective Nov. 25, 2005; para. (a) introductory text revised, 72 FR 2770, Jan. 23, 2007, effective Jan. 23, 2007; para. (c) revised, 72 FR 18892, Apr. 16, 2007, effective May 16, 2007]

§ 1.34 Acting in a representative capacity.

When a patent practitioner acting in a representative capacity appears in person or signs a paper in practice before the United States Patent and Trademark Office in a patent case, his or her personal appearance or signature shall constitute a representation to the United States Patent and Trademark Office that under the provisions of this subchapter and the law, he or she is authorized to represent the particular party on whose behalf he or she acts. In filing such a paper, the patent practitioner must set forth his or her registration number, his or her name and signature. Further proof of authority to act in a representative capacity may be required.

[46 FR 29181, May 29, 1981; para. (a), 50 FR 5171, Feb. 6, 1985, effective Mar. 6, 1985; revised, 65 FR 54604, Sept. 8, 2000, effective Nov. 7, 2000; revised, 69 FR 29865, May 26, 2004, effective June 25, 2004; revised, 70 FR 56119, Sept. 26, 2005, effective Nov. 25, 2005]

§ 1.36 Revocation of power of attorney; withdrawal of patent attorney or agent.

(a) A power of attorney, pursuant to § 1.32(b), may be revoked at any stage in the proceedings of a case by an applicant for patent (§ 1.41(b)) or an assignee of the entire interest of the applicant, or the owner of the entire interest of a patent. A power of attorney to the patent practitioners associated with a Customer Number will be treated as a request to revoke any powers of attorney previously given. Fewer than all of the applicants (or fewer than all of the assignees of the entire interest of the applicant or, in a reexamination proceeding, fewer than all the owners of the entire interest of a patent) may revoke the power of attorney only upon a showing of sufficient cause, and payment of the petition fee set forth in § 1.17(f). A patent practitioner will be notified of the revocation of the power of attorney. Where power of attorney is given to the patent practitioners associated with a Customer Number (§ 1.32(c)(2)), the practitioners so appointed will also be notified of the revocation of the power of attorney when the power of attorney to all of the practitioners associated with the Customer Number is revoked. The notice of revocation will be mailed to the correspondence address for the application (§ 1.33) in effect before the revocation. An assignment will not of itself operate as a revocation of a power previously given, but the assignee of the entire interest of the applicant may revoke previous powers of attorney and give another power of attorney of the assignee's own selection as provided in § 1.32(b).

(b)   A registered patent attorney or patent agent who has been given a power of attorney pursuant to § 1.32(b) may withdraw as attorney or agent of record upon application to and approval by the Director. The applicant or patent owner will be notified of the withdrawal of the registered patent attorney or patent agent. Where power of attorney is given to the patent practitioners associated with a Customer Number, a request to delete all of the patent practitioners associated with the Customer Number may not be granted if an applicant has given power of attorney to the patent practitioners associated with the Customer Number in an application that has an Office action to which a reply is due, but insufficient time remains for the applicant to file a reply. See § 41.5 of this title for withdrawal during proceedings before the Board of Patent Appeals and Interferences.

[49 FR 48416, Dec. 12, 1984, effective Feb. 11, 1985; revised, 65 FR 54604, Sept. 8, 2000, effective Nov. 7, 2000; revised, 68 FR 14332, Mar. 25, 2003, effective May 1, 2003; revised, 69 FR 29865, May 26, 2004, effective June 25, 2004; revised, 69 FR 49959, Aug. 12, 2004, effective Sept. 13, 2004; para. (a) revised, 70 FR 56119, Sept. 26, 2005, effective Nov. 25, 2005]

WHO MAY APPLY FOR A PATENT

§ 1.41   Applicant for patent.

(a)   A patent is applied for in the name or names of the actual inventor or inventors.

(1)   The inventorship of a nonprovisional application is that inventorship set forth in the oath or declaration as prescribed by § 1.63, except as provided for in §§ 1.53(d)(4) and 1.63(d). If an oath or declaration as prescribed by § 1.63 is not filed during the pendency of a nonprovisional application, the inventorship is that inventorship set forth in the application papers filed pursuant to § 1.53(b), unless applicant files a paper, including the processing fee set forth in § 1.17(i), supplying or changing the name or names of the inventor or inventors.

(2)   The inventorship of a provisional application is that inventorship set forth in the cover sheet as prescribed by § 1.51(c)(1). If a cover sheet as prescribed by § 1.51(c)(1) is not filed during the pendency of a provisional application, the inventorship is that inventorship set forth in the application papers filed pursuant to § 1.53(c), unless applicant files a paper including the processing fee set forth in § 1.17(q), supplying or changing the name or names of the inventor or inventors.

(3)   In a nonprovisional application filed without an oath or declaration as prescribed by § 1.63 or a provisional application filed without a cover sheet as prescribed by § 1.51(c)(1), the name, residence, and citizenship of each person believed to be an actual inventor should be provided when the application papers pursuant to § 1.53(b) or § 1.53(c) are filed.

(4)   The inventorship of an international application entering the national stage under 35 U.S.C. 371 is that inventorship set forth in the international application, which includes any change effected under PCT Rule 92bis. See § 1.497(d) and (f) for filing an oath or declaration naming an inventive entity different from the inventive entity named in the international application, or if a change to the inventive entity has been effected under PCT Rule 92bis subsequent to the execution of any declaration filed under PCT Rule 4.17(iv) (§ 1.48(f)(1) does not apply to an international application entering the national stage under 35 U.S.C. 371).

(b)   Unless the contrary is indicated the word "applicant" when used in these sections refers to the inventor or joint inventors who are applying for a patent, or to the person mentioned in §§ 1.42, 1.43 or 1.47 who is applying for a patent in place of the inventor.

(c)   Any person authorized by the applicant may physically or electronically deliver an application for patent to the Office on behalf of the inventor or inventors, but an oath or declaration for the application (§ 1.63) can only be made in accordance with § 1.64.

(d)   A showing may be required from the person filing the application that the filing was authorized where such authorization comes into question.

[48 FR 2708, Jan. 20, 1983; 48 FR 4285, Jan. 31, 1983; para. (a) revised, 62 FR 53131, Oct. 10, 1997, effective Dec. 1, 1997; paras. (a) and (c) revised, 65 FR 54604, Sept. 8, 2000, effective Nov. 7, 2000; para. (a)(4) revised, 67 FR 520, Jan. 4, 2002, effective Apr. 1, 2002]

§ 1.42   When the inventor is dead.

In case of the death of the inventor, the legal representative (executor, administrator, etc.) of the deceased inventor may make the necessary oath or declaration, and apply for and obtain the patent. Where the inventor dies during the time intervening between the filing of the application and the granting of a patent thereon, the letters patent may be issued to the legal representative upon proper intervention.

[48 FR 2709, Jan. 20, 1983, effective Feb. 27, 1983]

§ 1.43   When the inventor is insane or legally incapacitated.

In case an inventor is insane or otherwise legally incapacitated, the legal representative (guardian, conservator, etc.) of such inventor may make the necessary oath or declaration, and apply for and obtain the patent.

[48 FR 2709, Jan. 20, 1983, effective Feb. 27, 1983]

§ 1.44   [Reserved]

[Removed and reserved, 65 FR 54604, Sept. 8, 2000, effective Sept. 8, 2000]

§ 1.45   Joint inventors.

(a)   Joint inventors must apply for a patent jointly and each must make the required oath or declaration: neither of them alone, nor less than the entire number, can apply for a patent for an invention invented by them jointly, except as provided in § 1.47.

(b)   Inventors may apply for a patent jointly even though

(1)   They did not physically work together or at the same time,

(2)   Each inventor did not make the same type or amount of contribution, or

(3)   Each inventor did not make a contribution to the subject matter of every claim of the application.

(c)   If multiple inventors are named in a nonprovisional application, each named inventor must have made a contribution, individually or jointly, to the subject matter of at least one claim of the application and the application will be considered to be a joint application under 35 U.S.C. 116. If multiple inventors are named in a provisional application, each named inventor must have made a contribution, individually or jointly, to the subject matter disclosed in the provisional application and the provisional application will be considered to be a joint application under 35 U.S.C. 116.

[paras. (b) and (c), 47 FR 41274, Sept. 17, 1982, effective Oct. 1, 1982; 48 FR 2709, Jan. 20, 1983, effective Feb. 27, 1983; 50 FR 9379, Mar. 7, 1985, effective May 8, 1985; para. (c) revised, 60 FR 20195, Apr. 25, 1995, effective June 8, 1995]

§ 1.46   Assigned inventions and patents.

In case the whole or a part interest in the invention or in the patent to be issued is assigned, the application must still be made or authorized to be made, and an oath or declaration signed, by the inventor or one of the persons mentioned in §§ 1.42, 1.43, or 1.47. However, the patent may be issued to the assignee or jointly to the inventor and the assignee as provided in § 3.81.

[48 FR 2709, Jan. 20, 1983, effective Feb. 27, 1983; 57 FR 29642, July 6, 1992, effective Sept. 4, 1992]

§ 1.47   Filing when an inventor refuses to sign or cannot be reached.

(a)   If a joint inventor refuses to join in an application for patent or cannot be found or reached after diligent effort, the application may be made by the other inventor on behalf of himself or herself and the nonsigning inventor. The oath or declaration in such an application must be accompanied by a petition including proof of the pertinent facts, the fee set forth in § 1.17(g), and the last known address of the nonsigning inventor. The nonsigning inventor may subsequently join in the application by filing an oath or declaration complying with § 1.63.

(b)   Whenever all of the inventors refuse to execute an application for patent, or cannot be found or reached after diligent effort, a person to whom an inventor has assigned or agreed in writing to assign the invention, or who otherwise shows sufficient proprietary interest in the matter justifying such action, may make application for patent on behalf of and as agent for all the inventors. The oath or declaration in such an application must be accompanied by a petition including proof of the pertinent facts, a showing that such action is necessary to preserve the rights of the parties or to prevent irreparable damage, the fee set forth in § 1.17(g), and the last known address of all of the inventors. An inventor may subsequently join in the application by filing an oath or declaration complying with § 1.63.

(c)   The Office will send notice of the filing of the application to all inventors who have not joined in the application at the address(es) provided in the petition under this section, and publish notice of the filing of the application in the *Official Gazette*. The Office may dispense with this notice provision in a continuation or divisional application, if notice regarding the filing of the prior application was given to the nonsigning inventor(s).

[47 FR 41275, Sept. 17, 1982, effective Oct. 1, 1982; 48 FR 2709, Jan. 20, 1983, effective Feb. 27, 1983; revised, 62 FR 53131, Oct. 10, 1997, effective Dec. 1, 1997; revised, 65 FR 54604, Sept. 8, 2000, effective Nov. 7, 2000; paras. (a) and (b) revised, 69 FR 56481, Sept. 21, 2004, effective Nov. 22, 2004]

§ 1.48   Correction of inventorship in a patent application, other than a reissue application, pursuant to 35 U.S.C. 116.

(a)   *Nonprovisional application after oath/declaration filed.* If the inventive entity is set forth in error in an executed § 1.63 oath or declaration in a nonprovisional application, and such error arose without any deceptive intention on the part of the person named as an inventor in error or on the part of the person who through error was not named as an inventor, the inventorship of the nonprovisional application may be amended to name only the actual inventor or inventors. Amendment of the inventorship requires:

(1)   A request to correct the inventorship that sets forth the desired inventorship change;

(2)   A statement from each person being added as an inventor and from each person being deleted as an inventor that the error in inventorship occurred without deceptive intention on his or her part;

(3)   An oath or declaration by the actual inventor or inventors as required by § 1.63 or as permitted by §§ 1.42, 1.43 or § 1.47;

(4)   The processing fee set forth in § 1.17(i); and

(5)   If an assignment has been executed by any of the original named inventors, the written consent of the assignee (see § 3.73(b) of this chapter).

(b)   *Nonprovisional application—fewer inventors due to amendment or cancellation of claims.* If the correct inventors are named in a nonprovisional application, and the prosecution of the nonprovisional application results in the amendment or cancellation of claims so that fewer than all of the currently named inventors are the actual inventors of the invention being claimed in the nonprovisional application, an amendment must be filed requesting deletion of the name or names of the person or persons who are not inventors of the invention being claimed. Amendment of the inventorship requires:

(1)   A request, signed by a party set forth in § 1.33(b), to correct the inventorship that identifies the named inventor or inventors being deleted and acknowledges that the inventor's invention is no longer being claimed in the nonprovisional application; and

(2)   The processing fee set forth in § 1.17(i).

(c)   *Nonprovisional application—inventors added for claims to previously unclaimed subject matter.* If a nonprovisional application discloses unclaimed subject matter by an inventor or inventors not named in the application, the application may be amended to add claims to the subject matter and name the correct inventors for the application. Amendment of the inventorship requires:

(1)   A request to correct the inventorship that sets forth the desired inventorship change;

(2)   A statement from each person being added as an inventor that the addition is necessitated by amendment of the claims and that the inventorship error occurred without deceptive intention on his or her part;

(3)   An oath or declaration by the actual inventors as required by § 1.63 or as permitted by §§ 1.42, 1.43, or § 1.47;

(4)   The processing fee set forth in § 1.17(i); and

(5) If an assignment has been executed by any of the original named inventors, the written consent of the assignee (see § 3.73(b) of this chapter).

(d) *Provisional application—adding omitted inventors.* If the name or names of an inventor or inventors were omitted in a provisional application through error without any deceptive intention on the part of the omitted inventor or inventors, the provisional application may be amended to add the name or names of the omitted inventor or inventors. Amendment of the inventorship requires:

(1) A request, signed by a party set forth in § 1.33(b), to correct the inventorship that identifies the inventor or inventors being added and states that the inventorship error occurred without deceptive intention on the part of the omitted inventor or inventors; and

(2) The processing fee set forth in § 1.17(q).

(e) *Provisional application—deleting the name or names of the inventor or inventors.* If a person or persons were named as an inventor or inventors in a provisional application through error without any deceptive intention on the part of such person or persons, an amendment may be filed in the provisional application deleting the name or names of the person or persons who were erroneously named. Amendment of the inventorship requires:

(1) A request to correct the inventorship that sets forth the desired inventorship change;

(2) A statement by the person or persons whose name or names are being deleted that the inventorship error occurred without deceptive intention on the part of such person or persons;

(3) The processing fee set forth in § 1.17(q); and

(4) If an assignment has been executed by any of the original named inventors, the written consent of the assignee (see § 3.73(b) of this chapter).

(f)(1) *Nonprovisional application—filing executed oath/declaration corrects inventorship.* If the correct inventor or inventors are not named on filing a nonprovisional application under § 1.53(b) without an executed oath or declaration under § 1.63 by any of the inventors, the first submission of an executed oath or declaration under § 1.63 by any of the inventors during the pendency of the application will act to correct the earlier identification of inventorship. See §§ 1.41(a)(4) and 1.497(d) and (f) for submission of

an executed oath or declaration to enter the national stage under 35 U.S.C. 371 naming an inventive entity different from the inventive entity set forth in the international stage.

(2) *Provisional application filing cover sheet corrects inventorship.* If the correct inventor or inventors are not named on filing a provisional application without a cover sheet under § 1.51(c)(1), the later submission of a cover sheet under § 1.51(c)(1) during the pendency of the application will act to correct the earlier identification of inventorship.

(g) *Additional information may be required.* The Office may require such other information as may be deemed appropriate under the particular circumstances surrounding the correction of inventorship.

(h) *Reissue applications not covered.* The provisions of this section do not apply to reissue applications. See §§ 1.171 and 1.175 for correction of inventorship in a patent via a reissue application.

(i) *Correction of inventorship in patent.* See § 1.324 for correction of inventorship in a patent.

(j) *Correction of inventorship in a contested case before the Board of Patent Appeals and Interferences.* In a contested case under part 41, subpart D, of this title, a request for correction of an application must be in the form of a motion under § 41.121(a)(2) of this title and must comply with the requirements of this section.

[48 FR 2709, Jan. 20, 1983, effective Feb. 27, 1983; 49 FR 48416, Dec. 12, 1984, effective Feb. 11, 1985; 50 FR 9379, Mar. 7, 1985, effective May 8, 1985; para. (a), 57 FR 56446, Nov. 30, 1992, effective Jan. 4, 1993; revised, 60 FR 20195, Apr. 25, 1995, effective June 8, 1995; revised, 62 FR 53131, Oct. 10, 1997, effective Dec. 1, 1997; revised, 65 FR 54604, Sept. 8, 2000, effective Nov. 7, 2000; para. (f)(1) revised, 67 FR 520, Jan. 4, 2002, effective Apr. 1, 2002; paras. (a)-(c) and (i) revised and para. (j) added, 69 FR 49959, Aug. 12, 2004, effective Sept. 13, 2004]

THE APPLICATION

§ 1.51 General requisites of an application.

(a) Applications for patents must be made to the Director of the United States Patent and Trademark Office.

(b) A complete application filed under § 1.53(b) or § 1.53(d) comprises:

(1) A specification as prescribed by 35 U.S.C. 112, including a claim or claims, see §§ 1.71 to 1.77;

(2) An oath or declaration, see §§ 1.63 and 1.68;

(3) Drawings, when necessary, see §§ 1.81 to 1.85; and

(4) The prescribed filing fee, search fee, examination fee, and application size fee, see § 1.16.

(c) A complete provisional application filed under § 1.53(c) comprises:

(1) A cover sheet identifying:

(i) The application as a provisional application,

(ii) The name or names of the inventor or inventors, (see § 1.41(a)(2)),

(iii) The residence of each named inventor,

(iv) The title of the invention,

(v) The name and registration number of the attorney or agent (if applicable),

(vi) The docket number used by the person filing the application to identify the application (if applicable),

(vii) The correspondence address, and

(viii) The name of the U.S. Government agency and Government contract number (if the invention was made by an agency of the U.S. Government or under a contract with an agency of the U.S. Government);

(2) A specification as prescribed by the first paragraph of 35 U.S.C. 112, see § 1.71;

(3) Drawings, when necessary, see §§ 1.81 to 1.85; and

(4) The prescribed filing fee and application size fee, see § 1.16.

(d) Applicants are encouraged to file an information disclosure statement in nonprovisional applications. See § 1.97 and § 1.98. No information disclosure statement may be filed in a provisional application.

[42 FR 5593, Jan. 28, 1977; paras. (a) and (c), 47 FR 41275, Sept. 17, 1982, effective Oct. 1, 1982; paras. (a) and (b), 48 FR 2709, Jan. 20, 1983, effective Feb. 27, 1983; para. (b), 57 FR 2021, Jan. 17, 1992, effective Mar. 16, 1992; paras. (a) & (b) revised, 60 FR 20195, Apr. 25, 1995, effective June 8, 1995; revised, 62 FR 53131, Oct. 10, 1997, effective Dec. 1, 1997; para. (b) revised, 65 FR 54604, Sept. 8, 2000, effective Nov. 7, 2000; para. (a) revised, 68 FR 14332, Mar. 25, 2003, effective May 1, 2003; paras. (b)(4) and (c)(4) revised, 70 FR 3880, Jan. 27, 2005, effective Dec. 8, 2004]

§ 1.52 Language, paper, writing, margins, compact disc specifications.

(a) *Papers that are to become a part of the permanent United States Patent and Trademark Office records in the file of a patent application or a reexamination proceeding.*

(1) All papers, other than drawings, that are submitted on paper or by facsimile transmission, and are to become a part of the permanent United States Patent and Trademark Office records in the file of a patent application or reexamination proceeding, must be on sheets of paper that are the same size, not permanently bound together, and:

(i) Flexible, strong, smooth, non-shiny, durable, and white;

(ii) Either 21.0 cm by 29.7 cm (DIN size A4) or 21.6 cm by 27.9 cm (8 1/2 by 11 inches), with each sheet including a top margin of at least 2.0 cm (3/4 inch), a left side margin of at least 2.5 cm (1 inch), a right side margin of at least 2.0 cm (3/4 inch), and a bottom margin of at least 2.0 cm (3/4 inch);

(iii) Written on only one side in portrait orientation;

(iv) Plainly and legibly written either by a typewriter or machine printer in permanent dark ink or its equivalent; and

(v) Presented in a form having sufficient clarity and contrast between the paper and the writing thereon to permit the direct reproduction of readily legible copies in any number by use of photographic, electrostatic, photo-offset, and microfilming processes and electronic capture by use of digital imaging and optical character recognition.

(2) All papers that are submitted on paper or by facsimile transmission and are to become a part of the permanent records of the United States Patent and Trademark Office should have no holes in the sheets as submitted.

(3) The provisions of this paragraph and paragraph (b) of this section do not apply to the preprinted information on paper forms provided by the Office, or to the copy of the patent submitted on paper in double column format as the specification in a reissue application or request for reexamination.

(4) *See* § 1.58 for chemical and mathematical formulae and tables, and § 1.84 for drawings.

(5) Papers that are submitted electronically to the Office must be formatted and transmitted in compliance with the Office's electronic filing system requirements.

(b) *The application (specification, including the claims, drawings, and oath or declaration) or reexamination proceeding and any amendments or corrections to the application or reexamination proceeding.*

(1) The application or proceeding and any amendments or corrections to the application (including any translation submitted pursuant to paragraph (d) of this section) or proceeding, except as provided for in § 1.69 and paragraph (d) of this section, must:

(i) Comply with the requirements of paragraph (a) of this section; and

(ii) Be in the English language or be accompanied by a translation of the application and a translation of any corrections or amendments into the English language together with a statement that the translation is accurate.

(2) The specification (including the abstract and claims) for other than reissue applications and reexamination proceedings, and any amendments for applications (including reissue applications) and reexamination proceedings to the specification, except as provided for in §§ 1.821 through 1.825, must have:

(i) Lines that are 1 1/2 or double spaced;

(ii) Text written in a nonscript type font (*e.g.*, Arial, Times Roman, or Courier, preferably a font size of 12) lettering style having capital letters which should be at least 0.3175 cm. (0.125 inch) high, but may be no smaller than 0.21 cm. (0.08 inch) high (*e.g.*, a font size of 6); and

(iii) Only a single column of text.

(3) The claim or claims must commence on a separate physical sheet or electronic page (§ 1.75(h)).

(4) The abstract must commence on a separate physical sheet or electronic page or be submitted as the first page of the patent in a reissue application or reexamination proceeding (§ 1.72(b)).

(5) Other than in a reissue application or reexamination proceeding, the pages of the specification including claims and abstract must be numbered consecutively, starting with 1, the numbers being centrally located above or preferably below, the text.

(6) Other than in a reissue application or reexamination proceeding, the paragraphs of the specification, other than in the claims or abstract, may be numbered at the time the application is filed, and should be individually and consecutively numbered using Arabic numerals, so as to unambiguously identify each paragraph. The number should consist of at least four numerals enclosed in square brackets, including leading zeros (*e.g.*, [0001]). The numbers and enclosing brackets should appear to the right of the left margin as the first item in each paragraph, before the first word of the paragraph, and should be highlighted in bold. A gap, equivalent to approximately four spaces, should follow the number. Nontext elements (*e.g.*, tables, mathematical or chemical formulae, chemical structures, and sequence data) are considered part of the numbered paragraph around or above the elements, and should not be independently numbered. If a nontext element extends to the left margin, it should not be numbered as a separate and independent paragraph. A list is also treated as part of the paragraph around or above the list, and should not be independently numbered. Paragraph or section headers (titles), whether abutting the left margin or centered on the page, are not considered paragraphs and should not be numbered.

(c)(1) Any interlineation, erasure, cancellation or other alteration of the application papers filed must be made before the signing of any accompanying oath or declaration pursuant to § 1.63 referring to those application papers and should be dated and initialed or signed by the applicant on the same sheet of paper. Application papers containing alterations made after the signing of an oath or declaration referring to those application papers must be supported by a supplemental oath or declaration under § 1.67. In either situation, a substitute specification (§ 1.125) is required if the application papers do not comply with paragraphs (a) and (b) of this section.

(2) After the signing of the oath or declaration referring to the application papers, amendments may only be made in the manner provided by § 1.121.

(3) Notwithstanding the provisions of this paragraph, if an oath or declaration is a copy of the oath or declaration from a prior application, the application for which such copy is submitted may contain

alterations that do not introduce matter that would have been new matter in the prior application.

(d)　A nonprovisional or provisional application may be in a language other than English.

(1)　*Nonprovisional application.* If a nonprovisional application is filed in a language other than English, an English language translation of the non-English language application, a statement that the translation is accurate, and the processing fee set forth in § 1.17(i) are required. If these items are not filed with the application, applicant will be notified and given a period of time within which they must be filed in order to avoid abandonment.

(2)　*Provisional application.* If a provisional application is filed in a language other than English, an English language translation of the non-English language provisional application will not be required in the provisional application. *See* § 1.78(a) for the requirements for claiming the benefit of such provisional application in a nonprovisional application.

(e)　*Electronic documents that are to become part of the permanent United States Patent and Trademark Office records in the file of a patent application or reexamination proceeding.*

(1)　The following documents may be submitted to the Office on a compact disc in compliance with this paragraph:

(i)　A computer program listing (see § 1.96);

(ii)　A "Sequence Listing" (submitted under § 1.821(c)); or

(iii)　Any individual table (see § 1.58) if the table is more than 50 pages in length, or if the total number of pages of all of the tables in an application exceeds 100 pages in length, where a table page is a page printed on paper in conformance with paragraph (b) of this section and § 1.58(c).

(2)　A compact disc as used in this part means a Compact Disc-Read Only Memory (CD-ROM) or a Compact Disc-Recordable (CD-R) in compliance with this paragraph. A CD-ROM is a "read-only" medium on which the data is pressed into the disc so that it cannot be changed or erased. A CD-R is a "write once" medium on which once the data is recorded, it is permanent and cannot be changed or erased.

(3)(i) Each compact disc must conform to the International Standards Organization (ISO) 9660 standard, and the contents of each compact disc must be in compliance with the American Standard Code for Information Interchange (ASCII). CD-R discs must be finalized so that they are closed to further writing to the CD-R.

(ii)　Each compact disc must be enclosed in a hard compact disc case within an unsealed padded and protective mailing envelope and accompanied by a transmittal letter on paper in accordance with paragraph (a) of this section. The transmittal letter must list for each compact disc the machine format (*e.g.*, IBM-PC, Macintosh), the operating system compatibility (*e.g.*, MS-DOS, MS-Windows, Macintosh, Unix), a list of files contained on the compact disc including their names, sizes in bytes, and dates of creation, plus any other special information that is necessary to identify, maintain, and interpret (*e.g.*, tables in landscape orientation should be identified as landscape orientation or be identified when inquired about) the information on the compact disc. Compact discs submitted to the Office will not be returned to the applicant.

(4)　Any compact disc must be submitted in duplicate unless it contains only the "Sequence Listing" in computer readable form required by § 1.821(e). The compact disc and duplicate copy must be labeled "Copy 1" and "Copy 2," respectively. The transmittal letter which accompanies the compact disc must include a statement that the two compact discs are identical. In the event that the two compact discs are not identical, the Office will use the compact disc labeled "Copy 1" for further processing. Any amendment to the information on a compact disc must be by way of a replacement compact disc in compliance with this paragraph containing the substitute information, and must be accompanied by a statement that the replacement compact disc contains no new matter. The compact disc and copy must be labeled "COPY 1 REPLACEMENT MM/DD/YYYY" (with the month, day and year of creation indicated), and "COPY 2 REPLACEMENT MM/DD/YYYY," respectively.

(5)　The specification must contain an incorporation-by-reference of the material on the compact disc in a separate paragraph (§ 1.77(b)(5)), identifying each compact disc by the names of the files contained on each of the compact discs, their date of creation and their sizes in bytes. The Office may require applicant to amend the specification to include in the paper portion any part of the specification previously submitted on compact disc.

(6) A compact disc must also be labeled with the following information:

(i) The name of each inventor (if known);

(ii) Title of the invention;

(iii) The docket number, or application number if known, used by the person filing the application to identify the application; and

(iv) A creation date of the compact disc.

(v) If multiple compact discs are submitted, the label shall indicate their order (*e.g.* "1 of X").

(vi) An indication that the disk is "Copy 1" or "Copy 2" of the submission. See paragraph (b)(4) of this section.

(7) If a file is unreadable on both copies of the disc, the unreadable file will be treated as not having been submitted. A file is unreadable if, for example, it is of a format that does not comply with the requirements of paragraph (e)(3) of this section, it is corrupted by a computer virus, or it is written onto a defective compact disc.

(f)(1) Any sequence listing in an electronic medium in compliance with §§ 1.52(e) and 1.821(c) or (e), and any computer program listing filed in an electronic medium in compliance with §§ 1.52(e) and 1.96, will be excluded when determining the application size fee required by § 1.16(s) or § 1.492(j). For purposes of determining the application size fee required by § 1.16(s) or § 1.492(j), for an application the specification and drawings of which, excluding any sequence listing in compliance with § 1.821(c) or (e), and any computer program listing filed in an electronic medium in compliance with §§ 1.52(e) and 1.96, are submitted in whole or in part on an electronic medium other than the Office electronic filing system, each three kilobytes of content submitted on an electronic medium shall be counted as a sheet of paper.

(2) Except as otherwise provided in this paragraph, the paper size equivalent of the specification and drawings of an application submitted via the Office electronic filing system will be considered to be seventy-five percent of the number of sheets of paper present in the specification and drawings of the application when entered into the Office file wrapper after being rendered by the Office electronic filing system for purposes of determining the application

size fee required by § 1.16(s). Any sequence listing in compliance with § 1.821(c) or (e), and any computer program listing in compliance with § 1.96, submitted via the Office electronic filing system will be excluded when determining the application size fee required by § 1.16(s) if the listing is submitted in ASCII text as part of an associated file.

[43 FR 20462, May 11, 1978; paras. (a) and (d), 47 FR 41275, Sept. 17, 1982, effective Oct. 1, 1982; para. (c), 48 FR 2709, Jan. 20, 1983, effective Feb. 27, 1983; para. (d), 49 FR 554, Jan. 4, 1984, effective Apr. 1, 1984; para. (c), 57 FR 2021, Jan. 17, 1992, effective Mar. 16, 1992; paras. (a) and (b) amended, 61 FR 42790, Aug. 19, 1996, effective Sept. 23, 1996; paras. (a), (c) & (d) revised, 62 FR 53131, Oct. 10, 1997, effective Dec. 1, 1997; para. (e) added, 65 FR 54604, Sept. 8, 2000, effective Sept. 8, 2000 (effective date corrected, 65 FR 78958, Dec. 18, 2000); paras. (a), (b), and (c) revised, 65 FR 54604, Sept. 8, 2000, effective Nov. 7, 2000; para. (d) revised, 65 FR 57024, Sept. 20, 2000, effective Nov. 29, 2000; paras. (a) and (b) revised, 68 FR 38611, June 30, 2003, effective July 30, 2003; section heading and paras. (b)(2)(ii), (e)(1)(iii) and (e)(3)(i)-(ii) revised, 69 FR 56481, Sept. 21, 2004, effective Oct. 21, 2004; section heading revised and para. (f) added; 70 FR 3880, Jan. 27, 2005, effective Dec. 8, 2004; para. (f) revised, 70 FR 30360, May 26, 2005, effective July 1, 2005; para. (e)(5) revised, 70 FR 54259, Sept. 14, 2005, effective Sept. 14, 2005; paras. (a)(5), (a)(7), and (b)(7) removed and para. (a)(6) redesignated as (a)(5), 70 FR 56119, Sept. 26, 2005, effective Nov. 25, 2005; para. (d)(2) revised, 72 FR 46716, Aug. 21, 2007 (implementation enjoined and never became effective); para. (d)(2) revised, 74 FR 52686, Oct. 14, 2009, effective Oct. 14, 2009 (to remove changes made by the final rules in 72 FR 46716 from the CFR)]

§ 1.53 Application number, filing date, and completion of application.

(a) *Application number.* Any papers received in the Patent and Trademark Office which purport to be an application for a patent will be assigned an application number for identification purposes.

(b) *Application filing requirements - Nonprovisional application.* The filing date of an application for patent filed under this section, except for a provisional application under paragraph (c) of this section or a continued prosecution application under paragraph (d) of this section, is the date on which a specification as prescribed by 35 U.S.C. 112 containing a description pursuant to § 1.71 and at least one claim pursuant to § 1.75, and any drawing required by § 1.81(a) are filed in the Patent and Trademark Office. No new matter may be introduced into an application after its filing date. A continuing application, which may be a continuation, divisional, or continuation-in-part application, may be filed under the conditions specified in 35 U.S.C. 120, 121 or 365(c) and § 1.78(a).

(1) A continuation or divisional application that names as inventors the same or fewer than all of the inventors named in the prior application may be filed under this paragraph or paragraph (d) of this section.

(2) A continuation-in-part application (which may disclose and claim subject matter not disclosed in the prior application) or a continuation or divisional application naming an inventor not named in the prior application must be filed under this paragraph.

(c) *Application filing requirements - Provisional application.* The filing date of a provisional application is the date on which a specification as prescribed by the first paragraph of 35 U.S.C. 112, and any drawing required by § 1.81(a) are filed in the Patent and Trademark Office. No amendment, other than to make the provisional application comply with the patent statute and all applicable regulations, may be made to the provisional application after the filing date of the provisional application.

(1) A provisional application must also include the cover sheet required by § 1.51(c)(1), which may be an application data sheet (§ 1.76), or a cover letter identifying the application as a provisional application. Otherwise, the application will be treated as an application filed under paragraph (b) of this section.

(2) An application for patent filed under paragraph (b) of this section may be converted to a provisional application and be accorded the original filing date of the application filed under paragraph (b) of this section. The grant of such a request for conversion will not entitle applicant to a refund of the fees that were properly paid in the application filed under paragraph (b) of this section. Such a request for conversion must be accompanied by the processing fee set forth in § 1.17(q) and be filed prior to the earliest of:

(i) Abandonment of the application filed under paragraph (b) of this section;

(ii) Payment of the issue fee on the application filed under paragraph (b) of this section;

(iii) Expiration of twelve months after the filing date of the application filed under paragraph (b) of this section; or

(iv) The filing of a request for a statutory invention registration under § 1.293 in the application filed under paragraph (b) of this section.

(3) A provisional application filed under paragraph (c) of this section may be converted to a nonprovisional application filed under paragraph (b) of this section and accorded the original filing date of the provisional application. The conversion of a provisional application to a nonprovisional application will not result in either the refund of any fee properly paid in the provisional application or the application of any such fee to the filing fee, or any other fee, for the nonprovisional application. Conversion of a provisional application to a nonprovisional application under this paragraph will result in the term of any patent to issue from the application being measured from at least the filing date of the provisional application for which conversion is requested. Thus, applicants should consider avoiding this adverse patent term impact by filing a nonprovisional application claiming the benefit of the provisional application under 35 U.S.C. 119(e) (rather than converting the provisional application into a nonprovisional application pursuant to this paragraph). A request to convert a provisional application to a nonprovisional application must be accompanied by the fee set forth in § 1.17(i) and an amendment including at least one claim as prescribed by the second paragraph of 35 U.S.C. 112, unless the provisional application under paragraph (c) of this section otherwise contains at least one claim as prescribed by the second paragraph of 35 U.S.C.112. The nonprovisional application resulting from conversion of a provisional application must also include the filing fee, search fee, and examination fee for a nonprovisional application, an oath or declaration by the applicant pursuant to §§ 1.63, 1.162, or 1.175, and the surcharge required by § 1.16(f) if either the basic filing fee for a nonprovisional application or the oath or declaration was not present on the filing date accorded the resulting nonprovisional application (*i.e.*, the filing date of the original provisional application). A request to convert a

provisional application to a nonprovisional application must also be filed prior to the earliest of:

(i) Abandonment of the provisional application filed under paragraph (c) of this section; or

(ii) Expiration of twelve months after the filing date of the provisional application filed under paragraph (c) of this section.

(4) A provisional application is not entitled to the right of priority under 35 U.S.C. 119 or 365(a) or § 1.55, or to the benefit of an earlier filing date under 35 U.S.C. 120, 121 or 365(c) or § 1.78 of any other application. No claim for priority under 35 U.S.C. 119(e) or § 1.78(a)(4) may be made in a design application based on a provisional application. No request under § 1.293 for a statutory invention registration may be filed in a provisional application. The requirements of §§ 1.821 through 1.825 regarding application disclosures containing nucleotide and/or amino acid sequences are not mandatory for provisional applications.

(d) *Application filing requirements - Continued prosecution (nonprovisional) application.*

(1) A continuation or divisional application (but not a continuation-in-part) of a prior nonprovisional application may be filed as a continued prosecution application under this paragraph, provided that:

(i) The application is for a design patent;

(ii) The prior nonprovisional application is a design application that is complete as defined by § 1.51(b); and

(iii) The application under this paragraph is filed before the earliest of:

(A) Payment of the issue fee on the prior application, unless a petition under § 1.313(c) is granted in the prior application;

(B) Abandonment of the prior application; or

(C) Termination of proceedings on the prior application.

(2) The filing date of a continued prosecution application is the date on which a request on a separate paper for an application under this paragraph is filed. An application filed under this paragraph:

(i) Must identify the prior application;

(ii) Discloses and claims only subject matter disclosed in the prior application;

(iii) Names as inventors the same inventors named in the prior application on the date the applica-

tion under this paragraph was filed, except as provided in paragraph (d)(4) of this section;

(iv) Includes the request for an application under this paragraph, will utilize the file jacket and contents of the prior application, including the specification, drawings and oath or declaration from the prior application, to constitute the new application, and will be assigned the application number of the prior application for identification purposes; and

(v) Is a request to expressly abandon the prior application as of the filing date of the request for an application under this paragraph.

(3) The filing fee, search fee, and examination fee for a continued prosecution application filed under this paragraph are the basic filing fee as set forth in § 1.16(b), the search fee as set forth in § 1.16 (l), and the examination fee as set forth in § 1.16(p).

(4) An application filed under this paragraph may be filed by fewer than all the inventors named in the prior application, provided that the request for an application under this paragraph when filed is accompanied by a statement requesting deletion of the name or names of the person or persons who are not inventors of the invention being claimed in the new application. No person may be named as an inventor in an application filed under this paragraph who was not named as an inventor in the prior application on the date the application under this paragraph was filed, except by way of correction of inventorship under § 1.48.

(5) Any new change must be made in the form of an amendment to the prior application as it existed prior to the filing of an application under this paragraph. No amendment in an application under this paragraph (a continued prosecution application) may introduce new matter or matter that would have been new matter in the prior application. Any new specification filed with the request for an application under this paragraph will not be considered part of the original application papers, but will be treated as a substitute specification in accordance with § 1.125.

(6) The filing of a continued prosecution application under this paragraph will be construed to include a waiver of confidentiality by the applicant under 35 U.S.C. 122 to the extent that any member of the public, who is entitled under the provisions of § 1.14 to access to, copies of, or information concerning either the prior application or any continuing

application filed under the provisions of this paragraph, may be given similar access to, copies of, or similar information concerning the other application or applications in the file jacket.

(7) A request for an application under this paragraph is the specific reference required by 35 U.S.C. 120 to every application assigned the application number identified in such request. No amendment in an application under this paragraph may delete this specific reference to any prior application.

(8) In addition to identifying the application number of the prior application, applicant should furnish in the request for an application under this paragraph the following information relating to the prior application to the best of his or her ability:

    (i)   Title of invention;

    (ii)   Name of applicant(s); and

    (iii)   Correspondence address.

(9) See § 1.103(b) for requesting a limited suspension of action in an application filed under this paragraph.

(e)   *Failure to meet filing date requirements.*

(1) If an application deposited under paragraph (b), (c), or (d) of this section does not meet the requirements of such paragraph to be entitled to a filing date, applicant will be so notified, if a correspondence address has been provided, and given a period of time within which to correct the filing error. If, however, a request for an application under paragraph (d) of this section does not meet the requirements of that paragraph because the application in which the request was filed is not a design application, and if the application in which the request was filed was itself filed on or after June 8, 1995, the request for an application under paragraph (d) of this section will be treated as a request for continued examination under § 1.114.

(2) Any request for review of a notification pursuant to paragraph (e)(1) of this section, or a notification that the original application papers lack a portion of the specification or drawing(s), must be by way of a petition pursuant to this paragraph accompanied by the fee set forth in § 1.17(f). In the absence of a timely (§ 1.181(f)) petition pursuant to this paragraph, the filing date of an application in which the applicant was notified of a filing error pursuant to paragraph (e)(1) of this section will be the date the filing error is corrected.

(3) If an applicant is notified of a filing error pursuant to paragraph (e)(1) of this section, but fails to correct the filing error within the given time period or otherwise timely (§ 1.181(f)) take action pursuant to this paragraph, proceedings in the application will be considered terminated. Where proceedings in an application are terminated pursuant to this paragraph, the application may be disposed of, and any filing fees, less the handling fee set forth in § 1.21(n), will be refunded.

(f)   *Completion of application subsequent to filing—Nonprovisional (including continued prosecution or reissue) application.*

(1) If an application which has been accorded a filing date pursuant to paragraph (b) or (d) of this section does not include the basic filing fee, the search fee, or the examination fee, or if an application which has been accorded a filing date pursuant to paragraph (b) of this section does not include an oath or declaration by the applicant pursuant to §§ 1.63, 1.162 or § 1.175, and applicant has provided a correspondence address (§ 1.33(a)), applicant will be notified and given a period of time within which to pay the basic filing fee, search fee, and examination fee, file an oath or declaration in an application under paragraph (b) of this section, and pay the surcharge if required by § 1.16(f) to avoid abandonment.

(2) If an application which has been accorded a filing date pursuant to paragraph (b) of this section does not include the basic filing fee, the search fee, the examination fee, or an oath or declaration by the applicant pursuant to §§ 1.63, 1.162 or § 1.175, and applicant has not provided a correspondence address (§ 1.33(a)), applicant has two months from the filing date of the application within which to pay the basic filing fee, search fee, and examination fee, file an oath or declaration, and pay the surcharge required by § 1.16(f) to avoid abandonment.

(3) If the excess claims fees required by §§ 1.16(h) and (i) and multiple dependent claim fee required by § 1.16(j) are not paid on filing or on later presentation of the claims for which the excess claims or multiple dependent claim fees are due, the fees required by §§ 1.16(h), (i) and (j) must be paid or the claims canceled by amendment prior to the expiration of the time period set for reply by the Office in any notice of fee deficiency. If the application size fee required by § 1.16(s) (if any) is not paid on filing or

on later presentation of the amendment necessitating a fee or additional fee under § 1.16(s), the fee required by § 1.16(s) must be paid prior to the expiration of the time period set for reply by the Office in any notice of fee deficiency in order to avoid abandonment.

(4) This paragraph applies to continuation or divisional applications under paragraphs (b) or (d) of this section and to continuation-in-part applications under paragraph (b) of this section. See § 1.63(d) concerning the submission of a copy of the oath or declaration from the prior application for a continuation or divisional application under paragraph (b) of this section.

(5) If applicant does not pay the basic filing fee during the pendency of the application, the Office may dispose of the application.

(g) *Completion of application subsequent to filing—Provisional application.*

(1) If a provisional application which has been accorded a filing date pursuant to paragraph (c) of this section does not include the cover sheet required by § 1.51(c)(1) or the basic filing fee (§ 1.16(d)), and applicant has provided a correspondence address (§ 1.33(a)), applicant will be notified and given a period of time within which to pay the basic filing fee, file a cover sheet (§ 1.51(c)(1)), and pay the surcharge required by § 1.16(g) to avoid abandonment.

(2) If a provisional application which has been accorded a filing date pursuant to paragraph (c) of this section does not include the cover sheet required by § 1.51(c)(1) or the basic filing fee (§ 1.16(d)), and applicant has not provided a correspondence address (§ 1.33(a)), applicant has two months from the filing date of the application within which to pay the basic filing fee, file a cover sheet (§ 1.51(c)(1)), and pay the surcharge required by § 1.16(g) to avoid abandonment.

(3) If the application size fee required by § 1.16(s) (if any) is not paid on filing, the fee required by § 1.16(s) must be paid prior to the expiration of the time period set for reply by the Office in any notice of fee deficiency in order to avoid abandonment.

(4) If applicant does not pay the basic filing fee during the pendency of the application, the Office may dispose of the application.

(h) *Subsequent treatment of application - Nonprovisional (including continued prosecution) appli-* *cation.* An application for a patent filed under paragraphs (b) or (d) of this section will not be placed on the files for examination until all its required parts, complying with the rules relating thereto, are received, except that certain minor informalities may be waived subject to subsequent correction whenever required.

(i) *Subsequent treatment of application - Provisional application.* A provisional application for a patent filed under paragraph (c) of this section will not be placed on the files for examination and will become abandoned no later than twelve months after its filing date pursuant to 35 U.S.C. 111(b)(1).

(j) *Filing date of international application.* The filing date of an international application designating the United States of America is treated as the filing date in the United States of America under PCT Article 11(3), except as provided in 35 U.S.C. 102(e).

[48 FR 2709, Jan. 20, 1983, effective Feb. 27, 1983; paras. (b) and (d), 49 FR 554, Jan. 4, 1984, effective Apr. 1, 1984; para. (c), 50 FR 31826, Aug. 6, 1985, effective Oct. 5, 1985; paras. (c) and (d), 53 FR 47808, Nov. 28, 1988, effective Jan. 1, 1989; paras. (b) and (c), 54 FR 47518, Nov. 15, 1989, effective Jan. 16, 1990; paras. (a)-(e) revised, 60 FR 20195, Apr. 25, 1995, effective June 8, 1995; revised, 62 FR 53131, Oct. 10, 1997, effective Dec. 1, 1997; para. (d) revised, 63 FR 5734, Feb. 4, 1998, effective Feb. 4, 1998 (adopted as final, 63 FR 36184, Jul. 2, 1998); paras. (c)(3), (c)(4) and (d) revised, 65 FR 14865, Mar. 20, 2000, effective May 29, 2000 (paras. (c)(4) and (d) adopted as final, 65 FR 50092, Aug. 16, 2000); para. (c)(3) revised, 65 FR 50092, Aug. 16, 2000, effective Aug. 16, 2000; paras. (c)(1), (c)(2), (d)(4), (e)(2), (f), and (g) revised and para. (d)(10) added, 65 FR 54604, Sept. 8, 2000, effective Nov. 7, 2000; para. (c)(4) revised, 65 FR 78958, Dec. 18, 2000; para. (d)(9) revised, 68 FR 14332, Mar. 25, 2003, effective May 1, 2003; paras. (d)(1), (d)(3) and (e)(1) revised, 68 FR 32376, May 30, 2003, effective July 14, 2003; para. (d)(9) deleted and para. (d)(10) redesignated as para. (d)(9), 69 FR 29865, May 26, 2004, effective June 25, 2004; para. (e)(2) revised, 69 FR 56481, Sept. 21, 2004, effective Nov. 22, 2004; paras (c)(3), (f) and (g) revised, 70 FR 3880, Jan. 27, 2005, effective Dec., 8, 2004; paras. (d)(3) and (f)(5) revised, 70 FR 30360, May 26, 2005, effective July 1, 2005; paras. (b) and (c)(4) revised, 72 FR 46716, Aug. 21, 2007 (implementation enjoined and never became effective); paras. (b) and (c)(4) revised, 74 FR 52686, Oct. 14, 2009, effective Oct. 14, 2009 (to remove changes made by the final rules in 72 FR 46716 from the CFR)]

§ 1.54   Parts of application to be filed together; filing receipt.

(a)   It is desirable that all parts of the complete application be deposited in the Office together; otherwise, a letter must accompany each part, accurately and clearly connecting it with the other parts of the application. See § 1.53(f) and (g) with regard to completion of an application.

(b)   Applicant will be informed of the application number and filing date by a filing receipt, unless the application is an application filed under § 1.53(d).

[48 FR 2710, Jan. 20, 1983, effective Feb. 27, 1983; para. (b) amended, 61 FR 42790, Aug. 19, 1996, effective Sept. 23, 1996; revised, 62 FR 53131, Oct. 10, 1997, effective Dec. 1, 1997]

§ 1.55   Claim for foreign priority.

(a)   An applicant in a nonprovisional application may claim the benefit of the filing date of one or more prior foreign applications under the conditions specified in 35 U.S.C. 119(a) through (d) and (f), 172, and 365(a) and (b).

(1)(i)   In an original application filed under 35 U.S.C. 111(a), the claim for priority must be presented during the pendency of the application, and within the later of four months from the actual filing date of the application or sixteen months from the filing date of the prior foreign application. This time period is not extendable. The claim must identify the foreign application for which priority is claimed, as well as any foreign application for the same subject matter and having a filing date before that of the application for which priority is claimed, by specifying the application number, country (or intellectual property authority), day, month, and year of its filing. The time periods in this paragraph do not apply in an application under 35 U.S.C. 111(a) if the application is:

(A)   A design application; or

(B)   An application filed before November 29, 2000.

(ii)   In an application that entered the national stage from an international application after compliance with 35 U.S.C. 371, the claim for priority must be made during the pendency of the application and within the time limit set forth in the PCT and the Regulations under the PCT.

(2)   The claim for priority and the certified copy of the foreign application specified in 35 U.S.C. 119(b) or PCT Rule 17 must, in any event, be filed before the patent is granted. If the claim for priority or the certified copy of the foreign application is filed after the date the issue fee is paid, it must be accompanied by the processing fee set forth in § 1.17(i), but the patent will not include the priority claim unless corrected by a certificate of correction under 35 U.S.C. 255 and § 1.323

(3)   The Office may require that the claim for priority and the certified copy of the foreign application be filed earlier than provided in paragraphs (a)(1) or (a)(2) of this section:

(i)   When the application becomes involved in an interference (see § 41.202 of this title),

(ii)   When necessary to overcome the date of a reference relied upon by the examiner, or

(iii)   When deemed necessary by the examiner.

(4)(i) An English language translation of a non-English language foreign application is not required except:

(A)   When the application is involved in an interference (see § 41.202 of this title),

(B)   When necessary to overcome the date of a reference relied upon by the examiner, or

(C)   When specifically required by the examiner.

(ii)   If an English language translation is required, it must be filed together with a statement that the translation of the certified copy is accurate.

(b)   An applicant in a nonprovisional application may under certain circumstances claim priority on the basis of one or more applications for an inventor's certificate in a country granting both inventor's certificates and patents. To claim the right of priority on the basis of an application for an inventor's certificate in such a country under 35 U.S.C. 119(d), the applicant when submitting a claim for such right as specified in paragraph (a) of this section, shall include an affidavit or declaration. The affidavit or declaration must include a specific statement that, upon an investigation, he or she is satisfied that to the best of his or her knowledge, the applicant, when filing the application for the inventor's certificate, had the option to file an application for either a patent or an inventor's certificate as to the subject matter of the identified claim or claims forming the basis for the claim of priority.

(c) Unless such claim is accepted in accordance with the provisions of this paragraph, any claim for priority under 35 U.S.C. 119(a)-(d) or 365(a) not presented within the time period provided by paragraph (a) of this section is considered to have been waived. If a claim for priority under 35 U.S.C. 119(a)-(d) or 365(a) is presented after the time period provided by paragraph (a) of this section, the claim may be accepted if the claim identifying the prior foreign application by specifying its application number, country (or intellectual property authority), and the day, month, and year of its filing was unintentionally delayed. A petition to accept a delayed claim for priority under 35 U.S.C. 119(a)-(d) or 365(a) must be accompanied by:

(1) The claim under 35 U.S.C. 119(a)-(d) or 365(a) and this section to the prior foreign application, unless previously submitted;

(2) The surcharge set forth in § 1.17(t); and

(3) A statement that the entire delay between the date the claim was due under paragraph (a)(1) of this section and the date the claim was filed was unintentional. The Director may require additional information where there is a question whether the delay was unintentional.

(d)(1) The requirement in this section for the certified copy of the foreign application will be considered satisfied if:

(i) The applicant files a request, in a separate document, that the Office obtain a copy of the foreign application from a foreign intellectual property office participating with the Office in a bilateral or multilateral priority document exchange agreement (participating foreign intellectual property office (see § 1.14 (h)(1));

(ii) The foreign application is identified in the oath or declaration (Sec. 1.63(c)) or an application data sheet (§ 1.76 (a)(6)); and

(iii) The copy of the foreign application is received by the Office within the period set forth in paragraph (a) of this section. Such a request should be made within the later of four months from the filing date of the application or sixteen months from the filing date of the foreign application.

(2) If the foreign application was filed at a foreign intellectual property office that is not partici-

pating with the Office in a priority document exchange agreement, but a copy of the foreign application was filed in an application subsequently filed in a participating foreign intellectual property office, the request under paragraph (d)(1)(i) of this section must identify the participating foreign intellectual property office and the application number of the subsequent application in which a copy of the foreign application was filed.

[para. (b), 47 FR 41275, Sept. 17, 1982, effective Oct. 1 1982; 48 FR 2710, Jan. 20, 1983, effective Feb. 27, 1983; para. (b), 49 FR 554, Jan. 4, 1984, effective Apr. 1, 1984; para. (a), 49 FR 48416, Dec. 12, 1984, effective Feb. 11, 1985; para. (a), 54 FR 6893, Feb. 15, 1989, effective Apr. 17, 1989; para. (a) revised, 54 FR 9432, March 7, 1989, effective Apr. 17, 1989; para. (a), 54 FR 47518, Nov. 15, 1989, effective Jan. 16, 1990; para. (a) revised, 58 FR 54504, Oct. 22, 1993, effective Jan. 3, 1994; revised, 60 FR 20195, Apr.25, 1995, effective June 8, 1995; para. (a) revised, 62 FR 53131, Oct. 10, 1997, effective Dec. 1, 1997; para. (a) revised, 65 FR 54604, Sept. 8, 2000, effective Nov. 7, 2000; para. (a) revised and para. (c) added, 65 FR 57024, Sept. 20, 2000, effective Nov. 29, 2000; paras. (a) and (c) corrected, 65 FR 66502, Nov. 6, 2000, effective Nov. 29, 2000; paras.(a)(1) and (c) revised, 66 FR 67087, Dec. 28, 2001, effective Dec. 28, 2001; para. (c)(3) revised, 68 FR 14332, Mar. 25, 2003, effective May 1, 2003; paras. (a)(3) and (a)(4) revised, 69 FR 49959, Aug. 12, 2004, effective Sept. 13, 2004; para. (d) added, 72 FR 1664, Jan. 16, 2007, effective Jan. 16, 2007]

§ 1.56 Duty to disclose information material to patentability.

(a) A patent by its very nature is affected with a public interest. The public interest is best served, and the most effective patent examination occurs when, at the time an application is being examined, the Office is aware of and evaluates the teachings of all information material to patentability. Each individual associated with the filing and prosecution of a patent application has a duty of candor and good faith in dealing with the Office, which includes a duty to disclose to the Office all information known to that individual to be material to patentability as defined in this section. The duty to disclose information exists with respect to each pending claim until the claim is cancelled or withdrawn from consideration, or the application becomes abandoned. Information material to the patentability of a claim that is cancelled or withdrawn from consideration need not be submitted if the information is not material to the patentability of any claim remaining under consideration in the application. There is no duty to submit information which is not material to the patentability of any existing claim. The duty to disclose all information known to be material to patentability is deemed to be satisfied if all information known to be material to patentability of any claim issued in a patent was cited by the Office or submitted to the Office in the manner prescribed by §§ 1.97(b)-(d) and 1.98. However, no patent will be granted on an application in connection with which fraud on the Office was practiced or attempted or the duty of disclosure was violated through bad faith or intentional misconduct. The Office encourages applicants to carefully examine:

(1)   Prior art cited in search reports of a foreign patent office in a counterpart application, and

(2)   The closest information over which individuals associated with the filing or prosecution of a patent application believe any pending claim patentably defines, to make sure that any material information contained therein is disclosed to the Office.

(b)   Under this section, information is material to patentability when it is not cumulative to information already of record or being made of record in the application, and

(1)   It establishes, by itself or in combination with other information, a *prima facie* case of unpatentability of a claim; or

(2)   It refutes, or is inconsistent with, a position the applicant takes in:

(i)   Opposing an argument of unpatentability relied on by the Office, or

(ii)   Asserting an argument of patentability.

A *prima facie* case of unpatentability is established when the information compels a conclusion that a claim is unpatentable under the preponderance of evidence, burden-of-proof standard, giving each term in the claim its broadest reasonable construction consistent with the specification, and before any consideration is given to evidence which may be submitted in an attempt to establish a contrary conclusion of patentability.

(c)   Individuals associated with the filing or prosecution of a patent application within the meaning of this section are:

(1)   Each inventor named in the application;

(2)   Each attorney or agent who prepares or prosecutes the application; and

(3)   Every other person who is substantively involved in the preparation or prosecution of the application and who is associated with the inventor, with the assignee or with anyone to whom there is an obligation to assign the application.

(d)   Individuals other than the attorney, agent or inventor may comply with this section by disclosing information to the attorney, agent, or inventor.

(e)   In any continuation-in-part application, the duty under this section includes the duty to disclose to the Office all information known to the person to be material to patentability, as defined in paragraph (b) of this section, which became available between the filing date of the prior application and the national or PCT international filing date of the continuation-in-part application.

[42 FR 5593, Jan. 28, 1977; paras. (d) & (e) - (i), 47 FR 21751, May 19, 1982, effective July 1, 1982; para. (c), 48 FR 2710, Jan. 20, 1983, effective Feb. 27, 1983; paras. (b) and (j), 49 FR 554, Jan. 4, 1984, effective Apr. 1, 1984; paras. (d) and (h), 50 FR 5171, Feb. 6, 1985, effective Mar. 8, 1985; para. (e), 53 FR 47808, Nov. 28, 1988, effective Jan. 1, 1989; 57 FR 2021, Jan. 17, 1992, effective Mar. 16, 1992; para. (e) added, 65 FR 54604, Sept. 8, 2000, effective Nov. 7, 2000]

§ 1.57   Incorporation by reference.

(a)   Subject to the conditions and requirements of this paragraph, if all or a portion of the specification or drawing(s) is inadvertently omitted from an application, but the application contains a claim under § 1.55 for priority of a prior-filed foreign application, or a claim under § 1.78 for the benefit of a prior-filed provisional, nonprovisional, or international application, that was present on the filing date of the application, and the inadvertently omitted portion of the specification or drawing(s) is completely contained in the prior-filed application, the claim under § 1.55 or § 1.78 shall also be considered an incorporation by reference of the prior-filed application as to the inadvertently omitted portion of the specification or drawing(s).

(1)   The application must be amended to include the inadvertently omitted portion of the specification or drawing(s) within any time period set by the Office, but in no case later than the close of prose-

cution as defined by § 1.114(b), or abandonment of the application, whichever occurs earlier. The applicant is also required to:

(i) Supply a copy of the prior-filed application, except where the prior-filed application is an application filed under 35 U.S.C. 111;

(ii) Supply an English language translation of any prior-filed application that is in a language other than English; and

(iii) Identify where the inadvertently omitted portion of the specification or drawings can be found in the prior-filed application.

(2) Any amendment to an international application pursuant to this paragraph shall be effective only as to the United States, and shall have no effect on the international filing date of the application. In addition, no request under this section to add the inadvertently omitted portion of the specification or drawings in an international application designating the United States will be acted upon by the Office prior to the entry and commencement of the national stage (§ 1.491) or the filing of an application under 35 U.S.C. 111(a) which claims benefit of the international application. Any omitted portion of the international application which applicant desires to be effective as to all designated States, subject to PCT Rule 20.8(b), must be submitted in accordance with PCT Rule 20.

(3) If an application is not otherwise entitled to a filing date under § 1.53(b), the amendment must be by way of a petition pursuant to this paragraph accompanied by the fee set forth in § 1.17(f).

(b) Except as provided in paragraph (a) of this section, an incorporation by reference must be set forth in the specification and must:

(1) Express a clear intent to incorporate by reference by using the root words "incorporat(e)" and "reference" (e.g., "incorporate by reference"); and

(2) Clearly identify the referenced patent, application, or publication.

(c) "Essential material" may be incorporated by reference, but only by way of an incorporation by reference to a U.S. patent or U.S. patent application publication, which patent or patent application publication does not itself incorporate such essential material by reference. "Essential material" is material that is necessary to:

(1) Provide a written description of the claimed invention, and of the manner and process of making and using it, in such full, clear, concise, and exact terms as to enable any person skilled in the art to which it pertains, or with which it is most nearly connected, to make and use the same, and set forth the best mode contemplated by the inventor of carrying out the invention as required by the first paragraph of 35 U.S.C. 112;

(2) Describe the claimed invention in terms that particularly point out and distinctly claim the invention as required by the second paragraph of 35 U.S.C. 112; or

(3) Describe the structure, material, or acts that correspond to a claimed means or step for performing a specified function as required by the sixth paragraph of 35 U.S.C. 112.

(d) Other material ("Nonessential material") may be incorporated by reference to U.S. patents, U.S. patent application publications, foreign patents, foreign published applications, prior and concurrently filed commonly owned U.S. applications, or non-patent publications. An incorporation by reference by hyperlink or other form of browser executable code is not permitted.

(e) The examiner may require the applicant to supply a copy of the material incorporated by reference. If the Office requires the applicant to supply a copy of material incorporated by reference, the material must be accompanied by a statement that the copy supplied consists of the same material incorporated by reference in the referencing application.

(f) Any insertion of material incorporated by reference into the specification or drawings of an application must be by way of an amendment to the specification or drawings. Such an amendment must be accompanied by a statement that the material being inserted is the material previously incorporated by reference and that the amendment contains no new matter.

(g) An incorporation of material by reference that does not comply with paragraphs (b), (c), or (d) of this section is not effective to incorporate such material unless corrected within any time period set by the Office, but in no case later than the close of prosecution as defined by § 1.114(b), or abandonment of the application, whichever occurs earlier. In addition:

(1)   A correction to comply with paragraph (b)(1) of this section is permitted only if the application as filed clearly conveys an intent to incorporate the material by reference. A mere reference to material does not convey an intent to incorporate the material by reference.

(2)   A correction to comply with paragraph (b)(2) of this section is only permitted for material that was sufficiently described to uniquely identify the document.

[Added, 69 FR 56481, Sept. 21, 2004, effective Oct. 21, 2004; para. (a)(3) added, 69 FR 56481, Sept. 21, 2004, effective Nov. 22, 2004; para. (a)(2) revised, 72 FR 51559, Sept. 10, 2007, effective Sept. 10, 2007]

§ 1.58   Chemical and mathematical formulae and tables.

(a)   The specification, including the claims, may contain chemical and mathematical formulae, but shall not contain drawings or flow diagrams. The description portion of the specification may contain tables, but the same tables may only be included in both the drawings and description portion of the specification if the application was filed under 35 U.S.C. 371. Claims may contain tables either if necessary to conform to 35 U.S.C. 112 or if otherwise found to be desirable.

(b)   Tables that are submitted in electronic form (§§ 1.96(c) and 1.821(c)) must maintain the spatial relationships (e.g., alignment of columns and rows) of the table elements when displayed so as to visually preserve the relational information they convey. Chemical and mathematical formulae must be encoded to maintain the proper positioning of their characters when displayed in order to preserve their intended meaning.

(c)   Chemical and mathematical formulae and tables must be presented in compliance with § 1.52(a) and (b), except that chemical and mathematical formulae or tables may be placed in a landscape orientation if they cannot be presented satisfactorily in a portrait orientation. Typewritten characters used in such formulae and tables must be chosen from a block (nonscript) type font or lettering style having capital letters which should be at least 0.422 cm. (0.166 inch) high (e.g., preferably Arial, Times Roman, or Courier with a font size of 12), but may be no smaller than 0.21 cm. (0.08 inch) high (e.g., a font size of 6). A space at least 0.64 cm. (1/4 inch) high should be provided between complex formulae and tables and the text. Tables should have the lines and columns of data closely spaced to conserve space, consistent with a high degree of legibility.

[43 FR 20463, May 11, 1978; para. (b) removed and reserved, para. (c) amended, 61 FR 42790, Aug. 19, 1996, effective Sept. 23, 1996; para. (b) added, 65 FR 54604, Sept. 8, 2000, effective Nov. 7, 2000; revised, 69 FR 56481, Sept. 21, 2004, effective Oct. 21, 2004]

§ 1.59   Expungement of information or copy of papers in application file.

(a)(1) Information in an application will not be expunged, except as provided in paragraph (b) of this section or § 41.7(a) of this title.

(2)   Information forming part of the original disclosure (i.e., written specification including the claims, drawings, and any preliminary amendment specifically incorporated into an executed oath or declaration under §§ 1.63 and 1.175) will not be expunged from the application file.

(b)   An applicant may request that the Office expunge information, other than what is excluded by paragraph (a)(2) of this section, by filing a petition under this paragraph. Any petition to expunge information from an application must include the fee set forth in § 1.17(g) and establish to the satisfaction of the Director that the expungement of the information is appropriate in which case a notice granting the petition for expungement will be provided.

(c)   Upon request by an applicant and payment of the fee specified in § 1.19(b), the Office will furnish copies of an application, unless the application has been disposed of (see §§ 1.53(e), (f) and (g)). The Office cannot provide or certify copies of an application that has been disposed of.

[48 FR 2710, Jan. 20, 1983, effective Feb. 27, 1983; 49 FR 554, Jan. 4, 1984, effective Apr. 1, 1984; 49 FR 48416, Dec. 12, 1984, effective Feb. 11, 1985; 50 FR 23123, May 31, 1985, effective Feb. 11, 1985; revised, 60 FR 20195, Apr. 25, 1995, effective June 8, 1995; revised, 62 FR 53131, Oct. 10, 1997, effective Dec. 1, 1997; para. (b) revised, 65 FR 54604, Sept. 8, 2000, effective Nov. 7, 2000; para. (b) revised, 68 FR 14332, Mar. 25, 2003, effective May 1, 2003; revised, 68 FR 38611, June 30, 2003, effective July 30, 2003; para. (a)(1) revised, 69 FR 49959,

Aug. 12, 2004, effective Sept. 13, 2004; para. (b) revised, 69 FR 56481, Sept. 21, 2004, effective Nov. 22, 2004]

§ 1.60   [Reserved]

[48 FR 2710, Jan. 20, 1983, effective Feb. 27, 1983; 49 FR 554, Jan. 4, 1984, effective Apr. 1, 1984; 50 FR 9379, Mar. 7, 1985, effective May 8, 1985; paras. (a), (b) and (c), 54 FR 47519, Nov. 15, 1989, effective Jan. 16, 1990; paras. (b) and (c) revised, para. (d) added, 57 FR 56446, Nov. 30, 1992, effective Jan. 4, 1993; para. (b) revised, 60 FR 20195, Apr. 25, 1995, effective June 8, 1995; removed and reserved, 62 FR 53131, Oct. 10, 1997, effective Dec. 1, 1997]

§ 1.61   [Reserved]

(Editor's note: Substance is now in § 1.495)

§ 1.62   [Reserved]

[47 FR 47244, Oct. 25, 1982, added effective Feb. 27, 1983; 48 FR 2710, Jan. 20, 1983, effective date Feb. 27, 1983; paras. (a) and (d), 49 FR 555, Jan. 4, 1984, effective Apr. 1, 1984; paras. (a), (c), and (h), 50 FR 9380, Mar. 7, 1985, effective May 8, 1985; paras. (e) and (j), 54 FR 47519, Nov. 15, 1989, effective Jan. 16, 1990; paras. (a) and (e) revised, 60 FR 20195, Apr. 25, 1995, effective June 8, 1995; para. (f) revised, 61 FR 42790, Aug. 19, 1996, effective Sept. 23, 1996; removed and reserved, 62 FR 53131, Oct. 10, 1997, effective Dec. 1, 1997]

OATH OR DECLARATION

§ 1.63   Oath or declaration.

(a)   An oath or declaration filed under § 1.51(b)(2) as a part of a nonprovisional application must:

(1)   Be executed, *i.e.*, signed, in accordance with either § 1.66 or § 1.68. There is no minimum age for a person to be qualified to sign, but the person must be competent to sign, *i.e.*, understand the document that the person is signing;

(2)   Identify each inventor by full name, including the family name, and at least one given name without abbreviation together with any other given name or initial;

(3)   Identify the country of citizenship of each inventor; and

(4)   State that the person making the oath or declaration believes the named inventor or inventors to be the original and first inventor or inventors of the subject matter which is claimed and for which a patent is sought.

(b)   In addition to meeting the requirements of paragraph (a) of this section, the oath or declaration must also:

(1)   Identify the application to which it is directed;

(2)   State that the person making the oath or declaration has reviewed and understands the contents of the application, including the claims, as amended by any amendment specifically referred to in the oath or declaration; and

(3)   State that the person making the oath or declaration acknowledges the duty to disclose to the Office all information known to the person to be material to patentability as defined in § 1.56.

(c)   Unless such information is supplied on an application data sheet in accordance with § 1.76, the oath or declaration must also identify:

(1)   The mailing address, and the residence if an inventor lives at a location which is different from where the inventor customarily receives mail, of each inventor; and

(2)   Any foreign application for patent (or inventor's certificate) for which a claim for priority is made pursuant to § 1.55, and any foreign application having a filing date before that of the application on which priority is claimed, by specifying the application number, country, day, month, and year of its filing.

(d)(1)   A newly executed oath or declaration is not required under § 1.51(b)(2) and § 1.53(f) in a continuation or divisional application, provided that:

(i)   The prior nonprovisional application contained an oath or declaration as prescribed by paragraphs (a) through (c) of this section;

(ii)   The continuation or divisional application was filed by all or by fewer than all of the inventors named in the prior application;

(iii)   The specification and drawings filed in the continuation or divisional application contain no matter that would have been new matter in the prior application; and

(iv)   A copy of the executed oath or declaration filed in the prior application, showing the signature or an indication thereon that it was signed, is submitted for the continuation or divisional application.

(2) The copy of the executed oath or declaration submitted under this paragraph for a continuation or divisional application must be accompanied by a statement requesting the deletion of the name or names of the person or persons who are not inventors in the continuation or divisional application.

(3) Where the executed oath or declaration of which a copy is submitted for a continuation or divisional application was originally filed in a prior application accorded status under § 1.47, the copy of the executed oath or declaration for such prior application must be accompanied by:

(i) A copy of the decision granting a petition to accord § 1.47 status to the prior application, unless all inventors or legal representatives have filed an oath or declaration to join in an application accorded status under § 1.47 of which the continuation or divisional application claims a benefit under 35 U.S.C. 120, 121, or 365(c); and

(ii) If one or more inventor(s) or legal representative(s) who refused to join in the prior application or could not be found or reached has subsequently joined in the prior application or another application of which the continuation or divisional application claims a benefit under 35 U.S.C. 120, 121, or 365(c), a copy of the subsequently executed oath(s) or declaration(s) filed by the inventor or legal representative to join in the application.

(4) Where the power of attorney or correspondence address was changed during the prosecution of the prior application, the change in power of attorney or correspondence address must be identified in the continuation or divisional application. Otherwise, the Office may not recognize in the continuation or divisional application the change of power of attorney or correspondence address during the prosecution of the prior application.

(5) A newly executed oath or declaration must be filed in a continuation or divisional application naming an inventor not named in the prior application.

(e) A newly executed oath or declaration must be filed in any continuation-in-part application, which application may name all, more, or fewer than all of the inventors named in the prior application.

[48 FR 2711, Jan. 20, 1983, added effective Feb. 27, 1983; 48 FR 4285, Jan. 31, 1983; paras. (b)(3) and (d), 57 FR 2021, Jan. 17, 1992, effective Mar. 16, 1992; para. (a) revised, 60 FR 20195, Apr. 25, 1995, effective June 8, 1995; paras. (a) & (d) revised, para. (e) added, 62 FR 53131, Oct. 10, 1997, effective Dec. 1, 1997; paras. (a), (b), (c), and (e) revised, 65 FR 54604, Sept. 8, 2000, effective Nov. 7, 2000; para. (d)(4) revised, 69 FR 56481, Sept. 21, 2004, effective Oct. 21, 2004]

§ 1.64   Person making oath or declaration.

(a) The oath or declaration (§ 1.63), including any supplemental oath or declaration (§ 1.67), must be made by all of the actual inventors except as provided for in §§ 1.42, 1.43, 1.47, or § 1.67.

(b) If the person making the oath or declaration or any supplemental oath or declaration is not the inventor (§§ 1.42, 1.43, 1.47, or § 1.67), the oath or declaration shall state the relationship of the person to the inventor, and, upon information and belief, the facts which the inventor is required to state. If the person signing the oath or declaration is the legal representative of a deceased inventor, the oath or declaration shall also state that the person is a legal representative and the citizenship, residence, and mailing address of the legal representative.

[48 FR 2711, Jan. 20, 1983, added effective Feb. 27, 1983; revised, 65 FR 54604, Sept. 8, 2000, effective Nov. 7, 2000]

§ 1.66   Officers authorized to administer oaths.

(a) The oath or affirmation may be made before any person within the United States authorized by law to administer oaths. An oath made in a foreign country may be made before any diplomatic or consular officer of the United States authorized to administer oaths, or before any officer having an official seal and authorized to administer oaths in the foreign country in which the applicant may be, whose authority shall be proved by a certificate of a diplomatic or consular officer of the United States, or by an apostille of an official designated by a foreign country which, by treaty or convention, accords like effect to apostilles of designated officials in the United States. The oath shall be attested in all cases in this and other countries, by the proper official seal of the officer before whom the oath or affirmation is made. Such oath or affirmation shall be valid as to execution if it complies with the laws of the State or country where made. When the person before whom the oath or affirmation is made in this country is not provided with a seal, his official character shall be established by competent evidence, as by a certificate from a clerk of a court of record or other proper officer having a seal.

(b)   When the oath is taken before an officer in a country foreign to the United States, any accompanying application papers, except the drawings, must be attached together with the oath and a ribbon passed one or more times through all the sheets of the application, except the drawings, and the ends of said ribbon brought together under the seal before the latter is affixed and impressed, or each sheet must be impressed with the official seal of the officer before whom the oath is taken. If the papers as filed are not properly ribboned or each sheet impressed with the seal, the case will be accepted for examination, but before it is allowed, duplicate papers, prepared in compliance with the foregoing sentence, must be filed.

[47 FR 41275, Sept. 17, 1982, effective Oct. 1, 1982]

§ 1.67   Supplemental oath or declaration.

(a)   The Office may require, or inventors and applicants may submit, a supplemental oath or declaration meeting the requirements of § 1.63 or § 1.162 to correct any deficiencies or inaccuracies present in the earlier filed oath or declaration.

(1)   Deficiencies or inaccuracies relating to all the inventors or applicants (§§ 1.42, 1.43, or § 1.47) may be corrected with a supplemental oath or declaration signed by all the inventors or applicants.

(2)   Deficiencies or inaccuracies relating to fewer than all of the inventor(s) or applicant(s) (§§ 1.42, 1.43 or § 1.47) may be corrected with a supplemental oath or declaration identifying the entire inventive entity but signed only by the inventor(s) or applicant(s) to whom the error or deficiency relates.

(3)   Deficiencies or inaccuracies due to the failure to meet the requirements of § 1.63(c) (e.g., to correct the omission of a mailing address of an inventor) in an oath or declaration may be corrected with an application data sheet in accordance with § 1.76.

(4)   Submission of a supplemental oath or declaration or an application data sheet (§ 1.76), as opposed to who must sign the supplemental oath or declaration or an application data sheet, is governed by § 1.33(a)(2) and paragraph (b) of this section.

(b)   A supplemental oath or declaration meeting the requirements of § 1.63 must be filed when a claim is presented for matter originally shown or described but not substantially embraced in the statement of invention or claims originally presented or when an oath or declaration submitted in accordance with § 1.53(f) after the filing of the specification and any required drawings specifically and improperly refers to an amendment which includes new matter. No new matter may be introduced into a nonprovisional application after its filing date even if a supplemental oath or declaration is filed. In proper situations, the oath or declaration here required may be made on information and belief by an applicant other than the inventor.

(c)   [Reserved]

[48 FR 2711, Jan. 20, 1983, effective Feb. 27, 1983; para. (c) added, 57 FR 2021, Jan. 17, 1992, effective Mar. 16, 1992; para. (b) revised, 60 FR 20195, Apr. 25, 1995, effective June 8, 1995; para. (b) revised, 62 FR 53131, Oct. 10, 1997, effective Dec. 1, 1997; para. (a) revised and para. (c) removed and reserved, 65 FR 54604, Sept. 8, 2000, effective Nov. 7, 2000]

§ 1.68   Declaration in lieu of oath.

Any document to be filed in the Patent and Trademark Office and which is required by any law, rule, or other regulation to be under oath may be subscribed to by a written declaration. Such declaration may be used in lieu of the oath otherwise required, if, and only if, the declarant is on the same document, warned that willful false statements and the like are punishable by fine or imprisonment, or both (18 U.S.C. 1001) and may jeopardize the validity of the application or any patent issuing thereon. The declarant must set forth in the body of the declaration that all statements made of the declarant's own knowledge are true and that all statements made on information and belief are believed to be true.

[49 FR 48416, Dec. 12, 1984, effective Feb. 11, 1985]

§ 1.69   Foreign language oaths and declarations.

(a)   Whenever an individual making an oath or declaration cannot understand English, the oath or declaration must be in a language that such individual can understand and shall state that such individual understands the content of any documents to which the oath or declaration relates.

(b) Unless the text of any oath or declaration in a language other than English is in a form provided by the Patent and Trademark Office or in accordance with PCT Rule 4.17(iv), it must be accompanied by an English translation together with a statement that the translation is accurate, except that in the case of an oath or declaration filed under § 1.63, the translation may be filed in the Office no later than two months from the date applicant is notified to file the translation.

[42 FR 5594, Jan. 28, 1977; para. (b), 48 FR 2711, Jan. 20, 1983, effective Feb. 27, 1983; para. (b) revised, 62 FR 53131, Oct. 10, 1997, effective Dec. 1, 1997; para. (b) revised, 69 FR 56481, Sept. 21, 2004, effective Oct. 21, 2004; para. (b) revised, 70 FR 3880, Jan. 27, 2005, effective Dec. 8, 2004]

§ 1.70   [Reserved]

(Editor's note: Substance moved to § 1.497)

[52 FR 20046, May 28, 1987, effective July 1, 1987]

SPECIFICATION

§ 1.71   Detailed description and specification of the invention.

(a) The specification must include a written description of the invention or discovery and of the manner and process of making and using the same, and is required to be in such full, clear, concise, and exact terms as to enable any person skilled in the art or science to which the invention or discovery appertains, or with which it is most nearly connected, to make and use the same.

(b) The specification must set forth the precise invention for which a patent is solicited, in such manner as to distinguish it from other inventions and from what is old. It must describe completely a specific embodiment of the process, machine, manufacture, composition of matter or improvement invented, and must explain the mode of operation or principle whenever applicable. The best mode contemplated by the inventor of carrying out his invention must be set forth.

(c) In the case of an improvement, the specification must particularly point out the part or parts of the process, machine, manufacture, or composition of matter to which the improvement relates, and the description should be confined to the specific improvement and to such parts as necessarily cooperate with it or as may be necessary to a complete understanding or description of it.

(d) A copyright or mask work notice may be placed in a design or utility patent application adjacent to copyright and mask work material contained therein. The notice may appear at any appropriate portion of the patent application disclosure. For notices in drawings, see § 1.84(s). The content of the notice must be limited to only those elements provided for by law. For example, "©1983 John Doe"(17 U.S.C. 401) and "*M* John Doe" (17 U.S.C. 909) would be properly limited and, under current statutes, legally sufficient notices of copyright and mask work, respectively. Inclusion of a copyright or mask work notice will be permitted only if the authorization language set forth in paragraph (e) of this section is included at the beginning (preferably as the first paragraph) of the specification.

(e) The authorization shall read as follows:

A portion of the disclosure of this patent document contains material which is subject to (copyright or mask work) protection. The (copyright or mask work) owner has no objection to the facsimile reproduction by anyone of the patent document or the patent disclosure, as it appears in the Patent and Trademark Office patent file or records, but otherwise reserves all (copyright or mask work) rights whatsoever.

(f) The specification must commence on a separate sheet. Each sheet including part of the specification may not include other parts of the application or other information. The claim(s), abstract and sequence listing (if any) should not be included on a sheet including any other part of the application.

(g)(1) The specification may disclose or be amended to disclose the names of the parties to a joint research agreement (35 U.S.C. 103(c)(2)(C)).

(2) An amendment under paragraph (g)(1) of this section must be accompanied by the processing fee set forth § 1.17(i) if not filed within one of the following time periods:

(i) Within three months of the filing date of a national application;

(ii) Within three months of the date of entry of the national stage as set forth in § 1.491 in an international application;

(iii) Before the mailing of a first Office action on the merits; or

(iv) Before the mailing of a first Office action after the filing of a request for continued examination under § 1.114.

(3) If an amendment under paragraph (g)(1) of this section is filed after the date the issue fee is paid, the patent as issued may not necessarily include the names of the parties to the joint research agreement. If the patent as issued does not include the names of the parties to the joint research agreement, the patent must be corrected to include the names of the parties to the joint research agreement by a certificate of correction under 35 U.S.C. 255 and § 1.323 for the amendment to be effective.

[paras. (d) and (e), 53 FR 47808, Nov. 28, 1988, effective Jan. 1, 1989; para. (d), 58 FR 38719, July 20, 1993, effective Oct. 1, 1993; para. (f) added, 68 FR 38611, June 30, 2003, effective July 30, 2003; para. (g) added, 70 FR 1818, Jan. 11, 2005, effective Dec. 10, 2004; para. (g) revised, 70 FR 54259, Sept. 14, 2005, effective Sept. 14, 2005]

§ 1.72   Title and abstract.

(a) The title of the invention may not exceed 500 characters in length and must be as short and specific as possible. Characters that cannot be captured and recorded in the Office's automated information systems may not be reflected in the Office's records in such systems or in documents created by the Office. Unless the title is supplied in an application data sheet (§ 1.76), the title of the invention should appear as a heading on the first page of the specification.

(b) A brief abstract of the technical disclosure in the specification must commence on a separate sheet, preferably following the claims, under the heading "Abstract" or "Abstract of the Disclosure." The sheet or sheets presenting the abstract may not include other parts of the application or other material. The abstract in an application filed under 35 U.S.C. 111 may not exceed 150 words in length. The purpose of the abstract is to enable the United States Patent and Trademark Office and the public generally to determine quickly from a cursory inspection the nature and gist of the technical disclosure.

[31 FR 12922, Oct. 4, 1966; 43 FR 20464, May 11, 1978; para. (b) amended, 61 FR 42790, Aug. 19, 1996, effective Sept. 23, 1996; revised, 65 FR 54604, Sept. 8, 2000, effective Nov. 7, 2000; para. (a) revised, 65 FR 57024, Sept. 20, 2000, effective Nov. 29, 2000; para. (b) revised, 68 FR 38611, June 30, 2003, effective July 30, 2003]

§ 1.73   Summary of the invention.

A brief summary of the invention indicating its nature and substance, which may include a statement of the object of the invention, should precede the detailed description. Such summary should, when set forth, be commensurate with the invention as claimed and any object recited should be that of the invention as claimed.

§ 1.74   Reference to drawings.

When there are drawings, there shall be a brief description of the several views of the drawings and the detailed description of the invention shall refer to the different views by specifying the numbers of the figures and to the different parts by use of reference letters or numerals (preferably the latter).

§ 1.75   Claim(s).

(a) The specification must conclude with a claim particularly pointing out and distinctly claiming the subject matter which the applicant regards as his invention or discovery.

(b) More than one claim may be presented provided they differ substantially from each other and are not unduly multiplied.

(c) One or more claims may be presented in dependent form, referring back to and further limiting another claim or claims in the same application. Any dependent claim which refers to more than one other claim ("multiple dependent claim") shall refer to such other claims in the alternative only. A multiple dependent claim shall not serve as a basis for any other multiple dependent claim. For fee calculation purposes under § 1.16, a multiple dependent claim will be considered to be that number of claims to which direct reference is made therein. For fee calculation purposes also, any claim depending from a multiple dependent claim will be considered to be that number of claims to which direct reference is made in that multiple dependent claim. In addition to the other filing fees, any original application which is filed with, or is amended to include, multiple dependent claims must have paid therein the fee set forth in § 1.16(j). Claims in dependent form shall be construed to include all the limitations of the claim incorporated by reference into the dependent claim. A multiple dependent claim shall be construed to incorporate by reference all the limitations of each of the particular claims in relation to which it is being considered.

(d)(1)   The claim or claims must conform to the invention as set forth in the remainder of the specification and the terms and phrases used in the claims must find clear support or antecedent basis in the description so that the meaning of the terms in the claims may be ascertainable by reference to the description. (See § 1.58(a)).

(2)   See §§ 1.141 to 1.146 as to claiming different inventions in one application.

(e)   Where the nature of the case admits, as in the case of an improvement, any independent claim should contain in the following order:

(1)   A preamble comprising a general description of all the elements or steps of the claimed combination which are conventional or known,

(2)   A phrase such as "wherein the improvement comprises," and

(3)   Those elements, steps, and/or relationships which constitute that portion of the claimed combination which the applicant considers as the new or improved portion.

(f)   If there are several claims, they shall be numbered consecutively in Arabic numerals.

(g)   The least restrictive claim should be presented as claim number 1, and all dependent claims should be grouped together with the claim or claims to which they refer to the extent practicable.

(h)   The claim or claims must commence on a separate physical sheet or electronic page. Any sheet including a claim or portion of a claim may not contain any other parts of the application or other material.

(i)   Where a claim sets forth a plurality of elements or steps, each element or step of the claim should be separated by a line indentation.

[31 FR 12922, Oct. 4, 1966; 36 FR 12690, July 3, 1971; 37 FR 21995, Oct. 18, 1972; 43 FR 4015, Jan. 31, 1978; para. (c), 47 FR 41276, Sept. 17, 1982, effective Oct. 1, 1982; para. (g) amended, paras. (h) and (i) added, 61 FR 42790, Aug. 19, 1996, effective Sept. 23, 1996; para. (h) revised, 68 FR 38611, June 30, 2003, effective July 30, 2003; para. (h) revised, 68 FR 38611, June 30, 2003, effective July 30, 2003; para. (c) revised, 70 FR 3880, Jan. 27, 2005, effective Dec. 8, 2004; paras. (b) and (c) revised, 72 FR 46716, Aug. 21, 2007 (implementation enjoined and never became effective); paras. (b) and (c) revised, 74 FR 52686, Oct. 14, 2009, effective Oct. 14, 2009 (to remove changes made by the final rules in 72 FR 46716 from the CFR)]

§ 1.76   Application data sheet.

(a)   *Application data sheet.* An application data sheet is a sheet or sheets, that may be voluntarily submitted in either provisional or nonprovisional applications, which contains bibliographic data, arranged in a format specified by the Office. An application data sheet must be titled "Application Data Sheet" and must contain all of the section headings listed in paragraph (b) of this section, with any appropriate data for each section heading. If an application data sheet is provided, the application data sheet is part of the provisional or nonprovisional application for which it has been submitted.

(b)   *Bibliographic data.* Bibliographic data as used in paragraph (a) of this section includes:

(1)   *Applicant information.* This information includes the name, residence, mailing address, and citizenship of each applicant (§ 1.41(b)). The name of each applicant must include the family name, and at least one given name without abbreviation together with any other given name or initial. If the applicant is not an inventor, this information also includes the applicant's authority (§§ 1.42, 1.43, and 1.47) to apply for the patent on behalf of the inventor.

(2)   *Correspondence information.* This information includes the correspondence address, which may be indicated by reference to a customer number, to which correspondence is to be directed (see § 1.33(a)).

(3)   *Application information.* This information includes the title of the invention, a suggested classification, by class and subclass, the Technology Center to which the subject matter of the invention is assigned, the total number of drawing sheets, a suggested drawing figure for publication (in a nonprovisional application), any docket number assigned to the application, the type of application (*e.g.*, utility, plant, design, reissue, provisional), whether the application

discloses any significant part of the subject matter of an application under a secrecy order pursuant to § 5.2 of this chapter (see § 5.2(c)), and, for plant applications, the Latin name of the genus and species of the plant claimed, as well as the variety denomination. The suggested classification and Technology Center information should be supplied for provisional applications whether or not claims are present. If claims are not present in a provisional application, the suggested classification and Technology Center should be based upon the disclosure.

(4) *Representative information.* This information includes the registration number of each practitioner having a power of attorney in the application (preferably by reference to a customer number). Providing this information in the application data sheet does not constitute a power of attorney in the application (see § 1.32).

(5) *Domestic priority information.* This information includes the application number, the filing date, the status (including patent number if available), and relationship of each application for which a benefit is claimed under 35 U.S.C. 119(e), 120, 121, or 365(c). Providing this information in the application data sheet constitutes the specific reference required by 35 U.S.C. 119(e) or 120, and § 1.78(a)(2) or § 1.78(a)(5), and need not otherwise be made part of the specification.

(6) *Foreign priority information.* This information includes the application number, country, and filing date of each foreign application for which priority is claimed, as well as any foreign application having a filing date before that of the application for which priority is claimed. Providing this information in the application data sheet constitutes the claim for priority as required by 35 U.S.C. 119(b) and § 1.55(a).

(7) *Assignee information.* This information includes the name (either person or juristic entity) and address of the assignee of the entire right, title, and interest in an application. Providing this information in the application data sheet does not substitute for compliance with any requirement of part 3 of this chapter to have an assignment recorded by the Office.

(c) *Supplemental application data sheets.* Supplemental application data sheets:

(1) May be subsequently supplied prior to payment of the issue fee either to correct or update information in a previously submitted application data sheet, or an oath or declaration under § 1.63 or § 1.67, except that inventorship changes are governed by § 1.48, correspondence changes are governed by § 1.33(a), and citizenship changes are governed by § 1.63 or § 1.67; and

(2) Must be titled "Supplemental Application Data Sheet," include all of the section headings listed in paragraph (b) of this section, include all appropriate data for each section heading, and must identify the information that is being changed, preferably with underlining for insertions, and strike-through or brackets for text removed.

(d) *Inconsistencies between application data sheet and other documents.* For inconsistencies between information that is supplied by both an application data sheet under this section and other documents.

(1) The latest submitted information will govern notwithstanding whether supplied by an application data sheet, an amendment to the specification, a designation of a correspondence address, or by a § 1.63 or § 1.67 oath or declaration, except as provided by paragraph (d)(3) of this section;

(2) The information in the application data sheet will govern when the inconsistent information is supplied at the same time by an amendment to the specification, a designation of correspondence address, or a § 1.63 or § 1.67 oath or declaration, except as provided by paragraph (d)(3) of this section;

(3) The oath or declaration under § 1.63 or § 1.67 governs inconsistencies with the application data sheet in the naming of inventors (§ 1.41 (a)(1)) and setting forth their citizenship (35 U.S.C. 115);

(4) The Office will capture bibliographic information from the application data sheet (notwithstanding whether an oath or declaration governs the information). Thus, the Office shall generally, for example, not look to an oath or declaration under § 1.63 to see if the bibliographic information contained therein is consistent with the bibliographic information captured from an application data sheet (whether the oath or declaration is submitted prior to or subsequent to the application data sheet). Captured bibliographic information derived from an application data sheet containing errors may be corrected if applicant submits a request therefor and a supplemental application data sheet.

[Added, 65 FR 54604, Sept. 8, 2000, effective Nov. 7, 2000; para. (b)(7) added, 65 FR 57024, Sept. 20, 2000, effective Nov. 29, 2000; paras. (a), (b)(4), (c)(2) and (d) revised, 69 FR 56481, Sept. 21, 2004, effective Oct. 21, 2004; para. (b)(5) revised, 70 FR 54259, Sept. 14, 2005, effective Sept. 14, 2005; para. (b)(5) revised, 72 FR 46716, Aug. 21, 2007 (implementation enjoined and never became effective); para. (b)(5) revised, 74 FR 52686, Oct. 14, 2009, effective Oct. 14, 2009 (to remove changes made by the final rules in 72 FR 46716 from the CFR)]

§ 1.77　Arrangement of application elements.

(a)　The elements of the application, if applicable, should appear in the following order:

　　(1)　Utility application transmittal form.

　　(2)　Fee transmittal form.

　　(3)　Application data sheet (see § 1.76).

　　(4)　Specification.

　　(5)　Drawings.

　　(6)　Executed oath or declaration.

(b)　The specification should include the following sections in order:

　　(1)　Title of the invention, which may be accompanied by an introductory portion stating the name, citizenship, and residence of the applicant (unless included in the application data sheet).

　　(2)　Cross-reference to related applications (unless included in the application data sheet).

　　(3)　Statement regarding federally sponsored research or development.

　　(4)　The names of the parties to a joint research agreement.

　　(5)　Reference to a "Sequence Listing," a table, or a computer program listing appendix submitted on a compact disc and an incorporation-by-reference of the material on the compact disc (see § 1.52(e)(5)). The total number of compact discs including duplicates and the files on each compact disc shall be specified.

　　(6)　Background of the invention.

　　(7)　Brief summary of the invention.

　　(8)　Brief description of the several views of the drawing.

　　(9)　Detailed description of the invention.

　　(10)　A claim or claims.

　　(11)　Abstract of the disclosure.

　　(12)　"Sequence Listing," if on paper (see §§ 1.821 through 1.825).

(c)　The text of the specification sections defined in paragraphs (b)(1) through (b)(12) of this section, if applicable, should be preceded by a section heading in uppercase and without underlining or bold type.

[43 FR 20464, May 11, 1978; 46 FR 2612, Jan. 12, 1981; paras. (h) and (i), 48 FR 2712, Jan. 20, 1983, effective Feb. 27, 1983; revised, 61 FR 42790, Aug. 19, 1996, effective Sept. 23, 1996; revised, 65 FR 54604, Sept. 8, 2000, effective Nov. 7, 2000; paras. (b) and (c) revised, 70 FR 1818, Jan. 11, 2005, effective Dec. 10, 2004]

§ 1.78　Claiming benefit of earlier filing date and cross-references to other applications.

(a)(1) A nonprovisional application or international application designating the United States of America may claim an invention disclosed in one or more prior-filed copending nonprovisional applications or international applications designating the United States of America. In order for an application to claim the benefit of a prior-filed copending nonprovisional application or international application designating the United States of America, each prior-filed application must name as an inventor at least one inventor named in the later-filed application and disclose the named inventor's invention claimed in at least one claim of the later-filed application in the manner provided by the first paragraph of 35 U.S.C. 112. In addition, each prior-filed application must be:

　　(i)　An international application entitled to a filing date in accordance with PCT Article 11 and designating the United States of America; or

　　(ii)　Entitled to a filing date as set forth in § 1.53(b) or § 1.53(d) and have paid therein the basic filing fee set forth in § 1.16 within the pendency of the application.

　　(2)(i) Except for a continued prosecution application filed under § 1.53(d), any nonprovisional application or international application designating the United States of America claiming the benefit of one or more prior-filed copending nonprovisional applications or international applications designating the United States of America must contain or be amended to contain a reference to each such prior-filed application, identifying it by application number (consisting of the series code and serial number) or international application number and international filing date and indicating the relationship of the applications. Cross references to other related applications may be made when appropriate (*see* § 1.14).

(ii) This reference must be submitted during the pendency of the later-filed application. If the later-filed application is an application filed under 35 U.S.C. 111(a), this reference must also be submitted within the later of four months from the actual filing date of the later-filed application or sixteen months from the filing date of the prior-filed application. If the later-filed application is a nonprovisional application which entered the national stage from an international application after compliance with 35 U.S.C. 371, this reference must also be submitted within the later of four months from the date on which the national stage commenced under 35 U.S.C. 371 (b) or (f) in the later-filed international application or sixteen months from the filing date of the prior-filed application. These time periods are not extendable. Except as provided in paragraph (a)(3) of this section, the failure to timely submit the reference required by 35 U.S.C. 120 and paragraph (a)(2)(i) of this section is considered a waiver of any benefit under 35 U.S.C. 120, 121, or 365(c) to such prior-filed application. The time periods in this paragraph do not apply if the later-filed application is:

(A) An application for a design patent;

(B) An application filed under 35 U.S.C. 111 (a) before November 29, 2000; or

(C) A nonprovisional application which entered the national stage after compliance with 35 U.S.C. 371 from an international application filed under 35 U.S.C. 363 before November 29, 2000.

(iii) If the later-filed application is a nonprovisional application, the reference required by this paragraph must be included in an application data sheet (§ 1.76), or the specification must contain or be amended to contain such reference in the first sentence(s) following the title.

(iv) The request for a continued prosecution application under § 1.53(d) is the specific reference required by 35 U.S.C. 120 to the prior-filed application. The identification of an application by application number under this section is the identification of every application assigned that application number necessary for a specific reference required by 35 U.S.C. 120 to every such application assigned that application number.

(3) If the reference required by 35 U.S.C. 120 and paragraph (a)(2) of this section is presented after the time period provided by paragraph (a)(2)(ii) of this section, the claim under 35 U.S.C. 120, 121, or 365(c) for the benefit of a prior-filed copending nonprovisional application or international application designating the United States of America may be accepted if the reference identifying the prior-filed application by application number or international application number and international filing date was unintentionally delayed. A petition to accept an unintentionally delayed claim under 35 U.S.C. 120, 121, or 365(c) for the benefit of a prior-filed application must be accompanied by:

(i) The reference required by 35 U.S.C. 120 and paragraph (a)(2) of this section to the prior-filed application, unless previously submitted;

(ii) The surcharge set forth in § 1.17(t); and

(iii) A statement that the entire delay between the date the claim was due under paragraph (a)(2)(ii) of this section and the date the claim was filed was unintentional. The Director may require additional information where there is a question whether the delay was unintentional.

(4) A nonprovisional application, other than for a design patent, or an international application designating the United States of America may claim an invention disclosed in one or more prior-filed provisional applications. In order for an application to claim the benefit of one or more prior-filed provisional applications, each prior-filed provisional application must name as an inventor at least one inventor named in the later-filed application and disclose the named inventor's invention claimed in at least one claim of the later-filed application in the manner provided by the first paragraph of 35 U.S.C. 112. In addition, each prior-filed provisional application must be entitled to a filing date as set forth in § 1.53(c), and the basic filing fee set forth in § 1.16(d) must be paid within the time period set forth in § 1.53(g).

(5)(i) Any nonprovisional application or international application designating the United States of America claiming the benefit of one or more prior-filed provisional applications must contain or be amended to contain a reference to each such prior-filed provisional application, identifying it by the provisional application number (consisting of series code and serial number).

(ii)   This reference must be submitted during the pendency of the later-filed application. If the later-filed application is an application filed under 35 U.S.C. 111(a), this reference must also be submitted within the later of four months from the actual filing date of the later-filed application or sixteen months from the filing date of the prior-filed provisional application. If the later-filed application is a nonprovisional application which entered the national stage from an international application after compliance with 35 U.S.C. 371, this reference must also be submitted within the later of four months from the date on which the national stage commenced under 35 U.S.C. 371(b) or (f) in the later-filed international application or sixteen months from the filing date of the prior-filed provisional application. These time periods are not extendable. Except as provided in paragraph(a)(6) of this section, the failure to timely submit the reference is considered a waiver of any benefit under 35 U.S.C. 119(e) to such prior-filed provisional application. The time periods in this paragraph do not apply if the later-filed application is:

(A)   An application filed under 35 U.S.C. 111(a) before November 29, 2000; or

(B)   A nonprovisional application which entered the national stage after compliance with 35 U.S.C. 371 from an international application filed under 35 U.S.C. 363 before November 29, 2000.

(iii)   If the later-filed application is a nonprovisional application, the reference required by this paragraph must be included in an application data sheet (§ 1.76), or the specification must contain or be amended to contain such reference in the first sentence(s) following the title.

(iv)   If the prior-filed provisional application was filed in a language other than English and both an English-language translation of the prior-filed provisional application and a statement that the translation is accurate were not previously filed in the prior-filed provisional application, applicant will be notified and given a period of time within which to file, in the prior-filed provisional application, the translation and the statement. If the notice is mailed in a pending nonprovisional application, a timely reply to such a notice must include the filing in the nonprovisional application of either a confirmation that the translation and statement were filed in the provisional application, or an amendment or Supplemental Application Data Sheet withdrawing the benefit claim, or the nonprovisional application will be abandoned. The translation and statement may be filed in the provisional application, even if the provisional application has become abandoned.

(6)   If the reference required by 35 U.S.C. 119(e) and paragraph (a)(5) of this section is presented in a nonprovisional application after the time period provided by paragraph (a)(5)(ii) of this section, the claim under 35 U.S.C. 119(e) for the benefit of a prior filed provisional application may be accepted during the pendency of the later-filed application if the reference identifying the prior-filed application by provisional application number was unintentionally delayed. A petition to accept an unintentionally delayed claim under 35 U.S.C. 119(e) for the benefit of a prior-filed provisional application must be accompanied by:

(i)   The reference required by 35 U.S.C. 119(e) and paragraph (a)(5) of this section to the prior-filed provisional application, unless previously submitted;

(ii)   The surcharge set forth in § 1.17(t); and

(iii)   A statement that the entire delay between the date the claim was due under paragraph (a)(5)(ii) of this section and the date the claim was filed was unintentional. The Director may require additional information where there is a question whether the delay was unintentional.

(b)   Where two or more applications filed by the same applicant contain conflicting claims, elimination of such claims from all but one application may be required in the absence of good and sufficient reason for their retention during pendency in more than one application.

(c)   If an application or a patent under reexamination and at least one other application naming different inventors are owned by the same person and contain conflicting claims, and there is no statement of record indicating that the claimed inventions were commonly owned or subject to an obligation of assignment to the same person at the time the later invention was made, the Office may require the assignee to state whether the claimed inventions were commonly owned or subject to an obligation of assignment to the same person at the time the later invention was made, and if not, indicate which named inventor is the prior inventor. Even if the claimed inventions were commonly owned, or subject to an obligation of assignment to the same person, at the time the later invention was made, the conflicting claims may be rejected under the doctrine of double patenting in view of such commonly owned or assigned applications or patents under reexamination.

[36 FR 7312, Apr. 17, 1971; 49 FR 555, Jan. 4, 1984; paras. (a), (c) & (d), 50 FR 9380, Mar. 7, 1985, effective May 8, 1985; 50 FR 11366, Mar. 21, 1985; para. (a) revised 58 FR 54504, Oct. 22, 1993, effective Jan. 3, 1994; paras. (a)(1) and (a)(2) revised and paras. (a)(3) and (a)(4) added, 60 FR 20195, Apr. 25, 1995, effective June 8, 1995; para. (c) revised and para. (d) deleted, 61 FR 42790, Aug. 19, 1996, effective Sept. 23, 1996; para. (a) revised, 62 FR 53131, Oct. 10, 1997, effective Dec. 1, 1997; para. (a)(3) revised, 65 FR 14865, Mar. 20, 2000, effective May 29, 2000 (adopted as final, 65 FR 50092, Aug. 16, 2000); paras. (a)(2), (a)(4), and (c) revised, 65 FR 54604, Sept. 8, 2000, effective Sept. 8, 2000; paras. (a)(2), (a)(3), and (a)(4) revised and paras. (a)(5) and (a)(6) added, 65 FR 57024, Sept. 20, 2000, effective Nov. 29, 2000; para. (a) revised, 66 FR 67087, Dec. 28, 2001, effective Dec. 28, 2001; paras. (a)(3)(iii) & (a)(6)(iii) revised, 68 FR 14332, Mar. 25, 2003, effective May 1, 2003; para (a)(3) revised, 68 FR 70996, Dec. 22, 2003, effective Jan. 21, 2004; paras. (a)(1), (a)(2)(iii), (a)(5)(iii) and (c) revised, 69 FR 56481, Sept. 21, 2004, effective Sept. 21, 2004; para. (a)(4) revised, 70 FR 3880, Jan. 27, 2005, effective Dec. 8, 2004; para.(a)(1)(iii) removed and para. (a)(1)(ii) revised, 70 FR 30360, May 26, 2005, effective July 1, 2005; para. (a)(5)(iv) revised, 70 FR 56119, Sept. 26, 2005, effective Nov. 25, 2005; revised, 72 FR 46716, Aug. 21, 2007 (implementation enjoined and never became effective); revised, 74 FR 52686, Oct. 14, 2009, effective Oct. 14, 2009 (to remove changes made by the final rules in 72 FR 46716 from the CFR)]

§ 1.79   Reservation clauses not permitted.

A reservation for a future application of subject matter disclosed but not claimed in a pending application will not be permitted in the pending application, but an application disclosing unclaimed subject matter may contain a reference to a later filed application of the same applicant or owned by a common assignee disclosing and claiming that subject matter.

THE DRAWINGS

§ 1.81   Drawings required in patent application.

(a)   The applicant for a patent is required to furnish a drawing of his or her invention where necessary for the understanding of the subject matter sought to be patented; this drawing, or a high quality copy thereof, must be filed with the application. Since corrections are the responsibility of the applicant, the original drawing(s) should be retained by the applicant for any necessary future correction.

(b)   Drawings may include illustrations which facilitate an understanding of the invention (for example, flowsheets in cases of processes, and diagrammatic views).

(c)   Whenever the nature of the subject matter sought to be patented admits of illustration by a drawing without its being necessary for the understanding of the subject matter and the applicant has not furnished such a drawing, the examiner will require its submission within a time period of not less than two months from the date of the sending of a notice thereof.

(d)   Drawings submitted after the filing date of the application may not be used to overcome any insufficiency of the specification due to lack of an enabling disclosure or otherwise inadequate disclosure therein, or to supplement the original disclosure thereof for the purpose of interpretation of the scope of any claim.

[43 FR 4015, Jan. 31, 1978; para. (a), 53 FR 47809, Nov. 28, 1988, effective Jan. 1, 1989]

§ 1.83   Content of drawing.

(a)   The drawing in a nonprovisional application must show every feature of the invention specified in the claims. However, conventional features disclosed in the description and claims, where their detailed illustration is not essential for a proper understanding of the invention, should be illustrated in the drawing in the form of a graphical drawing symbol or a labeled representation (*e.g.*, a labeled rectangular box). In addition, tables and sequence listings that are included in the specification are, except for applications filed under 35 U.S.C. 371, not permitted to be included in the drawings.

(b)   When the invention consists of an improvement on an old machine the drawing must when possible exhibit, in one or more views, the improved portion itself, disconnected from the old structure, and also in another view, so much only of the old structure as will suffice to show the connection of the invention therewith.

(c) Where the drawings in a nonprovisional application do not comply with the requirements of paragraphs (a) and (b) of this section, the examiner shall require such additional illustration within a time period of not less than two months from the date of the sending of a notice thereof. Such corrections are subject to the requirements of § 1.81(d).

[31 FR 12923, Oct. 4, 1966; 43 FR 4015, Jan. 31, 1978; paras. (a) and (c) revised, 60 FR 20195, Apr. 25, 1995, effective June 8, 1995; para. (a) revised, 69 FR 56481, Sept. 21, 2004, effective Oct. 21, 2004]

§ 1.84   Standards for drawings.

(a) *Drawings*. There are two acceptable categories for presenting drawings in utility and design patent applications.

(1) *Black ink*. Black and white drawings are normally required. India ink, or its equivalent that secures solid black lines, must be used for drawings; or

(2) *Color*. On rare occasions, color drawings may be necessary as the only practical medium by which to disclose the subject matter sought to be patented in a utility or design patent application or the subject matter of a statutory invention registration. The color drawings must be of sufficient quality such that all details in the drawings are reproducible in black and white in the printed patent. Color drawings are not permitted in international applications (see PCT Rule 11.13), or in an application, or copy thereof, submitted under the Office electronic filing system. The Office will accept color drawings in utility or design patent applications and statutory invention registrations only after granting a petition filed under this paragraph explaining why the color drawings are necessary. Any such petition must include the following:

(i) The fee set forth in § 1.17(h);

(ii) Three (3) sets of color drawings;

(iii) An amendment to the specification to insert (unless the specification contains or has been previously amended to contain) the following

language as the first paragraph of the brief description of the drawings:

The patent or application file contains at least one drawing executed in color. Copies of this patent or patent application publication with color drawing(s) will be provided by the Office upon request and payment of the necessary fee.

(b) *Photographs.*—

(1) *Black and white*. Photographs, including photocopies of photographs, are not ordinarily permitted in utility and design patent applications. The Office will accept photographs in utility and design patent applications, however, if photographs are the only practicable medium for illustrating the claimed invention. For example, photographs or photomicrographs of: electrophoresis gels, blots (*e.g.*, immunological, western, Southern, and northern), autoradiographs, cell cultures (stained and unstained), histological tissue cross sections (stained and unstained), animals, plants, in vivo imaging, thin layer chromatography plates, crystalline structures, and, in a design patent application, ornamental effects, are acceptable. If the subject matter of the application admits of illustration by a drawing, the examiner may require a drawing in place of the photograph. The photographs must be of sufficient quality so that all details in the photographs are reproducible in the printed patent.

(2) *Color photographs*. Color photographs will be accepted in utility and design patent applications if the conditions for accepting color drawings and black and white photographs have been satisfied. See paragraphs (a)(2) and (b)(1) of this section.

(c) *Identification of drawings*. Identifying indicia should be provided, and if provided, should include the title of the invention, inventor's name, and application number, or docket number (if any) if an application number has not been assigned to the application. If this information is provided, it must be placed on the front of each sheet within the top margin. Each drawing sheet submitted after the filing date of an application must be identified as either "Replacement Sheet" or "New Sheet" pursuant to § 1.121(d). If a marked-up copy of any amended drawing figure including annotations indicating the changes made is filed, such marked-up copy must be clearly labeled as "Annotated Sheet" pursuant to § 1.121(d)(1).

(d) *Graphic forms in drawings.* Chemical or mathematical formulae, tables, and waveforms may be submitted as drawings and are subject to the same requirements as drawings. Each chemical or mathematical formula must be labeled as a separate figure, using brackets when necessary, to show that information is properly integrated. Each group of waveforms must be presented as a single figure, using a common vertical axis with time extending along the horizontal axis. Each individual waveform discussed in the specification must be identified with a separate letter designation adjacent to the vertical axis.

(e) *Type of paper.* Drawings submitted to the Office must be made on paper which is flexible, strong, white, smooth, non-shiny, and durable. All sheets must be reasonably free from cracks, creases, and folds. Only one side of the sheet may be used for the drawing. Each sheet must be reasonably free from erasures and must be free from alterations, overwritings, and interlineations. Photographs must be developed on paper meeting the sheet-size requirements of paragraph (f) of this section and the margin requirements of paragraph (g) of this section. See paragraph (b) of this section for other requirements for photographs.

(f) *Size of paper.* All drawing sheets in an application must be the same size. One of the shorter sides of the sheet is regarded as its top. The size of the sheets on which drawings are made must be:

(1)   21.0 cm. by 29.7 cm. (DIN size A4), or

(2)   21.6 cm. by 27.9 cm. (8 1/2 by 11 inches).

(g) *Margins.* The sheets must not contain frames around the sight (*i.e.*, the usable surface), but should have scan target points (*i.e.*, cross-hairs) printed on two cater-corner margin corners. Each sheet must include a top margin of at least 2.5 cm. (1 inch), a left side margin of at least 2.5 cm. (1 inch), a right side margin of at least 1.5 cm. (5/8 inch), and a bottom margin of at least 1.0 cm. (3/8 inch), thereby leaving a sight no greater than 17.0 cm. by 26.2 cm. on 21.0 cm. by 29.7 cm. (DIN size A4) drawing sheets, and a sight no greater than 17.6 cm. by 24.4 cm. (6 15/16 by 9 5/8 inches) on 21.6 cm. by 27.9 cm. (8 1/2 by 11 inch) drawing sheets.

(h) *Views.* The drawing must contain as many views as necessary to show the invention. The views may be plan, elevation, section, or perspective views. Detail views of portions of elements, on a larger scale if necessary, may also be used. All views of the drawing must be grouped together and arranged on the sheet(s) without wasting space, preferably in an upright position, clearly separated from one another, and must not be included in the sheets containing the specifications, claims, or abstract. Views must not be connected by projection lines and must not contain center lines. Waveforms of electrical signals may be connected by dashed lines to show the relative timing of the waveforms.

(1) *Exploded views.* Exploded views, with the separated parts embraced by a bracket, to show the relationship or order of assembly of various parts are permissible. When an exploded view is shown in a figure which is on the same sheet as another figure, the exploded view should be placed in brackets.

(2) *Partial views.* When necessary, a view of a large machine or device in its entirety may be broken into partial views on a single sheet, or extended over several sheets if there is no loss in facility of understanding the view. Partial views drawn on separate sheets must always be capable of being linked edge to edge so that no partial view contains parts of another partial view. A smaller scale view should be included showing the whole formed by the partial views and indicating the positions of the parts shown. When a portion of a view is enlarged for magnification purposes, the view and the enlarged view must each be labeled as separate views.

(i)   Where views on two or more sheets form, in effect, a single complete view, the views on the several sheets must be so arranged that the complete figure can be assembled without concealing any part of any of the views appearing on the various sheets.

(ii)   A very long view may be divided into several parts placed one above the other on a single sheet. However, the relationship between the different parts must be clear and unambiguous.

(3) *Sectional views.* The plane upon which a sectional view is taken should be indicated on the view from which the section is cut by a broken line. The ends of the broken line should be designated by Arabic or Roman numerals corresponding to the view number of the sectional view, and should have arrows to indicate the direction of sight. Hatching must be used to indicate section portions of an object, and must be made by regularly spaced oblique parallel

lines spaced sufficiently apart to enable the lines to be distinguished without difficulty. Hatching should not impede the clear reading of the reference characters and lead lines. If it is not possible to place reference characters outside the hatched area, the hatching may be broken off wherever reference characters are inserted. Hatching must be at a substantial angle to the surrounding axes or principal lines, preferably 45°. A cross section must be set out and drawn to show all of the materials as they are shown in the view from which the cross section was taken. The parts in cross section must show proper material(s) by hatching with regularly spaced parallel oblique strokes, the space between strokes being chosen on the basis of the total area to be hatched. The various parts of a cross section of the same item should be hatched in the same manner and should accurately and graphically indicate the nature of the material(s) that is illustrated in cross section. The hatching of juxtaposed different elements must be angled in a different way. In the case of large areas, hatching may be confined to an edging drawn around the entire inside of the outline of the area to be hatched. Different types of hatching should have different conventional meanings as regards the nature of a material seen in cross section.

(4)   *Alternate position.* A moved position may be shown by a broken line superimposed upon a suitable view if this can be done without crowding; otherwise, a separate view must be used for this purpose.

(5)   *Modified forms.* Modified forms of construction must be shown in separate views.

(i)   *Arrangement of views.* One view must not be placed upon another or within the outline of another. All views on the same sheet should stand in the same direction and, if possible, stand so that they can be read with the sheet held in an upright position. If views wider than the width of the sheet are necessary for the clearest illustration of the invention, the sheet may be turned on its side so that the top of the sheet, with the appropriate top margin to be used as the heading space, is on the right-hand side. Words must appear in a horizontal, left-to-right fashion when the page is either upright or turned so that the top becomes the right side, except for graphs utilizing standard scientific convention to denote the axis of abscissas (of X) and the axis of ordinates (of Y).

(j)   *Front page view.* The drawing must contain as many views as necessary to show the invention. One of the views should be suitable for inclusion on the front page of the patent application publication and patent as the illustration of the invention. Views must not be connected by projection lines and must not contain center lines. Applicant may suggest a single view (by figure number) for inclusion on the front page of the patent application publication and patent.

(k)   *Scale.* The scale to which a drawing is made must be large enough to show the mechanism without crowding when the drawing is reduced in size to two-thirds in reproduction. Indications such as "actual size" or "scale 1/2" on the drawings are not permitted since these lose their meaning with reproduction in a different format.

(l)   *Character of lines, numbers, and letters.* All drawings must be made by a process which will give them satisfactory reproduction characteristics. Every line, number, and letter must be durable, clean, black (except for color drawings), sufficiently dense and dark, and uniformly thick and well-defined. The weight of all lines and letters must be heavy enough to permit adequate reproduction. This requirement applies to all lines however fine, to shading, and to lines representing cut surfaces in sectional views. Lines and strokes of different thicknesses may be used in the same drawing where different thicknesses have a different meaning.

(m)   *Shading.* The use of shading in views is encouraged if it aids in understanding the invention and if it does not reduce legibility. Shading is used to indicate the surface or shape of spherical, cylindrical, and conical elements of an object. Flat parts may also be lightly shaded. Such shading is preferred in the case of parts shown in perspective, but not for cross sections. See paragraph (h)(3) of this section. Spaced lines for shading are preferred. These lines must be thin, as few in number as practicable, and they must contrast with the rest of the drawings. As a substitute for shading, heavy lines on the shade side of objects can be used except where they superimpose on each other or obscure reference characters. Light should come from the upper left corner at an angle of 45°. Surface delineations should preferably be shown by proper shading. Solid black shading areas are not permitted, except when used to represent bar graphs or color.

(n) *Symbols.* Graphical drawing symbols may be used for conventional elements when appropriate. The elements for which such symbols and labeled representations are used must be adequately identified in the specification. Known devices should be illustrated by symbols which have a universally recognized conventional meaning and are generally accepted in the art. Other symbols which are not universally recognized may be used, subject to approval by the Office, if they are not likely to be confused with existing conventional symbols, and if they are readily identifiable.

(o) *Legends.* Suitable descriptive legends may be used subject to approval by the Office, or may be required by the examiner where necessary for understanding of the drawing. They should contain as few words as possible.

(p) *Numbers, letters, and reference characters.*

(1) Reference characters (numerals are preferred), sheet numbers, and view numbers must be plain and legible, and must not be used in association with brackets or inverted commas, or enclosed within outlines, *e.g.,* encircled. They must be oriented in the same direction as the view so as to avoid having to rotate the sheet. Reference characters should be arranged to follow the profile of the object depicted.

(2) The English alphabet must be used for letters, except where another alphabet is customarily used, such as the Greek alphabet to indicate angles, wavelengths, and mathematical formulas.

(3) Numbers, letters, and reference characters must measure at least 32 cm. (1/8 inch) in height. They should not be placed in the drawing so as to interfere with its comprehension. Therefore, they should not cross or mingle with the lines. They should not be placed upon hatched or shaded surfaces. When necessary, such as indicating a surface or cross section, a reference character may be underlined and a blank space may be left in the hatching or shading where the character occurs so that it appears distinct.

(4) The same part of an invention appearing in more than one view of the drawing must always be designated by the same reference character, and the same reference character must never be used to designate different parts.

(5) Reference characters not mentioned in the description shall not appear in the drawings. Reference characters mentioned in the description must appear in the drawings.

(q) *Lead lines.* Lead lines are those lines between the reference characters and the details referred to. Such lines may be straight or curved and should be as short as possible. They must originate in the immediate proximity of the reference character and extend to the feature indicated. Lead lines must not cross each other. Lead lines are required for each reference character except for those which indicate the surface or cross section on which they are placed. Such a reference character must be underlined to make it clear that a lead line has not been left out by mistake. Lead lines must be executed in the same way as lines in the drawing. See paragraph (l) of this section.

(r) *Arrows.* Arrows may be used at the ends of lines, provided that their meaning is clear, as follows:

(1) On a lead line, a freestanding arrow to indicate the entire section towards which it points;

(2) On a lead line, an arrow touching a line to indicate the surface shown by the line looking along the direction of the arrow; or

(3) To show the direction of movement.

(s) *Copyright or Mask Work Notice.* A copyright or mask work notice may appear in the drawing, but must be placed within the sight of the drawing immediately below the figure representing the copyright or mask work material and be limited to letters having a print size of 32 cm. to 64 cm. (1/8 to 1/4 inches) high. The content of the notice must be limited to only those elements provided for by law. For example, "©1983 John Doe" (17 U.S.C. 401) and "*M* John Doe" (17 U.S.C. 909) would be properly limited and, under current statutes, legally sufficient notices of copyright and mask work, respectively. Inclusion of a copyright or mask work notice will be permitted only if the authorization language set forth in § 1.71(e) is included at the beginning (preferably as the first paragraph) of the specification.

(t) *Numbering of sheets of drawings.* The sheets of drawings should be numbered in consecutive Arabic numerals, starting with 1, within the sight as defined in paragraph (g) of this section. These numbers, if present, must be placed in the middle of the top of the sheet, but not in the margin. The numbers can be placed on the right-hand side if the drawing extends too close to the middle of the top edge of the usable surface. The drawing sheet numbering must be clear and larger than the numbers used as reference characters to avoid confusion. The number of each sheet should be shown by two Arabic numerals placed on either side of an oblique line, with the first being the sheet number and the second being the total number of sheets of drawings, with no other marking.

(u) *Numbering of views.*

(1) The different views must be numbered in consecutive Arabic numerals, starting with 1, independent of the numbering of the sheets and, if possible, in the order in which they appear on the drawing sheet(s). Partial views intended to form one complete view, on one or several sheets, must be identified by the same number followed by a capital letter. View numbers must be preceded by the abbreviation "FIG." Where only a single view is used in an application to illustrate the claimed invention, it must not be numbered and the abbreviation "FIG." must not appear.

(2) Numbers and letters identifying the views must be simple and clear and must not be used in association with brackets, circles, or inverted commas. The view numbers must be larger than the numbers used for reference characters.

(v) *Security markings.* Authorized security markings may be placed on the drawings provided they are outside the sight, preferably centered in the top margin.

(w) *Corrections.* Any corrections on drawings submitted to the Office must be durable and permanent.

(x) *Holes.* No holes should be made by applicant in the drawing sheets.

(y) *Types of drawings.* See § 1.152 for design drawings, § 1.165 for plant drawings, and § 1.173(a)(2) for reissue drawings.

[24 FR 10332, Dec. 22, 1959; 31 FR 12923, Oct. 4, 1966; 36 FR 9775, May 28, 1971; 43 FR 20464, May 11, 1978; 45 FR 73657, Nov. 6,1980; paras. (a), (b), (i), (j), and (l) amended, paras. (n), (o), and (p) added, 53 FR 47809, Nov. 28, 1988, effective Jan. 1, 1989; revised, 58 FR 38719, July 20, 1993, effective Oct. 1, 1993; paras. (c), (f), (g), and (x) revised, 61 FR 42790, Aug. 19, 1996, effective Sept. 23, 1996; paras. (a)(2)(i), (b), (c) & (g) revised, 62 FR 53131, Oct. 10, 1997, effective Dec. 1, 1997; paras. (a), (b), (c), (j), (k), (o), and (x) revised, and para. (y) added, 65 FR 54604, Sept. 8, 2000, effective Nov. 7, 2000; paras. (a)(2), (e), and (j) revised, 65 FR 57024, Sept. 20, 2000, effective Nov. 29, 2000; para. (c) revised, 69 FR 56481, Sept. 21, 2004, effective Sept. 21, 2004; para. (a)(2) revised, 69 FR 56481, Sept. 21, 2004, effective Nov. 22, 2004; para. (y) revised, 70 FR 3880, Jan. 27, 2005, effective Dec. 8, 2004]

§ 1.85 Corrections to drawings.

(a) A utility or plant application will not be placed on the files for examination until objections to the drawings have been corrected. Except as provided in § 1.215(c), any patent application publication will not include drawings filed after the application has been placed on the files for examination. Unless applicant is otherwise notified in an Office action, objections to the drawings in a utility or plant application will not be held in abeyance, and a request to hold objections to the drawings in abeyance will not be considered a *bona fide* attempt to advance the application to final action (§ 1.135(c)). If a drawing in a design application meets the requirements of § 1.84(e), (f), and (g) and is suitable for reproduction, but is not otherwise in compliance with § 1.84, the drawing may be admitted for examination.

(b) The Office will not release drawings for purposes of correction. If corrections are necessary, new corrected drawings must be submitted within the time set by the Office.

(c) If a corrected drawing is required or if a drawing does not comply with § 1.84 at the time an application is allowed, the Office may notify the applicant and set a three-month period of time from the mail date of the notice of allowability within which the applicant must file a corrected drawing in compliance with § 1.84 to avoid abandonment. This time period is not extendable under § 1.136(a) or § 1.136(b).

[47 FR 41276, Sept. 17, 1982, effective Oct. 1, 1982; 53 FR 47810, Nov. 28, 1988, effective Jan. 1, 1989; revised, 65 FR 54604, Sept. 8, 2000, effective Nov. 7, 2000; para. (a) revised, 65 FR 57024, Sept. 20, 2000, effective Nov. 29, 2000; para. (c) revised, 69 FR 56481, Sept. 21, 2004, effective Oct. 21, 2004]

§ 1.88 [Reserved]

[Deleted, 58 FR 38719, July 20, 1993, effective Oct. 1, 1993]

MODELS, EXHIBITS, SPECIMENS

§ 1.91 Models or exhibits not generally admitted as part of application or patent.

(a) A model or exhibit will not be admitted as part of the record of an application unless it:

(1) Substantially conforms to the requirements of § 1.52 or § 1.84;

(2) Is specifically required by the Office; or

(3) Is filed with a petition under this section including:

(i) The fee set forth in § 1.17(h); and

(ii) An explanation of why entry of the model or exhibit in the file record is necessary to demonstrate patentability.

(b) Notwithstanding the provisions of paragraph (a) of this section, a model, working model, or other physical exhibit may be required by the Office if deemed necessary for any purpose in examination of the application.

(c) Unless the model or exhibit substantially conforms to the requirements of § 1.52 or § 1.84 under paragraph (a)(1) of this section, it must be accompanied by photographs that show multiple views of the material features of the model or exhibit and that substantially conform to the requirements of § 1.84.

[Revised, 62 FR 53131, Oct. 10, 1997, effective Dec. 1, 1997; para. (a)(3)(i) revised, 65 FR 54604, Sept. 8, 2000, effective Nov. 7, 2000; para. (c) added, 69 FR 56481, Sept. 21, 2004, effective Oct. 21, 2004]

§ 1.92 [Reserved]

[Removed and reserved, 62 FR 53131, Oct. 10, 1997, effective Dec. 1, 1997]

§ 1.93 Specimens.

When the invention relates to a composition of matter, the applicant may be required to furnish specimens of the composition, or of its ingredients or intermediates, for the purpose of inspection or experiment.

§ 1.94 Return of models, exhibits or specimens.

(a) Models, exhibits, or specimens may be returned to the applicant if no longer necessary for the conduct of business before the Office. When applicant is notified that a model, exhibit, or specimen is no longer necessary for the conduct of business before the Office and will be returned, applicant must arrange for the return of the model, exhibit, or specimen at the applicant's expense. The Office will dispose of perishables without notice to applicant unless applicant notifies the Office upon submission of the model, exhibit or specimen that a return is desired and makes arrangements for its return promptly upon notification by the Office that the model, exhibit or specimen is no longer necessary for the conduct of business before the Office.

(b) Applicant is responsible for retaining the actual model, exhibit, or specimen for the enforceable life of any patent resulting from the application. The provisions of this paragraph do not apply to a model or exhibit that substantially conforms to the requirements of § 1.52 or § 1.84, where the model or exhibit has been described by photographs that substantially conform to § 1.84, or where the model, exhibit or specimen is perishable.

(c) Where applicant is notified, pursuant to paragraph (a) of this section, of the need to arrange for return of a model, exhibit or specimen, applicant must arrange for the return within the period set in such notice, to avoid disposal of the model, exhibit or specimen by the Office. Extensions of time are available under § 1.136, except in the case of perishables. Failure to establish that the return of the item has been arranged for within the period set or failure to have the item removed from Office storage within a reasonable amount of time notwithstanding any arrangement for return, will permit the Office to dispose of the model, exhibit or specimen.

[Revised, 68 FR 14332, Mar. 25, 2003, effective May 1, 2003; revised, 69 FR 56481, Sept. 21, 2004, effective Oct. 21, 2004]

§ 1.95 Copies of exhibits.

Copies of models or other physical exhibits will not ordinarily be furnished by the Office, and any model or exhibit in an application or patent shall not be taken from the Office except in the custody of an employee of the Office specially authorized by the Director.

[Revised, 68 FR 14332, Mar. 25, 2003, effective May 1, 2003]

§ 1.96   Submission of computer program listings.

(a)   *General.* Descriptions of the operation and general content of computer program listings should appear in the description portion of the specification. A computer program listing for the purpose of this section is defined as a printout that lists in appropriate sequence the instructions, routines, and other contents of a program for a computer. The program listing may be either in machine or machine-independent (object or source) language which will cause a computer to perform a desired procedure or task such as solve a problem, regulate the flow of work in a computer, or control or monitor events. Computer program listings may be submitted in patent applications as set forth in paragraphs (b) and (c) of this section.

(b)   *Material which will be printed in the patent*: If the computer program listing is contained in 300 lines or fewer, with each line of 72 characters or fewer, it may be submitted either as drawings or as part of the specification.

(1)   *Drawings.* If the listing is submitted as drawings, it must be submitted in the manner and complying with the requirements for drawings as provided in § 1.84. At least one figure numeral is required on each sheet of drawing.

(2)   *Specification.*

(i)   If the listing is submitted as part of the specification, it must be submitted in accordance with the provisions of § 1.52.

(ii)   Any listing having more than 60 lines of code that is submitted as part of the specification must be positioned at the end of the description but before the claims. Any amendment must be made by way of submission of a substitute sheet.

(c)   *As an appendix which will not be printed*: Any computer program listing may, and any computer program listing having over 300 lines (up to 72 characters per line) must, be submitted on a compact disc in compliance with § 1.52(e). A compact disc containing such a computer program listing is to be referred to as a "computer program listing appendix." The "computer program listing appendix" will not be part of the printed patent. The specification must include a reference to the "computer program listing appendix" at the location indicated in § 1.77(b)(5).

(1)   Multiple computer program listings for a single application may be placed on a single compact disc. Multiple compact discs may be submitted for a single application if necessary. A separate compact disc is required for each application containing a computer program listing that must be submitted on a "computer program listing appendix."

(2)   The "computer program listing appendix" must be submitted on a compact disc that complies with § 1.52(e) and the following specifications (no other format shall be allowed):

(i)   Computer Compatibility: IBM PC/XT/AT, or compatibles, or Apple Macintosh;

(ii)   Operating System Compatibility: MS-DOS, MS-Windows, Unix, or Macintosh;

(iii)   Line Terminator: ASCII Carriage Return plus ASCII Line Feed;

(iv)   Control Codes: the data must not be dependent on control characters or codes which are not defined in the ASCII character set; and

(v)   Compression: uncompressed data.

[46 FR 2612, Jan. 12, 1981; para. (b)(1), 54 FR 47519, Nov. 15, 1989, effective Jan. 16, 1990; revised, 61 FR 42790, Aug. 19, 1996, effective Sept. 23, 1996; paras. (b) and (c) revised, 65 FR 54604, Sept. 8, 2000, effective Sept. 8, 2000 (effective date corrected, 65 FR 78958, Dec. 18, 2000; para. (c) introductory text revised, 70 FR 54259, Sept. 14, 2005, effective Sept. 14, 2005]

INFORMATION DISCLOSURE STATEMENT

§ 1.97   Filing of information disclosure statement.

(a)   In order for an applicant for a patent or for a reissue of a patent to have an information disclosure statement in compliance with § 1.98 considered by the Office during the pendency of the application, the information disclosure statement must satisfy one of paragraphs (b), (c), or (d) of this section.

(b)   An information disclosure statement shall be considered by the Office if filed by the applicant within any one of the following time periods:

(1)   Within three months of the filing date of a national application other than a continued prosecution application under § 1.53(d);

(2)   Within three months of the date of entry of the national stage as set forth in § 1.491 in an international application;

(3)   Before the mailing of a first Office action on the merits; or

(4) Before the mailing of a first Office action after the filing of a request for continued examination under § 1.114.

(c) An information disclosure statement shall be considered by the Office if filed after the period specified in paragraph (b) of this section, provided that the information disclosure statement is filed before the mailing date of any of a final action under § 1.113, a notice of allowance under § 1.311, or an action that otherwise closes prosecution in the application, and it is accompanied by one of:

(1) The statement specified in paragraph (e) of this section; or

(2) The fee set forth in § 1.17(p).

(d) An information disclosure statement shall be considered by the Office if filed by the applicant after the period specified in paragraph (c) of this section, provided that the information disclosure statement is filed on or before payment of the issue fee and is accompanied by:

(1) The statement specified in paragraph (e) of this section; and

(2) The fee set forth in § 1.17(p).

(e) A statement under this section must state either:

(1) That each item of information contained in the information disclosure statement was first cited in any communication from a foreign patent office in a counterpart foreign application not more than three months prior to the filing of the information disclosure statement; or

(2) That no item of information contained in the information disclosure statement was cited in a communication from a foreign patent office in a counterpart foreign application, and, to the knowledge of the person signing the certification after making reasonable inquiry, no item of information contained in the information disclosure statement was known to any individual designated in § 1.56(c) more than three months prior to the filing of the information disclosure statement.

(f) No extensions of time for filing an information disclosure statement are permitted under § 1.136. If a *bona fide* attempt is made to comply with § 1.98, but part of the required content is inadvertently omitted, additional time may be given to enable full compliance.

(g) An information disclosure statement filed in accordance with this section shall not be construed as a representation that a search has been made.

(h) The filing of an information disclosure statement shall not be construed to be an admission that the information cited in the statement is, or is considered to be, material to patentability as defined in § 1.56(b).

(i) If an information disclosure statement does not comply with either this section or § 1.98, it will be placed in the file but will not be considered by the Office.

[48 FR 2712, Jan. 20, 1983, effective date Feb. 27, 1983; 57 FR 2021, Jan. 17, 1992, effective Mar. 16, 1992; para. (d) revised, 60 FR 20195, Apr. 25, 1995, effective June 8, 1995; paras. (a)- (d) revised, 61 FR 42790, Aug. 19, 1996, effective Sept. 23, 1996; paras. (c)-(e) revised, 62 FR 53131, Oct. 10, 1997, effective Dec. 1, 1997; para. (b) revised, 65 FR 14865, Mar. 20, 2000, effective May 29, 2000 (adopted as final, 65 FR 50092, Aug. 16, 2000); paras. (a) through (e) and (i) revised, 65 FR 54604, Sept. 8, 2000, effective Nov. 7, 2000]

§ 1.98 Content of information disclosure statement.

(a) Any information disclosure statement filed under § 1.97 shall include the items listed in paragraphs (a)(1), (a)(2) and (a)(3) of this section.

(1) A list of all patents, publications, applications, or other information submitted for consideration by the Office. U.S. patents and U.S. patent application publications must be listed in a section separately from citations of other documents. Each page of the list must include:

(i) The application number of the application in which the information disclosure statement is being submitted;

(ii) A column that provides a space, next to each document to be considered, for the examiner's initials; and

(iii) A heading that clearly indicates that the list is an information disclosure statement.

(2) A legible copy of:

(i) Each foreign patent;

(ii) Each publication or that portion which caused it to be listed, other than U.S. patents and U.S. patent application publications unless required by the Office;

(iii) For each cited pending unpublished U.S. application, the application specification including the claims, and any drawing of the application, or that portion of the application which caused it to be listed including any claims directed to that portion; and

(iv) All other information or that portion which caused it to be listed.

(3)(i) A concise explanation of the relevance, as it is presently understood by the individual designated in § 1.56(c) most knowledgeable about the content of the information, of each patent, publication, or other information listed that is not in the English language. The concise explanation may be either separate from applicant's specification or incorporated therein.

(ii) A copy of the translation if a written English-language translation of a non-English-language document, or portion thereof, is within the possession, custody, or control of, or is readily available to any individual designated in § 1.56(c).

(b)(1) Each U.S. patent listed in an information disclosure statement must be identified by inventor, patent number, and issue date.

(2) Each U.S. patent application publication listed in an information disclosure statement shall be identified by applicant, patent application publication number, and publication date.

(3) Each U.S. application listed in an information disclosure statement must be identified by the inventor, application number, and filing date.

(4) Each foreign patent or published foreign patent application listed in an information disclosure statement must be identified by the country or patent office which issued the patent or published the application, an appropriate document number, and the publication date indicated on the patent or published application.

(5) Each publication listed in an information disclosure statement must be identified by publisher, author (if any), title, relevant pages of the publication, date, and place of publication.

(c) When the disclosures of two or more patents or publications listed in an information disclosure statement are substantively cumulative, a copy of one of the patents or publications as specified in paragraph (a) of this section may be submitted without copies of the other patents or publications, provided that it is stated that these other patents or publications are cumulative.

(d) A copy of any patent, publication, pending U.S. application or other information, as specified in paragraph (a) of this section, listed in an information disclosure statement is required to be provided, even if the patent, publication, pending U.S. application or other information was previously submitted to, or cited by, the Office in an earlier application, unless:

(1) The earlier application is properly identified in the information disclosure statement and is relied on for an earlier effective filing date under 35 U.S.C. 120; and

(2) The information disclosure statement submitted in the earlier application complies with paragraphs (a) through (c) of this section.

[42 FR 5594, Jan. 28, 1977; para. (a) 48 FR 2712, Jan. 20, 1983, effective date Feb. 27, 1983; 57 FR 2021, Jan. 17, 1992, effective Mar. 16, 1992; revised, 65 FR 54604, Sept. 8, 2000, effective Nov. 7, 2000; paras. (a)(2) and (b) revised, 65 FR 57024, Sept. 20, 2000, effective Nov. 29, 2000; para. (e) added, 68 FR 38611, June 30, 2003, effective July 30, 2003; paras. (a) and (c) revised and para. (e) removed, 69 FR 56481, Sept. 21, 2004, effective Oct. 21, 2004]

§ 1.99 Third-party submission in published application.

(a) A submission by a member of the public of patents or publications relevant to a pending published application may be entered in the application file if the submission complies with the requirements of this section and the application is still pending when the submission and application file are brought before the examiner.

(b) A submission under this section must identify the application to which it is directed by application number and include:

(1) The fee set forth in § 1.17(p);

(2) A list of the patents or publications submitted for consideration by the Office, including the date of publication of each patent or publication;

(3) A copy of each listed patent or publication in written form or at least the pertinent portions; and

(4) An English language translation of all the necessary and pertinent parts of any non-English lan-

guage patent or publication in written form relied upon.

(c) The submission under this section must be served upon the applicant in accordance with § 1.248.

(d) A submission under this section shall not include any explanation of the patents or publications, or any other information. The Office will not enter such explanation or information if included in a submission under this section. A submission under this section is also limited to ten total patents or publications.

(e) A submission under this section must be filed within two months from the date of publication of the application (§ 1.215(a)) or prior to the mailing of a notice of allowance (§ 1.311), whichever is earlier. Any submission under this section not filed within this period is permitted only when the patents or publications could not have been submitted to the Office earlier, and must also be accompanied by the processing fee set forth in § 1.17(i). A submission by a member of the public to a pending published application that does not comply with the requirements of this section will not be entered.

(f) A member of the public may include a self-addressed postcard with a submission to receive an acknowledgment by the Office that the submission has been received. A member of the public filing a submission under this section will not receive any communications from the Office relating to the submission other than the return of a self-addressed postcard. In the absence of a request by the Office, an applicant has no duty to, and need not, reply to a submission under this section.

[48 FR 2712, Jan. 20, 1983; effective Feb. 27, 1983; removed and reserved, 57 FR 2021, Jan. 17, 1992, effective Mar. 16, 1992; added, 65 FR 57024, Sept. 20, 2000, effective Nov. 29, 2000; para. (f) corrected, 65 FR 66502, Nov. 6, 2000, effective Nov. 29, 2000; paras. (d) and (e) revised, 68 FR 38611, June 30, 2003, effective July 30, 2003]

EXAMINATION OF APPLICATIONS

§ 1.101 [Reserved]

[29 FR 13470, Sept. 30, 1964; para. (a), 48 FR 2712, Jan. 20, 1983, effective Feb. 27, 1983; para. (a), 50 FR 9381, Mar. 7, 1985, effective May 8, 1985; 52 FR 20046, May 28, 1987, effective July 1, 1987; para. (a) revised, 60 FR 20195, Apr. 25, 1995, effective June 8, 1995;

removed and reserved, 62 FR 53131, Oct. 10, 1997, effective Dec. 1, 1997]

§ 1.102 Advancement of examination.

(a) Applications will not be advanced out of turn for examination or for further action except as provided by this part, or upon order of the Director to expedite the business of the Office, or upon filing of a request under paragraph (b) of this section or upon filing a petition under paragraphs (c) or (d) of this section with a showing which, in the opinion of the Director, will justify so advancing it.

(b) Applications wherein the inventions are deemed of peculiar importance to some branch of the public service and the head of some department of the Government requests immediate action for that reason, may be advanced for examination.

(c) A petition to make an application special may be filed without a fee if the basis for the petition is:

(1) The applicant's age or health; or

(2) That the invention will materially:

(i) Enhance the quality of the environment;

(ii) Contribute to the development or conservation of energy resources; or

(iii) Contribute to countering terrorism.

(d) A petition to make an application special on grounds other than those referred to in paragraph (c) of this section must be accompanied by the fee set forth in § 1.17(h).

[24 FR 10332, Dec. 22, 1959; paras. (a), (c), and (d), 47 FR 41276, Sept. 17, 1982, effective Oct. 1, 1982; para. (d), 54 FR 6893, Feb. 15, 1989, effective Apr. 17, 1989; para. (d) revised, 60 FR 20195, Apr. 25, 1995, effective June 8, 1995; para. (a) revised, 62 FR 53131, Oct. 10, 1997, effective Dec. 1, 1997; para. (d) revised, 65 FR 54604, Sept. 8, 2000, effective Nov. 7, 2000; para. (a) revised, 68 FR 14332, Mar. 25, 2003, effective May 1, 2003; para. (c) revised, 69 FR 56481, Sept. 21, 2004, effective Oct. 21, 2004]

§ 1.103 Suspension of action by the Office.

(a) *Suspension for cause.* On request of the applicant, the Office may grant a suspension of action by the Office under this paragraph for good and sufficient cause. The Office will not suspend action if a reply by applicant to an Office action is outstanding.

Any petition for suspension of action under this paragraph must specify a period of suspension not exceeding six months. Any petition for suspension of action under this paragraph must also include:

(1) A showing of good and sufficient cause for suspension of action; and

(2) The fee set forth in § 1.17(g), unless such cause is the fault of the Office.

(b) *Limited suspension of action in a continued prosecution application (CPA) filed under § 1.53(d).* On request of the applicant, the Office may grant a suspension of action by the Office under this paragraph in a continued prosecution application filed under § 1.53(d) for a period not exceeding three months. Any request for suspension of action under this paragraph must be filed with the request for an application filed under § 1.53(d), specify the period of suspension, and include the processing fee set forth in § 1.17(i).

(c) *Limited suspension of action after a request for continued application (RCE) under § 1.114.* On request of the applicant, the Office may grant a suspension of action by the Office under this paragraph after the filing of a request for continued examination in compliance with § 1.114 for a period not exceeding three months. Any request for suspension of action under this paragraph must be filed with the request for continued examination under § 1.114, specify the period of suspension, and include the processing fee set forth in § 1.17(i).

(d) *Deferral of examination.* On request of the applicant, the Office may grant a deferral of examination under the conditions specified in this paragraph for a period not extending beyond three years from the earliest filing date for which a benefit is claimed under title 35, United States Code. A request for deferral of examination under this paragraph must include the publication fee set forth in § 1.18(d) and the processing fee set forth in § 1.17(i). A request for deferral of examination under this paragraph will not be granted unless:

(1) The application is an original utility or plant application filed under § 1.53(b) or resulting from entry of an international application into the national stage after compliance with § 1.495;

(2) The applicant has not filed a nonpublication request under § 1.213(a), or has filed a request under § 1.213(b) to rescind a previously filed nonpublication request;

(3) The application is in condition for publication as provided in § 1.211(c); and

(4) The Office has not issued either an Office action under 35 U.S.C. 132 or a notice of allowance under 35 U.S.C. 151.

(e) *Notice of suspension on initiative of the Office.* The Office will notify applicant if the Office suspends action by the Office on an application on its own initiative.

(f) *Suspension of action for public safety or defense.* The Office may suspend action by the Office by order of the Director if the following conditions are met:

(1) The application is owned by the United States;

(2) Publication of the invention may be detrimental to the public safety or defense; and

(3) The appropriate department or agency requests such suspension.

(g) *Statutory invention registration.* The Office will suspend action by the Office for the entire pendency of an application if the Office has accepted a request to publish a statutory invention registration in the application, except for purposes relating to patent interference proceedings under part 41, subpart D, of this title.

[24 FR 10332, Dec. 22, 1959; 33 FR 5624, Apr. 11, 1968; paras. (a) and (b), 47 FR 41276, Sept. 17, 1982, effective Oct. 1, 1982; para. (d), 49 FR 48416, Dec. 12, 1984, effective Feb. 11, 1985; para. (d), 50 FR 9381, Mar. 7, 1985, effective May 8, 1985; para. (a), 54 FR 6893, Feb. 15, 1989, effective Apr. 17, 1989; para. (a) revised, 60 FR 20195, Apr. 25, 1995, effective June 8, 1995; para. (a) revised, 62 FR 53131, Oct. 10, 1997, effective Dec. 1, 1997; revised, 65 FR 50092, Aug. 16, 2000, effective Aug. 16, 2000; paras. (d) through (f) redesignated as (e) through (g) and para. (d) added, 65 FR 57024, Sept. 20, 2000, effective Nov. 29, 2000; para. (d)(1) revised, 67 FR 520, Jan. 4, 2002, effective Apr. 1, 2002; para. (f) revised, 68 FR 14332, Mar. 25, 2003, effective May 1, 2003; para. (g) revised, 69 FR 49959, Aug. 12, 2004, effective Sept. 13, 2004; para. (a)(2) revised, 69 FR 56481, Sept. 21, 2004, effective Nov. 22, 2004]

§ 1.104 Nature of examination.

(a) *Examiner's action.*

(1) On taking up an application for examination or a patent in a reexamination proceeding, the examiner shall make a thorough study thereof and shall make a thorough investigation of the available prior art relating to the subject matter of the claimed invention. The examination shall be complete with respect both to compliance of the application or patent under reexamination with the applicable statutes and rules and to the patentability of the invention as claimed, as well as with respect to matters of form, unless otherwise indicated.

(2) The applicant, or in the case of a reexamination proceeding, both the patent owner and the requester, will be notified of the examiner's action. The reasons for any adverse action or any objection or requirement will be stated in an Office action and such information or references will be given as may be useful in aiding the applicant, or in the case of a reexamination proceeding the patent owner, to judge the propriety of continuing the prosecution.

(3) An international-type search will be made in all national applications filed on and after June 1, 1978.

(4) Any national application may also have an international-type search report prepared thereon at the time of the national examination on the merits, upon specific written request therefor and payment of the international-type search report fee set forth in § 1.21(e). The Patent and Trademark Office does not require that a formal report of an international-type search be prepared in order to obtain a search fee refund in a later filed international application.

(b) *Completeness of examiner's action.* The examiner's action will be complete as to all matters, except that in appropriate circumstances, such as misjoinder of invention, fundamental defects in the application, and the like, the action of the examiner may be limited to such matters before further action is made. However, matters of form need not be raised by the examiner until a claim is found allowable.

(c) *Rejection of claims.*

(1) If the invention is not considered patentable, or not considered patentable as claimed, the claims, or those considered unpatentable will be rejected.

(2) In rejecting claims for want of novelty or for obviousness, the examiner must cite the best references at his or her command. When a reference is complex or shows or describes inventions other than that claimed by the applicant, the particular part relied on must be designated as nearly as practicable. The pertinence of each reference, if not apparent, must be clearly explained and each rejected claim specified.

(3) In rejecting claims the examiner may rely upon admissions by the applicant, or the patent owner in a reexamination proceeding, as to any matter affecting patentability and, insofar as rejections in applications are concerned, may also rely upon facts within his or her knowledge pursuant to paragraph (d)(2) of this section.

(4) Subject matter which is developed by another person which qualifies as prior art only under 35 U.S.C. 102(e), (f) or (g) may be used as prior art under 35 U.S.C. 103 against a claimed invention unless the entire rights to the subject matter and the claimed invention were commonly owned by the same person or subject to an obligation of assignment to the same person at the time the claimed invention was made.

(i) Subject matter developed by another person and a claimed invention shall be deemed to have been commonly owned by the same person or subject to an obligation of assignment to the same person in any application and in any patent granted on or after December 10, 2004, if:

(A) The claimed invention and the subject matter was made by or on behalf of parties to a joint research agreement that was in effect on or before the date the claimed invention was made;

(B) The claimed invention was made as a result of activities undertaken within the scope of the joint research agreement; and

(C) The application for patent for the claimed invention discloses or is amended to disclose the names of the parties to the joint research agreement.

(ii) For purposes of paragraph (c)(4)(i) of this section, the term "joint research agreement" means a written contract, grant, or cooperative agreement entered into by two or more persons or entities for the performance of experimental, developmental, or research work in the field of the claimed invention.

(iii) To overcome a rejection under 35 U.S.C. 103(a) based upon subject matter which qualifies as prior art under only one or more of 35 U.S.C. 102(e), (f) or (g) via 35 U.S.C. 103(c)(2), the applicant must provide a statement to the effect that the prior art and the claimed invention were made by or on the behalf of parties to a joint research agreement, within the meaning of 35 U.S.C. 103(c)(3) and paragraph (c)(4)(ii) of this section, that was in effect on or before the date the claimed invention was made, and that the claimed invention was made as a result of activities undertaken within the scope of the joint research agreement.

(5) The claims in any original application naming an inventor will be rejected as being precluded by a waiver in a published statutory invention registration naming that inventor if the same subject matter is claimed in the application and the statutory invention registration. The claims in any reissue application naming an inventor will be rejected as being precluded by a waiver in a published statutory invention registration naming that inventor if the reissue application seeks to claim subject matter:

(i) Which was not covered by claims issued in the patent prior to the date of publication of the statutory invention registration; and

(ii) Which was the same subject matter waived in the statutory invention registration.

(d) *Citation of references.*

(1) If domestic patents are cited by the examiner, their numbers and dates, and the names of the patentees will be stated. If domestic patent application publications are cited by the examiner, their publication number, publication date, and the names of the applicants will be stated. If foreign published applications or patents are cited, their nationality or country, numbers and dates, and the names of the patentees will be stated, and such other data will be furnished as may be necessary to enable the applicant, or in the case of a reexamination proceeding, the patent owner, to identify the published applications or patents cited. In citing foreign published applications or patents, in case only a part of the document is involved, the particular pages and sheets containing the parts relied upon will be identified. If printed publications are cited, the author (if any), title, date, pages or plates, and place of publication, or place where a copy can be found, will be given.

(2) When a rejection in an application is based on facts within the personal knowledge of an employee of the Office, the data shall be as specific as possible, and the reference must be supported, when called for by the applicant, by the affidavit of such employee, and such affidavit shall be subject to contradiction or explanation by the affidavits of the applicant and other persons.

(e) *Reasons for allowance.* If the examiner believes that the record of the prosecution as a whole does not make clear his or her reasons for allowing a claim or claims, the examiner may set forth such reasoning. The reasons shall be incorporated into an Office action rejecting other claims of the application or patent under reexamination or be the subject of a separate communication to the applicant or patent owner. The applicant or patent owner may file a statement commenting on the reasons for allowance within such time as may be specified by the examiner. Failure by the examiner to respond to any statement commenting on reasons for allowance does not give rise to any implication.

[43 FR 20465, May 11, 1978; 46 FR 29182, May 29, 1981; para. (d), 47 FR 41276, Sept. 17, 1982, effective date Oct. 1, 1982; para. (e), 50 FR 9381, Mar. 7, 1985, effective May 8, 1985; para. (e), 57 FR 29642, July 6, 1992, effective Sept. 4, 1992; revised, 62 FR 53131, Oct. 10, 1997, effective Dec. 1, 1997; para. (c)(4) revised, 65 FR 14865, Mar. 20, 2000, effective May 29, 2000 (adopted as final, 65 FR 50092, Aug. 16, 2000); paras. (a)(2) and (e) revised, 65 FR 54604, Sept. 8, 2000, effective Nov. 7, 2000; para. (a)(5) removed and para. (d)(1) revised, 65 FR 57024, Sept. 20, 2000, effective Nov. 29, 2000; para. (c)(4) revised, 70 FR 1818, Jan. 11, 2005, effective Dec. 10, 2004; para. (c)(4) revised, 70 FR 54259, Sept. 14, 2005, effective Sept. 14, 2005; paras. (a)(1) and (b) revised, 72 FR 46716, Aug. 21, 2007 (implementation enjoined and never became effective); paras. (a)(1) and (b) revised, 74 FR 52686, Oct. 14, 2009, effective Oct. 14, 2009 (to remove changes made by the final rules in 72 FR 46716 from the CFR)]

§ 1.105   Requirements for information.

(a)(1) In the course of examining or treating a matter in a pending or abandoned application filed under 35 U.S.C. 111 or 371 (including a reissue application), in a patent, or in a reexamination proceeding, the examiner or other Office employee may require the submission, from individuals identified under § 1.56(c), or any assignee, of such information as may be reasonably necessary to properly examine or treat the matter, for example:

(i) *Commercial databases*: The existence of any particularly relevant commercial database known to any of the inventors that could be searched for a particular aspect of the invention.

(ii) *Search*: Whether a search of the prior art was made, and if so, what was searched.

(iii) *Related information*: A copy of any non-patent literature, published application, or patent (U.S. or foreign), by any of the inventors, that relates to the claimed invention.

(iv) *Information used to draft application*: A copy of any non-patent literature, published application, or patent (U.S. or foreign) that was used to draft the application.

(v) *Information used in invention process*: A copy of any non-patent literature, published application, or patent (U.S. or foreign) that was used in the invention process, such as by designing around or providing a solution to accomplish an invention result.

(vi) *Improvements*: Where the claimed invention is an improvement, identification of what is being improved.

(vii) *In Use*: Identification of any use of the claimed invention known to any of the inventors at the time the application was filed notwithstanding the date of the use.

(viii) *Technical information known to applicant*. Technical information known to applicant concerning the related art, the disclosure, the claimed subject matter, other factual information pertinent to patentability, or concerning the accuracy of the examiner's stated interpretation of such items.

(2) Where an assignee has asserted its right to prosecute pursuant to § 3.71(a) of this chapter, matters such as paragraphs (a)(1)(i), (iii), and (vii) of this section may also be applied to such assignee.

(3) Requirements for factual information known to applicant may be presented in any appropriate manner, for example:

(i) A requirement for factual information;

(ii) Interrogatories in the form of specific questions seeking applicant's factual knowledge; or

(iii) Stipulations as to facts with which the applicant may agree or disagree.

(4) Any reply to a requirement for information pursuant to this section that states either that the information required to be submitted is unknown to or is not readily available to the party or parties from which it was requested may be accepted as a complete reply.

(b) The requirement for information of paragraph (a)(1) of this section may be included in an Office action, or sent separately.

(c) A reply, or a failure to reply, to a requirement for information under this section will be governed by §§ 1.135 and 1.136.

[Removed and reserved, 62 FR 53131, Oct. 10, 1997, effective Dec.1, 1997; added, 65 FR 54604, Sept. 8, 2000, effective Nov. 7, 2000; para. (a)(3) revised and paras. (a)(1)(viii) and (a)(4) added, 69 FR 56481, Sept. 21, 2004, effective Oct. 21, 2004; para. (a)(1)(ix) added, 72 FR 46716, Aug. 21, 2007 (implementation enjoined and never became effective); para. (a)(1)(ix) removed, 74 FR 52686, Oct. 14, 2009, effective Oct. 14, 2009 (to remove changes made by the final rules in 72 FR 46716 from the CFR)]

§ 1.106 [Reserved]

[24 FR 10332, Dec. 22, 1959; 34 FR 18857, Nov. 26, 1969; para. (c) added, 47 FR 21752, May 19, 1982, effective July 1, 1982; paras. (d) and (e), 50 FR 9381, Mar. 7, 1985, effective May 8, 1985; removed and reserved, 62 FR 53131, Oct. 10, 1997, effective Dec. 1, 1997]

§ 1.107 [Reserved]

[46 FR 29182, May 29, 1981; para. (a) revised, 61 FR 42790, Aug. 19, 1996, effective Sept. 23, 1996; removed and reserved, 62 FR 53131, Oct. 10, 1997, effective Dec. 1, 1997]

§ 1.108 [Reserved]

[50 FR 9381, Mar. 7, 1985, effective May 8, 1985; removed and reserved, 62 FR 53131, Oct. 10, 1997, effective Dec. 1, 1997]

§ 1.109 [Reserved]

[Added 70 FR 1818, Jan. 11, 2005, effective Dec. 10, 2004; removed and reserved, 70 FR 54259, Sept. 14, 2005, effective Sept. 14, 2005]

§ 1.110 Inventorship and date of invention of the subject matter of individual claims.

When more than one inventor is named in an application or patent, the Patent and Trademark Office, when necessary for purposes of an Office proceeding, may require an applicant, patentee, or owner to identify the inventive entity of the subject matter of each claim in the application or patent. Where appropriate, the invention dates of the subject matter of each claim and the ownership of the subject matter on the date of invention may be required of the applicant, patentee or owner. *See* also §§ 1.78(c) and 1.130.

[50 FR 9381, Mar. 7, 1985, effective date May 8, 1985; revised, 61 FR 42790, Aug. 19, 1996, effective Sept. 23, 1996; revised, 72 FR 46716, Aug. 21, 2007 (implementation enjoined and never became effective); revised, 74 FR 52686, Oct. 14, 2009, effective Oct. 14, 2009 (to remove changes made by the final rules in 72 FR 46716 from the CFR)]

ACTION BY APPLICANT AND FURTHER CONSIDERATION

§ 1.111 Reply by applicant or patent owner to a non-final Office action.

(a)(1) If the Office action after the first examination (§ 1.104) is adverse in any respect, the applicant or patent owner, if he or she persists in his or her application for a patent or reexamination proceeding, must reply and request reconsideration or further examination, with or without amendment. See §§ 1.135 and 1.136 for time for reply to avoid abandonment.

(2) *Supplemental replies.* (i) A reply that is supplemental to a reply that is in compliance with § 1.111(b) will not be entered as a matter of right except as provided in paragraph (a)(2)(ii) of this section. The Office may enter a supplemental reply if the supplemental reply is clearly limited to:

(A) Cancellation of a claim(s);

(B) Adoption of the examiner suggestion(s);

(C) Placement of the application in condition for allowance;

(D) Reply to an Office requirement made after the first reply was filed;

(E) Correction of informalities (*e.g.*, typographical errors); or

(F) Simplification of issues for appeal.

(ii) A supplemental reply will be entered if the supplemental reply is filed within the period during which action by the Office is suspended under § 1.103(a) or (c).

(b) In order to be entitled to reconsideration or further examination, the applicant or patent owner must reply to the Office action. The reply by the applicant or patent owner must be reduced to a writing which distinctly and specifically points out the supposed errors in the examiner's action and must reply to every ground of objection and rejection in the prior Office action. The reply must present arguments pointing out the specific distinctions believed to render the claims, including any newly presented claims, patentable over any applied references. If the reply is with respect to an application, a request may be made that objections or requirements as to form not necessary to further consideration of the claims be held in abeyance until allowable subject matter is indicated. The applicant's or patent owner's reply must appear throughout to be a *bona fide* attempt to advance the application or the reexamination proceeding to final action. A general allegation that the claims define a patentable invention without specifically pointing out how the language of the claims patentably distinguishes them from the references does not comply with the requirements of this section.

(c) In amending in reply to a rejection of claims in an application or patent under reexamination, the applicant or patent owner must clearly point out the patentable novelty which he or she thinks the claims present in view of the state of the art disclosed by the references cited or the objections made. The applicant or patent owner must also show how the amendments avoid such references or objections.

[46 FR 29182, May 29, 1981; para. (b) revised, 62 FR 53131, Oct. 10, 1997, effective Dec. 1, 1997; paras. (a) and (c) revised, 65 FR 54604, Sept. 8, 2000, effective Nov. 7, 2000; para. (a)(2) revised, 68 FR 14332, Mar. 25, 2003, effective May 1, 2003; para. (a)(2) revised, 69 FR 56481, Sept. 21, 2004, effective Oct. 21, 2004; para. (a)(2)(i) revised, 70 FR 3880, Jan. 27, 2005, effective Dec. 8. 2004]

§ 1.112 Reconsideration before final action.

After reply by applicant or patent owner (§ 1.111 or § 1.945) to a non-final action and any comments by an inter partes reexamination requester (§ 1.947), the application or the patent under reexamination will be reconsidered and again examined. The applicant, or in the case of a reexamination proceeding the patent owner and any third party requester, will be notified if claims are rejected, objections or requirements made, or decisions favorable to patentability are made, in the same manner as after the first examination (§ 1.104). Applicant or patent owner may reply to such Office action in the same manner provided in § 1.111 or § 1.945, with or without amendment, unless such Office action indicates that it is made final (§ 1.113) or an appeal (§ 41.31 of this title) has been taken (§ 1.116), or in an inter partes reexamination, that it is an action closing prosecution (§ 1.949) or a right of appeal notice (§ 1.953).

[46 FR 29182, May 29, 1981; revised, 62 FR 53131, Oct. 10, 1997, effective Dec. 1, 1997; revised, 65 FR 54604, Sept. 8, 2000, effective Nov. 7, 2000; revised, 65 FR 76756, Dec. 7, 2000, effective Feb. 5, 2001; revised, 69 FR 49959, Aug. 12, 2004, effective Sept. 13, 2004]

§ 1.113 Final rejection or action.

(a)   On the second or any subsequent examination or consideration by the examiner the rejection or other action may be made final, whereupon applicant's, or for *ex parte* reexaminations filed under § 1.510, patent owner's reply is limited to appeal in the case of rejection of any claim (§ 41.31 of this title), or to amendment as specified in § 1.114 or § 1.116. Petition may be taken to the Director in the case of objections or requirements not involved in the rejection of any claim (§ 1.181). Reply to a final rejection or action must comply with § 1.114 or paragraph (c) of this section. For final actions in an inter partes reexamination filed under § 1.913, see § 1.953.

(b)   In making such final rejection, the examiner shall repeat or state all grounds of rejection then considered applicable to the claims in the application, clearly stating the reasons in support thereof.

(c)   Reply to a final rejection or action must include cancellation of, or appeal from the rejection of, each rejected claim. If any claim stands allowed, the reply to a final rejection or action must comply with any requirements or objections as to form.

[24 FR 10332, Dec. 22, 1959; 46 FR 29182, May 29, 1981; revised, 62 FR 53131, Oct. 10, 1997, effective Dec. 1, 1997; revised, 65 FR 14865, Mar. 20, 2000, effective May 29, 2000 (adopted as final, 65 FR 50092, Aug. 16, 2000); para. (a) revised, 65 FR 76756, Dec. 7, 2000, effective Feb. 5, 2001; para. (a) revised, 68 FR 14332, Mar. 25, 2003, effective May 1, 2003; para. (a) revised, 69 FR 49959, Aug. 12, 2004, effective Sept. 13, 2004]

§ 1.114 Request for continued examination.

(a)   If prosecution in an application is closed, an applicant may request continued examination of the application by filing a submission and the fee set forth in § 1.17(e) prior to the earliest of:

(1)   Payment of the issue fee, unless a petition under § 1.313 is granted;

(2)   Abandonment of the application; or

(3)   The filing of a notice of appeal to the U.S. Court of Appeals for the Federal Circuit under 35 U.S.C. 141, or the commencement of a civil action under 35 U.S.C. 145 or 146, unless the appeal or civil action is terminated.

(b)   Prosecution in an application is closed as used in this section means that the application is under appeal, or that the last Office action is a final action (§ 1.113), a notice of allowance (§ 1.311), or an action that otherwise closes prosecution in the application.

(c)   A submission as used in this section includes, but is not limited to, an information disclosure statement, an amendment to the written description, claims, or drawings, new arguments, or new evidence in support of patentability. If reply to an Office action under 35 U.S.C. 132 is outstanding, the submission must meet the reply requirements of § 1.111.

(d)   If an applicant timely files a submission and fee set forth in § 1.17(e), the Office will withdraw the finality of any Office action and the submission will be entered and considered. If an applicant files a request for continued examination under this section after appeal, but prior to a decision on the appeal, it will be treated as a request to withdraw the appeal and to reopen prosecution of the application before the examiner. An appeal brief (§ 41.37 of this title) or a reply brief (§ 41.41 of this title), or related papers, will not be considered a submission under this section.

(e)   The provisions of this section do not apply to:

(1)   A provisional application;

(2)   An application for a utility or plant patent filed under 35 U.S.C. 111(a) before June 8, 1995;

(3)   An international application filed under 35 U.S.C. 363 before June 8, 1995;

(4)   An application for a design patent; or

(5)   A patent under reexamination.

[Added 65 FR 14865, Mar. 20, 2000, effective May 29, 2000; revised 65 FR 50092, Aug. 16, 2000; para. (d) revised, 69 FR 49959, Aug. 12, 2004, effective Sept. 13, 2004; paras. (a) and (d) revised and (f), (g), and (h) added, 72 FR 46716, Aug. 21, 2007 (implementation enjoined and never became effective); paras. (a) and (d) revised and (f), (g), and (h) removed, 74 FR 52686, Oct. 14, 2009, effective Oct. 14, 2009 (to remove changes made by the final rules in 72 FR 46716 from the CFR)]

AMENDMENTS

§ 1.115   Preliminary amendments.

(a)   A preliminary amendment is an amendment that is received in the Office (§ 1.6) on or before the mail date of the first Office action under § 1.104. The patent application publication may include preliminary amendments (§ 1.215 (a)).

(1)   A preliminary amendment that is present on the filing date of an application is part of the original disclosure of the application.

(2)   A preliminary amendment filed after the filing date of the application is not part of the original disclosure of the application.

(b)   A preliminary amendment in compliance with § 1.121 will be entered unless disapproved by the Director.

(1)   A preliminary amendment seeking cancellation of all the claims without presenting any new or substitute claims will be disapproved.

(2)   A preliminary amendment may be disapproved if the preliminary amendment unduly interferes with the preparation of a first Office action in an application. Factors that will be considered in disapproving a preliminary amendment include:

(i)   The state of preparation of a first Office action as of the date of receipt (§ 1.6) of the preliminary amendment by the Office; and

(ii)   The nature of any changes to the specification or claims that would result from entry of the preliminary amendment.

(3)   A preliminary amendment will not be disapproved under (b)(2) of this section if it is filed no later than:

(i)   Three months from the filing date of an application under § 1.53 (b);

(ii)   The filing date of a continued prosecution application under § 1.53 (d); or

(iii)   Three months from the date the national stage is entered as set forth in § 1.491 in an international application.

(4)   The time periods specified in paragraph (b)(3) of this section are not extendable.

[46 FR 29183, May 29, 1981; removed and reserved, 62 FR 53131, Oct. 10, 1997, effective Dec. 1, 1997; added, 65 FR 54604, Sept. 8, 2000, effective Nov. 7, 2000; para. (b)(1) revised, 68 FR 14332, Mar. 25, 2003, effective May 1, 2003; revised, 69 FR 56481, Sept. 21, 2004, effective Sept. 21, 2004]

§ 1.116   Amendments and affidavits or other evidence after final action and prior to appeal.

(a)   An amendment after final action must comply with § 1.114 or this section.

(b)   After a final rejection or other final action (§ 1.113) in an application or in an *ex parte* reexamination filed under § 1.510, or an action closing prosecution (§ 1.949) in an *inter partes* reexamination filed under § 1.913, but before or on the same date of filing an appeal (§ 41.31 or § 41.61 of this title):

(1)   An amendment may be made canceling claims or complying with any requirement of form expressly set forth in a previous Office action;

(2)   An amendment presenting rejected claims in better form for consideration on appeal may be admitted; or

(3)   An amendment touching the merits of the application or patent under reexamination may be admitted upon a showing of good and sufficient reasons why the amendment is necessary and was not earlier presented.

(c)   The admission of, or refusal to admit, any amendment after a final rejection, a final action, an action closing prosecution, or any related proceedings will not operate to relieve the application or reexamination proceeding from its condition as subject to appeal or to save the application from abandonment under § 1.135, or the reexamination prosecution from termination under § 1.550(d) or § 1.957(b) or limitation of further prosecution under § 1.957(c).

(d)(1)Notwithstanding the provisions of paragraph (b) of this section, no amendment other than canceling claims, where such cancellation does not affect the scope of any other pending claim in the proceeding, can be made in an inter partes reexamination proceeding after the right of appeal notice under § 1.953 except as provided in § 1.981 or as permitted by § 41.77(b)(1) of this title.

(2) Notwithstanding the provisions of paragraph (b) of this section, an amendment made after a final rejection or other final action (§ 1.113) in an *ex parte* reexamination filed under §1.510, or an action closing prosecution (§ 1.949) in an inter partes reexamination filed under § 1.913 may not cancel claims where such cancellation affects the scope of any other pending claim in the reexamination proceeding except as provided in § 1.981 or as permitted by § 41.77(b)(1) of this title.

(e) An affidavit or other evidence submitted after a final rejection or other final action (§ 1.113) in an application or in an *ex parte* reexamination filed under § 1.510, or an action closing prosecution (§ 1.949) in an inter partes reexamination filed under § 1.913 but before or on the same date of filing an appeal (§ 41.31 or § 41.61 of this title), may be admitted upon a showing of good and sufficient reasons why the affidavit or other evidence is necessary and was not earlier presented.

(f) Notwithstanding the provisions of paragraph (e) of this section, no affidavit or other evidence can be made in an inter partes reexamination proceeding after the right of appeal notice under § 1.953 except as provided in § 1.981 or as permitted by § 41.77 (b)(1) of this title.

(g) After decision on appeal, amendments, affidavits and other evidence can only be made as provided in §§ 1.198 and 1.981, or to carry into effect a recommendation under § 41.50(c) of this title.

[24 FR 10332, Dec. 22, 1959; 46 FR 29183, May 29, 1981; para. (a) revised, 62 FR 53131, Oct. 10, 1997, effective Dec. 1, 1997; revised, 65 FR 14865, Mar. 20, 2000, effective May 29, 2000 (adopted as final, 65 FR 50092, Aug. 16, 2000); paras. (b) and (d) revised, 65 FR 76756, Dec. 7, 2000, effective Feb. 5, 2001; revised, 69 FR 49959, Aug. 12, 2004, effective Sept. 13, 2004]

§ 1.117 [Reserved]

[Removed and reserved, 62 FR 53131, Oct. 10, 1997, effective Dec. 1, 1997; added, 72 FR 46716, Aug. 21, 2007 (implementation enjoined and never became effective); removed, 74 FR 52686, Oct. 14, 2009, effective Oct. 14, 2009 (to remove changes made by the final rules in 72 FR 46716 from the CFR)]

§ 1.118 [Reserved]

[48 FR 2712, Jan. 20, 1983, effective Feb. 27, 1983; removed and reserved, 62 FR 53131, Oct. 10, 1997, effective Dec. 1, 1997]

§ 1.119 [Reserved]

[32 FR 13583, Sept. 28, 1967; removed and reserved, 62 FR 53131, Oct. 10, 1997, effective Dec. 1, 1997]

§ 1.121 Manner of making amendments in applications.

(a) *Amendments in applications, other than reissue applications.* Amendments in applications, other than reissue applications, are made by filing a paper, in compliance with § 1.52, directing that specified amendments be made.

(b) *Specification.* Amendments to the specification, other than the claims, computer listings (§ 1.96) and sequence listings (§ 1.825), must be made by adding, deleting or replacing a paragraph, by replacing a section, or by a substitute specification, in the manner specified in this section.

(1) *Amendment to delete, replace, or add a paragraph.* Amendments to the specification, including amendment to a section heading or the title of the invention which are considered for amendment purposes to be an amendment of a paragraph, must be made by submitting:

(i) An instruction, which unambiguously identifies the location, to delete one or more paragraphs of the specification, replace a paragraph with one or more replacement paragraphs, or add one or more paragraphs;

(ii) The full text of any replacement paragraph with markings to show all the changes relative to the previous version of the paragraph. The text of any added subject matter must be shown by underlining the added text. The text of any deleted matter must be shown by strike-through except that double brackets placed before and after the deleted characters may be used to show deletion of five or fewer consecutive characters. The text of any deleted subject matter must be shown by being placed within double brackets if strikethrough cannot be easily perceived;

(iii) The full text of any added paragraphs without any underlining; and

(iv) The text of a paragraph to be deleted must not be presented with strike-through or placed within double brackets. The instruction to delete may identify a paragraph by its paragraph number or include a few words from the beginning, and end, of the paragraph, if needed for paragraph identification purposes.

(2) *Amendment by replacement section.* If the sections of the specification contain section headings as provided in § 1.77(b), § 1.154(b), or § 1.163(c), amendments to the specification, other than the claims, may be made by submitting:

(i) A reference to the section heading along with an instruction, which unambiguously identifies the location, to delete that section of the specification and to replace such deleted section with a replacement section; and;

(ii) A replacement section with markings to show all changes relative to the previous version of the section. The text of any added subject matter must be shown by underlining the added text. The text of any deleted matter must be shown by strike-through except that double brackets placed before and after the deleted characters may be used to show deletion of five or fewer consecutive characters. The text of any deleted subject matter must be shown by being placed within double brackets if strike-through cannot be easily perceived.

(3) *Amendment by substitute specification.* The specification, other than the claims, may also be amended by submitting:

(i) An instruction to replace the specification; and

(ii) A substitute specification in compliance with §§ 1.125(b) and (c).

(4) *Reinstatement of previously deleted paragraph or section.* A previously deleted paragraph or section may be reinstated only by a subsequent amendment adding the previously deleted paragraph or section.

(5) *Presentation in subsequent amendment document.* Once a paragraph or section is amended in a first amendment document, the paragraph or section shall not be represented in a subsequent amendment document unless it is amended again or a substitute specification is provided.

(c) *Claims.* Amendments to a claim must be made by rewriting the entire claim with all changes (*e.g.*, additions and deletions) as indicated in this subsection, except when the claim is being canceled. Each amendment document that includes a change to an existing claim, cancellation of an existing claim or addition of a new claim, must include a complete listing of all claims ever presented, including the text of all pending and withdrawn claims, in the application. The claim listing, including the text of the claims, in the amendment document will serve to replace all prior versions of the claims, in the application. In the claim listing, the status of every claim must be indicated after its claim number by using one of the following identifiers in a parenthetical expression: (Original), (Currently amended), (Canceled), (Withdrawn), (Previously presented), (New), and (Not entered).

(1) *Claim listing.* All of the claims presented in a claim listing shall be presented in ascending numerical order. Consecutive claims having the same status of "canceled" or "not entered" may be aggregated into one statement (*e.g.*, Claims 1–5 (canceled)). The claim listing shall commence on a separate sheet of the amendment document and the sheet(s) that contain the text of any part of the claims shall not contain any other part of the amendment.

(2) *When claim text with markings is required.* All claims being currently amended in an amendment paper shall be presented in the claim listing, indicate a status of "currently amended," and be submitted with markings to indicate the changes that have been made relative to the immediate prior version of the claims. The text of any added subject matter must be shown by underlining the added text. The text of any deleted matter must be shown by strike-through except that double brackets placed before and after the deleted characters may be used to show deletion of five or fewer consecutive characters. The text of any deleted subject matter must be shown by being placed within double brackets if strike-through cannot be easily perceived. Only claims having the status of "currently amended," or "withdrawn" if also being amended, shall include markings. If a

withdrawn claim is currently amended, its status in the claim listing may be identified as "withdrawn—currently amended."

(3) *When claim text in clean version is required.* The text of all pending claims not being currently amended shall be presented in the claim listing in clean version, *i.e.*, without any markings in the presentation of text. The presentation of a clean version of any claim having the status of "original," "withdrawn" or "previously presented" will constitute an assertion that it has not been changed relative to the immediate prior version, except to omit markings that may have been present in the immediate prior version of the claims of the status of "withdrawn" or "previously presented." Any claim added by amendment must be indicated with the status of "new" and presented in clean version, *i.e.*, without any underlining.

(4) *When claim text shall not be presented; canceling a claim.*

(i) No claim text shall be presented for any claim in the claim listing with the status of "canceled" or "not entered."

(ii) Cancellation of a claim shall be effected by an instruction to cancel a particular claim number. Identifying the status of a claim in the claim listing as "canceled" will constitute an instruction to cancel the claim.

(5) *Reinstatement of previously canceled claim.* A claim which was previously canceled may be reinstated only by adding the claim as a "new" claim with a new claim number.

(d) *Drawings:* One or more application drawings shall be amended in the following manner: Any changes to an application drawing must be in compliance with § 1.84 and must be submitted on a replacement sheet of drawings which shall be an attachment to the amendment document and, in the top margin, labeled "Replacement Sheet". Any replacement sheet of drawings shall include all of the figures appearing on the immediate prior version of the sheet, even if only one figure is amended. Any new sheet of drawings containing an additional figure must be labeled in the top margin as "New Sheet". All changes to the drawings shall be explained, in detail, in either the drawing amendment or remarks section of the amendment paper.

(1) A marked-up copy of any amended drawing figure, including annotations indicating the changes made, may be included. The marked-up copy must be clearly labeled as "Annotated Sheet" and must be presented in the amendment or remarks section that explains the change to the drawings.

(2) A marked-up copy of any amended drawing figure, including annotations indicating the changes made, must be provided when required by the examiner.

(e) *Disclosure consistency.* The disclosure must be amended, when required by the Office, to correct inaccuracies of description and definition, and to secure substantial correspondence between the claims, the remainder of the specification, and the drawings.

(f) *No new matter.* No amendment may introduce new matter into the disclosure of an application.

(g) *Exception for examiner's amendments.* Changes to the specification, including the claims, of an application made by the Office in an examiner's amendment may be made by specific instructions to insert or delete subject matter set forth in the examiner's amendment by identifying the precise point in the specification or the claim(s) where the insertion or deletion is to be made. Compliance with paragraphs (b)(1), (b)(2), or (c) of this section is not required.

(h) *Amendment sections.* Each section of an amendment document (*e.g.*, amendment to the claims, amendment to the specification, replacement drawings, and remarks) must begin on a separate sheet.

(i) *Amendments in reissue applications.* Any amendment to the description and claims in reissue applications must be made in accordance with § 1.173.

(j) *Amendments in reexamination proceedings.* Any proposed amendment to the description and claims in patents involved in reexamination proceedings must be made in accordance with § 1.530.

(k) *Amendments in provisional applications.* Amendments in provisional applications are not usually made. If an amendment is made to a provisional application, however, it must comply with the provisions of this section. Any amendments to a provisional application shall be placed in the provisional application file but may not be entered.

[32 FR 13583, Sept. 28, 1967; 46 FR 29183, May 29, 1981; para. (e), 49 FR 555, Jan. 4, 1984, effective Apr. 1, 1984; revised, 62 FR 53131, Oct. 10, 1997, effective Dec. 1, 1997; revised, 65 FR 54604, Sept. 8, 2000, effective

Nov. 7, 2000; para. (i) revised, 65 FR 76756, Dec. 7, 2000, effective Feb. 5, 2001; revised, 68 FR 38611, June 30, 2003, effective July 30, 2003; para. (d) revised, 69 FR 56481, Sept. 21, 2004, effective Oct. 21, 2004]

§ 1.122 [Reserved]

[24 FR 10332, Dec. 22, 1959; para. (b), 49 FR 48416, Dec. 12, 1984, effective Feb. 11, 1985; removed and reserved, 62 FR 53131, Oct. 10, 1997, effective Dec. 1, 1997]

§ 1.123 [Reserved]

[48 FR 2712, Jan. 20, 1983, effective Feb. 27, 1983; 49 FR 555, Jan. 4, 1984, effective Apr. 1, 1984; amended, 58 FR 38719, July 20, 1993, effective Oct. 1, 1993; removed and reserved, 62 FR 53131, Oct. 10, 1997, effective Dec. 1, 1997]

§ 1.124 [Reserved]

[Removed and reserved, 62 FR 53131, Oct. 10, 1997, effective Dec. 1, 1997]

§ 1.125 Substitute specification.

(a) If the number or nature of the amendments or the legibility of the application papers renders it difficult to consider the application, or to arrange the papers for printing or copying, the Office may require the entire specification, including the claims, or any part thereof, be rewritten.

(b) Subject to § 1.312, a substitute specification, excluding the claims, may be filed at any point up to payment of the issue fee if it is accompanied by a statement that the substitute specification includes no new matter.

(c) A substitute specification submitted under this section must be submitted with markings showing all the changes relative to the immediate prior version of the specification of record. The text of any added subject matter must be shown by underlining the added text. The text of any deleted matter must be shown by strike-through except that double brackets placed before and after the deleted characters may be used to show deletion of five or fewer consecutive characters. The text of any deleted subject matter must be shown by being placed within double brackets if strike-through cannot be easily perceived. An accompanying clean version (without markings) must also be supplied. Numbering the paragraphs of the specification of record is not considered a change that must be shown pursuant to this paragraph.

(d) A substitute specification under this section is not permitted in a reissue application or in a reexamination proceeding.

[48 FR 2712, Jan. 20, 1983, effective Feb. 27, 1983; revised, 62 FR 53131, Oct. 10, 1997, effective Dec. 1, 1997; paras. (b)(2) and (c) revised, 65 FR 54604, Sept. 8, 2000, effective Nov. 7, 2000; paras. (b) and (c) revised, 68 FR 38611, June 30, 2003, effective July 30, 2003]

§ 1.126 Numbering of claims.

The original numbering of the claims must be preserved throughout the prosecution. When claims are canceled the remaining claims must not be renumbered. When claims are added, they must be numbered by the applicant consecutively beginning with the number next following the highest numbered claim previously presented (whether entered or not). When the application is ready for allowance, the examiner, if necessary, will renumber the claims consecutively in the order in which they appear or in such order as may have been requested by applicant.

[32 FR 13583, Sept. 28, 1967; revised, 62 FR 53131, Oct. 10, 1997, effective Dec. 1, 1997]

§ 1.127 Petition from refusal to admit amendment.

From the refusal of the primary examiner to admit an amendment, in whole or in part, a petition will lie to the Director under § 1.181.

[Revised, 68 FR 14332, Mar. 25, 2003, effective May 1, 2003]

TRANSITIONAL PROVISIONS

§ 1.129 Transitional procedures for limited examination after final rejection and restriction practice.

(a) An applicant in an application, other than for reissue or a design patent, that has been pending for at least two years as of June 8, 1995, taking into account any reference made in such application to any earlier filed application under 35 U.S.C. 120, 121 and

365(c), is entitled to have a first submission entered and considered on the merits after final rejection under the following circumstances: The Office will consider such a submission, if the first submission and the fee set forth in § 1.17(r) are filed prior to the filing of an appeal brief and prior to abandonment of the application. The finality of the final rejection is automatically withdrawn upon the timely filing of the submission and payment of the fee set forth in § 1.17(r). If a subsequent final rejection is made in the application, applicant is entitled to have a second submission entered and considered on the merits after the subsequent final rejection under the following circumstances: The Office will consider such a submission, if the second submission and a second fee set forth in § 1.17(r) are filed prior to the filing of an appeal brief and prior to abandonment of the application. The finality of the subsequent final rejection is automatically withdrawn upon the timely filing of the submission and payment of the second fee set forth in § 1.17(r). Any submission filed after a final rejection made in an application subsequent to the fee set forth in § 1.17(r) having been twice paid will be treated as set forth in § 1.116. A submission as used in this paragraph includes, but is not limited to, an information disclosure statement, an amendment to the written description, claims or drawings and a new substantive argument or new evidence in support of patentability.

(b)(1) In an application, other than for reissue or a design patent, that has been pending for at least three years as of June 8, 1995, taking into account any reference made in the application to any earlier filed application under 35 U.S.C. 120, 121 and 365(c), no requirement for restriction or for the filing of divisional applications shall be made or maintained in the application after June 8, 1995, except where:

(i) The requirement was first made in the application or any earlier filed application under 35 U.S.C. 120, 121 and 365(c) prior to April 8, 1995;

(ii) The examiner has not made a requirement for restriction in the present or parent application prior to April 8, 1995, due to actions by the applicant; or

(iii) The required fee for examination of each additional invention was not paid.

(2) If the application contains more than one independent and distinct invention and a requirement for restriction or for the filing of divisional applica-

tions cannot be made or maintained pursuant to this paragraph, applicant will be so notified and given a time period to:

(i) Elect the invention or inventions to be searched and examined, if no election has been made prior to the notice, and pay the fee set forth in 1.17(s) for each independent and distinct invention claimed in the application in excess of one which applicant elects;

(ii) Confirm an election made prior to the notice and pay the fee set forth in § 1.17(s) for each independent and distinct invention claimed in the application in addition to the one invention which applicant previously elected; or

(iii) File a petition under this section traversing the requirement. If the required petition is filed in a timely manner, the original time period for electing and paying the fee set forth in § 1.17(s) will be deferred and any decision on the petition affirming or modifying the requirement will set a new time period to elect the invention or inventions to be searched and examined and to pay the fee set forth in § 1.17(s) for each independent and distinct invention claimed in the application in excess of one which applicant elects.

(3) The additional inventions for which the required fee has not been paid will be withdrawn from consideration under § 1.142(b). An applicant who desires examination of an invention so withdrawn from consideration can file a divisional application under 35 U.S.C. 121.

(c) The provisions of this section shall not be applicable to any application filed after June 8, 1995.

[Added, 60 FR 20195, Apr. 25, 1995, effective June 8, 1995]

AFFIDAVITS OVERCOMING REJECTIONS

§ 1.130 Affidavit or declaration to disqualify commonly owned patent or published application as prior art.

(a) When any claim of an application or a patent under reexamination is rejected under 35 U.S.C. 103 on a U.S. patent or U.S. patent application publication which is not prior art under 35 U.S.C. 102(b), and the inventions defined by the claims in the application or patent under reexamination and by the claims in the patent or published application are not identical but are not patentably distinct, and the inventions are owned by the same party, the applicant or owner of the patent under reexamination may disqualify the patent or patent application publication as prior art. The patent or patent application publication can be disqualified as prior art by submission of:

(1)   A terminal disclaimer in accordance with § 1.321(c); and

(2)   An oath or declaration stating that the application or patent under reexamination and patent or published application are currently owned by the same party, and that the inventor named in the application or patent under reexamination is the prior inventor under 35 U.S.C. 104.

(b)   [Reserved]

[Added, 61 FR 42790, Aug. 19, 1996, effective Sept. 23, 1996; heading and para. (a) revised, 65 FR 57024, Sept. 20, 2000, effective Nov. 29, 2000; para. (b) removed and reserved, 70 FR 1818, Jan. 11, 2005, effective Dec. 10, 2004]

§ 1.131 Affidavit or declaration of prior invention.

(a)   When any claim of an application or a patent under reexamination is rejected, the inventor of the subject matter of the rejected claim, the owner of the patent under reexamination, or the party qualified under §§ 1.42, 1.43, or 1.47, may submit an appropriate oath or declaration to establish invention of the subject matter of the rejected claim prior to the effective date of the reference or activity on which the rejection is based. The effective date of a U.S. patent, U.S. patent application publication, or international application publication under PCT Article 21(2) is the earlier of its publication date or date that it is effective as a reference under 35 U.S.C. 102(e). Prior invention may not be established under this section in any country other than the United States, a NAFTA country, or a WTO member country. Prior invention may not be established under this section before December 8, 1993, in a NAFTA country other than the United States, or before January 1, 1996, in a WTO member country other than a NAFTA country. Prior invention may not be established under this section if either:

(1)   The rejection is based upon a U.S. patent or U.S. patent application publication of a pending or patented application to another or others which claims the same patentable invention as defined in §

41.203(a) of this title, in which case an applicant may suggest an interference pursuant to § 41.202(a) of this title; or

(2)   The rejection is based upon a statutory bar.

(b)   The showing of facts shall be such, in character and weight, as to establish reduction to practice prior to the effective date of the reference, or conception of the invention prior to the effective date of the reference coupled with due diligence from prior to said date to a subsequent reduction to practice or to the filing of the application. Original exhibits of drawings or records, or photocopies thereof, must accompany and form part of the affidavit or declaration or their absence must be satisfactorily explained.

[24 FR 10332, Dec. 22, 1959; 34 FR 18857, Nov. 26, 1969; para. (a), 48 FR 2713, Jan. 20, 1983, effective Feb. 27, 1983; para. (a), 50 FR 9381, Mar. 7, 1985, effective May 8, 1985; 50 FR 11366, Mar. 21, 1985; 53 FR 23733, June 23, 1988, effective Sept. 12, 1988; para. (a)(1) revised and para. (a)(2) added, 60 FR 21043, May 1, 1995, effective May 31, 1995; para. (a) revised, 61 FR 42790, Aug. 19, 1996, effective Sept. 23, 1996; heading and para. (a) revised, 65 FR 54604, Sept. 8, 2000, effective Sept. 8, 2000; para. (a) revised, 65 FR 57024, Sept. 20, 2000, effective Nov. 29, 2000; para. (a)(1) revised, 69 FR 49959, Aug. 12, 2004, effective Sept. 13, 2004; para. (b) revised, 69 FR 56481, Sept. 21, 2004, effective Oct. 21, 2004]

§ 1.132 Affidavits or declarations traversing rejections or objections.

When any claim of an application or a patent under reexamination is rejected or objected to, any evidence submitted to traverse the rejection or objection on a basis not otherwise provided for must be by way of an oath or declaration under this section.

[48 FR 2713, Jan. 20, 1983, effective Feb. 27, 1983; revised, 61 FR 42790, Aug. 19, 1996, effective Sept. 23, 1996; revised, 65 FR 54604, Sept. 8, 2000, effective Sept. 8, 2000; revised 65 FR 57024, Sept. 20, 2000, effective Nov. 29, 2000]

INTERVIEWS

§ 1.133 Interviews.

(a)(1)Interviews with examiners concerning applications and other matters pending before the Office must be conducted on Office premises and within Office hours, as the respective examiners may designate. Interviews will not be permitted at any other time or place without the authority of the Director.

(2) An interview for the discussion of the patentability of a pending application will not occur before the first Office action, unless the application is a continuing or substitute application or the examiner determines that such an interview would advance prosecution of the application.

(3) The examiner may require that an interview be scheduled in advance.

(b) In every instance where reconsideration is requested in view of an interview with an examiner, a complete written statement of the reasons presented at the interview as warranting favorable action must be filed by the applicant. An interview does not remove the necessity for reply to Office actions as specified in §§ 1.111 and 1.135.

[Para. (b) revised, 62 FR 53131, Oct. 10, 1997, effective Dec. 1, 1997; para. (a) revised, 65 FR 54604, Sept. 8, 2000, effective Nov. 7, 2000; para. (a)(1) revised, 68 FR 14332, Mar. 25, 2003, effective May 1, 2003; para. (a)(2) revised, 70 FR 56119, Sept. 26, 2005, effective Nov. 25, 2005]

TIME FOR REPLY BY APPLICANT; ABANDONMENT OF APPLICATION

§ 1.134 Time period for reply to an Office action.

An Office action will notify the applicant of any non-statutory or shortened statutory time period set for reply to an Office action. Unless the applicant is notified in writing that a reply is required in less than six months, a maximum period of six months is allowed.

[47 FR 41276, Sept. 17, 1982, effective Oct. 1, 1982; revised, 62 FR 53131, Oct. 10, 1997, effective Dec. 1, 1997]

§ 1.135 Abandonment for failure to reply within time period.

(a) If an applicant of a patent application fails to reply within the time period provided under § 1.134 and § 1.136, the application will become abandoned unless an Office action indicates otherwise.

(b) Prosecution of an application to save it from abandonment pursuant to paragraph (a) of this section must include such complete and proper reply as the condition of the application may require. The admission of, or refusal to admit, any amendment after final rejection or any amendment not responsive to the last action, or any related proceedings, will not operate to save the application from abandonment.

(c) When reply by the applicant is a *bona fide* attempt to advance the application to final action, and is substantially a complete reply to the non-final Office action, but consideration of some matter or compliance with some requirement has been inadvertently omitted, applicant may be given a new time period for reply under § 1.134 to supply the omission.

[Paras. (a), (b), and (c), 47 FR 41276, Sept. 17, 1982, effective Oct. 1, 1982; para. (d) deleted, 49 FR 555, Jan. 4, 1984, effective Apr. 1, 1984; revised, 62 FR 53131, Oct. 10, 1997, effective Dec. 1, 1997]

§ 1.136 Extensions of time.

(a)(1) If an applicant is required to reply within a nonstatutory or shortened statutory time period, applicant may extend the time period for reply up to the earlier of the expiration of any maximum period set by statute or five months after the time period set for reply, if a petition for an extension of time and the fee set in § 1.17(a) are filed, unless:

(i) Applicant is notified otherwise in an Office action;

(ii) The reply is a reply brief submitted pursuant to § 41.41 of this title;

(iii) The reply is a request for an oral hearing submitted pursuant to § 41.47(a) of this title;

(iv) The reply is to a decision by the Board of Patent Appeals and Interferences pursuant to § 1.304 or to § 41.50 or § 41.52 of this title; or

(v) The application is involved in a contested case (§ 41.101(a) of this title).

(2) The date on which the petition and the fee have been filed is the date for purposes of determining the period of extension and the corresponding amount of the fee. The expiration of the time period is determined by the amount of the fee paid. A reply must be filed prior to the expiration of the period of extension to avoid abandonment of the application (§ 1.135), but in no situation may an applicant reply later than the maximum time period set by statute, or be granted

an extension of time under paragraph (b) of this section when the provisions of this paragraph are available. See § 1.304 for extensions of time to appeal to the U.S. Court of Appeals for the Federal Circuit or to commence a civil action; § 1.550(c) for extensions of time in *ex parte* reexamination proceedings, § 1.956 for extensions of time in inter partes reexamination proceedings; and §§ 41.4(a) and 41.121(a)(3) of this title for extensions of time in contested cases before the Board of Patent Appeals and Interferences.

(3)   A written request may be submitted in an application that is an authorization to treat any concurrent or future reply, requiring a petition for an extension of time under this paragraph for its timely submission, as incorporating a petition for extension of time for the appropriate length of time. An authorization to charge all required fees, fees under § 1.17, or all required extension of time fees will be treated as a constructive petition for an extension of time in any concurrent or future reply requiring a petition for an extension of time under this paragraph for its timely submission. Submission of the fee set forth in § 1.17(a) will also be treated as a constructive petition for an extension of time in any concurrent reply requiring a petition for an extension of time under this paragraph for its timely submission.

(b)   When a reply cannot be filed within the time period set for such reply and the provisions of paragraph (a) of this section are not available, the period for reply will be extended only for sufficient cause and for a reasonable time specified. Any request for an extension of time under this paragraph must be filed on or before the day on which such reply is due, but the mere filing of such a request will not affect any extension under this paragraph. In no situation can any extension carry the date on which reply is due beyond the maximum time period set by statute. See § 1.304 for extensions of time to appeal to the U.S. Court of Appeals for the Federal Circuit or to commence a civil action; § 1.550(c) for extensions of time in *ex parte* reexamination proceedings; § 1.956 for extensions of time in *inter partes* reexamination proceedings; and §§ 41.4(a) and 41.121(a)(3) of this title for extensions of time in contested cases before the Board of Patent Appeals and Interferences. Any request under this section must be accompanied by the petition fee set forth in § 1.17(g).

(c)   If an applicant is notified in a "Notice of Allowability" that an application is otherwise in condition for allowance, the following time periods are not extendable if set in the "Notice of Allowability" or in an Office action having a mail date on or after the mail date of the "Notice of Allowability":

(1)   The period for submitting an oath or declaration in compliance with § 1.63;

(2)   The period for submitting formal drawings set under § 1.85(c); and

(3)   The period for making a deposit set under § 1.809(c).

[47 FR 41277, Sept. 17, 1982, effective Oct. 1, 1982; 49 FR 555, Jan. 4, 1984, effective Apr. 1, 1984; 49 FR 48416, Dec. 12, 1984, effective Feb. 11, 1985; 54 FR 29551, July 13, 1989, effective Aug. 20, 1989; para. (a) revised, 58 FR 54504, Oct. 22, 1993, effective Jan. 3, 1994; revised, 62 FR 53131, Oct. 10, 1997, effective Dec. 1, 1997; para. (c) added, 65 FR 54604, Sept. 8, 2000, effective Nov. 7, 2000; paras. (a)(2) and (b) revised, 65 FR 76756, Dec. 7, 2000, effective Feb. 5, 2001; para. (c) revised, 66 FR 21090, Apr. 27, 2001, effective May 29, 2001; paras. (a)(1), (a)(2), and (b) revised, 69 FR 49959, Aug. 12, 2004, effective Sept. 13, 2004; para. (b) revised, 69 FR 56481, Sept. 21, 2004, effective Nov. 22, 2004; para. (b) revised, 70 FR 3880, Jan. 27, 2005, effective Dec. 8, 2004; para. (a)(1) revised, 72 FR 46716, Aug. 21, 2007 (implementation enjoined and never became effective); para. (a)(1) revised, 74 FR 52686, Oct. 14, 2009, effective Oct. 14, 2009 (to remove changes made by the final rules in 72 FR 46716 from the CFR)]

§ 1.137   Revival of abandoned application, terminated or limited reexamination prosecution, or lapsed patent.

(a)   *Unavoidable.* If the delay in reply by applicant or patent owner was unavoidable, a petition may be filed pursuant to this paragraph to revive an abandoned application, a reexamination prosecution terminated under §§ 1.550(d) or 1.957(b) or limited under § 1.957(c), or a lapsed patent. A grantable petition pursuant to this paragraph must be accompanied by:

(1)   The reply required to the outstanding Office action or notice, unless previously filed;

(2)   The petition fee as set forth in § 1.17(l);

(3)   A showing to the satisfaction of the Director that the entire delay in filing the required reply from the due date for the reply until the filing of

a grantable petition pursuant to this paragraph was unavoidable; and

(4) Any terminal disclaimer (and fee as set forth in § 1.20(d)) required pursuant to paragraph (d) of this section.

(b) *Unintentional.* If the delay in reply by applicant or patent owner was unintentional, a petition may be filed pursuant to this paragraph to revive an abandoned application, a reexamination prosecution terminated under §§ 1.550(d) or 1.957(b) or limited under § 1.957(c), or a lapsed patent. A grantable petition pursuant to this paragraph must be accompanied by:

(1) The reply required to the outstanding Office action or notice, unless previously filed;

(2) The petition fee as set forth in § 1.17(m);

(3) A statement that the entire delay in filing the required reply from the due date for the reply until the filing of a grantable petition pursuant to this paragraph was unintentional. The Director may require additional information where there is a question whether the delay was unintentional; and

(4) Any terminal disclaimer (and fee as set forth in § 1.20(d)) required pursuant to paragraph (d) of this section.

(c) *Reply.* In a nonprovisional application abandoned for failure to prosecute, the required reply may be met by the filing of a continuing application. In a nonprovisional utility or plant application filed on or after June 8, 1995, and abandoned for failure to prosecute, the required reply may also be met by the filing of a request for continued examination in compliance with § 1.114. In an application or patent, abandoned or lapsed for failure to pay the issue fee or any portion thereof, the required reply must include payment of the issue fee or any outstanding balance. In an application, abandoned for failure to pay the publication fee, the required reply must include payment of the publication fee.

(d) *Terminal disclaimer.*

(1) Any petition to revive pursuant to this section in a design application must be accompanied by a terminal disclaimer and fee as set forth in § 1.321 dedicating to the public a terminal part of the term of any patent granted thereon equivalent to the period of abandonment of the application. Any petition to revive pursuant to this section in either a utility or plant application filed before June 8, 1995, must be accompanied by a terminal disclaimer and fee as set forth in § 1.321 dedicating to the public a terminal part of the term of any patent granted thereon equivalent to the lesser of:

(i) The period of abandonment of the application; or

(ii) The period extending beyond twenty years from the date on which the application for the patent was filed in the United States or, if the application contains a specific reference to an earlier filed application(s) under 35 U.S.C. 120, 121, or 365(c), from the date on which the earliest such application was filed.

(2) Any terminal disclaimer pursuant to paragraph (d)(1) of this section must also apply to any patent granted on a continuing utility or plant application filed before June 8, 1995, or a continuing design application, that contains a specific reference under 35 U.S.C. 120, 121, or 365(c) to the application for which revival is sought.

(3) The provisions of paragraph (d)(1) of this section do not apply to applications for which revival is sought solely for purposes of copendency with a utility or plant application filed on or after June 8, 1995, to lapsed patents, to reissue applications, or to reexamination proceedings.

(e) *Request for reconsideration.* Any request for reconsideration or review of a decision refusing to revive an abandoned application, a terminated or limited reexamination prosecution, or lapsed patent upon petition filed pursuant to this section, to be considered timely, must be filed within two months of the decision refusing to revive or within such time as set in the decision. Unless a decision indicates otherwise, this time period may be extended under:

(1) The provisions of § 1.136 for an abandoned application or lapsed patent;

(2) The provisions of § 1.550(c) for a terminated *ex parte* reexamination prosecution, where the *ex parte* reexamination was filed under § 1.510; or

(3) The provisions of § 1.956 for a terminated *inter partes* reexamination prosecution or an *inter partes* reexamination limited as to further prosecution, where the *inter partes* reexamination was filed under § 1.913.

(f) *Abandonment for failure to notify the Office of a foreign filing*: A nonprovisional application abandoned pursuant to 35 U.S.C. 122(b)(2)(B)(iii) for failure to timely notify the Office of the filing of an application in a foreign country or under a multinational treaty that requires publication of applications eighteen months after filing, may be revived only pursuant to paragraph (b) of this section. The reply requirement of paragraph (c) of this section is met by the notification of such filing in a foreign country or under a multinational treaty, but the filing of a petition under this section will not operate to stay any period for reply that may be running against the application.

(g) *Provisional applications:* A provisional application, abandoned for failure to timely respond to an Office requirement, may be revived pursuant to this section. Subject to the provisions of 35 U.S.C. 119(e)(3) and § 1.7(b), a provisional application will not be regarded as pending after twelve months from its filing date under any circumstances.

[47 FR 41277, Sept. 17, 1982, effective Oct. 1, 1982; para. (b) 48 FR 2713, Jan. 20, 1983, effective Feb. 27, 1983; paras. (a) - (c), paras. (d) & (e) added, 58 FR 44277, Aug. 20,1993, effective Sept. 20, 1993; para. (c) revised, 60 FR 20195, Apr. 25, 1995, effective June 8, 1995; revised, 62 FR 53131, Oct. 10, 1997, effective Dec. 1, 1997; para. (c) revised, 65 FR 54604, Sept. 8, 2000, effective Sept. 8, 2000; revised, 65 FR 57024, Sept. 20, 2000, effective Nov. 29, 2000; para. (d)(3) revised, 69 FR 56481, Sept. 21, 2004, effective Sept. 21, 2004; heading, paras. (a) introductory text, (b) introductory text, and (e) revised, 72 FR 18892, Apr. 16, 2007, effective May 16, 2007]

§ 1.138   Express abandonment.

(a)   An application may be expressly abandoned by filing a written declaration of abandonment identifying the application in the United States Patent and Trademark Office. Express abandonment of the application may not be recognized by the Office before the date of issue or publication unless it is actually received by appropriate officials in time to act.

(b)   A written declaration of abandonment must be signed by a party authorized under § 1.33(b)(1), (b)(3), or (b)(4) to sign a paper in the application, except as otherwise provided in this paragraph. A registered attorney or agent, not of record, who acts in a representative capacity under the provisions of § 1.34(a) when filing a continuing application, may expressly abandon the prior application as of the filing date granted to the continuing application.

(c)   An applicant seeking to abandon an application to avoid publication of the application (see §

1.211(a)(1)) must submit a declaration of express abandonment by way of a petition under this paragraph including the fee set forth in § 1.17(h) in sufficient time to permit the appropriate officials to recognize the abandonment and remove the application from the publication process. Applicants should expect that the petition will not be granted and the application will be published in regular course unless such declaration of express abandonment and petition are received by the appropriate officials more than four weeks prior to the projected date of publication.

(d)   An applicant seeking to abandon an application filed under 35 U.S.C. 111(a) and § 1.53(b) on or after December 8, 2004, to obtain a refund of the search fee and excess claims fee paid in the application, must submit a declaration of express abandonment by way of a petition under this paragraph before an examination has been made of the application. The date indicated on any certificate of mailing or transmission under § 1.8 will not be taken into account in determining whether a petition under § 1.138(d) was filed before an examination has been made of the application. If a request for refund of the search fee and excess claims fee paid in the application is not filed with the declaration of express abandonment under this paragraph or within two months from the date on which the declaration of express abandonment under this paragraph was filed, the Office may retain the entire search fee and excess claims fee paid in the application. This two-month period is not extendable. If a petition and declaration of express abandonment under this paragraph are not filed before an examination has been made of the application, the Office will not refund any part of the search fee and excess claims fee paid in the application except as provided in § 1.26.

[47 FR 47244, Oct. 25, 1982, effective Feb. 27, 1983; 49 FR 48416, Dec. 12, 1984, effective Feb. 11, 1985; revised, 65 FR 54604, Sept. 8, 2000, effective Nov. 7, 2000; para. (a) revised and para. (c) added, 65 FR 57024, Sept. 20, 2000, effective Nov. 29, 2000; para. (c) revised and para. (d) added, 71 FR 12284, Mar. 10, 2006, effective Mar. 10, 2006]

§ 1.139   [Reserved]

[Added, 60 FR 20195, Apr. 25, 1995, effective June 8, 1995; removed and reserved, 62 FR 53131, Oct. 10, 1997, effective Dec. 1, 1997]

JOINDER OF INVENTIONS IN ONE APPLICATION; RESTRICTION

§ 1.141 Different inventions in one national application.

(a) Two or more independent and distinct inventions may not be claimed in one national application, except that more than one species of an invention, not to exceed a reasonable number, may be specifically claimed in different claims in one national application, provided the application also includes an allowable claim generic to all the claimed species and all the claims to species in excess of one are written in dependent form (§ 1.75) or otherwise include all the limitations of the generic claim.

(b) Where claims to all three categories, product, process of making, and process of use, are included in a national application, a three way requirement for restriction can only be made where the process of making is distinct from the product. If the process of making and the product are not distinct, the process of using may be joined with the claims directed to the product and the process of making the product even though a showing of distinctness between the product and process of using the product can be made.

[52 FR 20046, May 28, 1987, effective July 1, 1987]

§ 1.142 Requirement for restriction.

(a) If two or more independent and distinct inventions are claimed in a single application, the examiner in an Office action will require the applicant in the reply to that action to elect an invention to which the claims will be restricted, this official action being called a requirement for restriction (also known as a requirement for division). Such requirement will normally be made before any action on the merits; however, it may be made at any time before final action.

(b) Claims to the invention or inventions not elected, if not canceled, are nevertheless withdrawn from further consideration by the examiner by the election, subject however to reinstatement in the event the requirement for restriction is withdrawn or overruled.

[Para (a) revised, 62 FR 53131, Oct. 10, 1997, effective Dec. 1, 1997; para. (a) revised and (c) added, 72 FR 46716, Aug. 21, 2007 (implementation enjoined and never became effective); para. (a) revised and (c) removed, 74 FR 52686, Oct. 14, 2009, effective Oct. 14, 2009 (to remove changes made by the final rules in 72 FR 46716 from the CFR)]

§ 1.143 Reconsideration of requirement.

If the applicant disagrees with the requirement for restriction, he may request reconsideration and withdrawal or modification of the requirement, giving the reasons therefor. (See § 1.111). In requesting reconsideration the applicant must indicate a provisional election of one invention for prosecution, which invention shall be the one elected in the event the requirement becomes final. The requirement for restriction will be reconsidered on such a request. If the requirement is repeated and made final, the examiner will at the same time act on the claims to the invention elected.

§ 1.144 Petition from requirement for restriction.

After a final requirement for restriction, the applicant, in addition to making any reply due on the remainder of the action, may petition the Director to review the requirement. Petition may be deferred until after final action on or allowance of claims to the invention elected, but must be filed not later than appeal. A petition will not be considered if reconsideration of the requirement was not requested (see § 1.181).

[Revised, 62 FR 53131, Oct. 10, 1997, effective Dec. 1, 1997; revised, 68 FR 14332, Mar. 25, 2003, effective May 1, 2003]

§ 1.145 Subsequent presentation of claims for different invention.

If, after an office action on an application, the applicant presents claims directed to an invention distinct from and independent of the invention previously claimed, the applicant will be required to restrict the claims to the invention previously claimed if the amendment is entered, subject to reconsideration and review as provided in §§ 1.143 and 1.144.

[Revised, 72 FR 46716, Aug. 21, 2007 (implementation enjoined and never became effective); revised, 74 FR 52686, Oct. 14, 2009, effective Oct. 14, 2009 (to remove changes made by the final rules in 72 FR 46716 from the CFR)]

§ 1.146 Election of species.

In the first action on an application containing a generic claim to a generic invention (genus) and claims to more than one patentably distinct species embraced thereby, the examiner may require the applicant in the reply to that action to elect a species of his or her invention to which his or her claim will be restricted if no claim to the genus is found to be allowable. However, if such application contains claims directed to more than a reasonable number of species, the examiner may require restriction of the claims to not more than a reasonable number of species before taking further action in the application.

[43 FR 20465, May 11, 1978; revised, 62 FR 53131, Oct. 10, 1997, effective Dec. 1, 1997]

DESIGN PATENTS

§ 1.151 Rules applicable.

The rules relating to applications for patents for other inventions or discoveries are also applicable to applications for patents for designs except as otherwise provided.

§ 1.152 Design drawings.

The design must be represented by a drawing that complies with the requirements of § 1.84 and must contain a sufficient number of views to constitute a complete disclosure of the appearance of the design. Appropriate and adequate surface shading should be used to show the character or contour of the surfaces represented. Solid black surface shading is not permitted except when used to represent the color black as well as color contrast. Broken lines may be used to show visible environmental structure, but may not be used to show hidden planes and surfaces that cannot be seen through opaque materials. Alternate positions of a design component, illustrated by full and broken lines in the same view are not permitted in a design drawing. Photographs and ink drawings are not permitted to be combined as formal drawings in one application. Photographs submitted in lieu of ink drawings in design patent applications must not dis-

close environmental structure but must be limited to the design claimed for the article.

[53 FR 47810, Nov. 28, 1988, effective Jan. 1, 1989; amended, 58 FR 38719, July 20, 1993, effective Oct. 1, 1993; revised, 62 FR 53131, Oct. 10, 1997, effective Dec. 1, 1997; revised, 65 FR 54604, Sept. 8, 2000, effective Sept. 8, 2000]

§ 1.153 Title, description and claim, oath or declaration.

(a) The title of the design must designate the particular article. No description, other than a reference to the drawing, is ordinarily required. The claim shall be in formal terms to the ornamental design for the article (specifying name) as shown, or as shown and described. More than one claim is neither required nor permitted.

(b) The oath or declaration required of the applicant must comply with § 1.63.

[24 FR 10332, Dec. 22, 1959; 29 FR 18503, Dec. 29, 1964; para. (b), 48 FR 2712, Jan. 20, 1983, effective Feb. 27, 1983]

§ 1.154 Arrangement of application elements in a design application.

(a) The elements of the design application, if applicable, should appear in the following order:

(1) Design application transmittal form.

(2) Fee transmittal form.

(3) Application data sheet (see § 1.76).

(4) Specification.

(5) Drawings or photographs.

(6) Executed oath or declaration (see § 1.153(b)).

(b) The specification should include the following sections in order:

(1) Preamble, stating the name of the applicant, title of the design, and a brief description of the nature and intended use of the article in which the design is embodied.

(2) Cross-reference to related applications (unless included in the application data sheet).

(3) Statement regarding federally sponsored research or development.

(4) Description of the figure or figures of the drawing.

(5)   Feature description.

(6)   A single claim.

(c)   The text of the specification sections defined in paragraph (b) of this section, if applicable, should be preceded by a section heading in uppercase letters without underlining or bold type.

[24 FR 10332, Dec. 22, 1959, para. (e), 48 FR 2713, Jan. 20, 1983, effective date Feb. 27, 1983; revised, 61 FR 42790, Aug. 19, 1996, effective Sept. 23, 1996; para. (a)(3) revised, 62 FR 53131, Oct. 10, 1997, effective Dec. 1, 1997; revised, 65 FR 54604, Sept. 8, 2000, effective Nov. 7, 2000]

§ 1.155   Expedited examination of design applications.

(a)   The applicant may request that the Office expedite the examination of a design application. To qualify for expedited examination:

(1)   The application must include drawings in compliance with § 1.84;

(2)   The applicant must have conducted a pre-examination search; and

(3)   The applicant must file a request for expedited examination including:

(i)   The fee set forth in § 1.17(k); and

(ii)   A statement that a preexamination search was conducted. The statement must also indicate the field of search and include an information disclosure statement in compliance with § 1.98.

(b)   The Office will not examine an application that is not in condition for examination (*e.g.*, missing basic filing fee) even if the applicant files a request for expedited examination under this section.

[47 FR 41277, Sept. 17, 1982, effective date Oct. 1, 1982; paras. (b)-(d) amended, paras. (e) and (f) added, 58 FR 44277, Aug. 20, 1993, effective Sept. 20, 1993; revised, 62 FR 53131, Oct. 10, 1997, effective Dec. 1, 1997; revised, 65 FR 54604, Sept. 8, 2000, effective Sept. 8, 2000]

PLANT PATENTS

§ 1.161   Rules applicable.

The rules relating to applications for patent for other inventions or discoveries are also applicable to applications for patents for plants except as otherwise provided.

§ 1.162   Applicant, oath or declaration.

The applicant for a plant patent must be the person who has invented or discovered and asexually reproduced the new and distinct variety of plant for which a patent is sought (or as provided in §§ 1.42, 1.43, and 1.47). The oath or declaration required of the applicant, in addition to the averments required by § 1.63, must state that he or she has asexually reproduced the plant. Where the plant is a newly found plant the oath or declaration must also state that it was found in a cultivated area.

[48 FR 2713, Jan. 20, 1983, effective Feb. 27, 1983]

§ 1.163   Specification and arrangement of application elements in a plant application.

(a)   The specification must contain as full and complete a disclosure as possible of the plant and the characteristics thereof that distinguish the same over related known varieties, and its antecedents, and must particularly point out where and in what manner the variety of plant has been asexually reproduced. For a newly found plant, the specification must particularly point out the location and character of the area where the plant was discovered.

(b)   The elements of the plant application, if applicable, should appear in the following order:

(1)   Plant application transmittal form.

(2)   Fee transmittal form.

(3)   Application data sheet (see § 1.76).

(4)   Specification.

(5)   Drawings (in duplicate).

(6)   Executed oath or declaration (§ 1.162).

(c)   The specification should include the following sections in order:

(1)   Title of the invention, which may include an introductory portion stating the name, citizenship, and residence of the applicant.

(2)   Cross-reference to related applications (unless included in the application data sheet).

(3)   Statement regarding federally sponsored research or development.

(4)   Latin name of the genus and species of the plant claimed.

(5)   Variety denomination.

(6)   Background of the invention.

(7)   Brief summary of the invention.

(8)   Brief description of the drawing.

(9)   Detailed botanical description.

(10)   A single claim.

(11)   Abstract of the disclosure.

(d)   The text of the specification or sections defined in paragraph (c) of this section, if applicable, should be preceded by a section heading in upper case, without underlining or bold type.

[24 FR 10332, Dec. 22, 1959; para. (b), 48 FR 2713, Jan. 20, 1983, effective Feb. 27, 1983; paras. (c) and (d) added, 61 FR 42790, Aug. 19, 1996, effective Sept. 23, 1996; para. (b) revised, 62 FR 53131, Oct. 10, 1997, effective Dec. 1, 1997; revised, 65 FR 54604, Sept. 8, 2000, effective Nov. 7, 2000]

§ 1.164   Claim.

The claim shall be in formal terms to the new and distinct variety of the specified plant as described and illustrated, and may also recite the principal distinguishing characteristics. More than one claim is not permitted.

§ 1.165   Plant Drawings.

(a)   Plant patent drawings should be artistically and competently executed and must comply with the requirements of § 1.84. View numbers and reference characters need not be employed unless required by the examiner. The drawing must disclose all the distinctive characteristics of the plant capable of visual representation.

(b)   The drawings may be in color. The drawing must be in color if color is a distinguishing characteristic of the new variety. Two copies of color drawings or photographs must be submitted.

[24 FR 10332, Dec. 22, 1959; para. (b), 47 FR 41277, Sept. 17, 1982, effective Oct. 1, 1982; paras. (a) and (b) amended, 58 FR 38719, July 20, 1993, effective Oct. 1, 1993; para. (b) revised, 65 FR 57024, Sept. 20, 2000, effective Nov. 29, 2000; para. (b) revised, 69 FR 56481, Sept. 21, 2004, effective Oct. 21, 2004]

§ 1.166   Specimens.

The applicant may be required to furnish specimens of the plant, or its flower or fruit, in a quantity and at a time in its stage of growth as may be designated, for study and inspection. Such specimens, properly packed, must be forwarded in conformity with instructions furnished to the applicant. When it is not possible to forward such specimens, plants must be made available for official inspection where grown.

§ 1.167   Examination.

Applications may be submitted by the Patent and Trademark Office to the Department of Agriculture for study and report.

[24 FR 10332, Dec. 22, 1959; 34 FR 18857, Nov. 26, 1969; revised, 62 FR 53131, Oct. 10, 1997, effective Dec. 1, 1997]

REISSUES

§ 1.171   Application for reissue.

An application for reissue must contain the same parts required for an application for an original patent, complying with all the rules relating thereto except as otherwise provided, and in addition, must comply with the requirements of the rules relating to reissue applications.

[47 FR 41278, Sept. 17, 1982, effective Oct. 1, 1982; revised, 54 FR 6893, Feb. 17, 1989, 54 FR 9432, March 7, 1989, effective Apr. 17, 1989; 56 FR 65142, Dec. 13, 1991, effective Dec. 16, 1991; revised, 62 FR 53131, Oct. 10, 1997, effective Dec. 1, 1997]

§ 1.172   Applicants, assignees.

(a)   A reissue oath must be signed and sworn to or declaration made by the inventor or inventors except as otherwise provided (see §§ 1.42, 1.43, 1.47), and must be accompanied by the written consent of all assignees, if any, owning an undivided interest in the patent, but a reissue oath may be made and sworn to or declaration made by the assignee of the entire interest if the application does not seek to enlarge the scope of the claims of the original patent. All assignees consenting to the reissue must establish their ownership interest in the patent by filing in the reissue application a submission in accordance with the provisions of § 3.73(b) of this chapter.

(b)   A reissue will be granted to the original patentee, his legal representatives or assigns as the interest may appear.

[24 FR 10332, Dec. 22, 1959; para. (a), 48 FR 2713, Jan. 20, 1983, effective Feb. 27, 1983; para. (a) revised, 62 FR 53131, Oct. 10, 1997, effective Dec. 1, 1997]

§1.173 Reissue specification, drawings, and amendments.

(a) *Contents of a reissue application.* An application for reissue must contain the entire specification, including the claims, and the drawings of the patent. No new matter shall be introduced into the application. No reissue patent shall be granted enlarging the scope of the claims of the original patent unless applied for within two years from the grant of the original patent, pursuant to 35 U.S.C. 251.

(1) *Specification, including claims.* The entire specification, including the claims, of the patent for which reissue is requested must be furnished in the form of a copy of the printed patent, in double column format, each page on only one side of a single sheet of paper. If an amendment of the reissue application is to be included, it must be made pursuant to paragraph (b) of this section. The formal requirements for papers making up the reissue application other than those set forth in this section are set out in §1.52. Additionally, a copy of any disclaimer (§1.321), certificate of correction (§§1.322 through 1.324), or reexamination certificate (§1.570) issued in the patent must be included. (See also §1.178).

(2) *Drawings.* Applicant must submit a clean copy of each drawing sheet of the printed patent at the time the reissue application is filed. If such copy complies with §1.84, no further drawings will be required. Where a drawing of the reissue application is to include any changes relative to the patent being reissued, the changes to the drawing must be made in accordance with paragraph (b)(3) of this section. The Office will not transfer the drawings from the patent file to the reissue application.

(b) *Making amendments in a reissue application.* An amendment in a reissue application is made either by physically incorporating the changes into the specification when the application is filed, or by a separate amendment paper. If amendment is made by incorporation, markings pursuant to paragraph (d) of this section must be used. If amendment is made by an amendment paper, the paper must direct that specified changes be made, as follows:

(1) *Specification other than the claims.* Changes to the specification, other than to the claims, must be made by submission of the entire text of an added or rewritten paragraph, including markings pursuant to paragraph (d) of this section, except that an entire paragraph may be deleted by a statement deleting the paragraph without presentation of the text of the paragraph. The precise point in the specification must be identified where any added or rewritten paragraph is located. This paragraph applies whether the amendment is submitted on paper or compact disc (see §§1.52(e)(1) and 1.821(c), but not for discs submitted under §1.821(e)).

(2) *Claims.* An amendment paper must include the entire text of each claim being changed by such amendment paper and of each claim being added by such amendment paper. For any claim changed by the amendment paper, a parenthetical expression "amended," "twice amended," *etc.*, should follow the claim number. Each changed patent claim and each added claim must include markings pursuant to paragraph (d) of this section, except that a patent claim or added claim should be canceled by a statement canceling the claim without presentation of the text of the claim.

(3) *Drawings.* One or more patent drawings shall be amended in the following manner: Any changes to a patent drawing must be submitted as a replacement sheet of drawings which shall be an attachment to the amendment document. Any replacement sheet of drawings must be in compliance with §1.84 and shall include all of the figures appearing on the original version of the sheet, even if only one figure is amended. Amended figures must be identified as "Amended," and any added figure must be identified as "New." In the event that a figure is canceled, the figure must be surrounded by brackets and identified as "Canceled." All changes to the drawing(s) shall be explained, in detail, beginning on a separate sheet accompanying the papers including the amendment to the drawings.

(i) A marked-up copy of any amended drawing figure, including annotations indicating the changes made, may be included. The marked-up copy must be clearly labeled as "Annotated Marked-up Drawings" and must be presented in the amendment or remarks section that explains the change to the drawings.

(ii) A marked-up copy of any amended drawing figure, including annotations indicating the changes made, must be provided when required by the examiner.

(c) *Status of claims and support for claim changes.* Whenever there is an amendment to the claims pursuant to paragraph (b) of this section, there must also be supplied, on pages separate from the pages containing the changes, the status (*i.e.,* pending or canceled), as of the date of the amendment, of all patent claims and of all added claims, and an explanation of the support in the disclosure of the patent for the changes made to the claims.

(d) *Changes shown by markings.* Any changes relative to the patent being reissued which are made to the specification, including the claims, upon filing, or by an amendment paper in the reissue application, must include the following markings:

(1) The matter to be omitted by reissue must be enclosed in brackets; and

(2) The matter to be added by reissue must be underlined, except for amendments submitted on compact discs (§§ 1.96 and 1.821(c)). Matter added by reissue on compact discs must be preceded with "<U>" and end with "</U>" to properly identify the material being added.

(e) *Numbering of patent claims preserved.* Patent claims may not be renumbered. The numbering of any claim added in the reissue application must follow the number of the highest numbered patent claim.

(f) *Amendment of disclosure may be required.* The disclosure must be amended, when required by the Office, to correct inaccuracies of description and definition, and to secure substantial correspondence between the claims, the remainder of the specification, and the drawings.

(g) *Amendments made relative to the patent.* All amendments must be made relative to the patent specification, including the claims, and drawings, which are in effect as of the date of filing of the reissue application.

[Revised, 65 FR 54604, Sept. 8, 2000, effective Nov. 7, 2000; para. (b)(3) revised, 68 FR 38611, June 30, 2003, effective July 30, 2003; para. (b) introductory text revised, 69 FR 56481, Sept. 21, 2004, effective Oct. 21, 2004]

§ 1.174 [Reserved]

[24 FR 10332, Dec. 22, 1959; para. (a), 48 FR 2713, Jan. 20, 1983, effective Feb. 27, 1983; removed and reserved, 65 FR 54604, Sept. 8, 2000, effective Nov. 7, 2000]

§ 1.175 Reissue oath or declaration.

(a) The reissue oath or declaration in addition to complying with the requirements of § 1.63, must also state that:

(1) The applicant believes the original patent to be wholly or partly inoperative or invalid by reason of a defective specification or drawing, or by reason of the patentee claiming more or less than the patentee had the right to claim in the patent, stating at least one error being relied upon as the basis for reissue; and

(2) All errors being corrected in the reissue application up to the time of filing of the oath or declaration under this paragraph arose without any deceptive intention on the part of the applicant.

(b)(1) For any error corrected, which is not covered by the oath or declaration submitted under paragraph (a) of this section, applicant must submit a supplemental oath or declaration stating that every such error arose without any deceptive intention on the part of the applicant. Any supplemental oath or declaration required by this paragraph must be submitted before allowance and may be submitted:

(i) With any amendment prior to allowance; or

(ii) In order to overcome a rejection under 35 U.S.C. 251 made by the examiner where it is indicated that the submission of a supplemental oath or declaration as required by this paragraph will overcome the rejection.

(2) For any error sought to be corrected after allowance, a supplemental oath or declaration must accompany the requested correction stating that the error(s) to be corrected arose without any deceptive intention on the part of the applicant.

(c) Having once stated an error upon which the reissue is based, as set forth in paragraph (a)(1), unless all errors previously stated in the oath or declaration are no longer being corrected, a subsequent oath or declaration under paragraph (b) of this section need not specifically identify any other error or errors being corrected.

(d) The oath or declaration required by paragraph (a) of this section may be submitted under the provisions of § 1.53(f).

(e) The filing of any continuing reissue application which does not replace its parent reissue application must include an oath or declaration which, pursuant to paragraph (a)(1) of this section, identifies at least one error in the original patent which has not been corrected by the parent reissue application or an earlier reissue application. All other requirements relating to oaths or declarations must also be met.

[24 FR 10332, Dec. 22, 1959; 29 FR 18503, Dec. 29, 1964; 34 FR 18857, Nov. 26, 1969; para. (a), 47 FR 21752, May 19, 1982, effective July 1,1982; para. (a), 48 FR 2713, Jan. 20, 1983, effective Feb. 27, 1983; para. (a)(7), 57 FR 2021, Jan. 17, 1992, effective Mar. 16, 1992; revised, 62 FR 53131, Oct. 10, 1997, effective Dec. 1, 1997; para. (e) added, 69 FR 56481, Sept. 21, 2004, effective Oct. 21, 2004]

§ 1.176 Examination of reissue.

(a) A reissue application will be examined in the same manner as a non-reissue, non-provisional application, and will be subject to all the requirements of the rules related to non-reissue applications. Applications for reissue will be acted on by the examiner in advance of other applications.

(b) Restriction between subject matter of the original patent claims and previously unclaimed subject matter may be required (restriction involving only subject matter of the original patent claims will not be required). If restriction is required, the subject matter of the original patent claims will be held to be constructively elected unless a disclaimer of all the patent claims is filed in the reissue application, which disclaimer cannot be withdrawn by applicant.

[42 FR 5595, Jan. 28, 1977; revised, 65 FR 54604, Sept. 8, 2000, effective Nov. 7, 2000]

§ 1.177 Issuance of multiple reissue patents.

(a) The Office may reissue a patent as multiple reissue patents. If applicant files more than one application for the reissue of a single patent, each such application must contain or be amended to contain in the first sentence of the specification a notice stating that more than one reissue application has been filed and identifying each of the reissue applications by relationship, application number and filing date. The Office may correct by certificate of correction under § 1.322 any reissue patent resulting from an application to which this paragraph applies that does not contain the required notice.

(b) If applicant files more than one application for the reissue of a single patent, each claim of the patent being reissued must be presented in each of the reissue applications as an amended, unamended, or canceled (shown in brackets) claim, with each such claim bearing the same number as in the patent being reissued. The same claim of the patent being reissued may not be presented in its original unamended form for examination in more than one of such multiple reissue applications. The numbering of any added claims in any of the multiple reissue applications must follow the number of the highest numbered original patent claim.

(c) If any one of the several reissue applications by itself fails to correct an error in the original patent as required by 35 U.S.C. 251 but is otherwise in condition for allowance, the Office may suspend action in the allowable application until all issues are resolved as to at least one of the remaining reissue applications. The Office may also merge two or more of the multiple reissue applications into a single reissue application. No reissue application containing only unamended patent claims and not correcting an error in the original patent will be passed to issue by itself.

[47 FR 41278, Sept. 17, 1982, effective date Oct. 1, 1982; revised, 54 FR 6893, Feb. 15, 1989, 54 FR 9432, March 7, 1989, effective Apr. 17, 1989; revised, 60 FR 20195, Apr. 25, 1995, effective June 8, 1995; revised, 65 FR 54604, Sept. 8, 2000, effective Nov. 7, 2000]

§ 1.178 Original patent; continuing duty of applicant.

(a) The application for reissue of a patent shall constitute an offer to surrender that patent, and the surrender shall take effect upon reissue of the patent. Until a reissue application is granted, the original patent shall remain in effect.

(b) In any reissue application before the Office, the applicant must call to the attention of the Office any prior or concurrent proceedings in which the patent (for which reissue is requested) is or was involved, such as interferences, reissues, reexaminations, or litigations and the results of such proceedings (see also § 1.173(a)(1)).

[24 FR 10332, Dec. 22, 1959; 34 FR 18857, Nov. 26, 1969; revised, 65 FR 54604, Sept. 8, 2000, effective Nov. 7, 2000; para. (a) revised, 69 FR 56481, Sept. 21, 2004, effective Sept. 21, 2004]

§ 1.179 [Reserved]

[Removed and reserved, 69 FR 56481, Sept. 21, 2004, effective Oct. 21, 2004]

PETITIONS AND ACTION BY THE DIRECTOR

§ 1.181 Petition to the Director.

(a)   Petition may be taken to the Director:

(1)   From any action or requirement of any examiner in the *ex parte* prosecution of an application, or in *ex parte* or *inter partes* prosecution of a reexamination proceeding which is not subject to appeal to the Board of Patent Appeals and Interferences or to the court;

(2)   In cases in which a statute or the rules specify that the matter is to be determined directly by or reviewed by the Director; and

(3)   To invoke the supervisory authority of the Director in appropriate circumstances. For petitions involving action of the Board of Patent Appeals and Interferences, see § 41.3 of this title.

(b)   Any such petition must contain a statement of the facts involved and the point or points to be reviewed and the action requested. Briefs or memoranda, if any, in support thereof should accompany or be embodied in the petition; and where facts are to be proven, the proof in the form of affidavits or declarations (and exhibits, if any) must accompany the petition.

(c)   When a petition is taken from an action or requirement of an examiner in the *ex parte* prosecution of an application, or in the *ex parte* or *inter partes* prosecution of a reexamination proceeding, it may be required that there have been a proper request for reconsideration (§ 1.111) and a repeated action by the examiner. The examiner may be directed by the Director to furnish a written statement, within a specified time, setting forth the reasons for his or her decision upon the matters averred in the petition, supplying a copy to the petitioner.

(d)   Where a fee is required for a petition to the Director the appropriate section of this part will so indicate. If any required fee does not accompany the petition, the petition will be dismissed.

(e)   Oral hearing will not be granted except when considered necessary by the Director.

(f)   The mere filing of a petition will not stay any period for reply that may be running against the application, nor act as a stay of other proceedings. Any petition under this part not filed within two months of the mailing date of the action or notice from which relief is requested may be dismissed as untimely, except as otherwise provided. This two-month period is not extendable.

(g)   The Director may delegate to appropriate Patent and Trademark Office officials the determination of petitions.

[24 FR 10332, Dec. 22, 1959; 34 FR 18857, Nov. 26, 1969; paras. (d) and (g), 47 FR 41278, Sept. 17, 1982, effective Oct. 1, 1982; para. (a), 49 FR 48416, Dec. 12, 1984, effective Feb. 11, 1985; para. (f) revised, 65 FR 54604, Sept. 8, 2000, effective Nov. 7, 2000; paras. (a) and (c) revised, 65 FR 76756, Dec. 7, 2000, effective Feb. 5, 2001; paras. (a), (a)(2)-(3), (c)-(e) & (g) revised, 68 FR 14332, Mar. 25, 2003, effective May 1, 2003; para. (a)(3) revised, 69 FR 49959, Aug. 12, 2004, effective Sept. 13, 2004]

§ 1.182 Questions not specifically provided for.

All situations not specifically provided for in the regulations of this part will be decided in accordance with the merits of each situation by or under the authority of the Director, subject to such other requirements as may be imposed, and such decision will be communicated to the interested parties in writing. Any petition seeking a decision under this section must be accompanied by the petition fee set forth in § 1.17(f).

[47 FR 41278, Sept. 17, 1982, effective date Oct. 1, 1982; revised, 62 FR 53131, Oct. 10, 1997, effective Dec. 1, 1997; revised, 68 FR 14332, Mar. 25, 2003, effective May 1, 2003; revised, 69 FR 56481, Sept. 21, 2004, effective Nov. 22, 2004]

§ 1.183 Suspension of rules.

In an extraordinary situation, when justice requires, any requirement of the regulations in this part which is not a requirement of the statutes may be suspended or waived by the Director or the Director's designee, *sua sponte*, or on petition of the interested party, subject to such other requirements as may be imposed. Any petition under this section must be accompanied by the petition fee set forth in § 1.17(f).

[47 FR 41278, Sept. 17, 1982, effective Oct. 1, 1982; revised, 68 FR 14332, Mar. 25, 2003, effective May 1, 2003; revised, 69 FR 56481, Sept. 21, 2004, effective Nov. 22, 2004]

§ 1.184 [Reserved]

[Removed and reserved, 62 FR 53131, Oct. 10, 1997, effective Dec. 1, 1997]

APPEAL TO THE BOARD OF PATENT APPEALS AND INTERFERENCES

§ 1.191 Appeal to Board of Patent Appeals and Interferences.

Appeals to the Board of Patent Appeals and Interferences under 35 U.S.C. 134(a) and (b) are conducted according to part 41 of this title.

[46 FR 29183, May 29, 1981; para. (a), 47 FR 41278, Sept. 17, 1982, effective Oct. 1, 1982; para. (d), 49 FR 555, Jan. 4, 1984, effective Apr. 1, 1984; 49 FR 48416, Dec. 12, 1984, effective Feb. 11, 1985; paras. (b) and (d) amended, para. (e) added, 54 FR 29553, July 13, 1989, effective Aug. 20, 1989; para. (d) revised, 58 FR 54504, Oct. 22, 1993, effective Jan. 3, 1994; paras. (a) and (b) revised, 62 FR 53131, Oct. 10, 1997, effective Dec. 1, 1997; para. (a) revised, 65 FR 76756, Dec. 7, 2000, effective Feb. 5, 2001; para. (e) revised, 68 FR 14332, Mar. 25, 2003, effective May 1, 2003; para. (a) revised, 68 FR 70996, Dec. 22, 2003, effective Jan. 21, 2004; revised, 69 FR 49959, Aug. 12, 2004, effective Sept. 13, 2004]

§ 1.192 [Reserved]

[36 FR 5850, Mar. 30, 1971; para. (a), 47 FR 41278, Sept. 17, 1982, effective Oct. 1, 1982; para. (a), 49 FR 556, Jan. 4, 1984, effective Apr. 1, 1984; 53 FR 23734, June 23, 1988, effective Sept. 12, 1988; para. (a), (c), and (d) revised, 58 FR 54504, Oct. 22, 1993, effective Jan. 3, 1994; paras. (a)-(c) revised, 60 FR 14488, Mar 17, 1995, effective Apr. 21, 1995; para. (a) revised, 62 FR 53131, Oct. 10, 1997, effective Dec. 1, 1997; removed and reserved, 69 FR 49959, Aug. 12, 2004, effective Sept. 13, 2004]

§ 1.193 [Reserved]

[24 FR 10332, Dec. 22, 1959; 34 FR 18858, Nov.26, 1969; para. (c), 47 FR 21752, May 19, 1982, added effective July 1, 1982; para. (b), 50 FR 9382, Mar. 7, 1985, effective May 8, 1985; 53 FR 23735, June 23, 1988, effec-

tive Sept. 12, 1988; para. (c) deleted, 57 FR 2021, Jan. 17, 1992, effective Mar. 16, 1992; para. (b) revised, 58 FR 54504, Oct. 22, 1993, effective Jan. 3, 1994; revised, 62 FR 53131, Oct. 10, 1997, effective Dec. 1, 1997; para. (b)(1) revised, 65 FR 54604, Sept. 8, 2000, effective Nov. 7, 2000; para. (a)(1) revised, 68 FR 14332, Mar. 25, 2003, effective May 1, 2003; removed and reserved, 69 FR 49959, Aug. 12, 2004, effective Sept. 13, 2004]

§ 1.194 [Reserved]

[42 FR 5595, Jan. 28, 1977; paras. (b) & (c), 47 FR 41278, Sept. 17, 1982, effective Oct. 1, 1982; para. (a), 49 FR 48416, Dec. 12, 1984, effective Feb. 11, 1985; para. (b) revised 53 FR 23735, June 23, 1988, effective Sept. 12, 1988; para. (b) revised, 58 FR 54504, Oct. 22, 1993, effective Jan. 3, 1994; revised, 62 FR 53131, Oct. 10, 1997, effective Dec. 1, 1997; removed and reserved, 69 FR 49959, Aug. 12, 2004, effective Sept. 13, 2004]

§ 1.195 [Reserved]

[34 FR 18858, Nov. 26, 1969; removed and reserved, 69 FR 49959, Aug. 12, 2004, effective Sept. 13, 2004]

§ 1.196 [Reserved]

[24 FR 10332, Dec. 12, 1959; 49 FR 29183, May 29, 1981; 49 FR 48416, Dec. 12, 1984, effective Feb. 12, 1985; para. (b) revised, 53 FR 23735, June 23, 1988, effective Sept. 12, 1988; paras. (a), (b) & (d) amended, paras. (e) & (f) added, 54 FR 29552, July 13, 1989, effective Aug. 20, 1989; para. (f) revised, 58 FR 54504, Oct. 22, 1993, effective Jan. 3, 1994; paras. (b) & (d) revised, 62 FR 53131, Oct. 10, 1997, effective Dec. 1, 1997; removed and reserved, 69 FR 49959, Aug. 12, 2004, effective Sept. 13, 2004]

§ 1.197 Return of jurisdiction from the Board of Patent Appeals and Interferences; termination of proceedings.

(a) *Return of jurisdiction from the Board of Patent Appeals and Interferences.* Jurisdiction over an application or patent under *ex parte* reexamination proceeding passes to the examiner after a decision by the Board of Patent Appeals and Interferences upon transmittal of the file to the examiner, subject to appellant's right of appeal or other review, for such further action by appellant or by the examiner, as the condition of the application or patent under *ex parte* reexamination proceeding may require, to carry into effect the decision of the Board of Patent Appeals and Interferences.

(b) *Termination of proceedings.*

(1) Proceedings on an application are considered terminated by the dismissal of an appeal or the failure to timely file an appeal to the court or a civil action (§ 1.304) except:

(i) Where claims stand allowed in an application; or

(ii) Where the nature of the decision requires further action by the examiner.

(2) The date of termination of proceedings on an application is the date on which the appeal is dismissed or the date on which the time for appeal to the U.S. Court of Appeals for the Federal Circuit or review by civil action (§ 1.304) expires in the absence of further appeal or review. If an appeal to the U.S. Court of Appeals for the Federal Circuit or a civil action has been filed, proceedings on an application are considered terminated when the appeal or civil action is terminated. A civil action is terminated when the time to appeal the judgment expires. An appeal to the U.S. Court of Appeals for the Federal Circuit, whether from a decision of the Board or a judgment in a civil action, is terminated when the mandate is issued by the Court.

[46 FR 29184, May 29, 1981; para. (a), 47 FR 41278, Sept. 17, 1982, effective Oct. 1, 1982; 49 FR 556, Jan. 4, 1984, effective Apr. 1, 1984; paras. (a) and (b), 49 FR 48416, Dec. 12, 1984, effective Feb. 11, 1985; paras. (b) and (c), 54 FR 29552, July 13, 1989, effective Aug. 20, 1989; para. (b) revised, 58 FR 54504, Oct. 22, 1993, effective Jan. 3, 1994; paras. (a) & (b) revised, 62 FR 53131, Oct. 10, 1997, effective Dec. 1, 1997; para. (c) revised, 68 FR 70996, Dec. 22, 2003, effective Jan. 21, 2004; revised, 69 FR 49959, Aug. 12, 2004, effective Sept. 13, 2004]

§ 1.198 Reopening after a final decision of the Board of Patent Appeals and Interferences.

When a decision by the Board of Patent Appeals and Interferences on appeal has become final for judicial review, prosecution of the proceeding before the primary examiner will not be reopened or reconsidered by the primary examiner except under the provisions of § 1.114 or § 41.50 of this title without the written authority of the Director, and then only for the consideration of matters not already adjudicated, sufficient cause being shown.

[49 FR 48416, Dec. 12, 1984, effective date Feb. 11, 1985; revised, 65 FR 14865, Mar. 20, 2000, effective May 29, 2000 (adopted as final, 65 FR 50092, Aug. 16, 2000); revised, 68 FR 14332, Mar. 25, 2003, effective May 1, 2003; revised, 69 FR 49959, Aug. 12, 2004, effective Sept. 13, 2004]

PUBLICATION OF APPLICATIONS

§ 1.211 Publication of applications.

(a) Each U.S. national application for patent filed in the Office under 35 U.S.C. 111(a) and each international application in compliance with 35 U.S.C. 371 will be published promptly after the expiration of a period of eighteen months from the earliest filing date for which a benefit is sought under title 35, United States Code, unless:

(1) The application is recognized by the Office as no longer pending;

(2) The application is national security classified (see § 5.2(c)), subject to a secrecy order under 35 U.S.C. 181, or under national security review;

(3) The application has issued as a patent in sufficient time to be removed from the publication process; or

(4) The application was filed with a nonpublication request in compliance with § 1.213(a).

(b) Provisional applications under 35 U.S.C. 111(b) shall not be published, and design applications under 35 U.S.C. chapter 16 and reissue applications under 35 U.S.C. chapter 25 shall not be published under this section.

(c) An application filed under 35 U.S.C. 111(a) will not be published until it includes the basic filing fee (§ 1.16(a) or 1.16(c)), any English translation required by § 1.52(d), and an executed oath or declaration under § 1.63. The Office may delay publishing any application until it includes any application size fee required by the Office under § 1.16(s) or § 1.492(j), a specification having papers in compliance with § 1.52 and an abstract (§ 1.72(b)), drawings in compliance with § 1.84, and a sequence listing in compliance with §§ 1.821 through 1.825 (if applicable), and until any petition under § 1.47 is granted.

(d) The Office may refuse to publish an application, or to include a portion of an application in the patent application publication (§ 1.215), if publication of the application or portion thereof would violate Federal or state law, or if the application or portion thereof contains offensive or disparaging material.

(e) The publication fee set forth in § 1.18(d) must be paid in each application published under this section before the patent will be granted. If an application is subject to publication under this section, the sum specified in the notice of allowance under § 1.311 will also include the publication fee which must be paid within three months from the date of mailing of the notice of allowance to avoid abandonment of the application. This three-month period is not extendable. If the application is not published under this section, the publication fee (if paid) will be refunded.

[Added, 65 FR 57024, Sept. 20, 2000, effective Nov. 29, 2000; para. (c) revised, 70 FR 3880, Jan. 27, 2005, effective Dec. 8, 2004]

§ 1.213 Nonpublication request.

(a) If the invention disclosed in an application has not been and will not be the subject of an application filed in another country, or under a multilateral international agreement, that requires publication of applications eighteen months after filing, the application will not be published under 35 U.S.C. 122(b) and § 1.211 provided:

(1) A request (nonpublication request) is submitted with the application upon filing;

(2) The request states in a conspicuous manner that the application is not to be published under 35 U.S.C. 122(b);

(3) The request contains a certification that the invention disclosed in the application has not been and will not be the subject of an application filed in another country, or under a multilateral international agreement, that requires publication at eighteen months after filing; and

(4) The request is signed in compliance with § 1.33(b).

(b) The applicant may rescind a nonpublication request at any time. A request to rescind a nonpublication request under paragraph (a) of this section must:

(1) Identify the application to which it is directed;

(2) State in a conspicuous manner that the request that the application is not to be published under 35 U.S.C. 122(b) is rescinded; and

(3) Be signed in compliance with § 1.33(b).

(c) If an applicant who has submitted a nonpublication request under paragraph (a) of this section subsequently files an application directed to the invention disclosed in the application in which the nonpublication request was submitted in another country, or under a multilateral international agreement, that requires publication of applications eighteen months after filing, the applicant must notify the Office of such filing within forty-five days after the date of the filing of such foreign or international application. The failure to timely notify the Office of the filing of such foreign or international application shall result in abandonment of the application in which the nonpublication request was submitted (35 U.S.C. 122(b)(2)(B)(iii)).

[Added, 65 FR 57024, Sept. 20, 2000, effective Nov. 29, 2000]

§ 1.215 Patent application publication.

(a) The publication of an application under 35 U.S.C. 122(b) shall include a patent application publication. The date of publication shall be indicated on the patent application publication. The patent application publication will be based upon the specification and drawings deposited on the filing date of the application, as well as the executed oath or declaration submitted to complete the application. The patent application publication may also be based upon amendments to the specification (other than the abstract or the claims) that are reflected in a substitute specification under § 1.125(b), amendments to the abstract under § 1.121(b), amendments to the claims that are reflected in a complete claim listing under § 1.121(c), and amendments to the drawings under § 1.121(d), provided that such substitute specification or amendment is submitted in sufficient time to be entered into the Office file wrapper of the application before technical preparations for publication of the application have begun. Technical preparations for publication of an application generally begin four months prior to the projected date of publication. The patent application publication of an application that has entered the national stage under 35 U.S.C. 371 may also include amendments made during the international stage. See paragraph (c) of this section for publication of an application based upon a copy of the application submitted via the Office electronic filing system.

(b)   If applicant wants the patent application publication to include assignee information, the applicant must include the assignee information on the application transmittal sheet or the application data sheet (§ 1.76). Assignee information may not be included on the patent application publication unless this information is provided on the application transmittal sheet or application data sheet included with the application on filing. Providing this information on the application transmittal sheet or the application data sheet does not substitute for compliance with any requirement of part 3 of this chapter to have an assignment recorded by the Office.

(c)   At applicant's option, the patent application publication will be based upon the copy of the application (specification, drawings, and oath or declaration) as amended, provided that applicant supplies such a copy in compliance with the Office electronic filing system requirements within one month of the mailing date of the first Office communication that includes a confirmation number for the application, or fourteen months of the earliest filing date for which a benefit is sought under title 35, United States Code, whichever is later.

(d)   If the copy of the application submitted pursuant to paragraph (c) of this section does not comply with the Office electronic filing system requirements, the Office will publish the application as provided in paragraph (a) of this section. If, however, the Office has not started the publication process, the Office may use an untimely filed copy of the application supplied by the applicant under paragraph (c) of this section in creating the patent application publication.

[Added, 65 FR 57024, Sept. 20, 2000, effective Nov. 29, 2000; paras. (a) and (c) revised, 69 FR 56481, Sept. 21, 2004, effective Oct. 21, 2004]

§ 1.217 Publication of a redacted copy of an application.

(a)   If an applicant has filed applications in one or more foreign countries, directly or through a multilateral international agreement, and such foreign-filed applications or the description of the invention in such foreign-filed applications is less extensive than the application or description of the invention in the application filed in the Office, the applicant may submit a redacted copy of the application filed in the Office for publication, eliminating any part or description of the invention that is not also contained in any of the corresponding applications filed in a foreign country. The Office will publish the application as provided in § 1.215(a) unless the applicant files a redacted copy of the application in compliance with this section within sixteen months after the earliest filing date for which a benefit is sought under title 35, United States Code.

(b)   The redacted copy of the application must be submitted in compliance with the Office electronic filing system requirements. The title of the invention in the redacted copy of the application must correspond to the title of the application at the time the redacted copy of the application is submitted to the Office. If the redacted copy of the application does not comply with the Office electronic filing system requirements, the Office will publish the application as provided in § 1.215(a).

(c)   The applicant must also concurrently submit in paper (§ 1.52(a)) to be filed in the application:

(1)   A certified copy of each foreign-filed application that corresponds to the application for which a redacted copy is submitted;

(2)   A translation of each such foreign-filed application that is in a language other than English, and a statement that the translation is accurate;

(3)   A marked-up copy of the application showing the redactions in brackets; and

(4)   A certification that the redacted copy of the application eliminates only the part or description of the invention that is not contained in any application filed in a foreign country, directly or through a multilateral international agreement, that corresponds to the application filed in the Office.

(d)   The Office will provide a copy of the complete file wrapper and contents of an application for which a redacted copy was submitted under this section to any person upon written request pursuant to § 1.14(c)(2), unless applicant complies with the requirements of paragraphs (d)(1), (d)(2), and (d)(3) of this section.

(1)   Applicant must accompany the submission required by paragraph (c) of this section with the following:

(i) A copy of any Office correspondence previously received by applicant including any desired redactions, and a second copy of all Office correspondence previously received by applicant showing the redacted material in brackets; and

(ii) A copy of each submission previously filed by the applicant including any desired redactions, and a second copy of each submission previously filed by the applicant showing the redacted material in brackets.

(2) In addition to providing the submission required by paragraphs (c) and (d)(1) of this section, applicant must:

(i) Within one month of the date of mailing of any correspondence from the Office, file a copy of such Office correspondence including any desired redactions, and a second copy of such Office correspondence showing the redacted material in brackets; and

(ii) With each submission by the applicant, include a copy of such submission including any desired redactions, and a second copy of such submission showing the redacted material in brackets.

(3) Each submission under paragraph (d)(1) or (d)(2) of this paragraph must also be accompanied by the processing fee set forth in § 1.17(i) and a certification that the redactions are limited to the elimination of material that is relevant only to the part or description of the invention that was not contained in the redacted copy of the application submitted for publication.

(e) The provisions of § 1.8 do not apply to the time periods set forth in this section.

[Added, 65 FR 57024, Sept. 20, 2000, effective Nov. 29, 2000]

§ 1.219 Early publication.

Applications that will be published under § 1.211 may be published earlier than as set forth in § 1.211(a) at the request of the applicant. Any request for early publication must be accompanied by the publication fee set forth in § 1.18(d). If the applicant does not submit a copy of the application in compliance with the Office electronic filing system requirements pursuant to § 1.215(c), the Office will publish the application as provided in § 1.215(a). No consideration will be given to requests for publication on a certain date, and such requests will be treated as a request for publication as soon as possible.

[Added, 65 FR 57024, Sept. 20, 2000, effective Nov. 29, 2000]

§ 1.221 Voluntary publication or republication of patent application publication.

(a) Any request for publication of an application filed before, but pending on, November 29, 2000, and any request for republication of an application previously published under § 1.211, must include a copy of the application in compliance with the Office electronic filing system requirements and be accompanied by the publication fee set forth in § 1.18(d) and the processing fee set forth in § 1.17(i). If the request does not comply with the requirements of this paragraph or the copy of the application does not comply with the Office electronic filing system requirements, the Office will not publish the application and will refund the publication fee.

(b) The Office will grant a request for a corrected or revised patent application publication other than as provided in paragraph (a) of this section only when the Office makes a material mistake which is apparent from Office records. Any request for a corrected or revised patent application publication other than as provided in paragraph (a) of this section must be filed within two months from the date of the patent application publication. This period is not extendable.

[Added, 65 FR 57024, Sept. 20, 2000, effective Nov. 29, 2000]

MISCELLANEOUS PROVISIONS

§ 1.248 Service of papers; manner of service; proof of service in cases other than interferences.

(a) Service of papers must be on the attorney or agent of the party if there be such or on the party if there is no attorney or agent, and may be made in any of the following ways:

(1) By delivering a copy of the paper to the person served;

(2) By leaving a copy at the usual place of business of the person served with someone in his employment;

(3)   When the person served has no usual place of business, by leaving a copy at the person's residence, with some person of suitable age and discretion who resides there;

(4)   Transmission by first class mail. When service is by mail the date of mailing will be regarded as the date of service;

(5)   Whenever it shall be satisfactorily shown to the Director that none of the above modes of obtaining or serving the paper is practicable, service may be by notice published in the *Official Gazette.*

(b)   Papers filed in the Patent and Trademark Office which are required to be served shall contain proof of service. Proof of service may appear on or be affixed to papers filed. Proof of service shall include the date and manner of service. In the case of personal service, proof of service shall also include the name of any person served, certified by the person who made service. Proof of service may be made by:

(1)   An acknowledgement of service by or on behalf of the person served or

(2)   A statement signed by the attorney or agent containing the information required by this section.

(c)   See § 41.106(e) of this title for service of papers in contested cases before the Board of Patent Appeals and Interferences.

[46 FR 29184, May 29, 1981; 49 FR 48416, Dec. 12, 1984, effective Feb. 11, 1985; para. (a)(5) revised, 68 FR 14332, Mar. 25, 2003, effective May 1, 2003; para. (c) revised, 69 FR 49959, Aug. 12, 2004, effective Sept. 13, 2004; para. (c) revised, 69 FR 49959, Aug. 12, 2004, effective Sept. 13, 2004; para. (c) revised, 69 FR 5 8260, Sept. 30, 2004, effective Sept. 30, 2004]

§ 1.251   Unlocatable file.

(a)   In the event that the Office cannot locate the file of an application, patent, or other patent-related proceeding after a reasonable search, the Office will notify the applicant or patentee and set a time period within which the applicant or patentee must comply with the notice in accordance with one of paragraphs (a)(1), (a)(2), or (a)(3) of this section.

(1)   Applicant or patentee may comply with a notice under this section by providing:

(i)   A copy of the applicant's or patentee's record (if any) of all of the correspondence between the Office and the applicant or patentee for such application, patent, or other proceeding (except for U.S. patent documents);

(ii)   A list of such correspondence; and

(iii)   A statement that the copy is a complete and accurate copy of the applicant's or patentee's record of all of the correspondence between the Office and the applicant or patentee for such application, patent, or other proceeding (except for U.S. patent documents), and whether applicant or patentee is aware of any correspondence between the Office and the applicant or patentee for such application, patent, or other proceeding that is not among applicant's or patentee's records.

(2)   Applicant or patentee may comply with a notice under this section by:

(i)   Producing the applicant's or patentee's record (if any) of all of the correspondence between the Office and the applicant or patentee for such application, patent, or other proceeding for the Office to copy (except for U.S. patent documents); and

(ii)   Providing a statement that the papers produced by applicant or patentee are applicant's or patentee's complete record of all of the correspondence between the Office and the applicant or patentee for such application, patent, or other proceeding (except for U.S. patent documents), and whether applicant or patentee is aware of any correspondence between the Office and the applicant or patentee for such application, patent, or other proceeding that is not among applicant's or patentee's records.

(3)   If applicant or patentee does not possess any record of the correspondence between the Office and the applicant or patentee for such application, patent, or other proceeding, applicant or patentee must comply with a notice under this section by providing a statement that applicant or patentee does not possess any record of the correspondence between the Office and the applicant or patentee for such application, patent, or other proceeding.

(b)   With regard to a pending application, failure to comply with one of paragraphs (a)(1), (a)(2), or (a)(3) of this section within the time period set in the notice will result in abandonment of the application.

[Added, 65 FR 69446, Nov. 17, 2000, effective Nov. 17, 2000]

§ 1.265 [Removed]

[Added, 72 FR 46716, Aug. 21, 2007 (implementation enjoined and never became effective); removed, 74 FR 52686, Oct. 14, 2009, effective Oct. 14, 2009 (to remove changes made by the final rules in 72 FR 46716 from the CFR)]

PROTESTS AND PUBLIC USE PROCEEDINGS

§ 1.291 Protests by the public against pending applications.

(a) A protest may be filed by a member of the public against a pending application, and it will be matched with the application file if it adequately identifies the patent application. A protest submitted within the time frame of paragraph (b) of this section, which is not matched in a timely manner to permit review by the examiner during prosecution, due to inadequate identification, may not be entered and may be returned to the protestor where practical, or, if return is not practical, discarded.

(b) The protest will be entered into the record of the application if, in addition to complying with paragraph (c) of this section, the protest has been served upon the applicant in accordance with § 1.248, or filed with the Office in duplicate in the event service is not possible; and, except for paragraph (b)(1) of this section, the protest was filed prior to the date the application was published under § 1.211, or a notice of allowance under § 1.311 was mailed, whichever occurs first:

(1) If a protest is accompanied by the written consent of the applicant, the protest will be considered if the protest is matched with the application in time to permit review during prosecution.

(2) A statement must accompany a protest that it is the first protest submitted in the application by the real party in interest who is submitting the protest; or the protest must comply with paragraph (c)(5) of this section. This section does not apply to the first protest filed in an application.

(c) In addition to compliance with paragraphs (a) and (b) of this section, a protest must include.

(1) A listing of the patents, publication, or other information relied upon;

(2) A concise explanation of the relevance of each item listed pursuant to paragraph (c)(1) of this section;

(3) A copy of each listed patent, publication, or other item of information in written form, or at least the pertinent portions thereof;

(4) An English language translation of all the necessary and pertinent parts of any non-English language patent, publication, or other item of information relied upon; and

(5) If it is a second or subsequent protest by the same party in interest, an explanation as to why the issue(s) raised in the second or subsequent protest are significantly different than those raised earlier and why the significantly different issue(s) were not presented earlier, and a processing fee under § 1.17(i) must be submitted.

(d) A member of the public filing a protest in an application under this section will not receive any communication from the Office relating to the protest, other than the return of a self-addressed postcard which the member of the public may include with the protest in order to receive an acknowledgement by the Office that the protest has been received. The limited involvement of the member of the public filing a protest pursuant to this section ends with the filing of the protest, and no further submission on behalf of the protestor will be considered, unless the submission is made pursuant to paragraph (c)(5) of this section.

(e) Where a protest raising inequitable conduct issues satisfies the provisions of this section for entry, it will be entered into the application file, generally without comment on the inequitable conduct issues raised in it.

(f) In the absence of a request by the Office, an applicant has no duty to, and need not, reply to a protest.

(g) Protests that fail to comply with paragraphs (b) or (c) of this section may not be entered, and if not entered, will be returned to the protestor, or discarded, at the option of the Office.

[47 FR 21752, May 19, 1982, effective July 1, 1982; paras. (a) and (c), 57 FR 2021, Jan. 17, 1992, effective Mar. 16, 1992; paras. (a) and (b) revised, 61 FR 42790, Aug. 19, 1996, effective Sept. 23, 1996; para. (c) revised, 62 FR 53131, Oct. 10, 1997, effective Dec. 1, 1997; para. (a)(1) revised, 65 FR 57024, Sept. 20, 2000, effective Nov. 29,

2000; revised, 69 FR 56481, Sept. 21, 2004, effective Nov. 22, 2004]

§ 1.292 Public use proceedings.

(a)   When a petition for the institution of public use proceedings, supported by affidavits or declarations is found, on reference to the examiner, to make a prima facie showing that the invention claimed in an application believed to be on file had been in public use or on sale more than one year before the filing of the application, a hearing may be had before the Director to determine whether a public use proceeding should be instituted. If instituted, the Director may designate an appropriate official to conduct the public use proceeding, including the setting of times for taking testimony, which shall be taken as provided by part 41, subpart D, of this title. The petitioner will be heard in the proceedings but after decision therein will not be heard further in the prosecution of the application for patent.

(b)   The petition and accompanying papers, or a notice that such a petition has been filed, shall be entered in the application file if:

(1)   The petition is accompanied by the fee set forth in § 1.17(j);

(2)   The petition is served on the applicant in accordance with § 1.248, or filed with the Office in duplicate in the event service is not possible; and

(3)   The petition is submitted prior to the date the application was published or the mailing of a notice of allowance under § 1.311, whichever occurs first.

(c)   A petition for institution of public use proceedings shall not be filed by a party to an interference as to an application involved in the interference. Public use and on sale issues in an interference shall be raised by a motion under § 41.121(a)(1) of this title.

[42 FR 5595, Jan. 28, 1977; para. (a), 47 FR 41279, Sept. 17, 1982; paras. (a) and (c), 49 FR 48416, Dec. 12, 1984, effective Feb. 12, 1985; paras. (a) and (b) revised, 61 FR 42790, Aug. 19, 1996, effective Sept. 23, 1996; para. (b)(3) revised, 65 FR 57024, Sept. 20, 2000, effective Nov. 29, 2000; para. (a) revised, 68 FR 14332, Mar. 25, 2003, effective May 1, 2003; paras. (a) and (c) revised, 69 FR 49959, Aug. 12, 2004, effective Sept. 13, 2004]

§ 1.293 Statutory invention registration.

(a)   An applicant for an original patent may request, at any time during the pendency of applicant's pending complete application, that the specification and drawings be published as a statutory invention registration. Any such request must be signed by (1) the applicant and any assignee of record or (2) an attorney or agent of record in the application.

(b)   Any request for publication of a statutory invention registration must include the following parts:

(1)   A waiver of the applicant's right to receive a patent on the invention claimed effective upon the date of publication of the statutory invention registration;

(2)   The required fee for filing a request for publication of a statutory invention registration as provided for in § 1.17(n) or (o);

(3)   A statement that, in the opinion of the requester, the application to which the request is directed meets the requirements of 35 U.S.C. 112; and

(4)   A statement that, in the opinion of the requester, the application to which the request is directed complies with the formal requirements of this part for printing as a patent.

(c)   A waiver filed with a request for a statutory invention registration will be effective, upon publication of the statutory invention registration, to waive the inventor's right to receive a patent on the invention claimed in the statutory invention registration, in any application for an original patent which is pending on, or filed after, the date of publication of the statutory invention registration. A waiver filed with a request for a statutory invention registration will not affect the rights of any other inventor even if the subject matter of the statutory invention registration and an application of another inventor are commonly owned. A waiver filed with a request for a statutory invention registration will not affect any rights in a patent to the inventor which issued prior to the date of publication of the statutory invention registration unless a reissue application is filed seeking to enlarge the scope of the claims of the patent. See also § 1.104(c)(5).

[50 FR 9382, Mar. 7, 1985, effective date May 8, 1985; para. (c) revised, 62 FR 53131, Oct. 10, 1997, effective Dec. 1, 1997]

§ 1.294 Examination of request for publication of a statutory invention registration and patent application to which the request is directed.

(a) Any request for a statutory invention registration will be examined to determine if the requirements of § 1.293 have been met. The application to which the request is directed will be examined to determine (1) if the subject matter of the application is appropriate for publication, (2) if the requirements for publication are met, and (3) if the requirements of 35 U.S.C. 112 and § 1.293 of this part are met.

(b) Applicant will be notified of the results of the examination set forth in paragraph (a) of this section. If the requirements of § 1.293 and this section are not met by the request filed, the notification to applicant will set a period of time within which to comply with the requirements in order to avoid abandonment of the application. If the application does not meet the requirements of 35 U.S.C. 112, the notification to applicant will include a rejection under the appropriate provisions of 35 U.S.C. 112. The periods for reply established pursuant to this section are subject to the extension of time provisions of § 1.136. After reply by the applicant, the application will again be considered for publication of a statutory invention registration. If the requirements of § 1.293 and this section are not timely met, the refusal to publish will be made final. If the requirements of 35 U.S.C. 112 are not met, the rejection pursuant to 35 U.S.C. 112 will be made final.

(c) If the examination pursuant to this section results in approval of the request for a statutory invention registration the applicant will be notified of the intent to publish a statutory invention registration.

[50 FR 9382, Mar. 7, 1985, effective date May 8, 1985; para. (b) revised, 62 FR 53131, Oct. 10, 1997, effective Dec. 1, 1997]

§ 1.295 Review of decision finally refusing to publish a statutory invention registration.

(a) Any requester who is dissatisfied with the final refusal to publish a statutory invention registration for reasons other than compliance with 35 U.S.C. 112 may obtain review of the refusal to publish the statutory invention registration by filing a petition to the Director accompanied by the fee set forth in § 1.17(g) within one month or such other time as is set in the decision refusing publication. Any such petition should comply with the requirements of § 1.181(b). The petition may include a request that the petition fee be refunded if the final refusal to publish a statutory invention registration for reasons other than compliance with 35 U.S.C. 112 is determined to result from an error by the Patent and Trademark Office.

(b) Any requester who is dissatisfied with a decision finally rejecting claims pursuant to 35 U.S.C. 112 may obtain review of the decision by filing an appeal to the Board of Patent Appeals and Interferences pursuant to § 41.31 of this title. If the decision rejecting claims pursuant to 35 U.S.C. 112 is reversed, the request for a statutory invention registration will be approved and the registration published if all of the other provisions of § 1.293 and this section are met.

[50 FR 9382, Mar. 7, 1985, effective May 8, 1985; para. (a) revised, 68 FR 14332, Mar. 25, 2003, effective May 1, 2003; para. (b) revised, 69 FR 49959, Aug. 12, 2004, effective Sept. 13, 2004; para. (a) revised, 69 FR 56481, Sept. 21, 2004, effective Nov. 22, 2004]

§ 1.296 Withdrawal of request for publication of statutory invention registration.

A request for a statutory invention registration, which has been filed, may be withdrawn prior to the date of the notice of the intent to publish a statutory invention registration issued pursuant to § 1.294(c) by filing a request to withdraw the request for publication of a statutory invention registration. The request to withdraw may also include a request for a refund of any amount paid in excess of the application filing fee and a handling fee of $130.00 which will be retained. Any request to withdraw the request for publication of a statutory invention registration filed on or after the date of the notice of intent to publish issued pursuant to § 1.294(c) must be in the form of a petition accompanied by the fee set forth in § 1.17(g).

[50 FR 9382, Mar. 7, 1985, effective date May 8, 1985; revised, 54 FR 6893, Feb. 15, 1989, effective Apr. 17, 1989; 56 FR 65142, Dec. 13, 1991, effective Dec. 16, 1991; revised, 69 FR 56481, Sept. 21, 2004, effective Nov. 22, 2004]

§ 1.297 Publication of statutory invention registration.

(a) If the request for a statutory invention registration is approved the statutory invention registration will be published. The statutory invention registration will be mailed to the requester at the correspondence address as provided for in § 1.33(a). A notice of the publication of each statutory invention registration will be published in the *Official Gazette*.

(b) Each statutory invention registration published will include a statement relating to the attributes of a statutory invention registration. The statement will read as follows:

A statutory invention registration is not a patent. It has the defensive attributes of a patent but does not have the enforceable attributes of a patent. No article or advertisement or the like may use the term patent, or any term suggestive of a patent, when referring to a statutory invention registration. For more specific information on the rights associated with a statutory invention registration see 35 U.S.C. 157.

[50 FR 9382, Mar. 7, 1985, effective May 8, 1985; 50 FR 31826, Aug. 6, 1985, effective Oct. 5, 1985]

REVIEW OF PATENT AND TRADEMARK OFFICE DECISIONS BY COURT

§ 1.301 Appeal to U.S. Court of Appeals for the Federal Circuit.

Any applicant, or any owner of a patent involved in any *ex parte* reexamination proceeding filed under § 1.510, dissatisfied with the decision of the Board of Patent Appeals and Interferences, and any party to an interference dissatisfied with the decision of the Board of Patent Appeals and Interferences, may appeal to the U.S. Court of Appeals for the Federal Circuit. The appellant must take the following steps in such an appeal: In the U. S. Patent and Trademark Office, file a written notice of appeal directed to the Director (§§ 1.302 and 1.304); and in the Court, file a copy of the notice of appeal and pay the fee for appeal as provided by the rules of the Court. For appeals by patent owners and third party requesters in *inter partes* reexamination proceedings filed under § 1.913, § 1.983 is controlling.

[47 FR 47381, Oct. 26, 1982, effective Oct. 26, 1982; 49 FR 48416, Dec. 12, 1984, effective Feb. 11, 1985; 50 FR 9383, Mar. 7, 1985, effective May 8, 1985; 54 FR 29552, July 13, 1989, effective Aug. 20, 1989; revised, 65 FR 76756, Dec. 7, 2000, effective Feb. 5, 2001; revised, 68 FR 14332, Mar. 25, 2003, effective May 1, 2003; revised, 68 FR 70996, Dec. 22, 2003, effective Jan. 21, 2004]

§ 1.302 Notice of appeal.

(a) When an appeal is taken to the U.S. Court of Appeals for the Federal Circuit, the appellant shall give notice thereof to the Director within the time specified in § 1.304.

(b) In interferences, the notice must be served as provided in § 41.106(e) of this title.

(c) In *ex parte* reexamination proceedings, the notice must be served as provided in § 1.550(f).

(d) In *inter partes* reexamination proceedings, the notice must be served as provided in § 1.903.

(e) Notices of appeal directed to the Director shall be mailed to or served by hand on the General Counsel as provided in § 104.2.

[24 FR 10332, Dec. 22, 1959; para. (a), 47 FR 47381, Oct. 26, 1982, effective Oct. 26, 1982; 49 FR 48416, Dec. 12, 1984, effective Feb. 11, 1985; 50 FR 9383, Mar. 7, 1985, effective May 8, 1985; para. (c) added, 53 FR 16414, May 8, 1988; paras. (a) & (c) revised, 68 FR 14332, Mar. 25, 2003, effective May 1, 2003; revised, 68 FR 70996, Dec. 22, 2003, effective Jan. 21, 2004; para. (b) revised, 69 FR 49959, Aug. 12, 2004, effective Sept. 13, 2004; para. (b) revised, 69 FR 58260, Sept. 30, 2004, effective Sept. 30, 2004]

§ 1.303 Civil action under 35 U.S.C. 145, 146, 306.

(a) Any applicant, or any owner of a patent involved in an *ex parte* reexamination proceeding filed before November 29, 1999, dissatisfied with the decision of the Board of Patent Appeals and Interferences, and any party to an interference dissatisfied with the decision of the Board of Patent Appeals and Interferences may, instead of appealing to the U.S. Court of Appeals for the Federal Circuit (§ 1.301), have remedy by civil action under 35 U.S.C. 145 or 146, as appropriate. Such civil action must be commenced within the time specified in § 1.304.

(b) If an applicant in an *ex parte* case, or an owner of a patent involved in an *ex parte* reexamination proceeding filed before November 29, 1999, has taken an appeal to the U.S. Court of Appeals for the Federal Circuit, he or she thereby waives his or her right to proceed under 35 U.S.C. 145.

(c)   A notice of election under 35 U.S.C. 141 to have all further proceedings on review conducted as provided in 35 U.S.C. 146 must be filed with the Office of the Solicitor and served as provided in § 41.106(e) of this title.

(d)   For an *ex parte* reexamination proceeding filed on or after November 29, 1999, and for any *inter partes* reexamination proceeding, no remedy by civil action under 35 U.S.C. 145 is available.

[47 FR 47381, Oct. 26, 1982, effective Oct. 26, 1982; 49 FR 48416, Dec. 12, 1984, effective Feb. 11, 1985; para. (c), 54 FR 29553, July 13, 1989, effective Aug. 20, 1989; para. (a) revised, 65 FR 54604, Sept. 8, 2000, effective Nov. 7, 2000; paras. (a) and (b) revised and para. (d) added, 65 FR 76756, Dec. 7, 2000, effective Feb. 5, 2001; para. (c) revised, 68 FR 14332, Mar. 25, 2003, effective May 1, 2003; paras. (a), (b), & (d) revised, 68 FR 70996, Dec. 22, 2003, effective Jan. 21, 2004; para. (c) revised, 69 FR 49959, Aug. 12, 2004, effective Sept. 13, 2004; para. (c) revised, 69 FR 58260, Sept. 30, 2004, effective Sept. 30, 2004]

§ 1.304   Time for appeal or civil action.

(a)(1)The time for filing the notice of appeal to the U.S. Court of Appeals for the Federal Circuit (§ 1.302) or for commencing a civil action (§ 1.303) is two months from the date of the decision of the Board of Patent Appeals and Interferences. If a request for rehearing or reconsideration of the decision is filed within the time period provided under § 41.52(a), § 41.79(a), or § 41.127(d) of this title, the time for filing an appeal or commencing a civil action shall expire two months after action on the request. In contested cases before the Board of Patent Appeals and Interferences, the time for filing a cross-appeal or cross-action expires:

(i)   Fourteen days after service of the notice of appeal or the summons and complaint; or

(ii)   Two months after the date of decision of the Board of Patent Appeals and Interferences, whichever is later.

(2)   The time periods set forth in this section are not subject to the provisions of § 1.136, § 1.550 (c), or § 1.956, or of § 41.4 of this title.

(3)   The Director may extend the time for filing an appeal or commencing a civil action:

(i)   For good cause shown if requested in writing before the expiration of the period for filing an appeal or commencing a civil action, or

(ii)   Upon written request after the expiration of the period for filing an appeal or commencing a civil action upon a showing that the failure to act was the result of excusable neglect.

(b)   The times specified in this section in days are calendar days. The time specified herein in months are calendar months except that one day shall be added to any two-month period which includes February 28. If the last day of the time specified for appeal or commencing a civil action falls on a Saturday, Sunday or Federal holiday in the District of Columbia, the time is extended to the next day which is neither a Saturday, Sunday nor a Federal holiday.

(c)   If a defeated party to an interference has taken an appeal to the U.S. Court of Appeals for the Federal Circuit and an adverse party has filed notice under 35 U.S.C. 141 electing to have all further proceedings conducted under 35 U.S.C. 146 (§ 1.303(c)), the time for filing a civil action thereafter is specified in 35 U.S.C. 141. The time for filing a cross-action expires 14 days after service of the summons and complaint.

[41 FR 758, Jan. 5, 1976; para. (a) and (c), 47 FR 47382, Oct. 26, 1982; para. (a), 49 FR 556, Jan. 4, 1984, effective Apr. 1, 1984; para. (a) 49 FR Dec. 12, 1984, effective Feb. 11, 1985; para. (a), 50 FR 9383, Mar. 7, 1985, effective May 8, 1985; 54 FR 29553, July 13, 1989, effective Aug. 20, 1989; paras. (a) and (c) revised 58 FR 54494, Oct. 22, 1993, effective Nov. 22, 1993; para. (a)(1) revised, 62 FR 53131, Oct. 10, 1997, effective Dec. 1, 1997; paras. (a)(1) and (a)(2) revised, 65 FR 76756, Dec. 7, 2000, effective Feb. 5, 2001; para. (a)(3) revised, 68 FR 14332, Mar. 25, 2003, effective May 1, 2003; para. (a)(1) revised, 68 FR 70996, Dec. 22, 2003, effective Jan. 21, 2004; paras. (a)(1) and (a)(2) revised, 69 FR 49959, Aug. 12, 2004, effective Sept. 13, 2004]

ALLOWANCE AND ISSUE OF PATENT

§ 1.311   Notice of Allowance.

(a)   If, on examination, it appears that the applicant is entitled to a patent under the law, a notice of allowance will be sent to the applicant at the correspondence address indicated in § 1.33. The notice of allowance shall specify a sum constituting the issue fee which must be paid within three months from the date of mailing of the notice of allowance to avoid abandonment of the application. The sum specified in the notice of allowance may also include the publication fee, in which case the issue fee and publication fee (§ 1.211(e)) must both be paid within three months from the date of mailing of the notice of allowance to avoid abandonment of the application. This three-month period is not extendable.

(b)   An authorization to charge the issue fee or other post-allowance fees set forth in § 1.18 to a deposit account may be filed in an individual application only after mailing of the notice of allowance. The submission of either of the following after the mailing of a notice of allowance will operate as a request to charge the correct issue fee or any publication fee due to any deposit account identified in a previously filed authorization to charge such fees:

(1)   An incorrect issue fee or publication fee; or

(2)   A fee transmittal form (or letter) for payment of issue fee or publication fee.

[47 FR 41279, Sept. 17, 1982, effective Oct. 1, 1982; para. (b) revised, 65 FR 54604, Sept. 8, 2000, effective Nov. 7, 2000; revised, 65 FR 57024, Sept. 20, 2000, effective Nov. 29, 2000; para. (a) revised, 66 FR 67087, Dec. 28, 2001, effective Dec. 28, 2001; para. (b) revised, 69 FR 56481, Sept. 21, 2004, effective Sept. 21, 2004]

§ 1.312 Amendments after allowance.

No amendment may be made as a matter of right in an application after the mailing of the notice of allowance. Any amendment filed pursuant to this section must be filed before or with the payment of the issue fee, and may be entered on the recommendation of the primary examiner, approved by the Director, without withdrawing the application from issue.

[Para. (b) revised, 58 FR 54504, Oct. 22, 1993, effective Jan. 3, 1994; para. (b) revised, 60 FR 20195, Apr. 25, 1995, effective June 8, 1995; para. (b) revised, 62 FR 53131, Oct. 10, 1997, effective Dec. 1, 1997; revised, 65 FR 14865, Mar. 20, 2000, effective May 29, 2000 (adopted as final, 65 FR 50092, Aug. 16, 2000); revised, 68 FR 14332, Mar. 25, 2003, effective May 1, 2003]

§ 1.313 Withdrawal from issue.

(a)   Applications may be withdrawn from issue for further action at the initiative of the Office or upon petition by the applicant. To request that the Office withdraw an application from issue, applicant must file a petition under this section including the fee set forth in § 1.17(h) and a showing of good and sufficient reasons why withdrawal of the application from issue is necessary. A petition under this section is not required if a request for continued examination under § 1.114 is filed prior to payment of the issue fee. If the Office withdraws the application from issue, the Office will issue a new notice of allowance if the Office again allows the application.

(b)   Once the issue fee has been paid, the Office will not withdraw the application from issue at its own initiative for any reason except:

(1)   A mistake on the part of the Office;

(2)   A violation of § 1.56 or illegality in the application;

(3)   Unpatentability of one or more claims; or

(4)   For interference.

(c)   Once the issue fee has been paid, the application will not be withdrawn from issue upon petition by the applicant for any reason except:

(1)   Unpatentability of one of more claims, which petition must be accompanied by an unequivocal statement that one or more claims are unpatentable, an amendment to such claim or claims, and an explanation as to how the amendment causes such claim or claims to be patentable;

(2)   Consideration of a request for continued examination in compliance with § 1.114; or

(3)   Express abandonment of the application. Such express abandonment may be in favor of a continuing application.

(d)   A petition under this section will not be effective to withdraw the application from issue unless it is actually received and granted by the appropriate officials before the date of issue. Withdrawal of an application from issue after payment of the issue fee may not be effective to avoid publication of application information.

[47 FR 41280, Sept. 17, 1982, effective Oct. 1, 1982; para. (a), 54 FR 6893, Feb. 15, 1989, 54 FR 9432, March 7, 1989, effective Apr. 17, 1989; para. (b), 57 FR 2021, Jan. 17, 1992, effective Mar. 16, 1992; para. (a) revised, 60 FR 20195, Apr. 25, 1995, effective June 8, 1995; revised,

65 FR 14865, Mar. 20, 2000, effective May 29, 2000 (paras. (b), (c)(1), (c)(3) and (d) adopted as final, 65 FR 50092, Aug. 16, 2000); paras. (a) and c(2) revised, 65 FR 50092, Aug. 16, 2000, effective Aug. 16, 2000)]

§ 1.314 Issuance of patent.

If applicant timely pays the issue fee, the Office will issue the patent in regular course unless the application is withdrawn from issue (§ 1.313) or the Office defers issuance of the patent. To request that the Office defer issuance of a patent, applicant must file a petition under this section including the fee set forth in § 1.17(h) and a showing of good and sufficient reasons why it is necessary to defer issuance of the patent.

[47 FR 41280, Sept. 17, 1982, effective date Oct. 1, 1982; revised, 54 FR 6893, Feb. 15, 1989, effective Apr. 17, 1989; revised, 60 FR 20195, Apr. 25, 1995, effective June 8, 1995; revised, 65 FR 54604, Sept. 8, 2000, effective Nov. 7, 2000]

§ 1.315 Delivery of patent.

The patent will be delivered or mailed upon issuance to the correspondence address of record. See § 1.33(a).

[Revised, 61 FR 42790, Aug. 19, 1996, effective Sept. 23, 1996]

§ 1.316 Application abandoned for failure to pay issue fee.

If the issue fee is not paid within three months from the date of the notice of allowance, the application will be regarded as abandoned. Such an abandoned application will not be considered as pending before the Patent and Trademark Office.

[47 FR 41280, Sept. 17, 1982, effective date Oct. 1, 1982; paras. (b)-(d) amended, paras. (e) and (f) added, 58 FR 44277, Aug. 20, 1993, effective Sept. 20, 1993; para. (d) revised, 60 FR 20195, Apr. 25, 1995, effective June 8, 1995; revised, 62 FR 53131, Oct. 10, 1997, effective Dec. 1, 1997]

§ 1.317 Lapsed patents; delayed payment of balance of issue fee.

If the issue fee paid is the amount specified in the notice of allowance, but a higher amount is required at the time the issue fee is paid, any remaining balance of the issue fee is to be paid within three months from the date of notice thereof and, if not paid, the patent will lapse at the termination of the three-month period.

[47 FR 41280, Sept. 17, 1982, effective date Oct. 1, 1982; paras. (a)-(d) amended, paras. (e) & (f) added, 58 FR 44277, Aug. 20, 1993, effective Sept. 20, 1993; para. (d) amended, 60 FR 20195, Apr. 25, 1995, effective June 8, 1995; revised, 62 FR 53131, Oct. 10, 1997, effective Dec. 1, 1997]

§ 1.318 [Reserved]

[43 FR 20465, May 11, 1978; removed and reserved, 62 FR 53131, Oct. 10, 1997, effective Dec. 1, 1997]

DISCLAIMER

§ 1.321 Statutory disclaimers, including terminal disclaimers.

(a) A patentee owning the whole or any sectional interest in a patent may disclaim any complete claim or claims in a patent. In like manner any patentee may disclaim or dedicate to the public the entire term, or any terminal part of the term, of the patent granted. Such disclaimer is binding upon the grantee and its successors or assigns. A notice of the disclaimer is published in the *Official Gazette* and attached to the printed copies of the specification. The disclaimer, to be recorded in the Patent and Trademark Office, must:

(1) Be signed by the patentee, or an attorney or agent of record;

(2) Identify the patent and complete claim or claims, or term being disclaimed. A disclaimer which is not a disclaimer of a complete claim or claims, or term will be refused recordation;

(3) State the present extent of patentee's ownership interest in the patent; and

(4) Be accompanied by the fee set forth in § 1.20(d).

(b) An applicant or assignee may disclaim or dedicate to the public the entire term, or any terminal part of the term, of a patent to be granted. Such terminal disclaimer is binding upon the grantee and its successors or assigns. The terminal disclaimer, to be recorded in the Patent and Trademark Office, must:

(1)   Be signed:

(i)   By the applicant, or

(ii)   If there is an assignee of record of an undivided part interest, by the applicant and such assignee, or

(iii)   If there is an assignee of record of the entire interest, by such assignee, or

(iv)   By an attorney or agent of record;

(2)   Specify the portion of the term of the patent being disclaimed;

(3)   State the present extent of applicant's or assignee's ownership interest in the patent to be granted; and

(4)   Be accompanied by the fee set forth in § 1.20(d).

(c)   A terminal disclaimer, when filed to obviate judicially created double patenting in a patent application or in a reexamination proceeding except as provided for in paragraph (d) of this section, must:

(1)   Comply with the provisions of paragraphs (b)(2) through (b)(4) of this section;

(2)   Be signed in accordance with paragraph (b)(1) of this section if filed in a patent application or in accordance with paragraph (a)(1) of this section if filed in a reexamination proceeding; and

(3)   Include a provision that any patent granted on that application or any patent subject to the reexamination proceeding shall be enforceable only for and during such period that said patent is commonly owned with the application or patent which formed the basis for the judicially created double patenting.

(d)   A terminal disclaimer, when filed in a patent application or in a reexamination proceeding to obviate double patenting based upon a patent or application that is not commonly owned but was disqualified under 35 U.S.C. 103(c) as resulting from activities undertaken within the scope of a joint research agreement, must:

(1)   Comply with the provisions of paragraphs (b)(2) through (b)(4) of this section;

(2)   Be signed in accordance with paragraph (b)(1) of this section if filed in a patent application or be signed in accordance with paragraph (a)(1) of this section if filed in a reexamination proceeding;

(3)   Include a provision waiving the right to separately enforce any patent granted on that application or any patent subject to the reexamination proceeding and the patent or any patent granted on the application which formed the basis for the double patenting, and that any patent granted on that application or any patent subject to the reexamination proceeding shall be enforceable only for and during such period that said patent and the patent, or any patent granted on the application, which formed the basis for the double patenting are not separately enforced.

[47 FR 41281, Sept. 17, 1982, effective Oct. 1, 1982; revised, 58 FR 54504, Oct. 22, 1993, effective Jan. 3, 1994; para. (c) revised, 61 FR 42790, Aug. 19, 1996, effective Sept. 23, 1996; para (d) added, 70 FR 1818, Jan. 11, 2005, effective Dec. 10, 2004; paras. (c) and (d) revised, 70 FR 54259, Sept. 14, 2005, effective Sept. 14, 2005]

CORRECTION OF ERRORS IN PATENT

§ 1.322   Certificate of correction of Office mistake.

(a)(1)   The Director may issue a certificate of correction pursuant to 35 U.S.C. 254 to correct a mistake in a patent, incurred through the fault of the Office, which mistake is clearly disclosed in the records of the Office:

(i)   At the request of the patentee or the patentee's assignee;

(ii)   Acting *sua sponte* for mistakes that the Office discovers; or

(iii)   Acting on information about a mistake supplied by a third party.

(2)(i) There is no obligation on the Office to act on or respond to a submission of information or request to issue a certificate of correction by a third party under paragraph (a)(1)(iii) of this section.

(ii)   Papers submitted by a third party under this section will not be made of record in the file that they relate to nor be retained by the Office.

(3)   If the request relates to a patent involved in an interference, the request must comply with the requirements of this section and be accompanied by a motion under § 41.121(a)(2) or § 41.121(a)(3) of this title.

(4)   The Office will not issue a certificate of correction under this section without first notifying the patentee (including any assignee of record) at the correspondence address of record as specified in § 1.33(a) and affording the patentee or an assignee an opportunity to be heard.

(b) If the nature of the mistake on the part of the Office is such that a certificate of correction is deemed inappropriate in form, the Director may issue a corrected patent in lieu thereof as a more appropriate form for certificate of correction, without expense to the patentee.

[24 FR 10332, Dec. 22, 1959; 34 FR 5550, Mar. 22, 1969; para. (a), 49 FR 48416, Dec. 12, 1984, effective Feb. 11, 1985; para. (a) revised, 65 FR 54604, Sept. 8, 2000, effective Nov. 7, 2000; paras. (a)(1) & (b) revised, 68 FR 14332, Mar. 25, 2003, effective May 1, 2003; para. (a)(3) revised, 69 FR 49959, Aug. 12, 2004, effective Sept. 13, 2004]

§ 1.323 Certificate of correction of applicant's mistake.

The Office may issue a certificate of correction under the conditions specified in 35 U.S.C. 255 at the request of the patentee or the patentee's assignee, upon payment of the fee set forth in § 1.20(a). If the request relates to a patent involved in an interference, the request must comply with the requirements of this section and be accompanied by a motion under § 41.121(a)(2) or § 41.121(a)(3) of this title.

[34 FR 5550, Mar. 22, 1969; 49 FR 48416, Dec. 12, 1984, effective Feb. 11, 1985; revised, 65 FR 54604, Sept. 8, 2000, effective Nov. 7, 2000; revised, 69 FR 49959, Aug. 12, 2004, effective Sept. 13, 2004]

§ 1.324 Correction of inventorship in patent, pursuant to 35 U.S.C. 256.

(a) Whenever through error a person is named in an issued patent as the inventor, or through error an inventor is not named in an issued patent and such error arose without any deceptive intention on his or her part, the Director, pursuant to 35 U.S.C. 256, may, on application of all the parties and assignees, or on order of a court before which such matter is called in question, issue a certificate naming only the actual inventor or inventors. A petition to correct inventorship of a patent involved in an interference must comply with the requirements of this section and must be accompanied by a motion under § 41.121(a)(2) or § 41.121(a)(3) of this title.

(b) Any request to correct inventorship of a patent pursuant to paragraph (a) of this section must be accompanied by:

(1) Where one or more persons are being added, a statement from each person who is being added as an inventor that the inventorship error occurred without any deceptive intention on his or her part;

(2) A statement from the current named inventors who have not submitted a statement under paragraph (b)(1) of this section either agreeing to the change of inventorship or stating that they have no disagreement in regard to the requested change;

(3) A statement from all assignees of the parties submitting a statement under paragraphs (b)(1) and (b)(2) of this section agreeing to the change of inventorship in the patent, which statement must comply with the requirements of § 3.73(b) of this chapter; and

(4) The fee set forth in § 1.20(b).

(c) For correction of inventorship in an application, see §§ 1.48 and 1.497.

(d) In a contested case before the Board of Patent Appeals and Interferences under part 41, subpart D, of this title, a request for correction of a patent must be in the form of a motion under § 41.121(a)(2) or § 41.121(a)(3) of this title.

[47 FR 41281, Sept. 17, 1982, effective Oct. 1, 1982; 48 FR 2713, Jan. 20, 1983, effective Feb. 27, 1983; 49 FR 48416, Dec. 12, 1984, 50 FR 23123, May 31, 1985, effective Feb. 11, 1985; revised, 62 FR 53131, Oct. 10, 1997, effective Dec. 1, 1997; heading and para. (b)(1) revised, 65 FR 54604, Sept. 8, 2000, effective Sept. 8, 2000; para. (c) added, 65 FR 54604, Sept. 8, 2000, effective Sept. 8, 2000; para. (a) revised, 68 FR 14332, Mar. 25, 2003, effective May 1, 2003; paras. (a) and (c) revised and para. (d) added, 69 FR 49959, Aug. 12, 2004, effective Sept. 13, 2004; para. (a) and para. (b) introductory text revised, 69 FR 56481, Sept. 21, 2004, effective Oct. 21, 2004; para. (a) revised, 70 FR 3880, Jan. 27, 2005, effective Dec. 8, 2004]

§ 1.325 Other mistakes not corrected.

Mistakes other than those provided for in §§ 1.322, 1.323, 1.324, and not affording legal grounds for reissue or for reexamination, will not be corrected after the date of the patent.

[48 FR 2714, Jan. 20, 1983, effective date Feb. 27, 1983]

ARBITRATION AWARDS

§ 1.331 [Reserved]

[24 FR 10332, Dec. 22, 1959; 43 FR 20465, May 11, 1978; 47 FR 41281, Sept. 17, 1982; deleted, 57 FR 29642, July 6, 1992, effective Sept. 4, 1992]

§ 1.332 [Reserved]

[47 FR 41281, Sept. 17, 1982; deleted, 57 FR 29642, July 6, 1992, effective Sept. 4, 1992]

§ 1.333 [Reserved]

[Deleted, 57 FR 29642, July 6, 1992, effective Sept. 4, 1992]

§ 1.334 [Reserved]

[47 FR 41281, Sept. 17, 1982, effective Oct. 1, 1982; para. (c), 54 FR 6893, Feb. 15, 1989, effective Apr. 17, 1989; deleted, 57 FR 29642, July 6, 1992, effective Sept. 4, 1992]

§ 1.335 Filing of notice of arbitration awards.

(a) Written notice of any award by an arbitrator pursuant to 35 U.S.C. 294 must be filed in the Patent and Trademark Office by the patentee or the patentee's assignee or licensee. If the award involves more than one patent a separate notice must be filed for placement in the file of each patent. The notice must set forth the patent number, the names of the inventor and patent owner, and the names and addresses of the parties to the arbitration. The notice must also include a copy of the award.

(b) If an award by an arbitrator pursuant to 35 U.S.C. 294 is modified by a court, the party requesting the modification must file in the Patent and Trademark Office, a notice of the modification for placement in the file of each patent to which the modification applies. The notice must set forth the patent number, the names of the inventor and patent owner, and the names and addresses of the parties to the arbitration. The notice must also include a copy of the court's order modifying the award.

(c) Any award by an arbitrator pursuant to 35 U.S.C. 294 shall be unenforceable until any notices required by paragraph (a) or (b) of this section are filed in the Patent and Trademark Office. If any required notice is not filed by the party designated in paragraph (a) or (b) of this section, any party to the arbitration proceeding may file such a notice.

[48 FR 2718, Jan. 20, 1983, effective Feb. 8, 1983]

AMENDMENT OF RULES

§ 1.351 Amendments to rules will be published.

All amendments to the regulations in this part will be published in the *Official Gazette* and in the *Federal Register*.

§ 1.352 [Reserved]

[Para. (a) amended, 58 FR 54504, Oct. 22, 1993, effective Jan. 3, 1994; removed and reserved, 62 FR 53131, Oct. 10, 1997, effective Dec. 1, 1997]

MAINTENANCE FEES

§ 1.362 Time for payment of maintenance fees.

(a) Maintenance fees as set forth in §§ 1.20(e) through (g) are required to be paid in all patents based on applications filed on or after December 12, 1980, except as noted in paragraph (b) of this section, to maintain a patent in force beyond 4, 8 and 12 years after the date of grant.

(b) Maintenance fees are not required for any plant patents or for any design patents. Maintenance fees are not required for a reissue patent if the patent being reissued did not require maintenance fees.

(c) The application filing dates for purposes of payment of maintenance fees are as follows:

(1) For an application not claiming benefit of an earlier application, the actual United States filing date of the application.

(2) For an application claiming benefit of an earlier foreign application under 35 U.S.C. 119, the United States filing date of the application.

(3) For a continuing (continuation, division, continuation-in-part) application claiming the benefit of a prior patent application under 35 U.S.C. 120, the actual United States filing date of the continuing application.

(4) For a reissue application, including a continuing reissue application claiming the benefit of a reissue application under 35 U.S.C. 120, the United

States filing date of the original non-reissue application on which the patent reissued is based.

(5) For an international application which has entered the United States as a Designated Office under 35 U.S.C. 371, the international filing date granted under Article 11(1) of the Patent Cooperation Treaty which is considered to be the United States filing date under 35 U.S.C. 363.

(d) Maintenance fees may be paid in patents without surcharge during the periods extending respectively from:

(1) 3 years through 3 years and 6 months after grant for the first maintenance fee,

(2) 7 years through 7 years and 6 months after grant for the second maintenance fee, and

(3) 11 years through 11 years and 6 months after grant for the third maintenance fee.

(e) Maintenance fees may be paid with the surcharge set forth in § 1.20(h) during the respective grace periods after:

(1) 3 years and 6 months and through the day of the 4th anniversary of the grant for the first maintenance fee.

(2) 7 years and 6 months and through the day of the 8th anniversary of the grant for the second maintenance fee, and

(3) 11 years and 6 months and through the day of the 12th anniversary of the grant for the third maintenance fee.

(f) If the last day for paying a maintenance fee without surcharge set forth in paragraph (d) of this section, or the last day for paying a maintenance fee with surcharge set forth in paragraph (e) of this section, falls on a Saturday, Sunday, or a federal holiday within the District of Columbia, the maintenance fee and any necessary surcharge may be paid under paragraph (d) or paragraph (e) respectively on the next succeeding day which is not a Saturday, Sunday, or Federal holiday.

(g) Unless the maintenance fee and any applicable surcharge is paid within the time periods set forth in paragraphs (d), (e) or (f) of this section, the patent will expire as of the end of the grace period set forth in paragraph (e) of this section. A patent which expires for the failure to pay the maintenance fee will expire at the end of the same date (anniversary date) the patent was granted in the 4th, 8th, or 12th year after grant.

(h) The periods specified in §§1.362(d) and (e) with respect to a reissue application, including a continuing reissue application thereof, are counted from the date of grant of the original non-reissue application on which the reissued patent is based.

[49 FR 34724, Aug. 31, 1984, added effective Nov. 1, 1984; paras. (a) and (e), 56 FR 65142, Dec. 13, 1991, effective Dec. 16, 1991; paras. (c)(4) and (e) revised and para. (h) added, 58 FR 54504, Oct. 22, 1993, effective Jan. 3, 1994]

§ 1.363 Fee address for maintenance fee purposes.

(a) All notices, receipts, refunds, and other communications relating to payment or refund of maintenance fees will be directed to the correspondence address used during prosecution of the application as indicated in § 1.33(a) unless:

(1) A fee address for purposes of payment of maintenance fees is set forth when submitting the issue fee, or

(2) A change in the correspondence address for all purposes is filed after payment of the issue fee, or

(3) A fee address or a change in the "fee address" is filed for purposes of receiving notices, receipts and other correspondence relating to the payment of maintenance fees after the payment of the issue fee, in which instance, the latest such address will be used.

(b) An assignment of a patent application or patent does not result in a change of the "correspondence address" or "fee address" for maintenance fee purposes.

(c) A fee address must be an address associated with a Customer Number.

[49 FR 34725, Aug. 31, 1984, added effective Nov. 1, 1984; para. (c) added, 69 FR 29865, May 26, 2004, effective June 25, 2004]

§ 1.366 Submission of maintenance fees.

(a) The patentee may pay maintenance fees and any necessary surcharges, or any person or organization may pay maintenance fees and any necessary surcharges on behalf of a patentee. Authorization by the patentee need not be filed in the Patent and Trademark

Office to pay maintenance fees and any necessary surcharges on behalf of the patentee.

(b) A maintenance fee and any necessary surcharge submitted for a patent must be submitted in the amount due on the date the maintenance fee and any necessary surcharge are paid. A maintenance fee or surcharge may be paid in the manner set forth in § 1.23 or by an authorization to charge a deposit account established pursuant to § 1.25. Payment of a maintenance fee and any necessary surcharge or the authorization to charge a deposit account must be submitted within the periods set forth in § 1.362(d), (e), or (f). Any payment or authorization of maintenance fees and surcharges filed at any other time will not be accepted and will not serve as a payment of the maintenance fee except insofar as a delayed payment of the maintenance fee is accepted by the Director in an expired patent pursuant to a petition filed under § 1.378. Any authorization to charge a deposit account must authorize the immediate charging of the maintenance fee and any necessary surcharge to the deposit account. Payment of less than the required amount, payment in a manner other than that set forth § 1.23, or in the filing of an authorization to charge a deposit account having insufficient funds will not constitute payment of a maintenance fee or surcharge on a patent. The procedures set forth in § 1.8 or § 1.10 may be utilized in paying maintenance fees and any necessary surcharges.

(c) In submitting maintenance fees and any necessary surcharges, identification of the patents for which maintenance fees are being paid must include the patent number, and the application number of the United States application for the patent on which the maintenance fee is being paid. If the payment includes identification of only the patent number (*i.e.*, does not identify the application number of the United States application for the patent on which the maintenance fee is being paid), the Office may apply the payment to the patent identified by patent number in the payment or may return the payment.

(d) Payment of maintenance fees and any surcharges should identify the fee being paid for each patent as to whether it is the 3 1/2-, 7 1/2-, or 11 1/2-year fee, whether small entity status is being changed or claimed, the amount of the maintenance fee and any surcharge being paid, and any assigned customer number. If the maintenance fee and any necessary sur-

charge is being paid on a reissue patent, the payment must identify the reissue patent by reissue patent number and reissue application number as required by paragraph (c) of this section and should also include the original patent number.

(e) Maintenance fee payments and surcharge payments relating thereto must be submitted separate from any other payments for fees or charges, whether submitted in the manner set forth in § 1.23 or by an authorization to charge a deposit account. If maintenance fee and surcharge payments for more than one patent are submitted together, they should be submitted on as few sheets as possible with the patent numbers listed in increasing patent number order. If the payment submitted is insufficient to cover the maintenance fees and surcharges for all the listed patents, the payment will be applied in the order the patents are listed, beginning at the top of the listing.

(f) Notification of any change in status resulting in loss of entitlement to small entity status must be filed in a patent prior to paying, or at the time of paying, the earliest maintenance fee due after the date on which status as a small entity is no longer appropriate. See § 1.27(g).

(g) Maintenance fees and surcharges relating thereto will not be refunded except in accordance with §§1.26 and 1.28(a).

[49 FR 34725, Aug. 31, 1984, added effective Nov. 1, 1984; para. (b) amended, 58 FR 54494, Oct. 22, 1993, effective Nov. 22, 1993; paras. (b) - (d) revised, 62 FR 53131, Oct. 10, 1997, effective Dec. 1, 1997; para. (c) revised, 65 FR 54604, Sept. 8, 2000, effective Sept. 8, 2000; para. (f) revised, 65 FR 78958, Dec. 18, 2000; para. (b) revised, 68 FR 14332, Mar. 25, 2003, effective May 1, 2003]

§ 1.377 Review of decision refusing to accept and record payment of a maintenance fee filed prior to expiration of patent.

(a) Any patentee who is dissatisfied with the refusal of the Patent and Trademark Office to accept and record a maintenance fee which was filed prior to the expiration of the patent may petition the Director to accept and record the maintenance fee.

(b) Any petition under this section must be filed within two months of the action complained of, or within such other time as may be set in the action complained of, and must be accompanied by the fee set forth in § 1.17(g). The petition may include a request that the petition fee be refunded if the refusal to accept and record the maintenance fee is determined to result from an error by the Patent and Trademark Office.

(c) Any petition filed under this section must comply with the requirements of § 1.181(b) and must be signed by an attorney or agent registered to practice before the Patent and Trademark Office, or by the patentee, the assignee, or other party in interest.

[49 FR 34725, Aug. 31, 1984, added effective Nov. 1, 1984; para. (c) revised, 62 FR 53131, Oct. 10, 1997, effective Dec. 1, 1997; para. (a) revised, 68 FR 14332, Mar. 25, 2003, effective May 1, 2003; para. (b) revised, 69 FR 56481, Sept. 21, 2004, effective Nov. 22, 2004]

§ 1.378 Acceptance of delayed payment of maintenance fee in expired patent to reinstate patent.

(a) The Director may accept the payment of any maintenance fee due on a patent after expiration of the patent if, upon petition, the delay in payment of the maintenance fee is shown to the satisfaction of the Director to have been unavoidable (paragraph (b) of this section) or unintentional (paragraph (c) of this section) and if the surcharge required by § 1.20(i) is paid as a condition of accepting payment of the maintenance fee. If the Director accepts payment of the maintenance fee upon petition, the patent shall be considered as not having expired, but will be subject to the conditions set forth in 35 U.S.C. 41(c)(2).

(b) Any petition to accept an unavoidably delayed payment of a maintenance fee filed under paragraph (a) of this section must include:

(1) The required maintenance fee set forth in § 1.20 (e) through (g);

(2) The surcharge set forth in § 1.20(i)(1); and

(3) A showing that the delay was unavoidable since reasonable care was taken to ensure that the maintenance fee would be paid timely and that the petition was filed promptly after the patentee was notified of, or otherwise became aware of, the expiration of the patent. The showing must enumerate the steps taken to ensure timely payment of the maintenance fee, the date and the manner in which patentee

became aware of the expiration of the patent, and the steps taken to file the petition promptly.

(c) Any petition to accept an unintentionally delayed payment of a maintenance fee filed under paragraph (a) of this section must be filed within twenty-four months after the six-month grace period provided in § 1.362(e) and must include:

(1) The required maintenance fee set forth in § 1.20 (e) through (g);

(2) The surcharge set forth in § 1.20(i)(2); and

(3) A statement that the delay in payment of the maintenance fee was unintentional.

(d) Any petition under this section must be signed by an attorney or agent registered to practice before the Patent and Trademark Office, or by the patentee, the assignee, or other party in interest.

(e) Reconsideration of a decision refusing to accept a maintenance fee upon petition filed pursuant to paragraph (a) of this section may be obtained by filing a petition for reconsideration within two months of, or such other time as set in the decision refusing to accept the delayed payment of the maintenance fee. Any such petition for reconsideration must be accompanied by the petition fee set forth in § 1.17(f). After the decision on the petition for reconsideration, no further reconsideration or review of the matter will be undertaken by the Director. If the delayed payment of the maintenance fee is not accepted, the maintenance fee and the surcharge set forth in § 1.20(i) will be refunded following the decision on the petition for reconsideration, or after the expiration of the time for filing such a petition for reconsideration, if none is filed. Any petition fee under this section will not be refunded unless the refusal to accept and record the maintenance fee is determined to result from an error by the Patent and Trademark Office.

[49 FR 34726, Aug. 31, 1984, added effective Nov. 1, 1984; para. (a), 50 FR 9383, Mar.7, 1985, effective May 8, 1985; paras. (b) and (c), 53 FR 47810, Nov. 28, 1988, effective Jan. 1, 1989; paras. (a) - (c) and (e), 56 FR 65142, Dec. 13, 1991, effective Dec. 16, 1991; paras. (a) - (c) and (e), 58 FR 44277, Aug. 20, 1993, effective Sept. 20, 1993; para. (d) revised, 62 FR 53131, Oct. 10, 1997, effective Dec. 1, 1997; paras. (a) & (e) revised, 68 FR 14332, Mar. 25, 2003, effective May 1, 2003; para. (e) revised, 69 FR 56536, Sept. 21, 2004, effective Nov. 22, 2004]

Subpart C — International Processing Provisions

GENERAL INFORMATION

§ 1.401 Definitions of terms under the Patent Cooperation Treaty.

(a) The abbreviation *PCT* and the term *Treaty* mean the Patent Cooperation Treaty.

(b) *International Bureau* means the World Intellectual Property Organization located in Geneva, Switzerland.

(c) *Administrative Instructions* means that body of instructions for operating under the Patent Cooperation Treaty referred to in PCT Rule 89.

(d) *Request,* when capitalized, means that element of the international application described in PCT Rules 3 and 4.

(e) *International application,* as used in this subchapter is defined in § 1.9(b).

(f) *Priority date* for the purpose of computing time limits under the Patent Cooperation Treaty is defined in PCT Art. 2(xi). Note also § 1.465.

(g) *Demand,* when capitalized, means that document filed with the International Preliminary Examining Authority which requests an international preliminary examination.

(h) *Annexes* means amendments made to the claims, description or the drawings before the International Preliminary Examining Authority.

(i) Other terms and expressions in this subpart C not defined in this section are to be taken in the sense indicated in PCT Art. 2 and 35 U.S.C. 351.

[43 FR 20466, May 11, 1978; 52 FR 20047, May 28, 1987]

§ 1.412 The United States Receiving Office.

(a) The United States Patent and Trademark Office is a Receiving Office only for applicants who are residents or nationals of the United States of America.

(b) The Patent and Trademark Office, when acting as a Receiving Office, will be identified by the full title "United States Receiving Office" or by the abbreviation "RO/US."

(c) The major functions of the Receiving Office include:

(1) According of international filing dates to international applications meeting the requirements of PCT Art. 11(1) and PCT Rule 20;

(2) Assuring that international applications meet the standards for format and content of PCT Art. 14(1), PCT Rule 9, 26, 29.1, 37, 38, 91, and portions of PCT Rules 3 through 11;

(3) Collecting and, when required, transmitting fees due for processing international applications (PCT Rule 14, 15, 16);

(4) Transmitting the record and search copies to the International Bureau and International Searching Authority, respectively (PCT Rules 22 and 23); and

(5) Determining compliance with applicable requirements of part 5 of this chapter.

(6) Reviewing and, unless prescriptions concerning national security prevent the application from being so transmitted (PCT Rule 19.4), transmitting the international application to the International Bureau for processing in its capacity as a Receiving Office:

(i) Where the United States Receiving Office is not the competent Receiving Office under PCT Rule 19.1 or 19.2 and § 1.421(a); or

(ii) Where the international application is not in English but is in a language accepted under PCT Rule 12.1(a) by the International Bureau as a Receiving Office; or

(iii) Where there is agreement and authorization in accordance with PCT Rule 19.4(a)(iii).

[Para. (c)(6) added, 60 FR 21438, May 2, 1995, effective June 1, 1995; para. (c)(6) revised, 63 FR 29614, June 1, 1998, effective July 1, 1998 (adopted as final, 63 FR 66040, Dec. 1, 1998)]

§ 1.413 The United States International Searching Authority.

(a) Pursuant to appointment by the Assembly, the United States Patent and Trademark Office will act as an International Searching Authority for international applications filed in the United States Receiving Office and in other Receiving Offices as may be agreed upon by the Director, in accordance with the agreement between the Patent and Trademark Office and the International Bureau (PCT Art. 16(3)(b)).

(b) The Patent and Trademark Office, when acting as an International Searching Authority, will be identified by the full title "United States International Searching Authority" or by the abbreviation "ISA/US."

(c) The major functions of the International Searching Authority include:

(1) Approving or establishing the title and abstract;

(2) Considering the matter of unity of invention;

(3) Conducting international and international-type searches and preparing international and international-type search reports (PCT Art. 15, 17 and 18, and PCT Rules 25, 33 to 45 and 47), and issuing declarations that no international search report will be established (PCT Article 17(2)(a));

(4) Preparing written opinions of the International Searching Authority in accordance with PCT Rule 43*bis* (when necessary); and

(5) Transmitting the international search report and the written opinion of the International Searching Authority to the applicant and the International Bureau.

[Para. (a) revised, 68 FR 14332, Mar. 25, 2003, effective May 1, 2003; paras. (a) & (c) revised, 68 FR 58991, Oct. 20, 2003, effective Jan. 1, 2004]

§ 1.414 The United States Patent and Trademark Office as a Designated Office or Elected Office.

(a) The United States Patent and Trademark Office will act as a Designated Office or Elected Office for international applications in which the United States of America has been designated or elected as a State in which patent protection is desired.

(b) The United States Patent and Trademark Office, when acting as a Designated Office or Elected Office during international processing will be identified by the full title "United States Designated Office" or by the abbreviation "DO/US" or by the full title "United States Elected Office" or by the abbreviation "EO/US."

(c) The major functions of the United States Designated Office or Elected Office in respect to international applications in which the United States of America has been designated or elected, include:

(1) Receiving various notifications throughout the international stage and

(2) Accepting for national stage examination international applications which satisfy the requirements of 35 U.S.C. 371.

[52 FR 20047, May 28, 1987, effective July 1, 1987]

§ 1.415 The International Bureau.

(a) The International Bureau is the World Intellectual Property Organization located at Geneva, Switzerland. It is the international intergovernmental organization which acts as the coordinating body under the Treaty and the Regulations (PCT Art. 2 (xix) and 35 U.S.C. 351(h)).

(b) The major functions of the International Bureau include:

(1) Publishing of international applications and the International Gazette;

(2) Transmitting copies of international applications to Designated Offices;

(3) Storing and maintaining record copies; and

(4) Transmitting information to authorities pertinent to the processing of specific international applications.

§ 1.416 The United States International Preliminary Examining Authority.

(a) Pursuant to appointment by the Assembly, the United States Patent and Trademark Office will act as an International Preliminary Examining Authority for international applications filed in the United States Receiving Office and in other Receiving Offices as may be agreed upon by the Director, in accordance with agreement between the Patent and Trademark Office and the International Bureau.

(b) The United States Patent and Trademark Office, when acting as an International Preliminary Examining Authority, will be identified by the full title "United States International Preliminary Examining Authority" or by the abbreviation "IPEA/US."

(c) The major functions of the International Preliminary Examining Authority include:

(1) Receiving and checking for defects in the Demand;

(2) Forwarding Demands in accordance with PCT Rule 59.3;

(3)   Collecting the handling fee for the International Bureau and the preliminary examination fee for the United States International Preliminary Examining Authority;

(4)   Informing applicant of receipt of the Demand;

(5)   Considering the matter of unity of invention;

(6)   Providing an international preliminary examination report which is a non-binding opinion on the questions of whether the claimed invention appears: to be novel, to involve an inventive step (to be nonobvious), and to be industrially applicable; and

(7)   Transmitting the international preliminary examination report to applicant and the International Bureau.

[Added 52 FR 20047, May 28, 1987; para. (c) revised, 63 FR 29614, June 1, 1998, effective July 1998 (adopted as final, 63 FR 66040, Dec. 1, 1998); para. (a) revised, 68 FR 14332, Mar. 25, 2003, effective May 1, 2003]

§ 1.417   Submission of translation of international publication.

The submission of an English language translation of the publication of an international application pursuant to 35 U.S.C. 154(d)(4) must clearly identify the international application to which it pertains (§ 1.5(a)) and be clearly identified as a submission pursuant to 35 U.S.C. 154(d)(4). Otherwise, the submission will be treated as a filing under 35 U.S.C. 111(a). Such submissions should be marked "Mail Stop PCT."

[Added 65 FR 57024, Sept. 20, 2000, effective Nov. 29, 2000; revised 67 FR 520, Jan. 4, 2002, effective Apr. 1, 2002; revised, 68 FR 14332, Mar. 25, 2003, effective May 1, 2003; revised, 68 FR 70996, Dec. 22, 2003, effective Jan. 21, 2004]

§ 1.419   Display of currently valid control number under the Paperwork Reduction Act.

(a)   Pursuant to the Paperwork Reduction Act of 1995 (44 U.S.C. 3501 *et seq.*), the collection of information in this subpart has been reviewed and approved by the Office of Management and Budget under control number 0651-0021.

(b)   Notwithstanding any other provision of law, no person is required to respond to nor shall a person be subject to a penalty for failure to comply with a collection of information subject to the requirements of the Paperwork Reduction Act unless that collection of information displays a currently valid Office of Management and Budget control number. This section constitutes the display required by 44 U.S.C. 3512(a) and 5 CFR 1320.5(b)(2)(i) for the collection of information under Office of Management and Budget control number 0651-0021 (see 5 CFR 1320.5(b)(2)(ii)(D)).

[Added, 63 FR 29614, June 1, 1998, effective July 1, 1998 (adopted as final, 63 FR 66040, Dec. 1, 1998)]

WHO MAY FILE AN INTERNATIONAL APPLICATION

§ 1.421   Applicant for international application.

(a)   Only residents or nationals of the United States of America may file international applications in the United States Receiving Office. If an international application does not include an applicant who is indicated as being a resident or national of the United States of America, and at least one applicant:

(1)   Has indicated a residence or nationality in a PCT Contracting State, or

(2)   Has no residence or nationality indicated, applicant will be so notified and, if the international application includes a fee amount equivalent to that required by § 1.445(a)(4), the international application will be forwarded for processing to the International Bureau acting as a Receiving Office (see also § 1.412(c)(6)).

(b)   Although the United States Receiving Office will accept international applications filed by any resident or national of the United States of America for international processing, for the purposes of the designation of the United States, an international application must be filed, and will be accepted by the Patent and Trademark Office for the national stage only if filed, by the inventor or as provided in §§ 1.422 or 1.423. Joint inventors must jointly apply for an international application.

(c)   For the purposes of designations other than the United States, international applications may be filed by the assignee or owner.

(d)   A registered attorney or agent of the applicant may sign the international application Request and file the international application for the applicant.

A separate power of attorney from each applicant may be required.

(e) Any indication of different applicants for the purpose of different Designated Offices must be shown on the Request portion of the international application.

(f) Requests for changes in the indications concerning the applicant, agent, or common representative of an international application shall be made in accordance with PCT Rule 92*bis* and may be required to be signed by all applicants.

(g) Requests for withdrawals of the international application, designations, priority claims, the Demand, or elections shall be made in accordance with PCT Rule 90*bis* and must be signed by all applicants. A separate power of attorney from the applicants will be required for the purposes of any request for a withdrawal in accordance with PCT Rule 90*bis* which is not signed by all applicants. The submission of a separate power of attorney may be excused upon the request of another applicant where one or more inventors cannot be found or reached after diligent effort. Such a request must be accompanied by a statement explaining to the satisfaction of the Director the lack of the signature concerned:

[Paras. (f) and (g), 53 FR 47810, Nov. 28, 1988, effective Jan. 1, 1989; para. (a) amended, 60 FR 21438, May 2, 1995, effective June 1, 1995; paras. (b)-(g) revised, 68 FR 58991, Oct. 20, 2003, effective Jan. 1, 2004; para. (a)(2) revised, 68 FR 67805, Dec. 4, 2003, effective Jan. 1, 2004]

§ 1.422 When the inventor is dead.

In case of the death of the inventor, the legal representative (executor, administrator, etc.) of the deceased inventor may file an international application which designates the United States of America.

§ 1.423 When the inventor is insane or legally incapacitated.

In case an inventor is insane or otherwise legally incapacitated, the legal representative (guardian, conservator, etc.) of such inventor may file an international application which designates the United States of America.

§ 1.424 [Reserved]

[Removed and reserved, 68 FR 58991, Oct. 20, 2003, effective Jan. 1, 2004]

§ 1.425 [Reserved]

[Removed and reserved, 68 FR 58991, Oct. 20, 2003, effective Jan. 1, 2004]

THE INTERNATIONAL APPLICATION

§ 1.431 International application requirements.

(a) An international application shall contain, as specified in the Treaty and the Regulations, a Request, a description, one or more claims, an abstract, and one or more drawings (where required). (PCT Art. 3(2) and Section 207 of the Administrative Instructions.)

(b) An international filing date will be accorded by the United States Receiving Office, at the time of receipt of the international application, provided that:

(1) At least one applicant is a United States resident or national and the papers filed at the time of receipt of the international application so indicate (35 U.S.C. 361(a), PCT Art. 11(1)(i)).

(2) The international application is in the English language (35 U.S.C. 361(c), PCT Art. 11(1)(ii)).

(3) The international application contains at least the following elements (PCT Art. 11(1)(iii)):

(i) An indication that it is intended as an international application (PCT Rule 4.2);

(ii) The designation of at least one Contracting State of the International Patent Cooperation Union (§ 1.432);

(iii) The name of the applicant, as prescribed (note §§ 1.421-1.423);

(iv) A part which on the face of it appears to be a description; and

(v) A part which on the face of it appears to be a claim.

(c) Payment of the international filing fee (PCT Rule 15.2) and the transmittal and search fees (§ 1.445) may be made in full at the time the international application papers required by paragraph (b) of this section are deposited or within one month thereafter. The international filing, transmittal, and search fee payable is the international filing, transmittal, and search fee in effect on the receipt date of the international application.

(1)   If the international filing, transmittal and search fees are not paid within one month from the date of receipt of the international application and prior to the sending of a notice of deficiency which imposes a late payment fee, applicant will be notified and given one month within which to pay the deficient fees plus the late payment fee. Subject to paragraph (c)(2) of this section, the late payment fee will be equal to the greater of:

(i)   Fifty percent of the amount of the deficient fees; or

(ii)   An amount equal to the transmittal fee.

(2)   The late payment fee shall not exceed an amount equal to fifty percent of the international filing fee not taking into account any fee for each sheet of the international application in excess of thirty sheets (PCT Rule 16*bis*).

(3)   The one-month time limit set pursuant to paragraph (c) of this section to pay deficient fees may not be extended.

(d)   If the payment needed to cover the transmittal fee, the international filing fee, the search fee, and the late payment fee pursuant to paragraph (c) of this section is not timely made in accordance with PCT Rule 16*bis*.1(e), the Receiving Office will declare the international application withdrawn under PCT Article 14(3)(a).

[43 FR 20486, May 11, 1978; paras. (b), (c), (d) and (e), 50 FR 9383, Mar. 7, 1985, effective May 8, 1985; para. (d) amended, 52 FR 20047, May 28, 1987; paras. (b)(1), (b)(3)(ii), (c) and (d) amended, para. (e) deleted, 58 FR 4335, Jan. 14, 1993, effective May 1, 1993; paras. (c) and (d) revised, 63 FR 29614, June 1, 1998, effective July 1, 1998 (adopted as final, 63 FR 66040, Dec. 1, 1998); paras. (b)(3), (c) & (d) revised, 68 FR 58991, Oct. 20, 2003, effective Jan. 1, 2004; para. (c)(2) corrected, 68 FR 67805, Dec. 4, 2003]

§ 1.432 Designation of States by filing an international application.

The filing of an international application request shall constitute:

(a)   The designation of all Contracting States that are bound by the Treaty on the international filing date;

(b)   An indication that the international application is, in respect of each designated State to which PCT Article 43 or 44 applies, for the grant of every kind of protection which is available by way of the designation of that State; and.

(c)   An indication that the international application is, in respect of each designated State to which PCT Article 45(1) applies, for the grant of a regional patent and also, unless PCT Article 45(2) applies, a national patent.

[43 FR 20486, May 11, 1978; para. (b) amended 52 FR 20047, May 28, 1987; paras. (a), (b) amended and para. (c) added, 58 FR 4335, Jan. 14, 1993, effective May 1, 1993; paras. (b) and (c) revised, para. (d) added, 63 FR 29614, June 1, 1998, effective July 1, 1998 (adopted as final, 63 FR 66040, Dec. 1, 1998); revised, 68 FR 58991, Oct. 20, 2003, effective Jan. 1, 2004]

§ 1.433 Physical requirements of international application.

(a)   The international application and each of the documents that may be referred to in the check list of the Request (PCT Rule 3.3(a)(ii)) shall be filed in one copy only.

(b)   All sheets of the international application must be on A4 size paper (21.0 x 29.7 cm.).

(c)   Other physical requirements for international applications are set forth in PCT Rule 11 and sections 201-207 of the Administrative Instructions.

§ 1.434 The request.

(a)   The request shall be made on a standardized form (PCT Rules 3 and 4). Copies of printed Request forms are available from the United States Patent and Trademark Office. Letters requesting printed forms should be marked "Mail Stop PCT."

(b)   The Check List portion of the Request form should indicate each document accompanying the international application on filing.

(c)   All information, for example, addresses, names of States and dates, shall be indicated in the Request as required by PCT Rule 4 and Administrative Instructions 110 and 201.

(d)   For the purposes of the designation of the United States of America, an international application shall include:

(1)   The name of the inventor; and

(2) A reference to any prior-filed national application or international application designating the United States of America, if the benefit of the filing date for the prior-filed application is to be claimed.

(e) An international application may also include in the Request a declaration of the inventors as provided for in PCT Rule 4.17(iv).

[Para. (a) amended, 58 FR 4335, Jan. 14, 1993, effective May 1, 1993; para. (d) revised, 66 FR 16004, Mar. 22, 2001, effective Mar. 1, 2001; para. (d)(2) revised, 66 FR 67087, Dec. 28, 2001, effective Dec. 28, 2001; paras. (a) & (d)(2) revised, 68 FR 14332, Mar. 25, 2003, effective May 1, 2003; para. (d) revised, para (e) added, 68 FR 58991, Oct. 20, 2003, effective Jan. 1, 2004]

§ 1.435 The description.

(a) The application must meet the requirements as to the content and form of the description set forth in PCT Rules 5, 9, 10, and 11 and sections 204 and 208 of the Administrative Instructions.

(b) In international applications designating the United States the description must contain upon filing an indication of the best mode contemplated by the inventor for carrying out the claimed invention.

[Para. (a) revised, 63 FR 29614, June 1, 1998, effective July 1, 1998 (adopted as final, 63 FR 66040, Dec. 1, 1998)]

§ 1.436 The claims.

The requirements as to the content and format of claims are set forth in PCT Art. 6 and PCT Rules 6, 9, 10 and 11 and shall be adhered to. The number of the claims shall be reasonable, considering the nature of the invention claimed.

§ 1.437 The drawings.

(a) Drawings are required when they are necessary for the understanding of the invention (PCT Art. 7).

(b) The physical requirements for drawings are set forth in PCT Rule 11 and shall be adhered to.

[Revised, 72 FR 51559, Sept. 10, 2007, effective Sept. 10, 2007]

§ 1.438 The abstract.

(a) Requirements as to the content and form of the abstract are set forth in PCT Rule 8, and shall be adhered to.

(b) Lack of an abstract upon filing of an international application will not affect the granting of a filing date. However, failure to furnish an abstract within one month from the date of the notification by the Receiving Office will result in the international application being declared withdrawn.

FEES

§ 1.445 International application filing, processing and search fees.

(a) The following fees and charges for international applications are established by the Director under the authority of 35 U.S.C. 376:

(1) A transmittal fee (see 35 U.S.C. 361 (d) and PCT Rule 14) $240.00

(2) A search fee (see 35 U.S.C. 361 (d) and PCT Rule 16) $2,080.00

(3) A supplemental search fee when required, per additional invention $2,080.00

(4) A fee equivalent to the transmittal fee in paragraph (a)(1) of this section for transmittal of an international application to the International Bureau for processing in its capacity as a Receiving Office (PCT Rule 19.4).

(b) The international filing fee shall be as prescribed in PCT Rule 15.

[43 FR 20466, May 11, 1978; para. (a), 47 FR 41282, Sept. 17, 1982, effective Oct. 1, 1982; para. (a)(4) - (6), 50 FR 9384, Mar. 7, 1985, effective May 8, 1985; 50 FR 31826, Aug. 6, 1985, effective Oct. 5, 1985; para. (a) amended 52 FR 20047, May 28, 1987; paras. (a)(2) and (3), 54 FR 6893, Feb. 15, 1989, 54 FR 9432, March 7, 1989, effective Apr. 17, 1989; para. (a), 56 FR 65142, Dec. 13, 1991, effective Dec. 27, 1991; para. (a), 57 FR 38190, Aug. 21, 1992, effective Oct. 1, 1992; para. (a)(4) added, 58 FR 4335, Jan. 14, 1993, effective May 1, 1993; paras. (a)(1)-(3), 59 FR 43736, Aug. 25, 1994, effective Oct. 1, 1994; para. (a)(5) added, 60 FR 21438, May 2, 1995, effective June 1, 1995; para. (a) amended, 60 FR 41018, Aug. 11, 1995, effective Oct. 1, 1995; para. (a) amended, 61 FR 39585, July 30, 1996, effective Oct. 1, 1996; para. (a) amended, 62 FR 40450, July 29, 1997, effective Oct. 1, 1997; para. (a) revised, 63 FR 29614, June 1, 1998, effective July 1,1998 (adopted as final, 63 FR 66040, Dec. 1,

1998); para. (a) revised, 68 FR 14332, Mar. 25, 2003, effective May 1, 2003; revised, 68 FR 58991, Oct. 20, 2003, effective Jan. 1, 2004; para. (a)(2) revised, 70 FR 3880, Jan. 27, 2005, effective Dec. 8, 2004; paras. (a)(2) and (a)(3) revised, 72 FR 51559, Sept. 10, 2007, effective Nov. 9, 2007; paras. (a)(1) through (a)(3) revised, 73 FR 67754, Nov. 12, 2008, effective Jan. 12, 2009]

§ 1.446 Refund of international application filing and processing fees.

(a) Money paid for international application fees, where paid by actual mistake or in excess, such as a payment not required by law or treaty and its regulations, may be refunded. A mere change of purpose after the payment of a fee will not entitle a party to a refund of such fee. The Office will not refund amounts of twenty-five dollars or less unless a refund is specifically requested and will not notify the payor of such amounts. If the payor or party requesting a refund does not provide the banking information necessary for making refunds by electronic funds transfer, the Office may use the banking information provided on the payment instrument to make any refund by electronic funds transfer.

(b) Any request for refund under paragraph (a) of this section must be filed within two years from the date the fee was paid. If the Office charges a deposit account by an amount other than an amount specifically indicated in an authorization under § 1.25(b), any request for refund based upon such charge must be filed within two years from the date of the deposit account statement indicating such charge and include a copy of that deposit account statement. The time periods set forth in this paragraph are not extendable.

(c) Refund of the supplemental search fees will be made if such refund is determined to be warranted by the Director or the Director's designee acting under PCT Rule 40.2(c).

(d) The international and search fees will be refunded if no international filing date is accorded or if the application is withdrawn before transmittal of the record copy to the International Bureau (PCT Rules 15.6 and 16.2). The search fee will be refunded if the application is withdrawn before transmittal of the search copy to the International Searching Authority. The transmittal fee will not be refunded.

(e) The handling fee (§ 1.482(b)) will be refunded (PCT Rule 57.6) only if:

(1) The Demand is withdrawn before the Demand has been sent by the International Preliminary Examining Authority to the International Bureau, or

(2) The Demand is considered not to have been submitted (PCT Rule 54.4(a)).

[43 FR 20466, May 11, 1978; para. (b), 47 FR 41282, Sept. 17, 1982, effective Oct. 1, 1982; para.(b), 50 FR 9384, Mar. 7, 1985, effective May 8, 1985; 50 FR 31826, Aug. 6, 1985, effective Oct. 5, 1985; para. (d) amended and para. (e) added, 58 FR 4335, Jan. 14, 1993, effective May 1, 1993; para (a) revised and para. (b) added, 65 FR 54604, Sept. 8, 2000, effective Nov. 7, 2000; para. (c) revised, 68 FR 14332, Mar. 25, 2003, effective May 1, 2003]

PRIORITY

§ 1.451 The priority claim and priority document in an international application.

(a) The claim for priority must, subject to paragraph (d) of this section, be made on the Request (PCT Rule 4.10) in a manner complying with sections 110 and 115 of the Administrative Instructions.

(b) Whenever the priority of an earlier United States national application or international application filed with the United States Receiving Office is claimed in an international application, the applicant may request in a letter of transmittal accompanying the international application upon filing with the United States Receiving Office or in a separate letter filed in the United States Receiving Office not later than 16 months after the priority date, that the United States Patent and Trademark Office prepare a certified copy of the prior application for transmittal to the International Bureau (PCT Article 8 and PCT Rule 17). The fee for preparing a certified copy is set forth in § 1.19(b)(1).

(c) If a certified copy of the priority document is not submitted together with the international application on filing, or, if the priority application was filed in the United States and a request and appropriate payment for preparation of such a certified copy do not accompany the international application on filing or are not filed within 16 months of the priority date, the certified copy of the priority document must be furnished by the applicant to the International Bureau or to the United States Receiving Office within the time limit specified in PCT Rule 17.1(a).

(d)   The applicant may correct or add a priority claim in accordance with PCT Rule 26*bis*.1.

[43 FR 20466, May 11, 1978; 47 FR 40140, Sept. 10, 1982, effective Oct. 1, 1982; para. (b), 47 FR 41282, Sept. 17, 1982, effective Oct. 1, 1982; paras. (b) & (c), 50 FR 9384, Mar. 7, 1985, effective May 8, 1985; para. (b), 54 FR 6893, Feb. 15, 1989, effective Apr. 17, 1989; para. (a) amended, 58 FR 4335, Jan. 14, 1993, effective May 1, 1993; para. (a) revised, para. (d) added, 63 FR 29614, June 1, 1998, effective July 1, 1998 (adopted as final, 63 FR 66040, Dec. 1, 1998); para. (b) revised, 66 FR 16004, Mar. 22, 2001, effective Mar. 1, 2001]

§ 1.452   Restoration of right of priority.

(a)   If the international application has an international filing date which is later than the expiration of the priority period as defined by PCT Rule 2.4 but within two months from the expiration of the priority period, the right of priority in the international application may be restored upon request if the delay in filing the international application within the priority period was unintentional.

(b)   A request to restore the right of priority in an international application under paragraph (a) of this section must be filed not later than two months from the expiration of the priority period and must include:

(1)   A notice under PCT Rule 26*bis*.1(a) adding the priority claim, if the priority claim in respect of the earlier application is not contained in the international application;

(2)   The fee set forth in § 1.17(t); and

(3)   A statement that the delay in filing the international application within the priority period was unintentional. The Director may require additional information where there is a question whether the delay was unintentional.

(c)   If the applicant makes a request for early publication under PCT Article 21(2)(b), any requirement under paragraph (b) of this section filed after the technical preparations for international publication have been completed by the International Bureau shall be considered as not having been submitted in time.

(d)   Restoration of a right of priority to a prior application by the United States Receiving Office under this section, or by any other Receiving Office under the provisions of PCT Rule 26*bis*.3, will not entitle applicants to a right of priority in any application which has entered the national stage under 35 U.S.C. 371, or in any application filed under 35 U.S.C. 111(a) which claims benefit under 35 U.S.C. 120 and 365(c) to an international application in which the right to priority has been restored.

[Added, 72 FR 51559 Sept. 10, 2007, effective Nov. 9, 2007]

REPRESENTATION

§ 1.455   Representation in international applications.

(a)   Applicants of international applications may be represented by attorneys or agents registered to practice before the United States Patent and Trademark Office or by an applicant appointed as a common representative (PCT Art. 49, Rules 4.8 and 90 and § 11.9). If applicants have not appointed an attorney or agent or one of the applicants to represent them, and there is more than one applicant, the applicant first named in the request and who is entitled to file in the U.S. Receiving Office shall be considered to be the common representative of all the applicants. An attorney or agent having the right to practice before a national office with which an international application is filed and for which the United States is an International Searching Authority or International Preliminary Examining Authority may be appointed to represent the applicants in the international application before that authority. An attorney or agent may appoint an associate attorney or agent who shall also then be of record (PCT Rule 90.1(d)). The appointment of an attorney or agent, or of a common representative, revokes any earlier appointment unless otherwise indicated (PCT Rule 90.6(b) and (c)).

(b)   Appointment of an agent, attorney or common representative (PCT Rule 4.8) must be effected either in the Request form, signed by applicant, in the Demand form, signed by applicant, or in a separate power of attorney submitted either to the United States Receiving Office or to the International Bureau.

(c)   Powers of attorney and revocations thereof should be submitted to the United States Receiving Office until the issuance of the international search report.

(d)   The addressee for correspondence will be as indicated in section 108 of the Administrative Instructions.

[43 FR 20466, May 11, 1978; 50 FR 5171, Feb. 6, 1985, effective Mar. 8, 1985; para. (a) amended, 58 FR 4335, Jan. 14, 1993, effective May 1, 1993; para. (b) revised, 68 FR 58991, Oct. 20, 2003, effective Jan. 1, 2004; para. (a) revised, 69 FR 35427, June 24, 2004, effective July 26, 2004]

TRANSMITTAL OF RECORD COPY

§ 1.461 Procedures for transmittal of record copy to the International Bureau.

(a)   Transmittal of the record copy of the international application to the International Bureau shall be made by the United States Receiving Office or as provided by PCT Rule 19.4.

(b)   [Reserved]

(c)   No copy of an international application may be transmitted to the International Bureau, a foreign Designated Office, or other foreign authority by the United States Receiving Office or the applicant, unless the applicable requirements of part 5 of this chapter have been satisfied.

[43 FR 20466, May 11, 1978; paras. (a) and (b), 50 FR 9384, Mar. 7, 1985, effective May 8, 1985; para. (a) revised, 63 FR 29614, June 1, 1998, effective July 1, 1998 (adopted as final, 63 FR 66040, Dec. 1, 1998)]

TIMING

§ 1.465 Timing of application processing based on the priority date.

(a)   For the purpose of computing time limits under the Treaty, the priority date shall be defined as in PCT Art. 2(xi).

(b)   When a claimed priority date is corrected under PCT Rule 26bis.1(a), or a priority claim is added under PCT Rule 26bis.1(a), withdrawn under PCT Rule 90bis.3, or considered not to have been made under PCT Rule 26bis.2, the priority date for the purposes of computing any non-expired time limits will be the filing date of the earliest remaining priority claim under PCT Article 8 of the international application, or if none, the international filing date.

(c)   When corrections under PCT Art. 11(2), Art. 14(2) or PCT Rule 20.2(a) (i) or (iii) are timely submitted, and the date of receipt of such corrections falls later than one year from the claimed priority date

or dates, the Receiving Office shall proceed under PCT Rule 26bis.2.

[Paras. (b) and (c) revised, 63 FR 29614, June 1, 1998, effective July 1, 1998 (adopted as final, 63 FR 66040, Dec. 1, 1998); para. (b) revised, 72 FR 51559, Sept. 10, 2007, effective Sept. 10, 2007]

§ 1.468 Delays in meeting time limits.

Delays in meeting time limits during international processing of international applications may only be excused as provided in PCT Rule 82. For delays in meeting time limits in a national application, see § 1.137.

AMENDMENTS

§ 1.471 Corrections and amendments during international processing.

(a)   Except as otherwise provided in this paragraph, all corrections submitted to the United States Receiving Office or United States International Searching Authority must be in English, in the form of replacement sheets in compliance with PCT Rules 10 and 11, and accompanied by a letter that draws attention to the differences between the replaced sheets and the replacement sheets. Replacement sheets are not required for the deletion of lines of text, the correction of simple typographical errors, and one addition or change of not more than five words per sheet. These changes may be stated in a letter and, if appropriate, the United States Receiving Office will make the deletion or transfer the correction to the international application, provided that such corrections do not adversely affect the clarity and direct reproducibility of the application (PCT Rule 26.4). Amendments that do not comply with PCT Rules 10 and 11.1 to 11.13 may not be entered.

(b)   Amendments of claims submitted to the International Bureau shall be as prescribed by PCT Rule 46.

(c)   Corrections or additions to the Request of any declarations under PCT Rule 4.17 should be submitted to the International Bureau as prescribed by PCT Rule 26ter.

[Para. (a) revised, 63 FR 29614, June 1, 1998, effective July 1, 1998 (adopted as final, 63 FR 66040, Dec. 1, 1998);

para. (c) added, 66 FR 16004, Mar. 22, 2001, effective Mar. 1, 2001]

§ 1.472 Changes in person, name, or address of applicants and inventors.

All requests for a change in person, name or address of applicants and inventor should be sent to the United States Receiving Office until the time of issuance of the international search report. Thereafter requests for such changes should be submitted to the International Bureau.

[43 FR 20466, May 11, 1978; redesignated at 52 FR 20047, May 28, 1987]

UNITY OF INVENTION

§ 1.475 Unity of invention before the International Searching Authority, the International Preliminary Examining Authority and during the national stage.

(a) An international and a national stage application shall relate to one invention only or to a group of inventions so linked as to form a single general inventive concept ("requirement of unity of invention"). Where a group of inventions is claimed in an application, the requirement of unity of invention shall be fulfilled only when there is a technical relationship among those inventions involving one or more of the same or corresponding special technical features. The expression "special technical features" shall mean those technical features that define a contribution which each of the claimed inventions, considered as a whole, makes over the prior art.

(b) An international or a national stage application containing claims to different categories of invention will be considered to have unity of invention if the claims are drawn only to one of the following combinations of categories:

(1) A product and a process specially adapted for the manufacture of said product; or

(2) A product and process of use of said product; or

(3) A product, a process specially adapted for the manufacture of the said product, and a use of the said product; or

(4) A process and an apparatus or means specifically designed for carrying out the said process; or

(5) A product, a process specially adapted for the manufacture of the said product, and an apparatus or means specifically designed for carrying out the said process.

(c) If an application contains claims to more or less than one of the combinations of categories of invention set forth in paragraph (b) of this section, unity of invention might not be present.

(d) If multiple products, processes of manufacture or uses are claimed, the first invention of the category first mentioned in the claims of the application and the first recited invention of each of the other categories related thereto will be considered as the main invention in the claims, see PCT Article 17(3)(a) and § 1.476(c).

(e) The determination whether a group of inventions is so linked as to form a single general inventive concept shall be made without regard to whether the inventions are claimed in separate claims or as alternatives within a single claim.

[Added 52 FR 20047, May 28, 1987, effective July 1, 1987; paras. (a) - (e) amended and para. (f) deleted, 58 FR 4335, Jan. 14, 1993, effective May 1, 1993]

§ 1.476 Determination of unity of invention before the International Searching Authority.

(a) Before establishing the international search report, the International Searching Authority will determine whether the international application complies with the requirement of unity of invention as set forth in § 1.475.

(b) If the International Searching Authority considers that the international application does not comply with the requirement of unity of invention, it shall inform the applicant accordingly and invite the payment of additional fees (note § 1.445 and PCT Art. 17(3)(a) and PCT Rule 40). The applicant will be given a time period in accordance with PCT Rule 40.3 to pay the additional fees due.

(c) In the case of non-compliance with unity of invention and where no additional fees are paid, the international search will be performed on the invention first mentioned ("main invention") in the claims.

(d) Lack of unity of invention may be directly evident before considering the claims in relation to any prior art, or after taking the prior art into consideration, as where a document discovered during the search shows the invention claimed in a generic or linking claim lacks novelty or is clearly obvious, leaving two or more claims joined thereby without a common inventive concept. In such a case the International Searching Authority may raise the objection of lack of unity of invention.

[43 FR 20466, May 11, 1978; redesignated and amended at 52 FR 20047, May 28, 1987; para. (a) amended, 58 FR 4335, Jan. 14, 1993, effective May 1, 1993]

§ 1.477 Protest to lack of unity of invention before the International Searching Authority.

(a)   If the applicant disagrees with the holding of lack of unity of invention by the International Searching Authority, additional fees may be paid under protest, accompanied by a request for refund and a statement setting forth reasons for disagreement or why the required additional fees are considered excessive, or both (PCT Rule 40.2(c)).

(b)   Protest under paragraph (a) of this section will be examined by the Director or the Director's designee. In the event that the applicant's protest is determined to be justified, the additional fees or a portion thereof will be refunded.

(c)   An applicant who desires that a copy of the protest and the decision thereon accompany the international search report when forwarded to the Designated Offices may notify the International Searching Authority to that effect any time prior to the issuance of the international search report. Thereafter, such notification should be directed to the International Bureau (PCT Rule 40.2(c)).

[43 FR 20466, May 11, 1978; redesignated and amended at 52 FR 20047, May 28, 1987; para. (b) revised, 68 FR 14332, Mar. 25, 2003, effective May 1, 2003]

INTERNATIONAL PRELIMINARY EXAMINATION

§ 1.480 Demand for international preliminary examination.

(a)   On the filing of a proper Demand in an application for which the United States International Preliminary Examining Authority is competent and for which the fees have been paid, the international

application shall be the subject of an international preliminary examination. The preliminary examination fee (§ 1.482(a)(1)) and the handling fee (§ 1.482(b)) shall be due within the applicable time limit set forth in PCT Rule 57.3.

(b)   The Demand shall be made on a standardized form (PCT Rule 53). Copies of the printed Demand forms are available from the United States Patent and Trademark Office. Letters requesting printed Demand forms should be marked "Mail Stop PCT."

(c)   Withdrawal of a proper Demand prior to the start of the international preliminary examination will entitle applicant to a refund of the preliminary examination fee minus the amount of the transmittal fee set forth in § 1.445(a)(1).

(d)   The filing of a Demand shall constitute the election of all Contracting States which are designated and are bound by Chapter II of the Treaty on the international filing date (PCT Rule 53.7).

(e)   Any Demand filed after the expiration of the applicable time limit set forth in PCT Rule 54*bis*.1(a) shall be considered as if it had not been submitted (PCT Rule 54*bis*.1(b)).

[52 FR 20048, May 28, 1987; para. (d), 53 FR 47810, Nov. 28, 1988, effective Jan. 1, 1989; para. (b) amended, 58 FR 4335, Jan. 14, 1993, effective May 1, 1993; para. (a) revised, 63 FR 29614, June 1, 1998, effective July 1, 1998 (adopted as final, 63 FR 66040, Dec. 1, 1998); para. (c) removed and para. (d) redesignated as para. (c), 67 FR 520, Jan. 4, 2002, effective Apr. 1, 2002; para. (b) revised, 68 FR 14332, Mar. 25, 2003, effective May 1, 2003; para. (a) revised, paras. (d) & (e) added, 68 FR 58991, Oct. 20, 2003, effective Jan. 1, 2004]

§ 1.481 Payment of international preliminary examination fees.

(a)   The handling and preliminary examination fees shall be paid within the time period set in PCT Rule 57.3. The handling fee or preliminary examination fee payable is the handling fee or preliminary examination fee in effect on the date of payment.

(1)   If the handling and preliminary examination fees are not paid within the time period set in PCT Rule 57.3, applicant will be notified and given one month within which to pay the deficient fees plus a late payment fee equal to the greater of:

(i)   Fifty percent of the amount of the deficient fees, but not exceeding an amount equal to double the handling fee; or

(ii)   An amount equal to the handling fee (PCT Rule 58*bis*.2).

(2)   The one-month time limit set in this paragraph to pay deficient fees may not be extended.

(b)   If the payment needed to cover the handling and preliminary examination fees, pursuant to paragraph (a) of this section, is not timely made in accordance with PCT Rule 58*bis*.1(d), the United States International Preliminary Examination Authority will declare the Demand to be considered as if it had not been submitted.

[63 FR 29614, June 1, 1998, effective July 1, 1998 (adopted as final, 63 FR 66040, Dec. 1, 1998); para. (a) revised, 68 FR 58991, Oct. 20, 2003, effective Jan. 1, 2004]

§ 1.482   International preliminary examination fees.

(a)   The following fees and charges for international preliminary examination are established by the Director under the authority of 35 U.S.C. 376:

(1)   The following preliminary examination fee is due on filing the Demand:

(i)   If an international search fee as set forth in § 1.445(a)(2) has been paid on the international application to the United States Patent and Trademark Office as an International Searching Authority $600.00

(ii)   If the International Searching Authority for the international application was an authority other than the United States Patent and Trademark Office $750.00

(2)   An additional preliminary examination fee when required, per additional invention . $600.00

(b)   The handling fee is due on filing the Demand and shall be as prescribed in PCT Rule 57.

[52 FR 20048, May 28, 1987; para. (a), 54 FR 6893, Feb. 15, 1989, effective Apr. 17, 1989; para. (a), 56 FR 65142, Dec. 13, 1991, effective Dec. 27, 1991; paras. (a)(1) and (a)(2)(ii), 57 FR 38190, Aug. 21, 1992, effective Oct. 1, 1992; paras. (a)(2)(i) and (b) amended, 58 FR 4335, Jan. 14, 1993, effective May 1, 1993; paras. (a)(1) and (a)(2)(ii), 59 FR 43736, Aug. 25, 1994, effective Oct. 1, 1994; paras. (a)(1)(i), (a)(1)(ii), & (a)(2)(ii) amended, 60 FR 41018, Aug. 11, 1995, effective Oct. 1, 1995; paras. (a)(1)(i), (a)(1)(ii), and (a)(2)(ii) amended, 61 FR 39585, July 30,

1996, effective Oct. 1, 1996; paras. (a)(1)(i), (a)(1)(ii), and (a)(2)(ii) amended, 62 FR 40450, July 29, 1997, effective Oct. 1, 1997; para. (a) revised, 68 FR 14332, Mar. 25, 2003, effective May 1, 2003; revised, 68 FR 58991, Oct. 20, 2003, effective Jan. 1, 2004; para. (b) & (e)-(g) revised, paras. (h) & (i) added, 68 FR 58991, Oct. 20, 2003, effective Jan. 1, 2004]

§ 1.484   Conduct of international preliminary examination.

(a)   An international preliminary examination will be conducted to formulate a non-binding opinion as to whether the claimed invention has novelty, involves an inventive step (is non-obvious) and is industrially applicable.

(b)   International preliminary examination will begin in accordance with PCT Rule 69.1.

(c)   No international preliminary examination will be conducted on inventions not previously searched by an International Searching Authority.

(d)   The International Preliminary Examining Authority will establish a written opinion if any defect exists or if the claimed invention lacks novelty, inventive step or industrial applicability and will set a non-extendable time limit in the written opinion for the applicant to reply.

(e)   The written opinion established by the International Searching Authority under PCT Rule 43*bis*.1 shall be considered to be a written opinion of the United States International Preliminary Examining Authority for the purposes of paragraph (d) of this section.

(f)   The International Preliminary Examining Authority may establish further written opinions under paragraph (d) of this section.

(g)   If no written opinion under paragraph (d) of this section is necessary, or if no further written opinion under paragraph (f) of this section is to be established, or after any written opinion and the reply thereto or the expiration of the time limit for reply to such written opinion, an international preliminary examination report will be established by the International Preliminary Examining Authority. One copy will be submitted to the International Bureau and one copy will be submitted to the applicant.

(h)   An applicant will be permitted a personal or telephone interview with the examiner, which may be requested after the filing of a Demand, and must be conducted during the period between the establishment of the written opinion and the establishment of the international preliminary examination report. Additional interviews may be conducted where the examiner determines that such additional interviews may be helpful to advancing the international preliminary examination procedure. A summary of any such personal or telephone interview must be filed by the applicant or, if not filed by applicant be made of record in the file by the examiner.

(i)   If the application whose priority is claimed in the international application is in a language other than English, the United States International Preliminary Examining Authority may, where the validity of the priority claim is relevant for the formulation of the opinion referred to in Article 33(1), invite the applicant to furnish an English translation of the priority document within two months from the date of the invitation. If the translation is not furnished within that time limit, the international preliminary report may be established as if the priority had not been claimed.

[52 FR 20049, May 28, 1987; para. (b) amended, 58 FR 4335, Jan. 14, 1993, effective May 1, 1993; paras. (d)-(f) revised, 62 FR 53131, Oct. 10, 1997, effective Dec. 1, 1997; para. (b) revised, 63 FR 29614, June 1, 1998, effective July 1, 1998 (adopted as final, 63 FR 66040, Dec. 1, 1998); para. (g) added, 66 FR 16004, Mar. 22, 2001, effective Mar. 1, 2001; para. (b) & (e)-(g) revised, paras. (h) & (i) added, 68 FR 58991, Oct. 20, 2003, effective Jan. 1, 2004]

§ 1.485   Amendments by applicant during international preliminary examination.

The applicant may make amendments at the time of filing the Demand. The applicant may also make amendments within the time limit set by the International Preliminary Examining Authority for reply to any notification under § 1.484(b) or to any written opinion. Any such amendments must be made in accordance with PCT Rule 66.8.

[Added 52 FR 20049, May 28, 1987; amended, 58 FR 4335, Jan. 14, 1993, effective May 1, 1993; para. (a) revised, 62 FR 53131, Oct. 10, 1997, effective Dec. 1, 1997; para. (a) revised, 63 FR 29614, June 1, 1998, effective July 1, 1998 (adopted as final, 63 FR 66040, Dec. 1, 1998); amended, 74 FR 31372, July 1, 2009, effective July 1, 2009]

§ 1.488   Determination of unity of invention before the International Preliminary Examining Authority.

(a)   Before establishing any written opinion or the international preliminary examination report, the International Preliminary Examining Authority will determine whether the international application complies with the requirement of unity of invention as set forth in § 1.475.

(b)   If the International Preliminary Examining Authority considers that the international application does not comply with the requirement of unity of invention, it may:

(1)   Issue a written opinion and/or an international preliminary examination report, in respect of the entire international application and indicate that unity of invention is lacking and specify the reasons therefor without extending an invitation to restrict or pay additional fees. No international preliminary examination will be conducted on inventions not previously searched by an International Searching Authority.

(2)   Invite the applicant to restrict the claims or pay additional fees, pointing out the categories of invention found, within a set time limit which will not be extended. No international preliminary examination will be conducted on inventions not previously searched by an International Searching Authority, or

(3)   If applicant fails to restrict the claims or pay additional fees within the time limit set for reply, the International Preliminary Examining Authority will issue a written opinion and/or establish an international preliminary examination report on the main invention and shall indicate the relevant facts in the said report. In case of any doubt as to which invention is the main invention, the invention first mentioned in the claims and previously searched by an International Searching Authority shall be considered the main invention.

(c)   Lack of unity of invention may be directly evident before considering the claims in relation to any prior art, or after taking the prior art into consideration, as where a document discovered during the search shows the invention claimed in a generic or linking claim lacks novelty or is clearly obvious, leaving two or more claims joined thereby without a common inventive concept. In such a case the

International Preliminary Examining Authority may raise the objection of lack of unity of invention.

[52 FR 20049, May 28, 1987; para. (a) amended, 58 FR 4335, Jan. 14, 1993, effective May 1, 1993; para. (b)(3) revised, 62 FR 53131, Oct. 10, 1997, effective Dec. 1, 1997]

§ 1.489 Protest to lack of unity of invention before the International Preliminary Examining Authority.

(a) If the applicant disagrees with the holding of lack of unity of invention by the International Preliminary Examining Authority, additional fees may be paid under protest, accompanied by a request for refund and a statement setting forth reasons for disagreement or why the required additional fees are considered excessive, or both.

(b) Protest under paragraph (a) of this section will be examined by the Director or the Director's designee. In the event that the applicant's protest is determined to be justified, the additional fees or a portion thereof will be refunded.

(c) An applicant who desires that a copy of the protest and the decision thereon accompany the international preliminary examination report when forwarded to the Elected Offices, may notify the International Preliminary Examining Authority to that effect any time prior to the issuance of the international preliminary examination report. Thereafter, such notification should be directed to the International Bureau.

[Added 52 FR 20050, May 28, 1987, effective July 1, 1987; para. (b) revised, 68 FR 14332, Mar. 25, 2003, effective May 1, 2003]

NATIONAL STAGE

§ 1.491 National stage commencement and entry.

(a) Subject to 35 U.S.C. 371(f), the national stage shall commence with the expiration of the applicable time limit under PCT Article 22(1) or (2), or under PCT Article 39(1)(a).

(b) An international application enters the national stage when the applicant has filed the documents and fees required by 35 U.S.C. 371(c) within the period set in § 1.495.

[Added, 52 FR 20050, May 28, 1987; revised, 66 FR 45775, Aug. 30, 2001; revised, 67 FR 520, Jan. 4, 2002, effective Apr. 1, 2002]

§ 1.492 National stage fees.

The following fees and charges are established for international applications entering the national stage under 35 U.S.C. 371:

(a) The basic national fee for an international application entering the national stage under 35 U.S.C. 371 if the basic national fee was not paid before December 8, 2004:

By a small entity (§ 1.27(a)) ... $165.00

By other than a small entity $330.00

(b) Search fee for an international application entering the national stage under 35 U.S.C. 371 if the basic national fee was not paid before December 8, 2004:

(1) If an international preliminary examination report on the international application prepared by the United States International Preliminary Examining Authority or a written opinion on the international application prepared by the United States International Searching Authority states that the criteria of novelty, inventive step (non-obviousness), and industrial applicability, as defined in PCT Article 33 (1) to (4) have been satisfied for all of the claims presented in the application entering the national stage:

By a small entity (§ 1.27(a)) $0.00

By other than a small entity $0.00

(2) If the search fee as set forth in § 1.445(a)(2) has been paid on the international application to the United States Patent and Trademark Office as an International Searching Authority:

By a small entity (§ 1.27(a)) $50.00

By other than a small entity $100.00

(3) If an international search report on the international application has been prepared by an International Searching Authority other than the United States International Searching Authority and is provided, or has been previously communicated by the International Bureau, to the Office:

By a small entity (§ 1.27(a)) ... $215.00

By other than a small entity $430.00

(4) In all situations not provided for in paragraphs (b)(1), (b)(2), or (b)(3) of this section:

By a small entity (§ 1.27(a)) ... $270.00

By other than a small entity $540.00

(c) The examination fee for an international application entering the national stage under 35 U.S.C. 371 if the basic national fee was not paid before December 8, 2004:

(1) If an international preliminary examination report on the international application prepared by the United States International Preliminary Examining Authority or a written opinion on the international application prepared by the United States International Searching Authority states that the criteria of novelty, inventive step (non-obviousness), and industrial applicability, as defined in PCT Article 33(1) to (4) have been satisfied for all of the claims presented in the application entering the national stage:

By a small entity (§ 1.27(a)) $0.00

By other than a small entity $0.00

(2) In all situations not provided for in paragraph (c)(1) of this section:

By a small entity (§ 1.27(a)) . . . $110.00

By other than a small entity $220.00

(d) In addition to the basic national fee, for filing or on later presentation at any other time of each claim in independent form in excess of 3:

By a small entity (§ 1.27(a)) . . . $110.00

By other than a small entity $220.00

(e) In addition to the basic national fee, for filing or on later presentation at any other time of each claim (whether dependent or independent) in excess of 20 (note that §1.75(c) indicates how multiple dependent claims are considered for fee calculation purposes):

By a small entity (§ 1.27(a)) $26.00

By other than a small entity $52.00

(f) In addition to the basic national fee, if the application contains, or is amended to contain, a multiple dependent claim, per application:

By a small entity (§ 1.27(a)) . . . $195.00

By other than a small entity $390.00

(g) If the excess claims fees required by paragraphs (d) and (e) of this section and multiple dependent claim fee required by paragraph (f) of this section are not paid with the basic national fee or on later presentation of the claims for which excess claims or multiple dependent claim fees are due, the fees required by paragraphs (d), (e), and (f) of this section must be paid or the claims canceled by amendment prior to the expiration of the time period set for reply by the Office in any notice of fee deficiency in order to avoid abandonment.

(h) Surcharge for filing any of the search fee, the examination fee, or the oath or declaration after the date of the commencement of the national stage (§ 1.491(a)) pursuant to § 1.495(c)

By a small entity (§ 1.27(a)). $65.00

By other than a small entity $130.00

(i) For filing an English translation of an international application or any annexes to an international preliminary examination report later than thirty months after the priority date (§§ 1.495(c) and (e)). . . . .$130.00.

(j) Application size fee for any international application for which the basic national fee was not paid before December 8, 2004, the specification and drawings of which exceed 100 sheets of paper, for each additional 50 sheets or fraction thereof:

By a small entity (§ 1.27(a)). . . . $135.00

By other than a small entity $270.00

[52 FR 20050, May 28, 1987, effective July 1, 1987; paras. (a)(1) - (3), (b), (d)- (f), 54 FR 6893, Feb. 15, 1989, effective Apr. 17, 1989; para. (a)(5) added, 56 FR 65142, Dec. 13, 1991, effective Dec. 16, 1991; revised, 56 FR 65142, Dec. 13, 1991, effective Dec. 16, 1991; paras. (a)(1)-(a)(3), (a)(5) and (b)-(d), 57 FR 38190, Aug. 21, 1992, effective Oct. 1, 1992; para. (e) amended, 58 FR 4335, Jan. 14, 1993, effective May 1, 1993; paras. (a), (b) and (d), 59 FR 43736, Aug. 25, 1994, effective Oct. 1, 1994; paras. (a), (b), & (d) amended, 60 FR 41018, Aug. 11, 1995, effective, Oct. 1, 1995; paras. (a), (b), & (d) amended, 61 FR 39585, July 30, 1996, effective Oct. 1, 1996; paras. (a), (b), & (d) amended, 62 FR 40450, July 29, 1997, effective Oct. 1, 1997; para. (g) added, 62 FR 53131, Oct. 10, 1997, effective Dec. 1, 1997; paras. (a)-(d) revised, 63 FR 67578, Dec. 8, 1998, effective Nov. 10, 1998; para. (a)(2) revised, 64 FR 67774, Dec. 3, 1999, effective Dec. 29, 1999; paras. (a), (b) and (d) revised, 65 FR 49193, Aug. 11, 2000, effective Oct. 1, 2000; paras. (a)-(e) revised, 65 FR 78958, Dec. 18, 2000; paras. (a)(1)-(a)(3), (a)(5), (b) and (d) revised, 66 FR 39447, July 31, 2001, effective Oct. 1, 2001; paras. (e) and (f) revised, 67 FR 520, Jan. 4, 2002, effective Apr. 1, 2002; paras. (a)(1) through (a)(3), and (a)(5) revised, 67 FR 70847, Nov. 27, 2002, effective Jan. 1, 2003; paras. (a)(1) through (a)(3), (a)(5), (b), and (d) revised, 68 FR 41532, July 14, 2003, effective Oct. 1, 2003; paras. (a)(1) through (a)(3), (a)(5), (b) and (d) revised, 69 F R 52604, Aug. 27, 2004, effective Oct. 1, 2004; revised, 70 FR 3880, Jan. 27, 2005, effective Dec. 8, 2004; paras. (b) and (c) revised, 70 FR 5053, Feb. 1, 2005, effective Feb. 1,

2005; paras. (h) and (j) revised, 70 FR 30360, May 26, 2005, effective July 1, 2005; paras. (b) and (c) revised, 70 FR 35375, June 20, 2005, effective July 1, 2005; paras. (a), (b)(2) through (b)(4), (c)(2), (d) through (f), and (j) revised, 72 FR 46899, Aug. 22, 2007, effective Sept. 30, 2007; paras. (b)(2) through (b)(4) corrected, 72 FR 55055, Sept. 28, 2007, effective Sept. 30, 2007; paras. (a), (b)(3), (b)(4), (c)(2), (d) through (f) and (j) revised, 73 FR 47534, Aug. 14, 2008, effective Oct. 2, 2008]

§ 1.494 [Reserved]

[Added 52 FR 20050, May 28, 1987; paras. (a) - (d) and (g) amended and para. (h) deleted, 58 FR 4335, Jan. 14, 1993, effective May 1, 1993; para. (c) revised, 62 FR 53131, Oct. 10, 1997, effective Dec. 1, 1997; para (c) revised, 63 FR 29614, June 1, 1998, effective, July 1, 1998 (adopted as final, 63 FR 66040, Dec. 1, 1998); para (f) revised, 65 FR 57024, Sept. 20, 2000, effective Nov. 29, 2000; para. (c)(2) revised, 66 FR 16004, Mar. 22, 2001, effective Mar. 1, 2000; para. (c)(2) corrected, 66 FR 28053, May 22, 2001, effective Mar. 22, 2001; removed and reserved, 67 FR 520, Jan. 4, 2002, effective Apr. 1, 2002]

§ 1.495 Entering the national stage in the United States of America.

(a) The applicant in an international application must fulfill the requirements of 35 U.S.C. 371 within the time periods set forth in paragraphs (b) and (c) of this section in order to prevent the abandonment of the international application as to the United States of America. The thirty-month time period set forth in paragraphs (b), (c), (d), (e) and (h) of this section may not be extended. International applications for which those requirements are timely fulfilled will enter the national stage and obtain an examination as to the patentability of the invention in the United States of America.

(b) To avoid abandonment of the application, the applicant shall furnish to the United States Patent and Trademark Office not later than the expiration of thirty months from the priority date:

(1) A copy of the international application, unless it has been previously communicated by the International Bureau or unless it was originally filed in the United States Patent and Trademark Office; and

(2) The basic national fee (see § 1.492(a)).

(c)(1) If applicant complies with paragraph (b) of this section before expiration of thirty months from the priority date, the Office will notify the applicant if he or she has omitted any of:

(i) A translation of the international application, as filed, into the English language, if it was originally filed in another language and if any English language translation of the publication of the international application previously submitted under 35 U.S.C. 154(d) (§ 1.417) is not also a translation of the international application as filed (35 U.S.C. 371(c)(2));

(ii) The oath or declaration of the inventor (35 U.S.C. 371(c)(4) and § 1.497), if a declaration of inventorship in compliance with § 1.497 has not been previously submitted in the international application under PCT Rule 4.17(iv) within the time limits provided for in PCT Rule 26ter.1;

(iii) The search fee set forth in § 1.492(b);

(iv) The examination fee set forth in § 1.492(c); and

(v) Any application size fee required by § 1.492(j);

(2) A notice under paragraph (c)(1) of this section will set a time period within which applicant must provide any omitted translation, oath or declaration of the inventor, search fee set forth in § 1.492(b), examination fee set forth in § 1.492(c), and any application size fee required by § 1.492(j) in order to avoid abandonment of the application.

(3) The payment of the processing fee set forth in § 1.492(i) is required for acceptance of an English translation later than the expiration of thirty months after the priority date. The payment of the surcharge set forth in § 1.492(h) is required for acceptance of any of the search fee, the examination fee, or the oath or declaration of the inventor after the date of the commencement of the national stage (§ 1.491(a)).

(4) A "Sequence Listing" need not be translated if the "Sequence Listing" complies with PCT Rule 12.1(d) and the description complies with PCT Rule 5.2(b).

(d) A copy of any amendments to the claims made under PCT Article 19, and a translation of those amendments into English, if they were made in another language, must be furnished not later than the expiration of thirty months from the priority date. Amendments under PCT Article 19 which are not received by the expiration of thirty months from the priority date will be considered to be canceled.

(e)   A translation into English of any annexes to an international preliminary examination report (if applicable), if the annexes were made in another language, must be furnished not later than the expiration of thirty months from the priority date. Translations of the annexes which are not received by the expiration of thirty months from the priority date may be submitted within any period set pursuant to paragraph (c) of this section accompanied by the processing fee set forth in § 1.492(f). Annexes for which translations are not timely received will be considered canceled.

(f)   Verification of the translation of the international application or any other document pertaining to an international application may be required where it is considered necessary, if the international application or other document was filed in a language other than English.

(g)   The documents and fees submitted under paragraphs (b) and (c) of this section must be clearly identified as a submission to enter the national stage under 35 U.S.C. 371. Otherwise, the submission will be considered as being made under 35 U.S.C. 111(a).

(h)   An international application becomes abandoned as to the United States thirty months from the priority date if the requirements of paragraph (b) of this section have not been complied with within thirty months from the priority date. If the requirements of paragraph (b) of this section are complied with within thirty months from the priority date but either of any required translation of the international application as filed or the oath or declaration are not timely filed, an international application will become abandoned as to the United States upon expiration of the time period set pursuant to paragraph (c) of this section.

[Added 52 FR 20051, May 28, 1987, effective July 1, 1987; paras. (a) -(e) & (h) amended and para. (i) deleted, 58 FR 4335, Jan. 14, 1993, effective May 1, 1993; para. (c) revised, 62 FR 53131, Oct. 10, 1997, effective Dec. 1, 1997; para (c) revised, 63 FR 29614, June 1, 1998, effective July 1, 1998 (adopted as final, 63 FR 66040, Dec. 1, 1998), para. (g) revised, 65 FR 57024, Sept. 20, 2000, effective Nov. 29, 2000; para. (c)(2) revised, 66 FR 16004, Mar. 22, 2001, effective Mar. 1, 2001 para. (c)(2) corrected, 66 FR 28053, May 22, 2001, effective Mar. 22, 2001; heading and paras. (a)-(e) and (h) revised, 67 FR 520, Jan. 4, 2002, effective Apr. 1, 2002; paras. (c) & (g) revised, 68 FR 70996, Dec. 22, 2003, effective Jan. 21, 2004; para. (c) revised, 70 FR 3880, Jan. 27, 2005, effective Dec. 8, 2004; paras. (c)(1)(i) and (c)(3) revised, 70 FR 30360, May 26, 2005, effective July 1, 2005; para. (g) revised, 72 FR 46716, Aug. 21, 2007 (implementation enjoined and never became effective); para. (g) revised, 74 FR 52686, Oct. 14, 2009, effective Oct. 14, 2009 (to remove changes made by the final rules in 72 FR 46716 from the CFR)]

§ 1.496 Examination of international applications in the national stage.

(a)   International applications which have complied with the requirements of 35 U.S.C. 371(c) will be taken up for action based on the date on which such requirements were met. However, unless an express request for early processing has been filed under 35 U.S.C. 371(f), no action may be taken prior to one month after entry into the national stage.

(b)   National stage applications having paid therein the search fee as set forth in § 1.492(b)(1) and the examination fee as set forth in § 1.492(c)(1) may be amended subsequent to the date of entry into the national stage only to the extent necessary to eliminate objections as to form or to cancel rejected claims. Such national stage applications will be advanced out of turn for examination.

[Added 52 FR 20051, May 28, 1987, effective July 1, 1987; para. (b) revised, 70 FR 5053, Feb. 1, 2005, effective Feb. 1, 2005; para. (b) revised, 70 FR 35375, June 20, 2005, effective July 1, 2005]

§ 1.497 Oath or declaration under 35 U.S.C. 371(c)(4).

(a)   When an applicant of an international application desires to enter the national stage under 35 U.S.C. 371 pursuant to § 1.495, and a declaration in compliance with this section has not been previously submitted in the international application under PCT Rule 4.17(iv) within the time limits provided for in PCT Rule 26ter.1, he or she must file an oath or declaration that:

(1)   Is executed in accordance with either §§ 1.66 or 1.68;

(2)   Identifies the specification to which it is directed;

(3)   Identifies each inventor and the country of citizenship of each inventor; and

(4)   States that the person making the oath or declaration believes the named inventor or inventors to be the original and first inventor or inventors of the

subject matter which is claimed and for which a patent is sought.

(b)(1) The oath or declaration must be made by all of the actual inventors except as provided for in §§ 1.42, 1.43 or 1.47.

(2) If the person making the oath or declaration or any supplemental oath or declaration is not the inventor (§§ 1.42, 1.43, or § 1.47), the oath or declaration shall state the relationship of the person to the inventor, and, upon information and belief, the facts which the inventor would have been required to state. If the person signing the oath or declaration is the legal representative of a deceased inventor, the oath or declaration shall also state that the person is a legal representative and the citizenship, residence and mailing address of the legal representative.

(c) Subject to paragraph (f) of this section, if the oath or declaration meets the requirements of paragraphs (a) and (b) of this section, the oath or declaration will be accepted as complying with 35 U.S.C. 371(c)(4) and § 1.495(c). However, if the oath or declaration does not also meet the requirements of § 1.63, a supplemental oath or declaration in compliance with § 1.63 or an application data sheet will be required in accordance with § 1.67.

(d) If the oath or declaration filed pursuant to 35 U.S.C. 371(c)(4) and this section names an inventive entity different from the inventive entity set forth in the international application, or if a change to the inventive entity has been effected under PCT Rule 92bis subsequent to the execution of any oath or declaration which was filed in the application under PCT Rule 4.17(iv) or this section and the inventive entity thus changed is different from the inventive entity identified in any such oath or declaration, applicant must submit:

(1) A statement from each person being added as an inventor and from each person being deleted as an inventor that any error in inventorship in the international application occurred without deceptive intention on his or her part;

(2) The processing fee set forth in § 1.17(i); and

(3) If an assignment has been executed by any of the original named inventors, the written consent of the assignee (see § 3.73(b) of this chapter); and

(4) Any new oath or declaration required by paragraph (f) of this section.

(e) The Office may require such other information as may be deemed appropriate under the particular circumstances surrounding the correction of inventorship.

(f) A new oath or declaration in accordance with this section must be filed to satisfy 35 U.S.C. 371(c)(4) if the declaration was filed under PCT Rule 4.17(iv), and:

(1) There was a change in the international filing date pursuant to PCT Rule 20.5(c) after the declaration was executed; or

(2) A change in the inventive entity was effected under PCT Rule 92bis after the declaration was executed and no declaration which sets forth and is executed by the inventive entity as so changed has been filed in the application.

(g) If a priority claim has been corrected or added pursuant to PCT Rule 26bis during the international stage after the declaration of inventorship was executed in the international application under PCT Rule 4.17(iv), applicant will be required to submit either a new oath or declaration or an application data sheet as set forth in § 1.76 correctly identifying the application upon which priority is claimed.

[Added 52 FR 20052, May 28, 1987, effective July 1, 1987; paras. (a) and (b) revised and para. (c) added, 61 FR 42790, Aug. 19, 1996, effective Sept. 23, 1996; para. (b)(2) revised and paras. (d) and (e) added, 65 FR 54604, Sept. 8, 2000, effective Nov. 7, 2000; paras. (a), (c), and (d) revised and paras. (f) and (g) added, 66 FR 16004, Mar. 22, 2001, effective Mar. 1, 2001; para. (a)(1) corrected, 66 FR 28053, May 22, 2001, effective Mar. 22, 2001; paras. (a), (c), (d), and (f) revised, 67 FR 520, Jan. 4, 2002, effective Apr. 1, 2002; para. (c) corrected, 67 FR 6075, Feb. 8, 2002; para. (f)(1), revised 72 FR 51559, Sept. 10, 2007, effective Sept. 10, 2007]

§ 1.499 Unity of invention during the national stage.

If the examiner finds that a national stage application lacks unity of invention under § 1.475, the examiner may in an Office action require the applicant in the response to that action to elect the invention to which the claims shall be restricted. Such requirement may be made before any action on the merits but may be made at any time before the final action at the discretion of the examiner. Review of any such requirement is provided under §§ 1.143 and 1.144.

[Added 52 FR 20052, May 28, 1987, effective July 1, 1987; amended, 58 FR 4335, Jan. 14, 1993, effective May 1, 1993]

Subpart D — *Ex Parte* Reexamination of Patents

CITATION OF PRIOR ART

§ 1.501 Citation of prior art in patent files.

(a) At any time during the period of enforceability of a patent, any person may cite, to the Office in writing, prior art consisting of patents or printed publications which that person states to be pertinent and applicable to the patent and believes to have a bearing on the patentability of any claim of the patent. If the citation is made by the patent owner, the explanation of pertinency and applicability may include an explanation of how the claims differ from the prior art. Such citations shall be entered in the patent file except as set forth in §§ 1.502 and 1.902.

(b) If the person making the citation wishes his or her identity to be excluded from the patent file and kept confidential, the citation papers must be submitted without any identification of the person making the submission.

(c) Citation of patents or printed publications by the public in patent files should either: (1) Reflect that a copy of the same has been mailed to the patent owner at the address as provided for in § 1.33(c); or in the event service is not possible (2) Be filed with the Office in duplicate.

[46 FR 29185, May 29, 1981, effective July 1, 1981; para. (a) revised, 65 FR 76756, Dec. 7, 2000, effective Feb. 5, 2001]

§ 1.502 Processing of prior art citations during an *ex parte* reexamination proceeding.

Citations by the patent owner under § 1.555 and by an *ex parte* reexamination requester under either § 1.510 or § 1.535 will be entered in the reexamination file during a reexamination proceeding. The entry in the patent file of citations submitted after the date of an order to reexamine pursuant to § 1.525 by persons other than the patent owner, or an *ex parte* reexamination requester under either § 1.510 or § 1.535, will be delayed until the reexamination proceeding has been concluded by the issuance and publication of a reexamination certificate. See § 1.902 for processing of prior art citations in patent and reexamination files during an *inter partes* reexamination proceeding filed under § 1.913.

[Added 65 FR 76756, Dec. 7, 2000, effective Feb. 5, 2001; revised, 72 FR 18892, Apr. 16, 2007, effective May 16, 2007]

REQUEST FOR *EX PARTE* REEXAMINATION

§ 1.510 Request for *ex parte* reexamination.

(a) Any person may, at any time during the period of enforceability of a patent, file a request for an *ex parte* reexamination by the Office of any claim of the patent on the basis of prior art patents or printed publications cited under § 1.501. The request must be accompanied by the fee for requesting reexamination set in § 1.20(c)(1).

(b) Any request for reexamination must include the following parts:

(1) A statement pointing out each substantial new question of patentability based on prior patents and printed publications.

(2) An identification of every claim for which reexamination is requested, and a detailed explanation of the pertinency and manner of applying the cited prior art to every claim for which reexamination is requested. If appropriate the party requesting reexamination may also point out how claims distinguish over cited prior art.

(3) A copy of every patent or printed publication relied upon or referred to in paragraph (b)(1) and (2) of this section accompanied by an English language translation of all the necessary and pertinent parts of any non-English language patent or printed publication.

(4) A copy of the entire patent including the front face, drawings, and specification/claims (in double column format) for which reexamination is requested, and a copy of any disclaimer, certificate of correction, or reexamination certificate issued in the patent. All copies must have each page plainly written on only one side of a sheet of paper.

(5) A certification that a copy of the request filed by a person other than the patent owner has been served in its entirety on the patent owner at the address as provided for in § 1.33(c). The name and

address of the party served must be indicated. If service was not possible, a duplicate copy must be supplied to the Office.

(c) If the request does not include the fee for requesting *ex parte* reexamination required by paragraph (a) of this section and meet all the requirements by paragraph (b) of this section, then the person identified as requesting reexamination will be so notified and will generally be given an opportunity to complete the request within a specified time. Failure to comply with the notice will result in the *ex parte* reexamination request not being granted a filing date, and will result in placement of the request in the patent file as a citation if it complies with the requirements of § 1.501.

(d) The filing date of the request for *ex parte* reexamination is the date on which the request satisfies all the requirements of this section.

(e) A request filed by the patent owner may include a proposed amendment in accordance with § 1.530.

(f) If a request is filed by an attorney or agent identifying another party on whose behalf the request is being filed, the attorney or agent must have a power of attorney from that party or be acting in a representative capacity pursuant to § 1.34.

[46 FR 29185, May 29, 1981, effective July 1, 1981; para. (a), 47 FR 41282, Sept. 17, 1982, effective Oct. 1, 1982; para. (e) revised, 62 FR 53131, Oct. 10, 1997, effective Dec. 1, 1997; paras. (b)(4) and (e) revised, 65 FR 54604, Sept. 8, 2000, effective Nov. 7, 2000; heading and para. (a) revised, 65 FR 76756, Dec. 7, 2000, effective Feb. 5, 2001; paras. (c) and (d) revised, 71 FR 9260, Feb. 23, 2006, effective Mar. 27, 2006; paras. (c) and (d) revised, 71 FR 44219, Aug. 4, 2006, effective Aug. 4, 2006; para. (f) revised, 72 FR 18892, Apr. 16, 2007, effective May 16, 2007]

§ 1.515 Determination of the request for *ex parte* reexamination.

(a) Within three months following the filing date of a request for an *ex parte* reexamination, an examiner will consider the request and determine whether or not a substantial new question of patentability affecting any claim of the patent is raised by the request and the prior art cited therein, with or without consideration of other patents or printed pub-

lications. The examiner's determination will be based on the claims in effect at the time of the determination, will become a part of the official file of the patent, and will be mailed to the patent owner at the address as provided for in § 1.33(c) and to the person requesting reexamination.

(b) Where no substantial new question of patentability has been found, a refund of a portion of the fee for requesting *ex parte* reexamination will be made to the requester in accordance with § 1.26(c).

(c) The requester may seek review by a petition to the Director under § 1.181 within one month of the mailing date of the examiner's determination refusing *ex parte* reexamination. Any such petition must comply with § 1.181(b). If no petition is timely filed or if the decision on petition affirms that no substantial new question of patentability has been raised, the determination shall be final and nonappealable.

[46 FR 29185, May 29, 1981, effective July 1, 1981; revised, 65 FR 76756, Dec. 7, 2000, effective Feb. 5, 2001; para. (c) revised, 68 FR 14332, Mar. 25, 2003, effective May 1, 2003]

§ 1.520 *Ex parte* reexamination at the initiative of the Director.

The Director, at any time during the period of enforceability of a patent, may determine whether or not a substantial new question of patentability is raised by patents or printed publications which have been discovered by the Director or which have been brought to the Director's attention, even though no request for reexamination has been filed in accordance with § 1.510 or § 1.913. The Director may initiate *ex parte* reexamination without a request for reexamination pursuant to § 1.510 or § 1.913. Normally requests from outside the Office that the Director undertake reexamination on his own initiative will not be considered. Any determination to initiate *ex parte* reexamination under this section will become a part of the official file of the patent and will be mailed to the patent owner at the address as provided for in § 1.33(c).

[46 FR 29186, May 29, 1981, effective July 1, 1981; revised, 65 FR 76756, Dec. 7, 2000, effective Feb. 5, 2001; revised, 68 FR 14332, Mar. 25, 2003, effective May 1, 2003]

EX PARTE REEXAMINATION

§ 1.525 Order for *ex parte* reexamination.

(a) If a substantial new question of patentability is found pursuant to § 1.515 or § 1.520, the determination will include an order for *ex parte* reexamination of the patent for resolution of the question. If the order for *ex parte* reexamination resulted from a petition pursuant to § 1.515(c), the *ex parte* reexamination will ordinarily be conducted by an examiner other than the examiner responsible for the initial determination under § 1.515(a).

(b) The notice published in the *Official Gazette* under § 1.11(c) will be considered to be constructive notice and *ex parte* reexamination will proceed.

[46 FR 29186, May 29, 1981, effective July 1, 1981; heading and paras. (a) and (b) revised, 65 FR 76756, Dec. 7, 2000, effective Feb. 5, 2001]

§ 1.530 Statement by patent owner in *ex parte* reexamination; amendment by patent owner in *ex parte* or *inter partes* reexamination; inventorship change in *ex parte* or *inter partes* reexamination.

(a) Except as provided in § 1.510(e), no statement or other response by the patent owner in an *ex parte* reexamination proceeding shall be filed prior to the determinations made in accordance with § 1.515 or § 1.520. If a premature statement or other response is filed by the patent owner, it will not be acknowledged or considered in making the determination, and it will be returned or discarded (at the Office's option).

(b) The order for *ex parte* reexamination will set a period of not less than two months from the date of the order within which the patent owner may file a statement on the new question of patentability, including any proposed amendments the patent owner wishes to make.

(c) Any statement filed by the patent owner shall clearly point out why the subject matter as claimed is not anticipated or rendered obvious by the prior art patents or printed publications, either alone or in any reasonable combinations. Where the reexamination request was filed by a third party requester, any statement filed by the patent owner must be served upon the *ex parte* reexamination requester in accordance with § 1.248.

(d) *Making amendments in a reexamination proceeding.* A proposed amendment in an *ex parte* or an *inter partes* reexamination proceeding is made by filing a paper directing that proposed specified changes be made to the patent specification, including the claims, or to the drawings. An amendment paper directing that proposed specified changes be made in a reexamination proceeding may be submitted as an accompaniment to a request filed by the patent owner in accordance with § 1.510(e), as part of a patent owner statement in accordance with paragraph (b) of this section, or, where permitted, during the prosecution of the reexamination proceeding pursuant to § 1.550(a) or § 1.937.

(1) *Specification other than the claims.* Changes to the specification, other than to the claims, must be made by submission of the entire text of an added or rewritten paragraph including markings pursuant to paragraph (f) of this section, except that an entire paragraph may be deleted by a statement deleting the paragraph, without presentation of the text of the paragraph. The precise point in the specification must be identified where any added or rewritten paragraph is located. This paragraph applies whether the amendment is submitted on paper or compact disc (*see* §§ 1.96 and 1.825).

(2) *Claims.* An amendment paper must include the entire text of each patent claim which is being proposed to be changed by such amendment paper and of each new claim being proposed to be added by such amendment paper. For any claim changed by the amendment paper, a parenthetical expression "amended," "twice amended," *etc.*, should follow the claim number. Each patent claim proposed to be changed and each proposed added claim must include markings pursuant to paragraph (f) of this section, except that a patent claim or proposed added claim should be canceled by a statement canceling the claim, without presentation of the text of the claim.

(3) *Drawings.* Any change to the patent drawings must be submitted as a sketch on a separate paper showing the proposed changes in red for approval by the examiner. Upon approval of the changes by the examiner, only new sheets of drawings including the changes and in compliance with § 1.84 must be filed. Amended figures must be identified as "Amended," and any added figure must be identified as "New." In the event a figure is canceled, the figure

must be surrounded by brackets and identified as "Canceled."

(4) The formal requirements for papers making up the reexamination proceeding other than those set forth in this section are set out in § 1.52.

(e) *Status of claims and support for claim changes.* Whenever there is an amendment to the claims pursuant to paragraph (d) of this section, there must also be supplied, on pages separate from the pages containing the changes, the status (*i.e.,* pending or canceled), as of the date of the amendment, of all patent claims and of all added claims, and an explanation of the support in the disclosure of the patent for the changes to the claims made by the amendment paper.

(f) *Changes shown by markings.* Any changes relative to the patent being reexamined which are made to the specification, including the claims, must include the following markings:

(1) The matter to be omitted by the reexamination proceeding must be enclosed in brackets; and

(2) The matter to be added by the reexamination proceeding must be underlined.

(g) *Numbering of patent claims preserved.* Patent claims may not be renumbered. The numbering of any claims added in the reexamination proceeding must follow the number of the highest numbered patent claim.

(h) *Amendment of disclosure may be required.* The disclosure must be amended, when required by the Office, to correct inaccuracies of description and definition, and to secure substantial correspondence between the claims, the remainder of the specification, and the drawings.

(i) *Amendments made relative to patent.* All amendments must be made relative to the patent specification, including the claims, and drawings, which are in effect as of the date of filing the request for reexamination.

(j) *No enlargement of claim scope.* No amendment may enlarge the scope of the claims of the patent or introduce new matter. No amendment may be proposed for entry in an expired patent. Moreover, no amendment, other than the cancellation of claims, will be incorporated into the patent by a certificate issued after the expiration of the patent.

(k) *Amendments not effective until certificate.* Although the Office actions will treat proposed amendments as though they have been entered, the proposed amendments will not be effective until the reexamination certificate is issued and published.

(l) *Correction of inventorship in an ex parte or inter partes reexamination proceeding.*

(1) When it appears in a patent being reexamined that the correct inventor or inventors were not named through error without deceptive intention on the part of the actual inventor or inventors, the Director may, on petition of all the parties set forth in § 1.324(b)(1)-(3), including the assignees, and satisfactory proof of the facts and payment of the fee set forth in § 1.20(b), or on order of a court before which such matter is called in question, include in the reexamination certificate to be issued under § 1.570 or § 1.997 an amendment naming only the actual inventor or inventors. The petition must be submitted as part of the reexamination proceeding and must satisfy the requirements of § 1.324.

(2) Notwithstanding paragraph (1)(1) of this section, if a petition to correct inventorship satisfying the requirements of § 1.324 is filed in a reexamination proceeding, and the reexamination proceeding is concluded other than by a reexamination certificate under § 1.570 or § 1.997, a certificate of correction indicating the change of inventorship stated in the petition will be issued upon request by the patentee.

[46 FR 29186, May 29, 1981, effective July 1, 1981; para. (d) revised, para. (e) removed, 62 FR 53131, Oct. 10, 1997, effective Dec. 1, 1997; heading and para. (d) revised, 65 FR 54604, Sept. 8, 2000, effective Nov. 7, 2000; paras. (e) through (l) added, 65 FR 54604, Sept. 8, 2000, effective Nov. 7, 2000; heading, paras. (a)-(c), para. (d) introductory text and para. (l) revised, 65 FR 76756, Dec. 7, 2000, effective Feb. 5, 2001; para. (l)(1) revised, 68 FR 14332, Mar. 25, 2003, effective May 1, 2003; paras. (a), (k), and (l) revised, 72 FR 18892, Apr. 16, 2007, effective May 16, 2007]

§ **1.535 Reply by third party requester in** *ex parte* **reexamination.**

A reply to the patent owner's statement under § 1.530 may be filed by the *ex parte* reexamination requester within two months from the date of service of the patent owner's statement. Any reply by the *ex parte* requester must be served upon the patent owner in accordance with § 1.248. If the patent owner does not file a statement under § 1.530, no reply or other submission from the *ex parte* reexamination requester will be considered.

[46 FR 29186, May 29, 1981, effective July 1, 1981; revised, 65 FR 76756, Dec. 7, 2000, effective Feb. 5, 2001]

§ 1.540 Consideration of responses in *ex parte* reexamination.

The failure to timely file or serve the documents set forth in § 1.530 or in § 1.535 may result in their being refused consideration. No submissions other than the statement pursuant to § 1.530 and the reply by the *ex parte* reexamination requester pursuant to § 1.535 will be considered prior to examination.

[46 FR 29186, May 29, 1981, effective July 1, 1981; revised, 65 FR 76756, Dec. 7, 2000, effective Feb. 5, 2001]

§ 1.550 Conduct of *ex parte* reexamination proceedings.

(a)   All *ex parte* reexamination proceedings, including any appeals to the Board of Patent Appeals and Interferences, will be conducted with special dispatch within the Office. After issuance of the *ex parte* reexamination order and expiration of the time for submitting any responses, the examination will be conducted in accordance with §§ 1.104 through 1.116 and will result in the issuance of an *ex parte* reexamination certificate under § 1.570.

(b)   The patent owner in an *ex parte* reexamination proceeding will be given at least thirty days to respond to any Office action. In response to any rejection, such response may include further statements and/or proposed amendments or new claims to place the patent in a condition where all claims, if amended as proposed, would be patentable.

(c)   The time for taking any action by a patent owner in an *ex parte* reexamination proceeding will be extended only for sufficient cause and for a reasonable time specified. Any request for such extension must be filed on or before the day on which action by the patent owner is due, but in no case will the mere filing of a request effect any extension. Any request for such extension must be accompanied by the petition fee set forth in § 1.17(g). See § 1.304(a) for extensions of time for filing a notice of appeal to the

U.S. Court of Appeals for the Federal Circuit or for commencing a civil action.

(d)   If the patent owner fails to file a timely and appropriate response to any Office action or any written statement of an interview required under § 1.560(b), the prosecution in the *ex parte* reexamination proceeding will be a terminated prosecution, and the Director will proceed to issue and publish a certificate concluding the reexamination proceeding under § 1.570 in accordance with the last action of the Office.

(e)   If a response by the patent owner is not timely filed in the Office,

(1)   The delay in filing such response may be excused if it is shown to the satisfaction of the Director that the delay was unavoidable; a petition to accept an unavoidably delayed response must be filed in compliance with § 1.137(a); or

(2)   The response may nevertheless be accepted if the delay was unintentional; a petition to accept an unintentionally delayed response must be filed in compliance with § 1.137(b).

(f)   The reexamination requester will be sent copies of Office actions issued during the *ex parte* reexamination proceeding. After filing of a request for *ex parte* reexamination by a third party requester, any document filed by either the patent owner or the third party requester must be served on the other party in the reexamination proceeding in the manner provided by § 1.248. The document must reflect service or the document may be refused consideration by the Office.

(g)   The active participation of the *ex parte* reexamination requester ends with the reply pursuant to § 1.535, and no further submissions on behalf of the reexamination requester will be acknowledged or considered. Further, no submissions on behalf of any third parties will be acknowledged or considered unless such submissions are:

(1)   in accordance with § 1.510 or § 1.535; or

(2)   entered in the patent file prior to the date of the order for *ex parte* reexamination pursuant to § 1.525.

(h)   Submissions by third parties, filed after the date of the order for *ex parte* reexamination pursuant to § 1.525, must meet the requirements of and will be treated in accordance with § 1.501(a).

[46 FR 29186, May 29, 1981, effective July 1, 1981; para. (c), 49 FR 556, Jan. 4, 1984, effective Apr. 1, 1984;

para. (a), 49 FR 48416, Dec. 12, 1984, effective Feb. 11, 1985; para. (c), 54 FR 29553, July 13, 1989, effective Aug. 20, 1989; paras. (a), (b), & (e) revised, 62 FR 53131, Oct. 10, 1997, effective Dec. 1, 1997; paras. (a) and (b) revised, 65 FR 54604, Sept. 8, 2000, effective Nov. 7, 2000; revised, 65 FR 76756, Dec. 7, 2000, effective Feb. 5, 2001; paras. (d) & (e)(1) revised, 68 FR 14332, Mar. 25, 2003, effective May 1, 2003; para. (c) revised, 69 FR 56481, Sept. 21, 2004, effective Nov. 22, 2004; para. (d) revised, 72 FR 18892, Apr. 16, 2007, effective May 16, 2007]

§ 1.552 Scope of reexamination in *ex parte* reexamination proceedings.

(a) Claims in an *ex parte* reexamination proceeding will be examined on the basis of patents or printed publications and, with respect to subject matter added or deleted in the reexamination proceeding, on the basis of the requirements of 35 U.S.C. 112.

(b) Claims in an *ex parte* reexamination proceeding will not be permitted to enlarge the scope of the claims of the patent.

(c) Issues other than those indicated in paragraphs (a) and (b) of this section will not be resolved in a reexamination proceeding. If such issues are raised by the patent owner or third party requester during a reexamination proceeding, the existence of such issues will be noted by the examiner in the next Office action, in which case the patent owner may consider the advisability of filing a reissue application to have such issues considered and resolved.

[46 FR 29186, May 29, 1981, effective July 1, 1981; revised, 65 FR 76756, Dec. 7, 2000, effective Feb. 5, 2001]

§ 1.555 Information material to patentability in *ex parte* reexamination and *inter partes* reexamination proceedings.

(a) A patent by its very nature is affected with a public interest. The public interest is best served, and the most effective reexamination occurs when, at the time a reexamination proceeding is being conducted, the Office is aware of and evaluates the teachings of all information material to patentability in a reexamination proceeding. Each individual associated with the patent owner in a reexamination proceeding has a duty of candor and good faith in dealing with the Office, which includes a duty to disclose to the Office all information known to that individual to be material to patentability in a reexamination proceeding. The individuals who have a duty to disclose to the Office all information known to them to be material to patentability in a reexamination proceeding are the patent owner, each attorney or agent who represents the patent owner, and every other individual who is substantively involved on behalf of the patent owner in a reexamination proceeding. The duty to disclose the information exists with respect to each claim pending in the reexamination proceeding until the claim is cancelled. Information material to the patentability of a cancelled claim need not be submitted if the information is not material to patentability of any claim remaining under consideration in the reexamination proceeding. The duty to disclose all information known to be material to patentability in a reexamination proceeding is deemed to be satisfied if all information known to be material to patentability of any claim in the patent after issuance of the reexamination certificate was cited by the Office or submitted to the Office in an information disclosure statement. However, the duties of candor, good faith, and disclosure have not been complied with if any fraud on the Office was practiced or attempted or the duty of disclosure was violated through bad faith or intentional misconduct by, or on behalf of, the patent owner in the reexamination proceeding. Any information disclosure statement must be filed with the items listed in § 1.98(a) as applied to individuals associated with the patent owner in a reexamination proceeding, and should be filed within two months of the date of the order for reexamination, or as soon thereafter as possible.

(b) Under this section, information is material to patentability in a reexamination proceeding when it is not cumulative to information of record or being made of record in the reexamination proceeding, and

(1) It is a patent or printed publication that establishes, by itself or in combination with other patents or printed publications, a *prima facie* case of unpatentability of a claim; or

(2) It refutes, or is inconsistent with, a position the patent owner takes in:

(i) Opposing an argument of unpatentability relied on by the Office, or

(ii) Asserting an argument of patentability.

A *prima facie* case of unpatentability of a claim pending in a reexamination proceeding is established when the information compels a conclusion that a claim is unpatentable under the preponderance of evidence, burden-of-proof standard, giving each term in the claim its broadest reasonable construction consistent with the specification, and before any consideration is given to evidence which may be submitted in an attempt to establish a contrary conclusion of patentability.

(c)   The responsibility for compliance with this section rests upon the individuals designated in paragraph (a) of this section and no evaluation will be made by the Office in the reexamination proceeding as to compliance with this section. If questions of compliance with this section are raised by the patent owner or the third party requester during a reexamination proceeding, they will be noted as unresolved questions in accordance with § 1.552(c).

[46 FR 29187, May 29, 1981, effective July 1, 1981; 47 FR 21752, May 19, 1982, effective July 1, 1982; paras. (a) and (b), 49 FR 556, Jan. 4, 1984, effective Apr. 1, 1984; revised 57 FR 2021, Jan. 17, 1992, effective Mar. 16, 1992; heading and para. (c) revised, 65 FR 76756, Dec. 7, 2000, effective Feb. 5, 2001]

§ 1.560   Interviews in *ex parte* reexamination proceedings.

(a)   Interviews in *ex parte* reexamination proceedings pending before the Office between examiners and the owners of such patents or their attorneys or agents of record must be conducted in the Office at such times, within Office hours, as the respective examiners may designate. Interviews will not be permitted at any other time or place without the authority of the Director. Interviews for the discussion of the patentability of claims in patents involved in *ex parte* reexamination proceedings will not be conducted prior to the first official action. Interviews should be arranged in advance. Requests that reexamination requesters participate in interviews with examiners will not be granted.

(b)   In every instance of an interview with an examiner in an *ex parte* reexamination proceeding, a complete written statement of the reasons presented at the interview as warranting favorable action must be filed by the patent owner. An interview does not remove the necessity for response to Office actions as specified in § 1.111. Patent owner's response to an outstanding Office action after the interview does not remove the necessity for filing the written statement. The written statement must be filed as a separate part of a response to an Office action outstanding at the time of the interview, or as a separate paper within one month from the date of the interview, whichever is later.

[46 FR 29187, May 29, 1981, effective July 1, 1981; revised, 65 FR 76756, Dec. 7, 2000, effective Feb. 5, 2001; para. (a) revised, 68 FR 14332, Mar. 25, 2003, effective May 1, 2003]

§ 1.565   Concurrent office proceedings which include an *ex parte* reexamination proceeding.

(a)   In an *ex parte* reexamination proceeding before the Office, the patent owner must inform the Office of any prior or concurrent proceedings in which the patent is or was involved such as interferences, reissues, *ex parte* reexaminations, *inter partes* reexaminations, or litigation and the results of such proceedings. See § 1.985 for notification of prior or concurrent proceedings in an *inter partes* reexamination proceeding.

(b)   If a patent in the process of *ex parte* reexamination is or becomes involved in litigation, the Director shall determine whether or not to suspend the reexamination. See § 1.987 for *inter partes* reexamination proceedings.

(c)   If *ex parte* reexamination is ordered while a prior *ex parte* reexamination proceeding is pending and prosecution in the prior *ex parte* reexamination proceeding has not been terminated, the *ex parte* reexamination proceedings will usually be merged and result in the issuance and publication of a single certificate under § 1.570. For merger of *inter partes* reexamination proceedings, see § 1.989(a). For merger of *ex parte* reexamination and *inter partes* reexamination proceedings, see § 1.989(b).

(d)   If a reissue application and an *ex parte* reexamination proceeding on which an order pursuant to § 1.525 has been mailed are pending concurrently on a patent, a decision will usually be made to merge the two proceedings or to suspend one of the two proceedings. Where merger of a reissue application and an *ex parte* reexamination proceeding is ordered, the merged examination will be conducted in accordance with §§ 1.171 through 1.179, and the patent owner will be required to place and maintain the same claims in the reissue application and the *ex parte* reexamination proceeding during the pendency of the merged proceeding. The examiner's actions and responses by the patent owner in a merged proceeding will apply to both the reissue application and the *ex parte* reexamination proceeding and will be physically entered into both files. Any *ex parte* reexamination proceeding merged with a reissue application shall be concluded by the grant of the reissued patent. For merger of a reissue application and an *inter partes* reexamination, see § 1.991.

(e)   If a patent in the process of *ex parte* reexamination is or becomes involved in an interference, the Director may suspend the reexamination or the interference. The Director will not consider a request to suspend an interference unless a motion (§ 41.121(a)(3) of this title) to suspend the interference has been presented to, and denied by, an administrative patent judge, and the request is filed within ten (10) days of a decision by an administrative patent judge denying the motion for suspension or such other time as the administrative patent judge may set. For concurrent inter partes reexamination and interference of a patent, see § 1.993.

[46 FR 29187, May 29, 1981, effective July 1, 1981; paras. (b) and (d), 47 FR 21753, May 19, 1982, effective July 1, 1982; paras. (b) & (e), 49 FR 48416, Dec. 12, 1984, 50 FR 23123, May 31, 1985, effective Feb. 11, 1985; para (a) revised, 65 FR 54604, Sept. 8, 2000, effective Nov. 7, 2000; revised, 65 FR 76756, Dec. 7, 2000, effective Feb. 5, 2001; paras. (b) & (e) revised, 68 FR 14332, Mar. 25, 2003, effective May 1, 2003; para. (e) revised, 69 FR 49959, Aug. 12, 2004, effective Sept. 13, 2004; paras. (c) and (d) revised, 72 FR 18892, Apr. 16, 2007, effective May 16, 2007]

CERTIFICATE

§ 1.570   Issuance and publication of *ex parte* reexamination certificate concludes *ex parte* reexamination proceeding.

(a)   To conclude an *ex parte* reexamination proceeding, the Director will issue and publish an *ex parte* reexamination certificate in accordance with 35 U.S.C. 307 setting forth the results of the *ex parte* reexamination proceeding and the content of the patent following the *ex parte* reexamination proceeding.

(b)   An *ex parte* reexamination certificate will be issued and published in each patent in which an *ex parte* reexamination proceeding has been ordered under § 1.525 and has not been merged with any *inter partes* reexamination proceeding pursuant to § 1.989(a). Any statutory disclaimer filed by the patent owner will be made part of the *ex parte* reexamination certificate.

(c)   The *ex parte* reexamination certificate will be mailed on the day of its date to the patent owner at the address as provided for in § 1.33(c). A copy of the *ex parte* reexamination certificate will also be mailed to the requester of the *ex parte* reexamination proceeding.

(d)   If an *ex parte* reexamination certificate has been issued and published which cancels all of the claims of the patent, no further Office proceedings will be conducted with that patent or any reissue applications or any reexamination requests relating thereto.

(e)   If the *ex parte* reexamination proceeding is terminated by the grant of a reissued patent as provided in § 1.565(d), the reissued patent will constitute the *ex parte* reexamination certificate required by this section and 35 U.S.C. 307.

(f)   A notice of the issuance of each *ex parte* reexamination certificate under this section will be published in the *Official Gazette* on its date of issuance.

[46 FR 29187, May 29, 1981, effective July 1, 1981; para. (e), 47 FR 21753, May 19, 1982, effective July 1, 1982; revised, 65 FR 76756, Dec. 7, 2000, effective Feb. 5, 2001; para. (a) revised, 68 FR 14332, Mar. 25, 2003, effective May 1, 2003; heading and paras. (a), (b), and (d) revised, 72 FR 18892, Apr. 16, 2007, effective May 16, 2007]

Subpart E — [Reserved]

Subpart F — Adjustment and Extension of Patent Term

ADJUSTMENT OF PATENT TERM DUE TO EXAMINATION DELAY

§ 1.701 Extension of patent term due to examination delay under the Uruguay Round Agreements Act (original applications, other than designs, filed on or after June 8, 1995, and before May 29, 2000).

(a) A patent, other than for designs, issued on an application filed on or after June 8, 1995, is entitled to extension of the patent term if the issuance of the patent was delayed due to:

(1) Interference proceedings under 35 U.S.C. 135(a); and/or

(2) The application being placed under a secrecy order under 35 U.S.C. 181; and/or

(3) Appellate review by the Board of Patent Appeals and Interferences or by a Federal court under 35 U.S.C. 141 or 145, if the patent was issued pursuant to a decision in the review reversing an adverse determination of patentability and if the patent is not subject to a terminal disclaimer due to the issuance of another patent claiming subject matter that is not patentably distinct from that under appellate review. If an application is remanded by a panel of the Board of Patent Appeals and Interferences and the remand is the last action by a panel of the Board of Patent Appeals and Interferences prior to the mailing of a notice of allowance under 35 U.S.C. 151 in the application, the remand shall be considered a decision in the review reversing an adverse determination of patentability as that phrase is used in 35 U.S.C. 154(b)(2) as amended by section 532(a) of the Uruguay Round Agreements Act, Public Law 103-465, 108 Stat. 4809, 4983-85 (1994), and a final decision in favor of the applicant under paragraph (c)(3) of this section. A remand by a panel of the Board of Patent Appeals and Interferences shall not be considered a decision in the review reversing an adverse determination of patentability as provided in this paragraph if there is filed a request for continued examination under 35 U.S.C. 132(b) that was not first preceded by the mailing, after such remand, of at least one of an action under 35 U.S.C. 132 or a notice of allowance under 35 U.S.C. 151.

(b) The term of a patent entitled to extension under paragraph (a) of this section shall be extended for the sum of the periods of delay calculated under paragraphs (c)(1), (c)(2), (c)(3) and (d) of this section, to the extent that these periods are not overlapping, up to a maximum of five years. The extension will run from the expiration date of the patent.

(c)(1) The period of delay under paragraph (a)(1) of this section for an application is the sum of the following periods, to the extent that the periods are not overlapping:

(i) With respect to each interference in which the application was involved, the number of days, if any, in the period beginning on the date the interference was declared or redeclared to involve the application in the interference and ending on the date that the interference was terminated with respect to the application; and

(ii) The number of days, if any, in the period beginning on the date prosecution in the application was suspended by the Patent and Trademark Office due to interference proceedings under 35 U.S.C. 135(a) not involving the application and ending on the date of the termination of the suspension.

(2) The period of delay under paragraph (a)(2) of this section for an application is the sum of the following periods, to the extent that the periods are not overlapping:

(i) The number of days, if any, the application was maintained in a sealed condition under 35 U.S.C. 181;

(ii) The number of days, if any, in the period beginning on the date of mailing of an examiner's answer under § 41.39 of this title in the application under secrecy order and ending on the date the secrecy order and any renewal thereof was removed;

(iii) The number of days, if any, in the period beginning on the date applicant was notified that an interference would be declared but for the secrecy order and ending on the date the secrecy order and any renewal thereof was removed; and

(iv) The number of days, if any, in the period beginning on the date of notification under § 5.3(c) and ending on the date of mailing of the notice of allowance under § 1.311.

(3) The period of delay under paragraph (a)(3) of this section is the sum of the number of days, if any, in the period beginning on the date on which an appeal to the Board of Patent Appeals and Interferences was filed under 35 U.S.C. 134 and ending on the date of a final decision in favor of the applicant by the Board of Patent Appeals and Interferences or by a

Federal court in an appeal under 35 U.S.C. 141 or a civil action under 35 U.S.C. 145.

(d) The period of delay set forth in paragraph (c)(3) shall be reduced by:

(1) Any time during the period of appellate review that occurred before three years from the filing of the first national application for patent presented for examination; and

(2) Any time during the period of appellate review, as determined by the Director, during which the applicant for patent did not act with due diligence. In determining the due diligence of an applicant, the Director may examine the facts and circumstances of the applicant's actions during the period of appellate review to determine whether the applicant exhibited that degree of timeliness as may reasonably be expected from, and which is ordinarily exercised by, a person during a period of appellate review.

(e) The provisions of this section apply only to original patents, except for design patents, issued on applications filed on or after June 8, 1995, and before May 29, 2000.

[Added, 60 FR 20195, Apr. 25, 1995, effective June 8, 1995; para. (e) added, 65 FR 56366, Sept. 18, 2000, effective Oct. 18, 2000; para. (d)(2) revised, 68 FR 14332, Mar. 25, 2003, effective May 1, 2003; para. (a)(3) revised, 69 FR 21704, Apr. 22, 2004, effective May 24, 2004; para. (c)(2)(ii) revised, 69 FR 49959, Aug. 12, 2004, effective Sept. 13, 2004]

§ 1.702 **Grounds for adjustment of patent term due to examination delay under the Patent Term Guarantee Act of 1999 (original applications, other than designs, filed on or after May 29, 2000).**

(a) *Failure to take certain actions within specified time frames.* Subject to the provisions of 35 U.S.C. 154(b) and this subpart, the term of an original patent shall be adjusted if the issuance of the patent was delayed due to the failure of the Office to:

(1) Mail at least one of a notification under 35 U.S.C. 132 or a notice of allowance under 35 U.S.C. 151 not later than fourteen months after the date on which the application was filed under 35 U.S.C. 111(a) or fulfilled the requirements of 35 U.S.C. 371 in an international application;

(2) Respond to a reply under 35 U.S.C. 132 or to an appeal taken under 35 U.S.C. 134 not later than four months after the date on which the reply was filed or the appeal was taken;

(3) Act on an application not later than four months after the date of a decision by the Board of Patent Appeals and Interferences under 35 U.S.C. 134 or 135 or a decision by a Federal court under 35 U.S.C. 141, 145, or 146 where at least one allowable claim remains in the application; or

(4) Issue a patent not later than four months after the date on which the issue fee was paid under 35 U.S.C. 151 and all outstanding requirements were satisfied.

(b) *Failure to issue a patent within three years of the actual filing date of the application.* Subject to the provisions of 35 U.S.C. 154(b) and this subpart, the term of an original patent shall be adjusted if the issuance of the patent was delayed due to the failure of the Office to issue a patent within three years after the date on which the application was filed under 35 U.S.C. 111(a) or the national stage commenced under 35 U.S.C. 371(b) or (f) in an international application, but not including:

(1) Any time consumed by continued examination of the application under 35 U.S.C. 132(b);

(2) Any time consumed by an interference proceeding under 35 U.S.C. 135(a);

(3) Any time consumed by the imposition of a secrecy order under 35 U.S.C. 181;

(4) Any time consumed by review by the Board of Patent Appeals and Interferences or a Federal court; or

(5) Any delay in the processing of the application by the Office that was requested by the applicant.

(c) *Delays caused by interference proceedings.* Subject to the provisions of 35 U.S.C. 154(b) and this subpart, the term of an original patent shall be adjusted if the issuance of the patent was delayed due to interference proceedings under 35 U.S.C. 135(a).

(d) *Delays caused by secrecy order.* Subject to the provisions of 35 U.S.C. 154(b) and this subpart, the term of an original patent shall be adjusted if the issuance of the patent was delayed due to the application being placed under a secrecy order under 35 U.S.C. 181.

(e) *Delays caused by successful appellate review.* Subject to the provisions of 35 U.S.C. 154(b) and this subpart, the term of an original patent shall be adjusted if the issuance of the patent was delayed due to review by the Board of Patent Appeals and Interferences under 35 U.S.C. 134 or by a Federal court under 35 U.S.C. 141 or 145, if the patent was issued under a decision in the review reversing an adverse determination of patentability. If an application is remanded by a panel of the Board of Patent Appeals and Interferences and the remand is the last action by a panel of the Board of Patent Appeals and Interferences prior to the mailing of a notice of allowance under 35 U.S.C. 151 in the application, the remand shall be considered a decision by the Board of Patent Appeals and Interferences as that phrase is used in 35 U.S.C. 154(b)(1)(A)(iii), a decision in the review reversing an adverse determination of patentability as that phrase is used in 35 U.S.C. 154(b)(1)(C)(iii), and a final decision in favor of the applicant under § 1.703(e). A remand by a panel of the Board of Patent Appeals and Interferences shall not be considered a decision in the review reversing an adverse determination of patentability as provided in this paragraph if there is filed a request for continued examination under 35 U.S.C. 132(b) that was not first preceded by the mailing, after such remand, of at least one of an action under 35 U.S.C. 132 or a notice of allowance under 35 U.S.C. 151.

(f)   The provisions of this section and §§1.703 through 1.705 apply only to original applications, except applications for a design patent, filed on or after May 29, 2000, and patents issued on such applications.

[Added, 65 FR 56366, Sept. 18, 2000, effective Oct. 18, 2000; para. (e) revised, 69 FR 21704, Apr. 22, 2004, effective May 24, 2004]

§ 1.703 Period of adjustment of patent term due to examination delay.

(a)   The period of adjustment under § 1.702(a) is the sum of the following periods:

(1)   The number of days, if any, in the period beginning on the day after the date that is fourteen months after the date on which the application was filed under 35 U.S.C. 111(a) or fulfilled the requirements of 35 U.S.C. 371 and ending on the date of mailing of either an action under 35 U.S.C. 132, or a notice of allowance under 35 U.S.C. 151, whichever occurs first;

(2)   The number of days, if any, in the period beginning on the day after the date that is four months after the date a reply under § 1.111 was filed and ending on the date of mailing of either an action under 35 U.S.C. 132, or a notice of allowance under 35 U.S.C. 151, whichever occurs first;

(3)   The number of days, if any, in the period beginning on the day after the date that is four months after the date a reply in compliance with § 1.113(c) was filed and ending on the date of mailing of either an action under 35 U.S.C. 132, or a notice of allowance under 35 U.S.C. 151, whichever occurs first;

(4)   The number of days, if any, in the period beginning on the day after the date that is four months after the date an appeal brief in compliance with § 41.37 of this title was filed and ending on the date of mailing of any of an examiner's answer under § 41.39 of this title, an action under 35 U.S.C. 132, or a notice of allowance under 35 U.S.C. 151, whichever occurs first;

(5)   The number of days, if any, in the period beginning on the day after the date that is four months after the date of a final decision by the Board of Patent Appeals and Interferences or by a Federal court in an appeal under 35 U.S.C. 141 or a civil action under 35 U.S.C. 145 or 146 where at least one allowable claim remains in the application and ending on the date of mailing of either an action under 35 U.S.C. 132 or a notice of allowance under 35 U.S.C. 151, whichever occurs first; and

(6)   The number of days, if any, in the period beginning on the day after the date that is four months after the date the issue fee was paid and all outstanding requirements were satisfied and ending on the date a patent was issued.

(b)   The period of adjustment under § 1.702(b) is the number of days, if any, in the period beginning on the day after the date that is three years after the date on which the application was filed under 35 U.S.C. 111(a) or the national stage commenced under 35 U.S.C. 371(b) or (f) in an international application and ending on the date a patent was issued, but not including the sum of the following periods:

(1)   The number of days, if any, in the period beginning on the date on which a request for continued examination of the application under 35 U.S.C.

132(b) was filed and ending on the date the patent was issued;

(2)(i) The number of days, if any, in the period beginning on the date an interference was declared or redeclared to involve the application in the interference and ending on the date that the interference was terminated with respect to the application; and

(ii) The number of days, if any, in the period beginning on the date prosecution in the application was suspended by the Office due to interference proceedings under 35 U.S.C. 135(a) not involving the application and ending on the date of the termination of the suspension;

(3)(i) The number of days, if any, the application was maintained in a sealed condition under 35 U.S.C. 181;

(ii) The number of days, if any, in the period beginning on the date of mailing of an examiner's answer under § 41.39 of this title in the application under secrecy order and ending on the date the secrecy order was removed;

(iii) The number of days, if any, in the period beginning on the date applicant was notified that an interference would be declared but for the secrecy order and ending on the date the secrecy order was removed; and

(iv) The number of days, if any, in the period beginning on the date of notification under § 5.3(c) of this chapter and ending on the date of mailing of the notice of allowance under 35 U.S.C. 151; and,

(4) The number of days, if any, in the period beginning on the date on which a notice of appeal to the Board of Patent Appeals and Interferences was filed under 35 U.S.C. 134 and § 41.31 of this title and ending on the date of the last decision by the Board of Patent Appeals and Interferences or by a Federal court in an appeal under 35 U.S.C. 141 or a civil action under 35 U.S.C. 145, or on the date of mailing of either an action under 35 U.S.C. 132, or a notice of allowance under 35 U.S.C. 151, whichever occurs first, if the appeal did not result in a decision by the Board of Patent Appeals and Interferences.

(c) The period of adjustment under § 1.702(c) is the sum of the following periods, to the extent that the periods are not overlapping:

(1) The number of days, if any, in the period beginning on the date an interference was declared or redeclared to involve the application in the interference and ending on the date that the interference was terminated with respect to the application; and

(2) The number of days, if any, in the period beginning on the date prosecution in the application was suspended by the Office due to interference proceedings under 35 U.S.C. 135(a) not involving the application and ending on the date of the termination of the suspension.

(d) The period of adjustment under § 1.702(d) is the sum of the following periods, to the extent that the periods are not overlapping:

(1) The number of days, if any, the application was maintained in a sealed condition under 35 U.S.C. 181;

(2) The number of days, if any, in the period beginning on the date of mailing of an examiner's answer under § 41.39 of this title in the application under secrecy order and ending on the date the secrecy order was removed;

(3) The number of days, if any, in the period beginning on the date applicant was notified that an interference would be declared but for the secrecy order and ending on the date the secrecy order was removed; and

(4) The number of days, if any, in the period beginning on the date of notification under § 5.3(c) of this chapter and ending on the date of mailing of the notice of allowance under 35 U.S.C. 151.

(e) The period of adjustment under § 1.702(e) is the sum of the number of days, if any, in the period beginning on the date on which a notice of appeal to the Board of Patent Appeals and Interferences was filed under 35 U.S.C. 134 and § 41.31 of this title and ending on the date of a final decision in favor of the applicant by the Board of Patent Appeals and Interferences or by a Federal court in an appeal under 35 U.S.C. 141 or a civil action under 35 U.S.C. 145.

(f) The adjustment will run from the expiration date of the patent as set forth in 35 U.S.C. 154(a)(2). To the extent that periods of delay attributable to the grounds specified in §1.702 overlap, the period of adjustment granted under this section shall not exceed the actual number of days the issuance of the patent was delayed. The term of a patent entitled to adjustment under § 1.702 and this section shall be adjusted for the sum of the periods calculated under paragraphs (a) through (e) of this section, to the extent that such periods are not overlapping, less the sum of the periods calculated under § 1.704. The date indicated on any certificate of mailing or transmission under § 1.8 shall not be taken into account in this calculation.

(g) No patent, the term of which has been disclaimed beyond a specified date, shall be adjusted under § 1.702 and this section beyond the expiration date specified in the disclaimer.

[Added, 65 FR 56366, Sept. 18, 2000, effective Oct. 18, 2000; para. (f) revised, 69 FR 21704, Apr. 22, 2004, effective May 24, 2004; paras. (a)(4), (b)(3)(ii), (b)(4), (d)(2), and (e) revised, 69 FR 49959, Aug. 12, 2004, effective Sept. 13, 2004]

§ 1.704 Reduction of period of adjustment of patent term.

(a) The period of adjustment of the term of a patent under § 1.703(a) through (e) shall be reduced by a period equal to the period of time during which the applicant failed to engage in reasonable efforts to conclude prosecution (processing or examination) of the application.

(b) With respect to the grounds for adjustment set forth in §§ 1.702(a) through (e), and in particular the ground of adjustment set forth in § 1.702(b), an applicant shall be deemed to have failed to engage in reasonable efforts to conclude processing or examination of an application for the cumulative total of any periods of time in excess of three months that are taken to reply to any notice or action by the Office making any rejection, objection, argument, or other request, measuring such three-month period from the date the notice or action was mailed or given to the applicant, in which case the period of adjustment set forth in § 1.703 shall be reduced by the number of days, if any, beginning on the day after the date that is three months after the date of mailing or transmission of the Office communication notifying the applicant of the rejection, objection, argument, or other request and ending on the date the reply was filed. The period, or shortened statutory period, for reply that is set in the Office action or notice has no effect on the three-month period set forth in this paragraph.

(c) Circumstances that constitute a failure of the applicant to engage in reasonable efforts to conclude processing or examination of an application

also include the following circumstances, which will result in the following reduction of the period of adjustment set forth in § 1.703 to the extent that the periods are not overlapping:

(1) Suspension of action under § 1.103 at the applicant's request, in which case the period of adjustment set forth in § 1.703 shall be reduced by the number of days, if any, beginning on the date a request for suspension of action under § 1.103 was filed and ending on the date of the termination of the suspension;

(2) Deferral of issuance of a patent under § 1.314, in which case the period of adjustment set forth in § 1.703 shall be reduced by the number of days, if any, beginning on the date a request for deferral of issuance of a patent under § 1.314 was filed and ending on the date the patent was issued;

(3) Abandonment of the application or late payment of the issue fee, in which case the period of adjustment set forth in §1.703 shall be reduced by the number of days, if any, beginning on the date of abandonment or the date after the date the issue fee was due and ending on the earlier of:

(i) The date of mailing of the decision reviving the application or accepting late payment of the issue fee; or

(ii) The date that is four months after the date the grantable petition to revive the application or accept late payment of the issue fee was filed;

(4) Failure to file a petition to withdraw the holding of abandonment or to revive an application within two months from the mailing date of a notice of abandonment, in which case the period of adjustment set forth in § 1.703 shall be reduced by the number of days, if any, beginning on the day after the date two months from the mailing date of a notice of abandonment and ending on the date a petition to withdraw the holding of abandonment or to revive the application was filed;

(5) Conversion of a provisional application under 35 U.S.C. 111(b) to a nonprovisional application under 35 U.S.C. 111(a) pursuant to 35 U.S.C. 111(b)(5), in which case the period of adjustment set forth in § 1.703 shall be reduced by the number of days, if any, beginning on the date the application was filed under 35 U.S.C. 111(b) and ending on the date a request in compliance with §1.53(c)(3) to convert the provisional application into a nonprovisional application was filed;

(6) Submission of a preliminary amendment or other preliminary paper less than one month before the mailing of an Office action under 35 U.S.C. 132 or notice of allowance under 35 U.S.C. 151 that requires the mailing of a supplemental Office action or notice of allowance, in which case the period of adjustment set forth in § 1.703 shall be reduced by the lesser of:

(i) The number of days, if any, beginning on the day after the mailing date of the original Office action or notice of allowance and ending on the date of mailing of the supplemental Office action or notice of allowance; or

(ii) Four months;

(7) Submission of a reply having an omission (§1.135(c)), in which case the period of adjustment set forth in § 1.703 shall be reduced by the number of days, if any, beginning on the day after the date the reply having an omission was filed and ending on the date that the reply or other paper correcting the omission was filed;

(8) Submission of a supplemental reply or other paper, other than a supplemental reply or other paper expressly requested by the examiner, after a reply has been filed, in which case the period of adjustment set forth in § 1.703 shall be reduced by the number of days, if any, beginning on the day after the date the initial reply was filed and ending on the date that the supplemental reply or other such paper was filed;

(9) Submission of an amendment or other paper after a decision by the Board of Patent Appeals and Interferences, other than a decision designated as containing a new ground of rejection under § 41.50 (b) of this title or statement under § 41.50(c) of this title, or a decision by a Federal court, less than one month before the mailing of an Office action under 35 U.S.C. 132 or notice of allowance under 35 U.S.C. 151 that requires the mailing of a supplemental Office action or supplemental notice of allowance, in which case the period of adjustment set forth in § 1.703 shall be reduced by the lesser of:

(i) The number of days, if any, beginning on the day after the mailing date of the original Office action or notice of allowance and ending on the mailing date of the supplemental Office action or notice of allowance; or

(ii) Four months;

(10) Submission of an amendment under § 1.312 or other paper after a notice of allowance has been given or mailed, in which case the period of adjustment set forth in § 1.703 shall be reduced by the lesser of:

(i) The number of days, if any, beginning on the date the amendment under § 1.312 or other paper was filed and ending on the mailing date of the Office action or notice in response to the amendment under § 1.312 or such other paper; or

(ii) Four months; and

(11) Further prosecution via a continuing application, in which case the period of adjustment set forth in § 1.703 shall not include any period that is prior to the actual filing date of the application that resulted in the patent.

(d) A paper containing only an information disclosure statement in compliance with §§ 1.97 and 1.98 will not be considered a failure to engage in reasonable efforts to conclude prosecution (processing or examination) of the application under paragraphs (c)(6), (c)(8), (c)(9), or (c)(10) of this section if it is accompanied by a statement that each item of information contained in the information disclosure statement was first cited in any communication from a foreign patent office in a counterpart application and that this communication was not received by any individual designated in § 1.56(c) more than thirty days prior to the filing of the information disclosure statement. This thirty-day period is not extendable.

(e) Submission of an application for patent term adjustment under § 1.705(b) (with or without request under § 1.705(c) for reinstatement of reduced patent term adjustment) will not be considered a failure to engage in reasonable efforts to conclude prosecution (processing or examination) of the application under paragraph (c)(10) of this section.

[Added, 65 FR 56366, Sept. 18, 2000, effective Oct. 18, 2000; para. (d) revised, 69 FR 21704, Apr. 22, 2004, effective May 24, 2004; para. (c)(9) revised, 69 FR 49959, Aug. 12, 2004, effective Sept. 13, 2004; para. (c)(11) redesignated as (c)(12) and (c)(11) added, 72 FR 46716, Aug. 21, 2007 (implementation enjoined and never became effective); para. (c)(11) removed and (c)(12) redesignated as (c)(11), 74 FR 52686, Oct. 14, 2009, effective Oct. 14, 2009 (to remove changes made by the final rules in 72 FR 46716 from the CFR)]

§ 1.705 Patent term adjustment determination.

(a) The notice of allowance will include notification of any patent term adjustment under 35 U.S.C. 154(b).

(b) Any request for reconsideration of the patent term adjustment indicated in the notice of allowance, except as provided in paragraph (d) of this section, and any request for reinstatement of all or part of the term reduced pursuant to § 1.704(b) must be by way of an application for patent term adjustment. An application for patent term adjustment under this section must be filed no later than the payment of the issue fee but may not be filed earlier than the date of mailing of the notice of allowance. An application for patent term adjustment under this section must be accompanied by:

(1) The fee set forth in § 1.18(e); and

(2) A statement of the facts involved, specifying:

(i) The correct patent term adjustment and the basis or bases under § 1.702 for the adjustment;

(ii) The relevant dates as specified in §§ 1.703(a) through (e) for which an adjustment is sought and the adjustment as specified in § 1.703(f) to which the patent is entitled;

(iii) Whether the patent is subject to a terminal disclaimer and any expiration date specified in the terminal disclaimer; and

(iv)(A) Any circumstances during the prosecution of the application resulting in the patent that constitute a failure to engage in reasonable efforts to conclude processing or examination of such application as set forth in § 1.704; or

(B) That there were no circumstances constituting a failure to engage in reasonable efforts to conclude processing or examination of such application as set forth in § 1.704.

(c) Any application for patent term adjustment under this section that requests reinstatement of all or part of the period of adjustment reduced pursuant to § 1.704(b) for failing to reply to a rejection, objection, argument, or other request within three months of the date of mailing of the Office communication notifying the applicant of the rejection, objection, argument, or other request must also be accompanied by:

(1) The fee set forth in § 1.18(f); and

(2) A showing to the satisfaction of the Director that, in spite of all due care, the applicant was unable to reply to the rejection, objection, argument, or other request within three months of the date of mailing of the Office communication notifying the applicant of the rejection, objection, argument, or other request. The Office shall not grant any request for reinstatement for more than three additional months for each reply beyond three months from the date of mailing of the Office communication notifying the applicant of the rejection, objection, argument, or other request.

(d) If there is a revision to the patent term adjustment indicated in the notice of allowance, the patent will indicate the revised patent term adjustment. If the patent indicates or should have indicated a revised patent term adjustment, any request for reconsideration of the patent term adjustment indicated in the patent must be filed within two months of the date the patent issued and must comply with the requirements of paragraphs (b)(1) and (b)(2) of this section. Any request for reconsideration under this section that raises issues that were raised, or could have been raised, in an application for patent term adjustment under paragraph (b) of this section shall be dismissed as untimely as to those issues.

(e) The periods set forth in this section are not extendable.

(f) No submission or petition on behalf of a third party concerning patent term adjustment under 35 U.S.C. 154(b) will be considered by the Office. Any such submission or petition will be returned to the third party, or otherwise disposed of, at the convenience of the Office.

[Added, 65 FR 56366, Sept. 18, 2000, effective Oct. 18, 2000; para. (c)(2) revised, 68 FR 14332, Mar. 25, 2003, effective May 1, 2003; para. (d) revised, 69 FR 21704, Apr. 22, 2004, effective May 24, 2004]

Subpart F — Adjustment and Extension of Patent Term

EXTENSION OF PATENT TERM DUE TO REGULATORY REVIEW

§ 1.710 Patents subject to extension of the patent term.

(a) A patent is eligible for extension of the patent term if the patent claims a product as defined in paragraph (b) of this section, either alone or in combination with other ingredients that read on a composition that received permission for commercial marketing or use, or a method of using such a product, or a method of manufacturing such a product, and meets all other conditions and requirements of this subpart.

(b) The term *product* referred to in paragraph (a) of this section means —

(1) The active ingredient of a new human drug, antibiotic drug, or human biological product (as those terms are used in the Federal Food, Drug, and Cosmetic Act and the Public Health Service Act) including any salt or ester of the active ingredient, as a single entity or in combination with another active ingredient; or

(2) The active ingredient of a new animal drug or veterinary biological product (as those terms are used in the Federal Food, Drug, and Cosmetic Act and the Virus-Serum-Toxin Act) that is not primarily manufactured using recombinant DNA, recombinant RNA, hybridoma technology, or other processes including site specific genetic manipulation techniques, including any salt or ester of the active ingredient, as a single entity or in combination with another active ingredient; or

(3) Any medical device, food additive, or color additive subject to regulation under the Federal Food, Drug, and Cosmetic Act.

[Added 52 FR 9394, Mar. 24, 1987, effective May 26, 1987; amended, 54 FR 30375, July 20, 1989, effective Aug. 22, 1989]

§ 1.720 **Conditions for extension of patent term.**

The term of a patent may be extended if:

(a) The patent claims a product or a method of using or manufacturing a product as defined in § 1.710;

(b) The term of the patent has never been previously extended, except for extensions issued pursuant to §§ 1.701, 1.760, or 1.790;

(c) An application for extension is submitted in compliance with § 1.740;

(d) The product has been subject to a regulatory review period as defined in 35 U.S.C. 156(g) before its commercial marketing or use;

(e) The product has received permission for commercial marketing or use and —

(1) The permission for the commercial marketing or use of the product is the first received permission for commercial marketing or use under the provision of law under which the applicable regulatory review occurred, or

(2) In the case of a patent other than one directed to subject matter within § 1.710(b)(2) claiming a method of manufacturing the product that primarily uses recombinant DNA technology in the manufacture of the product, the permission for the commercial marketing or use is the first received permission for the commercial marketing or use of a product manufactured under the process claimed in the patent, or

(3) In the case of a patent claiming a new animal drug or a veterinary biological product that is not covered by the claims in any other patent that has been extended, and has received permission for the commercial marketing or use in non-food-producing animals and in food-producing animals, and was not extended on the basis of the regulatory review period for use in non-food-producing animals, the permission for the commercial marketing or use of the drug or product after the regulatory review period for use in food-producing animals is the first permitted commercial marketing or use of the drug or product for administration to a food-producing animal.

(f) The application is submitted within the sixty-day period beginning on the date the product first received permission for commercial marketing or use under the provisions of law under which the applicable regulatory review period occurred; or in the case of a patent claiming a method of manufacturing the product which primarily uses recombinant DNA technology in the manufacture of the product, the application for extension is submitted within the sixty-day period beginning on the date of the first permitted commercial marketing or use of a product manufactured under the process claimed in the patent; or in the case of a patent that claims a new animal drug or a veterinary biological product that is not covered by the claims in any other patent that has been extended, and said drug or product has received permission for the commercial marketing or use in non-food-producing animals, the application for extension is submitted within the sixty-day period beginning on the date of the first permitted commercial marketing or use of the drug or product for administration to a food-producing animal;

(g) The term of the patent, including any interim extension issued pursuant to § 1.790, has not expired before the submission of an application in compliance with § 1.741; and

(h) No other patent term has been extended for the same regulatory review period for the product.

[Added 52 FR 9395, Mar. 24, 1987, effective May 26, 1987; paras. (e) & (f) amended, 54 FR 30375, July 20, 1989, effective Aug. 22, 1989; paras. (b) and (g) revised, 65 FR 54604, Sept. 8, 2000, effective Nov. 7, 2000]

§ 1.730 Applicant for extension of patent term; signature requirements.

(a) Any application for extension of a patent term must be submitted by the owner of record of the patent or its agent and must comply with the requirements of § 1.740.

(b) If the application is submitted by the patent owner, the application must be signed either by:

(1) The patent owner in compliance with § 3.73(b) of this chapter; or

(2) A registered practitioner on behalf of the patent owner.

(c) If the application is submitted on behalf of the patent owner by an agent of the patent owner (*e.g.*, a licensee of the patent owner), the application must be signed by a registered practitioner on behalf of the agent. The Office may require proof that the agent is authorized to act on behalf of the patent owner.

(d) If the application is signed by a registered practitioner, the Office may require proof that the practitioner is authorized to act on behalf of the patent owner or agent of the patent owner.

[Added 52 FR 9395, Mar. 24, 1987, effective May 26, 1987; revised, 65 FR 54604, Sept. 8, 2000, effective Nov. 7, 2000]

§ 1.740 Formal requirements for application for extension of patent term; correction of informalities.

(a) An application for extension of patent term must be made in writing to the Director. A formal application for the extension of patent term must include:

(1) A complete identification of the approved product as by appropriate chemical and generic name, physical structure or characteristics;

(2) A complete identification of the Federal statute including the applicable provision of law under which the regulatory review occurred;

(3) An identification of the date on which the product received permission for commercial marketing or use under the provision of law under which the applicable regulatory review period occurred;

(4) In the case of a drug product, an identification of each active ingredient in the product and as to each active ingredient, a statement that it has not been previously approved for commercial marketing or use under the Federal Food, Drug, and Cosmetic Act, the Public Health Service Act, or the Virus-Serum-Toxin Act, or a statement of when the active ingredient was approved for commercial marketing or use (either alone or in combination with other active ingredients), the use for which it was approved, and the provision of law under which it was approved.

(5) A statement that the application is being submitted within the sixty day period permitted for submission pursuant to § 1.720(f) and an identification of the date of the last day on which the application could be submitted;

(6) A complete identification of the patent for which an extension is being sought by the name of the inventor, the patent number, the date of issue, and the date of expiration;

(7) A copy of the patent for which an extension is being sought, including the entire specification (including claims) and drawings;

(8) A copy of any disclaimer, certificate of correction, receipt of maintenance fee payment, or reexamination certificate issued in the patent;

(9) A statement that the patent claims the approved product, or a method of using or manufacturing the approved product, and a showing which lists each applicable patent claim and demonstrates the manner in which at least one such patent claim reads on:

(i) The approved product, if the listed claims include any claim to the approved product;

(ii) The method of using the approved product, if the listed claims include any claim to the method of using the approved product; and

(iii) The method of manufacturing the approved product, if the listed claims include any claim to the method of manufacturing the approved product;

(10) A statement beginning on a new page of the relevant dates and information pursuant to 35 U.S.C.156(g) in order to enable the Secretary of Health and Human Services or the Secretary of Agriculture, as appropriate, to determine the applicable regulatory review period as follows:

(i) For a patent claiming a human drug, antibiotic, or human biological product:

(A) The effective date of the investigational new drug (IND) application and the IND number;

(B) The date on which a new drug application (NDA) or a Product License Application (PLA) was initially submitted and the NDA or PLA number; and

(C) The date on which the NDA was approved or the Product License issued;

(ii) For a patent claiming a new animal drug:

(A) The date a major health or environmental effects test on the drug was initiated, and any available substantiation of that date, or the date of an exemption under subsection (j) of Section 512 of the Federal Food, Drug, and Cosmetic Act became effective for such animal drug;

(B) The date on which a new animal drug application (NADA) was initially submitted and the NADA number; and

(C) The date on which the NADA was approved;

(iii) For a patent claiming a veterinary biological product:

(A) The date the authority to prepare an experimental biological product under the Virus-Serum-Toxin Act became effective;

(B) The date an application for a license was submitted under the Virus-Serum-Toxin Act; and

(C) The date the license issued;

(iv) For a patent claiming a food or color additive:

(A) The date a major health or environmental effects test on the additive was initiated and any available substantiation of that date;

(B) The date on which a petition for product approval under the Federal Food, Drug and Cosmetic Act was initially submitted and the petition number; and

(C) The date on which the FDA published a *Federal Register* notice listing the additive for use;

(v) For a patent claiming a medical device:

(A) The effective date of the investigational device exemption (IDE) and the IDE number, if applicable, or the date on which the applicant began the first clinical investigation involving the device, if no IDE was submitted, and any available substantiation of that date;

(B) The date on which the application for product approval or notice of completion of a product development protocol under Section 515 of the Federal Food, Drug and Cosmetic Act was initially submitted and the number of the application; and

(C) The date on which the application was approved or the protocol declared to be completed;

(11) A brief description beginning on a new page of the significant activities undertaken by the marketing applicant during the applicable regulatory review period with respect to the approved product and the significant dates applicable to such activities;

(12) A statement beginning on a new page that in the opinion of the applicant the patent is eligible for the extension and a statement as to the length of extension claimed, including how the length of extension was determined;

(13) A statement that applicant acknowledges a duty to disclose to the Director of the United States Patent and Trademark Office and the Secretary of Health and Human Services or the Secretary of Agriculture any information which is material to the determination of entitlement to the extension sought (*see* § 1.765);

(14) The prescribed fee for receiving and acting upon the application for extension (see § 1.20(j)); and

(15) The name, address, and telephone number of the person to whom inquiries and correspondence relating to the application for patent term extension are to be directed.

(b)   The application under this section must be accompanied by two additional copies of such application (for a total of three copies).

(c)   If an application for extension of patent term is informal under this section, the Office will so notify the applicant. The applicant has two months from the mail date of the notice, or such time as is set in the notice, within which to correct the informality. Unless the notice indicates otherwise, this time period may be extended under the provisions of § 1.136.

[Added 52 FR 9395, Mar. 24, 1987, effective May 26, 1987; para. (a) amended, 54 FR 30375, July 20, 1989, effective Aug. 22, 1989; para. (a)(14), 56 FR 65142, Dec. 13, 1991, effective Dec. 16, 1991; heading, introductory text of paragraph (a), and paras. (a)(9), (a)(10), (a)(14), (a)(15), (b) and (c) revised, 65 FR 54604, Sept. 8, 2000, effective Sept. 8, 2000; paras. (a)(16) and (a)(17) removed, 65 FR 54604, Sept. 8, 2000, effective Sept. 8, 2000; paras. (a) & (a)(13) revised, 68 FR 14332, Mar. 25, 2003, effective May 1, 2003]

§ 1.741   Complete application given a filing date; petition procedure.

(a)   The filing date of an application for extension of a patent term is the date on which a complete application is received in the Office or filed pursuant to the procedures set forth in §1.8 or § 1.10. A complete application must include:

(1)   An identification of the approved product;

(2)   An identification of each Federal statute under which regulatory review occurred;

(3)   An identification of the patent for which an extension is being sought;

(4)   An identification of each claim of the patent which claims the approved product or a method of using or manufacturing the approved product;

(5)   Sufficient information to enable the Director to determine under subsections (a) and (b) of 35 U.S.C. 156 the eligibility of a patent for extension, and the rights that will be derived from the extension, and information to enable the Director and the Secretary of Health and Human Services or the Secretary of Agriculture to determine the length of the regulatory review period; and

(6)   A brief description of the activities undertaken by the marketing applicant during the applicable regulatory review period with respect to the approved product and the significant dates applicable to such activities.

(b)   If an application for extension of patent term is incomplete under this section, the Office will so notify the applicant. If applicant requests review of a notice that an application is incomplete, or review of the filing date accorded an application under this section, applicant must file a petition pursuant to this paragraph accompanied by the fee set forth in § 1.17(f) within two months of the mail date of the notice that the application is incomplete, or the notice according the filing date complained of. Unless the notice indicates otherwise, this time period may be extended under the provisions of § 1.136.

[Added 52 FR 9396, Mar. 24, 1987, effective May 26, 1987; para. (a) amended, 54 FR 30375, July 20, 1989, effective Aug. 22, 1989; para. (a) amended, 58 FR 54494, Oct. 22, 1993, effective Nov. 22, 1993; para. (a) correcting amendment, 61 FR 64027, Dec. 3, 1996; heading, introductory text of paragraph (a), and paras. (a)(5) and (b) revised, 65 FR 54604, Sept. 8, 2000, effective Nov. 7, 2000; para. (a)(5) revised, 68 FR 14332, Mar. 25, 2003, effective May 1, 2003; para. (b) revised, 69 FR 56481, Sept. 21, 2004, effective Nov. 22, 2004]

§ 1.750   Determination of eligibility for extension of patent term.

A determination as to whether a patent is eligible for extension may be made by the Director solely on the basis of the representations contained in the application for extension filed in compliance with § 1.740 or § 1.790. This determination may be delegated to appropriate Patent and Trademark Office officials and may be made at any time before the certificate of extension is issued. The Director or other appropriate officials may require from applicant further information or make such independent inquiries as desired before a final determination is made on whether a patent is eligible for extension. In an application for extension filed in compliance with § 1.740, a notice will be mailed to applicant containing the determination as to the eligibility of the patent for extension and the period of time of the extension, if any. This notice shall constitute the final determination as to the eligibility and any period of extension of the patent. A single request for reconsideration of a final determination may be made if filed by the applicant within such time as may be set in the notice of final determination or, if no time is set, within one month from the date of the final determination. The time periods set forth herein are subject to the provisions of § 1.136.

[Added 52 FR 9396, Mar. 24, 1987, effective May 26, 1987; revised, 60 FR 25615, May 12, 1995, effective July 11, 1995; revised, 68 FR 14332, Mar. 25, 2003, effective May 1, 2003]

§ 1.760 Interim extension of patent term under 35 U.S.C. 156(e)(2).

An applicant who has filed a formal application for extension in compliance with § 1.740 may request one or more interim extensions for periods of up to one year each pending a final determination on the application pursuant to § 1.750. Any such request should be filed at least three months prior to the expiration date of the patent. The Director may issue interim extensions, without a request by the applicant, for periods of up to one year each until a final determination is made. The patent owner or agent will be notified when an interim extension is granted and notice of the extension will be published in the *Official Gazette of the United States Patent and Trademark Office*. The notice will be recorded in the official file of the patent and will be considered as part of the original patent. In no event will the interim extensions granted under this section be longer than the maximum period for extension to which the applicant would be eligible.

[Added, 52 FR 9396, Mar. 24, 1987, effective May 26, 1987; heading revised, 60 FR 25615, May 12, 1995, effective July 11, 1995; revised, 65 FR 54604, Sept. 8, 2000, effective Sept. 8, 2000; revised, 68 FR 14332, Mar. 25, 2003, effective May 1, 2003]

§ 1.765 Duty of disclosure in patent term extension proceedings.

(a)   A duty of candor and good faith toward the Patent and Trademark Office and the Secretary of Health and Human Services or the Secretary of Agriculture rests on the patent owner or its agent, on each attorney or agent who represents the patent owner and on every other individual who is substantively involved on behalf of the patent owner in a patent term extension proceeding. All such individuals who are aware, or become aware, of material information adverse to a determination of entitlement to the extension sought, which has not been previously made of record in the patent term extension proceeding must bring such information to the attention of the Office or the Secretary, as appropriate, in accordance with paragraph (b) of this section, as soon as it is practical to do so after the individual becomes aware of the information. Information is material where there is a substantial likelihood that the Office or the Secretary would consider it important in determinations to be made in the patent term extension proceeding.

(b)   Disclosures pursuant to this section must be accompanied by a copy of each written document which is being disclosed. The disclosure must be made to the Office or the Secretary, as appropriate, unless the disclosure is material to determinations to be made by both the Office and the Secretary, in which case duplicate copies, certified as such, must be filed in the Office and with the Secretary. Disclosures pursuant to this section may be made to the Office or the Secretary, as appropriate, through an attorney or agent having responsibility on behalf of the patent owner or its agent for the patent term extension proceeding or through a patent owner acting on his or her own behalf. Disclosure to such an attorney, agent or patent owner shall satisfy the duty of any other individual. Such an attorney, agent or patent owner has no duty to transmit information which is not material to the determination of entitlement to the extension sought.

(c)   No patent will be determined eligible for extension and no extension will be issued if it is determined that fraud on the Office or the Secretary was practiced or attempted or the duty of disclosure was violated through bad faith or gross negligence in connection with the patent term extension proceeding. If it is established by clear and convincing evidence that any fraud was practiced or attempted on the Office or the Secretary in connection with the patent term extension proceeding or that there was any violation of the duty of disclosure through bad faith or gross negligence in connection with the patent term extension proceeding, a final determination will be made pursuant to § 1.750 that the patent is not eligible for extension.

(d)   The duty of disclosure pursuant to this section rests on the individuals identified in paragraph (a) of this section and no submission on behalf of third parties, in the form of protests or otherwise, will be considered by the Office. Any such submissions by third parties to the Office will be returned to the party making the submission, or otherwise disposed of, without consideration by the Office.

[Added, 52 FR 9396, Mar. 24 1987, effective May 26, 1987, para. (a) amended, 54 FR 30375, July 20, 1989, effective Aug. 22, 1989; para. (a) revised, 60 FR 25615, May 12, 1995, effective July 11, 1995]

§ 1.770 Express withdrawal of application for extension of patent term.

An application for extension of patent term may be expressly withdrawn before a determination is made pursuant to § 1.750 by filing in the Office, in duplicate, a written declaration of withdrawal signed by the owner of record of the patent or its agent. An application may not be expressly withdrawn after the date permitted for reply to the final determination on the application. An express withdrawal pursuant to this section is effective when acknowledged in writing by the Office. The filing of an express withdrawal pursuant to this section and its acceptance by the Office does not entitle applicant to a refund of the filing fee (§ 1.20(j)) or any portion thereof.

[Added 52 FR 9397, Mar. 24 1987, effective May 26, 1987; 56 FR 65142, Dec. 13, 1991, effective Dec. 16, 1991; revised, 62 FR 53131, Oct. 10, 1997, effective Dec. 1, 1997]

§ 1.775 Calculation of patent term extension for a human drug, antibiotic drug, or human biological product.

(a)   If a determination is made pursuant to § 1.750 that a patent for a human drug, antibiotic drug, or human biological product is eligible for extension, the term shall be extended by the time as calculated in days in the manner indicated by this section. The patent term extension will run from the original expiration date of the patent or any earlier date set by terminal disclaimer (§ 1.321).

(b)   The term of the patent for a human drug, antibiotic drug or human biological product will be extended by the length of the regulatory review period for the product as determined by the Secretary of Health and Human Services, reduced as appropriate

pursuant to paragraphs (d)(1) through (d)(6) of this section.

(c)   The length of the regulatory review period for a human drug, antibiotic drug or human biological product will be determined by the Secretary of Health and Human Services. Under 35 U.S.C. 156(g)(1)(B), it is the sum of —

(1)   The number of days in the period beginning on the date an exemption under subsection (i) of section 505 or subsection (d) of section 507 of the Federal Food, Drug, and Cosmetic Act became effective for the approved product and ending on the date an application was initially submitted for such product under those sections or under section 351 of the Public Health Service Act; and

(2)   The number of days in the period beginning on the date the application was initially submitted for the approved product under section 351 of the Public Health Service Act, subsection (b) of section 505 or section 507 of the Federal Food, Drug, and Cosmetic Act and ending on the date such application was approved under such section.

(d)   The term of the patent as extended for a human drug, antibiotic drug or human biological product will be determined by—

(1)   Subtracting from the number of days determined by the Secretary of Health and Human Services to be in the regulatory review period:

(i)   The number of days in the periods of paragraphs (c)(1) and (c)(2) of this section which were on and before the date on which the patent issued;

(ii)   The number of days in the periods of paragraphs (c)(1) and (c)(2) of this section during which it is determined under 35 U.S.C. 156(d)(2)(B) by the Secretary of Health and Human Services that applicant did not act with due diligence;

(iii)   One-half the number of days remaining in the period defined by paragraph (c)(1) of this section after that period is reduced in accordance with paragraphs (d)(1)(i) and (ii) of this section; half days will be ignored for purposes of subtraction;

(2)   By adding the number of days determined in paragraph (d)(1) of this section to the original term of the patent as shortened by any terminal disclaimer;

(3)   By adding 14 years to the date of approval of the application under section 351 of the Public Health Service Act, or subsection (b) of section

505 or section 507 of the Federal Food, Drug, and Cosmetic Act;

(4) By comparing the dates for the ends of the periods obtained pursuant to paragraphs (d)(2) and (d)(3) of this section with each other and selecting the earlier date;

(5) If the original patent was issued after September 24, 1984,

(i) By adding 5 years to the original expiration date of the patent or any earlier date set by terminal disclaimer; and

(ii) By comparing the dates obtained pursuant to paragraphs (d)(4) and (d)(5)(i) of this section with each other and selecting the earlier date;

(6) If the original patent was issued before September 24, 1984, and

(i) If no request was submitted for an exemption under subsection (i) of section 505 or subsection (d) of section 507 of the Federal Food, Drug, and Cosmetic Act before September 24, 1984, by—

(A) Adding 5 years to the original expiration date of the patent or earlier date set by terminal disclaimer; and

(B) By comparing the dates obtained pursuant to paragraphs (d)(4) and (d)(6)(i)(A) of this section with each other and selecting the earlier date; or

(ii) If a request was submitted for an exemption under subsection (i) of section 505 or subsection (d) of section 507 of the Federal Food, Drug, or Cosmetic Act before September 24, 1984 and the commercial marketing or use of the product was not approved before September 24, 1984, by -

(A) Adding 2 years to the original expiration date of the patent or earlier date set by terminal disclaimer, and

(B) By comparing the dates obtained pursuant to paragraphs (d)(4) and (d)(6)(ii)(A) of this section with each other and selecting the earlier filing date.

[Added, 52 FR 9397, Mar. 24 1987, effective May 26, 1987]

§ 1.776 Calculation of patent term extension for a food additive or color additive.

(a) If a determination is made pursuant to § 1.750 that a patent for a food additive or color additive is eligible for extension, the term shall be extended by the time as calculated in days in the manner indicated by this section. The patent term extension will run from the original expiration date of the patent or earlier date set by terminal disclaimer (§ 1.321).

(b) The term of the patent for a food additive or color additive will be extended by the length of the regulatory review period for the product as determined by the Secretary of Health and Human Services, reduced as appropriate pursuant to paragraphs (d)(1) through (d)(6) of this section.

(c) The length of the regulatory review period for a food additive or color additive will be determined by the Secretary of Health and Human Services. Under 35 U.S.C. 156(g)(2)(B), it is the sum of -

(1) The number of days in the period beginning on the date a major health or environmental effects test on the additive was initiated and ending on the date a petition was initially submitted with respect to the approved product under the Federal Food, Drug, and Cosmetic Act requesting the issuance of a regulation for use of the product; and

(2) The number of days in the period beginning on the date a petition was initially submitted with respect to the approved product under the Federal Food, Drug and Cosmetic Act requesting the issuance of a regulation for use of the product, and ending on the date such regulation became effective or, if objections were filed to such regulation, ending on the date such objections were resolved and commercial marketing was permitted or, if commercial marketing was permitted and later revoked pending further proceedings as a result of such objections, ending on the date such proceedings were finally resolved and commercial marketing was permitted.

(d) The term of the patent as extended for a food additive or color additive will be determined by

(1) Subtracting from the number of days determined by the Secretary of Health and Human Services to be in the regulatory review period:

(i) The number of days in the periods of paragraphs (c)(1) and (c)(2) of this section which were on and before the date on which the patent issued;

(ii) The number of days in the periods of paragraphs (c)(1) and (c)(2) of this section during which it is determined under 35 U.S.C. 156(d)(2)(B) by the Secretary of Health and Human Services that applicant did not act with due diligence;

(iii) The number of days equal to one-half the number of days remaining in the period defined by paragraph (c)(1) of this section after that period is reduced in accordance with paragraphs (d)(1) (i) and (ii) of this section; half days will be ignored for purposes of subtraction;

(2) By adding the number of days determined in paragraph (d)(1) of this section to the original term of the patent as shortened by any terminal disclaimer;

(3) By adding 14 years to the date a regulation for use of the product became effective or, if objections were filed to such regulation, to the date such objections were resolved and commercial marketing was permitted or, if commercial marketing was permitted and later revoked pending further proceedings as a result of such objections, to the date such proceedings were finally resolved and commercial marketing was permitted;

(4) By comparing the dates for the ends of the periods obtained pursuant to paragraphs (d)(2) and (d)(3) of this section with each other and selecting the earlier date;

(5) If the original patent was issued after September 24, 1984,

(i) By adding 5 years to the original expiration date of the patent or earlier date set by terminal disclaimer; and

(ii) By comparing the dates obtained pursuant to paragraphs (d)(4) and (d)(5)(i) of this section with each other and selecting the earlier date;

(6) If the original patent was issued before September 24, 1984, and

(i) If no major health or environmental effects test was initiated and no petition for a regulation or application for registration was submitted before September 24, 1984, by

(A) Adding 5 years to the original expiration date of the patent or earlier date set by terminal disclaimer, and

(B) By comparing the dates obtained pursuant to paragraphs (d)(4) and (d)(6)(i)(A) of this section with each other and selecting the earlier date; or

(ii) If a major health or environmental effects test was initiated or a petition for a regulation or application for registration was submitted by Sep-

tember 24, 1984, and the commercial marketing or use of the product was not approved before September 24, 1984, by —

(A) Adding 2 years to the original expiration date of the patent or earlier date set by terminal disclaimer, and

(B) By comparing the dates obtained pursuant to paragraphs (d)(4) and (d)(6)(ii)(A) of this section with each other and selecting the earlier date.

[Added, 52 FR 9397, Mar. 24, 1987, effective May 26, 1987]

§ 1.777 Calculation of patent term extension for a medical device.

(a) If a determination is made pursuant to § 1.750 that a patent for a medical device is eligible for extension, the term shall be extended by the time as calculated in days in the manner indicated by this section. The patent term extension will run from the original expiration date of the patent or earlier date as set by terminal disclaimer (§ 1.321).

(b) The term of the patent for a medical device will be extended by the length of the regulatory review period for the product as determined by the Secretary of Health and Human Services, reduced as appropriate pursuant to paragraphs (d)(1) through (d)(6) of this section.

(c) The length of the regulatory review period for a medical device will be determined by the Secretary of Health and Human Services. Under 35 U.S.C. 156(g)(3)(B), it is the sum of

(1) The number of days in the period beginning on the date a clinical investigation on humans involving the device was begun and ending on the date an application was initially submitted with respect to the device under section 515 of the Federal Food, Drug, and Cosmetic Act; and

(2) The number of days in the period beginning on the date the application was initially submitted with respect to the device under section 515 of the Federal Food, Drug, and Cosmetic Act, and ending on the date such application was approved under such Act or the period beginning on the date a notice of completion of a product development protocol was initially submitted under section 515(f)(5) of the Act and ending on the date the protocol was declared completed under section 515(f)(6) of the Act.

(d) The term of the patent as extended for a medical device will be determined by —

(1) Subtracting from the number of days determined by the Secretary of Health and Human Services to be in the regulatory review period pursuant to paragraph (c) of this section:

(i) The number of days in the periods of paragraphs (c)(1) and (c)(2) of this section which were on and before the date on which the patent issued;

(ii) The number of days in the periods of paragraphs (c)(1) and (c)(2) of this section during which it is determined under 35 U.S.C. 156(d)(2)(B) by the Secretary of Health and Human Services that applicant did not act with due diligence;

(iii) One-half the number of days remaining in the period defined by paragraph (c)(1) of this section after that period is reduced in accordance with paragraphs (d)(1) (i) and (ii) of this section; half days will be ignored for purposes of subtraction;

(2) By adding the number of days determined in paragraph (d)(1) of this section to the original term of the patent as shortened by any terminal disclaimer;

(3) By adding 14 years to the date of approval of the application under section 515 of the Federal Food, Drug, and Cosmetic Act or the date a product development protocol was declared completed under section 515(f)(6) of the Act;

(4) By comparing the dates for the ends of the periods obtained pursuant to paragraphs (d)(2) and (d)(3) of this section with each other and selecting the earlier date;

(5) If the original patent was issued after September 24, 1984,

(i) By adding 5 years to the original expiration date of the patent or earlier date set by terminal disclaimer; and

(ii) By comparing the dates obtained pursuant to paragraphs (d)(4) and (d)(5)(i) of this section with each other and selecting the earlier date;

(6) If the original patent was issued before September 24, 1984, and

(i) If no clinical investigation on humans involving the device was begun or no product development protocol was submitted under section 515(f)(5) of the Federal Food, Drug, and Cosmetic Act before September 24, 1984, by —

(A) Adding 5 years to the original expiration date of the patent or earlier date set by terminal disclaimer and

(B) By comparing the dates obtained pursuant to paragraphs (d)(4) and (d)(6)(i)(A) of this section with each other and selecting the earlier date; or

(ii) If a clinical investigation on humans involving the device was begun or a product development protocol was submitted under section 515(f)(5) of the Federal Food, Drug, and Cosmetic Act before September 24, 1984 and the commercial marketing or use of the product was not approved before September 24, 1984, by

(A) Adding 2 years to the original expiration date of the patent or earlier date set by terminal disclaimer, and

(B) By comparing the dates obtained pursuant to paragraphs (d)(4) and (d)(6)(ii)(A) of this section with each other and selecting the earlier date.

[Added, 52 FR 9398, Mar. 24 1987, effective May 26, 1987]

§ 1.778 Calculation of patent term extension for an animal drug product.

(a) If a determination is made pursuant to § 1.750 that a patent for an animal drug is eligible for extension, the term shall be extended by the time as calculated in days in the manner indicated by this section. The patent term extension will run from the original expiration date of the patent or any earlier date set by terminal disclaimer (§ 1.321).

(b) The term of the patent for an animal drug will be extended by the length of the regulatory review period for the drug as determined by the Secretary of Health and Human Services, reduced as appropriate pursuant to paragraphs (d)(1) through (d)(6) of this section.

(c) The length of the regulatory review period for an animal drug will be determined by the Secretary of Health and Human Services. Under 35 U.S.C. 156(g)(4)(B), it is the sum of —

(1) The number of days in the period beginning on the earlier of the date a major health or environmental effects test on the drug was initiated or the date an exemption under subsection (j) of section 512 of the Federal Food, Drug, and Cosmetic Act became effective for the approved animal drug and ending on

the date an application was initially submitted for such animal drug under section 512 of the Federal Food, Drug, and Cosmetic Act; and

(2)   The number of days in the period beginning on the date the application was initially submitted for the approved animal drug under subsection (b) of section 512 of the Federal Food, Drug, and Cosmetic Act and ending on the date such application was approved under such section.

(d)   The term of the patent as extended for an animal drug will be determined by —

(1)   Subtracting from the number of days determined by the Secretary of Health and Human Services to be in the regulatory review period:

(i)   The number of days in the periods of paragraphs (c)(1) and (c)(2) of this section that were on and before the date on which the patent issued;

(ii)   The number of days in the periods of paragraphs (c)(1) and (c)(2) of this section during which it is determined under 35 U.S.C. 156(d)(2)(B) by the Secretary of Health and Human Services that applicant did not act with due diligence;

(iii)   One-half the number of days remaining in the period defined by paragraph (c)(1) of this section after that period is reduced in accordance with paragraphs (d)(1)(i) and (ii) of this section; half days will be ignored for purposes of subtraction;

(2)   By adding the number of days determined in paragraph (d)(1) of this section to the original term of the patent as shortened by any terminal disclaimer;

(3)   By adding 14 years to the date of approval of the application under section 512 of the Federal Food, Drug, and Cosmetic Act;

(4)   By comparing the dates for the ends of the periods obtained pursuant to paragraphs (d)(2) and (d)(3) of this section with each other and selecting the earlier date;

(5)   If the original patent was issued after November 16, 1988, by —

(i)   Adding 5 years to the original expiration date of the patent or any earlier date set by terminal disclaimer; and

(ii)   Comparing the dates obtained pursuant to paragraphs (d)(4) and (d)(5)(i) of this section with each other and selecting the earlier date;

(6)   If the original patent was issued before November 16, 1988, and

(i)   If no major health or environmental effects test on the drug was initiated and no request was submitted for an exemption under subsection (j) of section 512 of the Federal Food, Drug, and Cosmetic Act before November 16, 1988, by —

(A)   Adding 5 years to the original expiration date of the patent or earlier date set by terminal disclaimer; and

(B)   Comparing the dates obtained pursuant to paragraphs (d)(4) and (d)(6)(i)(A) of this section with each other and selecting the earlier date; or

(ii)   If a major health or environmental effects test was initiated or a request for an exemption under subsection (j) of section 512 of the Federal Food, Drug, and Cosmetic Act was submitted before November 16, 1988, and the application for commercial marketing or use of the animal drug was not approved before November 16, 1988, by —

(A)   Adding 3 years to the original expiration date of the patent or earlier date set by terminal disclaimer, and

(B)   Comparing the dates obtained pursuant to paragraphs (d)(4) and (d)(6)(ii)(A) of this section with each other and selecting the earlier date.

[Added, 54 FR 30375, July 20, 1989, effective Aug. 22, 1989]

§ 1.779   Calculation of patent term extension for a veterinary biological product.

(a)   If a determination is made pursuant to § 1.750 that a patent for a veterinary biological product is eligible for extension, the term shall be extended by the time as calculated in days in the manner indicated by this section. The patent term extension will run from the original expiration date of the patent or any earlier date set by terminal disclaimer (§ 1.321).

(b)   The term of the patent for a veterinary biological product will be extended by the length of the regulatory review period for the product as determined by the Secretary of Agriculture, reduced as appropriate pursuant to paragraphs (d)(1) through (d)(6) of this section.

(c)   The length of the regulatory review period for a veterinary biological product will be determined by the Secretary of Agriculture. Under 35 U.S.C. 156(g)(5)(B), it is the sum of —

(1) The number of days in the period beginning on the date the authority to prepare an experimental biological product under the Virus-Serum-Toxin Act became effective and ending on the date an application for a license was submitted under the Virus-Serum-Toxin Act; and

(2) The number of days in the period beginning on the date an application for a license was initially submitted for approval under the Virus-Serum-Toxin Act and ending on the date such license was issued.

(d) The term of the patent as extended for a veterinary biological product will be determined by —

(1) Subtracting from the number of days determined by the Secretary of Agriculture to be in the regulatory review period:

(i) The number of days in the periods of paragraphs (c)(1) and (c)(2) of this section that were on and before the date on which the patent issued;

(ii) The number of days in the periods of paragraphs (c)(1) and (c)(2) of this section during which it is determined under 35 U.S.C. 156(d)(2)(B) by the Secretary of Agriculture that applicant did not act with due diligence;

(iii) One-half the number of days remaining in the period defined by paragraph (c)(1) of this section after that period is reduced in accordance with paragraphs (d)(1)(i) and (ii) of this section; half days will be ignored for purposes of subtraction;

(2) By adding the number of days determined in paragraph (d)(1) of this section to the original term of the patent as shortened by any terminal disclaimer;

(3) By adding 14 years to the date of the issuance of a license under the Virus-Serum-Toxin Act;

(4) By comparing the dates for the ends of the periods obtained pursuant to paragraphs (d)(2) and (d)(3) of this section with each other and selecting the earlier date;

(5) If the original patent was issued after November 16, 1988, by —

(i) Adding 5 years to the original expiration date of the patent or any earlier date set by terminal disclaimer; and

(ii) Comparing the dates obtained pursuant to paragraphs (d)(4) and (d)(5)(i) of this section with each other and selecting the earlier date;

(6) If the original patent was issued before November 16, 1988, and

(i) If no request for the authority to prepare an experimental biological product under the Virus-Serum-Toxin Act was submitted before November 16, 1988, by —

(A) Adding 5 years to the original expiration date of the patent or earlier date set by terminal disclaimer; and

(B) Comparing the dates obtained pursuant to paragraphs (d)(4) and (d)(6)(i)(A) of this section with each other and selecting the earlier date; or

(ii) If a request for the authority to prepare an experimental biological product under the Virus-Serum-Toxin Act was submitted before November 16, 1988, and the commercial marketing or use of the product was not approved before November 16, 1988, by —

(A) Adding 3 years to the original expiration date of the patent or earlier date set by terminal disclaimer; and

(B) Comparing the dates obtained pursuant to paragraphs (d)(4) and (d)(6)(ii)(A) of this section with each other and selecting the earlier date.

[Added, 54 FR 30375, July 20, 1989, effective Aug. 22, 1989]

§ 1.780 Certificate or order of extension of patent term.

If a determination is made pursuant to § 1.750 that a patent is eligible for extension and that the term of the patent is to be extended, a certificate of extension, under seal, or an order granting interim extension under 35 U.S.C. 156(d)(5), will be issued to the applicant for the extension of the patent term. Such certificate or order will be recorded in the official file of the patent and will be considered as part of the original patent. Notification of the issuance of the certificate or order of extension will be published in the *Official Gazette of the United States Patent and Trademark Office*. Notification of the issuance of the order granting an interim extension under 35 U.S.C. 156(d)(5), including the identity of the product currently under regulatory review, will be published in the *Official Gazette of the United States Patent and Trademark Office* and in the *Federal Register*. No certificate of, or order granting, an extension will be issued if the term of the patent cannot be extended, even though the patent is otherwise determined to be eligible for extension. In such situations, the final determination made pursuant to § 1.750 will indicate that no certificate or order will issue.

[Added, 52 FR 9399, Mar. 24 1987, effective May 26, 1987; para. (a) revised, 60 FR 25615, May 12, 1995, effective July 11, 1995; revised, 65 FR 54604, Sept. 8, 2000, effective Nov. 7, 2000]

§ 1.785 Multiple applications for extension of term of the same patent or of different patents for the same regulatory review period for a product.

(a)   Only one patent may be extended for a regulatory review period for any product § 1.720 (h). If more than one application for extension of the same patent is filed, the certificate of extension of patent term, if appropriate, will be issued based upon the first filed application for extension.

(b)   If more than one application for extension is filed by a single applicant which seeks the extension of the term of two or more patents based upon the same regulatory review period, and the patents are otherwise eligible for extension pursuant to the requirements of this subpart, in the absence of an election by the applicant, the certificate of extension of patent term, if appropriate, will be issued upon the application for extension of the patent term having the earliest date of issuance of those patents for which extension is sought.

(c)   If an application for extension is filed which seeks the extension of the term of a patent based upon the same regulatory review period as that relied upon in one or more applications for extension pursuant to the requirements of this subpart, the certificate of extension of patent term will be issued on the application only if the patent owner or its agent is the holder of the regulatory approval granted with respect to the regulatory review period.

(d)   An application for extension shall be considered complete and formal regardless of whether it contains the identification of the holder of the regulatory approval granted with respect to the regulatory review period. When an application contains such information, or is amended to contain such information, it will be considered in determining whether an application is eligible for an extension under this section. A request may be made of any applicant to supply such information within a non-extendable period of not less than one month whenever multiple applications for extension of more than one patent are received and rely upon the same regulatory review period. Failure to provide such information within the period for reply set shall be regarded as conclusively establishing that the applicant is not the holder of the regulatory approval.

(e)   Determinations made under this section shall be included in the notice of final determination of eligibility for extension of the patent term pursuant to § 1.750 and shall be regarded as part of that determination.

[Added, 52 FR 9399, Mar. 24 1987, effective May 26, 1987; para. (b) amended, 54 FR 30375, July 20, 1989, effective Aug. 22, 1989; revised, 60 FR 25615, May 12, 1995, effective July 11, 1995; para. (d) revised, 62 FR 53131, Oct. 10, 1997, effective Dec. 1, 1997]

§ 1.790 Interim extension of patent term under 35 U.S.C. 156(d)(5).

(a)   An owner of record of a patent or its agent who reasonably expects that the applicable regulatory review period described in paragraph (1)(B)(ii), (2)(B)(ii), (3)(B)(ii), (4)(B)(ii), or (5)(B)(ii) of subsection (g) that began for a product that is the subject of such patent may extend beyond the expiration of the patent term in effect may submit one or more applications for interim extensions for periods of up to one year each. The initial application for interim extension must be filed during the period beginning 6 months and ending 15 days before the patent term is due to expire. Each subsequent application for interim extension must be filed during the period beginning 60 days before and ending 30 days before the expiration of the preceding interim extension. In no event will the interim extensions granted under this section be longer than the maximum period of extension to which the applicant would be entitled under 35 U.S.C. 156(c).

(b)   A complete application for interim extension under this section shall include all of the information required for a formal application under § 1.740 and a complete application under § 1.741. Sections (a)(1), (a)(2), (a)(4), and (a)(6) - (a)(17) of § 1.740 and § 1.741 shall be read in the context of a product currently undergoing regulatory review. Sections (a)(3) and (a)(5) of § 1.740 are not applicable to an application for interim extension under this section.

(c)   The content of each subsequent interim extension application may be limited to a request for a subsequent interim extension along with a statement that the regulatory review period has not been completed along with any materials or information required under §§ 1.740 and 1.741 that are not present in the preceding interim extension application.

[Added, 60 FR 25615, May 12, 1995, effective July 11, 1995]

§ 1.791   Termination of interim extension granted prior to regulatory approval of a product for commercial marketing or use.

Any interim extension granted under 35 U.S.C. 156(d)(5) terminates at the end of the 60-day period beginning on the date on which the product involved receives permission for commercial marketing or use. If within that 60-day period the patent owner or its agent files an application for extension under §§ 1.740 and 1.741 including any additional information required under 35 U.S.C. 156(d)(1) not contained in the application for interim extension, the patent shall be further extended in accordance with the provisions of 35 U.S.C. 156.

[Added, 60 FR 25615, May 12, 1995, effective July 11, 1995]

Subpart G — Biotechnology Invention Disclosures

DEPOSIT OF BIOLOGICAL MATERIAL

§ 1.801   Biological material.

For the purposes of these regulations pertaining to the deposit of biological material for purposes of patents for inventions under 35 U.S.C. 101, the term biological material shall include material that is capable of self-replication either directly or indirectly. Representative examples include bacteria, fungi including yeast, algae, protozoa, eukaryotic cells, cell lines, hybridomas, plasmids, viruses, plant tissue cells, lichens and seeds. Viruses, vectors, cell organelles and other non-living material existing in and reproducible from a living cell may be deposited by deposit of the host cell capable of reproducing the non-living material.

[Added, 54 FR 34880, Aug. 22, 1989, effective Jan. 1, 1990]

§ 1.802   Need or opportunity to make a deposit.

(a)   Where an invention is, or relies on, a biological material, the disclosure may include reference to a deposit of such biological material.

(b)   Biological material need not be deposited unless access to such material is necessary for the satisfaction of the statutory requirements for patentability under 35 U.S.C. 112. If a deposit is necessary, it shall be acceptable if made in accordance with these regulations. Biological material need not be deposited, *inter alia*, if it is known and readily available to the public or can be made or isolated without undue experimentation. Once deposited in a depository complying with these regulations, a biological material will be considered to be readily available even though some requirement of law or regulation of the United States or of the country in which the depository institution is located permits access to the material only under conditions imposed for safety, public health or similar reasons.

(c)   The reference to a biological material in a specification disclosure or the actual deposit of such material by an applicant or patent owner does not create any presumption that such material is necessary to satisfy 35 U.S.C. 112 or that deposit in accordance with these regulations is or was required.

[Added, 54 FR 34880, Aug. 22, 1989, effective Jan. 1, 1990]

§ 1.803   Acceptable depository.

(a)   A deposit shall be recognized for the purposes of these regulations if made in

(1)   Any International Depositary Authority (IDA) as established under the Budapest Treaty on the International Recognition of the Deposit of Microorganisms for the Purposes of Patent Procedure, or

(2)   Any other depository recognized to be suitable by the Office. Suitability will be determined by the Director on the basis of the administrative and technical competence, and agreement of the depository to comply with the terms and conditions applicable to deposits for patent purposes. The Director may seek the advice of impartial consultants on the suitability of a depository. The depository must:

(i)   Have a continuous existence;

(ii)   Exist independent of the control of the depositor;

(iii)   Possess the staff and facilities sufficient to examine the viability of a deposit and store the deposit in a manner which ensures that it is kept viable and uncontaminated;

(iv)   Provide for sufficient safety measures to minimize the risk of losing biological material deposited with it;

(v)   Be impartial and objective;

(vi)   Furnish samples of the deposited material in an expeditious and proper manner; and

(vii)   Promptly notify depositors of its inability to furnish samples, and the reasons why.

(b)   A depository seeking status under paragraph (a)(2) of this section must direct a communication to the Director which shall:

(1)   Indicate the name and address of the depository to which the communication relates;

(2)   Contain detailed information as to the capacity of the depository to comply with the requirements of paragraph (a)(2) of this section, including information on its legal status, scientific standing, staff, and facilities;

(3)   Indicate that the depository intends to be available, for the purposes of deposit, to any depositor under these same conditions;

(4)   Where the depository intends to accept for deposit only certain kinds of biological material, specify such kinds;

(5)   Indicate the amount of any fees that the depository will, upon acquiring the status of suitable depository under paragraph (a)(2) of this section, charge for storage, viability statements and furnishings of samples of the deposit.

(c)   A depository having status under paragraph (a)(2) of this section limited to certain kinds of biological material may extend such status to additional kinds of biological material by directing a communication to the Director in accordance with paragraph (b) of this section. If a previous communication under paragraph (b) of this section is of record, items in common with the previous communication may be incorporated by reference.

(d)   Once a depository is recognized to be suitable by the Director or has defaulted or discontinued its performance under this section, notice thereof will

be published in the *Official Gazette* of the Patent and Trademark Office.

[Added, 54 FR 34881, Aug. 22, 1989, effective Jan. 1, 199; paras. (a)(2) & (b)-(d) revised, 68 FR 14332, Mar. 25, 2003, effective May 1, 2003]

§ 1.804   Time of making an original deposit.

(a)   Whenever a biological material is specifically identified in an application for patent as filed, an original deposit thereof may be made at any time before filing the application for patent or, subject to § 1.809, during pendency of the application for patent.

(b)   When the original deposit is made after the effective filing date of an application for patent, the applicant must promptly submit a statement from a person in a position to corroborate the fact, stating that the biological material which is deposited is a biological material specifically identified in the application as filed.

[Added, 54 FR 34881, Aug. 22, 1989, effective Jan. 1, 1990; para. (b) revised, 62 FR 53131, Oct. 10, 1997, effective Dec. 1, 1997]

§ 1.805   Replacement or supplement of deposit.

(a)   A depositor, after receiving notice during the pendency of an application for patent, application for reissue patent or reexamination proceeding, that the depository possessing a deposit either cannot furnish samples thereof or can furnish samples thereof but the deposit has become contaminated or has lost its capability to function as described in the specification, shall notify the Office in writing, in each application for patent or patent affected. In such a case, or where the Office otherwise learns, during the pendency of an application for patent, application for reissue patent or reexamination proceeding, that the depository possessing a deposit either cannot furnish samples thereof or can furnish samples thereof but the deposit has become contaminated or has lost its capability to function as described in the specification, the need for making a replacement or supplemental deposit will be governed by the same considerations governing the need for making an original deposit under the provisions set forth in § 1.802(b). A replacement or supplemental deposit made during the pendency of an application for patent shall not be accepted unless it meets the requirements for making an original deposit under these regulations, including the requirement set forth under § 1.804(b). A replacement or supplemental deposit made in connection with a patent, whether or not made during the pendency of an application for reissue patent or a reexamination proceeding or both, shall not be accepted unless a certificate of correction under § 1.323 is requested by the patent owner which meets the terms of paragraphs (b) and (c) of this section.

(b)   A request for certificate of correction under this section shall not be granted unless the certificate identifies:

(1)   The accession number for the replacement or supplemental deposit;

(2)   The date of the deposit; and

(3)   The name and address of the depository.

(c)   A request for a certificate of correction under this section shall not be granted unless the request is made promptly after the replacement or supplemental deposit has been made and the request:

(1)   Includes a statement of the reason for making the replacement or supplemental deposit;

(2)   Includes a statement from a person in a position to corroborate the fact, and stating that the replacement or supplemental deposit is of a biological material which is identical to that originally deposited;

(3)   Includes a showing that the patent owner acted diligently —

(i)   In the case of a replacement deposit, in making the deposit after receiving notice that samples could no longer be furnished from an earlier deposit; or

(ii)   In the case of a supplemental deposit, in making the deposit after receiving notice that the earlier deposit had become contaminated or had lost its capability to function as described in the specification;

(4)   Includes a statement that the term of the replacement or supplemental deposit expires no earlier than the term of the deposit being replaced or supplemented; and

(5)   Otherwise establishes compliance with these regulations.

(d)   A depositor's failure to replace a deposit, or in the case of a patent, to diligently replace a deposit and promptly thereafter request a certificate of correction which meets the terms of paragraphs (b) and (c) of this section, after being notified that the depository possessing the deposit cannot furnish samples thereof, shall cause the application or patent involved to be treated in any Office proceeding as if no deposit were made.

(e)   In the event a deposit is replaced according to these regulations, the Office will apply a rebuttable presumption of identity between the original and the replacement deposit where a patent making reference to the deposit is relied upon during any Office proceeding.

(f)   A replacement or supplemental deposit made during the pendency of an application for patent may be made for any reason.

(g)   In no case is a replacement or supplemental deposit of a biological material necessary where the biological material, in accordance with § 1.802(b), need not be deposited.

(h)   No replacement deposit of a biological material is necessary where a depository can furnish samples thereof but the depository for national security, health or environmental safety reasons is unable to provide samples to requesters outside of the jurisdiction where the depository is located.

(i)   The Office will not recognize in any Office proceeding a replacement deposit of a biological material made by a patent owner where the depository could furnish samples of the deposit being replaced.

[Added, 54 FR 34881, Aug. 22, 1989, effective Jan. 1, 1990; para. (c) revised, 62 FR 53131, Oct. 10, 1997, effective Dec. 1, 1997]

§ 1.806   Term of deposit.

A deposit made before or during pendency of an application for patent shall be made for a term of at least thirty (30) years and at least five (5) years after the most recent request for the furnishing of a sample of the deposit was received by the depository. In any case, samples must be stored under agreements that would make them available beyond the enforceable life of the patent for which the deposit was made.

[Added, 54 FR 34882, Aug. 22, 1989, effective Jan. 1, 1990]

§ 1.807 Viability of deposit.

(a)   A deposit of biological material that is capable of self-replication either directly or indirectly must be viable at the time of deposit and during the term of deposit. Viability may be tested by the depository. The test must conclude only that the deposited material is capable of reproduction. No evidence is necessarily required regarding the ability of the deposited material to perform any function described in the patent application.

(b)   A viability statement for each deposit of a biological material defined in paragraph (a) of this section not made under the Budapest Treaty on the International Recognition of the Deposit of Microorganisms for the Purposes of Patent Procedure must be filed in the application and must contain:

(1)   The name and address of the depository;

(2)   The name and address of the depositor;

(3)   The date of deposit;

(4)   The identity of the deposit and the accession number given by the depository;

(5)   The date of the viability test;

(6)   The procedures used to obtain a sample if the test is not done by the depository; and

(7)   A statement that the deposit is capable of reproduction.

(c)   If a viability test indicates that the deposit is not viable upon receipt, or the examiner cannot, for scientific or other valid reasons, accept the statement of viability received from the applicant, the examiner shall proceed as if no deposit has been made. The examiner will accept the conclusion set forth in a viability statement issued by a depository recognized under § 1.803(a).

[Added, 54 FR 34882, Aug. 22, 1989, effective Jan. 1, 1990]

§ 1.808 Furnishing of samples.

(a)   A deposit must be made under conditions that assure that:

(1)   Access to the deposit will be available during pendency of the patent application making reference to the deposit to one determined by the Director to be entitled thereto under § 1.14 and 35 U.S.C. 122, and

(2)   Subject to paragraph (b) of this section, all restrictions imposed by the depositor on the availability to the public of the deposited material will be irrevocably removed upon the granting of the patent.

(b)   The depositor may contract with the depository to require that samples of a deposited biological material shall be furnished only if a request for a sample, during the term of the patent:

(1)   Is in writing or other tangible form and dated;

(2)   Contains the name and address of the requesting party and the accession number of the deposit; and

(3)   Is communicated in writing by the depository to the depositor along with the date on which the sample was furnished and the name and address of the party to whom the sample was furnished.

(c)   Upon request made to the Office, the Office will certify whether a deposit has been stated to have been made under conditions which make it available to the public as of the issue date of the patent grant provided the request contains:

(1)   The name and address of the depository;

(2)   The accession number given to the deposit;

(3)   The patent number and issue date of the patent referring to the deposit; and

(4)   The name and address of the requesting party.

[Added, 54 FR 34882, Aug. 22, 1989, effective Jan. 1, 199; para. (a)(1) revised, 68 FR 14332, Mar. 25, 2003, effective May 1, 2003]

§ 1.809 Examination procedures.

(a)   The examiner shall determine pursuant to § 1.104 in each application for patent, application for reissue patent or reexamination proceeding if a deposit is needed, and if needed, if a deposit actually made is acceptable for patent purposes. If a deposit is needed and has not been made or replaced or supplemented in accordance with these regulations, the examiner, where appropriate, shall reject the affected claims under the appropriate provision of 35 U.S.C. 112, explaining why a deposit is needed and/or why a deposit actually made cannot be accepted.

(b)   The applicant for patent or patent owner shall reply to a rejection under paragraph (a) of this section by—

(1)   In the case of an applicant for patent, either making an acceptable original, replacement, or

supplemental deposit, or assuring the Office in writing that an acceptable deposit will be made; or, in the case of a patent owner, requesting a certificate of correction of the patent which meets the terms of paragraphs (b) and (c) of § 1.805, or

(2) Arguing why a deposit is not needed under the circumstances of the application or patent considered and/or why a deposit actually made should be accepted. Other replies to the examiner's action shall be considered nonresponsive. The rejection will be repeated until either paragraph (b)(1) of this section is satisfied or the examiner is convinced that a deposit is not needed.

(c) If an application for patent is otherwise in condition for allowance except for a needed deposit and the Office has received a written assurance that an acceptable deposit will be made, applicant will be notified and given a period of time within which the deposit must be made in order to avoid abandonment. This time period is not extendable under § 1.136(a) or (b) if set forth in a "Notice of Allowability" or in an Office action having a mail date on or after the mail date of a "Notice of Allowability" (see § 1.136(c)).

(d) For each deposit made pursuant to these regulations, the specification shall contain:

(1) The accession number for the deposit;

(2) The date of the deposit;

(3) A description of the deposited biological material sufficient to specifically identify it and to permit examination; and

(4) The name and address of the depository.

(e) Any amendment required by paragraphs (d)(1), (d)(2) or (d)(4) of this section must be filed before or with the payment of the issue fee (see § 1.312).

[Added, 54 FR 34882, Aug. 22, 1989, effective Jan. 1, 1990; paras. (b) and (c) revised and para. (e) added, 66 FR 21092, Apr. 27, 2001, effective May 29, 2001]

APPLICATION DISCLOSURES CONTAINING NUCLEOTIDE AND/OR AMINO ACID SEQUENCES

§ 1.821 Nucleotide and/or amino acid sequence disclosures in patent applications.

(a) Nucleotide and/or amino acid sequences as used in §§ 1.821 through 1.825 are interpreted to mean an unbranched sequence of four or more amino acids or an unbranched sequence of ten or more nucleotides. Branched sequences are specifically excluded from this definition. Sequences with fewer than four specifically defined nucleotides or amino acids are specifically excluded from this section. "Specifically defined" means those amino acids other than "Xaa" and those nucleotide bases other than "n" defined in accordance with the World Intellectual Property Organization (WIPO) Handbook on Industrial Property Information and Documentation, Standard ST.25: Standard for the Presentation of Nucleotide and Amino Acid Sequence Listings in Patent Applications (1998), including Tables 1 through 6 in Appendix 2, herein incorporated by reference. (Hereinafter "WIPO Standard ST.25 (1998)"). This incorporation by reference was approved by the Director of the Federal Register in accordance with 5 U.S.C. 552(a) and 1 CFR part 51. Copies of WIPO Standard ST.25 (1998) may be obtained from the World Intellectual Property Organization; 34 chemin des Colombettes; 1211 Geneva 20 Switzerland. Copies may also be inspected at the National Archives and Records Administration (NARA). For information on the availability of this material at NARA, call 202-741-6030, or go to: *http://www.archives.gov/federal_register/code_of_federal_regulations/ibr_locations.html.* Nucleotides and amino acids are further defined as follows:

(1) *Nucleotides:* Nucleotides are intended to embrace only those nucleotides that can be represented using the symbols set forth in WIPO Standard ST.25 (1998), Appendix 2, Table 1. Modifications, *e.g.,* methylated bases, may be described as set forth in WIPO Standard ST.25 (1998), Appendix 2, Table 2, but shall not be shown explicitly in the nucleotide sequence.

(2) *Amino acids:* Amino acids are those L-amino acids commonly found in naturally occurring proteins and are listed in WIPO Standard ST.25 (1998), Appendix 2, Table 3. Those amino acid sequences containing D-amino acids are not intended to be embraced by this definition. Any amino acid sequence that contains post-translationally modified amino acids may be described as the amino acid sequence that is initially translated using the symbols shown in WIPO Standard ST.25 (1998), Appendix 2, Table 3 with the modified positions; *e.g.,* hydroxyla-

tions or glycosylations, being described as set forth in WIPO Standard ST.25 (1998), Appendix 2, Table 4, but these modifications shall not be shown explicitly in the amino acid sequence. Any peptide or protein that can be expressed as a sequence using the symbols in WIPO Standard ST.25 (1998), Appendix 2, Table 3 in conjunction with a description in the Feature section to describe, for example, modified linkages, cross links and end caps, non-peptidyl bonds, etc., is embraced by this definition.

(b) Patent applications which contain disclosures of nucleotide and/or amino acid sequences, in accordance with the definition in paragraph (a) of this section, shall, with regard to the manner in which the nucleotide and/or amino acid sequences are presented and described, conform exclusively to the requirements of §§ 1.821 through 1.825.

(c) Patent applications which contain disclosures of nucleotide and/or amino acid sequences must contain, as a separate part of the disclosure, a paper or compact disc copy (*see* § 1.52(e)) disclosing the nucleotide and/or amino acid sequences and associated information using the symbols and format in accordance with the requirements of §§ 1.822 and 1.823. This paper or compact disc copy is referred to elsewhere in this subpart as the "Sequence Listing." Each sequence disclosed must appear separately in the "Sequence Listing." Each sequence set forth in the "Sequence Listing" must be assigned a separate sequence identifier. The sequence identifiers must begin with 1 and increase sequentially by integers. If no sequence is present for a sequence identifier, the code "000" must be used in place of the sequence. The response for the numeric identifier <160> must include the total number of SEQ ID NOs, whether followed by a sequence or by the code "000."

(d) Where the description or claims of a patent application discuss a sequence that is set forth in the "Sequence Listing" in accordance with paragraph (c) of this section, reference must be made to the sequence by use of the sequence identifier, preceded by "SEQ ID NO:" in the text of the description or claims, even if the sequence is also embedded in the text of the description or claims of the patent application.

(e) A copy of the "Sequence Listing" referred to in paragraph (c) of this section must also be submitted in computer readable form (CRF) in accordance with the requirements of § 1.824. The computer readable form must be a copy of the "Sequence Listing" and may not be retained as a part of the patent application file. If the computer readable form of a new application is to be identical with the computer readable form of another application of the applicant on file in the Office, reference may be made to the other application and computer readable form in lieu of filing a duplicate computer readable form in the new application if the computer readable form in the other application was compliant with all of the requirements of this subpart. The new application must be accompanied by a letter making such reference to the other application and computer readable form, both of which shall be completely identified. In the new application, applicant must also request the use of the compliant computer readable "Sequence Listing" that is already on file for the other application and must state that the paper or compact disc copy of the "Sequence Listing" in the new application is identical to the computer readable copy filed for the other application.

(f) In addition to the paper or compact disc copy required by paragraph (c) of this section and the computer readable form required by paragraph (e) of this section, a statement that the "Sequence Listing" content of the paper or compact disc copy and the computer readable copy are the same must be submitted with the computer readable form, *e.g.*, a statement that "the sequence listing information recorded in computer readable form is identical to the written (on paper or compact disc) sequence listing."

(g) If any of the requirements of paragraphs (b) through (f) of this section are not satisfied at the time of filing under 35 U.S.C. 111(a) or at the time of entering the national stage under 35 U.S.C. 371, applicant will be notified and given a period of time within which to comply with such requirements in order to prevent abandonment of the application. Any submission in reply to a requirement under this paragraph must be accompanied by a statement that the submission includes no new matter.

(h) If any of the requirements of paragraphs (b) through (f) of this section are not satisfied at the time of filing an international application under the Patent Cooperation Treaty (PCT), which application is to be searched by the United States International Searching Authority or examined by the United States

International Preliminary Examining Authority, applicant will be sent a notice necessitating compliance with the requirements within a prescribed time period. Any submission in reply to a requirement under this paragraph must be accompanied by a statement that the submission does not include matter which goes beyond the disclosure in the international application as filed. If applicant fails to timely provide the required computer readable form, the United States International Searching Authority shall search only to the extent that a meaningful search can be performed without the computer readable form and the United States International Preliminary Examining Authority shall examine only to the extent that a meaningful examination can be performed without the computer readable form.

[Added, 55 FR 18230, May 1, 1990, effective Oct. 1, 1990; para. (h) amended, 58 FR 9335, Jan. 14, 1993, effective May 1, 1993; revised, 63 FR 29620, June 1, 1998, effective July 1, 1998; paras. (c), (e), and (f) revised, 65 FR 54604, Sept. 8, 2000, effective Sept. 8, 2000 (effective date corrected, 65 FR 78958, Dec. 18, 2000); para. (a) revised, 70 FR 10488, Mar. 4, 2005, effective Mar. 4, 2005]

§ 1.822   Symbols and format to be used for nucleotide and/or amino acid sequence data.

(a)   The symbols and format to be used for nucleotide and/or amino acid sequence data shall conform to the requirements of paragraphs (b) through (e) of this section.

(b)   The code for representing the nucleotide and/or amino acid sequence characters shall conform to the code set forth in the tables in WIPO Standard ST.25 (1998), Appendix 2, Tables 1 and 3. This incorporation by reference was approved by the Director of the Federal Register in accordance with 5 U.S.C. 552(a) and 1 CFR part 51. Copies of ST.25 may be obtained from the World Intellectual Property Organization; 34 chemin des Colombettes; 1211 Geneva 20 Switzerland. Copies may also be inspected at the National Archives and Records Administration (NARA). For information on the availability of this material at NARA, call 202-741-6030, or go to: *http:/ /www.archives.gov/federal_register/ code_of_federal_regulations/ibr_locations.html*. No code other than that specified in these sections shall be used in nucleotide and amino acid sequences. A modified base or modified or unusual amino acid may be presented in a given sequence as the corresponding unmodified base or amino acid if the modified base or modified or unusual amino acid is one of those listed in WIPO Standard ST.25 (1998), Appendix 2, Tables 2 and 4, and the modification is also set forth in the Feature section. Otherwise, each occurrence of a base or amino acid not appearing in WIPO Standard ST.25 (1998), Appendix 2, Tables 1 and 3, shall be listed in a given sequence as "n" or "Xaa," respectively, with further information, as appropriate, given in the Feature section, preferably by including one or more feature keys listed in WIPO Standard ST.25 (1998), Appendix 2, Tables 5 and 6.

(c)   *Format representation of nucleotides.* (1) A nucleotide sequence shall be listed using the lower-case letter for representing the one-letter code for the nucleotide bases set forth in WIPO Standard ST.25 (1998), Appendix 2, Table 1.

(2)   The bases in a nucleotide sequence (including introns) shall be listed in groups of 10 bases except in the coding parts of the sequence. Leftover bases, fewer than 10 in number, at the end of noncoding parts of a sequence shall be grouped together and separated from adjacent groups of 10 or 3 bases by a space.

(3)   The bases in the coding parts of a nucleotide sequence shall be listed as triplets (codons). The amino acids corresponding to the codons in the coding parts of a nucleotide sequence shall be typed immediately below the corresponding codons. Where a codon spans an intron, the amino acid symbol shall be typed below the portion of the codon containing two nucleotides.

(4)   A nucleotide sequence shall be listed with a maximum of 16 codons or 60 bases per line, with a space provided between each codon or group of 10 bases.

(5)   A nucleotide sequence shall be presented, only by a single strand, in the 5 to 3 direction, from left to right.

(6)   The enumeration of nucleotide bases shall start at the first base of the sequence with number 1. The enumeration shall be continuous through the whole sequence in the direction 5 to 3. The enumeration shall be marked in the right margin, next to the line containing the one-letter codes for the bases, and giving the number of the last base of that line.

(7)   For those nucleotide sequences that are circular in configuration, the enumeration method set forth in paragraph (c)(6) of this section remains applicable with the exception that the designation of the first base of the nucleotide sequence may be made at the option of the applicant.

(d)   *Representation of amino acids.* (1) The amino acids in a protein or peptide sequence shall be listed using the three-letter abbreviation with the first letter as an upper case character, as in WIPO Standard ST.25 (1998), Appendix 2, Table 3.

(2)   A protein or peptide sequence shall be listed with a maximum of 16 amino acids per line, with a space provided between each amino acid.

(3)   An amino acid sequence shall be presented in the amino to carboxy direction, from left to right, and the amino and carboxy groups shall not be presented in the sequence.

(4)   The enumeration of amino acids may start at the first amino acid of the first mature protein, with the number 1. When presented, the amino acids preceding the mature protein, *e.g.*, pre-sequences, pro-sequences, pre-pro-sequences and signal sequences, shall have negative numbers, counting backwards starting with the amino acid next to number 1. Otherwise, the enumeration of amino acids shall start at the first amino acid at the amino terminal as number 1. It shall be marked below the sequence every 5 amino acids. The enumeration method for amino acid sequences that is set forth in this section remains applicable for amino acid sequences that are circular in configuration, with the exception that the designation of the first amino acid of the sequence may be made at the option of the applicant.

(5)   An amino acid sequence that contains internal terminator symbols (*e.g.*, "Ter", "*", or ".", etc.) may not be represented as a single amino acid sequence, but shall be presented as separate amino acid sequences.

(e)   A sequence with a gap or gaps shall be presented as a plurality of separate sequences, with separate sequence identifiers, with the number of separate sequences being equal in number to the number of continuous strings of sequence data. A sequence that is made up of one or more noncontiguous segments of a larger sequence or segments from different sequences shall be presented as a separate sequence.

[Added, 55 FR 18230, May 1, 1990, effective Oct. 1, 1990; revised, 63 FR 29620, June 1, 1998, effective, July 1, 1998; para. (b) revised, 70 FR 10488, Mar. 4, 2005, effective Mar. 4, 2005]

§ 1.823 Requirements for nucleotide and/or amino acid sequences as part of the application.

(a)(1) If the "Sequence Listing" required by § 1.821(c) is submitted on paper: The "Sequence Listing," setting forth the nucleotide and/or amino acid sequence and associated information in accordance with paragraph (b) of this section, must begin on a new page and must be titled "Sequence Listing." The pages of the "Sequence Listing" preferably should be numbered independently of the numbering of the remainder of the application. Each page of the "Sequence Listing" shall contain no more than 66 lines and each line shall contain no more than 72 characters. The sheet or sheets presenting a sequence listing may not include material other than part of the sequence listing. A fixed-width font should be used exclusively throughout the "Sequence Listing."

(2)   If the "Sequence Listing" required by § 1.821(c) is submitted on compact disc: The "Sequence Listing" must be submitted on a compact disc in compliance with § 1.52(e). The compact disc may also contain table information if the application contains table information that may be submitted on a compact disc (§ 1.52(e)(1)(iii)). The specification must contain an incorporation-by-reference of the Sequence Listing as required by § 1.52(e)(5). The presentation of the "Sequence Listing" and other materials on compact disc under § 1.821(c) does not substitute for the Computer Readable Form that must be submitted on disk, compact disc, or tape in accordance with § 1.824.

(b)   The "Sequence Listing" shall, except as otherwise indicated, include the actual nucleotide and/or amino acid sequence, the numeric identifiers and their accompanying information as shown in the following table. The numeric identifier shall be used only in the "Sequence Listing." The order and presentation of the items of information in the "Sequence Listing" shall conform to the arrangement given below. Each item of information shall begin on a new line and shall begin with the numeric identifier enclosed in angle brackets as shown. The submission of those items of information designated with an "M" is mandatory. The submission of those items of information designated with an "O" is optional. Numeric identifiers <110> through <170> shall only be set forth at the beginning of the "Sequence Listing." The following table illustrates the numeric identifiers.

Numeric Identifier	Definition	Comments and format	Mandatory (M) or Optional (O)
<110>	Applicant......................	Preferably max. of 10 names; one name per line; preferable format: Surname, Other Names and/or Initials.	M.
<120>	Title of Invention..........	....	M.
<130>	File Reference...............	Personal file reference........................	M when filed prior to assignment or appl. number
<140>	Current Application Number.	Specify as: US 07/999,999 or PCT/US96/99999.	M, if available.
<141>	Current Filing Date.......	Specify as: yyyy-mm-dd.....................	M, if available.
<150>	Prior Application Number.	Specify as: US 07/999,999 or PCT/US96/99999.	M, if applicable include priority documents under 35 U.S.C. 119 and 120
<151>	Prior Application Filing Date.	Specify as: yyyy-mm-dd	M, if applicable
<160>	Number of SEQ ID NOs.	Count includes total number of SEQ ID NOs...................................	M.
<170>	Software......................	Name of software used to create the Sequence Listing.	O.
<210>	SEQ ID NO:#:..............	Response shall be an integer representing the SEQ ID NO shown.	M.
<211>	Length.........................	Respond with an integer expressing the number of bases or amino acid residues.	M.
<212>	Type............................	Whether presented sequence molecule is DNA, RNA, or PRT (protein). If a nucleotide sequence contains both DNA and RNA fragments, the type shall be "DNA." In addition, the combined DNA/ RNA molecule shall be further described in the <220> to <223> feature section.	M.
<213>	Organism.....................	Scientific name, i.e. Genus/ species, Unknown or Artificial Sequence. In addition, the "Unknown" or "Artificial Sequence" organisms shall be further described in the <220> to <223> feature section.	M.

Numeric Identifier	Definition	Comments and format	Mandatory (M) or Optional (O)
<220>	Feature..........................	Leave blank after <220>. <221-223> provide for a description of points of biological significance in the sequence.	M, under the following conditions: if "n," "Xaa," or a modified or unusual L-amino acid or modified base was used in a sequence; if ORGANISM is "Artificial Sequence" or "Unknown"; if molecule is combined DNA/RNA.
<221>	Name/Key....................	Provide appropriate identifier for feature, preferably from WIPO Standard ST.25 (1998), Appendix 2, Tables 5 and 6.	M, under the following conditions: if "n," "Xaa," or a modified or unusual L-amino acid or modified base was used in a sequence.
Numeric Identifier	Definition	Comments and format	Mandatory (M) or Optional (O)
<222>	Location.......................	Specify location within sequence; where appropriate state number of first and last bases/amino acids in feature.	M, under the following conditions: if "n," "Xaa," or a modified or unusual L-amino acid or modified base was used in a sequence.
<223>	Other Information.........	Other relevant information; four lines maximum...	M, under the following conditions: if "n," "Xaa," or a modified or unusual L-amino acid or modified base was used in a sequence; if ORGANISM is "Artificial Sequence" or "Unknown"; if molecule is combined DNA/RNA.
<300>	Publication Information	Leave blank after <300>	O.
<301>	Authors.........................	Preferably max. of ten named authors of publication; specify one name per line; preferable format: Surname, Other Names and/or Initials.	O.
<302>	Title.............................	....	O.
<303>	Journal.........................	....	O.
<304>	Volume	....	O.
<305>	Issue	....	O.
<306>	Pages	....	O.
<307>	Date..............	Journal date on which data published; specify as yyyy-mm-dd, MMM-yyyy or Season-yyyy.	O.
<308>	Database Accession Number.	Accession number assigned by database including database name.	O.
<309>	Database Entry Date........	Date of entry in database; specify as yyyy-mm-dd or MMM-yyyy.	O.

Numeric Identifier	Definition	Comments and format	Mandatory (M) or Optional (O)
<310>	Patent Document Number.	Document number; for patent-type citations only. Specify as, for example, US 07/ 999,999.	O.
<311>	Patent Filing Date..............	Document filing date, for patent-type citations only; specify as yyyy-mm-dd.	O.
<312>	Publication Date...............	Document publication date, for patent-type citations only; specify as yyyy-mm-dd.	O.
<313>	Relevant Residues............	FROM (position) TO (position)...........	O.
<400>	Sequence......................	SEQ ID NO should follow the numeric identifier and should appear on the line preceding the actual sequence.	M.

[Added, 55 FR 18230, May 1, 1990, effective Oct. 1, 1990; revised, 63 FR 29620, June 1, 1998, effective July 1, 1998; heading and para. (a) revised, 65 FR 54604, Sept. 8, 2000, effective Sept. 8, 2000 (effective date corrected, 65 FR 78958, Dec. 18, 2000); para. (a)(1) revised, 68 FR 38611, June 30, 2003, effective July 30, 2003]

§ 1.824 Form and format for nucleotide and/or amino acid sequence submissions in computer readable form.

(a)   The computer readable form required by § 1.821(e) shall meet the following requirements:

(1)   The computer readable form shall contain a single "Sequence Listing" as either a diskette, series of diskettes, or other permissible media outlined in paragraph (c) of this section.

(2)   The "Sequence Listing" in paragraph (a)(l) of this section shall be submitted in American Standard Code for Information Interchange (ASCII) text. No other formats shall be allowed.

(3)   The computer readable form may be created by any means, such as word processors, nucleotide/amino acid sequence editors' or other custom computer programs; however, it shall conform to all requirements detailed in this section.

(4)   File compression is acceptable when using diskette media, so long as the compressed file is in a self-extracting format that will decompress on one of the systems described in paragraph (b) of this section.

(5)   Page numbering must not appear within the computer readable form version of the "Sequence Listing" file.

(6)   All computer readable forms must have a label permanently affixed thereto on which has been hand-printed or typed: the name of the applicant, the title of the invention, the date on which the data were recorded on the computer readable form, the operating system used, a reference number, and an application number and filing date, if known. If multiple diskettes are submitted, the diskette labels must indicate their order (e.g., "1 of X").

(b)   Computer readable form submissions must meet these format requirements:

(1)   Computer Compatibility: IBM PC/XT/ AT or Apple Macintosh;

(2)   Operating System Compatibility: MS-DOS, MS-Windows, Unix or Macintosh;

(3)   Line Terminator: ASCII Carriage Return plus ASCII Line Feed; and

(4)   Pagination: Continuous file (no "hard page break" codes permitted).

(c)   Computer readable form files submitted may be in any of the following media:

(1) Diskette: 3.50 inch, 1.44 Mb storage; 3.50 inch, 720 Kb storage; 5.25 inch, 1.2 Mb storage; 5.25 inch, 360 Kb storage.

(2) Magnetic tape: 0.5 inch, up to 24000 feet; Density: 1600 or 6250 bits per inch, 9 track; Format: Unix tar command; specify blocking factor (not "block size"); Line Terminator: ASCII Carriage Return plus ASCII Line Feed.

(3) 8mm Data Cartridge: Format: Unix tar command; specify blocking factor (not "block size"); Line Terminator: ASCII Carriage Return plus ASCII Line Feed.

(4) Compact disc: Format: ISO 9660 or High Sierra Format.

(5) Magneto Optical Disk: Size/Storage Specifications: 5.25 inch, 640 Mb.

(d) Computer readable forms that are submitted to the Office will not be returned to the applicant.

[Added, 55 FR 18230, May 1, 1990, effective Oct. 1, 1990; revised, 63 FR 29620, June 1, 1998, effective July 1, 1998; revised, 65 FR 54604, Sept. 8, 2000, effective Sept. 8, 2000 (effective date corrected, 65 FR 78958, Dec. 18, 2000)]

§ 1.825   Amendments to or replacement of sequence listing and computer readable copy thereof.

(a) Any amendment to a paper copy of the "Sequence Listing" (§ 1.821(c)) must be made by the submission of substitute sheets and include a statement that the substitute sheets include no new matter. Any amendment to a compact disc copy of the "Sequence Listing" (§ 1.821(c)) must be made by the submission of a replacement compact disc (2 copies) in compliance with § 1.52(e). Amendments must also be accompanied by a statement that indicates support for the amendment in the application, as filed, and a statement that the replacement compact disc includes no new matter.

(b) Any amendment to the paper or compact disc copy of the "Sequence Listing," in accordance with paragraph (a) of this section, must be accompanied by a substitute copy of the computer readable form (§ 1.821(e)) including all previously submitted data with the amendment incorporated therein, accompanied by a statement that the copy in computer readable form is the same as the substitute copy of the "Sequence Listing."

(c) Any appropriate amendments to the "Sequence Listing" in a patent; e.g., by reason of reissue or certificate of correction, must comply with the requirements of paragraphs (a) and (b) of this section.

(d) If, upon receipt, the computer readable form is found to be damaged or unreadable, applicant must provide, within such time as set by the Director, a substitute copy of the data in computer readable form accompanied by a statement that the substitute data is identical to that originally filed.

[Added 55 FR 18230, May 1, 1990, effective Oct. 1, 1990; revised, 63 FR 29620, June 1, 1998, effective July 1, 1998; paras. (a) and (b) revised, 65 FR 54604, Sept. 8, 2000, effective Sept. 8, 2000 (effective date corrected, 65 FR 78958, Dec. 18, 2000); para. (d) revised, 68 FR 14332, Mar. 25, 2003, effective May 1, 2003]

APPENDIX A TO SUBPART G TO PART 1 —
SAMPLE SEQUENCE LISTING

```
<110> Smith, John
      Smith, Jane

<120> Example of a Sequence Listing

<130> 01-00001

<140> US 08/999,999

<141> 1998-02-28

<150> EP 91000000
<151> 1997-12-31

<160> 2

<170> PatentIn ver. 2.0

<210> 1
<211> 403
<212> DNA
<213> Paramecium aurelia

<220>
<221> CDS
<222> 341..394

<300>
<301> Doe, Richard
<302> Isolation and Characterization of a Gene Encoding a
      Protease from Paramecium sp.
<303> Journal of Fictional Genes
<304> 1
<305> 4
<306> 1 - 7
<307> 1988-06-20

<400> 1
ctactctact  ctactctcat  ctactatctt  ctttggatct  ctgagtctgc  ctgagtggta    60

ctcttgagtc  ctggagatct  ctcctctcac  atgtgatcgt  cgagactgac  cgatagatcg   120

ctgactgact  ctgagatagt  cgagcccgta  cgagacccgt  cgagggtgac  agagagtggg   180

cgcgtgcgcg  cagagcgccg  cgccggtgcg  cgcgcgagtg  cgcggtgggc  cgcgcgaggg   240

ctttcgcggc  agcggcggcg  ctttccggcg  cgcgcccgtc  cgcccctaga  cctgagaggt   300

cttctcttcc  ctcctcttca  ctagagaggt  ctatatatac  atg gtt tca atg ttc     355

                                                Met Val Ser Met Phe
                                                1               5
```

```
agc ttg tct ttc aaa tgg cct gga ttt tgt ttg ttt gtt tgtttgctc    403
Ser Leu Ser Phe Lys Trp Pro Gly Phe Cys Leu Phe Val
                10                      15
```

<210> 2
<211> 18
<212> PRT
<213> Paramecium aurelia

<400> 2

```
Met Val Ser Met Phe Ser Leu Ser Phe Lys Trp Pro Gly Phe Cys Leu
1               5                 10                      15

Phe Val
```

Subpart H — *Inter Partes* Reexamination of Patents That Issued From an Original Application Filed in the United States on or After November 29, 1999

PRIOR ART CITATIONS

§ 1.902 Processing of prior art citations during an *inter partes* reexamination proceeding.

Citations by the patent owner in accordance with § 1.933 and by an *inter partes* reexamination third party requester under § 1.915 or § 1.948 will be entered in the *inter partes* reexamination file. The entry in the patent file of other citations submitted after the date of an order for reexamination pursuant to § 1.931 by persons other than the patent owner, or the third party requester under either § 1.913 or § 1.948, will be delayed until the *inter partes* reexamination proceeding has been concluded by the issuance and publication of a reexamination certificate. See § 1.502 for processing of prior art citations in patent and reexamination files during an *ex parte* reexamination proceeding filed under § 1.510.

[Added, 65 FR 76756, Dec. 7, 2000, effective Feb. 5, 2001; revised, 72 FR 18892, Apr. 16, 2007, effective May 16, 2007]

REQUIREMENTS FOR *INTER PARTES* REEXAMINATION PROCEEDINGS

§ 1.903 Service of papers on parties in *inter partes* reexamination.

The patent owner and the third party requester will be sent copies of Office actions issued during the *inter partes* reexamination proceeding. After filing of a request for *inter partes* reexamination by a third party requester, any document filed by either the patent owner or the third party requester must be served on every other party in the reexamination proceeding in the manner provided in § 1.248. Any document must reflect service or the document may be refused consideration by the Office. The failure of the patent owner or the third party requester to serve documents may result in their being refused consideration.

[Added, 65 FR 76756, Dec. 7, 2000, effective Feb. 5, 2001]

§ 1.904 Notice of *inter partes* reexamination in *Official Gazette.*

A notice of the filing of an *inter partes* reexamination request will be published in the *Official Gazette.* The notice published in the *Official Gazette* under § 1.11(c) will be considered to be constructive notice of the *inter partes* reexamination proceeding and *inter partes* reexamination will proceed.

[Added, 65 FR 76756, Dec. 7, 2000, effective Feb. 5, 2001]

§ 1.905 Submission of papers by the public in *inter partes* reexamination.

Unless specifically provided for, no submissions on behalf of any third parties other than third party requesters as defined in 35 U.S.C. 100(e) will be considered unless such submissions are in accordance with § 1.915 or entered in the patent file prior to the date of the order for reexamination pursuant to § 1.931. Submissions by third parties, other than third party requesters, filed after the date of the order for reexamination pursuant to § 1.931, must meet the requirements of § 1.501 and will be treated in accordance with § 1.902. Submissions which do not meet the requirements of § 1.501 will be returned.

[Added, 65 FR 76756, Dec. 7, 2000, effective Feb. 5, 2001]

§ 1.906 Scope of reexamination in *inter partes* reexamination proceeding.

(a)   Claims in an *inter partes* reexamination proceeding will be examined on the basis of patents or printed publications and, with respect to subject matter added or deleted in the reexamination proceeding, on the basis of the requirements of 35 U.S.C. 112.

(b)   Claims in an *inter partes* reexamination proceeding will not be permitted to enlarge the scope of the claims of the patent.

(c)   Issues other than those indicated in paragraphs (a) and (b) of this section will not be resolved in an *inter partes* reexamination proceeding. If such issues are raised by the patent owner or the third party requester during a reexamination proceeding, the existence of such issues will be noted by the examiner in the next Office action, in which case the patent owner may desire to consider the advisability of filing a reissue application to have such issues considered and resolved.

[Added, 65 FR 76756, Dec. 7, 2000, effective Feb. 5, 2001]

§ 1.907 *Inter partes* reexamination prohibited.

(a) Once an order to reexamine has been issued under § 1.931, neither the third party requester, nor its privies, may file a subsequent request for *inter partes* reexamination of the patent until an *inter partes* reexamination certificate is issued under § 1.997, unless authorized by the Director.

(b) Once a final decision has been entered against a party in a civil action arising in whole or in part under 28 U.S.C. 1338 that the party has not sustained its burden of proving invalidity of any patent claim-in-suit, then neither that party nor its privies may thereafter request *inter partes* reexamination of any such patent claim on the basis of issues which that party, or its privies, raised or could have raised in such civil action, and an *inter partes* reexamination requested by that party, or its privies, on the basis of such issues may not thereafter be maintained by the Office.

(c) If a final decision in an *inter partes* reexamination proceeding instituted by a third party requester is favorable to patentability of any original, proposed amended, or new claims of the patent, then neither that party nor its privies may thereafter request *inter partes* reexamination of any such patent claims on the basis of issues which that party, or its privies, raised or could have raised in such *inter partes* reexamination proceeding.

[Added, 65 FR 76756, Dec. 7, 2000, effective Feb. 5, 2001; para. (a) revised, 68 FR 14332, Mar. 25, 2003, effective May 1, 2003]

§ 1.913 Persons eligible to file request for *inter partes* reexamination.

Except as provided for in § 1.907, any person other than the patent owner or its privies may, at any time during the period of enforceability of a patent which issued from an original application filed in the United States on or after November 29, 1999, file a request for *inter partes* reexamination by the Office of any claim of the patent on the basis of prior art patents or printed publications cited under § 1.501.

[Added, 65 FR 76756, Dec. 7, 2000, effective Feb. 5, 2001; revised, 68 FR 70996, Dec. 22, 2003, effective Jan. 21, 2004]

§ 1.915 Content of request for *inter partes* reexamination.

(a) The request must be accompanied by the fee for requesting *inter partes* reexamination set forth in § 1.20(c)(2).

(b) A request for *inter partes* reexamination must include the following parts:

(1) An identification of the patent by patent number and every claim for which reexamination is requested.

(2) A citation of the patents and printed publications which are presented to provide a substantial new question of patentability.

(3) A statement pointing out each substantial new question of patentability based on the cited patents and printed publications, and a detailed explanation of the pertinency and manner of applying the patents and printed publications to every claim for which reexamination is requested.

(4) A copy of every patent or printed publication relied upon or referred to in paragraphs (b)(1) through (3) of this section, accompanied by an English language translation of all the necessary and pertinent parts of any non-English language document.

(5) A copy of the entire patent including the front face, drawings, and specification/claims (in double column format) for which reexamination is requested, and a copy of any disclaimer, certificate of correction, or reexamination certificate issued in the patent. All copies must have each page plainly written on only one side of a sheet of paper.

(6) A certification by the third party requester that a copy of the request has been served in its entirety on the patent owner at the address provided for in § 1.33(c). The name and address of the party served must be indicated. If service was not possible, a duplicate copy of the request must be supplied to the Office.

(7) A certification by the third party requester that the estoppel provisions of § 1.907 do not prohibit the *inter partes* reexamination.

(8) A statement identifying the real party in interest to the extent necessary for a subsequent person filing an *inter partes* reexamination request to determine whether that person is a privy.

(c) If an *inter partes* request is filed by an attorney or agent identifying another party on whose behalf the request is being filed, the attorney or agent must have a power of attorney from that party or be acting in a representative capacity pursuant to § 1.34.

(d) If the *inter partes* request does not include the fee for requesting *inter partes* reexamination required by paragraph (a) of this section and meet all the requirements of paragraph (b) of this section, then the person identified as requesting *inter partes* reexamination will be so notified and will generally be given an opportunity to complete the request within a specified time. Failure to comply with the notice will result in the *inter partes* reexamination request not being granted a filing date, and will result in placement of the request in the patent file as a citation if it complies with the requirements of § 1.501.

[Added, 65 FR 76756, Dec. 7, 2000, effective Feb. 5, 2001; para. (d) revised, 71 FR 9260, Feb. 23, 2006, effective Mar. 27, 2006; para. (d) revised, 71 FR 44219, Aug. 4, 2006, effective Aug. 4, 2006; para. (c) revised, 72 FR 18892, Apr. 16, 2007, effective May 16, 2007]

§ 1.919 Filing date of request for *inter partes* reexamination.

(a) The filing date of a request for *inter partes* reexamination is the date on which the request satisfies all the requirements for the request set forth in § 1.915.

(b) If the request is not granted a filing date, the request will be placed in the patent file as a citation of prior art if it complies with the requirements of § 1.501.

[Added, 65 FR 76756, Dec. 7, 2000, effective Feb. 5, 2001; para. (a) revised, 71 FR 9260, Feb. 23, 2006, effective Mar. 27, 2006]

§ 1.923 Examiner's determination on the request for *inter partes* reexamination.

Within three months following the filing date of a request for *inter partes* reexamination under § 1.915, the examiner will consider the request and determine whether or not a substantial new question of patentability affecting any claim of the patent is raised by the request and the prior art citation. The examiner's determination will be based on the claims in effect at the time of the determination, will become a part of the official file of the patent, and will be mailed to the patent owner at the address as provided for in § 1.33(c) and to the third party requester. If the examiner determines that no substantial new question of patentability is present, the examiner shall refuse the request and shall not order *inter partes* reexamination.

[Added, 65 FR 76756, Dec. 7, 2000, effective Feb. 5, 2001; revised, 72 FR 18892, Apr. 16, 2007, effective May 16, 2007]

§ 1.925 Partial refund if request for *inter partes* reexamination is not ordered.

Where *inter partes* reexamination is not ordered, a refund of a portion of the fee for requesting *inter partes* reexamination will be made to the requester in accordance with § 1.26(c).

[Added, 65 FR 76756, Dec. 7, 2000, effective Feb. 5, 2001]

§ 1.927 Petition to review refusal to order *inter partes* reexamination.

The third party requester may seek review by a petition to the Director under § 1.181 within one month of the mailing date of the examiner's determination refusing to order *inter partes* reexamination. Any such petition must comply with § 1.181(b). If no petition is timely filed or if the decision on petition affirms that no substantial new question of patentability has been raised, the determination shall be final and nonappealable.

[Added, 65 FR 76756, Dec. 7, 2000, effective Feb. 5, 2001; revised, 68 FR 14332, Mar. 25, 2003, effective May 1, 2003]

INTER PARTES REEXAMINATION OF PATENTS

§ 1.931 Order for *inter partes* reexamination.

(a) If a substantial new question of patentability is found, the determination will include an order for *inter partes* reexamination of the patent for resolution of the question.

(b) If the order for *inter partes* reexamination resulted from a petition pursuant to § 1.927, the *inter partes* reexamination will ordinarily be conducted by an examiner other than the examiner responsible for the initial determination under § 1.923.

[Added, 65 FR 76756, Dec. 7, 2000, effective Feb. 5, 2001]

INFORMATION DISCLOSURE IN *INTER PARTES* REEXAMINATION

§ 1.933 Patent owner duty of disclosure in *inter partes* reexamination proceedings.

(a) Each individual associated with the patent owner in an *inter partes* reexamination proceeding has a duty of candor and good faith in dealing with the Office, which includes a duty to disclose to the Office all information known to that individual to be material to patentability in a reexamination proceeding as set forth in § 1.555(a) and (b). The duty to disclose all information known to be material to patentability in an *inter partes* reexamination proceeding is deemed to be satisfied by filing a paper in compliance with the requirements set forth in § 1.555(a) and (b).

(b) The responsibility for compliance with this section rests upon the individuals designated in paragraph (a) of this section, and no evaluation will be made by the Office in the reexamination proceeding as to compliance with this section. If questions of compliance with this section are raised by the patent owner or the third party requester during a reexamination proceeding, they will be noted as unresolved questions in accordance with § 1.906(c).

[Added, 65 FR 76756, Dec. 7, 2000, effective Feb. 5, 2001]

OFFICE ACTIONS AND RESPONSES (BEFORE THE EXAMINER) IN *INTER PARTES* REEXAMINATION

§ 1.935 Initial Office action usually accompanies order for *inter partes* reexamination.

The order for *inter partes* reexamination will usually be accompanied by the initial Office action on the merits of the reexamination.

[Added, 65 FR 76756, Dec. 7, 2000, effective Feb. 5, 2001]

§ 1.937 Conduct of *inter partes* reexamination.

(a) All *inter partes* reexamination proceedings, including any appeals to the Board of Patent Appeals and Interferences, will be conducted with special dispatch within the Office, unless the Director makes a determination that there is good cause for suspending the reexamination proceeding.

(b) The *inter partes* reexamination proceeding will be conducted in accordance with §§ 1.104 through 1.116, the sections governing the application examination process, and will result in the issuance of an *inter partes* reexamination certificate under § 1.997, except as otherwise provided.

(c) All communications between the Office and the parties to the *inter partes* reexamination which are directed to the merits of the proceeding must be in writing and filed with the Office for entry into the record of the proceeding.

[Added, 65 FR 76756, Dec. 7, 2000, effective Feb. 5, 2001; para. (a) revised, 68 FR 14332, Mar. 25, 2003, effective May 1, 2003]

§ 1.939 Unauthorized papers in *inter partes* reexamination

(a) If an unauthorized paper is filed by any party at any time during the *inter partes* reexamination proceeding it will not be considered and may be returned.

(b) Unless otherwise authorized, no paper shall be filed prior to the initial Office action on the merits of the *inter partes* reexamination.

[Added, 65 FR 76756, Dec. 7, 2000, effective Feb. 5, 2001]

§ 1.941 Amendments by patent owner in *inter partes* reexamination.

Amendments by patent owner in *inter partes* reexamination proceedings are made by filing a paper in compliance with §§ 1.530(d)-(k) and 1.943.

[Added, 65 FR 76756, Dec. 7, 2000, effective Feb. 5, 2001]

§ 1.943 Requirements of responses, written comments, and briefs in *inter partes* reexamination.

(a) The form of responses, written comments, briefs, appendices, and other papers must be in accordance with the requirements of § 1.52.

(b) Responses by the patent owner and written comments by the third party requester shall not exceed 50 pages in length, excluding amendments, appendices of claims, and reference materials such as prior art references.

(c) Appellant's briefs filed by the patent owner and the third party requester shall not exceed thirty pages or 14,000 words in length, excluding appendices of claims and reference materials such as prior art references. All other briefs filed by any party shall not exceed fifteen pages in length or 7,000 words. If the page limit for any brief is exceeded, a certificate is required stating the number of words contained in the brief.

[Added, 65 FR 76756, Dec. 7, 2000, effective Feb. 5, 2001]

§ 1.945 Response to Office action by patent owner in *inter partes* reexamination.

(a) The patent owner will be given at least thirty days to file a response to any Office action on the merits of the *inter partes* reexamination.

(b) Any supplemental response to the Office action will be entered only where the supplemental response is accompanied by a showing of sufficient cause why the supplemental response should be entered. The showing of sufficient cause must include:

(1) An explanation of how the requirements of § 1.111(a)(2)(i) are satisfied;

(2) An explanation of why the supplemental response was not presented together with the original response to the Office action; and

(3) A compelling reason to enter the supplemental response.

[Added, 65 FR 76756, Dec. 7, 2000, effective Feb. 5, 2001; revised, 72 FR 18892, Apr. 16, 2007, effective May 16, 2007]

§ 1.947 Comments by third party requester to patent owner's response in *inter partes* reexamination.

Each time the patent owner files a response to an Office action on the merits pursuant to § 1.945, a third party requester may once file written comments within a period of 30 days from the date of service of the patent owner's response. These comments shall be limited to issues raised by the Office action or the patent owner's response. The time for submitting comments by the third party requester may not be extended. For the purpose of filing the written comments by the third party requester, the comments will be considered as having been received in the Office as of the date of deposit specified in the certificate under § 1.8.

[Added, 65 FR 76756, Dec. 7, 2000, effective Feb. 5, 2001]

§ 1.948 Limitations on submission of prior art by third party requester following the order for *inter partes* reexamination.

(a) After the *inter partes* reexamination order, the third party requester may only cite additional prior art as defined under § 1.501 if it is filed as part of a comments submission under § 1.947 or § 1.951(b) and is limited to prior art:

(1) which is necessary to rebut a finding of fact by the examiner;

(2) which is necessary to rebut a response of the patent owner; or

(3) which for the first time became known or available to the third party requester after the filing of the request for *inter partes* reexamination proceeding. Prior art submitted under paragraph (a)(3) of this section must be accompanied by a statement as to when the prior art first became known or available to the third party requester and must include a discussion of the pertinency of each reference to the patentability of at least one claim.

(b) [Reserved]

[Added, 65 FR 76756, Dec. 7, 2000, effective Feb. 5, 2001]

§ 1.949 Examiner's Office action closing prosecution in *inter partes* reexamination.

Upon consideration of the issues a second or subsequent time, or upon a determination of patentability of all claims, the examiner shall issue an Office action treating all claims present in the *inter partes* reexamination, which may be an action closing prosecution. The Office action shall set forth all rejections and determinations not to make a proposed rejection, and the grounds therefor. An Office action will not usually close prosecution if it includes a new ground of rejection which was not previously addressed by the patent owner, unless the new ground was necessitated by an amendment.

[Added, 65 FR 76756, Dec. 7, 2000, effective Feb. 5, 2001]

§ 1.951 Options after Office action closing prosecution in *inter partes* reexamination.

(a) After an Office action closing prosecution in an *inter partes* reexamination, the patent owner may once file comments limited to the issues raised in the Office action closing prosecution. The comments can include a proposed amendment to the claims, which amendment will be subject to the criteria of § 1.116 as to whether or not it shall be admitted. The comments must be filed within the time set for response in the Office action closing prosecution.

(b) When the patent owner does file comments, a third party requester may once file comments responsive to the patent owner's comments within 30 days from the date of service of patent owner's comments on the third party requester.

[Added, 65 FR 76756, Dec. 7, 2000, effective Feb. 5, 2001]

§ 1.953 Examiner's Right of Appeal Notice in *inter partes* reexamination.

(a) Upon considering the comments of the patent owner and the third party requester subsequent to the Office action closing prosecution in an *inter partes* reexamination, or upon expiration of the time for submitting such comments, the examiner shall issue a Right of Appeal Notice, unless the examiner reopens prosecution and issues another Office action on the merits.

(b) Expedited Right of Appeal Notice: At any time after the patent owner's response to the initial Office action on the merits in an *inter partes* reexamination, the patent owner and all third party requesters may stipulate that the issues are appropriate for a final action, which would include a final rejection and/or a final determination favorable to patentability, and may request the issuance of a Right of Appeal Notice. The request must have the concurrence of the patent owner and all third party requesters present in the proceeding and must identify all of the appealable issues and the positions of the patent owner and all third party requesters on those issues. If the examiner determines that no other issues are present or should be raised, a Right of Appeal Notice limited to the identified issues shall be issued.

(c) The Right of Appeal Notice shall be a final action, which comprises a final rejection setting forth each ground of rejection and/or final decision favorable to patentability including each determination not to make a proposed rejection, an identification of the status of each claim, and the reasons for decisions favorable to patentability and/or the grounds of rejection for each claim. No amendment can be made in response to the Right of Appeal Notice. The Right of Appeal Notice shall set a one-month time period for either party to appeal. If no notice of appeal is filed, prosecution in the *inter partes* reexamination proceeding will be terminated, and the Director will proceed to issue and publish a certificate under § 1.997 in accordance with the Right of Appeal Notice.

[Added, 65 FR 76756, Dec. 7, 2000, effective Feb. 5, 2001; para. (c) revised, 68 FR 14332, Mar. 25, 2003, effective May 1, 2003; paras. (b) and (c) revised, 72 FR 18892, Apr. 16, 2007, effective May 16, 2007]

INTERVIEWS PROHIBITED IN *INTER PARTES* REEXAMINATION

§ 1.955 Interviews prohibited in *inter partes* reexamination proceedings.

There will be no interviews in an *inter partes* reexamination proceeding which discuss the merits of the proceeding.

[Added, 65 FR 76756, Dec. 7, 2000, effective Feb. 5, 2001]

EXTENSIONS OF TIME, TERMINATING OF REEXAMINATION PROSECUTION, AND PETITIONS TO REVIVE IN *INTER PARTES* REEXAMINATION

§ 1.956   Patent owner extensions of time in *inter partes* reexamination.

The time for taking any action by a patent owner in an *inter partes* reexamination proceeding will be extended only for sufficient cause and for a reasonable time specified. Any request for such extension must be filed on or before the day on which action by the patent owner is due, but in no case will the mere filing of a request effect any extension. Any request for such extension must be accompanied by the petition set forth in § 1.17(g). See § 1.304(a) for extensions of time for filing a notice of appeal to the U.S. Court of Appeals for the Federal Circuit.

[Added, 65 FR 76756, Dec. 7, 2000, effective Feb. 5, 2001; revised, 69 FR 56481, Sept. 21, 2004, effective Nov. 22, 2004]

§ 1.957   Failure to file a timely, appropriate or complete response or comment in *inter partes* reexamination.

(a)   If the third party requester files an untimely or inappropriate comment, notice of appeal or brief in an *inter partes* reexamination, the paper will be refused consideration.

(b)   If no claims are found patentable, and the patent owner fails to file a timely and appropriate response in an *inter partes* reexamination proceeding, the prosecution in the reexamination proceeding will be a terminated prosecution and the Director will proceed to issue and publish a certificate concluding the reexamination proceeding under § 1.997 in accordance with the last action of the Office.

(c)   If claims are found patentable and the patent owner fails to file a timely and appropriate response to any Office action in an *inter partes* reexamination proceeding, further prosecution will be limited to the claims found patentable at the time of the failure to respond, and to any claims added thereafter which do not expand the scope of the claims which were found patentable at that time.

(d)   When action by the patent owner is a *bona fide* attempt to respond and to advance the prosecution and is substantially a complete response to the Office action, but consideration of some matter or compliance with some requirement has been inadvertently omitted, an opportunity to explain and supply the omission may be given.

[Added, 65 FR 76756, Dec. 7, 2000, effective Feb. 5, 2001; para. (b) revised, 68 FR 14332, Mar. 25, 2003, effective May 1, 2003; para. (b) revised, 72 FR 18892, Apr. 16, 2007, effective May 16, 2007]

§ 1.958   Petition to revive *inter partes* reexamination prosecution terminated for lack of patent owner response.

(a)   If a response by the patent owner is not timely filed in the Office, the delay in filing such response may be excused if it is shown to the satisfaction of the Director that the delay was unavoidable. A grantable petition to accept an unavoidably delayed response must be filed in compliance with § 1.137(a).

(b)   Any response by the patent owner not timely filed in the Office may be accepted if the delay was unintentional. A grantable petition to accept an unintentionally delayed response must be filed in compliance with § 1.137(b).

[Added, 65 FR 76756, Dec. 7, 2000, effective Feb. 5, 2001; para. (a) revised, 68 FR 14332, Mar. 25, 2003, effective May 1, 2003; heading revised, 72 FR 18892, Apr. 16, 2007, effective May 16, 2007]

APPEAL TO THE BOARD OF PATENT APPEALS AND INTERFERENCES IN *INTER PARTES* REEXAMINATION

§ 1.959   Appeal in *inter partes* reexamination.

Appeals to the Board of Patent Appeals and Interferences under 35 U.S.C. 134(c) are conducted according to part 41 of this title.

[Added, 65 FR 76756, Dec. 7, 2000, effective Feb. 5, 2001; para (f) added, 68 FR 70996, Dec. 22, 2003, effective Jan. 21, 2004; revised, 69 FR 49959, Aug. 12, 2004, effective Sept. 13, 2004]

§ 1.961 - 1.977 [Reserved]

§ 1.979 Return of Jurisdiction from the Board of Patent Appeals and Interferences; termination of appeal proceedings.

(a) Jurisdiction over an *inter partes* reexamination proceeding passes to the examiner after a decision by the Board of Patent Appeals and Interferences upon transmittal of the file to the examiner, subject to each appellant's right of appeal or other review, for such further action as the condition of the *inter partes* reexamination proceeding may require, to carry into effect the decision of the Board of Patent Appeals and Interferences.

(b) Upon judgment in the appeal before the Board of Patent Appeals and Interferences, if no further appeal has been taken (§ 1.983), the prosecution in the *inter partes* reexamination proceeding will be terminated and the Director will issue and publish a certificate under § 1.997 concluding the proceeding. If an appeal to the U.S. Court of Appeals for the Federal Circuit has been filed, that appeal is considered terminated when the mandate is issued by the Court.

[Added, 65 FR 76756, Dec. 7, 2000, effective Feb. 5, 2001; para. (f) revised, 68 FR 14332, Mar. 25, 2003, effective May 1, 2003; paras. (e) & (f) revised, 68 FR 70996, Dec. 22, 2003, effective Jan. 21, 2004; revised, 69 FR 49959, Aug. 12, 2004, effective Sept. 13, 2004; heading and para. (b) revised, 72 FR 18892, Apr. 16, 2007, effective May 16, 2007]

§ 1.981 Reopening after a final decision of the Board of Patent Appeals and Interferences.

When a decision by the Board of Patent Appeals and Interferences on appeal has become final for judicial review, prosecution of the *inter partes* reexamination proceeding will not be reopened or reconsidered by the primary examiner except under the provisions of § 41.77 of this title without the written authority of the Director, and then only for the consideration of matters not already adjudicated, sufficient cause being shown.

[Added, 65 FR 76756, Dec. 7, 2000, effective Feb. 5, 2001; revised, 68 FR 14332, Mar. 25, 2003, effective May 1, 2003; revised, 69 FR 49959, Aug. 12, 2004, effective Sept. 13, 2004]

APPEAL TO THE UNITED STATES COURT OF APPEALS FOR THE FEDERAL CIRCUIT IN *INTER PARTES* REEXAMINATION

§ 1.983 Appeal to the United States Court of Appeals for the Federal Circuit in *inter partes* reexamination.

(a) The patent owner or third party requester in an *inter partes* reexamination proceeding who is a party to an appeal to the Board of Patent Appeals and Interferences and who is dissatisfied with the decision of the Board of Patent Appeals and Interferences may, subject to § 41.81, appeal to the U.S. Court of Appeals for the Federal Circuit and may be a party to any appeal thereto taken from a reexamination decision of the Board of Patent Appeals and Interferences.

(b) The appellant must take the following steps in such an appeal:

(1) In the U.S. Patent and Trademark Office, timely file a written notice of appeal directed to the Director in accordance with §§ 1.302 and 1.304;

(2) In the U.S. Court of Appeals for the Federal Circuit, file a copy of the notice of appeal and pay the fee, as provided for in the rules of the U.S. Court of Appeals for the Federal Circuit; and

(3) Serve a copy of the notice of appeal on every other party in the reexamination proceeding in the manner provided in § 1.248.

(c) If the patent owner has filed a notice of appeal to the U.S. Court of Appeals for the Federal Circuit, the third party requester may cross appeal to the U.S. Court of Appeals for the Federal Circuit if also dissatisfied with the decision of the Board of Patent Appeals and Interferences.

(d) If the third party requester has filed a notice of appeal to the U.S. Court of Appeals for the Federal Circuit, the patent owner may cross appeal to the U.S. Court of Appeals for the Federal Circuit if also dissatisfied with the decision of the Board of Patent Appeals and Interferences.

(e) A party electing to participate in an appellant's appeal must, within fourteen days of service of the appellant's notice of appeal under paragraph (b) of this section, or notice of cross appeal under paragraphs (c) or (d) of this section, take the following steps:

(1) In the U.S. Patent and Trademark Office, timely file a written notice directed to the Director

electing to participate in the appellant's appeal to the U.S. Court of Appeals for the Federal Circuit by mail to, or hand service on, the General Counsel as provided in § 104.2;

    (2)   In the U.S. Court of Appeals for the Federal Circuit, file a copy of the notice electing to participate in accordance with the rules of the U.S. Court of Appeals for the Federal Circuit; and

    (3)   Serve a copy of the notice electing to participate on every other party in the reexamination proceeding in the manner provided in § 1.248.

    (f)   Notwithstanding any provision of the rules, in any reexamination proceeding commenced prior to November 2, 2002, the third party requester is precluded from appealing and cross appealing any decision of the Board of Patent Appeals and Interferences to the U.S. Court of Appeals for the Federal Circuit, and the third party requester is precluded from participating in any appeal taken by the patent owner to the U.S. Court of Appeals for the Federal Circuit.

[Added, 65 FR 76756, Dec. 7, 2000, effective Feb. 5, 2001; para. (a)(1) revised, 68 FR 14332, Mar. 25, 2003, effective May 1, 2003; revised, 68 FR 70996, Dec. 22, 2003, effective Jan. 21, 2004; para. (a) revised, 72 FR 18892, Apr. 16, 2007, effective May 16, 2007]

CONCURRENT PROCEEDINGS INVOLVING SAME PATENT IN *INTER PARTES* REEXAMINATION

§ 1.985   Notification of prior or concurrent proceedings in *inter partes* reexamination.

    (a)   In any *inter partes* reexamination proceeding, the patent owner shall call the attention of the Office to any prior or concurrent proceedings in which the patent is or was involved, including but not limited to interference, reissue, reexamination, or litigation and the results of such proceedings.

    (b)   Notwithstanding any provision of the rules, any person at any time may file a paper in an *inter partes* reexamination proceeding notifying the Office of a prior or concurrent proceedings in which the same patent is or was involved, including but not limited to interference, reissue, reexamination, or litigation and the results of such proceedings. Such paper must be limited to merely providing notice of the other proceeding without discussion of issues of the current *inter partes* reexamination proceeding.

Any paper not so limited will be returned to the sender.

[Added, 65 FR 76756, Dec. 7, 2000, effective Feb. 5, 2001]

§ 1.987   Suspension of *inter partes* reexamination proceeding due to litigation.

If a patent in the process of *inter partes* reexamination is or becomes involved in litigation, the Director shall determine whether or not to suspend the *inter partes* reexamination proceeding.

[Added, 65 FR 76756, Dec. 7, 2000, effective Feb. 5, 2001; revised, 68 FR 14332, Mar. 25, 2003, effective May 1, 2003]

§ 1.989   Merger of concurrent reexamination proceedings.

    (a)   If any reexamination is ordered while a prior *inter partes* reexamination proceeding is pending for the same patent and prosecution in the prior *inter partes* reexamination proceeding has not been terminated, a decision may be made to merge the two proceedings or to suspend one of the two proceedings. Where merger is ordered, the merged examination will normally result in the issuance and publication of a single reexamination certificate under § 1.997.

    (b)   An *inter partes* reexamination proceeding filed under § 1.913 which is merged with an *ex parte* reexamination proceeding filed under § 1.510 will result in the merged proceeding being governed by §§ 1.902 through 1.997, except that the rights of any third party requester of the *ex parte* reexamination shall be governed by §§ 1.510 through 1.560.

[Added, 65 FR 76756, Dec. 7, 2000, effective Feb. 5, 2001; para. (a) revised, 72 FR 18892, Apr. 16, 2007, effective May 16, 2007]

§ 1.991   Merger of concurrent reissue application and *inter partes* reexamination proceeding.

If a reissue application and an *inter partes* reexamination proceeding on which an order pursuant to § 1.931 has been mailed are pending concurrently on a patent, a decision may be made to merge the two proceedings or to suspend one of the two proceedings. Where merger of a reissue application and an *inter partes* reexamination proceeding is ordered, the merged proceeding will be conducted in accordance with §§ 1.171 through 1.179, and the patent owner will be required to place and maintain the same claims in the reissue application and the *inter partes* reexamination proceeding during the pendency of the merged proceeding. In a merged proceeding the third party requester may participate to the extent provided under §§ 1.902 through 1.997 and 41.60 through 41.81, except that such participation shall be limited to issues within the scope of *inter partes* reexamination. The examiner's actions and any responses by the patent owner or third party requester in a merged proceeding will apply to both the reissue application and the *inter partes* reexamination proceeding and be physically entered into both files. Any *inter partes* reexamination proceeding merged with a reissue application shall be concluded by the grant of the reissued patent.

[Added, 65 FR 76756, Dec. 7, 2000, effective Feb. 5, 2001; revised, 72 FR 18892, Apr. 16, 2007, effective May 16, 2007]

§ 1.993 Suspension of concurrent interference and inter partes reexamination proceeding.

If a patent in the process of inter partes reexamination is or becomes involved in an interference, the Director may suspend the inter partes reexamination or the interference. The Director will not consider a request to suspend an interference unless a motion under § 41.121(a)(3) of this title to suspend the interference has been presented to, and denied by, an administrative patent judge and the request is filed within ten (10) days of a decision by an administrative patent judge denying the motion for suspension or such other time as the administrative patent judge may set.

[Added, 65 FR 76756, Dec. 7, 2000, effective Feb. 5, 2001; revised, 68 FR 14332, Mar. 25, 2003, effective May 1, 2003; revised, 69 FR 49959, Aug. 12, 2004, effective Sept. 13, 2004]

§ 1.995 Third party requester's participation rights preserved in merged proceeding.

When a third party requester is involved in one or more proceedings, including an *inter partes* reexamination proceeding, the merger of such proceedings will be accomplished so as to preserve the third party requester's right to participate to the extent specifically provided for in these regulations. In merged proceedings involving different requesters, any paper filed by one party in the merged proceeding shall be served on all other parties of the merged proceeding.

[Added, 65 FR 76756, Dec. 7, 2000, effective Feb. 5, 2001]

REEXAMINATION CERTIFICATE IN *INTER PARTES* REEXAMINATION

§ 1.997 Issuance and publication of *inter partes* reexamination certificate concludes *inter partes* reexamination proceeding.

(a) To conclude an *inter partes* reexamination proceeding, the Director will issue and publish an *inter partes* reexamination certificate in accordance with 35 U.S.C. 316 setting forth the results of the *inter partes* reexamination proceeding and the content of the patent following the *inter partes* reexamination proceeding.

(b) A certificate will be issued and published in each patent in which an *inter partes* reexamination proceeding has been ordered under § 1.931. Any statutory disclaimer filed by the patent owner will be made part of the certificate.

(c) The certificate will be sent to the patent owner at the address as provided for in § 1.33(c). A copy of the certificate will also be sent to the third party requester of the *inter partes* reexamination proceeding.

(d) If a certificate has been issued and published which cancels all of the claims of the patent, no further Office proceedings will be conducted with that patent or any reissue applications or any reexamination requests relating thereto.

(e) If the *inter partes* reexamination proceeding is terminated by the grant of a reissued patent as provided in § 1.991, the reissued patent will constitute the reexamination certificate required by this section and 35 U.S.C. 316.

(f) A notice of the issuance of each certificate under this section will be published in the *Official Gazette*.

[Added, 65 FR 76756, Dec. 7, 2000, effective Feb. 5, 2001; para. (a) revised, 68 FR 14332, Mar. 25, 2003, effective May 1, 2003; heading and paras. (a), (b), and (d) revised, 72 FR 18892, Apr. 16, 2007, effective May 16, 2007]

PART 3 — ASSIGNMENT, RECORDING AND RIGHTS OF ASSIGNEE

Sec.
3.1 Definitions.

DOCUMENTS ELIGIBLE FOR RECORDING

3.11   Documents which will be recorded.

3.16   Assignability of trademarks prior to filing an allegation of use.

REQUIREMENTS FOR RECORDING

3.21   Identification of patents and patent applications.

3.24   Requirements for documents and cover sheets relating to patents and patent applications.

3.25   Recording requirements for trademark applications and registrations.

3.26   English language requirement.

3.27   Mailing address for submitting documents to be recorded.

3.28   Requests for recording.

COVER SHEET REQUIREMENTS

3.31   Cover sheet content.

3.34   Correction of cover sheet errors.

FEES

3.41   Recording fees.

DATE AND EFFECT OF RECORDING

3.51   Recording date.

3.54   Effect of recording.

3.56   Conditional assignments.

3.58   Governmental registers.

DOMESTIC REPRESENTATIVE

3.61   Domestic representative.

ACTION TAKEN BY ASSIGNEE

3.71   Prosecution by assignee.

3.73   Establishing right of assignee to take action.

ISSUANCE TO ASSIGNEE

3.81   Issue of patent to assignee.

3.85   Issue of registration to assignee.

§ 3.1   Definitions.

For purposes of this part, the following definitions shall apply:

Application means a national application for patent, an international patent application that designates the United States of America, or an application to register a trademark under section 1 or 44 of the Trademark Act, 15 U.S.C. 1051 or 15 U.S.C. 1126, unless otherwise indicated.

Assignment means a transfer by a party of all or part of its right, title and interest in a patent, patent application, registered mark or a mark for which an application to register has been filed.

Document means a document which a party requests to be recorded in the Office pursuant to § 3.11 and which affects some interest in an application, patent, or registration.

Office means the United States Patent and Trademark Office.

Recorded document means a document which has been recorded in the Office pursuant to § 3.11.

Registration means a trademark registration issued by the Office.

[Added, 57 FR 29634, July 6, 1992, effective Sept. 4, 1992; revised, 69 FR 29865, May 26, 2004, effective June 25, 2004]

DOCUMENTS ELIGIBLE FOR RECORDING

§ 3.11   Documents which will be recorded.

(a)   Assignments of applications, patents, and registrations, accompanied by completed cover sheets as specified in §§ 3.28 and 3.31, will be recorded in the Office. Other documents, accompanied by completed cover sheets as specified in §§ 3.28 and 3.31, affecting title to applications, patents, or registrations, will be recorded as provided in this part or at the discretion of the Director.

(b) Executive Order 9424 of February 18, 1944 (9 FR 1959, 3 CFR 1943-1948 Comp., p. 303) requires the several departments and other executive agencies of the Government, including Government-owned or Government-controlled corporations, to forward promptly to the Director for recording all licenses, assignments, or other interests of the Government in or under patents or patent applications. Assignments and other documents affecting title to patents or patent applications and documents not affecting title to patents or patent applications required by Executive Order 9424 to be filed will be recorded as provided in this part.

(c) A joint research agreement or an excerpt of a joint research agreement will also be recorded as provided in this part.

[Added, 57 FR 29634, July 6, 1992, effective Sept. 4, 1992; revised, 62 FR 53131, Oct. 10, 1997, effective Dec. 1, 1997; revised, 68 FR 14332, Mar. 25, 2003, effective May 1, 2003; para. (c) added, 70 FR 1818, Jan. 11, 2005, effective Dec. 10, 2004; para. (c) revised, 70 FR 54259, Sept. 14, 2005, effective Sept. 14, 2005]

§ 3.16 Assignability of trademarks prior to filing an allegation of use.

Before an allegation of use under either 15 U.S.C. 1051(c) or 15 U.S.C. 1051(d) is filed, an applicant may only assign an application to register a mark under 15 U.S.C. 1051(b) to a successor to the applicant's business, or portion of the business to which the mark pertains, if that business is ongoing and existing.

[Added, 57 FR 29634, July 6, 1992, effective Sept. 4, 1992; revised, 64 FR 48900, Sept. 8, 1999, effective Oct. 30, 1999]

REQUIREMENTS FOR RECORDING

§ 3.21 Identification of patents and patent applications.

An assignment relating to a patent must identify the patent by the patent number. An assignment relating to a national patent application must identify the national patent application by the application number (consisting of the series code and the serial number, e.g., 07/123,456). An assignment relating to an international patent application which designates the United States of America must identify the international application by the international application number (e.g., PCT/US90/01234). If an assignment of a patent application filed under § 1.53(b) is executed concurrently with, or subsequent to, the execution of the patent application, but before the patent application is filed, it must identify the patent application by the name of each inventor and the title of the invention so that there can be no mistake as to the patent application intended. If an assignment of a provisional application under § 1.53(c) is executed before the provisional application is filed, it must identify the provisional application by the name of each inventor and the title of the invention so that there can be no mistake as to the provisional application intended.

[Added, 57 FR 29634, July 6, 1992, effective Sept. 4, 1992; amended, 60 FR 20195, Apr. 25, 1995, effective June 8, 1995; revised, 62 FR 53131, Oct. 10, 1997, effective Dec. 1, 1997; revised, 69 FR 29865, May 26, 2004, effective June 25, 2004]

§ 3.24 Requirements for documents and cover sheets relating to patents and patent applications.

(a) *For electronic submissions:* Either a copy of the original document or an extract of the original document may be submitted for recording. All documents must be submitted as digitized images in Tagged Image File Format (TIFF) or another form as prescribed by the Director. When printed to a paper size of either 21.6 by 27.9 cm (8 1/2 inches by 11 inches) or 21.0 by 29.7 cm (DIN size A4), the document must be legible and a 2.5 cm (one-inch) margin must be present on all sides.

(b) *For paper or facsimile submissions*: Either a copy of the original document or an extract of the original document must be submitted for recording. Only one side of each page may be used. The paper size must be either 21.6 by 27.9 cm (8 1/2 inches by 11 inches) or 21.0 by 29.7 cm (DIN size A4), and in either case, a 2.5 cm (one-inch) margin must be present on all sides. For paper submissions, the paper used should be flexible, strong white, non-shiny, and durable. The Office will not return recorded documents, so original documents must not be submitted for recording.

[Added, 57 FR 29634, July 6, 1992, effective Sept. 4, 1992; heading revised, 64 FR 48900, Sept. 8, 1999, effective Oct. 30, 1999; revised, 69 FR 29865, May 26, 2004, effective June 25, 2004; revised, 69 FR 29865, May 26, 2004, effective June 25, 2004]

§ 3.25   Recording requirements for trademark applications and registrations.

(a) *Documents affecting title.* To record documents affecting title to a trademark application or registration, a legible cover sheet (*see* § 3.31) and one of the following must be submitted:

(1)   A copy of the original document;

(2)   A copy of an extract from the document evidencing the effect on title; or

(3)   A statement signed by both the party conveying the interest and the party receiving the interest explaining how the conveyance affects title.

(b) *Name changes.* Only a legible cover sheet is required (*See* § 3.31).

(c) *All documents.* (1) *For electronic submissions*: All documents must be submitted as digitized images in Tagged Image File Format (TIFF) or another form as prescribed by the Director. When printed to a paper size of either 21.6 by 27.9 cm (8 1/2 by 11 inches) or 21.0 by 29.7 cm (DIN size A4), a 2.5 cm (one-inch) margin must be present on all sides.

(2)   *For paper or facsimile submissions*: All documents should be submitted on white and non-shiny paper that is either 8 1/2 by 11 inches (21.6 by 27.9 cm) or DIN size A4 (21.0 by 29.7 cm) with a one-inch (2.5 cm) margin on all sides in either case. Only one side of each page may be used. The Office will not return recorded documents, so original documents should not be submitted for recording.

[Added, 64 FR 48900, Sept. 8, 1999, effective Oct. 30, 1999; revised, 69 FR 29865, May 26, 2004, effective June 25, 2004]

§ 3.26   English language requirement.

The Office will accept and record non-English language documents only if accompanied by an English translation signed by the individual making the translation.

[Added, 57 FR 29634, July 6, 1992, effective Sept. 4, 1992; revised, 62 FR 53131, Oct. 10, 1997, effective Dec. 1, 1997]

§ 3.27   Mailing address for submitting documents to be recorded.

Documents and cover sheets submitted by mail for recordation should be addressed to Mail Stop Assignment Recordation Services, Director of the United States Patent and Trademark Office, P.O. Box 1450, Alexandria, Virginia 22313-1450, unless they are filed together with new applications.

[Added, 57 FR 29634, July 6, 1992, effective Sept. 4, 1992; revised, 62 FR 53131, Oct. 10, 1997, effective Dec. 1, 1997; revised, 65 FR 54604, Sept. 8, 2000, effective Nov. 7, 2000; revised, 68 FR 14332, Mar. 25, 2003, effective May 1, 2003; revised, 69 FR 29865, May 26, 2004, effective June 25, 2004]

§ 3.28   Requests for recording.

Each document submitted to the Office for recording must include a single cover sheet (as specified in § 3.31) referring either to those patent applications and patents, or to those trademark applications and registrations, against which the document is to be recorded. If a document to be recorded includes interests in, or transactions involving, both patents and trademarks, then separate patent and trademark cover sheets, each accompanied by a copy of the document to be recorded, must be submitted. If a document to be recorded is not accompanied by a completed cover sheet, the document and the incomplete cover sheet will be returned pursuant to § 3.51 for proper completion, in which case the document and a completed cover sheet should be resubmitted.

[Added, 57 FR 29634, July 6, 1992, effective Sept. 4, 1992; revised, 64 FR 48900, Sept. 8, 1999, effective Oct. 30, 1999; revised, 70 FR 56119, Sept. 26, 2005, effective Nov. 25, 2005]

COVER SHEET REQUIREMENTS

§ 3.31   Cover sheet content.

(a)   Each patent or trademark cover sheet required by § 3.28 must contain:

(1)   The name of the party conveying the interest;

(2) The name and address of the party receiving the interest;

(3) A description of the interest conveyed or transaction to be recorded;

(4) Identification of the interests involved:

(i) For trademark assignments and trademark name changes: Each trademark registration number and each trademark application number, if known, against which the Office is to record the document. If the trademark application number is not known, a copy of the application or a reproduction of the trademark must be submitted, along with an estimate of the date that the Office received the application; or

(ii) For any other document affecting title to a trademark or patent application, registration or patent: Each trademark or patent application number or each trademark registration number or patent against which the document is to be recorded, or an indication that the document is filed together with a patent application;

(5) The name and address of the party to whom correspondence concerning the request to record the document should be mailed;

(6) The date the document was executed;

(7) The signature of the party submitting the document. For an assignment document or name change filed electronically, the person who signs the cover sheet must either:

(i) Place a symbol comprised of letters, numbers, and/or punctuation marks between forward slash marks (*e.g.* Thomas O'Malley III) in the signature block on the electronic submission; or

(ii) Sign the cover sheet using some other form of electronic signature specified by the Director.

(8) For trademark assignments, the entity and citizenship of the party receiving the interest. In addition, if the party receiving the interest is a domestic partnership or domestic joint venture, the cover sheet must set forth the names, legal entities, and national citizenship (or the state or country of organization) of all general partners or active members that compose the partnership or joint venture.

(b) A cover sheet should not refer to both patents and trademarks, since any information, including information about pending patent applications, submitted with a request for recordation of a document against a trademark application or trademark registration will become public record upon recordation.

(c) Each patent cover sheet required by § 3.28 seeking to record a governmental interest as provided by § 3.11(b) must:

(1) Indicate that the document relates to a Government interest; and

(2) Indicate, if applicable, that the document to be recorded is not a document affecting title (see § 3.41(b)).

(d) Each trademark cover sheet required by § 3.28 seeking to record a document against a trademark application or registration should include, in addition to the serial number or registration number of the trademark, identification of the trademark or a description of the trademark, against which the Office is to record the document.

(e) Each patent or trademark cover sheet required by § 3.28 should contain the number of applications, patents or registrations identified in the cover sheet and the total fee.

(f) Each trademark cover sheet should include the citizenship of the party conveying the interest.

(g) The cover sheet required by § 3.28 seeking to record a joint research agreement or an excerpt of a joint research agreement as provided by § 3.11(c) must:

(1) Identify the document as a "joint research agreement" (in the space provided for the description of the interest conveyed or transaction to be recorded if using an Office-provided form);

(2) Indicate the name of the owner of the application or patent (in the space provided for the name and address of the party receiving the interest if using an Office-provided form);

(3) Indicate the name of each other party to the joint research agreement party (in the space provided for the name of the party conveying the interest if using an Office-provided form); and

(4) Indicate the date the joint research agreement was executed.

[Added, 57 FR 29634, July 6, 1992, effective Sept. 4, 1992; para. (c) added, 62 FR 53131, Oct. 10, 1997, effective Dec. 1, 1997; paras. (a)-(b) revised, paras. (d)-(e) added, 64 FR 48900, Sept. 8, 1999, effective Oct. 30, 1999; para. (a)(7) deleted and para. (a)(8) redesignated as para. (a)(7), 67 FR 79520, Dec. 30, 2002, effective Dec. 30, 2002; paras. (a)(7) & (c)(1) revised and para. (f) added, 69

FR 29865, May 26, 2004, effective June 25, 2004; para (g) added, 70 FR 1818, Jan. 11, 2005, effective Dec. 10, 2004; para. (a)(7)(i) revised, 70 FR 56119, Sept. 26, 2005, effective Nov. 25, 2005; para. (a)(8) added and para. (f) revised, 73 FR 67759, Nov. 17, 2008, effective Jan. 16, 2009]

§ 3.34   Correction of cover sheet errors.

(a)   An error in a cover sheet recorded pursuant to § 3.11 will be corrected only if:

(1)   The error is apparent when the cover sheet is compared with the recorded document to which it pertains and

(2)   A corrected cover sheet is filed for recordation.

(b)   The corrected cover sheet must be accompanied by a copy of the document originally submitted for recording and by the recording fee as set forth in § 3.41.

[Added, 57 FR 29634, July 6, 1992, effective Sept. 4, 1992; para. (b) revised, 69 FR 29865, May 26, 2004, effective June 25, 2004]

FEES

§ 3.41   Recording fees.

(a)   All requests to record documents must be accompanied by the appropriate fee. Except as provided in paragraph (b) of this section, a fee is required for each application, patent and registration against which the document is recorded as identified in the cover sheet. The recording fee is set in § 1.21(h) of this chapter for patents and in § 2.6(b)(6) of this chapter for trademarks.

(b)   No fee is required for each patent application and patent against which a document required by Executive Order 9424 is to be filed if:

(1)   The document does not affect title and is so identified in the cover sheet (see § 3.31(c)(2)); and

(2)   The document and cover sheet are either: Faxed or electronically submitted as prescribed by the Director, or mailed to the Office in compliance with § 3.27.

[Added, 57 FR 29634, July 6, 1992, effective Sept. 4, 1992; revised, 62 FR 53131, Oct. 10, 1997, effective Dec. 1, 1997; para. (a) amended, 63 FR 48081, Sept. 9, 1998, effective October 9, 1998; para. (a) corrected, 63 FR 52158, Sept. 10, 1998; para. (b)(2) revised, 69 FR 29865, May 26, 2004, effective June 25, 2004]

DATE AND EFFECT OF RECORDING

§ 3.51   Recording date.

The date of recording of a document is the date the document meeting the requirements for recording set forth in this part is filed in the Office. A document which does not comply with the identification requirements of § 3.21 will not be recorded. Documents not meeting the other requirements for recording, for example, a document submitted without a completed cover sheet or without the required fee, will be returned for correction to the sender where a correspondence address is available. The returned papers, stamped with the original date of receipt by the Office, will be accompanied by a letter which will indicate that if the returned papers are corrected and resubmitted to the Office within the time specified in the letter, the Office will consider the original date of filing of the papers as the date of recording of the document. The procedure set forth in § 1.8 or § 1.10 of this chapter may be used for resubmissions of returned papers to have the benefit of the date of deposit in the United States Postal Service. If the returned papers are not corrected and resubmitted within the specified period, the date of filing of the corrected papers will be considered to be the date of recording of the document. The specified period to resubmit the returned papers will not be extended.

[Added, 57 FR 29634, July 6, 1992, effective Sept. 4, 1992; revised, 62 FR 53131, Oct. 10, 1997, effective Dec. 1, 1997]

§ 3.54   Effect of recording.

The recording of a document pursuant to § 3.11 is not a determination by the Office of the validity of the document or the effect that document has on the title to an application, a patent, or a registration. When necessary, the Office will determine what effect a document has, including whether a party has the authority to take an action in a matter pending before the Office.

[Added, 57 FR 29634, July 6, 1992, effective Sept. 4, 1992]

§ 3.56 Conditional assignments.

Assignments which are made conditional on the performance of certain acts or events, such as the payment of money or other condition subsequent, if recorded in the Office, are regarded as absolute assignments for Office purposes until cancelled with the written consent of all parties or by the decree of a court of competent jurisdiction. The Office does not determine whether such conditions have been fulfilled.

[Added, 57 FR 29634, July 6, 1992, effective Sept. 4, 1992]

§ 3.58 Governmental registers.

(a)   The Office will maintain a Departmental Register to record governmental interests required to be recorded by Executive Order 9424. This Departmental Register will not be open to public inspection but will be available for examination and inspection by duly authorized representatives of the Government. Governmental interests recorded on the Departmental Register will be available for public inspection as provided in § 1.12.

(b)   The Office will maintain a Secret Register to record governmental interests required to be recorded by Executive Order 9424. Any instrument to be recorded will be placed on this Secret Register at the request of the department or agency submitting the same. No information will be given concerning any instrument in such record or register, and no examination or inspection thereof or of the index thereto will be permitted, except on the written authority of the head of the department or agency which submitted the instrument and requested secrecy, and the approval of such authority by the Director. No instrument or record other than the one specified may be examined, and the examination must take place in the presence of a designated official of the Patent and Trademark Office. When the department or agency which submitted an instrument no longer requires secrecy with respect to that instrument, it must be recorded anew in the Departmental Register.

[Added, 62 FR 53131, Oct. 10, 1997, effective Dec. 1, 1997; para. (b) revised, 68 FR 14332, Mar. 25, 2003, effective May 1, 2003]

DOMESTIC REPRESENTATIVE

§ 3.61 Domestic representative.

If the assignee of a patent, patent application, trademark application or trademark registration is not domiciled in the United States, the assignee may designate a domestic representative in a document filed in the United States Patent and Trademark Office. The designation should state the name and address of a person residing within the United States on whom may be served process or notice of proceedings affecting the application, patent or registration or rights thereunder.

[Added, 57 FR 29634, July 6, 1992, effective Sept. 4, 1992; revised, 67 FR 79520, Dec. 30, 2002, effective Dec. 30, 2002]

ACTION TAKEN BY ASSIGNEE

§ 3.71 Prosecution by assignee.

(a)   *Patents — conducting of prosecution.* One or more assignees as defined in paragraph (b) of this section may, after becoming of record pursuant to paragraph (c) of this section, conduct prosecution of a national patent application or a reexamination proceeding to the exclusion of either the inventive entity, or the assignee(s) previously entitled to conduct prosecution.

(b)   *Patents —* assignee(s) who can prosecute. The assignee(s) who may conduct either the prosecution of a national application for patent or a reexamination proceeding are:

(1)   *A single assignee.* An assignee of the entire right, title and interest in the application or patent being reexamined who is of record, or

(2)   *Partial assignee(s) together or with inventor(s).* All partial assignees, or all partial assignees and inventors who have not assigned their right, title and interest in the application or patent being reexamined, who together own the entire right, title and interest in the application or patent being reexamined. A partial assignee is any assignee of record having less than the entire right, title and interest in the application or patent being reexamined.

(c)   *Patents — Becoming of record.* An assignee becomes of record either in a national patent application or a reexamination proceeding by filing a statement in compliance with § 3.73(b) that is signed by a party who is authorized to act on behalf of the assignee.

(d) *Trademarks*. The assignee of a trademark application or registration may prosecute a trademark application, submit documents to maintain a trademark registration, or file papers against a third party in reliance on the assignee's trademark application or registration, to the exclusion of the original applicant or previous assignee. The assignee must establish ownership in compliance with § 3.73(b).

[Added, 57 FR 29634, July 6, 1992, effective Sept. 4, 1992; revised, 65 FR 54604, Sept. 8, 2000, effective Nov. 7, 2000]

§ 3.73   Establishing right of assignee to take action.

(a)   The inventor is presumed to be the owner of a patent application, and any patent that may issue therefrom, unless there is an assignment. The original applicant is presumed to be the owner of a trademark application or registration, unless there is an assignment.

(b)(1)   In order to request or take action in a patent or trademark matter, the assignee must establish its ownership of the patent or trademark property of paragraph (a) of this section to the satisfaction of the Director. The establishment of ownership by the assignee may be combined with the paper that requests or takes the action. Ownership is established by submitting to the Office a signed statement identifying the assignee, accompanied by either:

(i)   Documentary evidence of a chain of title from the original owner to the assignee (*e.g.*, copy of an executed assignment). For trademark matters only, the documents submitted to establish ownership may be required to be recorded pursuant to § 3.11 in the assignment records of the Office as a condition to permitting the assignee to take action in a matter pending before the Office. For patent matters only, the submission of the documentary evidence must be accompanied by a statement affirming that the documentary evidence of the chain of title from the original owner to the assignee was or concurrently is being submitted for recordation pursuant to § 3.11; or

(ii)   A statement specifying where documentary evidence of a chain of title from the original owner to the assignee is recorded in the assignment records of the Office (*e.g.*, reel and frame number).

(2)   The submission establishing ownership must show that the person signing the submission is a person authorized to act on behalf of the assignee by:

(i)   Including a statement that the person signing the submission is authorized to act on behalf of the assignee; or

(ii)   Being signed by a person having apparent authority to sign on behalf of the assignee, *e.g.*, an officer of the assignee.

(c)   For patent matters only:

(1)   Establishment of ownership by the assignee must be submitted prior to, or at the same time as, the paper requesting or taking action is submitted.

(2)   If the submission under this section is by an assignee of less than the entire right, title and interest, such assignee must indicate the extent (by percentage) of its ownership interest, or the Office may refuse to accept the submission as an establishment of ownership.

[Added, 57 FR 29634, July 6, 1992, effective Sept. 4, 1992; para. (b) revised, 62 FR 53131, Oct. 10, 1997, effective Dec. 1, 1997; revised, 65 FR 54604, Sept. 8, 2000, effective Nov. 7, 2000; para. (b)(1) revised, 68 FR 14332, Mar. 25, 2003, effective May 1, 2003; para. (b)(1)(i) revised, 70 FR 56119, Sept. 26, 2005, effective Nov. 25, 2005.]

ISSUANCE TO ASSIGNEE

§ 3.81   Issue of patent to assignee.

(a)   *With payment of the issue fee:* An application may issue in the name of the assignee consistent with the application's assignment where a request for such issuance is submitted with payment of the issue fee, provided the assignment has been previously recorded in the Office. If the assignment has not been previously recorded, the request must state that the document has been filed for recordation as set forth in § 3.11.

(b)   *After payment of the issue fee:* Any request for issuance of an application in the name of the assignee submitted after the date of payment of the issue fee, and any request for a patent to be corrected to state the name of the assignee, must state that the assignment was submitted for recordation as set forth in § 3.11 before issuance of the patent, and must include a request for a certificate of correction under §

1.323 of this chapter (accompanied by the fee set forth in § 1.20(a)) and the processing fee set forth in § 1.17 (i) of this chapter.

(c) *Partial assignees.* (1) If one or more assignee, together with one or more inventor, holds the entire right, title, and interest in the application, the patent may issue in the names of the assignee and the inventor.

(2) If multiple assignees hold the entire right, title, and interest to the exclusion of all the inventors, the patent may issue in the names of the multiple assignees.

[Added, 57 FR 29634, July 6, 1992, effective Sept. 4, 1992; amended, 60 FR 20195, Apr. 25, 1995, effective June 8, 1995; revised, 65 FR 54604, Sept. 8, 2000, effective Nov. 7, 2000; revised, 69 FR 29865, May 26, 2004, effective June 25, 2004]

§ 3.85　Issue of registration to assignee.

The certificate of registration may be issued to the assignee of the applicant, or in a new name of the applicant, provided that the party files a written request in the trademark application by the time the application is being prepared for issuance of the certificate of registration, and the appropriate document is recorded in the Office. If the assignment or name change document has not been recorded in the Office, then the written request must state that the document has been filed for recordation. The address of the assignee must be made of record in the application file.

[Added, 57 FR 29634, July 6, 1992, effective Sept. 4, 1992]

PART 4 — COMPLAINTS REGARDING INVENTION PROMOTERS

Sec.

4.1 Complaints Regarding Invention Promoters.

4.2 Definitions.

4.3 Submitting Complaints

4.4 Invention Promoter Reply.

4.5 Notice by Publication.

4.6 Attorneys and Agents

§ 4.1　Complaints Regarding Invention Promoters.

These regulations govern the Patent and Trademark Office's (Office) responsibilities under the Inventors' Rights Act of 1999, which can be found in the U.S. Code at 35 U.S.C. 297. The Act requires the Office to provide a forum for the publication of complaints concerning invention promoters. The Office will not conduct any independent investigation of the invention promoter. Although the Act provides additional civil remedies for persons injured by invention promoters, those remedies must be pursued by the injured party without the involvement of the Office.

[Added, 65 FR 3127, Jan. 20, 2000, effective Jan. 28, 2000]

§ 4.2　Definitions.

(a) *Invention Promoter* means any person, firm, partnership, corporation, or other entity who offers to perform or performs invention promotion services for, or on behalf of, a customer, and who holds itself out through advertising in any mass media as providing such services, but does not include—

(1) Any department or agency of the Federal Government or of a State or local government;

(2) Any nonprofit, charitable, scientific, or educational organization qualified under applicable State law or described under section 170(b)(1)(A) of the Internal Revenue Code of 1986;

(3) Any person or entity involved in the evaluation to determine commercial potential of, or offering to license or sell, a utility patent or a previously filed nonprovisional utility patent application;

(4) Any party participating in a transaction involving the sale of the stock or assets of a business; or

(5) Any party who directly engages in the business of retail sales of products or the distribution of products.

(b) *Customer* means any individual who enters into a contract with an invention promoter for invention promotion services.

(c) *Contract for Invention Promotion Services* means a contract by which an invention promoter undertakes invention promotion services for a customer.

(d) *Invention Promotion Services* means the procurement or attempted procurement for a customer of a firm, corporation, or other entity to develop and market products or services that include the invention of the customer.

[Added, 65 FR 3127, Jan. 20, 2000, effective Jan. 28, 2000]

§ 4.3   Submitting Complaints.

(a) A person may submit a complaint concerning an invention promoter with the Office. A person submitting a complaint should understand that the complaint may be forwarded to the invention promoter and may become publicly available. The Office will not accept any complaint that requests that it be kept confidential.

(b) A complaint must be clearly marked, or otherwise identified, as a complaint under these rules. The complaint must include:

(1) The name and address of the complainant;

(2) The name and address of the invention promoter;

(3) The name of the customer;

(4) The invention promotion services offered or performed by the invention promoter;

(5) The name of the mass media in which the invention promoter advertised providing such services;

(6) An explanation of the relationship between the customer and the invention promoter, and

(7) A signature of the complainant.

(c) The complaint should fairly summarize the action of the invention promoter about which the person complains. Additionally, the complaint should include names and addresses of persons believed to be associated with the invention promoter. Complaints, and any replies, must be addressed to: Mail Stop 24, Commissioner for Patents, P.O. Box 1450, Alexandria, Virginia 22313-1450.

(d) Complaints that do not provide the information requested in paragraphs (b) and (c) of this section will be returned. If complainant's address is not provided, the complaint will be destroyed.

(e) No originals of documents should be included with the complaint.

(f) A complaint can be withdrawn by the complainant or the named customer at any time prior to its publication.

[Para. (c) revised, 68 FR 14332, Mar. 25, 2003, effective May 1, 2003]

§ 4.4   Invention Promoter Reply.

(a) If a submission appears to meet the requirements of a complaint, the invention promoter named in the complaint will be notified of the complaint and given 30 days to respond. The invention promoter's response will be made available to the public along with the complaint. If the invention promoter fails to reply within the 30-day time period set by the Office, the complaint will be made available to the public. Replies sent after the complaint is made available to the public will also be published.

(b) A response must be clearly marked, or otherwise identified, as a response by an invention promoter. The response must contain:

(1) The name and address of the invention promoter;

(2) A reference to a complaint forwarded to the invention promoter or a complaint previously published;

(3) The name of the individual signing the response; and

(4) The title or authority of the individual signing the response.

[Added, 65 FR 3127, Jan. 20, 2000, effective Jan. 28, 2000]

§ 4.5   Notice by Publication.

If the copy of the complaint that is mailed to the invention promoter is returned undelivered, then the Office will publish a Notice of Complaint Received in the *Official Gazette*, the Federal Register, or on the Office's Internet home page. The invention promoter will be given 30 days from such notice to submit a reply to the complaint. If the Office does not receive a reply from the invention promoter within 30 days, the complaint alone will become publicly available.

[Added, 65 FR 3127, Jan. 20, 2000, effective Jan. 28, 2000]

§ 4.6   Attorneys and Agents.

Complaints against registered patent attorneys and agents will not be treated under this section, unless a complaint fairly demonstrates that invention promotion services are involved. Persons having complaints about registered patent attorneys or agents should contact the Office of Enrollment and Discipline at Mail Stop OED, Director of the United States Patent and Trademark Office, PO Box 1450, Alexandria, Virginia 22313-1450, and the attorney discipline section of the attorney's state licensing bar if an attorney is involved.

[Added, 65 FR 3127, Jan. 20, 2000, effective Jan. 28, 2000; revised, 68 FR 14332, Mar. 25, 2003, effective May 1, 2003]

PART 5 — SECRECY OF CERTAIN INVENTIONS AND LICENSES TO EXPORT AND FILE APPLICATIONS IN FOREIGN COUNTRIES

SECRECY

Sec.

5.1   Applications and correspondence involving national security.

5.2   Secrecy order.

5.3   Prosecution of application under secrecy orders; withholding patent.

5.4   Petition for rescission of secrecy order.

5.5   Permit to disclose or modification of secrecy order.

5.6   [Reserved]

5.7   [Reserved]

5.8   [Reserved]

LICENSES FOR FOREIGN EXPORTING AND FILING

5.11   License for filing in a foreign country an application on an invention made in the United States or for transmitting international application.

5.12   Petition for license.

5.13   Petition for license; no corresponding application.

5.14   Petition for license; corresponding U.S. application.

5.15   Scope of license.

5.16   [Reserved]

5.17   [Reserved]

5.18   Arms, ammunition, and implements of war.

5.19   Export of technical data.

5.20   Export of technical data relating to sensitive nuclear technology.

5.25   Petition for retroactive license.

GENERAL

5.31   [Reserved]

5.32   [Reserved]

5.33   [Reserved]

SECRECY

§ 5.1   **Applications and correspondence involving national security.**

(a)   All correspondence in connection with this part, including petitions, should be addressed to: Mail Stop L&R, Commissioner for Patents, P.O. Box 1450, Alexandria, Virginia 22313-1450.

(b)   Application as used in this part includes provisional applications filed under 35 U.S.C. 111(b) (§ 1.9(a)(2) of this chapter), nonprovisional applications filed under 35 U.S.C. 111(a) or entering the national stage from an international application after compliance with 35 U.S.C. 371 (§ 1.9(a)(3)), or international applications filed under the Patent Cooperation Treaty prior to entering the national stage of processing (§ 1.9(b)).

(c)   Patent applications and documents relating thereto that are national security classified (see § 1.9(i) of this chapter) and contain authorized national security markings (*e.g.*, "Confidential," "Secret" or "Top Secret") are accepted by the Office. National security classified documents filed in the Office must be either hand-carried to Licensing and Review or mailed to the Office in compliance with paragraph (a) of this section.

(d)   The applicant in a national security classified patent application must obtain a secrecy order pursuant to § 5.2(a). If a national security classified patent application is filed without a notification pursuant to § 5.2(a), the Office will set a time period within which either the application must be declassified, or the application must be placed under a secrecy order pursuant to § 5.2(a), or the applicant must submit evidence of a good faith effort to obtain a secrecy order pursuant to § 5.2(a) from the relevant department or agency in order to prevent abandonment of the application. If evidence of a good faith effort to obtain a secrecy order pursuant to § 5.2(a) from the relevant department or agency is submitted by the applicant within the time period set by the Office, but the application has not been declassified or placed under a secrecy order pursuant to § 5.2(a), the Office will again set a time period within which either the application must be declassified, or the application must be placed under a secrecy order pursuant to § 5.2(a), or the applicant must submit evidence of a good faith effort to again obtain a secrecy order pursuant to § 5.2(a) from the relevant department or agency in order to prevent abandonment of the application.

(e)   An application will not be published under § 1.211 of this chapter or allowed under § 1.311 of this chapter if publication or disclosure of the application would be detrimental to national security. An application under national security review will not be published at least until six months from its filing date or three months from the date the application was referred to a defense agency, whichever is later. A national security classified patent application will not be published under § 1.211 of this chapter or allowed under § 1.311 of this chapter until the application is declassified and any secrecy order under § 5.2(a) has been rescinded.

(f)   Applications on inventions made outside the United States and on inventions in which a U.S. Government defense agency has a property interest will not be made available to defense agencies.

[43 FR 20470, May 11, 1978; revised, 62 FR 53131, Oct. 10, 1997, effective Dec. 1, 1997; revised, 65 FR 54604, Sept. 8, 2000, effective Nov. 7, 2000; para. (e) revised, 65 FR 57024, Sept. 20, 2000, effective Nov. 29, 2000; para. (a) revised, 68 FR 14332, Mar. 25, 2003, effective May 1, 2003; para. (a) revised, 69 FR 29865, May 26, 2004, effective June 25, 2004]

§ 5.2   Secrecy order.

(a)   When notified by the chief officer of a defense agency that publication or disclosure of the invention by the granting of a patent would be detrimental to the national security, an order that the invention be kept secret will be issued by the Commissioner for Patents.

(b)   Any request for compensation as provided in 35 U.S.C. 183 must not be made to the Patent and Trademark Office, but directly to the department or agency which caused the secrecy order to be issued.

(c)   An application disclosing any significant part of the subject matter of an application under a secrecy order pursuant to paragraph (a) of this section also falls within the scope of such secrecy order. Any

such application that is pending before the Office must be promptly brought to the attention of Licensing and Review, unless such application is itself under a secrecy order pursuant to paragraph (a) of this section. Any subsequently filed application containing any significant part of the subject matter of an application under a secrecy order pursuant to paragraph (a) of this section must either be hand-carried to Licensing and Review or mailed to the Office in compliance with § 5.1(a).

[24 FR 10381, Dec. 22, 1959; para. (b) revised, paras. (c) and (d) removed, 62 FR 53131, Oct. 10, 1997, effective Dec. 1, 1997; para. (c) added, 65 FR 54604, Sept. 8, 2000, effective Nov. 7, 2000; para. (a) revised, 68 FR 14332, Mar. 25, 2003, effective May 1, 2003; revised, 69 FR 49959, Aug. 12, 2004, effective Sept. 13, 2004]

§ 5.3   Prosecution of application under secrecy orders; withholding patent.

Unless specifically ordered otherwise, action on the application by the Office and prosecution by the applicant will proceed during the time an application is under secrecy order to the point indicated in this section:

(a)   National applications under secrecy order which come to a final rejection must be appealed or otherwise prosecuted to avoid abandonment. Appeals in such cases must be completed by the applicant but unless otherwise specifically ordered by the Commissioner for Patents will not be set for hearing until the secrecy order is removed.

(b)   An interference will not be declared involving a national application under secrecy order. An applicant whose application is under secrecy order may suggest an interference (§ 41.202(a) of this title), but the Office will not act on the request while the application remains under a secrecy order.

(c)   When the national application is found to be in condition for allowance except for the secrecy order the applicant and the agency which caused the secrecy order to be issued will be notified. This notice (which is not a notice of allowance under § 1.311 of this chapter) does not require reply by the applicant and places the national application in a condition of suspension until the secrecy order is removed. When the secrecy order is removed the Patent and Trademark Office will issue a notice of allowance under

§ 1.311 of this chapter, or take such other action as may then be warranted.

(d) International applications under secrecy order will not be mailed, delivered, or otherwise transmitted to the international authorities or the applicant. International applications under secrecy order will be processed up to the point where, if it were not for the secrecy order, record and search copies would be transmitted to the international authorities or the applicant.

[43 FR 20470, May 11, 1978; amended 43 FR 28479, June 30, 1978; para. (b) amended 53 FR 23736, June 23, 1988, effective Sept. 12, 1988; para. (c) revised, 62 FR 53131, Oct. 10, 1997, effective Dec. 1, 1997; para. (a) revised, 68 FR 14332, Mar. 25, 2003, effective May 1, 2003; revised, 69 FR 49959, Aug. 12, 2004, effective Sept. 13, 2004]

§ 5.4   Petition for rescission of secrecy order.

(a)   A petition for rescission or removal of a secrecy order may be filed by, or on behalf of, any principal affected thereby. Such petition may be in letter form, and it must be in duplicate.

(b)   The petition must recite any and all facts that purport to render the order ineffectual or futile if this is the basis of the petition. When prior publications or patents are alleged the petition must give complete data as to such publications or patents and should be accompanied by copies thereof.

(c)   The petition must identify any contract between the Government and any of the principals under which the subject matter of the application or any significant part thereof was developed or to which the subject matter is otherwise related. If there is no such contract, the petition must so state.

(d)   Appeal to the Secretary of Commerce, as provided by 35 U.S.C. 181, from a secrecy order cannot be taken until after a petition for rescission of the secrecy order has been made and denied. Appeal must be taken within sixty days from the date of the denial, and the party appealing, as well as the department or agency which caused the order to be issued, will be notified of the time and place of hearing.

[24 FR 10381, Dec. 22, 1959; paras. (a) and (d) revised, 62 FR 53131, Oct. 10, 1997, effective Dec. 1, 1997; revised, 69 FR 49959, Aug. 12, 2004, effective Sept. 13, 2004]

§ 5.5   Permit to disclose or modification of secrecy order.

(a)   Consent to disclosure, or to the filing of an application abroad, as provided in 35 U.S.C. 182, shall be made by a "permit" or "modification" of the secrecy order.

(b)   Petitions for a permit or modification must fully recite the reason or purpose for the proposed disclosure. Where any proposed disclose is known to be cleared by a defense agency to receive classified information, adequate explanation of such clearance should be made in the petition including the name of the agency or department granting the clearance and the date and degree thereof. The petition must be filed in duplicate.

(c)   In a petition for modification of a secrecy order to permit filing abroad, all countries in which it is proposed to file must be made known, as well as all attorneys, agents and others to whom the material will be consigned prior to being lodged in the foreign patent office. The petition should include a statement vouching for the loyalty and integrity of the proposed disclosees and where their clearance status in this or the foreign country is known all details should be given.

(d)   Consent to the disclosure of subject matter from one application under secrecy order may be deemed to be consent to the disclosure of common subject matter in other applications under secrecy order so long as the subject matter is not taken out of context in a manner disclosing material beyond the modification granted in the first application.

(e)   Organizations requiring consent for disclosure of applications under secrecy order to persons or organizations in connection with repeated routine operation may petition for such consent in the form of a general permit. To be successful such petitions must ordinarily recite the security clearance status of the disclosees as sufficient for the highest classification of material that may be involved.

[24 FR 10381, Dec. 22, 1959; paras. (b) and (e) revised, 62 FR 53131, Oct. 10, 1997, effective Dec. 1, 1997]

§ 5.6   [Reserved]

[Removed and reserved, 62 FR 53131, Oct. 10, 1997, effective Dec. 1, 1997]

§ 5.7   [Reserved]

[Removed and reserved, 62 FR 53131, Oct. 10, 1997, effective Dec. 1, 1997]

§ 5.8   [Reserved]

[Removed and reserved, 62 FR 53131, Oct. 10, 1997, effective Dec. 1, 1997]

LICENSES FOR FOREIGN EXPORTING AND FILING

§ 5.11   License for filing in a foreign country an application on an invention made in the United States or for transmitting international application.

(a)   A license from the Commissioner for Patents under 35 U.S.C. 184 is required before filing any application for patent including any modifications, amendments, or supplements thereto or divisions thereof or for the registration of a utility model, industrial design, or model, in a foreign patent office or any foreign patent agency or any international agency other than the United States Receiving Office, if the invention was made in the United States and:

(1)   An application on the invention has been filed in the United States less than six months prior to the date on which the application is to be filed, or

(2)   No application on the invention has been filed in the United States.

(b)   The license from the Commissioner for Patents referred to in paragraph (a) would also authorize the export of technical data abroad for purposes relating to the preparation, filing or possible filing and prosecution of a foreign patent application without separately complying with the regulations contained in 22 CFR parts 121 through 130 (International Traffic in Arms Regulations of the Department of State), 15 CFR parts 730-774 (Regulations of the Bureau of Industry and Security, Department of Commerce) and 10 CFR part 810 (Foreign Atomic Energy Programs of the Department of Energy).

(c)   Where technical data in the form of a patent application, or in any form, are being exported for purposes related to the preparation, filing or possible filing and prosecution of a foreign patent application, without the license from the Commissioner for Patents referred to in paragraphs (a) or (b) of this section, or on an invention not made in the United States, the export regulations contained in 22 CFR parts 120 through 130 (International Traffic in Arms Regulations of the Department of State), 15 CFR parts 730-774 (Bureau of Industry and Security Regulations, Department of Commerce) and 10 CFR part 810 (Assistance to Foreign Atomic Energy Activities Regulations of the Department of Energy) must be complied with unless a license is not required because a United States application was on file at the time of export for at least six months without a secrecy order under § 5.2 being placed thereon. The term "exported" means export as it is defined in 22 CFR part 120, 15 CFR part 734 and activities covered by 10 CFR part 810.

(d)   If a secrecy order has been issued under § 5.2, an application cannot be exported to, or filed in, a foreign country (including an international agency in a foreign country), except in accordance with § 5.5.

(e)   No license pursuant to paragraph (a) of this section is required:

(1)   If the invention was not made in the United States, or

(2)   If the corresponding United States application is not subject to a secrecy order under § 5.2, and was filed at least six months prior to the date on which the application is filed in a foreign country, or

(3)   For subsequent modifications, amendments and supplements containing additional subject matter to, or divisions of, a foreign patent application if:

(i)   A license is not, or was not, required under paragraph (e)(2) of this section for the foreign patent application;

(ii)   The corresponding United States application was not required to be made available for inspection under 35 U.S.C. 181; and

(iii)   Such modifications, amendments, and supplements do not, or did not, change the general nature of the invention in a manner which would require any corresponding United States application to be or have been available for inspection under 35 U.S.C. 181.

(f)   A license pursuant to paragraph (a) of this section can be revoked at any time upon written notification by the Patent and Trademark Office. An authorization to file a foreign patent application resulting from the passage of six months from the date of filing of a United States patent application may be revoked by the imposition of a secrecy order.

[49 FR 13461, Apr. 4, 1984; paras. (a) and (e), 56 FR 1924, Jan. 18, 1991, effective Feb. 19, 1991; paras. (b), (c), and (e)(3) revised, 62 FR 53131, Oct. 10, 1997, effective Dec. 1, 1997; paras. (a)-(c) revised, 68 FR 14332, Mar. 25, 2003, effective May 1, 2003; paras. (b) and (c) revised, 70 FR 56119, Sept. 26, 2005, effective Nov. 25, 2005]

§ 5.12   Petition for license.

(a)   Filing of an application for patent for inventions made in the United States will be considered to include a petition for license under 35 U.S.C. 184 for the subject matter of the application. The filing receipt will indicate if a license is granted. If the initial automatic petition is not granted, a subsequent petition may be filed under paragraph (b) of this section.

(b)   A petition for license must include the fee set forth in § 1.17(g) of this chapter, the petitioner's address, and full instructions for delivery of the requested license when it is to be delivered to other than the petitioner. The petition should be presented in letter form.

[48 FR 2714, Jan. 20, 1983; amended 49 FR 13462, Apr. 4, 1984; para. (b) revised, 62 FR 53131, Oct. 10, 1997, effective Dec. 1, 1997; para. (b) revised, 65 FR 54604, Sept. 8, 2000, effective Nov. 7, 2000; para. (b) revised, 69 FR 56481, Sept. 21, 2004, effective Nov. 22, 2004]

§ 5.13   Petition for license; no corresponding application.

If no corresponding national or international application has been filed in the United States, the petition for license under § 5.12(b) must also be accompanied by a legible copy of the material upon which a license is desired. This copy will be retained as a measure of the license granted.

[43 FR 20471, May 11, 1978; 49 FR 13462, Apr. 4, 1984; revised, 62 FR 53131, Oct. 10, 1997, effective Dec. 1, 1997]

§ 5.14   Petition for license; corresponding U.S. application.

(a)   When there is a corresponding United States application on file, a petition for license under § 5.12(b) must also identify this application by application number, filing date, inventor, and title, but

a copy of the material upon which the license is desired is not required. The subject matter licensed will be measured by the disclosure of the United States application.

(b)   Two or more United States applications should not be referred to in the same petition for license unless they are to be combined in the foreign or international application, in which event the petition should so state and the identification of each United States application should be in separate paragraphs.

(c)   Where the application to be filed or exported abroad contains matter not disclosed in the United States application or applications, including the case where the combining of two or more United States applications introduces subject matter not disclosed in any of them, a copy of the application as it is to be filed in the foreign country or international application which is to be transmitted to a foreign international or national agency for filing in the Receiving Office, must be furnished with the petition. If however, all new matter in the foreign or international application to be filed is readily identifiable, the new matter may be submitted in detail and the remainder by reference to the pertinent United States application or applications.

[43 FR 20471, May 11, 1978; 49 FR 13462, Apr. 4, 1984; para. (a) revised, 62 FR 53131, Oct. 10, 1997, effective Dec. 1, 1997]

§ 5.15   Scope of license.

(a)   Applications or other materials reviewed pursuant to §§ 5.12 through 5.14, which were not required to be made available for inspection by defense agencies under 35 U.S.C. 181, will be eligible for a license of the scope provided in this paragraph. This license permits subsequent modifications, amendments, and supplements containing additional subject matter to, or divisions of, a foreign patent application, if such changes to the application do not alter the general nature of the invention in a manner which would require the United States application to have been made available for inspection under 35 U.S.C. 181. Grant of this license authorizing the export and filing of an application in a foreign country or the transmitting of an international application to any foreign patent agency or international patent agency when the subject matter of the foreign or international application corresponds to that of the domestic application. This license includes authority:

(1)   To export and file all duplicate and formal application papers in foreign countries or with international agencies;

(2)   To make amendments, modifications, and supplements, including divisions, changes or supporting matter consisting of the illustration, exemplification, comparison, or explanation of subject matter disclosed in the application; and

(3)   To take any action in the prosecution of the foreign or international application provided that the adding of subject matter or taking of any action under paragraphs (a)(1) or (2) of this section does not change the general nature of the invention disclosed in the application in a manner which would require such application to have been made available for inspection under 35 U.S.C. 181 by including technical data pertaining to:

(i)   Defense services or articles designated in the United States Munitions List applicable at the time of foreign filing, the unlicensed exportation of which is prohibited pursuant to the Arms Export Control Act, as amended, and 22 CFR parts 121 through 130; or

(ii)   Restricted Data, sensitive nuclear technology or technology useful in the production or utilization of special nuclear material or atomic energy, dissemination of which is subject to restrictions of the Atomic Energy Act of 1954, as amended, and the Nuclear Non-Proliferation Act of 1978, as implemented by the regulations for Unclassified Activities in Foreign Atomic Energy Programs, 10 CFR part 810, in effect at the time of foreign filing.

(b)   Applications or other materials which were required to be made available for inspection under 35 U.S.C. 181 will be eligible for a license of the scope provided in this paragraph. Grant of this license authorizes the export and filing of an application in a foreign country or the transmitting of an international application to any foreign patent agency or international patent agency. Further, this license includes authority to export and file all duplicate and formal papers in foreign countries or with foreign and international patent agencies and to make amendments, modifications, and supplements to, file divisions of, and take any action in the prosecution of the foreign or international application, provided subject matter additional to that covered by the license is not involved.

(c)   A license granted under § 5.12(b) pursuant to § 5.13 or § 5.14 shall have the scope indicated in paragraph (a) of this section, if it is so specified in the license. A petition, accompanied by the required fee (§ 1.17(g) of this chapter), may also be filed to change a license having the scope indicated in paragraph (b) of this section to a license having the scope indicated in paragraph (a) of this section. No such petition will be granted if the copy of the material filed pursuant to § 5.13 or any corresponding United States application was required to be made available for inspection under 35 U.S.C. 181. The change in the scope of a license will be effective as of the date of the grant of the petition.

(d)   In those cases in which no license is required to file the foreign application or transmit the international application, no license is required to file papers in connection with the prosecution of the foreign or international application not involving the disclosure of additional subject matter.

(e)   Any paper filed abroad or transmitted to an international patent agency following the filing of a foreign or international application which changes the general nature of the subject matter disclosed at the time of filing in a manner which would require such application to have been made available for inspection under 35 U.S.C. 181 or which involves the disclosure of subject matter listed in paragraphs (a)(3)(i) or (ii) of this section must be separately licensed in the same manner as a foreign or international application. Further, if no license has been granted under § 5.12(a) on filing the corresponding United States application, any paper filed abroad or with an international patent agency which involves the disclosure of additional subject matter must be licensed in the same manner as a foreign or international application.

(f)   Licenses separately granted in connection with two or more United States applications may be exercised by combining or dividing the disclosures, as desired, provided:

(1)   Subject matter which changes the general nature of the subject matter disclosed at the time of filing or which involves subject matter listed in paragraphs (a)(3) (i) or (ii) of this section is not introduced and,

(2)   In the case where at least one of the licenses was obtained under § 5.12(b), additional subject matter is not introduced.

(g)   A license does not apply to acts done before the license was granted. See § 5.25 for petitions for retroactive licenses.

[49 FR 13462, Apr. 4, 1984; paras. (a) - (c), (e) and (f), 56 FR 1924, Jan. 18, 1991, effective Feb. 19, 1991; paras. (a)-(c) and (e) revised, 62 FR 53131, Oct. 10, 1997, effective Dec. 1, 1997; para. (c) revised, 69 FR 56481, Sept. 21, 2004, effective Nov. 22, 2004]

§ 5.16   [Reserved]

[Removed and reserved, 62 FR 53131, Oct. 10, 1997, effective Dec. 1, 1997]

§ 5.17   [Reserved]

[49 FR 13463, Apr. 4, 1984; removed and reserved, 62 FR 53131, Oct. 10, 1997, effective Dec. 1, 1997]

§ 5.18   Arms, ammunition, and implements of war.

(a)   The exportation of technical data relating to arms, ammunition, and implements of war generally is subject to the International Traffic in Arms Regulations of the Department of State (22 CFR parts 120 through 130); the articles designated as arms, ammunitions, and implements of war are enumerated in the U.S. Munitions List (22 CFR part 121). However, if a patent applicant complies with regulations issued by the Commissioner for Patents under 35 U.S.C. 184, no separate approval from the Department of State is required unless the applicant seeks to export technical data exceeding that used to support a patent application in a foreign country. This exemption from Department of State regulations is applicable regardless of whether a license from the Commissioner for Patents is required by the provisions of §§ 5.11 and 5.12 (22 CFR part 125).

(b)   When a patent application containing subject matter on the Munitions List (22 CFR part 121) is subject to a secrecy order under § 5.2 and a petition is made under § 5.5 for a modification of the secrecy order to permit filing abroad, a separate request to the Department of State for authority to export classified information is not required (22 CFR part 125).

[35 FR 6430., Apr. 22, 1970; revised, 62 FR 53131, Oct. 10, 1997, effective Dec. 1, 1997; para. (a) revised, 68 FR 14332, Mar. 25, 2003, effective May 1, 2003]

§ 5.19   Export of technical data.

(a)   Under regulations (15 CFR 734.3(b)(1)(v)) established by the Department of Commerce, a license is not required in any case to file a patent application or part thereof in a foreign country if the foreign filing is in accordance with the regulations (§§ 5.11 through 5.25) of the U.S. Patent and Trademark Office.

(b)   An export license is not required for data contained in a patent application prepared wholly from foreign-origin technical data where such application is being sent to the foreign inventor to be executed and returned to the United States for subsequent filing in the U.S. Patent and Trademark Office (15 CFR 734.10(a)).

[45 FR 72654, Nov. 3, 1980; para. (a) revised, 58 FR 54504, Oct. 22, 1993, effective Jan. 3, 1994; revised, 62 FR 53131, Oct. 10, 1997, effective Dec. 1, 1997; revised, 70 FR 56119, Sept. 26, 2005, effective Nov. 25, 2005]

§ 5.20   Export of technical data relating to sensitive nuclear technology.

Under regulations (10 CFR 810.7) established by the United States Department of Energy, an application filed in accordance with the regulations (§§ 5.11 through 5.25) of the Patent and Trademark Office and eligible for foreign filing under 35 U.S.C. 184, is considered to be information available to the public in published form and a generally authorized activity for the purposes of the Department of Energy regulations.

[49 FR 13463, Apr. 4, 1984; revised, 62 FR 53131, Oct. 10, 1997, effective Dec. 1, 1997]

§ 5.25   Petition for retroactive license.

(a)   A petition for retroactive license under 35 U.S.C. 184 shall be presented in accordance with § 5.13 or § 5.14(a), and shall include:

(1)   A listing of each of the foreign countries in which the unlicensed patent application material was filed,

(2)   The dates on which the material was filed in each country,

(3)   A verified statement (oath or declaration) containing:

(i)   An averment that the subject matter in question was not under a secrecy order at the time it was filed abroad, and that it is not currently under a secrecy order,

(ii)   A showing that the license has been diligently sought after discovery of the proscribed foreign filing, and

(iii)   An explanation of why the material was filed abroad through error and without deceptive intent without the required license under § 5.11 first having been obtained, and

(4)   The required fee (§ 1.17(g) of this chapter).

(b)   The explanation in paragraph (a) of this section must include a showing of facts rather than a mere allegation of action through error and without deceptive intent. The showing of facts as to the nature of the error should include statements by those persons having personal knowledge of the acts regarding filing in a foreign country and should be accompanied by copies of any necessary supporting documents such as letters of transmittal or instructions for filing. The acts which are alleged to constitute error without deceptive intent should cover the period leading up to and including each of the proscribed foreign filings.

(c)   If a petition for a retroactive license is denied, a time period of not less than thirty days shall be set, during which the petition may be renewed. Failure to renew the petition within the set time period will result in a final denial of the petition. A final denial of a petition stands unless a petition is filed under § 1.181 within two months of the date of the denial. If the petition for a retroactive license is denied with respect to the invention of a pending application and no petition under § 1.181 has been filed, a final rejection of the application under 35 U.S.C. 185 will be made.

[49 FR 13463, Apr. 4, 1984; para. (a), 56 FR 1924, Jan. 18, 1991, effective Feb. 19, 1991; para. (c) removed, 62 FR 53131, Oct. 10, 1997, effective Dec. 1, 1997; para. (a)(4) revised, para. (b) redesignated as para. (c) and para. (b) added, 69 FR 56481, Sept. 21, 2004, effective Nov. 22, 2004]

GENERAL

§ 5.31   [Reserved]

[24 FR 10381, Dec. 22, 1959; Redesignated at 49 FR 13463, Apr. 4, 1984; removed and reserved, 62 FR 53131, Oct. 10, 1997, effective Dec. 1, 1997]

§ 5.32   [Reserved]

[24 FR 10381, Dec. 22, 1959; Redesignated at 49 FR 13463, Apr. 4, 1984; removed and reserved, 62 FR 53131, Oct. 10, 1997, effective Dec. 1, 1997]

§ 5.33   [Reserved]

[49 FR 13463, Apr. 4, 1984; amended, 61 FR 56439, Nov. 1, 1996, effective Dec. 2, 1996; removed and reserved, 62 FR 53131, Oct. 10, 1997, effective Dec. 1, 1997]

Index I – RULES RELATING TO PATENTS

A

Abandoned applications:
  Abandonment by failure to reply 1.135
  Abandonment during interference 41.127
  Abandonment for failure to pay issue fee 1.316
  Express abandonment 1.138
  Processing and retention fee . . . . 1.21(l)
  Referred to in issued patents 1.14
  Revival of 1.137
  When open to public inspection 1.14
Abandonment of application. (See Abandoned
  applications.)
Abstract of the disclosure 1.72, 1.77, 1.163
Access to pending applications (limited) 1.14
Action by applicant . . . . 1.111 - 1.138
Addresses for correspondence with the
  United States Patent and Trademark Office 1.1
  Board of Patent Appeals and Interferences . 1.1(a)(1),
     41.10
  Deposit account replenishment . . . . 1.25(c)(3),
     1.25(c)(4)
  Director of the United States Patent and
    Trademark Office . . . . 1.1(a)
  FOIA Officer . . . . 102.1(b), 102.4(a)
  Generally . . . . 1.1(a)
  Licensing and Review . . . . 5.1(a)
  Office of the General Counsel . . . . 1.1(a)(3),
     102.10(b), 102.29(b)
  Office of the Solicitor . . . . 1.1(a)(3),
  Mail Stops
    Mail Stop 4 . . . . 150.6
    Mail Stop 8 . . . . 1.1(a)(3)
    Mail Stop 24 . . . . 4.3(c)
    Mail Stop Assignment Recordation
     Services . . . . 1.1(a)(4), 3.27
    Mail Stop CPA . . . . 1.53(d)(9)
    Mail Stop Document Services . . . . 1.1(a)(4)
    Mail Stop *Ex parte* Reexam . . . . 1.1(c)(1)
    Mail Stop *Inter partes* Reexam . . . . 1.1(c)(2)
    Mail Stop Interference . . . . 41.10(b)
    Mail Stop M Correspondence . . . . 1.1(d)(2)
    Mail Stop OED 4.6
    Mail Stop Patent Ext . . . . 1.1(e)
    Mail Stop PCT . . . 1.1(b), 1.417, 1.434(a), 1.480(b)
  Maintenance fee payments . . . . 1.1(d)(1)
  Patent correspondence . . . . 1.1(a)(1)
  Privacy Officer . . . . 102.23(a), 102.24(a)
  Trademark correspondence 2.190
Adjustment of patent term. (see Patent term
  adjustment due to examination delay.)

Administrator, executor, or other legal
  representative may make
  application and receive patent 1.42, 1.43, 1.64
Admission to practice. (See Attorneys and
  agents.)
Affidavit (See also Oath in patent application):
  After appeal 41.33
  As evidence in a contested case 41.154
  To disqualify commonly owned patent or
    published application as prior art 1.130
  Traversing rejections or objections 1.132
Agents. (See Attorneys and agents.)
Allowance and issue of patent:
  Amendment after allowance 1.312
  Application abandoned for nonpayment
    of issue fee 1.316
  Deferral of issuance 1.314
  Delayed payment of issue fee 1.137
  Delivery of patent 1.315
  Failure to pay issue fee . . . . 1.137(c), 1.316
  Issuance of patent 1.314
  Notice of allowance 1.311
  Patent to issue upon payment of issue fee 1.311, 1.314
  Patent to lapse if issue fee is not paid in full . . . 1.317
  Reasons for 1.104
  Withdrawal from issue 1.313
Allowed claims, rejection of by Board of
  Patent Appeals and Interferences . . . . 41.50(b)
Amendment:
  Adding or substituting claims 1.121
  After appeal 41.33, 41.63
  After decision on appeal, based on new
    rejection of Board of Patent Appeals
    and Interferences . . . . 41.50(b)(1)
  After final action 1.116
  After final action (transitional procedures) 1.129
  After notice of allowance 1.312
  Copying claim of another application
    for interference 41.202
  Copying claim of issued patent 41.202
  Deletions and insertions 1.121
  Drawings 1.121
  Manner of making 1.121
  Not covered by original oath 1.67
  Numbering of claims 1.126
  Of amendments 1.121
  Of claims 1.121
  Of disclosure 1.121
  Of drawing 1.121
  Of specification 1.121
  Paper and writing 1.52
  Petition from refusal to admit 1.127

Preliminary. 1.115
Proposed during interference. 41.121
Provisional application . . . . 1.53(c)
Reexamination proceedings. . . 1.121(j), 1.530, 1.941
Reissue. . . . . 1.121(i), 1.173
Requisites of 1.33, 1.111, 1.116, 1.121, 1.125
Right to amend. 1.111, 1.116, 1.127
Signature to 1.33
Substitute specification 1.125
Time for 1.134
To applications in interference. 41.121
To correct inaccuracies 1.121
To correspond to original drawing or specifica-
 tion. 1.121
To reissues. 1.173
To save from abandonment 1.135
Amino acid sequences. (See Nucleotide and/or
 amino acid sequences.)
Appeals:
 Civil Actions under 35 U.S.C. 145, 146, 306 . . 1.303,
 1.304
 To the Board of Patent Appeals and
  Interferences 41.30-41.54
  Affidavits after appeal 41.33
  Brief 41.37
  Decision/Action by Board 41.50
   Return of jurisdiction to examiner . . . . . 1.197(a)
   Termination of proceedings . . . . 1.197(b)
  Examiner's answer 41.39
  Fees. 41.20
  Hearing of. 41.47
  Inter partes reexamination 41.61
  New grounds of rejection . . . . 41.39(a)(2), 41.50(b)
  Notice of appeal 41.31
  Public inspection or publication of decisions. . 1.14
  Rehearing . . . . 41.50(b)(2), 41.52
  Reopening after final Board decision. 1.198
  Reply brief 41.41
  Sanctions 41.128
  What may be appealed 41.31
  Who may appeal. 41.31
 To Court of Appeals for the Federal Circuit:
  Fee provided by rules of court 1.301
  From Board of Patent Appeals and Interfer-
   ences. 1.301
  Notice and reasons of appeal 1.302
  Time for filing notice of appeal 1.302, 1.304
Applicant for patent:
 Actual inventor or inventors to make
  application for patent 1.41, 1.45
 Assignee . . . . 1.47(b)
 Change of (see Correction of inventorship)

Correspondence address 1.33
Daytime telephone number 1.33
Deceased or insane inventor. 1.42, 1.43
Executor or administrator 1.42
In a continued prosecution application . . . 1.53(b)(1),
 1.53(d)(4)
In an international application 1.421-1.425
Informed of application number 1.54
Inventorship in a provisional application . 1.41(a)(2)
Mailing address and residence of inventors
 may be provided in oath/declaration or in
 application data sheet 1.63, 1.76
May be represented by an attorney or agent 1.31
Person making oath or declaration 1.64
Personal attendance unnecessary 1.2
Required to conduct business with decorum
 and courtesy 1.3
Required to report assistance received 1.4
Who may apply for a patent 1.41-1.48
Application Data sheet 1.76
Application for patent (See also Abandoned
 applications, Claims, Drawing, Examination
 of applications, Provisional applications,
 Publication of application, Published
 application, Reissues, Specification):
 Access to. 1.14
 Acknowledgment of filing 1.54
 Alteration after execution 1.52
 Alteration before execution 1.52
 Application number and filing date 1.54
 Arrangement 1.77
 Compact disc submissions (see Electronic
  documents)
 Confidentiality of applications 1.14
 Continuation or division, reexecution not
  required. 1.63
 Continued prosecution application . . . . 1.53(d)
  Filed by facsimile 1.6, 1.8
 Copies of, furnished to applicants 1.59
 Cross-references to related applications 1.78
 Deceased or insane inventor 1.42, 1.43
 Declaration 1.68
 Duty of disclosure. 1.56
 Examined only when complete. 1.53
 Filed by other than inventor 1.42, 1.43, 1.47,
              1.64, 1.421(b)
 Filing date 1.53
 Filing requirements. 1.53
 Foreign language oath or declaration 1.69
 Formulas and tables 1.58
 General requisites 1.51
 Identification required in letters concerning. 1.5

Incomplete papers not filed for examination. . . . 1.53
Interlineations, etc., to be indicated. 1.52
Involving national security 5.1
Language, paper, writing, margin 1.52
Later filing of oath and filing fee. 1.53
Missing pages when application filed . . . . 1.53(e)
Must be made by actual inventor, with excep-
    tions. 1.41, 1.46, 1.47
Naming of inventors:
    Application data sheet . . . . 1.76(b)(1)
    In a continued prosecution application . 1.53(d)(4)
    In a provisional application . 1.41(a)(2), 1.51(c)(1),
        1.53(c)(1)
    In an international application 1.421
        National stage 1.497
    Inconsistencies between application data
        sheet and oath or declaration . . . . 1.76(d)
    Joint inventors 1.45
    Oath/declaration. . . . . 1.63(a)(2)
Non-English language 1.52
Nonpublication request 1.213
Numbering of claims 1.126
Numbering of paragraphs 1.52, 1.125
Original disclosure not expunged . . . . 1.59(a)(2)
Parts filed separately 1.54
Parts of application desirably filed together 1.54
Parts of complete application 1.51
Processing fees 1.17
Provisional application 1.9, 1.51, 1.53
Publication of 1.211, 1.219
Published 1.9, 1.215
Relating to atomic energy 1.14
Reservation for future application not permit-
    ted 1.79
Retention fee . . . . 1.53(f)
Secrecy order. 5.1-5.5
Status information 1.14
Tables and formulas. 1.58
To contain but one invention unless connected. 1.141
To whom made 1.51
Two or more by same party with conflicting
    claims. 1.78
Application number. . . . . 1.5(a), 1.53, 1.54
Arbitration award filing. 1.335
Arbitration in a contested case before the Board . 41.126
Assignee:
    Correspondence held with assignee(s) of
        entire interest. 3.71, 3.73
    Establishing ownership . . . . 3.73(b)
    May conduct prosecution of application . . . 3.71, 3.73
    May make application on behalf of
        inventor(s). . . . . 1.47(b)

May take action in Board proceeding. 41.9
Must consent to application for reissue of
    patent 1.171, 1.172
Partial assignee(s). 1.46, 3.71, 3.73, 3.81
Assignments and recording:
    Abstracts of title, fee for. . . . . 1.19(b)(5)
    Conditional assignments. 3.56
    Cover sheet required. 3.28, 3.31
    Corrections 3.34
    Date of receipt is date of record 3.51
    Definitions 1.332
    Effect of recording 3.54
    Fees. . . . . 1.21(h)
    Formal requirements. 3.21-3.28
    If recorded before payment of issue fee,
        patent may issue to assignee. 3.81
    Joint research agreements. . . . . 3.11(c), 3.31(g)
    Mailing address for submitting
        documents. . . . . 1.1(a)(4), 3.27
    Must be recorded in Patent and
        Trademark Office to issue patent to assignee. . . 3.81
    Must identify patent or application. 3.21
    Orders for copies of 1.12
    Patent may issue to assignee. 3.81
    Recording of assignments. 3.11
    Records open to public inspection 1.12
    Requirements for recording 3.21-3.41
    What will be accepted for recording. 3.11
Atomic energy applications reported to Depart-
    ment of Energy 1.14
Attorneys and agents:
    Acting in representative capacity 1.33, 1.34
    Annual practitioner maintenance fee:
        Registered attorney or agent . . . . 1.21(a)(7), 11.8(d)
        Individual granted limited recognition . . 1.21(a)(8)
    Assignment will not operate as a revocation
        of power 1.36
    Certificate of good standing . . . . 1.21(a)
    Complaints 4.6
    Fee on admission . . . . 1.21(a)
    Office cannot aid in selection of. 1.31
    Personal interviews with examiners 1.133
    Power of attorney 1.32
    Power to inspect 1.14
    Representative capacity 1.33, 1.34
    Required to conduct business with
        decorum and courtesy. 1.3
    Revocation of power. . . . . 1.36(a)
    Signature and certificate of attorney. 1.4, 11.18
    Withdrawal of. 1.36(b), 41.5

Rev. 8, July 2010

Authorization of agents. (See Attorneys
    and agents.)
Award in arbitration 1.335

B

Balance in deposit account 1.25
Basic filing fee 1.16
Benefit of earlier application 1.78
Bill in equity. (See Civil action.)
Biological material. (See Deposit of biological
    material.)
Board of Patent Appeals and Interferences.
    (See Appeal to Board of Patent Appeals and
    Interferences.)
Briefs:
    In petitions to Director 1.181
    On appeal to Board 41.37
Business to be conducted with decorum and
    courtesy 1.3
Business to be transacted in writing 1.2

C

Certificate of correction 1.322, 1.323
    Fees 1.20
    Mistakes not corrected 1.325
Certificate of mailing (First Class) or transmission . . 1.8
Certification effect of presentation
    to Office . . . . 1.4(d), 11.18
Certified copies of records, papers, etc. . . . . . 1.4(f), 1.13
    Fee for certification . . . . 1.19(b)
Chemical and mathematical formulae and tables . . . 1.58
Citation of prior art in patented file 1.501
Citation of references 1.104
Civil action 1.303, 1.304
Claims (See also Examination of applications):
    Amendment of 1.121
    Commence on separate sheet or
        electronic page . . . . 1.52(b), 1.75(h)
    Conflicting, same applicant or owner 1.78
    Date of invention of 1.110
    Dependent 1.75
    Design patent 1.153
    May be in dependent form 1.75
    More than one permitted 1.75
    Multiple dependent 1.75
    Must conform to invention and specification . . . 1.75
    Notice of rejection of 1.104
    Numbering of 1.126
    Part of complete application 1.51
    Plant patent 1.164
    Rejection of 1.104

Required 1.75
    Separate from other parts of application . . . . . 1.75(h)
    Twice rejected before appeal 41.31
Color drawing . . . . 1.6(d)(4), 1.84(a)(2)
Commissioner of Patents and Trademarks (See
    Director of the USPTO.)
Common ownership, statement by assignee may
    be required . . . . 1.78(c)
Compact disc submissions. (See Electronic docu-
    ments.)
Complaints against examiners, how presented 1.3
Complaints regarding invention promoters (See
    Invention promoters.)
Composition of matter, specimens of ingredients
    may be required 1.93
Computer program listing appendix 1.96
Concurrent office proceedings 1.565
Conflicting claims, same applicant or owner in
    two or more applications 1.78
Contested cases before the Board of Patent
    Appeals and Interferences 41.100-41.208
Continued examination, request for 1.114
    Fee 1.17
    Suspension of action after 1.103
Continued prosecution application . . . . 1.53(d)
    Suspension of action in 1.103
Continuing application for invention disclosed
    and claimed in prior application 1.53, 1.63
Control number, display of 1.419
Copies of patents, published applications, records,
    etc. 1.11, 1.12, 1.13
Copies of records, fees . . . . 1.19(b), 1.59
Copyright notice in specification . . . . 1.71(d)
Copyright notice on drawings . . . . 1.84(s)
Correction, certificate of 1.322, 1.323
Correction of inventorship:
    In a nonprovisional application 1.48
        Before filing oath/declaration . . . 1.41(a)(1), 1.76(c)
        By filing oath/declaration . . . . 1.76(d)(3)
        When filing a continuation or divisional
            application . . . . 1.63(d)
        When filing a continued prosecution
            application . . . . 1.53(d)(4)
    In a provisional application 1.48
        By filing a cover sheet . . . . 1.48(f)(2)
        Without filing a cover sheet . . . . 1.41(a)(2)
    In a reexamination proceeding 1.530
    In an international application 1.472
        When entering the national stage 1.497
    In an issued patent 1.324
    In other than a reissue application 1.48

Inconsistencies between application data sheet
and oath or declaration . . . . 1.76(d)
Motion to correct inventorship in an
interference . . . . 41.121(a)(2)
Supplemental application data sheet(s) . . . . 1.76(c)
Correspondence:
Address:
Change of correspondence address . . . . 1.33(a)
Established by the office if more than one is
specified . . . . 1.33(a)
Of the U.S. Patent and Trademark Office 1.1
Business with the Office to be transacted by. 1.2
Discourteous communications not entered 1.3
Double, with different parties in interest not
allowed 1.33
Duplicate copies disposed of. 1.4
Facsimile transmission . . . . 1.6(d)
Held with attorney or agent 1.33
Identification of application or patent in letter
relating to. 1.5
Involving national security 5.1
May be held exclusively with assignee(s) of
entire interest 3.71
Nature of 1.4
Patent owners in reexamination. . . . . 1.33(c)
Receipt of letters and papers 1.6
Rules for conducting in general. 1.1-1.8
Separate letter for each subject or inquiry 1.4
Signature requirements . . . . 1.4(d)
When no attorney or agent. 1.33
With attorney or agent after power or authori-
zation is filed 1.33
Court of Appeals for the Federal Circuit, appeal
to. (See Appeal to Court of Appeals for the Fed-
eral Circuit.)
Credit card payment 1.23
Cross-reference to related applications 1.76-1.78
Customer Number
Defined . . . . 1.32(a)(4)
Required to establish a Fee Address . . . . 1.363(c)

D

Date of invention of subject matter of individual
claims. 1.110
Day for taking any action or paying any fee falling
on Saturday, Sunday, or Federal holiday 1.7
Death or insanity of inventor. 1.42, 1.43
In an international application 1.422, 1.423
Decision by the Board of Patent Appeals and
Interferences. 41.50
Return of jurisdiction to examiner. . . . . 1.197(a)
Termination of proceedings. . . . . 1.197(b)

Declaration (See also Oath in patent application):
Foreign language 1.69
In lieu of oath 1.68
In patent application 1.68
Deferral of examination 1.103
Definitions:
Assignment. 3.1
Customer Number. . . . . 1.32(a)(4)
Document 3.1
Federal holiday within the District of
Columbia 1.9
National and international applications 1.9
National security classified 1.9
Nonprofit organization 1.27
Person (for small entity purposes) 1.27
Power of Attorney . . . . 1.32(a)(1)
Principal . . . . 1.32(a)(2)
Published application 1.9
Recorded document 3.1
Revocation . . . . 1.32(a)(3)
Service of process. . . . . 15 CFR Part 15
Small business concern. 1.27
Small entity. 1.27
Terms under Patent Cooperation Treaty 1.401
Testimony by employees . . . . 15 CFR Part 15a
Delivery of patent. 1.315
Deposit accounts. 1.25
Fees. . . . . 1.21(b)
Deposit of biological material:
Acceptable depository 1.803
Biological material 1.801
Examination procedures. 1.809
Furnishing of samples. 1.808
Need or opportunity to make a deposit. 1.802
Replacement or supplemental deposit 1.805
Term of deposit. 1.806
Time of making original deposit. 1.804
Viability of deposit 1.807
Deposit of computer program listings . . . . . 1.52(e), 1.96
Depositions (See also Testimony in contested
cases before the Board):
Certificate of officer to accompany . . . . 41.157(e)
Original filed as exhibit . . . . 41.157(e)
Person before whom taken . . . . 41.157(e)
Transcripts of . . . . 41.154(a), 41.157
Description of invention. (See Specification.)
Design Patent Applications:
Arrangement of application elements. 1.154
Claim 1.153
Drawing 1.152
Expedited examination 1.155
Filing fee. . . . . 1.16(b)

Rev. 8, July 2010

Issue fee . . . . 1.18(b)
Oath 1.153
Rules applicable. 1.151
Title, description and claim 1.153
Determination of request for *ex parte*
reexamination. 1.515
Director of the USPTO (See also Petition to the
Director):
    Address of 1.1
    Availability of decisions by 1.14
    Initiates *ex parte* reexamination. 1.520
Disclaimer, statutory:
    Fee . . . . 1.20(d)
    Requirements of. 1.321
    Terminal. 1.321
Disclosure, amendments to add new matter not
permitted 1.121
Discovery in contested cases before the Board . . . 41.150-
41.158
Division. (See Restriction of application.)
Document supply fees 1.19
Drawing:
    Amendment of. 1.121
    Arrangement of views . . . . 1.84(i)
    Arrows . . . . 1.84(r)
    Character of lines. . . . . 1.84(l)
    Color . . . . 1.6(d)(4), 1.84(a)(2), 1.165(b)
    Content of drawing 1.83
    Copyright notice . . . . 1.84(s)
    Correction . . . . 1.84(w), 1.85(c), 1.121
    Cost of copies of 1.19
    Design application 1.152
    Figure for front page . . . . 1.76, 1.84(j)
    Filed with application 1.81
    Graphics. . . . . 1.84(d)
    Hatching and shading. . . . . 1.84(m)
    Holes . . . . 1.84(x)
    Identification . . . . 1.84(c)
    If of an improvement, must show connection
    with old structure. 1.83
    Informal drawings 1.85
    Ink . . . . 1.84(a)(1)
    Lead lines. . . . . 1.84(q)
    Legends . . . . 1.84(o)
    Letters . . . . 1.84(p)
    Location of names . . . . 1.84(c)
    Mask work notice. . . . . 1.84(s)
    Must be described in and referred to specifica-
    tion. 1.74
    Must show every feature of the invention 1.83
    No return or release . . . . 1.85(b)
    Numbering of sheets . . . . 1.84(t)

Numbering of views . . . . 1.84(u)
Numbers . . . . 1.84(p)
Original should be retained by applicant . . . . . 1.81(a)
Paper. . . . . 1.84(e)
Part of application papers 1.52
Photographs . . . . 1.84(b)
Plant patent application. 1.81, 1.165
Reference characters. . . . . 1.74, 1.84(p)
Reissue 1.173
Release not permitted . . . . 1.85(b)
Required by law when necessary for under-
    standing. 1.81
Scale . . . . 1.84(k)
Security markings . . . . 1.84(v)
Shading. . . . . 1.84(m)
Size of sheet and margins . . . . 1.84(f),(g)
Standards for drawings 1.84
Symbols . . . . 1.84(n)
Views . . . . 1.84(h)
When necessary, part of complete application . . . 1.51
Duty of disclosure. 1.56, 1.555
    Patent term extension 1.765

E

Election of species 1.146
Electronic documents:
    Compact disc submissions:
        Amino acid sequences 1.821, 1.823, 1.825
        Computer program listings 1.96
        Incorporation by reference in specification . . . 1.52
        Nuclide acid sequences 1.821, 1.823, 1.825
        Requirements 1.52
        Submitted as part of permanent record 1.52, 1.58,
        1.96, 1.821, 1.823, 1.825
        Tables 1.58
Employee testimony. (See Testimony by Office
employees.)
Establishing small entity status 1.27, 1.28
Evidence in contested cases before the Board
. . . . 41.154
Ex parte reexamination. (See Reexamination.)
Examination of applications:
    Advancement of examination. 1.102
    As to form. 1.104
    Citation of references 1.104
    Completeness of examiner's action 1.104
    Deferral of. 1.103
    Examiner's action 1.104
    International-type search. 1.104
    Nature of examination 1.104
    Reasons for allowance 1.104
    Reconsideration after rejection if requested . . . 1.111

Reissue. 1.176
Rejection of claims 1.104
Request for continued examination. 1.114
Requirements for information by examiner . . . 1.105
Suspension of. 1.103
Examiners:
   Answers on appeal. 41.39
   Complaints against 1.3
   Interviews with 1.133
Executors. 1.42
Exhibits. (See Models and exhibits.)
Export of technical data. 5.19, 5.20
Express abandonment 1.138
"Express Mail" 1.6, 1.10
   Date of receipt of. 1.6
   Petition in regard to 1.10
Expungement. 1.59
Extension of patent term (See also Patent term
   adjustment):
   Due to examination delay under the URAA
     (35 U.S.C. 154) 1.701
   Due to regulatory review period (35 U.S.C.
     156):
     Applicant for 1.730
     Application for. 1.740
     Calculation of term:
       Animal drug product. 1.778
       Food or color additive. 1.776
       Human drug product. 1.775
       Medical device 1.777
       Veterinary biological product 1.779
     Certificate of extension 1.780
     Conditions for. 1.720
     Correction of informalities 1.740
     Determination of eligibility 1.750
     Duty of disclosure 1.765
     Filing date of application 1.741
     Formal requirements 1.740
     Incomplete application 1.741
     Interim extension under 35 U.S.C. 156(d)(5) 1.790
     Interim extension under 35 U.S.C. 156(e)(2). 1.760
     Multiple applications 1.785
     Order granting interim extension 1.780
     Patents subject to 1.710
     Signature requirements for application 1.730
     Termination of interim extension granted
       under 35 U.S.C. 156(d)(5) 1.791
     Withdrawal of application 1.770

Extension of time 1.136
   Fees. 1.17
   Interference proceedings. 41.4

F

Facsimile transmission . . . . 1.6(d), 1.8
Federal holiday within the District of Columbia . . . 1.9(h)
Federal Register, publication of rules in. 1.351
Fees and payment of money:
   Credit card 1.23
   Deposit accounts. 1.25
   Document supply fees 1.19
   Extension of time 1.17
   Fee on appeal to the Court of Appeals for the
     Federal Circuit provided by rules of court 1.301
   Fees payable in advance 1.22
   Foreign filing license petition. . . . . 1.17(g)
   For international-type search report . . . . 1.21(e)
   Itemization required 1.22
   Method of payment. 1.23
   Money by mail at risk of sender 1.23
   Money paid by mistake. 1.26
   Necessary for application to be complete. 1.51
   Petition fees 1.17, 1.181, 41.20
   Post allowance 1.18
   Processing fees 1.17
   Reexamination request . . . . 1.20(c)
   Refunds. 1.26
   Relating to international applications 1.25(b), 1.445,
     1.481, 1.482, 1.492
   Schedule of fees and charges 1.16-1.21
Files open to the public 1.11
Filing date of application 1.53
Filing, search, and examination fees 1.16
Filing in Post Office. 1.10
Filing of interference settlement agreements 41.205
Final rejection:
   Appeal from 41.31
   Response to. 1.113, 1.116
   When and how given 1.113
First Class Mail (includes Priority Mail and
   Express Mail) 1.8
Foreign application. 1.55
   License to file 5.11-5.25
Foreign country:
   Taking oath in 1.66
   Taking testimony in . . . . 41.156(b)
Foreign mask work protection . . . . Part 150
   Evaluation of request 150.4
   Definition 150.1
   Duration of proclamation 150.5
   Initiation of evaluation 150.2

Mailing address 150.6
Submission of requests 150.3
Formulas and tables in patent applications.. . . . . 1.58
Fraud practiced or attempted on Office. 1.56
Freedom of Information Act (FOIA) . . . . Part 102
   Appeals from initial determinations or
     untimely delays 102.10
   Business information 102.9
   Correspondence address 102.1, 102.4
   Expedited processing 102.6
   Fees 102.11
   Public reference facilities 102.2
   Records 102.3
   Responses to requests 102.7
     Responsibility for responding 102.5
     Time limits 102.6
   Requirements for making requests 102.4

G

Gazette. (See *Official Gazette.*)
General authorization to charge deposit account1.25, 1.136
General information and correspondence 1.1-1.8
Government acquisition of foreign patent rights. Part 501
Government employee invention . . . . Part 501
Government interest in patent, recording of . 3.11, 3.31,
   3.41, 3.58
Governmental registers 3.58
Guardian of insane person may apply for patent. . . . 1.43

H

Hearings:
   Before the Board of Patents Appeals and Inter-
     ferences 41.47
   Fee for appeal hearing 41.20
Holiday, time for action expiring on 1.6, 1.7

I

Identification of application, patent or registration . . . 1.5
Inconsistencies between application data sheet
   and oath or declaration . . . . 1.76(d)
Incorporation by reference. 1.57
Information disclosure statement:
   At time of filing application. 1.51
   Content of 1.98
   Not permitted in provisional applications 1.51
   Reexamination. 1.555, 1.902
   Suspension of action to provide time for
     consideration of an IDS in a CPA . . . . 1.103(b)
   Third party submission of 1.99
   To comply with duty of disclosure 1.97

Information, Public. . . . . .Part 102
Insane inventor, application by guardian of 1.43
Inter partes reexamination. (See Reexamination.)
Interferences:
   Abandonment of the contest 41.127
   Access to applications. . . . . 1.11(e)
   Addition of patent or application. 41.203
   Amendment during 41.121
   Appeal to the Court of Appeals for the Federal
     Circuit. 1.301, 1.302
   Applicant requests 41.202
   Arbitration. 41.126
   Burden of proof. 41.207
   Civil action 1.303
   Common interests in the invention. 41.206
   Concession of priority. 41.127
   Copying claims from patent 41.121, 41.202
   Declaration of interference 41.203
   Definitions 41.201
   Disclaimer to avoid interference. 41.127
   Discovery 41.150
   Extension of time 41.4
   In what cases declared 41.203
   Junior party fails to overcome filing date of
     senior party 41.204
   Jurisdiction over involved files. 41.103
   Manner of service of papers 41.106
   Motions. 41.121
   Notice to file civil action 1.303
   Notice of declaration. 41.203
   Petitions 41.3
   Presumption as to order of invention 41.207
   Priority Statement 41.204
   Prosecution by owner of entire interest 41.9
   Records of, when open to public . . . . 1.11(e)
   Requests by applicants 41.202
   Review of decision by civil action 1.303
   Same party 41.206
   Sanctions 41.128
   Secrecy order cases. . . . . 5.3(b)
   Service of papers. 41.106
   Statutory disclaimer by patentee during 41.127
   Suggestion of claims for interference 41.202
   Suspension of other proceedings 41.103
   Time period for completion 41.200
   Translation of document in foreign language . . 41.154
International application. (See Patent Cooperation
   Treaty.)
International Preliminary Examining Authority. . . . 1.416
Interview summary 1.133
Interviews with examiner 1.133, 1.560

Invention promoters:
 Complaints regarding 4.1-4.6
  Publication of. 4.1, 4.3, 4.5
  Reply to 4.4
  Submission of. 4.3
  Withdrawal of. 4.3
 Definition. 4.2
 Reply to complaint. 4.4
Inventor (See also Applicant for patent,
 Application for patent):
 Death or insanity of inventor. 1.42, 1.43
  In an international application 1.422, 1.423
 Refuses to sign application 1.47
 To make application. 1.41, 1.45
 Unavailable 1.47
Inventor's certificate priority benefit. 1.55
Inventorship and date of invention of the subject
 matter of individual claims 1.110
Issue fee. 1.18
Issue of patent. (See Allowance and issue of
 patent.)

J

Joinder of inventions in one application 1.141
Joint inventors 1.45, 1.47, 1.324
Joint patent to inventor and assignee. 1.46, 3.81
Jurisdiction:
 After decision by Board of Patent Appeals and
  Interferences 1.197, 1.198
 After notice of allowance 1.312
 Over involved files 41.103

L

Lapsed patents. 1.317
Legal representative of deceased or
 incapacitated inventor 1.42-1.43, 1.64
Legibility of papers 1.52
Letters to the Office. (See Correspondence.)
Library service fee. . . . . 1.19(c)
License and assignment of government
 interest in patent. 3.11, 3.31, 3.41
License for foreign filing. 5.11-5.15
List of U.S. patents classified in a subclass,
 cost of. . . . . 1.19(d)
Local delivery box rental. . . . . 1.21(d)
Lost files 1.251

M

Mail Stops
 Mail Stop 4 . . . . 150.6
 Mail Stop 8 . . . . 1.1(a)(3)
 Mail Stop 24 . . . . 4.3(c)
 Mail Stop Assignment Recordation
  Services . . . . 1.1(a)(4), 3.27
 Mail Stop Document Services . . . . 1.1(a)(4)
 Mail Stop *Ex parte* Reexam . . . . 1.1(c)(1)
 Mail Stop *Inter partes* Reexam . . . . 1.1(c)(2)
 Mail Stop Interference . . . . .41.10(b)
 Mail Stop L&R 5.1
 Mail Stop M Correspondence . . . . 1.1(d)(2)
 Mail Stop OED 4.6
 Mail Stop Patent Ext . . . . 1.1(e)
 Mail Stop PCT . . . . 1.1(b), 1.417, 1.434(a), 1.480(b)
Maintenance fees 1.20
 Acceptance of delayed payment of. 1.378
 Address for payments . . . . 1.1(d)(1)
 Address for correspondence (at PTO). . . . . . 1.1(d)(2)
 Address for correspondence (applicant's) 1.363
 Review of decision refusing to accept 1.377
 Submission of. 1.366
 Time for payment of. 1.362
Mask work notice in specification . . . . 1.71(d)
Mask work notice on drawing . . . . 1.84(s)
Mask work protection, foreign. . . . . .Part 150
Microorganisms. (See Deposit of biological
 material.)
Minimum balance in deposit accounts. 1.25
Missing pages when application filed . . . . 1.53(e)
Mistake in patent, certificate thereof issued. 1.322, 1.323
Models and exhibits:
 Copies of. 1.95
 Disposal without notice unless return
  arrangements made. 1.94
 If on examination model found necessary
  request therefor will be made. 1.91
 In contested cases 41.154
 May be required 1.91
 Model not generally admitted in application or
  patent 1.91
 Not to be taken from the Office except in
  custody of sworn employee 1.95
 Return of. 1.94
 Working model may be required 1.91
Money. (See Fees and payment of money.)
Motions in interferences. 41.121
 To take testimony in foreign country . . . . . .41.156(b)

N

Name of Applicant or Inventor (see Applicant
 for patent, Application for patent, Inventor)
New matter inadmissible in application. 1.121
New matter inadmissible in reissue 1.173
Non-English language specification fee. . . . . 1.17(i)

Nonprofit organization:
    Definition............................. 1.27
    Small entity status 1.27
Notice:
    Of allowance of application............... 1.311
    Of appeal to the Court of Appeals for
       the Federal Circuit................1.301, 1.302
    Of arbitration award..................... 1.335
    Of defective *ex parte* reexamination request. 1.510(c)
    Of declaration of interference 41.203
    Of oral hearings before the Board of
       Patent Appeals and Interferences 41.47
    Of rejection of an application 1.104
    Of taking testimony .... 41.157(c)
Nucleotide and/or amino acid sequences:
    Amendments to 1.825
    Disclosure in patent applications........... 1.821
    Form and format for computer readable form .. 1.824
    Format for sequence data................. 1.822
    Replacement of 1.825
    Requirements.......................... 1.823
    Submission on compact disc 1.52, 1.821, 1.823
    Symbols.............................. 1.822

O

Oath in patent application. (See also Declaration):
    Apostles................................ 1.66
    Before whom taken in foreign countries 1.66
    Before whom taken in United States 1.66
    By administrator or executor 1.42, 1.63, 1.64
    By guardian of insane person. 1.43, 1.63, 1.64
    Certificate of Officer administering........... 1.66
    Continuation-in-part..................... 1.63(e)
    Declaration............................. 1.68
    Foreign language 1.69
    International application 1.497
    Inventor's Certificate..................... 1.63
    Made by inventor....................1.41, 1.63
    Made by someone other than inventor ...... 1.64(b)
    Officers authorized to administer oaths........ 1.66
    Part of complete application 1.51
    Person making 1.64
    Plant patent application 1.162
    Requirements of......................... 1.63
    Ribboned to other papers.................. 1.66
    Sealed................................. 1.66
    Signature to 1.63, 1.64, 1.67
    Supplemental 1.67
    To acknowledge duty of disclosure 1.63
    When taken abroad to seal all papers......... 1.66
Oath or declaration in reissue application 1.175

Oath or declaration
    Plant patent application................... 1.162
    When international application enters
       national stage 1.497
Object of the invention....................... 1.73
Office action time for reply 1.134
Office fees. (See Fees and payment of money.)
Official action, based exclusively upon the
    written record 1.2
Official business, should be transacted in writing 1.2
Official Gazette:
    Amendments to rules published in 1.351
    Announces request for reexamination . . 1.11(c), 1.904
    Notice of filing application to
       nonsigning inventor 1.47
    Notice of issuance of *ex parte*
       reexamination certificate .... 1.570(f)
    Notice of issuance of *inter partes*
       reexamination certificate 1.997
Oral statements............................... 1.2

P

Payment of fees, Method 1.23
Paper, definition of........................... 1.9
Papers (requirements to become part of
    Office permanent records)................. 1.52
Papers not received on Saturday, Sunday,
    or holidays.............................. 1.6
Patent application. (See Application for patent
    and Provisional patent applications.)
Patent application publication. (See Published
    application.)
Patent attorneys and agents. (See Attorneys and
    agents.)
Patent Cooperation Treaty:
    Access to international application files ... 1.14(g)
    Amendments and corrections during
       international processing 1.471
    Amendments during international
       preliminary examination................. 1.485
    Applicant for international application........ 1.421
    Changes in person, name or address,
       where filed .... 1.421(f), 1.472
    Conduct of international preliminary
       examination 1.484
    Copies of international application files .... 1.14(g)
    Definition of terms 1.401
    Delays in meeting time limits.............. 1.468
    Demand for international preliminary
       examination 1.480
    Designation of States 1.432
    Entry into national stage............. 1.491, 1.495

Examination at national stage 1.496
Fees:
   Authorization to charge fees under
    37 CFR 1.16 . . . . 1.25(b)
   Due on filing of international application. . 1.431(c)
   Failure to pay results in withdrawal of
    application . . . . 1.431(d), 1.432
   Filing, processing and search fees 1.445
   International Filing Fee . . . . 1.431(c), 1.445(b)
   International preliminary
    examination 1.481, 1.482
   National stage. . . . . 1.25(b), 1.492
   Refunds 1.446
Filing by other than inventor . . . . 1.421(b)
International application requirements 1.431
   Abstract 1.438
   Claims 1.436
   Description. 1.435
   Drawings 1.437
   Physical requirements 1.433
   Request. 1.434
International Bureau 1.415
International Preliminary Examining
   Authority 1.416
Inventor deceased 1.422
Inventor insane or legally incapacitated 1.423
Inventors, joint. . . . . 1.421(b), 1.497
National stage in the United States:
   Commencement 1.491
   Entry. 1.491, 1.495
   Examination 1.496
   Fees . . . . 1.25(b); 1.492
Oath or declaration at national stage 1.497
Priority, claim for. 1.55, 1.451, 1.452
Record copy to International Bureau,
   transmittal procedures 1.461
Representation by attorney or agent 1.455
Time limits for processing applications. . 1.465, 1.468
United States as:
   Designated or Elected Office 1.414
   International Searching Authority 1.413
   Receiving Office 1.412
Unity of invention:
   Before International Searching
    Authority 1.475, 1.476
   Before International Preliminary
    Examining Authority 1.488
   National stage. 1.475, 1.499
   Protest to lack of. 1.477, 1.489

Patent term adjustment due to examination
   delay 1.702-1.705
   Application for 1.705
   Determination 1.705
   Grounds for 1.702
   Period of adjustment 1.703
   Reduction of period of adjustment 1.704
Patent term extension due to examination delay . . 1.701
Patent term extension due to regulatory review
   period. (See Extension of patent term due to
   regulatory review period (35 U.S.C. 156).)
Patents (See also Allowance and issue of patent):
   Available for license or sale, publication of
    notice . . . . 1.21(i)
   Certified copies of 1.13
   Correction of errors in . . . 1.171, 1.322, 1.323, 1.324
   Delivery of 1.315
   Disclaimer. 1.321
   Identification required in letters concerning. 1.5
   Lapsed, for nonpayment of issue fee 1.317
   Obtainable by civil action. 1.303
   Price of copies 1.19
   Records of, open to public 1.11, 1.12
   Reissuing of, when defective 1.171-1.178
Payment of fees 1.23
Personal attendance unnecessary 1.2
Petition for reissue 1.171, 1.172
Petition to the Director:
   Fees. 1.17
   For delayed payment of issue fee 1.137
   For expungement of papers 1.59
   For extension of time 1.136
   For license for foreign filing. 5.12
   For the revival of an abandoned application . . . 1.137
   From formal objections or requirements 1.113, 1.181
   From requirement for restriction 1.129, 1.144
   General requirements 1.181
   In interferences. 41.3
   In reexamination. 1.181
    If examiner refused the *ex parte* request. . . 1.515(c)
   On refusal of examiner to admit amendment . . . 1.127
   Questions not specifically provided for 1.182
   Suspension of rules. 1.183
   Petition to accept an
    unintentionally delayed claim for domes-
    tic
    priority . . . . 1.78(a)(3), 1.78(a)(6)
   Petition to accept an unintentionally
    delayed claim for foreign priority . . . . 1.55(c)
   To exercise supervisory authority. 1.181
   To make special 1.102
   Untimely unless filed within two months 1.181

Photographs . . . . 1.84(b), 1.152
Plant patent applications:
   Applicant 1.162
   Claim 1.164
   Declaration. 1.162
   Description. 1.162
   Drawings 1.165
   Examination. 1.167
   Fee for copies. 1.19
   Filing fee . . . . 1.16(c)
   Issue fee . . . . 1.18(c)
   Oath 1.162
   Rules applicable. 1.161
   Specification and arrangement of application
     elements 1.163
   Specimens 1.166
Post issuance and reexamination fees 1.20
Post Office receipt as filing date 1.10
Postal emergency or interruption. . . . . 1.10(g)-(i)
Power of attorney. (See Attorneys or agents.)
Power to inspect . . . . 1.14(c)
Preliminary amendments 1.115
Preliminary Examining Authority, International. . . 1.416
Preserved in confidence, applications 1.12, 1.14
   Exceptions (status, access or copies available) . . 1.14
Prior art citation in patented files 1.501
Prior art statement:
   Content of 1.98
   To comply with duty of disclosure. 1.97
Prior invention, affidavit or declaration of to
   overcome rejection. 1.130, 1.131
Priority, right of, under treaty or law:
   Domestic benefit claim:
     Cross-reference to related
       application(s) 1.76-1.78
     Filing fee must be paid in provisional
       application 1.78
     Indication of whether international
       application was published in English . 1.78(a)(2)
     May be in first sentence of application
       or on application data sheet 1.78
     Petition to accept, unintentionally delayed . . . 1.78
     Translation of non-English language
       provisional application required 1.78
     Waived if not timely 1.78
   Foreign priority claim:
     Filed after issue fee has been paid 1.55
     May be on application data sheet or in
       oath/declaration . . . . 1.63(c)
     Petition to accept, unintentionally delayed . . 1.55
     Priority document 1.55
     Time for claiming. 1.55

Privacy Act . . . . Part 102
   Denial of access to records 102.25
   Definitions 102.22
   Disclosure of records 102.25, 102.30
   Exemptions 102.33, 102.34
   Fees. 102.31
   Grant of access to records 102.25
   Inquiries 102.23
   Medical records 102.26
   Penalties 102.32
   Requests for records 102.24
   Requests for correction or amendment 102.27
     Appeal of initial adverse determination . . . 102.29
     Review of requests 102.28
Processing and retention fee. . . . . 1.21(l), 1.53(f)
Proclamation as to protection of foreign
   mask works . . . . Part 150
Protests to grants of patent 1.291
Provisional applications:
   Claiming the benefit of. 1.78
   Converting a nonprovisional to a provisional. . 1.53(c)
   Converting a provisional to a
     nonprovisional . . . . 1.53(c)
   Cover sheet required by § 1.51(c)(1) may
     be a § 1.76 application data sheet . . . . . . 1.53(c)(1)
   Filing date. . . . . 1.53(c)
   Filing fee. . . . . 1.16(d)
   General requisites . . . . 1.51(c)
   Later filing of fee and cover sheet . . . . 1.53(g)
   Names of inventor(s) . . . . 1.41(a)(2)
     Application data sheet . . . . 1.53(c)(1), 1.76
     Correction of 1.48
     Cover sheet . . . . 1.51(c)(1), 1.53(c)(1)
     Joint inventors 1.45
   No right of priority . . . . 1.53(c)
   No examination. . . . . 1.53(i)
   Papers concerning, should identify provisional
     application as such, by application number . . . 1.5(f)
   Parts of complete provisional application. . . . . 1.51(c)
   Processing fees 1.17
   Revival of 1.137
   When abandoned . . . . 1.53(i)
Provisional rights
   Submission of international publication
     or English translation thereof pursuant
     to 35 U.S.C. 154(d)(4) 1.417
Public Information . . . . Part 102
Public use proceedings 1.292
   Fee. . . . . 1.17(j)
Publication of application 1.211
   Early publication 1.219
   Express abandonment to avoid publication . . . 1.138

Fee 1.18
Nonpublication request 1.213
Publication of redacted copy 1.217
Republication 1.221
Voluntary publication 1.221
Published application
    Access to 1.11, 1.14
    Certified copies of 1.13
    Contents 1.215
    Definition 1.9
    Records of, open to public 1.11, 1.12
    Republication of 1.221
    Third party submission in 1.99

R

Reasons for allowance 1.104
Reconsideration of Office action 1.112
Reconstruction of lost files 1.251
Recording of assignments. (See Assignments and
    recording.)
Records of the Patent and Trademark Office . . 1.11-1.15
Reexamination:
    Announcement in O.G. . . . . 1.11(c)
    Correction of inventorship 1.530
    Correspondence address . . . . 1.33(c)
    Ex parte proceedings:
        Amendments, manner of making . . . 1.121(j), 1.530
        Appeal to Board 41.31
        Appeal to C.A.F.C. 1.301
        Civil action under 35 U.S.C. 145 . . . . 1.303
        Concurrent with interference, reissue, other
            reexamination, litigation, or office
            proceeding(s) 1.565
        Conduct of 1.550
        Duty of disclosure in 1.555
        Examiner's determination to grant or
            refuse request for 1.515
        Extensions of time in . . . . 1.550(c)
        Initiated by the Director 1.520
        Interviews in 1.560
        Issuance and publication of certificate
            concludes 1.570
        Order for reexamination by examiner 1.525
        Patent owner's statement 1.530, 1.540
        Processing of prior art citations during 1.502
        Reply to patent owner's statement to
            third party requester 1.535, 1.540
        Request for 1.510
        Scope of 1.552
        Service of papers 1.248
    Examiner's action 1.104
    Fee . . . . 1.20(c)

Fees may be charged to deposit account 1.25
Identification in letter . . . . 1.5(d)
Inter partes proceedings 1.902-1.997
    Amendments, manner of making . . 1.121(j), 1.530,
        1.941
    Appeal to Board 41.61
    Appeal to C.A.F.C. 1.983
    Civil action under 35 U.S.C. 145 not
        available . . . . 1.303(d)
    Concurrent with interference, reissue, other
        reexamination, litigation, or office
        proceeding(s) 1.565, 1.985
    Conduct of 1.937
    Duty of disclosure in 1.555, 1.923
    Examiner's determination to grant or
        refuse request for 1.923-1.927
    Extensions of time in 1.956
    Filing date of request for 1.919
    Issuance of certificate at conclusion of 1.997
    Merged with concurrent reexamination
        proceedings 1.989
    Merged with reissue application 1.991
    Notice of, in the *Official Gazette* 1.904
    Persons eligible to file request for 1.903
    Processing of prior art citations during 1.902
    Scope of 1.906
    Service of papers 1.248, 1.903
    Submission of papers by the public 1.905
    Subsequent requests for 1.907
    Suspension due to concurrent interference . . . 1.993
    Suspension due to litigation 1.987
Information Disclosure Statements 1.98, 1.555
Open to public . . . . 1.11(d)
Reconsideration before final action 1.112
Refund of fee 1.26
Reply to action 1.111
Revival of terminated or limited
    reexamination prosecution 1.137
Reference characters in drawings . . . . 1.74, 1.84(p)
References cited on examination 1.104
Refund of money paid by mistake 1.26
    International applications 1.446
    Later establishment of small entity status 1.28
    Time period for requesting 1.26
Register of Government interest in patents 3.58
Rehearing:
    On appeal to Board 41.52
    Request for, time for appeal after action on . . . 1.304
Reissues:
    Amendments 1.173
    Applicants, assignees 1.172
    Application for reissue 1.171

Application made and sworn to by inventor,
      if living 1.172
Continuing duty of applicant.............. 1.178
Declaration........................... 1.175
Drawings 1.173
Examination of reissue................... 1.176
Filed during *ex parte* reexamination 1.565
Filed during *inter partes* reexamination 1.985
Filing fee 1.16
Filing of announcement in *Official Gazette*..... 1.11
Grounds for and requirements 1.171-1.178
Issue fee.............................. 1.18(a)
Multiple applications for reissue of a
      single patent 1.177
Oath 1.175
Open to public 1.11
Original patent surrendered 1.178
Restriction 1.176
Specification 1.173
Take precedence in order of examination 1.176
To contain no new matter................. 1.173
What must accompany application 1.171, 1.172
Rejection:
      After two rejections appeal may be taken
         from examiner to Board................. 41.31
      Applicant will be notified of rejection
         with reasons and references............ 1.104
      Based on commonly owned prior art,
         how overcome 1.130
      Examiner may rely on admissions by applicant
         or patent owner, or facts within examiner's
         knowledge.......................... 1.104
      Final............................... 1.113
      Formal objections 1.104
      On account of invention shown by others but
         not claimed, how overcome.............. 1.131
      References will be cited................ 1.104
      Requisites of notice of.................. 1.104
Reply brief.............................. 41.41
Reply to Office action:
      Abandonment for failure to 1.135
      By applicant or patent owner.............. 1.111
      Substantially complete.................. 1.135
      Supplemental....................... 1.111
      Time for 1.134
Representative capacity..................... 1.34(a)
Request for continued examination............ 1.114
      Fee 1.17
      Suspension of action after 1.103
Request for reconsideration.................. 1.112
Request for *ex parte* reexamination............ 1.510
Request for *inter partes* reexamination 1.913-1.927

Requirement for submission of information....... 1.105
Reservation clauses not permitted 1.79
Restriction of application. 1.141-1.146, 1.176
      Claims to nonelected invention withdrawn 1.142
      Constructive election 1.145
      Petition from requirements for 1.129, 1.144
      Provisional election 1.143
      Reconsideration of requirement 1.143
      Requirement for 1.142
      Subsequent presentation of claims for
         different invention 1.145
Retention fee..................... 1.21(l), 1.53(f)
Return of correspondence................... 1.5(a)
Revival of abandoned application, terminated
      or limited reexamination prosecution, or
      lapsed patent 1.137
      Unavoidable abandonment fee .... 1.17(l)
      Unintentional abandonment fee .... 1.17(m)
Revocation of power of attorney or
      authorization of agent .... 1.36(a)
Rules of Practice:
      Amendments to rules will be published 1.351

S

Saturday, when last day falls on 1.7
Secrecy order 5.1-5.5
Sequences:
      Amendments to sequence listing and computer
         readable copy 1.825
      Disclosure requirements 1.821, 1.823
      Sequence data, symbols and format 1.822
      Submissions in computer readable form....... 1.824
      Submissions on compact disc in lieu of paper .. 1.52,
         1.821, 1.823
Serial number of application 1.5
Service of notices:
      In interference cases 41.106
      Of appeal to the U.S. Court of Appeals for the
         Federal Circuit 1.301
Service of papers 1.248
Service of process................... 15 CFR Part 15
Shortened period for reply 1.134
Signature:
      EFS character coded................... 1.4(d)(3)
      Handwritten .... 1.4(d)(1)
      Implicit certifications .... 1.4(d), 11.18
      S-signature .... 1.4(d)(2)
      To a written assertion of small entity status   1.27(c)(2)
      To amendments and other papers .... 1.33(b)
      To an application for extension of patent term   .1.730
      To express abandonment.................. 1.138
      To oath 1.63

To reissue oath or declaration 1.172
When copy is acceptable 1.4
Small business concern:
    Definition. 1.27
    Small entity status 1.27
Small entity:
    Definition. 1.27
    Errors in status excused 1.28
    Fraud on the office 1.27
    License to Federal agency 1.27
    Statement 1.27
    Statement in parent application 1.27
    Status establishment. 1.27, 1.28
    Status update 1.27, 1.28
Solicitor's address . . . . 1.1(a)(3), 1.302(c)
Species of invention claimed. 1.141, 1.146
Specification (See also Application for
    patent, Claims):
    Abstract 1.72
    Amendments to 1.121, 1.125
    Arrangement of 1.77, 1.154, 1.163
    Best mode 1.71
    Claim 1.75
    Commence on separate sheet. . . . . 1.71(f)
    Contents of. 1.71-1.75
    Copyright notice . . . . 1.71(d)
    Cross-references to other applications. 1.78
    Description of the invention 1.71
    If defective, reissue to correct 1.171-1.178
    Mask work notice . . . . 1.71(d)
    Must conclude with specific and distinct claim. . 1.75
    Must point out new improvements specifically. . 1.71
    Must refer by figures to drawings 1.74
    Must set forth the precise invention 1.71
    Object of the invention 1.73
    Order of arrangement in framing. 1.77
    Paper, writing, margins 1.52
    Paragraph numbering. 1.52
    Part of complete application 1.51
    Reference to drawings. 1.74
    Requirements of. 1.71-1.75
    Reservation clauses not permitted. 1.79
    Separate from other parts of application . . . . . 1.71(f)
    Substitute 1.125
    Summary of the invention 1.73
    Title of the invention 1.72
    To be rewritten, if necessary 1.125
Specimens. (See Models and exhibits.)
Specimens of composition of matter to be
    furnished when required 1.93
Specimens of plants. 1.166
Statement of status as small entity. 1.27

Status information 1.14
Statutory disclaimer fee . . . . 1.20(d)
Statutory invention registrations. 1.293
    Examination. 1.294
    Publication of 1.297
    Review of decision finally refusing to publish. . 1.295
    Withdrawal of request for publication of 1.296
Submission of international publication or English
    translation thereof pursuant to 35 U.S.C.
    154(d)(4) 1.417
Sufficient funds in deposit account 1.25
Suit in equity. (See Civil action.)
Summary of invention 1.73
Sunday, when last day falls on 1.7
Supervisory authority, petition to
    Director to exercise. 1.181
Supplemental oath /declaration 1.67
Surcharge for oath or basic filing fee filed
    after filing date . . . . 1.16(f), 1.53(f)
Suspension of action. 1.103
Suspension of rules. 1.183
Symbols for drawings. 1.84(n)
Symbols for nucleotide and/or amino acid
    sequence data 1.822

T

Tables in patent applications 1.58
Terminal disclaimer 1.321
Testimony by Office employees. . . . . . . 15 CFR Part 15a
Testimony in contested cases before the Board
    . . . . 41.156-41.158
    Compelling testimony and production 41.156
    Expert testimony. 41.158
    Taking testimony 41.157
Third party submission in published application . . . 1.99
Time expiring on Saturday, Sunday, or holiday 1.7
Time for claiming benefit of prior (domestic)
    application 1.78
Time for claiming foreign priority 1.55
Time for filing preliminary amendment to ensure
    entry thereof 1.115
Time for payment of issue fee 1.311
Time for payment of publication fee 1.311
Time for reply by applicant 1.134, 1.135, 1.136
Time for reply to Office action. 1.134, 1.136
Time for requesting a refund 1.26
Time, periods of. 1.7
Timely filing of correspondence 1.8, 1.10
Title of invention 1.72
Title reports, fee for . . . . 1.19(b)
Transitional procedures 1.129

U

Unavoidable abandonment 1.137
Unintentional abandonment. 1.137
United States as
    Designated Office 1.414
    Elected Office 1.414
    International Preliminary Examining
      Authority 1.416
    International Searching Authority 1.413
    Receiving Office 1.412

Unlocatable files. 1.251
Unsigned continuation or divisional application 1.53, 1.63
Use of file of parent application . . . . 1.53(d)

W

Waiver of confidentiality . . . . 1.53(d)(6)
Withdrawal from issue 1.313
Withdrawal of attorney or agent. . . . . 1.36(b)
Withdrawal of request for statutory invention
    registration 1.296

PRACTICE BEFORE THE PATENT AND TRADEMARK OFFICE

PART 10 — REPRESENTATION OF OTHERS BEFORE THE PATENT AND TRADEMARK OFFICE

Sec.

10.1   Definitions.
10.2   [Reserved]
10.3   [Reserved]
10.4   [Reserved]

INDIVIDUALS ENTITLED TO PRACTICE BEFORE THE PATENT AND TRADEMARK OFFICE

10.5   [Reserved]
10.6   [Reserved]
10.7   [Reserved]
10.8   [Reserved]
10.9   [Reserved]
10.10   [Reserved]
10.11   Removing names from the register.
10.12 - 10.19 [Reserved]

PATENT AND TRADEMARK OFFICE CODE OF PROFESSIONAL RESPONSIBILITY

10.20   Canons and Disciplinary Rules.
10.21   Canon 1.
10.22   Maintaining integrity and competence of the legal profession.
10.23   Misconduct.
10.24   Disclosure of information to authorities.
10.25 - 10.29 [Reserved]
10.30   Canon 2.
10.31   Communications concerning a practitioner's services.
10.32   Advertising.
10.33   Direct contact with prospective clients.
10.34   Communication of fields of practice.
10.35   Firm names and letterheads.
10.36   Fees for legal services.
10.37   Division of fees among practitioners.
10.38   Agreements restricting the practice of a practitioner.
10.39   Acceptance of employment.
10.40   Withdrawal from employment.
10.41 - 10.45 [Reserved]
10.46   Canon 3.
10.47   Aiding unauthorized practice of law.
10.48   Sharing legal fees.
10.49   Forming a partnership with a non-practitioner.
10.50 - 10.55 [Reserved]
10.56   Canon 4.
10.57   Preservation of confidences and secrets of a client.
10.58 - 10.60 [Reserved]
10.61   Canon 5.
10.62   Refusing employment when the interest of the practitioner may impair the practitioner's independent professional judgment.
10.63   Withdrawal when the practitioner becomes a witness.
10.64   Avoiding acquisition of interest in litigation or proceeding before the Office.
10.65   Limiting business relations with a client.
10.66   Refusing to accept or continue employment if the interests of another client may impair the independent professional judgment of the practitioner.
10.67   Settling similar claims of clients.
10.68   Avoiding influence by others than the client.
10.69 - 10.75 [Reserved]
10.76   Canon 6.
10.77   Failing to act competently.
10.78   Limiting liability to client.
10.79 - 10.82 [Reserved]
10.83   Canon 7.
10.84   Representing a client zealously.
10.85   Representing a client within the bounds of the law.
10.86   [Reserved]
10.87   Communicating with one of adverse interest.
10.88   Threatening criminal prosecution.
10.89   Conduct in proceedings.
10.90 - 10.91 [Reserved]
10.92   Contact with witnesses.
10.93   Contact with officials.
10.94 - 10.99 [Reserved]
10.100 Canon 8.
10.101 Action as a public official.
10.102 Statements concerning officials.
10.103 Practitioner candidate for judicial office.
10.104 - 10.109 [Reserved]
10.110 Canon 9.
10.111 Avoiding even the appearance of impropriety.

10.112   Preserving identity of funds and property of client.
10.113 - 10.170 [Reserved]

§ 10.1   Definitions.

This part governs solely the practice of patent, trademark, and other law before the Patent and Trademark Office. Nothing in this part shall be construed to preempt the authority of each State to regulate the practice of law, except to the extent necessary for the Patent and Trademark Office to accomplish its federal objectives. Unless otherwise clear from the context, the following definitions apply to this part:

(a)   *Affidavit* means affidavit, declaration under 35 U.S.C. 25 (see § 1.68 and § 2.20 of this subchapter), or statutory declaration under 28 U.S.C. 1746.

(b)   *Application* includes an application for a design, plant, or utility patent, an application to reissue any patent, and an application to register a trademark.

(c)   *Attorney* or *lawyer* means an individual who is a member in good standing of the bar of any United States court or the highest court of any State. A "non-lawyer" is a person who is not an attorney or lawyer.

(d)   *Canon* is defined in § 10.20(a).

(e)   *Confidence* is defined in § 10.57(a).

(f)   *Differing interests* include every interest that may adversely affect either the judgment or the loyalty of a practitioner to a client, whether it be a conflicting, inconsistent, diverse, or other interest.

(g)   *Director* means the Director of Enrollment and Discipline.

(h)   *Disciplinary Rule* is defined in § 10.20(b).

(i)   *Employee of a tribunal* includes all employees of courts, the Office, and other adjudicatory bodies.

(j)   *Giving information* within the meaning of § 10.23(c) (2) includes making (1) a written statement or representation or (2) an oral statement or representation.

(k)   *Law firm* includes a professional legal corporation or a partnership.

(l)   *Legal counsel* means practitioner.

(m)   *Legal profession* includes the individuals who are lawfully engaged in practice of patent, trademark, and other law before the Office.

(n)   *Legal service* means any legal service which may lawfully be performed by a practitioner before the Office.

(o)   *Legal System* includes the Office and courts and adjudicatory bodies which review matters on which the Office has acted.

(p)   *Office* means Patent and Trademark Office.

(q)   *Person* includes a corporation, an association, a trust, a partnership, and any other organization or legal entity.

(r)   *Practitioner* means (1) an attorney or agent registered to practice before the Office in patent cases or (2) an individual authorized under 5 U.S.C. 500(b) or otherwise as provided by this subchapter, to practice before the Office in trademark cases or other non-patent cases. A "suspended or excluded practitioner" is a practitioner who is suspended or excluded under § 10.156. A "non-practitioner" is an individual who is not a practitioner.

(s)   A *proceeding before the Office* includes an application, a reexamination, a protest, a public use proceeding, a patent interference, an *inter partes* trademark proceeding, or any other proceeding which is pending before the Office.

(t)   *Professional legal corporation* means a corporation authorized by law to practice law for profit.

(u)   *Registration* means registration to practice before the Office in patent cases.

(v)   *Respondent* is defined in § 10.134(a)(1).

(w)   *Secret* is defined in § 10.57(a).

(x)   *Solicit* is defined in § 10.33.

(y)   *State* includes the District of Columbia, Puerto Rico, and other federal territories and possessions.

(z)   *Tribunal* includes courts, the Office, and other adjudicatory bodies.

(aa)   *United States* means the United States of America, its territories and possessions.

[Added 50 FR 5172, Feb. 6, 1985, effective Mar. 8, 1985]

§ 10.2   [Reserved]

[Added 50 FR 5173, Feb. 6, 1985, effective Mar. 8, 1985; removed and reserved, 69 FR 35427, June 24, 2004, effective July 26, 2004]

§ 10.3   [Reserved]

[Added 50 FR 5173, Feb. 6, 1985, effective Mar. 8, 1985; removed and reserved, 69 FR 35427, June 24, 2004, effective July 26, 2004]

§ 10.4 [Reserved]

[Added 50 FR 5173, Feb. 6, 1985, effective Mar. 8, 1985; removed and reserved, 73 FR 59513, Oct. 9, 2008, effective Oct. 9, 2008]

INDIVIDUALS ENTITLED TO PRACTICE BEFORE THE PATENT AND TRADEMARK OFFICE

§ 10.5 [Reserved]

[Added 50 FR 5173, Feb. 6, 1985, effective Mar. 8, 1985; removed and reserved, 69 FR 35427, June 24, 2004, effective July 26, 2004]

§ 10.6 [Reserved]

[Added 50 FR 5173, Feb. 6, 1985, effective Mar. 8, 1985; paras. (d) & (e) removed 53 FR 38948, Oct. 4, 1988, effective Nov. 4, 1988; removed and reserved, 69 FR 35427, June 24, 2004, effective July 26, 2004]

§ 10.7 [Reserved]

[Added 50 FR 5174, Feb. 6, 1985, effective Mar. 8, 1985; removed and reserved, 69 FR 35427, June 24, 2004, effective July 26, 2004]

§ 10.8 [Reserved]

[Added 50 FR 5174, Feb. 6, 1985, effective Mar. 8, 1985; removed and reserved, 69 FR 35427, June 24, 2004, effective July 26, 2004]

§ 10.9 [Reserved]

[Added 50 FR 5174, Feb. 6, 1985, effective Mar. 8, 1985; para. (c) added, 58 FR 4335, Jan. 14, 1993, effective May 1, 1993; para. (c) amended, 60 FR 21438, May 2, 1995, effective June 1, 1995; removed and reserved, 69 FR 35427, June 24, 2004, effective July 26, 2004]

§ 10.10 [Reserved]

[Added 50 FR 5175, Feb. 6, 1985, effective Mar. 8, 1985; revised 53 FR 38950, Oct. 4, 1988, effective Nov. 4, 1988; corrected 53 FR 41278, Oct. 20, 1988; removed and reserved, 69 FR 35427, June 24, 2004, effective July 26, 2004]

§ 10.11 Removing names from the register.

A letter may be addressed to any individual on the register, at the address of which separate notice was last received by the Director, for the purpose of ascertaining whether such individual desires to remain on the register. The name of any individual failing to reply and give any information requested by the Director within a time limit specified will be removed from the register and the names of individuals so removed will be published in the Official Gazette. The name of any individual so removed may be reinstated on the register as may be appropriate and upon payment of the fee set forth in § 1.21(a)(3) of this subchapter.

[Added 50 FR 5175, Feb. 6, 1985, effective Mar. 8, 1985; revised, 69 FR 35427, June 24, 2004, effective July 26, 2004]

§ 10.12 - 10.19 [Reserved]

PATENT AND TRADEMARK OFFICE CODE OF PROFESSIONAL RESPONSIBILITY

§ 10.20 Canons and Disciplinary Rules.

(a) Canons are set out in §§ 10.21, 10.30, 10.46, 10.56, 10.61, 10.76, 10.83, 10.100, and 10.110. Canons are statements of axiomatic norms, expressing in general terms the standards of professional conduct expected of practitioners in their relationships with the public, with the legal system, and with the legal profession.

(b) Disciplinary Rules are set out in §§ 10.22-10.24, 10.31-10.40, 10.47-10.57, 10.62-10.68, 10.77, 10.78, 10.84, 10.85, 10.87-10.89, 10.92, 10.93, 10.101-10.103, 10.111, and 10.112. Disciplinary Rules are mandatory in character and state the minimum level of conduct below which no practitioner can fall without being subjected to disciplinary action.

[Added 50 FR 5175, Feb. 6, 1985, effective Mar. 8, 1985]

§ 10.21 Canon 1.

A practitioner should assist in maintaining the integrity and competence of the legal profession.

[Added 50 FR 5175, Feb. 6, 1985, effective Mar. 8, 1985]

§ 10.22 Maintaining integrity and competence of the legal profession.

(a) A practitioner is subject to discipline if the practitioner has made a materially false statement in, or if the practitioner has deliberately failed to disclose a material fact requested in connection with, the practitioner's application for registration or membership in the bar of any United States court or any State court or his or her authority to otherwise practice before the Office in trademark and other non-patent cases.

(b) A practitioner shall not further the application for registration or membership in the bar of any United States court, State court, or administrative agency of another person known by the practitioner to be unqualified in respect to character, education, or other relevant attribute.

[Added 50 FR 5175, Feb. 6, 1985, effective Mar. 8, 1985]

§ 10.23 Misconduct.

(a) A practitioner shall not engage in disreputable or gross misconduct.

(b) A practitioner shall not:

(1) Violate a Disciplinary Rule.

(2) Circumvent a Disciplinary Rule through actions of another.

(3) Engage in illegal conduct involving moral turpitude.

(4) Engage in conduct involving dishonesty, fraud, deceit, or misrepresentation.

(5) Engage in conduct that is prejudicial to the administration of justice.

(6) Engage in any other conduct that adversely reflects on the practitioner's fitness to practice before the Office.

(c) Conduct which constitutes a violation of paragraphs (a) and (b) of this section includes, but is not limited to:

(1) Conviction of a criminal offense involving moral turpitude, dishonesty, or breach of trust.

(2) Knowingly giving false or misleading information or knowingly participating in a material way in giving false or misleading information, to:

(i) A client in connection with any immediate, prospective, or pending business before the Office.

(ii) The Office or any employee of the Office.

(3) Misappropriation of, or failure to properly or timely remit, funds received by a practitioner or the practitioner's firm from a client to pay a fee which the client is required by law to pay to the Office.

(4) Directly or indirectly improperly influencing, attempting to improperly influence, offering or agreeing to improperly influence, or attempting to offer or agree to improperly influence an official action of any employee of the Office by:

(i) Use of threats, false accusations, duress, or coercion,

(ii) An offer of any special inducement or promise of advantage, or

(iii) Improperly bestowing of any gift, favor, or thing of value.

(5) Suspension or disbarment from practice as an attorney or agent on ethical grounds by any duly constituted authority of a State or the United States or, in the case of a practitioner who resides in a foreign country or is registered under § 11.6(c), by any duly constituted authority of:

(i) A State,

(ii) The United States, or

(iii) The country in which the practitioner resides.

(6) Knowingly aiding or abetting a practitioner suspended or excluded from practice before the Office in engaging in unauthorized practice before the Office under § 11.58.

(7) Knowingly withholding from the Office information identifying a patent or patent application of another from which one or more claims have been copied. See § 41.202(a)(1) of this title.

(8) Failing to inform a client or former client or failing to timely notify the Office of an inability to notify a client or former client of correspondence received from the Office or the client's or former client's opponent in an *inter partes* proceeding before the Office when the correspondence (i) could have a significant effect on a matter pending before the Office, (ii) is received by the practitioner on behalf of a client or former client and (iii) is correspondence of which a reasonable practitioner would believe under the circumstances the client or former client should be notified.

(9) Knowingly misusing a "Certificate of Mailing or Transmission" under § 1.8 of this chapter.

(10) Knowingly violating or causing to be violated the requirements of § 1.56 or § 1.555 of this subchapter.

(11) Except as permitted by § 1.52(c) of this chapter, knowingly filing or causing to be filed an application containing any material alteration made in the application papers after the signing of the accompanying oath or declaration without identifying the alteration at the time of filing the application papers.

(12) Knowingly filing, or causing to be filed, a frivolous complaint alleging a violation by a practitioner of the Patent and Trademark Office Code of Professional Responsibility.

(13) Knowingly preparing or prosecuting or providing assistance in the preparation or prosecution of a patent application in violation of an undertaking signed under § 11.10(b).

(14) Knowingly failing to advise the Director in writing of any change which would preclude continued registration under § 11.6.

(15) Signing a paper filed in the Office in violation of the provisions of § 11.18 or making a scandalous or indecent statement in a paper filed in the Office.

(16) Willfully refusing to reveal or report knowledge or evidence to the Director contrary to § 10.24 or § 11.22(b).

(17) Representing before the Office in a patent case either a joint venture comprising an inventor and an invention developer or an inventor referred to the registered practitioner by an invention developer when (i) the registered practitioner knows, or has been advised by the Office, that a formal complaint filed by a Federal or State agency, based on any violation of any law relating to securities, unfair methods of competition, unfair or deceptive acts or practices, mail fraud, or other civil or criminal conduct, is pending before a Federal or State court or Federal or State agency, or has been resolved unfavorably by such court or agency, against the invention developer in connection with invention development services and (ii) the registered practitioner fails to fully advise the inventor of the existence of the pending complaint or unfavorable resolution thereof prior to undertaking or continuing representation of the joint venture or inventor. "Invention developer" means any person, and any agent, employee, officer, partner, or independent contractor thereof, who is not a registered practitioner and who advertises invention development services in media of general circulation or who enters into contracts for invention development services with customers as a result of such advertisement. "Invention development services" means acts of invention development required or promised to be performed, or actually performed, or both, by an invention developer for a customer. "Invention development" means the evaluation, perfection, marketing, brokering, or promotion of an invention on behalf of a customer by an invention developer, including a patent search, preparation of a patent application, or any other act done by an invention developer for consideration toward the end of procuring or attempting to procure a license, buyer, or patent for an invention. "Customer" means any individual who has made an invention and who enters into a contract for invention development services with an invention developer with respect to the invention by which the inventor becomes obligated to pay the invention developer less than $5,000 (not to include any additional sums which the invention developer is to receive as a result of successful development of the invention). "Contract for invention development services" means a contract for invention development services with an invention developer with respect to an invention made by a customer by which the inventor becomes obligated to pay the invention developer less than $5,000 (not to include any additional sums which the invention developer is to receive as a result of successful development of the invention).

(18) In the absence of information sufficient to establish a reasonable belief that fraud or inequitable conduct has occurred, alleging before a tribunal that anyone has committed a fraud on the Office or engaged in inequitable conduct in a proceeding before the Office.

(19) Action by an employee of the Office contrary to the provisions set forth in § 11.10(d).

(20) Knowing practice by a Government employee contrary to applicable Federal conflict of interest laws, or regulations of the Department, agency, or commission employing said individual.

(d) A practitioner who acts with reckless indifference to whether a representation is true or false is chargeable with knowledge of its falsity. Deceitful statements of half-truths or concealment of material facts shall be deemed actual fraud within the meaning of this part.

[Added 50 FR 5175, Feb. 6, 1985, effective Mar. 8, 1985; amended 50 FR 25073, June 17, 1985; 50 FR 25980, June 24, 1985; paras. (c)(13), (19) & (20), 53 FR 38950, Oct. 4, 1988, effective Nov. 4, 1988; corrected 53 FR 41278, Oct. 20, 1988; paras. (c)(10) & (c)(11), 57 FR 2021, Jan. 17, 1992, effective Mar. 16, 1992; para. (c)(9) amended, 58 FR 54494, Oct. 22, 1993, effective Nov. 22, 1993; para. (c)(9) amended, 61 FR 56439, Nov. 1, 1996, effective Dec. 2, 1996; para. (c)(15) amended, 62 FR 53131, Oct. 10, 1997, effective Dec. 1, 1997; para. (c)(11) revised, 65 FR 54604, Sept. 8, 2000, effective Nov. 7, 2000; para (c)(7) revised, 69 FR 49959, Aug. 12, 2004, effective Sept. 13, 2004; paras. (c)(5), (c)(6), (c)(13) through (c)(16), and (c)(19) revised, 73 FR 59513, Oct. 9, 2008, effective Oct. 9, 2008]

§ 10.24　Disclosure of information to authorities.

(a) A practitioner possessing unprivileged knowledge of a violation of a Disciplinary Rule shall report such knowledge to the Director.

(b) A practitioner possessing unprivileged knowledge or evidence concerning another practitioner, employee of the Office, or a judge shall reveal fully such knowledge or evidence upon proper request of a tribunal or other authority empowered to investigate or act upon the conduct of practitioners, employees of the Office, or judges.

[Added 50 FR 5176, Feb. 6, 1985, effective Mar. 8, 1985]

§ 10.25 - 10.29　[Reserved]

§ 10.30　Canon 2.

A practitioner should assist the legal profession in fulfilling its duty to make legal counsel available.

[Added 50 FR 5177, Feb. 6, 1985, effective Mar. 8, 1985]

§ 10.31　Communications concerning a practitioner's services.

(a) No practitioner shall with respect to any prospective business before the Office, by word, circular, letter, or advertising, with intent to defraud in any manner, deceive, mislead, or threaten any pro-spective applicant or other person having immediate or prospective business before the Office.

(b) A practitioner may not use the name of a Member of either House of Congress or of an individual in the service of the United States in advertising the practitioner's practice before the Office.

(c) Unless authorized under § 11.14(b), a non-lawyer practitioner shall not hold himself or herself out as authorized to practice before the Office in trademark cases.

(d) Unless a practitioner is an attorney, the practitioner shall not hold himself or herself out:

(1) To be an attorney or lawyer or

(2) As authorized to practice before the Office in non-patent and trademark cases.

[Added 50 FR 5177, Feb. 6, 1985, effective Mar. 8, 1985; para. (c) revised, 73 FR 59513, Oct. 9, 2008, effective Oct. 9, 2008]

§ 10.32　Advertising.

(a) Subject to § 10.31, a practitioner may advertise services through public media, including a telephone directory, legal directory, newspaper, or other periodical, radio, or television, or through written communications not involving solicitation as defined by § 10.33.

(b) A practitioner shall not give anything of value to a person for recommending the practitioner's services, except that a practitioner may pay the reasonable cost of advertising or written communication permitted by this section and may pay the usual charges of a not-for-profit lawyer referral service or other legal service organization.

(c) Any communication made pursuant to this section shall include the name of at least one practitioner responsible for its content.

[Added 50 FR 5177, Feb. 6, 1985, effective Mar. 8, 1985]

§ 10.33　Direct contact with prospective clients.

A practitioner may not solicit professional employment from a prospective client with whom the practitioner has no family or prior professional relationship, by mail, in-person, or otherwise, when a significant motive for the practitioner's doing so is the practitioner's pecuniary gain under circumstances evidencing undue influence, intimidation, or overreaching. The term "solicit" includes contact in person, by telephone or telegraph, by letter or other writing, or by other communication directed to a specific recipient, but does not include letters addressed or advertising circulars distributed generally to persons not specifically known to need legal services of the kind provided by the practitioner in a particular matter, but who are so situated that they might in general find such services useful.

[Added 50 FR 5177, Feb.6, 1985, effective Mar. 8, 1985]

§ 10.34 Communication of fields of practice.

A registered practitioner may state or imply that the practitioner is a specialist as follows:

(a) A registered practitioner who is an attorney may use the designation "Patents," "Patent Attorney," "Patent Lawyer," "Registered Patent Attorney," or a substantially similar designation.

(b) A registered practitioner who is not an attorney may use the designation "Patents," "Patent Agent," "Registered Patent Agent," or a substantially similar designation, except that any practitioner who was registered prior to November 15, 1938, may refer to himself or herself as a "patent attorney."

[Added 50 FR 5177, Feb. 6, 1985, effective Mar. 8, 1985]

§ 10.35 Firm names and letterheads.

(a) A practitioner shall not use a firm name, letterhead, or other professional designation that violates § 10.31. A trade name may be used by a practitioner in private practice if it does not imply a current connection with a government agency or with a public or charitable legal services organization and is not otherwise in violation of § 10.31.

(b) Practitioners may state or imply that they practice in a partnership or other organization only when that is the fact.

[Added 50 FR 5177, Feb. 6, 1985, effective Mar. 8, 1985]

§ 10.36 Fees for legal services.

(a) A practitioner shall not enter into an agreement for, charge, or collect an illegal or clearly excessive fee.

(b) A fee is clearly excessive when, after a review of the facts, a practitioner of ordinary prudence would be left with a definite and firm conviction that the fee is in excess of a reasonable fee. Factors to be considered as guides in determining the reasonableness of a fee include the following:

(1) The time and labor required, the novelty and difficulty of the questions involved, and the skill requisite to perform the legal service properly.

(2) The likelihood, if apparent to the client, that the acceptance of the particular employment will preclude other employment by the practitioner.

(3) The fee customarily charged for similar legal services.

(4) The amount involved and the results obtained.

(5) The time limitations imposed by the client or by the circumstances.

(6) The nature and length of the professional relationship with the client.

(7) The experience, reputation, and ability of the practitioner or practitioners performing the services.

(8) Whether the fee is fixed or contingent.

[Added 50 FR 5177, Feb. 6, 1985, effective Mar. 8, 1985]

§ 10.37 Division of fees among practitioners.

(a) A practitioner shall not divide a fee for legal services with another practitioner who is not a partner in or associate of the practitioner's law firm or law office, unless:

(1) The client consents to employment of the other practitioner after a full disclosure that a division of fees will be made.

(2) The division is made in proportion to the services performed and responsibility assumed by each.

(3) The total fee of the practitioners does not clearly exceed reasonable compensation for all legal services rendered to the client.

(b) This section does not prohibit payment to a former partner or associate pursuant to a separation or retirement agreement.

[Added 50 FR 5177, Feb. 6, 1985, effective Mar. 8, 1985]

§ 10.38 Agreements restricting the practice of a practitioner.

(a) A practitioner shall not be a party to or participate in a partnership or employment agreement with another practitioner that restricts the right of a practitioner to practice before the Office after the termination of a relationship created by the agreement, except as a condition to payment of retirement benefits.

(b) In connection with the settlement of a controversy or suit, a practitioner shall not enter into an agreement that restricts the practitioner's right to practice before the Office.

[Added 50 FR 5177, Feb. 6, 1985, effective Mar. 8, 1985]

§ 10.39 Acceptance of employment.

A practitioner shall not accept employment on behalf of a person if the practitioner knows or it is obvious that such person wishes to:

(a) Bring a legal action, commence a proceeding before the Office, conduct a defense, assert a position in any proceeding pending before the Office, or otherwise have steps taken for the person, merely for the purpose of harassing or maliciously injuring any other person.

(b) Present a claim or defense in litigation or any proceeding before the Office that it is not warranted under existing law, unless it can be supported by good faith argument for an extension, modification, or reversal of existing law.

[Added 50 FR 5177, Feb. 6, 1985, effective Mar. 8, 1985]

§ 10.40 Withdrawal from employment.

(a) A practitioner shall not withdraw from employment in a proceeding before the Office without permission from the Office (see §§ 1.36 and 2.19 of this subchapter). In any event, a practitioner shall not withdraw from employment until the practitioner has taken reasonable steps to avoid foreseeable prejudice to the rights of the client, including giving due notice to his or her client, allowing time for employment of another practitioner, delivering to the client all papers and property to which the client is entitled, and complying with applicable laws and rules. A practitioner who withdraws from employment shall refund promptly any part of a fee paid in advance that has not been earned.

(b) *Mandatory withdrawal.* A practitioner representing a client before the Office shall withdraw from employment if:

(1) The practitioner knows or it is obvious that the client is bringing a legal action, commencing a proceeding before the Office, conducting a defense, or asserting a position in litigation or any proceeding pending before the Office, or is otherwise having steps taken for the client, merely for the purpose of harassing or maliciously injuring any person;

(2) The practitioner knows or it is obvious that the practitioner's continued employment will result in violation of a Disciplinary Rule;

(3) The practitioner's mental or physical condition renders it unreasonably difficult for the practitioner to carry out the employment effectively; or

(4) The practitioner is discharged by the client.

(c) *Permissive withdrawal.* If paragraph (b) of this section is not applicable, a practitioner may not request permission to withdraw in matters pending before the Office unless such request or such withdrawal is because:

(1) The petitioner's client:

(i) Insists upon presenting a claim or defense that is not warranted under existing law and cannot be supported by good faith argument for an extension, modification, or reversal of existing law;

(ii) Personally seeks to pursue an illegal course of conduct;

(iii) Insists that the practitioner pursue a course of conduct that is illegal or that is prohibited under a Disciplinary Rule;

(iv) By other conduct renders it unreasonably difficult for the practitioner to carry out the employment effectively;

(v) Insists, in a matter not pending before a tribunal, that the practitioner engage in conduct that is contrary to the judgment and advice of the practitioner but not prohibited under the Disciplinary Rule; or

(vi) Has failed to pay one or more bills rendered by the practitioner for an unreasonable period of time or has failed to honor an agreement to pay a retainer in advance of the performance of legal services.

(2) The practitioner's continued employment is likely to result in a violation of a Disciplinary Rule;

(3) The practitioner's inability to work with co-counsel indicates that the best interests of the client likely will be served by withdrawal;

(4) The practitioner's mental or physical condition renders it difficult for the practitioner to carry out the employment effectively;

(5) The practitioner's client knowingly and freely assents to termination of the employment; or

(6) The practitioner believes in good faith, in a proceeding pending before the Office, that the Office will find the existence of other good cause for withdrawal.

[Added 50 FR 5178, Feb. 6, 1985, effective Mar. 8, 1985]

§ 10.41 - 10.45 [Reserved]

§ 10.46 Canon 3.

A practitioner should assist in preventing the unauthorized practice of law.

[Added 50 FR 5178, Feb. 6, 1985, effective Mar. 8, 1985]

§ 10.47 Aiding unauthorized practice of law.

(a) A practitioner shall not aid a non-practitioner in the unauthorized practice of law before the Office.

(b) A practitioner shall not aid a suspended or excluded practitioner in the practice of law before the Office.

(c) A practitioner shall not aid a non-lawyer in the unauthorized practice of law.

[Added 50 FR 5178, Feb. 6, 1985, effective Mar. 8, 1985]

§ 10.48 Sharing legal fees.

A practitioner or a firm of practitioners shall not share legal fees with a non-practitioner except that:

(a) An agreement by a practitioner with the practitioner's firm, partner, or associate may provide for the payment of money, over a reasonable period of time after the practitioner's death, to the practitioner's estate or to one or more specified persons.

(b) A practitioner who undertakes to complete unfinished legal business of a deceased practitioner may pay to the estate of the deceased practitioner that proportion of the total compensation which fairly represents the services rendered by the deceased practitioner.

(c) A practitioner or firm of practitioners may include non-practitioner employees in a compensation or retirement plan, even though the plan is based in whole or in part on a profit-sharing arrangement, providing such plan does not circumvent another Disciplinary Rule.

[Added 50 FR 5178, Feb. 6, 1985, effective Mar. 8, 1985; para. (b) revised, 58 FR 54511, Oct. 22, 1993, effective June 3, 1994]

§ 10.49 Forming a partnership with a non-practitioner.

A practitioner shall not form a partnership with a nonpractitioner if any of the activities of the partnership consist of the practice of patent, trademark, or other law before the Office.

[Added 50 FR 5178, Feb. 6, 1985, effective Mar. 8, 1985]

§ 10.50 - 10.55 [Reserved]

§ 10.56 Canon 4.

A practitioner should preserve the confidences and secrets of a client.

[Added 50 FR 5178, Feb. 6, 1985, effective Mar. 8, 1985]

§ 10.57 Preservation of confidences and secrets of a client.

(a) "Confidence" refers to information protected by the attorney-client or agent-client privilege under applicable law. "Secret" refers to other information gained in the professional relationship that the client has requested be held inviolate or the disclosure of which would be embarrassing or would be likely to be detrimental to the client.

(b) Except when permitted under paragraph (c) of this section, a practitioner shall not knowingly:

(1)   Reveal a confidence or secret of a client.

(2)   Use a confidence or secret of a client to the disadvantage of the client.

(3)   Use a confidence or secret of a client for the advantage of the practitioner or of a third person, unless the client consents after full disclosure.

(c)   A practitioner may reveal:

(1)   Confidences or secrets with the consent of the client affected but only after a full disclosure to the client.

(2)   Confidences or secrets when permitted under Disciplinary Rules or required by law or court order.

(3)   The intention of a client to commit a crime and the information necessary to prevent the crime.

(4)   Confidences or secrets necessary to establish or collect the practitioner's fee or to defend the practitioner or the practitioner's employees or associates against an accusation of wrongful conduct.

(d)   A practitioner shall exercise reasonable care to prevent the practitioner's employees, associates, and others whose services are utilized by the practitioner from disclosing or using confidences or secrets of a client, except that a practitioner may reveal the information allowed by paragraph (c) of this section through an employee.

[Added 50 FR 5178, Feb. 6, 1985, effective Mar. 8, 1985]

§ 10.58 - 10.60 [Reserved]

§ 10.61   Canon 5.

A practitioner should exercise independent professional judgment on behalf of a client.

[Added 50 FR 5179, Feb. 6, 1985, effective Mar. 8, 1985]

§ 10.62   Refusing employment when the interest of the practitioner may impair the practitioner's independent professional judgment.

(a)   Except with the consent of a client after full disclosure, a practitioner shall not accept employment if the exercise of the practitioner's professional judgment on behalf of the client will be or reasonably may be affected by the practitioner's own financial, business, property, or personal interests.

(b)   A practitioner shall not accept employment in a proceeding before the Office if the practitioner knows or it is obvious that the practitioner or another practitioner in the practitioner's firm ought to sign an affidavit to be filed in the Office or be called as a witness, except that the practitioner may undertake the employment and the practitioner or another practitioner in the practitioner's firm may testify:

(1)   If the testimony will relate solely to an uncontested matter.

(2)   If the testimony will relate solely to a matter of formality and there is no reason to believe that substantial evidence will be offered in opposition to the testimony.

(3)   If the testimony will relate solely to the nature and value of legal services rendered in the case by the practitioner or the practitioner's firm to the client.

(4)   As to any matter, if refusal would work a substantial hardship on the client because of the distinctive value of the practitioner or the practitioner's firm as counsel in the particular case.

[Added 50 FR 5179, Feb. 6, 1985, effective Mar. 8, 1985]

§ 10.63   Withdrawal when the practitioner becomes a witness.

(a)   If, after undertaking employment in a proceeding in the Office, a practitioner learns or it is obvious that the practitioner or another practitioner in the practitioner's firm ought to sign an affidavit to be filed in the Office or be called as a witness on behalf of a practitioner's client, the practitioner shall withdraw from the conduct of the proceeding and the practitioner's firm, if any, shall not continue representation in the proceeding, except that the practitioner may continue the representation and the practitioner or another practitioner in the practitioner's firm may testify in the circumstances enumerated in paragraphs (1) through (4) of § 10.62(b).

(b)   If, after undertaking employment in a proceeding before the Office, a practitioner learns or it is obvious that the practitioner or another practitioner in the practitioner's firm may be asked to sign an affidavit to be filed in the Office or be called as a witness other than on behalf of the practitioner's client, the practitioner may continue the representation until it is apparent that the practitioner's affidavit or testimony is or may be prejudicial to the practitioner's client.

[Added 50 FR 5179, Feb. 6, 1985, effective Mar. 8, 1985]

§ 10.64 Avoiding acquisition of interest in litigation or proceeding before the Office.

(a) A practitioner shall not acquire a proprietary interest in the subject matter of a proceeding before the Office which the practitioner is conducting for a client, except that the practitioner may:

(1) Acquire a lien granted by law to secure the practitioner's fee or expenses; or

(2) Contract with a client for a reasonable contingent fee; or

(3) In a patent case, take an interest in the patent as part or all of his or her fee.

(b) While representing a client in connection with a contemplated or pending proceeding before the Office, a practitioner shall not advance or guarantee financial assistance to a client, except that a practitioner may advance or guarantee the expenses of going forward in a proceeding before the Office including fees required by law to be paid to the Office, expenses of investigation, expenses of medical examination, and costs of obtaining and presenting evidence, provided the client remains ultimately liable for such expenses. A practitioner may, however, advance any fee required to prevent or remedy an abandonment of a client's application by reason of an act or omission attributable to the practitioner and not to the client, whether or not the client is ultimately liable for such fee.

[Added 50 FR 5179, Feb. 6, 1985, effective Mar. 8, 1985]

§ 10.65 Limiting business relations with a client.

A practitioner shall not enter into a business transaction with a client if they have differing interests therein and if the client expects the practitioner to exercise professional judgment therein for the protection of the client, unless the client has consented after full disclosure.

[Added 50 FR 5179, Feb. 6, 1985, effective Mar. 8, 1985]

§ 10.66 Refusing to accept or continue employment if the interests of another client may impair the independent professional judgment of the practitioner.

(a) A practitioner shall decline proffered employment if the exercise of the practitioner's independent professional judgment in behalf of a client will be or is likely to be adversely affected by the acceptance of the proffered employment, or if it would be likely to involve the practitioner in representing differing interests, except to the extent permitted under paragraph (c) of this section.

(b) A practitioner shall not continue multiple employment if the exercise of the practitioner's independent professional judgment in behalf of a client will be or is likely to be adversely affected by the practitioner's representation of another client, or if it would be likely to involve the practitioner in representing differing interests, except to the extent permitted under paragraph (c) of this section.

(c) In the situations covered by paragraphs (a) and (b) of this section, a practitioner may represent multiple clients if it is obvious that the practitioner can adequately represent the interest of each and if each consents to the representation after full disclosure of the possible effect of such representation on the exercise of the practitioner's independent professional judgment on behalf of each.

(d) If a practitioner is required to decline employment or to withdraw from employment under a Disciplinary Rule, no partner, or associate, or any other practitioner affiliated with the practitioner or the practitioner's firm, may accept or continue such employment unless otherwise ordered by the Director or Commissioner.

[Added 50 FR 5179, Feb. 6, 1985, effective Mar. 8, 1985]

§ 10.67 Settling similar claims of clients.

A practitioner who represents two or more clients shall not make or participate in the making of an aggregate settlement of the claims of or against the practitioner's clients, unless each client has consented to the settlement after being advised of the existence and nature of all the claims involved in the proposed settlement, of the total amount of the settlement, and of the participation of each person in the settlement.

[Added 50 FR 5179, Feb. 6, 1985, effective Mar. 8, 1985]

§ 10.68 Avoiding influence by others than the client.

(a) Except with the consent of the practitioner's client after full disclosure, a practitioner shall not:

(1) Accept compensation from one other than the practitioner's client for the practitioner's legal services to or for the client.

(2) Accept from one other than the practitioner's client any thing of value related to the practitioner's representation of or the practitioner's employment by the client.

(b) A practitioner shall not permit a person who recommends, employs, or pays the practitioner to render legal services for another, to direct or regulate the practitioner's professional judgment in rendering such legal services.

(c) A practitioner shall not practice with or in the form of a professional corporation or association authorized to practice law for a profit, if a non-practitioner has the right to direct or control the professional judgment of a practitioner.

[Added 50 FR 5180, Feb. 6, 1985, effective Mar. 8, 1985]

§ 10.69 - 10.75 [Reserved]

§ 10.76 Canon 6.

A practitioner should represent a client competently.

[Added 50 FR 5180, Feb. 6, 1985, effective Mar. 8, 1985]

§ 10.77 Failing to act competently.

A practitioner shall not:

(a) Handle a legal matter which the practitioner knows or should know that the practitioner is not competent to handle, without associating with the practitioner another practitioner who is competent to handle it.

(b) Handle a legal matter without preparation adequate in the circumstances.

(c) Neglect a legal matter entrusted to the practitioner.

[Added 50 FR 5180, Feb. 6, 1985, effective Mar. 8, 1985]

§ 10.78 Limiting liability to client.

A practitioner shall not attempt to exonerate himself or herself from, or limit his or her liability to, a client for his or her personal malpractice.

[Added 50 FR 5180, Feb. 6, 1985, effective Mar. 8, 1985]

§ 10.79 - 10.82 [Reserved]

§ 10.83 Canon 7.

A practitioner should represent a client zealously within the bounds of the law.

[Added 50 FR 5180, Feb. 6, 1985, effective Mar. 8, 1985]

§ 10.84 Representing a client zealously.

(a) A practitioner shall not intentionally:

(1) Fail to seek the lawful objectives of a client through reasonable available means permitted by law and the Disciplinary Rules, except as provided by paragraph (b) of this section. A practitioner does not violate the provisions of this section, however, by acceding to reasonable requests of opposing counsel which do not prejudice the rights of the client, by being punctual in fulfilling all professional commitments, by avoiding offensive tactics, or by treating with courtesy and consideration all persons involved in the legal process.

(2) Fail to carry out a contract of employment entered into with a client for professional services, but a practitioner may withdraw as permitted under §§ 10.40, 10.63, and 10.66.

(3) Prejudice or damage a client during the course of a professional relationship, except as required under this part.

(b) In representation of a client, a practitioner may:

(1) Where permissible, exercise professional judgment to waive or fail to assert a right or position of the client.

(2) Refuse to aid or participate in conduct that the practitioner believes to be unlawful, even

though there is some support for an argument that the conduct is legal.

[Added 50 FR 5180, Feb. 6, 1985, effective Mar. 8, 1985]

§ 10.85 Representing a client within the bounds of the law.

(a) In representation of a client, a practitioner shall not:

(1) Initiate or defend any proceeding before the Office, assert a position, conduct a defense, delay a trial or proceeding before the Office, or take other action on behalf of the practitioner's client when the practitioner knows or when it is obvious that such action would serve merely to harass or maliciously injure another.

(2) Knowingly advance a claim or defense that is unwarranted under existing law, except that a practitioner may advance such claim or defense if it can be supported by good faith argument for an extension, modification, or reversal of existing law.

(3) Conceal or knowingly fail to disclose that which the practitioner is required by law to reveal.

(4) Knowingly use perjured testimony or false evidence.

(5) Knowingly make a false statement of law or fact.

(6) Participate in the creation or preservation of evidence when the practitioner knows or it is obvious that the evidence is false.

(7) Counsel or assist a client in conduct that the practitioner knows to be illegal or fraudulent.

(8) Knowingly engage in other illegal conduct or conduct contrary to a Disciplinary Rule.

(b) A practitioner who receives information clearly establishing that:

(1) A client has, in the course of the representation, perpetrated a fraud upon a person or tribunal shall promptly call upon the client to rectify the same, and if the client refuses or is unable to do so the practitioner shall reveal the fraud to the affected person or tribunal.

(2) A person other than a client has perpetrated a fraud upon a tribunal shall promptly reveal the fraud to the tribunal.

[Added 50 FR 5180, Feb. 6, 1985, effective Mar. 8, 1985]

§ 10.86 [Reserved]

§ 10.87 Communicating with one of adverse interest.

During the course of representation of a client, a practitioner shall not:

(a) Communicate or cause another to communicate on the subject of the representation with a party the practitioner knows to be represented by another practitioner in that matter unless the practitioner has the prior consent of the other practitioner representing such other party or is authorized by law to do so. It is not improper, however, for a practitioner to encourage a client to meet with an opposing party for settlement discussions.

(b) Give advice to a person who is not represented by a practitioner other than the advice to secure counsel, if the interests of such person are or have a reasonable possibility of being in conflict with the interests of the practitioner's client.

[Added 50 FR 5180, Feb. 6, 1985, effective Mar. 8, 1985]

§ 10.88 Threatening criminal prosecution.

A practitioner shall not present, participate in presenting, or threaten to present criminal charges solely to obtain an advantage in any prospective or pending proceeding before the Office.

[Added 50 FR 5180, Feb. 6, 1985, effective Mar. 8, 1985]

§ 10.89 Conduct in proceedings.

(a) A practitioner shall not disregard or advise a client to disregard any provision of this Subchapter or a decision of the Office made in the course of a proceeding before the Office, but the practitioner may take appropriate steps in good faith to test the validity of such provision or decision.

(b) In presenting a matter to the Office, a practitioner shall disclose:

(1) Controlling legal authority known to the practitioner to be directly adverse to the position of the client and which is not disclosed by opposing counsel or an employee of the Office.

(2)   Unless privileged or irrelevant, the identities of the client the practitioner represents and of the persons who employed the practitioner.

(c)   In appearing in a professional capacity before a tribunal, a practitioner shall not:

(1)   State or allude to any matter that the practitioner has no reasonable basis to believe is relevant to the case or that will not be supported by admissible evidence.

(2)   Ask any question that the practitioner has no reasonable basis to believe is relevant to the case and that is intended to degrade a witness or other person.

(3)   Assert the practitioner's personal knowledge of the facts in issue, except when testifying as a witness.

(4)   Assert the practitioner's personal opinion as to the justness of a cause, as to the credibility of a witness, as to the culpability of a civil litigant, or as to the guilt or innocence of an accused; but the practitioner may argue, on the practitioner's analysis of the evidence, for any position or conclusion with respect to the matters stated herein.

(5)   Engage in undignified or discourteous conduct before the Office (see § 1.3 of the subchapter).

(6)   Intentionally or habitually violate any provision of this subchapter or established rule of evidence.

[Added 50 FR 5180, Feb. 6, 1985, effective Mar. 8, 1985]

§ 10.90 - 10.91 [Reserved]

§ 10.92 Contact with witnesses.

(a)   A practitioner shall not suppress any evidence that the practitioner or the practitioner's client has a legal obligation to reveal or produce.

(b)   A practitioner shall not advise or cause a person to be secreted or to leave the jurisdiction of a tribunal for the purpose of making the person unavailable as a witness therein.

(c)   A practitioner shall not pay, offer to pay, or acquiesce in payment of compensation to a witness contingent upon the content of the witness' affidavit, testimony or the outcome of the case. But a practitioner may advance, guarantee, or acquiesce in the payment of:

(1)   Expenses reasonably incurred by a witness in attending, testifying, or making an affidavit.

(2)   Reasonable compensation to a witness for the witness' loss of time in attending, testifying, or making an affidavit.

(3)   A reasonable fee for the professional services of an expert witness.

[Added 50 FR 5181, Feb. 6, 1985, effective Mar. 8, 1985]

§ 10.93 Contact with officials.

(a)   A practitioner shall not give or lend anything of value to a judge, official, or employee of a tribunal under circumstances which might give the appearance that the gift or loan is made to influence official action.

(b)   In an adversary proceeding, including any *inter partes* proceeding before the Office, a practitioner shall not communicate, or cause another to communicate, as to the merits of the cause with a judge, official, or Office employee before whom the proceeding is pending, except:

(1)   In the course of official proceedings in the cause.

(2)   In writing if the practitioner promptly delivers a copy of the writing to opposing counsel or to the adverse party if the adverse party is not represented by a practitioner.

(3)   Orally upon adequate notice to opposing counsel or to the adverse party if the adverse party is not represented by a practitioner.

(4)   As otherwise authorized by law.

[Added 50 FR 5181, Feb. 6, 1985, effective Mar. 8, 1985]

§ 10.94 - 10.99 [Reserved]

§ 10.100 Canon 8.

A practitioner should assist in improving the legal system.

[Added 50 FR 5181, Feb. 6, 1985, effective Mar. 8, 1985]

§ 10.101 Action as a public official.

(a) A practitioner who holds public office shall not:

(1) Use the practitioner's public position to obtain, or attempt to obtain, a special advantage in legislative matters for the practitioner or for a client under circumstances where the practitioner knows or it is obvious that such action is not in the public interest.

(2) Use the practitioner's public position to influence, or attempt to influence, a tribunal to act in favor of the practitioner or of a client.

(3) Accept any thing of value from any person when the practitioner knows or it is obvious that the offer is for the purpose of influencing the practitioner's action as a public official.

(b) A practitioner who is an officer or employee of the United States shall not practice before the Office in patent cases except as provided in § 10.10(c) and (d).

[Added 50 FR 5181, Feb. 6, 1985, effective Mar. 8, 1985; para. (b) amended, 54 FR 6520, Feb. 13, 1989]

§ 10.102 Statements concerning officials.

(a) A practitioner shall not knowingly make false statements of fact concerning the qualifications of a candidate for election or appointment to a judicial office or to a position in the Office.

(b) A practitioner shall not knowingly make false accusations against a judge, other adjudicatory officer, or employee of the Office.

[Added 50 FR 5181, Feb. 6, 1985, effective Mar. 8, 1985]

§ 10.103 Practitioner candidate for judicial office.

A practitioner who is a candidate for judicial office shall comply with applicable provisions of law.

[Added 50 FR 5181, Feb. 6, 1985, effective Mar. 8, 1985]

§ 10.104 - 10.109 [Reserved]

§ 10.110 Canon 9.

A practitioner should avoid even the appearance of professional impropriety.

[Added 50 FR 5181, Feb. 6, 1985, effective Mar. 8, 1985]

§ 10.111 Avoiding even the appearance of impropriety.

(a) A practitioner shall not accept private employment in a matter upon the merits of which he or she has acted in a judicial capacity.

(b) A practitioner shall not accept private employment in a matter in which he or she had personal responsibility while a public employee.

(c) A practitioner shall not state or imply that the practitioner is able to influence improperly or upon irrelevant grounds any tribunal, legislative body, or public official.

[Added 50 FR 5181, Feb. 6, 1985, effective Mar. 8, 1985]

§ 10.112 Preserving identity of funds and property of client.

(a) All funds of clients paid to a practitioner or a practitioner's firm, other than advances for costs and expenses, shall be deposited in one or more identifiable bank accounts maintained in the United States or, in the case of a practitioner having an office in a foreign country or registered under § 11.6(c), in the United States or the foreign country.

(b) No funds belonging to the practitioner or the practitioner's firm shall be deposited in the bank accounts required by paragraph (a) of this section except as follows:

(1) Funds reasonably sufficient to pay bank charges may be deposited therein.

(2) Funds belonging in part to a client and in part presently or potentially to the practitioner or the practitioner's firm must be deposited therein, but the portion belonging to the practitioner or the practitioner's firm may be withdrawn when due unless the right of the practitioner or the practitioner's firm to receive it is disputed by the client, in which event the disputed portion shall not be withdrawn until the dispute is finally resolved.

(c) A practitioner shall:

(1) Promptly notify a client of the receipt of the client's funds, securities, or other properties.

(2) Identify and label securities and properties of a client promptly upon receipt and place them

in a safe deposit box or other place of safekeeping as soon as practicable.

    (3)   Maintain complete records of all funds, securities, and other properties of a client coming into the possession of the practitioner and render appropriate accounts to the client regarding the funds, securities, or other properties.

    (4)   Promptly pay or deliver to the client as requested by a client the funds, securities, or other properties in the possession of the practitioner which the client is entitled to receive.

[Added 50 FR 5181, Feb. 6, 1985, effective Mar. 8, 1985; para. (a) revised, 70 FR 56119, Sept. 26, 2005, effective Nov. 25, 2005]

§ 10.113 - 10.170 [Reserved]

PART 11 — REPRESENTATION OF OTHERS BEFORE THE UNITED STATES PATENT AND TRADEMARK OFFICE

Subpart A—General Provisions

GENERAL INFORMATION

Sec.

11.1   Definitions.
11.2   Director of the Office of Enrollment and Discipline.
11.3   Suspension of rules.

Subpart B—Recognition To Practice Before the USPTO

PATENTS, TRADEMARKS, AND OTHER NON-PATENT LAW

11.4   [Reserved]
11.5   Register of attorneys and agents in patent matters; practice before the office.
11.6   Registration of attorneys and agents.
11.7   Requirements for registration.
11.8   Oath and registration fee.
11.9   Limited recognition in patent matters.
11.10   Restrictions on practice in patent matters.
11.11   Administrative suspension, inactivation, resignation, and readmission.
11.12 - 11.13 [Reserved]
11.14   Individuals who may practice before the Office in trademarks and other non-patent matters.
11.15   Refusal to recognize a practitioner.
11.16 - 11.17 [Reserved]
11.18   Signature and certificate for correspondence filed in the Office.

Subpart C—Investigations and Disciplinary Proceedings, Jurisdiction, Sanctions, Investigations, Proceedings

11.19   Disciplinary jurisdiction; Jurisdiction to transfer to disability inactive status.
11.20   Disciplinary sanctions; Transfer to disability inactive status.
11.21   Warnings.
11.22   Investigations.
11.23   Committee on Discipline.
11.24   Reciprocal discipline.
11.25   Interim suspension and discipline based upon conviction of committing a serious crime.
11.26   Settlement.
11.27   Exclusion on consent.
11.28   Incapacitated practitioners in a disciplinary proceeding.
11.29   Reciprocal transfer or initial transfer to disability inactive status.
11.30-11.31 [Reserved]
11.32   Initiating a disciplinary proceeding.
11.33   [Reserved]
11.34   Complaint.
11.35   Service of complaint.
11.36   Answer to complaint.
11.37   [Reserved]
11.38   Contested case.
11.39   Hearing officer; appointment; responsibilities; review of interlocutory orders; stays.
11.40   Representative for OED Director or respondent.
11.41   Filing of papers.
11.42   Service of papers.
11.43   Motions.
11.44   Hearings.
11.45   Amendment of pleadings.
11.46-11.48 [Reserved]

11.49 Burden of proof.

11.50 Evidence.

11.51 Depositions.

11.52 Discovery.

11.53 Proposed findings and conclusions; post-hearing memorandum.

11.54 Initial decision of hearing officer.

11.55 Appeal to the USPTO Director.

11.56 Decision of the USPTO Director.

11.57 Review of final decision of the USPTO Director.

11.58 Duties of disciplined or resigned practitioner.

11.59 Dissemination of disciplinary and other information.

11.60 Petition for reinstatement.

11.61 Savings clause.

11.62-11.99 [Reserved]

Subpart A — General Provisions

GENERAL INFORMATION

§ 11.1 Definitions.

This part governs solely the practice of patent, trademark, and other law before the United States Patent and Trademark Office. Nothing in this part shall be construed to preempt the authority of each State to regulate the practice of law, except to the extent necessary for the United States Patent and Trademark Office to accomplish its Federal objectives. Unless otherwise clear from the context, the following definitions apply to this part:

Attorney or *lawyer* means an individual who is a member in good standing of the highest court of any State, including an individual who is in good standing of the highest court of one State and not under an order of any court or Federal agency suspending, enjoining, restraining, disbarring or otherwise restricting the attorney from practice before the bar of another State or Federal agency. A *non-lawyer* means a person who is not an attorney or lawyer.

Belief or *believes* means that the person involved actually supposed the fact in question to be true. A person's belief may be inferred from circumstances.

Conviction or *convicted* means any confession to a crime; a verdict or judgment finding a person guilty of a crime; any entered plea, including *nolo contendre* or Alford plea, to a crime; or receipt of deferred adjudication (whether judgment or sentence has been entered or not) for an accused or pled crime.

Crime means any offense declared to be a felony or misdemeanor by Federal or State law in the jurisdiction where the act occurs.

Data sheet means a form used to collect the name, address, and telephone information from individuals recognized to practice before the Office in patent matters.

Disqualified means any action that prohibits a practitioner from participating in or appearing before the program or agency, regardless of how long the prohibition lasts or the specific terminology used.

Federal agency means any authority of the executive branch of the Government of the United States.

Federal program means any program established by an Act of Congress or administered by a Federal agency.

Fiscal year means the time period from October 1st through the ensuing September 30th.

Fraud or *fraudulent* means conduct having a purpose to deceive and not merely negligent misrepresentation or failure to apprise another of relevant information.

Good moral character and reputation means the possession of honesty and truthfulness, trustworthiness and reliability, and a professional commitment to the legal process and the administration of justice, as well as the condition of being regarded as possessing such qualities.

Knowingly, known, or *knows* means actual knowledge of the fact in question. A person's knowledge may be inferred from circumstances.

Mandatory Disciplinary Rule is a rule identified in § 10.20(b) of this chapter as a Disciplinary Rule.

Matter means any litigation, administrative proceeding, lobbying activity, application, claim, investigation, controversy, arrest, charge, accusation, contract, negotiation, estate or family relations practice issue, request for a ruling or other determination, or any other matter covered by the conflict of interest rules of the appropriate Government entity.

OED means the Office of Enrollment and Discipline.

OED Director means the Director of the Office of Enrollment and Discipline.

OED Director's representatives means attorneys within the USPTO Office of General Counsel who act as representatives of the OED Director.

Office means the United States Patent and Trademark Office.

Practitioner means:

(1) An attorney or agent registered to practice before the Office in patent matters,

(2) An individual authorized under 5 U.S.C. 500(b) or otherwise as provided by § 10.14(b), (c), and (e) of this subchapter, to practice before the Office in trademark matters or other non-patent matters, or

(3) An individual authorized to practice before the Office in a patent case or matters under § 11.9(a) or (b).

Proceeding before the Office means an application for patent, an application for reissue, a reexamination, a protest, a public use matter, an *inter partes* patent matter, correction of a patent, correction of inventorship, an application to register a trademark, an *inter partes* trademark matter, an appeal, a petition, and any other matter that is pending before the Office.

Reasonable or *reasonably* when used in relation to conduct by a practitioner means the conduct of a reasonably prudent and competent practitioner.

Registration means registration to practice before the Office in patent proceedings.

Roster means a list of individuals who have been registered as either a patent attorney or patent agent.

Serious crime means:

(1) Any criminal offense classified as a felony under the laws of the United States, any state or any foreign country where the crime occurred; or

(2) Any crime a necessary element of which, as determined by the statutory or common law definition of such crime in the jurisdiction where the crime occurred, includes interference with the administration of justice, false swearing, misrepresentation, fraud, willful failure to file income tax returns, deceit, bribery, extortion, misappropriation, theft, or an attempt or a conspiracy or solicitation of another to commit a "serious crime."

Significant evidence of rehabilitation means satisfactory evidence that is significantly more probable than not that there will be no recurrence in the foreseeable future of the practitioner's prior disability or addiction.

State means any of the 50 states of the United States of America, the District of Columbia, and any Commonwealth or territory of the United States of America.

Substantial when used in reference to degree or extent means a material matter of clear and weighty importance.

Suspend or *suspension* means a temporary debarring from practice before the Office or other jurisdiction.

United States means the United States of America, and the territories and possessions the United States of America.

USPTO Director means the Director of the United States Patent and Trademark Office, or an employee of the Office delegated authority to act for the Director of the United States Patent and Trademark Office in matters arising under this part.

[Added, 69 FR 35427, June 24, 2004, effective July 26, 2004; revised, 73 FR 47650, Aug. 14, 2008, effective Sept. 15, 2008]

§ 11.2   Director of the Office of Enrollment and Discipline.

(a) *Appointment.* The USPTO Director shall appoint a Director of the Office of Enrollment and Discipline (OED Director). In the event of a vacancy in the office of the OED Director, the USPTO Director may designate an employee of the Office to serve as acting OED Director. The OED Director shall be an active member in good standing of the bar of the highest court of a State.

(b) *Duties.* The OED Director shall:

(1) Supervise staff as may be necessary for the performance of the OED Director's duties.

(2) Receive and act upon applications for registration, prepare and grade the examination provided for in § 11.7(b), maintain the register provided for in § 11.5, and perform such other duties in connection with enrollment and recognition of attorneys and agents as may be necessary.

(3) Conduct investigations into the moral character and reputation of any individual seeking to be registered as an attorney or agent, or of any individual seeking limited recognition, deny registration or recognition of individuals failing to demonstrate possession of good moral character and reputation, and perform such other duties in connection with enrollment matters and investigations as may be necessary.

(4) Conduct investigations of matters involving possible grounds for discipline of practitioners coming to the attention of the OED Director. Except in matters meriting summary dismissal, no disposition under § 11.22(h) shall be recommended or undertaken by the OED Director until the accused practitioner shall have been afforded an opportunity to respond to a reasonable inquiry by the OED Director.

(5) With the consent of a panel of three members of the Committee on Discipline, initiate disciplinary proceedings under § 11.32 and perform such other duties in connection with investigations and disciplinary proceedings as may be necessary.

(6) Oversee the preliminary screening of information and close investigations as provided for in § 11.22.

(7) [Reserved]

(c) *Petition to OED Director regarding enrollment or recognition.* Any petition from any action or requirement of the staff of OED reporting to the OED Director shall be taken to the OED Director accompanied by payment of the fee set forth in § 1.21(a)(5)(i) of this chapter. Any such petition not filed within sixty days from the mailing date of the action or notice from which relief is requested will be dismissed as untimely. The filing of a petition will neither stay the period for taking other action which may be running, nor stay other proceedings. The petitioner may file a single request for reconsideration of a decision within thirty days of the date of the decision. Filing a request for reconsideration stays the period for seeking review of the OED Director's decision until a final decision on the request for reconsideration is issued. A final decision by the OED Director may be reviewed in accordance with the provisions of paragraph (d) of this section.

(d) *Review of OED Director's decision regarding enrollment or recognition.* A party dissatisfied with a final decision of the OED Director regarding enrollment or recognition may seek review of the decision upon petition to the USPTO Director accompanied by payment of the fee set forth in § 1.21(a)(5)(ii) of this chapter. Any such petition to the USPTO Director waives a right to seek reconsideration from the OED Director. Any petition not filed within thirty days after the final decision of the OED Director may be dismissed as untimely. Briefs or memoranda, if any, in support of the petition shall accompany the petition. The petition will be decided on the basis of the record made before the OED Director. The USPTO Director in deciding the petition will consider no new evidence. Copies of documents already of record before the OED Director shall not be submitted with the petition. An oral hearing will not be granted except when considered necessary by the USPTO Director. Any request for reconsideration of the decision of the USPTO Director may be dismissed as untimely if not filed within thirty days after the date of said decision.

(e) *Petition to USPTO Director in disciplinary matters.* Petition may be taken to the USPTO Director to invoke the supervisory authority of the USPTO Director in appropriate circumstances in disciplinary matters. Any such petition must contain a statement of the facts involved and the point or points to be reviewed and the action requested. Briefs or memoranda, if any, in support of the petition must accompany the petition. Where facts are to be proven, the proof in the form of affidavits or declarations (and exhibits, if any) must accompany the petition. The OED Director may be directed by the USPTO Director to file a reply to the petition, supplying a copy to the petitioner. An oral hearing will not be granted except when considered necessary by the USPTO Director. The mere filing of a petition will not stay an investigation, disciplinary proceeding or other proceedings. Any petition under this part not filed within thirty days of the mailing date of the action or notice from which relief is requested may be dismissed as untimely. Any request for reconsideration of the decision of the USPTO Director may be dismissed as untimely if not filed within thirty days after the date of said decision.

[Added, 69 FR 35427, June 24, 2004, effective July 26, 2004; paras. (a), (b)(4), (c) and (d) revised, paras. (b)(5), (b)(6) and (e) added, 73 FR 47650, Aug. 14, 2008, effective Sept. 15, 2008]

§ 11.3 Suspension of rules.

(a) In an extraordinary situation, when justice requires, any requirement of the regulations of this Part which is not a requirement of statute may be suspended or waived by the USPTO Director or the designee of the USPTO Director, *sua sponte*, or on petition by any party, including the OED Director or the OED Director's representative, subject to such other requirements as may be imposed.

(b)   No petition under this section shall stay a disciplinary proceeding unless ordered by the USPTO Director or a hearing officer.

[Added, 69 FR 35427, June 24, 2004, effective July 26, 2004; revised, 73 FR 47650, Aug. 14, 2008, effective Sept. 15, 2008]

Subpart B — Recognition To Practice Before the USPTO

PATENTS, TRADEMARKS, AND OTHER NON-PATENT LAW

§ 11.4   [Reserved]

[Reserved, 69 FR 35427, June 24, 2004, effective July 26, 2004]

§ 11.5   Register of attorneys and agents in patent matters; practice before the office.

(a)   A register of attorneys and agents is kept in the Office on which are entered the names of all individuals recognized as entitled to represent applicants having prospective or immediate business before the Office in the preparation and prosecution of patent applications. Registration in the Office under the provisions of this part shall entitle the individuals so registered to practice before the Office only in patent matters.

(b)   *Practice before the Office.* Practice before the Office includes, but is not limited to, law-related service that comprehends any matter connected with the presentation to the Office or any of its officers or employees relating to a client's rights, privileges, duties, or responsibilities under the laws or regulations administered by the Office for the grant of a patent or registration of a trademark, or for enrollment or disciplinary matters. Such presentations include preparing necessary documents in contemplation of filing the documents with the Office, corresponding and communicating with the Office, and representing a client through documents or at interviews, hearings, and meetings, as well as communicating with and advising a client concerning matters pending or contemplated to be presented before the Office. Nothing in this section proscribes a practitioner from employ-

ing or retaining non-practitioner assistants under the supervision of the practitioner to assist the practitioner in matters pending or contemplated to be presented before the Office.

(1)   *Practice before the Office in patent matters.* Practice before the Office in patent matters includes, but is not limited to, preparing and prosecuting any patent application, consulting with or giving advice to a client in contemplation of filing a patent application or other document with the Office, drafting the specification or claims of a patent application; drafting an amendment or reply to a communication from the Office that may require written argument to establish the patentability of a claimed invention; drafting a reply to a communication from the Office regarding a patent application; and drafting a communication for a public use, interference, reexamination proceeding, petition, appeal to or any other proceeding before the Board of Patent Appeals and Interferences, or other proceeding. Registration to practice before the Office in patent cases sanctions the performance of those services which are reasonably necessary and incident to the preparation and prosecution of patent applications or other proceeding before the Office involving a patent application or patent in which the practitioner is authorized to participate. The services include:

(i)   Considering the advisability of relying upon alternative forms of protection which may be available under state law, and

(ii)   Drafting an assignment or causing an assignment to be executed for the patent owner in contemplation of filing or prosecution of a patent application for the patent owner, where the practitioner represents the patent owner after a patent issues in a proceeding before the Office, and when drafting the assignment the practitioner does no more than replicate the terms of a previously existing oral or written obligation of assignment from one person or party to another person or party.

(2)   *Practice before the Office in trademark matters.* Practice before the Office in trademark matters includes, but is not limited to, consulting with or giving advice to a client in contemplation of filing a trademark application or other document with the Office; preparing and prosecuting an application for trademark registration; preparing an amendment which may require written argument to establish the

registrability of the mark; and conducting an opposition, cancellation, or concurrent use proceeding; or conducting an appeal to the Trademark Trial and Appeal Board.

[Added, 69 FR 35427, June 24, 2004, effective July 26, 2004; revised, 73 FR 47650, Aug. 14, 2008, effective Sept. 15, 2008]

§ 11.6   Registration of attorneys and agents.

(a)   *Attorneys.* Any citizen of the United States who is an attorney and who fulfills the requirements of this part may be registered as a patent attorney to practice before the Office. When appropriate, any alien who is an attorney, who lawfully resides in the United States, and who fulfills the requirements of this part may be registered as a patent attorney to practice before the Office, provided that such registration is not inconsistent with the terms upon which the alien was admitted to, and resides in, the United States and further provided that the alien may remain registered only:

(1)   If the alien continues to lawfully reside in the United States and registration does not become inconsistent with the terms upon which the alien continues to lawfully reside in the United States, or

(2)   If the alien ceases to reside in the United States, the alien is qualified to be registered under paragraph (c) of this section. See also § 11.9(b).

(b)   *Agents.* Any citizen of the United States who is not an attorney, and who fulfills the requirements of this part may be registered as a patent agent to practice before the Office. When appropriate, any alien who is not an attorney, who lawfully resides in the United States, and who fulfills the requirements of this part may be registered as a patent agent to practice before the Office, provided that such registration is not inconsistent with the terms upon which the alien was admitted to, and resides in, the United States, and further provided that the alien may remain registered only:

(1)   If the alien continues to lawfully reside in the United States and registration does not become inconsistent with the terms upon which the alien continues to lawfully reside in the United States or

(2)   If the alien ceases to reside in the United States, the alien is qualified to be registered under paragraph (c) of this section. See also § 11.9(b).

(c)   *Foreigners.* Any foreigner not a resident of the United States who shall file proof to the satisfaction of the OED Director that he or she is registered and in good standing before the patent office of the country in which he or she resides and practices, and who is possessed of the qualifications stated in § 11.7, may be registered as a patent agent to practice before the Office for the limited purpose of presenting and prosecuting patent applications of applicants located in such country, provided that the patent office of such country allows substantially reciprocal privileges to those admitted to practice before the Office. Registration as a patent agent under this paragraph shall continue only during the period that the conditions specified in this paragraph obtain. Upon notice by the patent office of such country that a patent agent registered under this section is no longer registered or no longer in good standing before the patent office of such country, and absent a showing of cause why his or her name should not be removed from the register, the OED Director shall promptly remove the name of the patent agent from the register and publish the fact of removal. Upon ceasing to reside in such country, the patent agent registered under this section is no longer qualified to be registered under this section, and the OED Director shall promptly remove the name of the patent agent from the register and publish the fact of removal.

(d)   *Board of Patent Appeals and Interferences matters.* For action by a person who is not registered in a proceeding before the Board of Patent Appeals and Interferences, see § 41.5(a) of this title.

[Added, 69 FR 35427, June 24, 2004, effective July 26, 2004; para. (d) revised, 69 FR 49959, Aug. 12, 2004, effective Sept. 13, 2004]

§ 11.7   Requirements for registration.

(a)   No individual will be registered to practice before the Office unless he or she has:

(1)   Applied to the USPTO Director in writing by completing an application for registration form supplied by the OED Director and furnishing all requested information and material; and

(2)   Established to the satisfaction of the OED Director that he or she:

(i)   Possesses good moral character and reputation;

(ii) Possesses the legal, scientific, and technical qualifications necessary for him or her to render applicants valuable service; and

(iii) Is competent to advise and assist patent applicants in the presentation and prosecution of their applications before the Office.

(b)(1) To enable the OED Director to determine whether an individual has the qualifications specified in paragraph (a)(2) of this section, the individual shall:

(i) File a complete application for registration each time admission to the registration examination is requested. A complete application for registration includes:

(A) An application for registration form supplied by the OED Director wherein all requested information and supporting documents are furnished,

(B) Payment of the fees required by § 1.21(a)(1) of this subchapter,

(C) Satisfactory proof of scientific and technical qualifications, and

(D) For aliens, provide proof that recognition is not inconsistent with the terms of their visa or entry into the United States;

(ii) Pass the registration examination, unless the taking and passing of the examination is waived as provided in paragraph (d) of this section. Unless examination is waived pursuant to paragraph (d) of this section, each individual seeking registration must take and pass the registration examination to enable the OED Director to determine whether the individual possesses the legal and competence qualifications specified in paragraphs (a)(2)(ii) and (a)(2)(iii) of this section. An individual failing the examination may, upon receipt of notice of failure from OED, reapply for admission to the examination. An individual failing the examination must wait thirty days after the date the individual last took the examination before retaking the examination. An individual reapplying shall:

(A) File a completed application for registration form wherein all requested information and supporting documents are furnished,

(B) Pay the fees required by § 1.21 (a)(1) of this subchapter, and

(C) For aliens, provide proof that recognition is not inconsistent with the terms of their visa or entry into the United States; and

(iii) Provide satisfactory proof of possession of good moral character and reputation.

(2) An individual failing to file a complete application for registration will not be admitted to the examination and will be notified of the incompleteness. Applications for registration that are incomplete as originally submitted will be considered only when they have been completed and received by OED, provided that this occurs within sixty days of the mailing date of the notice of incompleteness. Thereafter, a new and complete application for registration must be filed. Only an individual approved as satisfying the requirements of paragraphs (b)(1)(i)(A), (b)(1)(i)(B), (b)(1)(i)(C) and (b)(1)(i)(D) of this sect i on may be admitted to the examination.

(3) If an individual does not reapply until more than one year after the mailing date of a notice of failure, that individual must again comply with paragraph (b)(1)(i) of this section.

(c) Each individual seeking registration is responsible for updating all information and answers submitted in or with the application for registration based upon anything occurring between the date the application for registration is signed by the individual, and the date he or she is registered or recognized to practice before the Office in patent matters. The update shall be filed within thirty days after the date of the occasion that necessitates the update.

(d) *Waiver of the Registration Examination for Former Office Employees.* (1) *Former patent examiners who by July 26, 2004, had not actively served four years in the patent examining corps, and were serving in the corps at the time of their separation.* The OED Director may waive the taking of a registration examination in the case of any individual meeting the requirements of paragraph (b)(1)(i)(C) of this section who is a former patent examiner but by July 26, 2004, had not served four years in the patent examining corps, if the individual demonstrates that he or she:

(i) Actively served in the patent examining corps of the Office and was serving in the corps at the time of separation from the Office,

(ii) Received a certificate of legal competency and negotiation authority;

(iii) After receiving the certificate of legal competency and negotiation authority, was rated at least fully successful in each quality performance element of his or her performance plan for the last two complete fiscal years as a patent examiner; and

(iv) Was not under an oral or written warning regarding the quality performance elements at the time of separation from the patent examining corps.

(2) *Former patent examiners who on July 26, 2004, had actively served four years in the patent examining corps, and were serving in the corps at the time of their separation.* The OED Director may waive the taking of a registration examination in the case of any individual meeting the requirements of paragraph (b)(1)(i)(C) of this section who is a former patent examiner and by July 26, 2004, had served four years in the patent examining corps, if the individual demonstrates that he or she:

(i) Actively served for at least four years in the patent examining corps of the Office by July 26, 2004, and was serving in the corps at the time of separation from the Office;

(ii) Was rated at least fully successful in each quality performance element of his or her performance plan for the last two complete fiscal years as a patent examiner in the Office; and

(iii) Was not under an oral or written warning regarding the quality performance elements at the time of separation from the patent examining corps.

(3) *Certain former Office employees who were not serving in the patent examining corps upon their separation from the Office.* The OED Director may waive the taking of a registration examination in the case of a former Office employee meeting the requirements of paragraph (b)(1)(i)(C) of this section who by petition demonstrates possession of the necessary legal qualifications to render to patent applicants and others valuable service and assistance in the preparation and prosecution of their applications or other business before the Office by showing that he or she has:

(i) Exhibited comprehensive knowledge of patent law equivalent to that shown by passing the registration examination as a result of having been in a position of responsibility in the Office in which he or she:

(A) Provided substantial guidance on patent examination policy, including the development of rule or procedure changes, patent examination guidelines, changes to the Manual of Patent Examining Procedure, development of training or testing materials for the patent examining corps, or development of materials for the registration examination or continuing legal education; or

(B) Represented the Office in patent cases before Federal courts; and

(ii) Was rated at least fully successful in each quality performance element of his or her performance plan for said position for the last two complete rating periods in the Office, and was not under an oral or written warning regarding such performance elements at the time of separation from the Office.

(4) To be eligible for consideration for waiver, an individual formerly employed by the Office within the scope of one of paragraphs (d)(1), (d)(2) or (d)(3) of this section must file a complete application for registration and pay the fee required by § 1.21(a)(1)(i) of this subchapter within two years of the individual's date of separation from the Office. All other individuals formerly employed by the Office, including former examiners, filing an application for registration or fee more than two years after separation from the Office, are required to take and pass the registration examination. The individual or former examiner must pay the examination fee required by § 1.21(a)(1)(ii) of this subchapter within thirty days after notice of non-waiver.

(e) *Examination results.* Notification of the examination results is final. Within sixty days of the mailing date of a notice of failure, the individual is entitled to inspect, but not copy, the questions and answers he or she incorrectly answered. Review will be under supervision. No notes may be taken during such review. Substantive review of the answers or questions may not be pursued by petition for regrade. An individual who failed the examination has the right to retake the examination an unlimited number of times upon payment of the fees required by § 1.21 (a)(1)(i) and (ii) of this subchapter, and a fee charged by a commercial entity administering the examination.

(f) *Application for reciprocal recognition.* An individual seeking reciprocal recognition under § 11.6 (c), in addition to satisfying the provisions of paragraphs (a) and (b) of this section, and the provisions of § 11.8(c), shall pay the application fee required by § 1.21(a)(1)(i) of this subchapter upon filing an application for registration.

(g) *Investigation of good moral character and reputation.* (1) Every individual seeking recognition shall answer all questions in the application for registration and request(s) for comments issued by OED; disclose all relevant facts, dates and information; and provide verified copies of documents relevant to his or her good moral character and reputation. An individual who is an attorney shall submit a certified copy of each of his or her State bar applications and moral character determinations, if available.

(2)(i) If the OED Director receives information from any source that reflects adversely on the good moral character or reputation of an individual seeking registration or recognition, the OED Director shall conduct an investigation into the good moral character and reputation of that individual. The investigation will be conducted after the individual has passed the registration examination, or after the registration examination has been waived for the individual, as applicable. An individual failing to timely answer questions or respond to an inquiry by OED shall be deemed to have withdrawn his or her application, and shall be required to reapply, pass the examination, and otherwise satisfy all the requirements of this section. No individual shall be certified for registration or recognition by the OED Director until, to the satisfaction of the OED Director, the individual demonstrates his or her possession of good moral character and reputation.

(ii) The OED Director, in considering an application for registration by an attorney, may accept a State bar's character determination as meeting the requirements set forth in paragraph (g) of this section if, after review, the Office finds no substantial discrepancy between the information provided with his or her application for registration and the State bar application and moral character determination, provided that acceptance is not inconsistent with other rules and the requirements of 35 U.S.C. 2(b)(2)(D).

(h) *Good moral character and reputation.* Evidence showing lack of good moral character and reputation may include, but is not limited to, conviction of a felony or a misdemeanor identified in paragraph (h)(1) of this section, drug or alcohol abuse; lack of candor; suspension or disbarment on ethical grounds from a State bar; and resignation from a State bar while under investigation.

(1) *Conviction of felony or misdemeanor.* An individual who has been convicted of a felony or a misdemeanor involving moral turpitude, breach of trust, interference with the administration of justice, false swearing, misrepresentation, fraud, deceit, bribery, extortion, misappropriation, theft, or conspiracy to commit any felony or misdemeanor, is presumed not to be of good moral character and reputation in the absence of a pardon or a satisfactory showing of reform and rehabilitation, and shall file with his or her application for registration the fees required by § 1.21(a)(1)(ii) and (a)(10) of this subchapter. The OED Director shall determine whether individuals convicted of said felony or misdemeanor provided satisfactory proof of reform and rehabilitation.

(i) An individual who has been convicted of a felony or a misdemeanor identified in paragraph (h)(1) of this section shall not be eligible to apply for registration during the time of any sentence (including confinement or commitment to imprisonment), deferred adjudication, and period of probation or parole as a result of the conviction, and for a period of two years after the date of completion of the sentence, deferred adjudication, and period of probation or parole, whichever is later.

(ii) The following presumptions apply to the determination of good moral character and reputation of an individual convicted of said felony or misdemeanor:

(A) The court record or docket entry of conviction is conclusive evidence of guilt in the absence of a pardon or a satisfactory showing of reform or rehabilitation; and

(B) An individual convicted of a felony or any misdemeanor identified in paragraph (h)(1) of this section is conclusively deemed not to have good moral character and reputation, and shall not be eligible to apply for registration for a period of two years after completion of the sentence, deferred adjudication, and period of probation or parole, whichever is later.

(iii) The individual, upon applying for registration, shall provide satisfactory evidence that he or she is of good moral character and reputation.

(iv) Upon proof that a conviction has been set aside or reversed, the individual shall be eligible to file a complete application for registration and the fee required by § 1.21(a)(1)(ii) of this subchapter and, upon passing the registration examination, have the OED Director determine, in accordance with paragraph (h)(1) of this section, whether, absent the conviction, the individual possesses good moral character and reputation.

(2) *Good moral character and reputation involving drug or alcohol abuse.* An individual's record is reviewed as a whole to see if there is a drug or alcohol abuse issue. An individual appearing to abuse drugs or alcohol may be asked to undergo an evaluation, at the individual's expense, by a qualified professional approved by the OED Director. In instances where, before an investigation commences, there is evidence of a present abuse or an individual has not established a record of recovery, the OED Director may request the individual to withdraw his or her application, and require the individual to satisfactorily demonstrate that he or she is complying with treatment and undergoing recovery.

(3) *Moral character and reputation involving lack of candor.* An individual's lack of candor in disclosing facts bearing on or relevant to issues concerning good moral character and reputation when completing the application or any time thereafter may be found to be cause to deny registration on moral character and reputation grounds.

(4) *Moral character and reputation involving suspension, disbarment, or resignation from a profession.* (i) An individual who has been disbarred or suspended from practice of law or other profession, or has resigned in lieu of a disciplinary proceeding (excluded or disbarred on consent) shall be ineligible to apply for registration as follows:

(A) An individual who has been disbarred from practice of law or other profession, or has resigned in lieu of a disciplinary proceeding (excluded or disbarred on consent) shall be ineligible to apply for registration for a period of five years from the date of disbarment or resignation.

(B) An individual who has been suspended on ethical grounds from the practice of law or other profession shall be ineligible to apply for registration until expiration of the period of suspension.

(C) An individual who was not only disbarred, suspended or resigned in lieu of a disciplinary proceeding, but also convicted in a court of a felony, or of a crime involving moral turpitude or breach of trust, shall be ineligible to apply for registration until

the conditions in paragraphs (h)(1) and (h)(4) of this section are fully satisfied.

(ii) An individual who has been disbarred or suspended, or who resigned in lieu of a disciplinary proceeding shall file an application for registration and the fees required by § 1.21(a)(1)(ii) and (a)(10) of this subchapter; provide a full and complete copy of the proceedings that led to the disbarment, suspension, or resignation; and provide satisfactory proof that he or she possesses good moral character and reputation. The following presumptions shall govern the determination of good moral character and reputation of an individual who has been licensed to practice law or other profession in any jurisdiction and has been disbarred, suspended on ethical grounds, or allowed to resign in lieu of discipline, in that jurisdiction.

(A) A copy of the record resulting in disbarment, suspension or resignation is *prima facie* evidence of the matters contained in the record, and the imposition of disbarment or suspension, or the acceptance of the resignation of the individual shall be deemed conclusive that the individual has committed professional misconduct.

(B) The individual is ineligible for registration and is deemed not to have good moral character and reputation during the period of the imposed discipline.

(iii) The only defenses available with regard to an underlying disciplinary matter resulting in disbarment, suspension on ethical grounds, or resignation in lieu of a disciplinary proceeding are set out below, and must be shown to the satisfaction of the OED Director:

(A) The procedure in the disciplinary court was so lacking in notice or opportunity to be heard as to constitute a deprivation of due process;

(B) There was such infirmity of proof establishing the misconduct as to give rise to the clear conviction that the Office could not, consistently with its duty, accept as final the conclusion on that subject; or

(C) The finding of lack of good moral character and reputation by the Office would result in grave injustice.

(i) *Factors that may be taken into consideration when evaluating rehabilitation of an individual seeking a moral character and reputation determination.* The factors enumerated below are guidelines to assist the OED Director in determining whether an individual has demonstrated rehabilitation from an act of misconduct or moral turpitude. The factors include:

(1) The nature of the act of misconduct, including whether it involved moral turpitude, whether there were aggravating or mitigating circumstances, and whether the activity was an isolated event or part of a pattern;

(2) The age and education of the individual at the time of the misconduct and the age and education of the individual at the present time;

(3) The length of time that has passed between the misconduct and the present, absent any involvement in any further acts of moral turpitude, the amount of time and the extent of rehabilitation being dependent upon the nature and seriousness of the act of misconduct under consideration;

(4) Restitution by the individual to any person who suffered monetary losses through acts or omissions of the individual;

(5) Expungement of a conviction;

(6) Successful completion or early discharge from probation or parole;

(7) Abstinence from the use of controlled substances or alcohol for not less than two years if the specific misconduct was attributable in part to the use of a controlled substance or alcohol, where abstinence may be demonstrated by, but is not necessarily limited to, enrolling in and complying with a self-help or professional treatment program;

(8) If the specific misconduct was attributable in part to a medically recognized mental disease, disorder or illness, proof that the individual sought professional assistance, and complied with the treatment program prescribed by the professional, and submitted letters from the treating psychiatrist/psychologist verifying that the medically recognized mental disease, disorder or illness will not impede the individual's ability to competently practice before the Office;

(9) Payment of the fine imposed in connection with any criminal conviction;

(10) Correction of behavior responsible in some degree for the misconduct;

(11) Significant and conscientious involvement in programs designed to provide social benefits or to ameliorate social problems; and

(12) Change in attitude from that which existed at the time of the act of misconduct in question as evidenced by any or all of the following:

(i) Statements of the individual;

(ii) Statements from persons familiar with the individual's previous misconduct and with subsequent attitudes and behavioral patterns;

(iii) Statements from probation or parole officers or law enforcement officials as to the individual's social adjustments; and

(iv) Statements from persons competent to testify with regard to neuropsychiatry or emotional disturbances.

(j) *Notice to Show Cause.* The OED Director shall inquire into the good moral character and reputation of an individual seeking registration, providing the individual with the opportunity to create a record on which a decision is made. If, following inquiry and consideration of the record, the OED Director is of the opinion that the individual seeking registration has not satisfactorily established that he or she possesses good moral character and reputation, the OED Director shall issue to the individual a notice to show cause why the individual's application for registration should not be denied.

(1) The individual shall be given no less than ten days from the date of the notice to reply. The notice shall be given by certified mail at the address appearing on the application if the address is in the United States, and by any other reasonable means if the address is outside the United States.

(2) Following receipt of the individual's response, or in the absence of a response, the OED Director shall consider the individual's response, if any, and the record, and determine whether, in the OED Director's opinion, the individual has sustained his or her burden of satisfactorily demonstrating that he or she possesses good moral character and reputation.

(k) *Reapplication for registration.* An individual who has been refused registration for lack of good moral character or reputation may reapply for registration two years after the date of the decision, unless a shorter period is otherwise ordered by the USPTO Director. An individual, who has been notified that he or she is under investigation for good moral character and reputation may elect to withdraw his or her application for registration, and may reapply for registration two years after the date of withdrawal. Upon reapplication for registration, the individual shall pay the fees required by § 1.21(a)(1)(ii) and (a)(10) of this subchapter, and has the burden of showing to the satisfaction of the OED Director his or her possession of good moral character and reputation as prescribed in paragraph (b) of this section. Upon reapplication for registration, the individual also shall complete successfully the examination prescribed in paragraph (b) of this section, even though the individual has previously passed a registration examination.

[Added, 69 FR 35427, June 24, 2004, effective July 26, 2004]

§ 11.8 Oath and registration fee.

(a) After an individual passes the examination, or the examination is waived, the OED Director shall promptly publish a solicitation for information concerning the individual's good moral character and reputation. The solicitation shall include the individual's name, and business or communication postal address.

(b) An individual shall not be registered as an attorney under § 11.6(a), registered as an agent under § 11.6(b) or (c), or granted limited recognition under § 11.9(b) unless within two years of the mailing date of a notice of passing registration examination or of waiver of the examination the individual files with the OED Director a completed Data Sheet, an oath or declaration prescribed by the USPTO Director, and the registration fee set forth in § 1.21(a)(2) of this subchapter. An individual seeking registration as an attorney under § 11.6(a) must provide a certificate of good standing of the bar of the highest court of a State that is no more than six months old.

(c) An individual who does not comply with the requirements of paragraph (b) of this section within the two-year period will be required to retake the registration examination.

(d) *Annual practitioner maintenance fee.* A registered patent attorney or agent shall annually pay to the USPTO Director a practitioner maintenance fee in the amount set forth in § 1.21(a)(7) of this subchapter. Individuals granted limited recognition under paragraph (b) of § 11.9 shall annually pay to the USPTO Director a practitioner maintenance fee in the amount set forth in § 1.21(a)(8) of this subchapter. Adequate notice shall be published and sent to practitioners in advance of the due date for payment of the annual

practitioner maintenance fee. Payment shall be for the fiscal year in which the annual practitioner maintenance fee is assessed. Payment shall be due by the last day of the payment period. Persons newly registered or granted limited recognition shall not be liable for the annual practitioner maintenance fee during the fiscal year in which they are first registered or granted limited recognition. Failure to comply with the provisions of this paragraph (d) shall require the OED Director to subject a practitioner to a delinquency fee penalty set forth in § 11.11(b)(1), and further financial penalties and administrative suspension as set forth in § 11.11(b)(2) and (b)(3).

[Added, 69 FR 35427, June 24, 2004, effective July 26, 2004; para. (d) added, 73 FR 67750, Nov. 17, 2008, effective Dec. 17, 2008]

§ 11.9 Limited recognition in patent matters.

(a) Any individual not registered under § 11.6 may, upon a showing of circumstances which render it necessary or justifiable, and that the individual is of good moral character and reputation, be given limited recognition by the OED Director to prosecute as attorney or agent a specified patent application or specified patent applications. Limited recognition under this paragraph shall not extend further than the application or applications specified. Limited recognition shall not be granted while individuals who have passed the examination or for whom the examination has been waived are awaiting registration to practice before the Office in patent matters.

(b) A nonimmigrant alien residing in the United States and fulfilling the provisions of § 11.7(a) and (b) may be granted limited recognition if the nonimmigrant alien is authorized by the Bureau of Citizenship and Immigration Services to be employed or trained in the United States in the capacity of representing a patent applicant by presenting or prosecuting a patent application. Limited recognition shall be granted for a period consistent with the terms of authorized employment or training. Limited recognition shall not be granted or extended to a non-United States citizen residing abroad. If granted, limited recognition shall automatically expire upon the nonimmigrant alien's departure from the United States.

(c) An individual not registered under § 11.6 may, if appointed by an applicant, prosecute an international patent application only before the United

States International Searching Authority and the United States International Preliminary Examining Authority, provided that the individual has the right to practice before the national office with which the international application is filed as provided in PCT Art. 49, Rule 90 and § 1.455 of this subchapter, or before the International Bureau when the USPTO is acting as Receiving Office pursuant to PCT Rules 83.1*bis* and 90.1.

[Added, 69 FR 35427, June 24, 2004, effective July 26, 2004]

§ 11.10   Restrictions on practice in patent matters.

(a)   Only practitioners who are registered under § 11.6 or individuals given limited recognition under § 11.9(a) or (b) are permitted to prosecute patent applications of others before the Office; or represent others in any proceedings before the Office.

(b)   *Post employment agreement of former Office employee.* No individual who has served in the patent examining corps or elsewhere in the Office may practice before the Office after termination of his or her service, unless he or she signs a written undertaking agreeing:

(1)   To not knowingly act as agent or attorney for, or otherwise represent, or assist in any manner the representation of, any other person:

(i)   Before the Office,

(ii)   In connection with any particular patent or patent application,

(iii)   In which said employee participated personally and substantially as an employee of the Office; and

(2)   To not knowingly act within two years after terminating employment by the Office as agent or attorney for, or otherwise represent, or assist in any manner the representation of any other person:

(i)   Before the Office,

(ii)   In connection with any particular patent or patent application,

(iii)   If such patent or patent application was pending under the employee's official responsibility as an officer or employee within a period of one year prior to the termination of such responsibility.

(3)   The words and phrases in paragraphs (b)(1) and (b)(2) of this section are construed as follows:

(i)   *Represent* and *representation* mean acting as patent attorney or patent agent or other representative in any appearance before the Office, or communicating with an employee of the Office with intent to influence.

(ii)   *Assist in any manner* means aid or help another person on a particular patent or patent application involving representation.

(iii)   *Particular patent or patent application* means any patent or patent application, including, but not limited to, a provisional, substitute, international, continuation, divisional, continuation-in-part, or reissue patent application, as well as any protest, reexamination, petition, appeal, or interference based on the patent or patent application.

(iv)   *Participate personally and substantially.* (A) Basic requirements. The restrictions of § 11.10(a)(1) apply only to those patents and patent applications in which a former Office employee had "personal and substantial participation," exercised "through decision, approval, disapproval, recommendation, the rendering of advice, investigation or otherwise." To *participate personally* means directly, and includes the participation of a subordinate when actually directed by the former Office employee in the patent or patent application. *Substantially* means that the employee's involvement must be of significance to the matter, or form a basis for a reasonable appearance of such significance. It requires more than official responsibility, knowledge, perfunctory involvement, or involvement on an administrative or peripheral issue. A finding of substantiality should be based not only on the effort devoted to a patent or patent application, but also on the importance of the effort. While a series of peripheral involvements may be insubstantial, the single act of approving or participation in a critical step may be substantial. It is essential that the participation be related to a "particular patent or patent application." (*See* paragraph (b)(3)(iii) of this section.)

(B)   Participation on ancillary matters. An Office employee's participation on subjects not directly involving the substantive merits of a patent or patent application may not be "substantial," even if it is time-consuming. An employee whose official responsibility is the review of a patent or patent application solely for compliance with administrative control or budgetary considerations and who reviews a particular patent or patent application for such a purpose should not be regarded as having participated substantially in the patent or patent application, except when such considerations also are the subject of the employee's proposed representation.

(C) Role of official responsibility in determining substantial participation. *Official responsibility* is defined in paragraph (b)(3)(v) of this section. "Personal and substantial participation" is different from "official responsibility." One's responsibility may, however, play a role in determining the "substantiality" of an Office employee's participation.

(v) *Official responsibility* means the direct administrative or operating authority, whether intermediate or final, and either exercisable alone or with others, and either personally or through subordinates, to approve, disapprove, or otherwise direct Government actions.

(A) Determining official responsibility. Ordinarily, those areas assigned by statute, regulation, Executive Order, job description, or delegation of authority determine the scope of an employee's "official responsibility". All particular matters under consideration in the Office are under the "official responsibility" of the Director of the Office, and each is under that of any intermediate supervisor having responsibility for an employee who actually participates in the patent or patent application within the scope of his or her duties. A patent examiner would have "official responsibility" for the patent applications assigned to him or her.

(B) Ancillary matters and official responsibility. *Administrative* authority as used in paragraph (v) of this section means authority for planning, organizing and controlling a patent or patent application rather than authority to review or make decisions on ancillary aspects of a patent or patent application such as the regularity of budgeting procedures, public or community relations aspects, or equal employment opportunity considerations. Responsibility for such an ancillary consideration does not constitute official responsibility for the particular patent or patent application, except when such a consideration is also the subject of the employee's proposed representation.

(C) Duty to inquire. In order for a former employee, *e.g.*, former patent examiner, to be barred from representing or assisting in representing another

as to a particular patent or patent application, he or she need not have known, while employed by the Office, that the patent or patent application was pending under his or her official responsibility. The former employee has a reasonable duty of inquiry to learn whether the patent or patent application had been under his or her official responsibility. Ordinarily, a former employee who is asked to represent another on a patent or patent application will become aware of facts sufficient to suggest the relationship of the prior matter to his or her former office, *e.g.*, technology center, group or art unit. If so, he or she is under a duty to make further inquiry. It would be prudent for an employee to maintain a record of only patent application numbers of the applications actually acted upon by decision or recommendation, as well as those applications under the employee's official responsibility which he or she has not acted upon.

(D) Self-disqualification. A former employee, *e.g.*, former patent examiner, cannot avoid the restrictions of this section through self-disqualification with respect to a patent or patent application for which he or she otherwise had official responsibility. However, an employee who through self-disqualification does not participate personally and substantially in a particular patent or patent application is not subject to the lifetime restriction of paragraph (b)(1) of this section.

(vi) *Pending* means that the matter was in fact referred to or under consideration by persons within the employee's area of official responsibility.

(4) Measurement of the two-year restriction period. The two-year period under paragraph (b)(2) of this section is measured from the date when the employee's official responsibility in a particular area ends, not from the termination of service in the Office, unless the two occur simultaneously. The prohibition applies to all particular patents or patent applications subject to such official responsibility in the one-year period before termination of such responsibility.

(c) *Former employees of the Office.* This section imposes restrictions generally parallel to those imposed in 18 U.S.C. 207(a) and (b)(1). This section, however, does not interpret these statutory provisions or any other post-employment restrictions that may apply to former Office employees, and such former employees should not assume that conduct not prohibited by this section is otherwise permissible.

Former employees of the Office, whether or not they are practitioners, are encouraged to contact the Department of Commerce for information concerning applicable post-employment restrictions.

(d) An employee of the Office may not prosecute or aid in any manner in the prosecution of any patent application before the Office.

(e) Practice before the Office by Government employees is subject to any applicable conflict of interest laws, regulations or codes of professional responsibility.

[Added, 69 FR 35427, June 24, 2004, effective July 26, 2004]

§ 11.11 Administrative suspension, inactivation, resignation, and readmission.

(a) A registered attorney or agent must notify the OED Director of his or her postal address for his or her office, up to three e-mail addresses where he or she receives e-mail, and business telephone number, as well as every change to any of said addresses or telephone numbers within thirty days of the date of the change. A registered attorney or agent shall, in addition to any notice of change of address and telephone number filed in individual patent applications, separately file written notice of the change of address or telephone number to the OED Director. A registered practitioner who is an attorney in good standing with the bar of the highest court of one or more States shall provide the OED Director with the State bar identification number associated with each membership. The OED Director shall publish from the roster a list containing the name, postal business addresses, business telephone number, registration number, and registration status as an attorney or agent of each registered practitioner recognized to practice before the Office in patent cases.

(b) *Administrative suspension.* (1) Whenever it appears that a registered patent attorney, a registered patent agent or a person granted limited recognition under § 11.9(b) has failed to comply with § 11.8(d), the OED Director shall publish and send a notice to the attorney, agent or person granted limited recognition advising of the noncompliance, the consequence of being administratively suspended under paragraph (b)(5) of this section if noncompliance is not timely remedied, and the requirements for reinstatement under paragraph (f) of this section. The notice shall be published and sent to the attorney, agent or person granted limited recognition by mail to the last postal address furnished under paragraph (a) of this section or by e-mail addressed to the last e-mail addresses furnished under paragraph (a) of this section. The notice shall demand compliance and payment of a delinquency fee set forth in § 1.21(a)(9)(i) of this subchapter within sixty days after the date of such notice.

(2) In the event a registered patent attorney, registered patent agent or person granted limited recognition fails to comply with the notice of paragraph (b)(1) of this section within the time allowed, the OED Director shall publish and send in the manner provided for in paragraph (b)(1) of this section to the attorney, agent, or person granted limited recognition a Rule to Show Cause why his or her registration or recognition should not be administratively suspended, and he or she no longer be permitted to practice before the Office in patent matters or in any way hold himself or herself out as being registered or authorized to practice before the Office in patent matters. The OED Director shall file a copy of the Rule to Show Cause with the USPTO Director.

(3) Within 30 days of the OED Director's sending the Rule to Show Cause identified in § 11.11(b)(2), the registered patent attorney, registered patent agent or person granted limited recognition may file a response to the Rule to Show Cause with the USPTO Director. The response must set forth the factual and legal bases why the person should not be administratively suspended. The registered patent attorney, registered patent agent or person granted limited recognition shall serve the OED Director with a copy of the response at the time it is filed with the USPTO Director. Within ten days of receiving a copy of the response, the OED Director may file a reply with the USPTO Director that includes documents demonstrating that the notice identified in § 11.11(b)(1) was published and sent to the practitioner in accordance with § 11.11(b)(1). A copy of the reply by the OED Director shall be served on the registered patent attorney, registered patent agent or person granted limited recognition. When acting on the Rule to Show Cause, if the USPTO Director determines that there are no genuine issues of material fact regarding the Office's compliance with the notice requirements under this section or the failure of the person to pay the requisite fees, the USPTO Director

shall enter an order administratively suspending the registered patent attorney, registered patent agent or person granted limited recognition. Otherwise, the USPTO Director shall enter an appropriate order dismissing the Rule to Show Cause. Nothing herein shall permit an administratively suspended registered patent attorney, registered patent agent or person granted limited recognition to seek a stay of the administrative suspension during the pendency of any review of the USPTO Director's final decision.

(4) An administratively suspended attorney, agent or person granted limited recognition remains responsible for paying his or her annual practitioner maintenance fee required by § 11.8(d).

(5) An administratively suspended attorney, agent or person granted limited recognition is subject to investigation and discipline for his or her conduct prior to, during, or after the period he or she was administratively suspended.

(6) An administratively suspended attorney, agent or person granted limited recognition is prohibited from practicing before the Office in patent cases while administratively suspended. An attorney, agent or person granted limited recognition who knows he or she has been administratively suspended under this section will be subject to discipline for failing to comply with the provisions of this paragraph.

(c) *Administrative Inactivation.* (1) Any registered practitioner who shall become employed by the Office shall comply with § 10.40 of this subchapter for withdrawal from the applications, patents, and trademark matters wherein he or she represents an applicant or other person, and notify the OED Director in writing of said employment on the first day of said employment. The name of any registered practitioner employed by the Office shall be endorsed on the roster as administratively inactive. The practitioner shall not be responsible for payments of the annual practitioner maintenance fee each complete fiscal year while the practitioner is in administratively inactive status. Upon separation from the Office, the practitioner may request reactivation by completing and filing an application, Data Sheet, signing a written undertaking required by § 11.10, and paying the fee set forth in § 1.21(a)(1)(i) of this subchapter. Upon restoration to active status, the practitioner shall be responsible for paying the annual practitioner maintenance fee for the fiscal year in which the practitioner

is restored to active status. An administratively inactive practitioner remains subject to the provisions of the Mandatory Disciplinary Rules identified in § 10.20(b) of this subchapter, and to proceedings and sanctions under §§ 11.19 through 11.58 for conduct that violates a provision of the Mandatory Disciplinary Rules identified in § 10.20(b) of this subchapter prior to or during employment at the Office. If, within 30 days after separation from the Office, the practitioner does not request active status or another status, the practitioner will be endorsed on the roster as voluntarily inactive and be subject to the provisions of paragraph (d) of this section.

(2) Any registered practitioner who is a judge of a court of record, full-time court commissioner, U.S. bankruptcy judge, U.S. magistrate judge, or a retired judge who is eligible for temporary judicial assignment and is not engaged in the practice of law may request, in writing, that his or her name be endorsed on the roster as administratively inactive. Upon acceptance of the request, the OED Director shall endorse the name of the practitioner as administratively inactive. The practitioner shall not be responsible for payment of the annual practitioner maintenance fee for each complete fiscal year the practitioner is in administratively inactive status. Following separation from the bench, the practitioner may request restoration to active status by completing and filing an application, Data Sheet, signing a written undertaking required by § 11.10, and paying the fee set forth in § 1.21(a)(1)(i) of this subchapter. Upon restoration to active status, the practitioner shall be responsible for paying the annual practitioner maintenance fee for the fiscal year in which the practitioner is restored to active status.

(d) *Voluntary Inactivation.* (1) Except as provided in paragraph (d)(4) of this section, any registered practitioner may voluntarily enter inactive status by filing a request, in writing, that his or her name be endorsed on the roster as voluntarily inactive. Upon acceptance of the request, the OED Director shall endorse the name as voluntarily inactive.

(2) A registered practitioner in voluntary inactive status shall be responsible for payment of the annual practitioner maintenance fee for voluntary inactive status set forth in § 1.21(a)(7)(ii) of this subchapter for each complete fiscal year the practitioner continues to be in voluntary inactive status.

(3) A registered practitioner who seeks or enters into voluntary inactive status is subject to investigation and discipline for his or her conduct prior to, during, or after the period of his or her inactivation.

(4) A registered practitioner who is in arrears in paying annual practitioner maintenance fees or under administrative suspension for annual practitioner maintenance fee delinquency is ineligible to seek or enter into voluntary inactive status.

(5) A registered practitioner in voluntary inactive status is prohibited from practicing before the Office in patent cases while in voluntary inactive status. A practitioner in voluntary inactive status will be subject to discipline for failing to comply with the provisions of this paragraph. Upon acceptance of the request for voluntary inactive status, the practitioner must comply with the provisions of § 10.40 of this subchapter.

(6) Any registered practitioner whose name has been endorsed as voluntarily inactive pursuant to paragraph (d)(1) of this section and is not under investigation, not subject to a disciplinary proceeding, and not in arrears for the annual practitioner maintenance fee for voluntary inactive status may be restored to active status on the register as may be appropriate provided that the practitioner files a written request for restoration, a completed application for registration on a form supplied by the OED Director furnishing all requested information and material, including information and material pertaining to the practitioner's moral character and reputation under § 11.7(a)(2)(i) during the period of inactivation, a declaration or affidavit attesting to the fact that the practitioner has read the most recent revisions of the patent laws and the rules of practice before the Office, and pays the fees set forth in §§ 1.21(a)(7)(iii) and (iv) of this subchapter.

(e) *Resignation.* A registered practitioner or a practitioner recognized under § 11.14(c), who is neither under investigation under § 11.22 for a possible violation of the Mandatory Disciplinary Rules identified in § 10.20(b) of Part 10 of this subchapter, subject to discipline under §§ 11.24 or 11.25, nor a practitioner against whom no probable cause has been found by a panel of the Committee on Discipline under § 11.23(b), may resign by notifying the OED Director in writing that he or she desires to resign. Upon accep-

tance in writing by the OED Director of such notice, that registered practitioner or practitioner under § 11.14 shall no longer be eligible to practice before the Office but shall continue to file a change of address for five years thereafter in order that he or she may be located in the event information regarding the practitioner's conduct comes to the attention of the OED Director or any grievance is made about his or her conduct while he or she engaged in practice before the Office. The name of any registered practitioner whose resignation is accepted shall be removed from the register, endorsed as resigned, and notice thereof published in the Official Gazette. Upon acceptance of the resignation by the OED Director, the practitioner must comply with the provisions of § 10.40 of this subchapter.

(f) *Administrative reinstatement.* (1) Any registered practitioner who has been administratively suspended pursuant to paragraph (b) of this section, or who has resigned pursuant to paragraph (e) of this section, may be reinstated on the register provided the practitioner has applied for reinstatement on an application form supplied by the OED Director, demonstrated compliance with the provisions of §§ 11.7(a)(2)(i) and (iii), and paid the fees set forth in §§ 1.21(a)(7)(i), (a)(9)(i) and (a)(9)(ii) of this subchapter. Any person granted limited recognition who has been administratively suspended pursuant to paragraph (b) of this section may have their recognition reactivated provided the practitioner has applied for reinstatement on an application form supplied by the OED Director, demonstrated compliance with the provisions of §§ 11.7(a)(2)(i) and (iii), and paid the fees set forth in §§ 1.21(a)(8)(i), (a)(9)(i) and (a)(9)(ii) of this subchapter. A practitioner who has resigned or was administratively suspended for two or more years before the date the Office receives a completed application from the person who resigned or was administratively suspended must also pass the registration examination under § 11.7(b)(1)(ii). Any reinstated practitioner is subject to investigation and discipline for his or her conduct that occurred prior to, during, or after the period of his or her administrative suspension or resignation.

(2) Any registered practitioner whose registration has been administratively inactivated pursuant to paragraph (c) of this section may be reinstated to the register as may be appropriate provided within

two years after his or her employment with the Office ceases or within two years after his or her employment in a judicial capacity ceases the following is filed with the OED Director: a request for reinstatement, a completed application for registration on a form supplied by the OED Director furnishing all requested information and material, and the fee set forth in § 1.21(a)(9)(ii) of this subchapter. Any registered practitioner inactivated or reinstated is subject to investigation and discipline for his or her conduct before, during, or after the period of his or her inactivation.

[Added, 69 FR 35427, June 24, 2004, effective July 26, 2004; revised, 73 FR 67750, Nov. 17, 2008, effective Dec. 17, 2008]

§ 11.12 - 11.13 [Reserved]

§ 11.14 Individuals who may practice before the Office in trademarks and other non-patent matters.

(a) *Attorneys.* Any individual who is an attorney as defined in § 11.1 may represent others before the Office in trademark and other non-patent matters. An attorney is not required to apply for registration or recognition to practice before the Office in trademark and other non-patent matters. Registration as a patent practitioner does not itself entitle an individual to practice before the Office in trademark matters.

(b) *Non-lawyers.* Individuals who are not attorneys are not recognized to practice before the Office in trademark and other non-patent matters, except that individuals not attorneys who were recognized to practice before the Office in trademark matters under this chapter prior to January 1, 1957, will be recognized as agents to continue practice before the Office in trademark matters. Except as provided in the preceding sentence, registration as a patent agent does not itself entitle an individual to practice before the Office in trademark matters.

(c) *Foreigners.* Any foreign attorney or agent not a resident of the United States who shall file a written application for reciprocal recognition under paragraph (f) of this section and prove to the satisfaction of the OED Director that he or she is registered or in good standing before the patent or trademark office of the country in which he or she resides and practices

and is possessed of good moral character and reputation, may be recognized for the limited purpose of representing parties located in such country before the Office in the presentation and prosecution of trademark matters, provided: the patent or trademark office of such country allows substantially reciprocal privileges to those permitted to practice in trademark matters before the Office. Recognition under this paragraph shall continue only during the period that the conditions specified in this paragraph obtain.

(d) Recognition of any individual under this section shall not be construed as sanctioning or authorizing the performance of any act regarded in the jurisdiction where performed as the unauthorized practice of law.

(e) No individual other than those specified in paragraphs (a), (b), and (c) of this section will be permitted to practice before the Office in trademark matters on behalf of a client. Any individual may appear in a trademark or other non-patent matter in his or her own behalf. Any individual may appear in a trademark matter for:

(1) A firm of which he or she is a member,

(2) A partnership of which he or she is a partner, or

(3) A corporation or association of which he or she is an officer and which he or she is authorized to represent, if such firm, partnership, corporation, or association is a party to a trademark proceeding pending before the Office.

(f) *Application for reciprocal recognition.* An individual seeking reciprocal recognition under paragraph (c) of this section, in addition to providing evidence satisfying the provisions of paragraph (c) of this section, shall apply in writing to the OED Director for reciprocal recognition, and shall pay the application fee required by § 1.21(a)(1)(i) of this subchapter.

[Added, 73 FR 47650, Aug. 14, 2008, effective Sept. 15, 2008]

§ 11.15 Refusal to recognize a practitioner.

Any practitioner authorized to appear before the Office may be suspended, excluded, or reprimanded in accordance with the provisions of this Part. Any practitioner who is suspended or excluded under this Part shall not be entitled to practice before the Office in patent, trademark, or other non-patent matters while suspended or excluded.

[Added, 73 FR 47650, Aug. 14, 2008, effective Sept. 15, 2008]

§ 11.16 - 11.17 [Reserved]

§ 11.18 Signature and certificate for correspondence filed in the Office.

(a)   For all documents filed in the Office in patent, trademark, and other non-patent matters, and all documents filed with a hearing officer in a disciplinary proceeding, except for correspondence that is required to be signed by the applicant or party, each piece of correspondence filed by a practitioner in the Office must bear a signature, personally signed by such practitioner, in compliance with § 1.4(d)(1) of this subchapter.

(b)   By presenting to the Office or hearing officer in a disciplinary proceeding (whether by signing, filing, submitting, or later advocating) any paper, the party presenting such paper, whether a practitioner or non-practitioner, is certifying that—

(1)   All statements made therein of the party's own knowledge are true, all statements made therein on information and belief are believed to be true, and all statements made therein are made with the knowledge that whoever, in any matter within the jurisdiction of the Office, knowingly and willfully falsifies, conceals, or covers up by any trick, scheme, or device a material fact, or knowingly and willfully makes any false, fictitious, or fraudulent statements or representations, or knowingly and willfully makes or uses any false writing or document knowing the same to contain any false, fictitious, or fraudulent statement or entry, shall be subject to the penalties set forth under 18 U.S.C. 1001 and any other applicable criminal statute, and violations of the provisions of this section may jeopardize the probative value of the paper; and

(2)   To the best of the party's knowledge, information and belief, formed after an inquiry reasonable under the circumstances,

(i)   The paper is not being presented for any improper purpose, such as to harass someone or to cause unnecessary delay or needless increase in the cost of any proceeding before the Office;

(ii)   The other legal contentions therein are warranted by existing law or by a nonfrivolous argument for the extension, modification, or reversal of existing law or the establishment of new law;

(iii)   The allegations and other factual contentions have evidentiary support or, if specifically so identified, are likely to have evidentiary support after a reasonable opportunity for further investigation or discovery; and

(iv)   The denials of factual contentions are warranted on the evidence, or if specifically so identified, are reasonably based on a lack of information or belief.

(c)   Violations of any of paragraphs (b)(2)(i) through (iv) of this section are, after notice and reasonable opportunity to respond, subject to such sanctions or actions as deemed appropriate by the USPTO Director, which may include, but are not limited to, any combination of—

(1)   Striking the offending paper;

(2)   Referring a practitioner's conduct to the Director of Enrollment and Discipline for appropriate action;

(3)   Precluding a party or practitioner from submitting a paper, or presenting or contesting an issue;

(4)   Affecting the weight given to the offending paper; or

(5)   Terminating the proceedings in the Office.

(d)   Any practitioner violating the provisions of this section may also be subject to disciplinary action.

[Added, 73 FR 47650, Aug. 14, 2008, effective Sept. 15, 2008]

Subpart C — Investigations and Disciplinary Proceedings; Jurisdiction, Sanctions, Investigations, and Proceedings

§ 11.19 Disciplinary jurisdiction; Jurisdiction to transfer to disability inactive status.

(a)   All practitioners engaged in practice before the Office; all practitioners administratively suspended; all practitioners registered to practice before the Office in patent cases; all practitioners inactivated; all practitioners authorized under § 11.6(d) to take testimony; and all practitioners transferred to disability inactive status, reprimanded, suspended, or excluded from the practice of law by a duly constituted authority, including by the USPTO Director, are subject to the disciplinary jurisdiction of the Office. Practitioners who have resigned shall also be subject to such jurisdiction with respect to conduct undertaken prior to the resignation and conduct in regard to any practice before the Office following the resignation.

(b) *Grounds for discipline; Grounds for transfer to disability inactive status.* The following, whether done individually by a practitioner or in concert with any other person or persons and whether or not done in the course of providing legal services to a client, or in a matter pending before the Office, constitute grounds for discipline or grounds for transfer to disability inactive status.

(1) Grounds for discipline include:

(i) Conviction of a serious crime;

(ii) Discipline on ethical grounds imposed in another jurisdiction or disciplinary disqualification from participating in or appearing before any Federal program or agency;

(iii) Failure to comply with any order of a Court disciplining a practitioner, or any final decision of the USPTO Director in a disciplinary matter;

(iv) Violation of a Mandatory Disciplinary Rule identified in § 10.20(b) of Part 10 of this Subchapter; or

(v) Violation of the oath or declaration taken by the practitioner. See § 11.8.

(2) Grounds for transfer to disability inactive status include:

(i) Being transferred to disability inactive status in another jurisdiction;

(ii) Being judicially declared incompetent, being judicially ordered to be involuntarily committed after a hearing on the grounds of insanity, incompetency or disability, or being placed by court order under guardianship or conservatorship; or

(iii) Filing a motion requesting a disciplinary proceeding be held in abeyance because the practitioner is suffering from a disability or addiction that makes it impossible for the practitioner to adequately defend the charges in the disciplinary proceeding.

(c) Petitions to disqualify a practitioner in ex parte or inter partes matters in the Office are not governed by §§ 11.19 through 11.60 and will be handled on a case-by-case basis under such conditions as the USPTO Director deems appropriate.

(d) The OED Director may refer the existence of circumstances suggesting unauthorized practice of law to the authorities in the appropriate jurisdiction(s).

[Added, 73 FR 47650, Aug. 14, 2008, effective Sept. 15, 2008]

§ 11.20 Disciplinary sanctions; Transfer to disability inactive status.

(a) *Types of discipline.* The USPTO Director, after notice and opportunity for a hearing, and where grounds for discipline exist, may impose on a practitioner the following types of discipline:

(1) Exclusion from practice before the Office;

(2) Suspension from practice before the Office for an appropriate period of time;

(3) Reprimand or censure; or

(4) *Probation.* Probation may be imposed *in lieu* of or in addition to any other disciplinary sanction. Any conditions of probation shall be stated in writing in the order imposing probation. The order shall also state whether, and to what extent, the practitioner shall be required to notify clients of the probation. The order shall establish procedures for the supervision of probation. Violation of any condition of probation shall be cause for the probation to be revoked, and the disciplinary sanction to be imposed for the remainder of the probation period. Revocation of probation shall occur only after an order to show cause why probation should not be revoked is resolved adversely to the practitioner.

(b) *Conditions imposed with discipline.* When the USPTO Director imposes discipline, the practitioner may be required to make restitution either to persons financially injured by the practitioner's conduct or to an appropriate client's security trust fund, or both, as a condition of probation or of reinstatement. Such restitution shall be limited to the return of unearned practitioner fees or misappropriated client funds. Any other reasonable condition may also be imposed, including a requirement that the practitioner take and pass a professional responsibility examination.

(c) *Transfer to disability inactive status.* The USPTO Director, after notice and opportunity for a hearing may, and where grounds exist to believe a practitioner has been transferred to disability inactive status in another jurisdiction, or has been judicially declared incompetent; judicially ordered to be involuntarily committed after a hearing on the grounds of incompetency or disability, or placed by court order under guardianship or conservatorship, transfer the practitioner to disability inactive status.

[Added, 73 FR 47650, Aug. 14, 2008, effective Sept. 15, 2008]

§ 11.21 Warnings.

A warning is neither public nor a disciplinary sanction. The OED Director may conclude an investigation with the issuance of a warning. The warning shall contain a brief statement of facts and Mandatory Disciplinary Rules identified in § 10.20(b) of Part 10 of this Subchapter relevant to the facts.

[Added, 73 FR 47650, Aug. 14, 2008, effective Sept. 15, 2008]

§ 11.22 Investigations.

(a)   The OED Director is authorized to investigate possible grounds for discipline. An investigation may be initiated when the OED Director receives a grievance, information or evidence from any source suggesting possible grounds for discipline. Neither unwillingness nor neglect by a grievant to prosecute a charge, nor settlement, compromise, or restitution with the grievant, shall in itself justify abatement of an investigation.

(b)   Any person possessing information or evidence concerning possible grounds for discipline of a practitioner may report the information or evidence to the OED Director. The OED Director may request that the report be presented in the form of an affidavit or declaration.

(c)   Information or evidence coming from any source which presents or alleges facts suggesting possible grounds for discipline of a practitioner will be deemed a grievance.

(d)   *Preliminary screening of information or evidence.* The OED Director shall examine all information or evidence concerning possible grounds for discipline of a practitioner.

(e)   *Notification of investigation.* The OED Director shall notify the practitioner in writing of the initiation of an investigation into whether a practitioner has engaged in conduct constituting possible grounds for discipline.

(f)   *Request for information and evidence by OED Director.*

(1)   In the course of the investigation, the OED Director may request information and evidence regarding possible grounds for discipline of a practitioner from:

(i)   The grievant,

(ii)   The practitioner, or

(iii)   Any person who may reasonably be expected to provide information and evidence needed in connection with the grievance or investigation.

(2)   The OED Director may request information and evidence regarding possible grounds for discipline of a practitioner from a non-grieving client either after obtaining the consent of the practitioner or upon a finding by a Contact Member of the Committee on Discipline, appointed in accordance with § 11.23(d), that good cause exists to believe that the possible ground for discipline alleged has occurred with respect to non-grieving clients. Neither a request for, nor disclosure of, such information shall constitute a violation of any of the Mandatory Disciplinary Rules identified in § 10.20(b) of this subchapter.

(g)   Where the OED Director makes a request under paragraph (f)(2) of this section to a Contact Member of the Committee on Discipline, such Contact Member shall not, with respect to the practitioner connected to the OED Director's request, participate in the Committee on Discipline panel that renders a probable cause determination under paragraph (b)(1) of this section concerning such practitioner, and that forwards the probable cause finding and recommendation to the OED Director under paragraph (b)(2) of this section.

(h)   *Disposition of investigation.* Upon the conclusion of an investigation, the OED Director may:

(1)   Close the investigation without issuing a warning, or taking disciplinary action;

(2)   Issue a warning to the practitioner;

(3)   Institute formal charges upon the approval of the Committee on Discipline; or

(4) Enter into a settlement agreement with the practitioner and submit the same for approval of the USPTO Director.

(i) *Closing investigation without issuing a warning or taking disciplinary action.* The OED Director shall terminate an investigation and decline to refer a matter to the Committee on Discipline if the OED Director determines that:

(1) The information or evidence is unfounded;

(2) The information or evidence relates to matters not within the jurisdiction of the Office;

(3) As a matter of law, the conduct about which information or evidence has been obtained does not constitute grounds for discipline, even if the conduct may involve a legal dispute; or

(4) The available evidence is insufficient to conclude that there is probable cause to believe that grounds exist for discipline.

[Added, 73 FR 47650, Aug. 14, 2008, effective Sept. 15, 2008]

§ 11.23 Committee on Discipline.

(a) The USPTO Director shall appoint a Committee on Discipline. The Committee on Discipline shall consist of at least three employees of the Office. None of the Committee members shall report directly or indirectly to the OED Director or any employee designated by the USPTO Director to decide disciplinary matters. Each Committee member shall be a member in good standing of the bar of the highest court of a State. The Committee members shall select a Chairperson from among themselves. Three Committee members will constitute a panel of the Committee.

(b) *Powers and duties of the Committee on Discipline.* The Committee shall have the power and duty to:

(1) Meet in panels at the request of the OED Director and, after reviewing evidence presented by the OED Director, by majority vote of the panel, determine whether there is probable cause to bring charges under § 11.32 against a practitioner; and

(2) Prepare and forward its own probable cause findings and recommendations to the OED Director.

(c) No discovery shall be authorized of, and no member of the Committee on Discipline shall be required to testify about deliberations of, the Committee on Discipline or of any panel.

(d) The Chairperson shall appoint the members of the panels and a Contact Member of the Committee on Discipline.

[Added, 73 FR 47650, Aug. 14, 2008, effective Sept. 15, 2008]

§ 11.24 Reciprocal discipline.

(a) *Notification of OED Director.* Within thirty days of being publicly censured, publicly reprimanded, subjected to probation, disbarred or suspended by another jurisdiction, or being disciplinarily disqualified from participating in or appearing before any Federal program or agency, a practitioner subject to the disciplinary jurisdiction of the Office shall notify the OED Director in writing of the same. A practitioner is deemed to be disbarred if he or she is disbarred, excluded on consent, or has resigned in lieu of a disciplinary proceeding. Upon receiving notification from any source or otherwise learning that a practitioner subject to the disciplinary jurisdiction of the Office has been so publicly censured, publicly reprimanded, subjected to probation, disbarred, suspended or disciplinarily disqualified, the OED Director shall obtain a certified copy of the record or order regarding the public censure, public reprimand, probation, disbarment, suspension or disciplinary disqualification and file the same with the USPTO Director. The OED Director shall, in addition, without Committee on Discipline authorization, file with the USPTO Director a complaint complying with § 11.34 against the practitioner predicated upon the public censure, public reprimand, probation, disbarment, suspension or disciplinary disqualification. The OED Director shall request the USPTO Director to issue a notice and order as set forth in paragraph (b) of this section.

(b) *Notification served on practitioner.* Upon receipt of a certified copy of the record or order regarding the practitioner being so publicly censured, publicly reprimanded, subjected to probation, disbarred, suspended or disciplinarily disqualified together with the complaint, the USPTO Director shall issue a notice directed to the practitioner in accordance with § 11.35 and to the OED Director containing:

(1) A copy of the record or order regarding the public censure, public reprimand, probation, disbarment, suspension or disciplinary disqualification;

(2) A copy of the complaint; and

(3) An order directing the practitioner to file a response with the USPTO Director and the OED Director, within forty days of the date of the notice establishing a genuine issue of material fact predicated upon the grounds set forth in paragraphs (d)(1)(i) through (d)(1)(iv) of this section that the imposition of the identical public censure, public reprimand, probation, disbarment, suspension or disciplinary disqualification would be unwarranted and the reasons for that claim.

(c) *Effect of stay in another jurisdiction.* In the event the public censure, public reprimand, probation, disbarment, suspension imposed by another jurisdiction or disciplinary disqualification imposed in the Federal program or agency has been stayed, any reciprocal discipline imposed by the USPTO may be deferred until the stay expires.

(d) *Hearing and discipline to be imposed.* (1) The USPTO Director shall hear the matter on the documentary record unless the USPTO Director determines that an oral hearing is necessary. After expiration of the forty days from the date of the notice pursuant to provisions of paragraph (b) of this section, the USPTO Director shall consider any timely filed response and shall impose the identical public censure, public reprimand, probation, disbarment, suspension or disciplinary disqualification unless the practitioner clearly and convincingly demonstrates, and the USPTO Director finds there is a genuine issue of material fact that:

(i) The procedure elsewhere was so lacking in notice or opportunity to be heard as to constitute a deprivation of due process;

(ii) There was such infirmity of proof establishing the conduct as to give rise to the clear conviction that the Office could not, consistently with its duty, accept as final the conclusion on that subject;

(iii) The imposition of the same public censure, public reprimand, probation, disbarment, suspension or disciplinary disqualification by the Office would result in grave injustice; or

(iv) Any argument that the practitioner was not publicly censured, publicly reprimanded, placed on probation, disbarred, suspended or disciplinarily disqualified.

(2) If the USPTO Director determines that there is no genuine issue of material fact, the USPTO Director shall enter an appropriate final order. If the USPTO Director is unable to make such determination because there is a genuine issue of material fact, the USPTO Director shall enter an appropriate order:

(i) Referring the complaint to a hearing officer for a formal hearing and entry of an initial decision in accordance with the other rules in this part, and

(ii) Directing the practitioner to file an answer to the complaint in accordance with § 11.36.

(e) *Adjudication in another jurisdiction or Federal agency or program.* In all other respects, a final adjudication in another jurisdiction or Federal agency or program that a practitioner, whether or not admitted in that jurisdiction, has been guilty of misconduct shall establish a prima facie case by clear and convincing evidence that the practitioner violated 37 CFR 10.23, as further identified under 37 CFR 10.23(c)(5), (or any successor regulation identifying such public censure, public reprimand, probation, disbarment, suspension or disciplinary disqualification as a basis for a disciplinary proceeding in this Office).

(f) *Reciprocal discipline—action where practice has ceased.* Upon request by the practitioner, reciprocal discipline may be imposed *nunc pro tunc* only if the practitioner promptly notified the OED Director of his or her censure, public reprimand, probation, disbarment, suspension or disciplinary disqualification in another jurisdiction, and establishes by clear and convincing evidence that the practitioner voluntarily ceased all activities related to practice before the Office and complied with all provisions of § 11.58. The effective date of any public censure, public reprimand, probation, suspension, disbarment or disciplinary disqualification imposed nunc pro tunc shall be the date the practitioner voluntarily ceased all activities related to practice before the Office and complied with all provisions of § 11.58.

(g) *Reinstatement following reciprocal discipline proceeding.* A practitioner may petition for reinstatement under conditions set forth in § 11.60 no sooner than completion of the period of reciprocal discipline imposed, and compliance with all provisions of § 11.58.

[Added, 73 FR 47650, Aug. 14, 2008, effective Sept. 15, 2008]

§ 11.25 Interim suspension and discipline based upon conviction of committing a serious crime.

(a) *Notification of OED Director.* Upon being convicted of a crime in a court of the United States or any State, or violating a criminal law of a foreign country, a practitioner subject to the disciplinary jurisdiction of the Office shall notify the OED Director in writing of the same within thirty days from the date of such conviction. Upon being advised or learning that a practitioner subject to the disciplinary jurisdiction of the Office has been convicted of a crime, the OED Director shall make a preliminary determination whether the crime constitutes a serious crime warranting interim suspension. If the crime is a serious crime, the OED Director shall file with the USPTO Director proof of the conviction and request the USPTO Director to issue a notice and order set forth in paragraph (b)(2) of this section. The OED Director shall in addition, without Committee on Discipline authorization, file with the USPTO Director a complaint against the practitioner complying with § 11.34 predicated upon the conviction of a serious crime. If the crime is not a serious crime, the OED Director shall process the matter in the same manner as any other information or evidence of a possible violation of a Mandatory Disciplinary Rule identified in § 10.20 (b) of this subchapter coming to the attention of the OED Director.

(b) *Interim suspension and referral for disciplinary proceeding.* All proceedings under this section shall be handled as expeditiously as possible.

(1) The USPTO Director has authority to place a practitioner on interim suspension after hearing the request for interim suspension on the documentary record.

(2) *Notification served on practitioner.* Upon receipt of a certified copy of the court record, docket entry or judgment demonstrating that the practitioner has been so convicted together with the complaint, the USPTO Director shall forthwith issue a notice directed to the practitioner in accordance with §§ 11.35(a), (b) or (c), and to the OED Director, containing:

(i) A copy of the court record, docket entry, or judgment of conviction;

(ii) A copy of the complaint; and

(iii) An order directing the practitioner to file a response with the USPTO Director and the OED Director, within forty days of the date of the notice, establishing that there is a genuine issue of material fact that the crime did not constitute a serious crime, the practitioner is not the individual found guilty of the crime, or that the conviction was so lacking in notice or opportunity to be heard as to constitute a deprivation of due process.

(3) *Hearing and final order on request for interim suspension.* The request for interim suspension shall be heard by the USPTO Director on the documentary record unless the USPTO Director determines that the practitioner's response establishes a genuine issue of material fact that: The crime did not constitute a serious crime, the practitioner is not the person who committed the crime, or that the conviction was so lacking in notice or opportunity to be heard as to constitute a deprivation of due process. If the USPTO Director determines that there is no genuine issue of material fact regarding the defenses set forth in the preceding sentence, the USPTO Director shall enter an appropriate final order regarding the OED Director's request for interim suspension regardless of the pendency of any criminal appeal. If the USPTO Director is unable to make such determination because there is a genuine issue of material fact, the USPTO Director shall enter a final order dismissing the request and enter a further order referring the complaint to a hearing officer for a hearing and entry of an initial decision in accordance with the other rules in this part and directing the practitioner to file an answer to the complaint in accordance with § 11.36.

(4) *Termination.* The USPTO Director has authority to terminate an interim suspension. In the interest of justice, the USPTO Director may terminate an interim suspension at any time upon a showing of extraordinary circumstances, after affording the OED Director an opportunity to respond to the request to terminate interim suspension.

(5) *Referral for disciplinary proceeding.* Upon entering a final order imposing interim suspension, the USPTO Director shall refer the complaint to a hearing officer to conduct a formal disciplinary proceeding. The formal disciplinary proceeding, however, shall be stayed by the hearing officer until all

direct appeals from the conviction are concluded. Review of the initial decision of the hearing officer shall be pursuant to § 11.55.

(c) Proof *of conviction and guilt*—(1) *Conviction in the United States.* For purposes of a hearing for interim suspension and a hearing on the formal charges in a complaint filed as a consequence of the conviction, a certified copy of the court record, docket entry, or judgment of conviction in a court of the United States or any State shall establish a prima facie case by clear and convincing evidence that the practitioner was convicted of a serious crime and that the conviction was not lacking in notice or opportunity to be heard as to constitute a deprivation of due process.

(2) *Conviction in a foreign country.* For purposes of a hearing for interim suspension and on the formal charges filed as a result of a finding of guilt, a certified copy of the court record, docket entry, or judgment of conviction in a court of a foreign country shall establish a prima facie case by clear and convincing evidence that the practitioner was convicted of a serious crime and that the conviction was not lacking in notice or opportunity to be heard as to constitute a deprivation of due process. However, nothing in this paragraph shall preclude the practitioner from demonstrating by clear and convincing evidence in any hearing on a request for interim suspension there is a genuine issue of material fact to be considered when determining if the elements of a serious crime were committed in violating the criminal law of the foreign country and whether a disciplinary sanction should be entered.

(d) *Crime determined not to be serious crime.* If the USPTO Director determines that the crime is not a serious crime, the complaint shall be referred to the OED Director for investigation under § 11.22 and processing as is appropriate.

(e) *Reinstatement*—(1) *Upon reversal or setting aside a finding of guilt or a conviction.* If a practitioner suspended solely under the provisions of paragraph (b) of this section demonstrates that the underlying finding of guilt or conviction of serious crimes has been reversed or vacated, the order for interim suspension shall be vacated and the practitioner shall be placed on active status unless the finding of guilt was reversed or the conviction was set aside with respect to less than all serious crimes for which the practitioner was found guilty or convicted. The

vacating of the interim suspension will not terminate any other disciplinary proceeding then pending against the practitioner, the disposition of which shall be determined by the hearing officer before whom the matter is pending, on the basis of all available evidence other than the finding of guilt or conviction.

(2) *Following conviction of a serious crime.* Any practitioner convicted of a serious crime and disciplined in whole or in part in regard to that conviction, may petition for reinstatement under conditions set forth in § 11.60 no sooner than five years after being discharged following completion of service of his or her sentence, or after completion of service under probation or parole, whichever is later.

(f) *Notice to clients and others of interim suspension.* An interim suspension under this section shall constitute a suspension of the practitioner for the purpose of § 11.58.

[Added, 73 FR 47650, Aug. 14, 2008, effective Sept. 15, 2008]

§ 11.26   Settlement.

Before or after a complaint under § 11.34 is filed, a settlement conference may occur between the OED Director and the practitioner. Any offers of compromise and any statements made during the course of settlement discussions shall not be admissible in subsequent proceedings. The OED Director may recommend to the USPTO Director any settlement terms deemed appropriate, including steps taken to correct or mitigate the matter forming the basis of the action, or to prevent recurrence of the same or similar conduct. A settlement agreement shall be effective only upon entry of a final decision by the USPTO Director.

[Added, 73 FR 47650, Aug. 14, 2008, effective Sept. 15, 2008]

§ 11.27   Exclusion on consent.

(a) *Required affidavit.* The OED Director may confer with a practitioner concerning possible violations by the practitioner of the Rules of Professional Conduct whether or not a disciplinary proceeding has been instituted. A practitioner who is the subject of an investigation or a pending disciplinary proceeding based on allegations of grounds for discipline, and who desires to resign, may only do so by consenting to exclusion and delivering to the OED Director an affidavit declaring the consent of the practitioner to exclusion and stating:

(1) That the practitioner's consent is freely and voluntarily rendered, that the practitioner is not being subjected to coercion or duress, and that the practitioner is fully aware of the implications of consenting to exclusion;

(2) That the practitioner is aware that there is currently pending an investigation into, or a proceeding involving allegations of misconduct, the nature of which shall be specifically set forth in the affidavit to the satisfaction of the OED Director;

(3) That the practitioner acknowledges that, if and when he or she applies for reinstatement under § 11.60, the OED Director will conclusively presume, for the limited purpose of determining the application for reinstatement, that:

(i) The facts upon which the investigation or complaint is based are true, and

(ii) The practitioner could not have successfully defended himself or herself against the allegations in the investigation or charges in the complaint.

(b) *Action by the USPTO Director.* Upon receipt of the required affidavit, the OED Director shall file the affidavit and any related papers with the USPTO Director for review and approval. Upon such approval, the USPTO Director will enter an order excluding the practitioner on consent and providing other appropriate actions. Upon entry of the order, the excluded practitioner shall comply with the requirements set forth in § 11.58.

(c) When an affidavit under paragraph (a) of this section is received after a complaint under § 11.34 has been filed, the OED Director shall notify the hearing officer. The hearing officer shall enter an order transferring the disciplinary proceeding to the USPTO Director, who may enter an order excluding the practitioner on consent.

(d) *Reinstatement.* Any practitioner excluded on consent under this section may not petition for reinstatement for five years. A practitioner excluded on consent who intends to reapply for admission to practice before the Office must comply with the provisions of § 11.58, and apply for reinstatement in accordance with § 11.60. Failure to comply with the provisions of § 11.58 constitutes grounds for denying an application for reinstatement.

[Added, 73 FR 47650, Aug. 14, 2008, effective Sept. 15, 2008]

§ 11.28 Incapacitated practitioners in a disciplinary proceeding.

(a) *Holding in abeyance a disciplinary proceeding because of incapacitation due to a current disability or addiction*—(1) *Practitioner's motion.* In the course of a disciplinary proceeding under § 11.32, but before the date set by the hearing officer for a hearing, the practitioner may file a motion requesting the hearing officer to enter an order holding such proceeding in abeyance based on the contention that the practitioner is suffering from a disability or addiction that makes it impossible for the practitioner to adequately defend the charges in the disciplinary proceeding.

(i) *Content of practitioner's motion.* The practitioner's motion shall, in addition to any other requirement of § 11.43, include or have attached thereto:

(A) A brief statement of all material facts;

(B) Affidavits, medical reports, official records, or other documents and the opinion of at least one medical expert setting forth and establishing any of the material facts on which the practitioner is relying;

(C) A statement that the practitioner acknowledges the alleged incapacity by reason of disability or addiction;

(D) Written consent that the practitioner be transferred to disability inactive status if the motion is granted; and

(E) A written agreement by the practitioner to not practice before the Office in patent, trademark or other non-patent cases while on disability inactive status.

(ii) *Response.* The OED Director's response to any motion hereunder shall be served and filed within thirty days after service of the practitioner's motion unless such time is shortened or enlarged by the hearing officer for good cause shown, and shall set forth the following:

(A) All objections, if any, to the actions requested in the motion;

(B) An admission, denial or allegation of lack of knowledge with respect to each of the material facts in the practitioner's motion and accompanying documents; and

(C) Affidavits, medical reports, official records, or other documents setting forth facts on which the OED Director intends to rely for purposes of disputing or denying any material fact set forth in the practitioner's papers.

(2) *Disposition of practitioner's motion.* The hearing officer shall decide the motion and any response thereto. The motion shall be granted upon a showing of good cause to believe the practitioner to be incapacitated as alleged. If the required showing is made, the hearing officer shall enter an order holding the disciplinary proceeding in abeyance. In the case of addiction to drugs or intoxicants, the order may provide that the practitioner will not be returned to active status absent satisfaction of specified conditions. Upon receipt of the order, the OED Director shall transfer the practitioner to disability inactive status, give notice to the practitioner, cause notice to be published, and give notice to appropriate authorities in the Office that the practitioner has been placed on disability inactive status. The practitioner shall comply with the provisions of § 11.58, and shall not engage in practice before the Office in patent, trademark and other non-patent law until a determination is made of the practitioner's capability to resume practice before the Office in a proceeding under paragraph (c) or paragraph (d) of this section. A practitioner on disability inactive status must seek permission from the OED Director to engage in an activity authorized under § 11.58(e). Permission will be granted only if the practitioner has complied with all the conditions of §§ 11.58(a) through 11.58(d) applicable to disability inactive status. In the event that permission is granted, the practitioner shall fully comply with the provisions of § 11.58(e).

(b) *Motion for reactivation.* Any practitioner transferred to disability inactive status in a disciplinary proceeding may file with the hearing officer a motion for reactivation once a year beginning at any time not less than one year after the initial effective date of inactivation, or once during any shorter interval provided by the order issued pursuant to paragraph (a)(2) of this section or any modification thereof. If the motion is granted, the disciplinary proceeding shall resume under such schedule as may be established by the hearing officer.

(c) *Contents of motion for reactivation.* A motion by the practitioner for reactivation alleging that a practitioner has recovered from a prior disability or addiction shall be accompanied by all available medical reports or similar documents relating thereto. The hearing officer may require the practitioner to present such other information as is necessary.

(d) *OED Director's motion to resume disciplinary proceeding held in abeyance.* (1) The OED Director, having good cause to believe a practitioner is no longer incapacitated, may file a motion requesting the hearing officer to terminate a prior order holding in abeyance any pending proceeding because of the practitioner's disability or addiction. The hearing officer shall decide the matter presented by the OED Director's motion hereunder based on the affidavits and other admissible evidence attached to the OED Director's motion and the practitioner's response. The OED Director bears the burden of showing by clear and convincing evidence that the practitioner is able to defend himself or herself. If there is any genuine issue as to one or more material facts, the hearing officer will hold an evidentiary hearing.

(2) The hearing officer, upon receipt of the OED Director's motion under paragraph (d)(1) of this section, may direct the practitioner to file a response. If the hearing officer requires the practitioner to file a response, the practitioner must present clear and convincing evidence that the prior self-alleged disability or addiction continues to make it impossible for the practitioner to defend himself or herself in the underlying proceeding being held in abeyance.

(e) *Action by the hearing officer.* If, in deciding a motion under paragraph (b) or (d) of this section, the hearing officer determines that there is good cause to believe the practitioner is not incapacitated from defending himself or herself, or is not incapacitated from practicing before the Office, the hearing officer shall take such action as is deemed appropriate, including the entry of an order directing the reactivation of the practitioner and resumption of the disciplinary proceeding.

[Added, 73 FR 47650, Aug. 14, 2008, effective Sept. 15, 2008]

§ 11.29 Reciprocal transfer or initial transfer to disability inactive status.

(a) *Notification of OED Director.* (1) Transfer to disability inactive status in another jurisdiction as grounds for reciprocal transfer by the Office. Within thirty days of being transferred to disability inactive status in another jurisdiction, a practitioner subject to the disciplinary jurisdiction of the Office shall notify the OED Director in writing of the transfer. Upon notification from any source that a practitioner subject to the disciplinary jurisdiction of the Office has been transferred to disability inactive status in another jurisdiction, the OED Director shall obtain a certified copy of the order. The OED Director shall file with the USPTO Director:

(i) The order;

(ii) A request that the practitioner be transferred to disability inactive status, including the specific grounds therefor; and

(iii) A request that the USPTO Director issue a notice and order as set forth in paragraph (b) of this section.

(2) *Involuntary commitment, adjudication of incompetency or court ordered placement under guardianship or conservatorship as grounds for initial transfer to disability inactive status.* Within thirty days of being judicially declared incompetent, being judicially ordered to be involuntarily committed after a hearing on the grounds of incompetency or disability, or being placed by court order under guardianship or conservatorship in another jurisdiction, a practitioner subject to the disciplinary jurisdiction of the Office shall notify the OED Director in writing of such judicial action. Upon notification from any source that a practitioner subject to the disciplinary jurisdiction of the Office has been subject to such judicial action, the OED Director shall obtain a certified copy of the order. The OED Director shall file with the USPTO Director:

(i) The order;

(ii) A request that the practitioner be transferred to disability inactive status, including the specific grounds therefor; and

(iii) A request that the USPTO Director issue a notice and order as set forth in paragraph (b) of this section.

(b) *Notice served on practitioner.* Upon receipt of a certified copy of an order or declaration issued by another jurisdiction demonstrating that a practitioner subject to the disciplinary jurisdiction of the Office has been transferred to disability inactive status, judicially declared incompetent, judicially ordered to be involuntarily committed after a judicial hearing on the grounds of incompetency or disability, or placed by court order under guardianship or conservatorship, together with the OED Director's request, the USPTO Director shall issue a notice, comporting with § 11.35, directed to the practitioner containing:

(1) A copy of the order or declaration from the other jurisdiction,

(2) A copy of the OED Director's request; and

(3) An order directing the practitioner to file a response with the USPTO Director and the OED Director, within 30 days from the date of the notice, establishing a genuine issue of material fact supported by an affidavit and predicated upon the grounds set forth in § 11.29(d)(1) through (4) that a transfer to disability inactive status would be unwarranted and the reasons therefor.

(c) *Effect of stay of transfer, judicially declared incompetence, judicially ordered involuntarily commitment on the grounds of incompetency or disability, or court-ordered placement under guardianship or conservatorship.* In the event the transfer, judicially declared incompetence, judicially ordered involuntary commitment on the grounds of incompetency or disability, or court-ordered placement under guardianship or conservatorship in the other jurisdiction has been stayed there, any reciprocal transfer or transfer by the Office may be deferred until the stay expires.

(d) *Hearing and transfer to disability inactive status.* The request for transfer to disability inactive status shall be heard by the USPTO Director on the documentary record unless the USPTO Director determines that there is a genuine issue of material fact, in which case the USPTO Director may deny the request. Upon the expiration of 30 days from the date of the notice pursuant to the provisions of paragraph (b) of this section, the USPTO Director shall consider any timely filed response and impose the identical transfer to disability inactive status based on the practitioner's transfer to disability status in another jurisdiction, or shall transfer the practitioner to disability inactive status based on judicially declared incompetence, judicially ordered involuntary commitment on the grounds of incompetency or disability, or court-ordered placement under guardianship or conservatorship, unless the practitioner demonstrates by clear and convincing evidence, or the USPTO Director finds there is a genuine issue of material fact by clear and convincing evidence that:

(1) The procedure was so lacking in notice or opportunity to be heard as to constitute a deprivation of due process;

(2) There was such infirmity of proof establishing the transfer to disability status, judicial declaration of incompetence, judicial order for involuntary commitment on the grounds of incompetency or disability, or placement by court order under guardianship or conservatorship that the USPTO Director could not, consistent with Office's duty, accept as final the conclusion on that subject;

(3) The imposition of the same disability status or transfer to disability status by the USPTO Director would result in grave injustice; or

(4) The practitioner is not the individual transferred to disability status, judicially declared incompetent, judicially ordered for involuntary commitment on the grounds of incompetency or disability, or placed by court order under guardianship or conservatorship.

(5) If the USPTO Director determines that there is no genuine issue of material fact with regard to any of the elements of paragraphs (d)(1) through (4) of this section, the USPTO Director shall enter an appropriate final order. If the USPTO Director is unable to make that determination because there is a genuine issue of material fact, the USPTO Director shall enter an appropriate order dismissing the OED Director's request for such reason.

(e) *Adjudication in other jurisdiction.* In all other aspects, a final adjudication in another jurisdiction that a practitioner be transferred to disability inactive status, is judicially declared incompetent, is judicially ordered to be involuntarily committed on the grounds of incompetency or disability, or is placed by court order under guardianship or conservatorship shall establish the disability for purposes of a reciprocal transfer to or transfer to disability status before the Office.

(f) A practitioner who is transferred to disability inactive status under this section shall be deemed to have been refused recognition to practice before the Office for purposes of 35 U.S.C. 32.

(g) *Order imposing reciprocal transfer to disability inactive status or order imposing initial transfer to disability inactive status.* An order by the USPTO Director imposing reciprocal transfer to disability inactive status, or transferring a practitioner to disability inactive status shall be effective immediately, and shall be for an indefinite period until further order of the USPTO Director. A copy of the order transferring a practitioner to disability inactive status shall be served upon the practitioner, the practitioner's guardian, and/or the director of the institution to which the practitioner has been committed in the manner the USPTO Director may direct. A practitioner reciprocally transferred or transferred to disability inactive status shall comply with the provisions of § 11.58, and shall not engage in practice before the Office in patent, trademark and other non-patent law unless and until reinstated to active status.

(h) *Confidentiality of proceeding; Orders to be public*—(1) *Confidentiality of proceeding.* All proceedings under this section involving allegations of disability of a practitioner shall be kept confidential until and unless the USPTO Director enters an order reciprocally transferring or transferring the practitioner to disability inactive status.

(2) *Orders to be public.* The OED Director shall publicize any reciprocal transfer to disability inactive status or transfer to disability inactive status in the same manner as for the imposition of public discipline.

(i) *Employment of practitioners on disability inactive status.* A practitioner on disability inactive status must seek permission from the OED Director to engage in an activity authorized under § 11.58(e). Permission will be granted only if the practitioner has complied with all the conditions of §§ 11.58(a) through 11.58(d) applicable to disability inactive status. In the event that permission is granted, the practitioner shall fully comply with the provisions of § 11.58(e).

(j) *Reinstatement from disability inactive status.* (1) *Generally.* No practitioner reciprocally transferred or transferred to disability inactive status under this section may resume active status except by order of the OED Director.

(2) *Petition*. A practitioner reciprocally transferred or transferred to disability inactive status shall be entitled to petition the OED Director for transfer to active status once a year, or at whatever shorter intervals the USPTO Director may direct in the order transferring or reciprocally transferring the practitioner to disability inactive status or any modification thereof.

(3) *Examination*. Upon the filing of a petition for transfer to active status, the OED Director may take or direct whatever action is deemed necessary or proper to determine whether the incapacity has been removed, including a direction for an examination of the practitioner by qualified medical or psychological experts designated by the OED Director. The expense of the examination shall be paid and borne by the practitioner.

(4) *Required disclosure, waiver of privilege*. With the filing of a petition for reinstatement to active status, the practitioner shall be required to disclose the name of each psychiatrist, psychologist, physician and hospital or other institution by whom or in which the practitioner has been examined or treated for the disability since the transfer to disability inactive status. The practitioner shall furnish to the OED Director written consent to the release of information and records relating to the incapacity if requested by the OED Director.

(5) *Learning in the law, examination*. The OED Director may direct that the practitioner establish proof of competence and learning in law, which proof may include passing the registration examination.

(6) *Granting of petition for transfer to active status*. The OED Director shall grant the petition for transfer to active status upon a showing by clear and convincing evidence that the incapacity has been removed.

(7) *Reinstatement in other jurisdiction*. If a practitioner is reciprocally transferred to disability inactive status on the basis of a transfer to disability inactive status in another jurisdiction, the OED Director may dispense with further evidence that the disability has been removed and may immediately direct reinstatement to active status upon such terms as are deemed proper and advisable.

(8) *Judicial declaration of competency*. If a practitioner is transferred to disability inactive status on the basis of a judicially declared incompetence, judicially ordered involuntary commitment on the grounds of incompetency or disability, or court-ordered placement under guardianship or conservatorship has been declared to be competent, the OED Director may dispense with further evidence that the incapacity to practice law has been removed and may immediately direct reinstatement to active status.

[Added, 73 FR 47650, Aug. 14, 2008, effective Sept. 15, 2008]

§ 11.30 - 11.31 [Reserved]

§ 11.32 Instituting a disciplinary proceeding.

If after conducting an investigation under § 11.22(a), the OED Director is of the opinion that grounds exist for discipline under §§ 11.19(b)(3) through (5), the OED Director, after complying where necessary with the provisions of 5 U.S.C. 558(c), shall convene a meeting of a panel of the Committee on Discipline. The panel of the Committee on Discipline shall then determine as specified in § 11.23(b) whether a disciplinary proceeding shall be instituted. If the panel of the Committee on Discipline determines that probable cause exists to bring charges under §§ 11.19(b)(3) through (5), the OED Director shall institute a disciplinary proceeding by filing a complaint under § 11.34.

[Added, 73 FR 47650, Aug. 14, 2008, effective Sept. 15, 2008]

§ 11.33 [Reserved]

§ 11.34 Complaint.

(a) A complaint instituting a disciplinary proceeding under §§ 11.25(b)(4) or 11.32 shall:

(1) Name the practitioner who may then be referred to as the "respondent";

(2) Give a plain and concise description of the respondent's alleged grounds for discipline;

(3) State the place and time, not less than thirty days from the date the complaint is filed, for filing an answer by the respondent;

(4) State that a decision by default may be entered if an answer is not timely filed by the respondent; and

(5)   Be signed by the OED Director.

(b)   A complaint will be deemed sufficient if it fairly informs the respondent of any grounds for discipline, and where applicable, the Mandatory Disciplinary Rules identified in § 10.20(b) of this subchapter that form the basis for the disciplinary proceeding so that the respondent is able to adequately prepare a defense.

(c)   The complaint shall be filed in the manner prescribed by the USPTO Director.

[Added, 73 FR 47650, Aug. 14, 2008, effective Sept. 15, 2008]

§ 11.35   Service of complaint.

(a)   A complaint may be served on a respondent in any of the following methods:

(1)   By delivering a copy of the complaint personally to the respondent, in which case the individual who gives the complaint to the respondent shall file an affidavit with the OED Director indicating the time and place the complaint was delivered to the respondent.

(2)   By mailing a copy of the complaint by "Express Mail," first-class mail, or any delivery service that provides ability to confirm delivery or attempted delivery to:

(i)   A respondent who is a registered practitioner at the address provided to OED pursuant to § 11.11, or

(ii)   A respondent who is a nonregistered practitioner at the last address for the respondent known to the OED Director.

(3)   By any method mutually agreeable to the OED Director and the respondent.

(4)   In the case of a respondent who resides outside the United States, by sending a copy of the complaint by any delivery service that provides ability to confirm delivery or attempted delivery, to:

(i)   A respondent who is a registered practitioner at the address provided to OED pursuant to § 11.11; or

(ii)   A respondent who is a nonregistered practitioner at the last address for the respondent known to the OED Director.

(b)   If a copy of the complaint cannot be delivered to the respondent through any one of the procedures in paragraph (a) of this section, the OED Director shall serve the respondent by causing an appropriate notice to be published in the Official Gazette for two consecutive weeks, in which case, the time for filing an answer shall be thirty days from the second publication of the notice. Failure to timely file an answer will constitute an admission of the allegations in the complaint in accordance with paragraph (d) of § 11.36, and the hearing officer may enter an initial decision on default.

(c)   If the respondent is known to the OED Director to be represented by an attorney under § 11.40(a), a copy of the complaint shall be served on the attorney in lieu of service on the respondent in the manner provided for in paragraph (a) or (b) of this section.

[Added, 73 FR 47650, Aug. 14, 2008, effective Sept. 15, 2008]

§ 11.36   Answer to complaint.

(a)   *Time for answer*. An answer to a complaint shall be filed within the time set in the complaint but in no event shall that time be less than thirty days from the date the complaint is filed.

(b)   *With whom filed*. The answer shall be filed in writing with the hearing officer at the address specified in the complaint. The hearing officer may extend the time for filing an answer once for a period of no more than thirty days upon a showing of good cause, provided a motion requesting an extension of time is filed within thirty days after the date the complaint is served on respondent. A copy of the answer, and any exhibits or attachments thereto, shall be served on the OED Director.

(c)   *Content*. The respondent shall include in the answer a statement of the facts that constitute the grounds of defense and shall specifically admit or deny each allegation set forth in the complaint. The respondent shall not deny a material allegation in the complaint that the respondent knows to be true or state that respondent is without sufficient information to form a belief as to the truth of an allegation, when in fact the respondent possesses that information. The respondent shall also state affirmatively in the answer special matters of defense and any intent to raise a disability as a mitigating factor. If respondent intends to raise a special matter of defense or disability, the answer shall specify the defense or disability, its nexus to the misconduct, and the reason it provides a defense or mitigation. A respondent who fails to do so cannot rely on a special matter of defense or disability. The hearing officer may, for good cause, allow the respondent to file the statement late, grant additional hearing preparation time, or make other appropriate orders.

(d) *Failure to deny allegations in complaint.* Every allegation in the complaint that is not denied by a respondent in the answer shall be deemed to be admitted and may be considered proven. The hearing officer at any hearing need receive no further evidence with respect to that allegation.

(e) *Default judgment.* Failure to timely file an answer will constitute an admission of the allegations in the complaint and may result in entry of default judgment.

[Added, 73 FR 47650, Aug. 14, 2008, effective Sept. 15, 2008]

§ 11.37 [Reserved]

§ 11.38 Contested case.

Upon the filing of an answer by the respondent, a disciplinary proceeding shall be regarded as a contested case within the meaning of 35 U.S.C. 24. Evidence obtained by a subpoena issued under 35 U.S.C. 24 shall not be admitted into the record or considered unless leave to proceed under 35 U.S.C. 24 was previously authorized by the hearing officer.

[Added, 73 FR 47650, Aug. 14, 2008, effective Sept. 15, 2008]

§ 11.39 Hearing officer; appointment; responsibilities; review of interlocutory orders; stays.

(a) *Appointment.* A hearing officer, appointed by the USPTO Director under 5 U.S.C. 3105 or 35 U.S.C. 32, shall conduct disciplinary proceedings as provided by this Part.

(b) *Independence of the Hearing Officer.*

(1) A hearing officer appointed in accordance with paragraph (a) of this section shall not be subject to first level or second level supervision by either the USPTO Director or OED Director, or his or her designee.

(2) A hearing officer appointed in accordance with paragraph (a) of this section shall not be subject to supervision of the person(s) investigating or prosecuting the case.

(3) A hearing officer appointed in accordance with paragraph (a) of this section shall be impartial, shall not be an individual who has participated in any manner in the decision to initiate the proceedings, and shall not have been employed under the immediate supervision of the practitioner.

(4) A hearing officer appointed in accordance with paragraph (a) of this section shall be admitted to practice law and have suitable experience and training conducting hearings, reaching a determination, and rendering an initial decision in an equitable manner.

(c) *Responsibilities.* The hearing officer shall have authority, consistent with specific provisions of these regulations, to:

(1) Administer oaths and affirmations;

(2) Make rulings upon motions and other requests;

(3) Rule upon offers of proof, receive relevant evidence, and examine witnesses;

(4) Authorize the taking of a deposition of a witness in lieu of personal appearance of the witness before the hearing officer;

(5) Determine the time and place of any hearing and regulate its course and conduct;

(6) Hold or provide for the holding of conferences to settle or simplify the issues;

(7) Receive and consider oral or written arguments on facts or law;

(8) Adopt procedures and modify procedures for the orderly disposition of proceedings;

(9) Make initial decisions under §§ 11.25 and 11.54; and

(10) Perform acts and take measures as necessary to promote the efficient, timely, and impartial conduct of any disciplinary proceeding.

(d) *Time for making initial decision.* The hearing officer shall set times and exercise control over a disciplinary proceeding such that an initial decision under § 11.54 is normally issued within nine months of the date a complaint is filed. The hearing officer may, however, issue an initial decision more than nine months after a complaint is filed if there exist circumstances, in his or her opinion, that preclude issuance of an initial decision within nine months of the filing of the complaint.

(e)   *Review of interlocutory orders.* The USPTO Director will not review an interlocutory order of a hearing officer except:

(1)   When the hearing officer shall be of the opinion:

(i)   That the interlocutory order involves a controlling question of procedure or law as to which there is a substantial ground for a difference of opinion, and

(ii)   That an immediate decision by the USPTO Director may materially advance the ultimate termination of the disciplinary proceeding, or

(2)   In an extraordinary situation where the USPTO Director deems that justice requires review.

(f)   *Stays pending review of interlocutory order.* If the OED Director or a respondent seeks review of an interlocutory order of a hearing officer under paragraph (b)(2) of this section, any time period set by the hearing officer for taking action shall not be stayed unless ordered by the USPTO Director or the hearing officer.

(g)   The hearing officer shall engage in no ex parte discussions with any party on the merits of the complaint, beginning with appointment and ending when the final agency decision is issued.

[Added, 73 FR 47650, Aug. 14, 2008, effective Sept. 15, 2008]

§ 11.40   Representative for OED Director or respondent.

(a)   A respondent may represent himself or herself, or be represented by an attorney before the Office in connection with an investigation or disciplinary proceeding. The attorney shall file a written declaration that he or she is an attorney within the meaning of § 11.1 and shall state:

(1)   The address to which the attorney wants correspondence related to the investigation or disciplinary proceeding sent, and

(2)   A telephone number where the attorney may be reached during normal business hours.

(b)   The Deputy General Counsel for Intellectual Property and Solicitor, and attorneys in the Office of the Solicitor shall represent the OED Director. The attorneys representing the OED Director in disciplinary proceedings shall not consult with the USPTO Director, the General Counsel, the Deputy General

Counsel for General Law, or an individual designated by the USPTO Director to decide disciplinary matters regarding the proceeding. The General Counsel and the Deputy General Counsel for General Law shall remain screened from the investigation and prosecution of all disciplinary proceedings in order that they shall be available as counsel to the USPTO Director in deciding disciplinary proceedings unless access is appropriate to perform their duties. After a final decision is entered in a disciplinary proceeding, the OED Director and attorneys representing the OED Director shall be available to counsel the USPTO Director, the General Counsel, and the Deputy General Counsel for General Law in any further proceedings.

[Added, 73 FR 47650, Aug. 14, 2008, effective Sept. 15, 2008]

§ 11.41   Filing of papers.

(a)   The provisions of §§ 1.8 and 2.197 of this subchapter do not apply to disciplinary proceedings. All papers filed after the complaint and prior to entry of an initial decision by the hearing officer shall be filed with the hearing officer at an address or place designated by the hearing officer.

(b)   All papers filed after entry of an initial decision by the hearing officer shall be filed with the USPTO Director. A copy of the paper shall be served on the OED Director. The hearing officer or the OED Director may provide for filing papers and other matters by hand, by "Express Mail," or by other means.

[Added, 73 FR 47650, Aug. 14, 2008, effective Sept. 15, 2008]

§ 11.42   Service of papers.

(a)   All papers other than a complaint shall be served on a respondent who is represented by an attorney by:

(1)   Delivering a copy of the paper to the office of the attorney; or

(2)   Mailing a copy of the paper by first-class mail, "Express Mail," or other delivery service to the attorney at the address provided by the attorney under § 11.40(a)(1); or

(3)   Any other method mutually agreeable to the attorney and a representative for the OED Director.

(b) All papers other than a complaint shall be served on a respondent who is not represented by an attorney by:

(1) Delivering a copy of the paper to the respondent; or

(2) Mailing a copy of the paper by first-class mail, "Express Mail," or other delivery service to the respondent at the address to which a complaint may be served or such other address as may be designated in writing by the respondent; or

(3) Any other method mutually agreeable to the respondent and a representative of the OED Director.

(c) A respondent shall serve on the representative for the OED Director one copy of each paper filed with the hearing officer or the OED Director. A paper may be served on the representative for the OED Director by:

(1) Delivering a copy of the paper to the representative; or

(2) Mailing a copy of the paper by first-class mail, "Express Mail," or other delivery service to an address designated in writing by the representative; or

(3) Any other method mutually agreeable to the respondent and the representative.

(d) Each paper filed in a disciplinary proceeding shall contain therein a certificate of service indicating:

(1) The date on which service was made; and

(2) The method by which service was made.

(e) The hearing officer or the USPTO Director may require that a paper be served by hand or by "Express Mail."

(f) Service by mail is completed when the paper mailed in the United States is placed into the custody of the U.S. Postal Service.

[Added, 73 FR 47650, Aug. 14, 2008, effective Sept. 15, 2008]

§ 11.43 Motions.

Motions, including all prehearing motions commonly filed under the Federal Rules of Civil Procedure, shall be filed with the hearing officer. The hearing officer will determine whether replies to responses will be authorized and the time period for filing such a response. No motion shall be filed with the hearing officer unless such motion is supported by a written statement by the moving party that the mov-

ing party or attorney for the moving party has conferred with the opposing party or attorney for the opposing party in an effort in good faith to resolve by agreement the issues raised by the motion and has been unable to reach agreement. If, prior to a decision on the motion, the parties resolve issues raised by a motion presented to the hearing officer, the parties shall promptly notify the hearing officer.

[Added, 73 FR 47650, Aug. 14, 2008, effective Sept. 15, 2008]

§ 11.44 Hearings.

(a) The hearing officer shall preside over hearings in disciplinary proceedings. The hearing officer shall set the time and place for the hearing. In cases involving an incarcerated respondent, any necessary oral hearing may be held at the location of incarceration. Oral hearings will be stenographically recorded and transcribed, and the testimony of witnesses will be received under oath or affirmation. The hearing officer shall conduct the hearing as if the proceeding were subject to 5 U.S.C. 556. A copy of the transcript of the hearing shall become part of the record. A copy of the transcript shall be provided to the OED Director and the respondent at the expense of the Office.

(b) If the respondent to a disciplinary proceeding fails to appear at the hearing after a notice of hearing has been given by the hearing officer, the hearing officer may deem the respondent to have waived the right to a hearing and may proceed with the hearing in the absence of the respondent.

(c) A hearing under this section will not be open to the public except that the hearing officer may grant a request by a respondent to open his or her hearing to the public and make the record of the disciplinary proceeding available for public inspection, *provided*, a protective order is entered to exclude from public disclosure information which is privileged or confidential under applicable laws or regulations.

[Added, 73 FR 47650, Aug. 14, 2008, effective Sept. 15, 2008]

§ 11.45 Amendment of pleadings.

The OED Director may, without Committee on Discipline authorization, but with the authorization of the hearing officer, amend the complaint to include additional charges based upon conduct committed before or after the complaint was filed. If amendment of the complaint is authorized, the hearing officer shall authorize amendment of the answer. Any party who would otherwise be prejudiced by the amendment will be given reasonable opportunity to meet the allegations in the complaint or answer as amended, and the hearing officer shall make findings on any issue presented by the complaint or answer as amended.

[Added, 73 FR 47650, Aug. 14, 2008, effective Sept. 15, 2008]

§ 11.46 - 11.48 [Reserved]

§ 11.49   Burden of proof.

In a disciplinary proceeding, the OED Director shall have the burden of proving the violation by clear and convincing evidence and a respondent shall have the burden of proving any affirmative defense by clear and convincing evidence.

[Added, 73 FR 47650, Aug. 14, 2008, effective Sept. 15, 2008]

§ 11.50   Evidence.

(a)   *Rules of evidence.* The rules of evidence prevailing in courts of law and equity are not controlling in hearings in disciplinary proceedings. However, the hearing officer shall exclude evidence that is irrelevant, immaterial, or unduly repetitious.

(b)   *Depositions.* Depositions of witnesses taken pursuant to § 11.51 may be admitted as evidence.

(c)   *Government documents.* Official documents, records, and papers of the Office, including, but not limited to, all papers in the file of a disciplinary investigation, are admissible without extrinsic evidence of authenticity. These documents, records, and papers may be evidenced by a copy certified as correct by an employee of the Office.

(d)   *Exhibits.* If any document, record, or other paper is introduced in evidence as an exhibit, the hearing officer may authorize the withdrawal of the exhibit subject to any conditions the hearing officer deems appropriate.

(e)   *Objections.* Objections to evidence will be in short form, stating the grounds of objection. Objections and rulings on objections will be a part of the record. No exception to the ruling is necessary to preserve the rights of the parties.

[Added, 73 FR 47650, Aug. 14, 2008, effective Sept. 15, 2008]

§ 11.51   Depositions.

(a)   Depositions for use at the hearing in lieu of personal appearance of a witness before the hearing officer may be taken by respondent or the OED Director upon a showing of good cause and with the approval of, and under such conditions as may be deemed appropriate by, the hearing officer. Depositions may be taken upon oral or written questions, upon not less than ten days' written notice to the other party, before any officer authorized to administer an oath or affirmation in the place where the deposition is to be taken. The parties may waive the requirement of ten days' notice and depositions may then be taken of a witness at a time and place mutually agreed to by the parties. When a deposition is taken upon written questions, copies of the written questions will be served upon the other party with the notice, and copies of any written cross-questions will be served by hand or "Express Mail" not less than five days before the date of the taking of the deposition unless the parties mutually agree otherwise. A party on whose behalf a deposition is taken shall file a copy of a transcript of the deposition signed by a court reporter with the hearing officer and shall serve one copy upon the opposing party. Expenses for a court reporter and preparing, serving, and filing depositions shall be borne by the party at whose instance the deposition is taken. Depositions may not be taken to obtain discovery, except as provided for in paragraph (b) of this section.

(b)   When the OED Director and the respondent agree in writing, a deposition of any witness who will appear voluntarily may be taken under such terms and conditions as may be mutually agreeable to the OED Director and the respondent. The deposition shall not be filed with the hearing officer and may not be admitted in evidence before the hearing officer unless he or she orders the deposition admitted in evidence. The admissibility of the deposition shall lie within the discretion of the hearing officer who may reject the deposition on any reasonable basis including the fact that demeanor is involved and that the witness should have been called to appear personally before the hearing officer.

[Added, 73 FR 47650, Aug. 14, 2008, effective Sept. 15, 2008

§ 11.52 Discovery.

Discovery shall not be authorized except as follows:

(a) After an answer is filed under § 11.36 and when a party establishes that discovery is reasonable and relevant, the hearing officer, under such conditions as he or she deems appropriate, may order an opposing party to:

(1) Answer a reasonable number of written requests for admission or interrogatories;

(2) Produce for inspection and copying a reasonable number of documents; and

(3) Produce for inspection a reasonable number of things other than documents.

(b) Discovery shall not be authorized under paragraph (a) of this section of any matter which:

(1) Will be used by another party solely for impeachment;

(2) Is not available to the party under 35 U.S.C. 122;

(3) Relates to any other disciplinary proceeding;

(4) Relates to experts except as the hearing officer may require under paragraph (e) of this section;

(5) Is privileged; or

(6) Relates to mental impressions, conclusions, opinions, or legal theories of any attorney or other representative of a party.

(c) The hearing officer may deny discovery requested under paragraph (a) of this section if the discovery sought:

(1) Will unduly delay the disciplinary proceeding;

(2) Will place an undue burden on the party required to produce the discovery sought; or

(3) Consists of information that is available:

(i) Generally to the public;

(i) Equally to the parties; or

(iii) To the party seeking the discovery through another source.

(d) Prior to authorizing discovery under paragraph (a) of this section, the hearing officer shall require the party seeking discovery to file a motion (§ 11.43) and explain in detail, for each request made, how the discovery sought is reasonable and relevant to an issue actually raised in the complaint or the answer.

(e) The hearing officer may require parties to file and serve, prior to any hearing, a pre-hearing statement that contains:

(1) A list (together with a copy) of all proposed exhibits to be used in connection with a party's case-in-chief;

(2) A list of proposed witnesses;

(3) As to each proposed expert witness:

(i) An identification of the field in which the individual will be qualified as an expert;

(ii) A statement as to the subject matter on which the expert is expected to testify; and

(iii) A statement of the substance of the facts and opinions to which the expert is expected to testify;

(4) Copies of memoranda reflecting respondent's own statements to administrative representatives.

[Added, 73 FR 47650, Aug. 14, 2008, effective Sept. 15, 2008]

§ 11.53 Proposed findings and conclusions; post-hearing memorandum.

Except in cases in which the respondent has failed to answer the complaint or amended complaint, the hearing officer, prior to making an initial decision, shall afford the parties a reasonable opportunity to submit proposed findings and conclusions and a post-hearing memorandum in support of the proposed findings and conclusions.

[Added, 73 FR 47650, Aug. 14, 2008, effective Sept. 15, 2008]

§ 11.54 Initial decision of hearing officer.

(a) The hearing officer shall make an initial decision in the case. The decision will include:

(1) A statement of findings of fact and conclusions of law, as well as the reasons or bases for those findings and conclusions with appropriate references to the record, upon all the material issues of fact, law, or discretion presented on the record, and

(2) An order of default judgment, of suspension or exclusion from practice, of reprimand, or an order dismissing the complaint. The hearing officer

shall transmit a copy of the decision to the OED Director and to the respondent. After issuing the decision, the hearing officer shall transmit the entire record to the OED Director. In the absence of an appeal to the USPTO Director, the decision of the hearing officer, including a default judgment, will, without further proceedings, become the decision of the USPTO Director thirty days from the date of the decision of the hearing officer.

(b)   The initial decision of the hearing officer shall explain the reason for any default judgment, reprimand, suspension, or exclusion. In determining any sanction, the following four factors must be considered if they are applicable:

(1)   Whether the practitioner has violated a duty owed to a client, to the public, to the legal system, or to the profession;

(2)   Whether the practitioner acted intentionally, knowingly, or negligently;

(3)   The amount of the actual or potential injury caused by the practitioner's misconduct; and

(4)   The existence of any aggravating or mitigating factors.

[Added, 73 FR 47650, Aug. 14, 2008, effective Sept. 15, 2008]

§ 11.55   Appeal to the USPTO Director.

(a)   Within thirty days after the date of the initial decision of the hearing officer under §§ 11.25 or 11.54, either party may appeal to the USPTO Director. The appeal shall include the appellant's brief. If more than one appeal is filed, the party who files the appeal first is the appellant for purpose of this rule. If appeals are filed on the same day, the respondent is the appellant. If an appeal is filed, then the OED Director shall transmit the entire record to the USPTO Director. Any cross-appeal shall be filed within fourteen days after the date of service of the appeal pursuant to § 11.42, or thirty days after the date of the initial decision of the hearing officer, whichever is later. The cross-appeal shall include the cross-appellant's brief. Any appellee or cross-appellee brief must be filed within thirty days after the date of service pursuant to § 11.42 of an appeal or cross-appeal. Any reply brief must be filed within fourteen days after the date of service of any appellee or cross-appellee brief.

(b)   An appeal or cross-appeal must include exceptions to the decisions of the hearing officer and supporting reasons for those exceptions. Any exception not raised will be deemed to have been waived and will be disregarded by the USPTO Director in reviewing the initial decision.

(c)   All briefs shall:

(1)   Be filed with the USPTO Director at the address set forth in § 1.1(a)(3)(ii) of this subchapter and served on the opposing party;

(2)   Include separate sections containing a concise statement of the disputed facts and disputed points of law; and

(3)   Be typed on 8 1/2 by 11-inch paper, and comply with Rule 32(a)(4)-(6) of the Federal Rules of Appellate Procedure.

(d)   An appellant's, cross-appellant's, appellee's, and cross-appellee's brief shall be no more than thirty pages in length, and comply with Rule 28(a)(2), (3), and (5) through (10) of the Federal Rules of Appellate Procedure. Any reply brief shall be no more than fifteen pages in length, and shall comply with Rule 28 (a)(2), (3), (8), and (9) of the Federal Rules of Appellate Procedure.

(e)   The USPTO Director may refuse entry of a nonconforming brief.

(f)   The USPTO Director will decide the appeal on the record made before the hearing officer.

(g)   Unless the USPTO Director permits, no further briefs or motions shall be filed.

(h)   The USPTO Director may order reopening of a disciplinary proceeding in accordance with the principles that govern the granting of new trials. Any request to reopen a disciplinary proceeding on the basis of newly discovered evidence must demonstrate that the newly discovered evidence could not have been discovered by due diligence.

(i)   In the absence of an appeal by the OED Director, failure by the respondent to appeal under the provisions of this section shall result in the initial decision being final and effective thirty days from the date of the initial decision of the hearing officer.

[Added, 73 FR 47650, Aug. 14, 2008, effective Sept. 15, 2008]

§ 11.56   Decision of the USPTO Director.

(a)   The USPTO Director shall decide an appeal from an initial decision of the hearing officer. On appeal from the initial decision, the USPTO Director has authority to conduct a de novo review of the factual record. The USPTO Director may affirm, reverse, or modify the initial decision or remand the matter to the hearing officer for such further proceedings as the USPTO Director may deem appropriate. In making a final decision, the USPTO Director shall review the record or the portions of the record designated by the parties. The USPTO Director shall transmit a copy of the final decision to the OED Director and to the respondent.

(b) A final decision of the USPTO Director may dismiss a disciplinary proceeding, reverse or modify the initial decision, reprimand a practitioner, or may suspend or exclude the practitioner from practice before the Office. A final decision suspending or excluding a practitioner shall require compliance with the provisions of § 11.58. The final decision may also condition the reinstatement of the practitioner upon a showing that the practitioner has taken steps to correct or mitigate the matter forming the basis of the action, or to prevent recurrence of the same or similar conduct.

(c) The respondent or the OED Director may make a single request for reconsideration or modification of the decision by the USPTO Director if filed within twenty days from the date of entry of the decision. No request for reconsideration or modification shall be granted unless the request is based on newly discovered evidence or error of law or fact, and the requestor must demonstrate that any newly discovered evidence could not have been discovered any earlier by due diligence. Such a request shall have the effect of staying the effective date of the order of discipline in the final decision. The decision by the USPTO Director is effective on its date of entry.

[Added, 73 FR 47650, Aug. 14, 2008, effective Sept. 15, 2008]

§ 11.57 Review of final decision of the USPTO Director.

(a) Review of the final decision by the USPTO Director in a disciplinary case may be had, subject to § 11.55(d), by a petition filed in accordance with 35 U.S.C. 32. The Respondent must serve the USPTO Director with the petition. Respondent must serve the petition in accordance with Rule 4 of the Federal Rules of Civil Procedure and § 104.2 of this Title.

(b) Except as provided for in § 11.56(c), an order for discipline in a final decision will not be stayed except on proof of exceptional circumstances.

[Added, 73 FR 47650, Aug. 14, 2008, effective Sept. 15, 2008]

§ 11.58 Duties of disciplined or resigned practitioner, or practitioner on disability inactive status.

(a) An excluded, suspended or resigned practitioner, or practitioner transferred to disability inactive status shall not engage in any practice of patent, trademark and other non-patent law before the Office. An excluded, suspended or resigned practitioner will not be automatically reinstated at the end of his or her period of exclusion or suspension. An excluded, suspended or resigned practitioner, or practitioner transferred to disability inactive status must comply with the provisions of this section and § 11.60 to be reinstated. Failure to comply with the provisions of this section may constitute both grounds for denying reinstatement or readmission; and cause for further action, including seeking further exclusion, suspension, and for revocation of any pending probation.

(b) Unless otherwise ordered by the USPTO Director, any excluded, suspended or resigned practitioner, or practitioner transferred to disability inactive status shall:

(1) Within thirty days after the date of entry of the order of exclusion, suspension, acceptance of resignation, or transfer to disability inactive status:

(i) File a notice of withdrawal as of the effective date of the exclusion, suspension, acceptance of resignation, or transfer to disability inactive status in each pending patent and trademark application, each pending reexamination and interference proceeding, and every other matter pending in the Office, together with a copy of the notices sent pursuant to paragraphs (b) and (c) of this section;

(ii) Provide notice to all State and Federal jurisdictions and administrative agencies to which the practitioner is admitted to practice and all clients the practitioner represents having immediate or prospective business before the Office in patent, trademark and other non-patent matters of the order of exclusion, suspension, acceptance of resignation, or transferred to disability inactive status and of the practitioner's consequent inability to act as a practitioner after the effective date of the order; and that, if not represented by another practitioner, the client should act promptly to substitute another practitioner, or to seek legal advice elsewhere, calling attention to any urgency arising from the circumstances of the case;

(iii) Provide notice to the practitioner(s) for all opposing parties (or, to the parties in the absence of a practitioner representing the parties) in matters pending before the Office of the practitioner's exclusion, suspension, resignation, or transfer to disability inactive status and, that as a consequence, the practitioner is disqualified from acting as a practitioner regarding matters before the Office after the effective date of the suspension, exclusion, resignation or transfer to disability inactive status, and state in the notice the mailing address of each client of the excluded, suspended or resigned practitioner, or practitioner transferred to disability inactive status who is a party in the pending matter;

(iv) Deliver to all clients having immediate or prospective business before the Office in patent, trademark or other non-patent matters any papers or other property to which the clients are entitled, or shall notify the clients and any co-practitioner of a suitable time and place where the papers and other property may be obtained, calling attention to any urgency for obtaining the papers or other property;

(v) Relinquish to the client, or other practitioner designated by the client, all funds for practice before the Office, including any legal fees paid in advance that have not been earned and any advanced costs not expended;

(vi) Take any necessary and appropriate steps to remove from any telephone, legal, or other directory any advertisement, statement, or representation which would reasonably suggest that the practitioner is authorized to practice patent, trademark, or other non-patent law before the Office; and

(vii) Serve all notices required by paragraphs (b)(1)(ii) and (b)(1)(iii) of this section by certified mail, return receipt requested, unless mailed abroad. If mailed abroad, all notices shall be served with a receipt to be signed and returned to the practitioner.

(2) Within forty-five days after entry of the order of suspension, exclusion, or of acceptance of resignation, the practitioner shall file with the OED Director an affidavit of compliance certifying that the practitioner has fully complied with the provisions of the order, this section, and with the Mandatory Disciplinary Rules identified in § 10.20(b) of this subchapter for withdrawal from representation. Appended to the affidavit of compliance shall be:

(i) A copy of each form of notice, the names and addresses of the clients, practitioners, courts, and agencies to which notices were sent, and all return receipts or returned mail received up to the date of the affidavit. Supplemental affidavits shall be filed covering subsequent return receipts and returned mail. Such names and addresses of clients shall remain confidential unless otherwise ordered by the USPTO Director;

(ii) A schedule showing the location, title and account number of every bank account designated as a client or trust account, deposit account in the Office, or other fiduciary account, and of every account in which the practitioner holds or held as of the entry date of the order any client, trust, or fiduciary funds for practice before the Office;

(iii) A schedule describing the practitioner's disposition of all client and fiduciary funds for practice before the Office in the practitioner's possession, custody or control as of the date of the order or thereafter;

(iv) Such proof of the proper distribution of said funds and the closing of such accounts as has been requested by the OED Director, including copies of checks and other instruments;

(v) A list of all other State, Federal, and administrative jurisdictions to which the practitioner is admitted to practice; and

(vi) An affidavit describing the precise nature of the steps taken to remove from any telephone, legal, or other directory any advertisement, statement, or representation which would reasonably suggest that the practitioner is authorized to practice patent, trademark, or other non-patent law before the Office. The affidavit shall also state the residence or other address of the practitioner to which communications may thereafter be directed, and list all State and Federal jurisdictions, and administrative agencies to which the practitioner is admitted to practice. The OED Director may require such additional proof as is deemed necessary. In addition, for the period of discipline, an excluded or suspended practitioner, or a practitioner transferred to disability inactive status shall continue to file a statement in accordance with § 11.11, regarding any change of residence or other address to which communications may thereafter be directed, so that the excluded or suspended practitioner, or practitioner transferred to disability inactive status may be located if a grievance is received regarding any conduct occurring before or after the exclusion or suspension. The practitioner shall retain copies of all notices sent and shall maintain complete records of the steps taken to comply with the notice requirements.

(3) Not hold himself or herself out as authorized to practice law before the Office.

(4) Not advertise the practitioner's availability or ability to perform or render legal services for any person having immediate or prospective business before the Office as to that business.

(5) Not render legal advice or services to any person having immediate or prospective business before the Office as to that business.

(6) Promptly take steps to change any sign identifying the practitioner's or the practitioner's firm's office and the practitioner's or the practitioner's firm's stationery to delete therefrom any advertisement, statement, or representation which would reasonably suggest that the practitioner is authorized to practice law before the Office.

(c) An excluded, suspended or resigned practitioner, or practitioner transferred to disability inactive status after entry of the order of exclusion or suspension, acceptance of resignation, or transfer to disability inactive status shall not accept any new retainer regarding immediate or prospective business before the Office, or engage as a practitioner for another in any new case or legal matter regarding practice before the Office. The excluded, suspended or resigned practitioner, or practitioner transferred to disability inactive status shall be granted limited recognition for a period of thirty days. During the thirty-day period of limited recognition, the excluded, suspended or resigned practitioner, or practitioner transferred to disability inactive status shall conclude work on behalf of a client on any matters that were pending before the Office on the date of entry of the order of exclusion or suspension, or acceptance of resignation. If such work cannot be concluded, the excluded, suspended or resigned practitioner, or practitioner transferred to dis-

ability inactive status shall so advise the client so that the client may make other arrangements.

(d) *Required records.* An excluded, suspended or resigned practitioner, or practitioner transferred to disability inactive status shall keep and maintain records of the various steps taken under this section, so that in any subsequent proceeding proof of compliance with this section and with the exclusion or suspension order will be available. The OED Director will require the practitioner to submit such proof as a condition precedent to the granting of any petition for reinstatement.

(e) An excluded, suspended or resigned practitioner, or practitioner on disability inactive status who aids another practitioner in any way in the other practitioner's practice of law before the Office, may, under the direct supervision of the other practitioner, act as a paralegal for the other practitioner or perform other services for the other practitioner which are normally performed by laypersons, provided:

(1) The excluded, suspended or resigned practitioner, or practitioner transferred to disability inactive status is a salaried employee of:

(i) The other practitioner;

(ii) The other practitioner's law firm; or

(iii) A client-employer who employs the other practitioner as a salaried employee;

(2) The other practitioner assumes full professional responsibility to any client and the Office for any work performed by the excluded, suspended or resigned practitioner for the other practitioner;

(3) The excluded, suspended or resigned practitioner, or practitioner transferred to disability inactive status does not:

(i) Communicate directly in writing, orally, or otherwise with a client of the other practitioner in regard to any immediate or prospective business before the Office;

(ii) Render any legal advice or any legal services to a client of the other practitioner in regard to any immediate or prospective business before the Office; or

(iii) Meet in person or in the presence of the other practitioner in regard to any immediate or prospective business before the Office, with:

(A) Any Office employee in connection with the prosecution of any patent, trademark, or other case;

(B) Any client of the other practitioner, the other practitioner's law firm, or the client-employer of the other practitioner; or

(C) Any witness or potential witness whom the other practitioner, the other practitioner's law firm, or the other practitioner's client-employer may or intends to call as a witness in any proceeding before the Office. The term "witness" includes individuals who will testify orally in a proceeding before, or sign an affidavit or any other document to be filed in, the Office.

(f) When an excluded, suspended or resigned practitioner, or practitioner transferred to disability inactive status acts as a paralegal or performs services under paragraph (e) of this section, the practitioner shall not thereafter be reinstated to practice before the Office unless:

(1) The practitioner shall have filed with the OED Director an affidavit which:

(i) Explains in detail the precise nature of all paralegal or other services performed by the excluded, suspended or resigned practitioner, or practitioner transferred to disability inactive status, and

(ii) Shows by clear and convincing evidence that the excluded, suspended or resigned practitioner, or practitioner transferred to disability inactive status has complied with the provisions of this section and all Mandatory Disciplinary Rules identified in § 10.20(b) of this subchapter; and

(2) The other practitioner shall have filed with the OED Director a written statement which:

(i) Shows that the other practitioner has read the affidavit required by paragraph (d)(1) of this section and that the other practitioner believes every statement in the affidavit to be true, and

(ii) States why the other practitioner believes that the excluded, suspended or resigned practitioner, or practitioner transferred to disability inactive status has complied with paragraph (c) of this section.

[Added, 73 FR 47650, Aug. 14, 2008, effective Sept. 15, 2008]

§ 11.59 Dissemination of disciplinary and other information.

(a) The OED Director shall inform the public of the disposition of each matter in which public discipline has been imposed, and of any other changes in a practitioner's registration status. Public discipline includes exclusion, as well as exclusion on consent; suspension; and public reprimand. Unless otherwise ordered by the USPTO Director, the OED Director shall give notice of public discipline and the reasons for the discipline to disciplinary enforcement agencies in the State where the practitioner is admitted to practice, to courts where the practitioner is known to be admitted, and the public. If public discipline is imposed, the OED Director shall cause a final decision of the USPTO Director to be published. Final decisions of the USPTO Director include default judgments. See § 11.54(a)(2). If a private reprimand is imposed, the OED Director shall cause a redacted version of the final decision to be published.

(b) *Records available to the public.* Unless the USPTO Director orders that the proceeding or a portion of the record be kept confidential, the OED Director's records of every disciplinary proceeding where a practitioner is reprimanded, suspended, or excluded, including when said sanction is imposed by default judgment, shall be made available to the public upon written request, except that information may be withheld as necessary to protect the privacy of third parties or as directed in a protective order issued pursuant to § 11.44(c). The record of a proceeding that results in a practitioner's transfer to disability inactive status shall not be available to the public.

(c) *Access to records of exclusion by consent.* Unless the USPTO Director orders that the proceeding or a portion of the record be kept confidential, an order excluding a practitioner on consent under § 11.27 and the affidavit required under paragraph (a) of § 11.27 shall be available to the public, except that information in the order or affidavit may be withheld as necessary to protect the privacy of third parties or as directed in a protective order under § 11.44(c). The affidavit required under paragraph (a) of § 11.27 shall not be used in any other proceeding except by order of the USPTO Director or upon written consent of the practitioner.

[Added, 73 FR 47650, Aug. 14, 2008, effective Sept. 15, 2008]

§ 11.60 Petition for reinstatement.

(a) *Restrictions on reinstatement.* An excluded, suspended or resigned practitioner shall not resume practice of patent, trademark, or other non-patent law before the Office until reinstated by order of the OED Director or the USPTO Director.

(b) *Petition for reinstatement.* An excluded or suspended practitioner shall be eligible to apply for reinstatement only upon expiration of the period of suspension or exclusion and the practitioner's full compliance with § 11.58. An excluded practitioner shall be eligible to apply for reinstatement no earlier than at least five years from the effective date of the exclusion. A resigned practitioner shall be eligible to petition for reinstatement and must show compliance with § 11.58 no earlier than at least five years from the date the practitioner's resignation is accepted and an order is entered excluding the practitioner on consent.

(c) *Review of reinstatement petition.* An excluded, suspended or resigned practitioner shall file a petition for reinstatement accompanied by the fee required by § 1.21(a)(10) of this subchapter. The petition for reinstatement shall be filed with the OED Director. An excluded or suspended practitioner who has violated any provision of § 11.58 shall not be eligible for reinstatement until a continuous period of the time in compliance with § 11.58 that is equal to the period of suspension or exclusion has elapsed. A resigned practitioner shall not be eligible for reinstatement until compliance with § 11.58 is shown. If the excluded, suspended or resigned practitioner is not eligible for reinstatement, or if the OED Director determines that the petition is insufficient or defective on its face, the OED Director may dismiss the petition. Otherwise the OED Director shall consider the petition for reinstatement. The excluded, suspended or resigned practitioner seeking reinstatement shall have the burden of proof by clear and convincing evidence. Such proof shall be included in or accompany the petition, and shall establish:

(1) That the excluded, suspended or resigned practitioner has the good moral character and reputation, competency, and learning in law required under § 11.7 for admission;

(2) That the resumption of practice before the Office will not be detrimental to the administration of justice or subversive to the public interest; and

(3) That the suspended practitioner has complied with the provisions of § 11.58 for the full period of suspension, that the excluded practitioner has complied with the provisions of § 11.58 for at least five

continuous years, or that the resigned practitioner has complied with § 11.58 upon acceptance of the resignation.

(d) *Petitions for reinstatement — Action by the OED Director granting reinstatement.* (1) If the excluded, suspended or resigned practitioner is found to have complied with paragraphs(c)(1) through (c)(3) of this section, the OED Director shall enter an order of reinstatement, which shall be conditioned on payment of the costs of the disciplinary proceeding to the extent set forth in paragraphs (d)(2) and (3) of this section.

(2) *Payment of costs of disciplinary proceedings.* Prior to reinstatement to practice, the excluded or suspended practitioner shall pay the costs of the disciplinary proceeding. The costs imposed pursuant to this section include all of the following:

(i) The actual expense incurred by the OED Director or the Office for the original and copies of any reporter's transcripts of the disciplinary proceeding, and any fee paid for the services of the reporter;

(ii) All expenses paid by the OED Director or the Office which would qualify as taxable costs recoverable in civil proceedings; and

(iii) The charges determined by the OED Director to be "reasonable costs" of investigation, hearing, and review. These amounts shall serve to defray the costs, other than fees for services of attorneys and experts, of the Office of Enrollment and Discipline in the preparation or hearing of the disciplinary proceeding, and costs incurred in the administrative processing of the disciplinary proceeding.

(3) An excluded or suspended practitioner may be granted relief, in whole or in part, only from an order assessing costs under this section or may be granted an extension of time to pay these costs, in the discretion of the OED Director, upon grounds of hardship, special circumstances, or other good cause.

(e) *Petitions for reinstatement — Action by the OED Director denying reinstatement.* If the excluded, suspended or resigned practitioner is found unfit to resume the practice of patent law before the Office, the OED Director shall first provide the excluded, suspended or resigned practitioner with an opportunity to show cause in writing why the petition should not be denied. Failure to comply with § 11.12 (c) shall constitute unfitness. If unpersuaded by the showing, the OED Director shall deny the petition. The OED Director may require the excluded, suspended or resigned practitioner, in meeting the requirements of § 11.7, to take and pass an examination under § 11.7 (b), ethics courses, and/or the Multistate Professional Responsibility Examination. The OED Director shall provide findings, together with the record. The findings shall include on the first page, immediately beneath the caption of the case, a separate section entitled "Prior Proceedings" which shall state the docket number of the original disciplinary proceeding in which the exclusion or suspension was ordered.

(f)   *Resubmission of petitions for reinstatement.* If a petition for reinstatement is denied, no further petition for reinstatement may be filed until the expiration of at least one year following the denial unless the order of denial provides otherwise.

(g)   *Reinstatement proceedings open to public.* Proceedings on any petition for reinstatement shall be open to the public. Before reinstating any excluded or suspended practitioner, the OED Director shall publish a notice of the excluded or suspended practitioner's petition for reinstatement and shall permit the public a reasonable opportunity to comment or submit evidence with respect to the petition for reinstatement.

[Added, 73 FR 47650, Aug. 14, 2008, effective Sept. 15, 2008]

§ 11.61 Savings clause.

(a)   A disciplinary proceeding based on conduct engaged in prior to September 15, 2008 may be instituted subsequent to such effective date, if such conduct would continue to justify suspension or exclusion under the provisions of this part.

(b)   No practitioner shall be subject to a disciplinary proceeding under this part based on conduct engaged in before the effective date hereof if such conduct would not have been subject to disciplinary action before September 15, 2008.

(c)   Sections 11.24, 11.25, 11.28 and 11.34 through 11.57 shall apply to all proceedings in which the complaint is filed on or after the effective date of these regulations. Section 11.26 and 11.27 shall apply to matters pending on or after September 15, 2008.

(d)   Sections 11.58 through 11.60 shall apply to all cases in which an order of suspension or exclusion is entered or resignation is accepted on or after September 15, 2008.

[Added, 73 FR 47650, Aug. 14, 2008, effective Sept. 15, 2008]

§ 11.62 -11.99 [Reserved]

Index II – RULES RELATING TO REPRESENTATION OF OTHERS BEFORE THE UNITED STATES PATENT AND TRADEMARK OFFICE

A

Address change 10.11, 11.11
Advertising 10.31, 10.32
Agents, registration of 11.6
Agreements restricting practice 10.38
Aliens 11.6, 11.9
Applicant for patent, representation of 1.31, 11.10
Attorneys, recognition of to practice in trademark cases 11.14
Attorneys, registration of to practice in patent cases 11.6, 11.7

B

Breach of trust 10.23
Business transactions or relations with client 10.65

C

Candidate for judicial office 10.103
Canons and disciplinary rules . . . . 10.20 - 10.112
Certificate of mailing 1.8, 10.23
Certification effect of signature 11.18
Circumventing a disciplinary rule, amendment . . . 10.23
Code of Professional Responsibility . . . . . 10.20 - 10.112
Coercion, Use of 10.23
Committee on Discipline 10.4
Communicating with person having adverse interest 10.67
Communications concerning practitioner's service 10.31
Compensation for legal services 10.68
Competence 10.76, 10.77
Complaint instituting disciplinary proceedings 11.34
Concealment of material information 10.23
Conduct in proceeding before Office 10.89
Conduct prejudicial to the administration of justice 10.23
Conflict of interest 10.66
Conviction of criminal offense 10.23

D

Deceit 10.23
Decisions of the USPTO Director 11.56, 11.57
Definitions:
    Affidavit 10.1
    Agent 11.6
    Application 10.1

Attorney or lawyer 11.1
Canon 10.20
Confidence 10.57
Differing interests 10.1
Director of Enrollment and Discipline 10.1
Disciplinary rule 10.20
Disqualified 11.1
Excessive legal fees 10.36
Excluded practitioner 10.1
Federal agency 11.1
Federal program 11.1
Giving information 10.1
Invention development services 10.23
Law firm 10.1
Legal counsel 10.1
Legal profession 10.1
Legal service 10.1
Legal system 10.1
Mandatory Disciplinary Rule 11.1
Non-practitioner 10.1
Office 10.1
Person 10.1
Practitioner 10.1
Proceeding before the Office 10.1
Professional legal corporation 10.1
Registration 10.1
Respondent 11.34
Secret 10.33, 10.57
Serious crime 11.1
State 10.1, 11.1
Suspended practitioner 10.1
Tribunal 10.1
United States 10.1
Designation as registered attorney or agent 10.34
Direct contact with prospective clients 10.33
Director of Enrollment and Discipline:
    Appointment 11.2
    Duties 11.2
    Review of decisions of OED Director 11.2
Discharge of attorney or agent by client 10.40
Disciplinary proceedings and investigations:
    Amendment of pleadings 11.45
    Answer to complaint 11.36
    Appeal to the USPTO Director 11.55
    Burden of proof 11.49
    Certificate of mailing 1.8
    Committee on Discipline 11.23
    Complaint 11.34
    Contested case 11.38
    Deliberations of Committee on Discipline 10.4
    Discovery in Disciplinary Proceedings 11.52
    Duties of disciplined or resigned practitioner . . . 11.58

Rev. 8, July 2010

Exclusion on consent 11.27
Filing papers after complaint filed 11.41
Hearing officer 11.39
Hearings 11.44
Incapacitated practitioners 11.28
Initial decision of hearing officer 11.54
Instituting disciplinary proceeding 11.32
Investigations of violations of
    disciplinary rules 11.22
Post hearing memorandum 11.53
Reciprocal discipline 11.24
Reciprocal transfer 11.29
Reinstatement of suspended or excluded
    practitioner 11.60
Representative for OED Director/respondent . . 11.40
Review of decision denying reinstatement
    of practitioner 11.2
Review of interlocutory orders by hearing
    officer 11.39
Savings clause 11.61
Service of complaint 11.35
Service of papers 11.42
Settlement of complaint 11.26
Warnings 11.21
Disciplinary rule violation
    Disclosure of 10.23, 10.24, 10.84, 10.85
Discourteous conduct 10.89
Discovery in disciplinary proceedings:
    Deliberations of committee on discipline 10.4
    Depositions 11.51
    Discovery 11.52
    Evidence 11.50
    Motions filed with hearing officer 11.43
Division of legal fees 10.37
Duress, use of 10.23
Duty to make counsel available 10.30

E

Employment:
    Acceptance 10.39
    Failure to carry out contract 10.84
    Refusing employment 10.62, 10.63, 10.66
    Withdrawal from employment . . . 10.40, 10.63, 10.66
Excessive legal fees 10.36

F

Failure to disclose material fact with regard
    to registration 10.22
Failure to notify client 10.23
False accusations 10.23
False statements concerning officials 10.102

Favors, improperly bestowing 10.23
Fees:
    Annual practitioner maintenance fee:
        Registered attorney or agent . . . 1.21(a)(7), 11.8(d)
        Individual granted limited recognition . . 1.21(a)(8)
        Delinquency . . . . 1.21(a)(9)(i)
    Petition to review decision of Director
        of Enrollment and Discipline . . . . 1.21(a)(5)
    Registration for admission to
        examination . . . . 1.21(a)(1)
    Registration to practice . . . . 1.21(a)(2)
    Reinstatement . . . . 1.21(a)(9)(ii)
Firm name, use of 10.35
Fitness to practice before the Office 10.23
Foreigners 11.6, 11.9, 11.14
Former Patent and Trademark Office
    employees 10.23, 11.7, 11.10
Fraud or inequitable conduct 10.23, 10.85
Frivolous complaint 10.23
Funds of client, preserving identity of 10.112

G

Gift, improperly bestowing 10.23
Government employees, registration of to practice
    in patent cases 11.10

I

Illegal conduct involving moral turpitude 10.23
Illegal fees for services 10.36
Improper alteration of patent application 10.23
Improper execution of oath or declaration 10.23
Improper influence 10.23
Improper signature 10.23
Improperly bestowing thing of value 10.23
Incompetence 10.77, 10.78
Indecent statement, making of 10.23
Independent professional judgment,
    exercise of 10.61, 10.62, 10.66, 10.68
Individual unqualified in respect to
    character, education, etc. 10.22, 11.7
Influence by others than client 10.68
Information precluding registration, failure
    to disclose 10.22
Integrity and competence of the legal profession,
    maintaining of 10.22
Interest in litigation or proceeding before Office,
    acquiring of 10.64

J

Joint venture 10.23
Judicial office, candidate for 10.103

L

Legal fees:
Division of.................................... 10.37
Failure to pay................................ 10.40
Sharing of 10.48
Legal system, assistance in improving the 10.100
Letterheads, use of........................... 10.35
Limited recognition to practice in patent matters ... 11.9

M

Malpractice, limiting client's liability.......... 10.78
Materially false statements in application for
registration................................ 10.22
Misappropriation of funds.................... 10.23
Misconduct 10.23
Misrepresentations.................. 10.22, 10.23
Multiple employment 10.66

N

Neglecting legal matters 10.77
Non-practitioner, formation of partnership with ... 10.49

O

Oath requirement............................ 11.8
Officials, contact with 10.93

P

Petitions:
Reinstatement 11.60
Review of final decision of USPTO Director .. 11.57
Review decision of Director of Enrollment
and Discipline 11.2
Suspension of rules 10.170
Preserve secrets and confidence of client ... 10.56, 10.57
Professional impropriety, avoiding
appearance of.................... 10.110, 10.111
Promise of advantage, offer of 10.23
Property of client........................... 10.112
Proprietary interest in subject matter........... 10.64
Publication in *Official Gazette* 10.11

R

Recognition to practice before the Patent and
Trademark Office:
Agents 11.5, 11.6, 11.7, 11.14
Aliens.................... 11.6, 11.7, 11.14
Attorneys 11.5, 11.6, 11.7, 11.14
Change of address, requirement to
notify Director.................... 10.11, 11.11

Examination for registration in patent cases..... 11.7
Examination fees 1.21, 11.7
Foreigners.................... 11.6, 11.9, 11.14
Former Patent and Trademark Office
employees.................. 10.23, 11.7, 11.10
Government employees 10.23, 11.10
Limited recognition in patent cases 11.9
Non-lawyers, recognition in trademark cases... 11.14
Recognition for representation 1.34, 11.14
Refusal to recognize practitioner 11.15
Register of attorneys and agents in patent
cases 11.5
Registration fee............................. 1.21
Registration number 1.34
Removal of attorneys and agents from the
register 10.11
Representation by registered attorney or agent
in patent cases........................... 1.31
Requirements for registration............... 11.7
Review of Director's decision refusing
registration 11.2
Trademark cases 11.14
Unauthorized representation by an
agent.......................... 10.31, 11.10
Records, property and funds of client,
maintaining of.......................... 10.112
Reinstatement after removal from the
register................................. 10.11
Reinstatement of excluded or suspended
practitioner 11.60
Representing client within bounds of the law 10.85

S

Scandalous statements, making of 10.23
Secrets and confidence, preservation
of clients 10.56, 10.57
Settlement of claims of clients............... 10.67
Sharing legal fees........................... 10.48
Signature and certificate of practitioner.......... 11.18
Solicitation 10.32, 10.33
Statement concerning officials, making
false..................................... 10.102
Suspension of practitioner 10.23
Based on conviction of a serious crime 11.25
Rules.................................... 11.3

T

Threats of criminal prosecution 10.88
Threats, use of 10.23

 Rev. 8, July 2010

U

Unauthorized practice 10.23, 10.31, 10.46, 10.47
Undignified conduct 10.89

V

Violating duty of candor and good faith 10.23
Violation of disciplinary rule, misconduct 10.23

W

Withdrawal from employment 10.40
Witnesses 10.63, 10.92

Z

Zealously representing the client 10.83, 10.84

PART 15 — [Reserved]

[Part 15 removed and reserved, 61 FR 42807, Aug. 19, 1996]

PART 15a — [Reserved]

[Part 15a removed and reserved, 61 FR 42807, Aug. 19, 1996]

PART 41 — PRACTICE BEFORE THE BOARD OF PATENT APPEALS AND INTERFERENCES

Subpart A—General Provisions

GENERAL INFORMATION

Sec.
41.1   Policy.
41.2   Definitions.
41.3   Petitions.
41.4   Timeliness.
41.5   Counsel.
41.6   Public availability of Board records.
41.7   Management of the record.
41.8   Mandatory notices.
41.9   Action by owner.
41.10   Correspondence addresses.
41.11   Ex parte communications in inter partes proceedings.
41.12   Citation of authority.
41.20   Fees.

Subpart B—Ex Parte Appeals

41.30   Definitions.
41.31   Appeal to Board.
41.33   Amendments and affidavits or other evidence after appeal.
41.35   Jurisdiction over appeal.
41.37   Appeal brief.
41.39   Examiner's answer.
41.41   Reply brief.
41.43   Examiner's response to reply brief.
41.47   Oral hearing.
41.50   Decisions and other actions by the Board.
41.52   Rehearing.
41.54   Action following decision.

Subpart C—Inter Partes Appeals

41.60   Definitions.
41.61   Notice of appeal and cross appeal to Board.
41.63   Amendments and affidavits or other evidence after appeal.
41.64   Jurisdiction over appeal in inter partes reexamination.
41.66   Time for filing briefs.
41.67   Appellant's brief.
41.68   Respondent's brief.
41.69   Examiner's answer.
41.71   Rebuttal brief.
41.73   Oral hearing.
41.77   Decisions and other actions by the Board.
41.79   Rehearing.
41.81   Action following decision.

Subpart D—Contested Cases

41.100 Definitions.
41.101 Notice of proceeding.
41.102 Completion of examination.
41.103 Jurisdiction over involved files.
41.104 Conduct of contested case.
41.106 Filing and service.
41.108 Lead counsel.
41.109 Access to and copies of Office records.
41.110 Filing claim information.
41.120 Notice of basis for relief.
41.121 Motions.
41.122 Oppositions and replies.
41.123 Default filing times.
41.124 Oral argument.
41.125 Decision on motions.
41.126 Arbitration.
41.127 Judgment.
41.128 Sanctions.
41.150 Discovery.
41.151 Admissibility.
41.152 Applicability of the Federal Rules of Evidence.
41.153 Records of the Office.
41.154 Form of evidence.
41.155 Objection; motion to exclude; motion in limine.

41.156 Compelling testimony and production.

41.157 Taking testimony.

41.158 Expert testimony; tests and data.

Subpart E—Patent Interferences

41.200 Procedure; pendency.

41.201 Definitions.

41.202 Suggesting an interference.

41.203 Declaration.

41.204 Notice of basis for relief.

41.205 Settlement agreements.

41.206 Common interests in the invention.

41.207 Presumptions.

41.208 Content of substantive and responsive motions.

Subpart A — General Provisions

§ 41.1   Policy.

(a)   *Scope.* Part 41 governs proceedings before the Board of Patent Appeals and Interferences. Sections 1.1 to 1.36 and 1.181 to 1.183 of this title also apply to practice before the Board, as do other sections of part 1 of this title that are incorporated by reference into part 41.

(b)   *Construction.* The provisions of Part 41 shall be construed to secure the just, speedy, and inexpensive resolution of every proceeding before the Board.

(c)   *Decorum.* Each party must act with courtesy and decorum in all proceedings before the Board, including interactions with other parties.

[Added, 65 FR 52916, Aug. 31, 2000, effective Oct. 2, 2000]

§ 41.2   Definitions.

Unless otherwise clear from the context, the following definitions apply to proceedings under this part:

Affidavit means affidavit, declaration under § 1.68 of this title, or statutory declaration under 28 U.S.C. 1746. A transcript of an ex parte deposition may be used as an affidavit in a contested case.

Board means the Board of Patent Appeals and Interferences and includes:

     (1)   For a final Board action:

     (i)   In an appeal or contested case, a panel of the Board.

     (ii)   In a proceeding under § 41.3, the Chief Administrative Patent Judge or another official acting under an express delegation from the Chief Administrative Patent Judge.

     (2)   For non-final actions, a Board member or employee acting with the authority of the Board.

Board member means the Under Secretary of Commerce for Intellectual Property and Director of the United States Patent and Trademark Office, the Deputy Under Secretary of Commerce for Intellectual Property and Deputy Director of the United States Patent and Trademark Office, the Commissioner for Patents, the Commissioner for Trademarks, and the administrative patent judges.

Contested case means a Board proceeding other than an appeal under 35 U.S.C. 134 or a petition under § 41.3. An appeal in an *inter partes* reexamination is not a contested case.

Final means, with regard to a Board action, final for the purposes of judicial review. A decision is final only if:

     (1)   *In a panel proceeding.* The decision is rendered by a panel, disposes of all issues with regard to the party seeking judicial review, and does not indicate that further action is required; and

     (2)   *In other proceedings.* The decision disposes of all issues or the decision states it is final.

Hearing means consideration of the issues of record. *Rehearing* means reconsideration.

Office means United States Patent and Trademark Office.

Panel means at least three Board members acting in a panel proceeding.

Panel proceeding means a proceeding in which final action is reserved by statute to at least three Board members, but includes a non-final portion of such a proceeding whether administered by a panel or not.

Party, in this part, means any entity participating in a Board proceeding, other than officers and employees of the Office, including:

     (1)   An appellant;

     (2)   A participant in a contested case;

     (3)   A petitioner; and

     (4)   Counsel for any of the above, where context permits.

[Added, 69 FR 49959, Aug. 12, 2004, effective Sept. 13, 2004]

§ 41.3   Petitions.

(a)   *Deciding official.* Petitions must be addressed to the Chief Administrative Patent Judge. A panel or an administrative patent judge may certify a question of policy to the Chief Administrative Patent Judge for decision. The Chief Administrative Patent Judge may delegate authority to decide petitions.

(b)   *Scope.* This section covers petitions on matters pending before the Board (§§ 41.35, 41.64, 41.103, and 41.205); otherwise, see §§ 1.181 to 1.183 of this title. The following matters are not subject to petition:

(1)   Issues committed by statute to a panel, and

(2)   In pending contested cases, procedural issues. See § 41.121(a)(3) and § 41.125(c).

(c)   *Petition fee.* The fee set in § 41.20(a) must accompany any petition under this section except no fee is required for a petition under this section seeking supervisory review.

(d)   *Effect on proceeding.* The filing of a petition does not stay the time for any other action in a Board proceeding.

(e)   *Time for action.* (1) Except as otherwise provided in this part or as the Board may authorize in writing, a party may:

(i) File the petition within 14 days from the date of the action from which the party is requesting relief, and

(ii)   File any request for reconsideration of a petition decision within 14 days of the decision on petition or such other time as the Board may set.

(2)   A party may not file an opposition or a reply to a petition without Board authorization.

[Added, 69 FR 49959, Aug. 12, 2004, effective Sept. 13, 2004; para. (e)(1) revised, 69 FR 58260, Sept. 30, 2004, effective Sept. 30, 2004]

§ 41.4   Timeliness.

(a)   *Extensions of time.* Extensions of time will be granted only on a showing of good cause except as otherwise provided by rule.

(b)   *Late filings.* (1) A late filing that results in either an application becoming abandoned or a reex- amination prosecution becoming terminated under §§ 1.550(d) or 1.957(b) of this title or limited under § 1.957(c) of this title may be revived as set forth in § 1.137 of this title.

(2)   A late filing that does not result in either an application becoming abandoned or a reexamination prosecution becoming terminated under §§ 1.550(d) or 1.957(b) of this title or limited under § 1.957(c) of this title will be excused upon a showing of excusable neglect or a Board determination that consideration on the merits would be in the interest of justice.

(c)   *Scope.* This section governs all proceedings before the Board, but does not apply to filings related to Board proceedings before or after the Board has jurisdiction, such as:

(1)   Extensions during prosecution (see § 1.136 of this title),

(2)   Filing of a brief or request for oral hear- ing (see §§ 41.37, 41.41, 41.47, 41.67, 41.68, 41.71 and 41.73), or

(3)   Seeking judicial review (see §§1.301 to 1.304 of this title).

[Added, 69 FR 49959, Aug. 12, 2004, effective Sept. 13, 2004; para. (b) revised, 72 FR 18892, Apr. 16, 2007, effective May 16, 2007]

§ 41.5   Counsel.

While the Board has jurisdiction:

(a)   *Appearance pro hac vice.* The Board may authorize a person other than a registered practitioner to appear as counsel in a specific proceeding.

(b)   *Disqualification.* (1) The Board may dis- qualify counsel in a specific proceeding after notice and an opportunity to be heard.

(2)   A decision to disqualify is not final for the purposes of judicial review until certified by the Chief Administrative Patent Judge.

(c)   *Withdrawal.* Counsel may not withdraw from a proceeding before the Board unless the Board authorizes such withdrawal. See § 10.40 of this title regarding conditions for withdrawal.

(d)   *Procedure.* The Board may institute a proceeding under this section on its own or a party in a contested case may request relief under this section.

(e)   *Referral to the Director of Enrollment and Discipline.* Possible violations of the disciplinary rules in part 11 of this subchapter may be referred to the Office of Enrollment and Discipline for investigation. See § 11.22 of this subchapter.

[Added, 69 FR 49959, Aug. 12, 2004, effective Sept. 13, 2004; para. (e) revised, 73 FR 47650, Aug. 14, 2008, effective Sept. 15, 2008]

§ 41.6   Public availability of Board records.

(a)   *Publication.* (1) *Generally.* Any Board action is available for public inspection without a party's permission if rendered in a file open to the public pursuant to § 1.11 of this title or in an application that has been published in accordance with §§ 1.211 to 1.221 of this title. The Office may independently publish any Board action that is available for public inspection.

(2)   *Determination of special circumstances.* Any Board action not publishable under paragraph (a)(1) of this section may be published or made available for public inspection if the Director believes that special circumstances warrant publication and a party does not, within two months after being notified of the intention to make the action public, object in writing on the ground that the action discloses the objecting party's trade secret or other confidential information and states with specificity that such information is not otherwise publicly available. If the action discloses such information, the party shall identify the deletions in the text of the action considered necessary to protect the information. If the affected party considers that the entire action must be withheld from the public to protect such information, the party must explain why. The party will be given time, not less than twenty days, to request reconsideration and seek court review before any contested portion of the action is made public over its objection.

(b)   *Record of proceeding.* (1) The record of a Board proceeding is available to the public unless a patent application not otherwise available to the public is involved.

(2)   Notwithstanding paragraph (b)(1) of this section, after a final Board action in or judgment in a Board proceeding, the record of the Board proceeding will be made available to the public if any involved file is or becomes open to the public under § 1.11 of this title or an involved application is or becomes published under §§ 1.211 to 1.221 of this title.

[Added, 69 FR 49959, Aug. 12, 2004, effective Sept. 13, 2004]

§ 41.7   Management of the record.

(a)   The Board may expunge any paper directed to a Board proceeding, or filed while an application or patent is under the jurisdiction of the Board, that is not authorized under this part or in a Board order, or that is filed contrary to a Board order.

(b)   A party may not file a paper previously filed in the same Board proceeding, not even as an exhibit or appendix, without Board authorization or as required by rule.

[Added, 69 FR 49959, Aug. 12, 2004, effective Sept. 13, 2004]

§ 41.8   Mandatory notices.

(a)   In an appeal brief (§§ 41.37, 41.67, or 41.68) or at the initiation of a contested case (§ 41.101), and within 20 days of any change during the proceeding, a party must identify:

(1)   Its real party-in-interest, and

(2)   Each judicial or administrative proceeding that could affect, or be affected by, the Board proceeding.

(b)   For contested cases, a party seeking judicial review of a Board proceeding must file a notice with the Board of the judicial review within 20 days of the filing of the complaint or the notice of appeal. The notice to the Board must include a copy of the complaint or notice of appeal. See also §§ 1.301 to 1.304 of this title.

[Added, 69 FR 49959, Aug. 12, 2004, effective Sept. 13, 2004]

§ 41.9   Action by owner.

(a)   *Entire interest.* An owner of the entire interest in an application or patent involved in a Board proceeding may act in the proceeding to the exclusion of the inventor (see 3.73 (b) of this title).

(b)   *Part interest.* An owner of a part interest in an application or patent involved in a Board proceeding may petition to act in the proceeding to the exclusion of an inventor or a co-owner. The petition must show the inability or refusal of an inventor or co-owner to prosecute the proceeding or other cause why it is in the interest of justice to permit the owner of a part interest to act in the proceeding. An order granting the petition may set conditions on the actions of the parties during the proceeding.

[Added, 69 FR 49959, Aug. 12, 2004, effective Sept. 13, 2004]

§ 41.10 Correspondence addresses.

Except as the Board may otherwise direct,

(a) *Appeals.* Correspondence in an application or a patent involved in an appeal (subparts B and C of this part) during the period beginning when an appeal docketing notice is issued and ending when a decision has been rendered by the Board, as well as any request for rehearing of a decision by the Board, shall be mailed to: Board of Patent Appeals and Interferences, United States Patent and Trademark Office, PO Box 1450, Alexandria, Virginia 22313-1450. Notices of appeal, appeal briefs, reply briefs, requests for oral hearing, as well as all other correspondence in an application or a patent involved in an appeal to the Board for which an address is not otherwise specified, should be addressed as set out in § 1.1 (a)(1)(i) of this title.

(b) *Contested cases.* Mailed correspondence in contested cases (subpart D of this part) shall be sent to Mail Stop INTERFERENCE, Board of Patent Appeals and Interferences, United States Patent and Trademark Office, PO Box 1450, Alexandria, Virginia 22313-1450.

[Added, 69 FR 49959, Aug. 12, 2004, effective Sept. 13, 2004]

§ 41.11 *Ex parte* communications in *inter partes* proceedings.

An *ex parte* communication about an inter partes reexamination (subpart C of this part) or about a contested case (subparts D and E of this part) with a Board member, or with a Board employee assigned to the proceeding, is not permitted.

[Added, 69 FR 49959, Aug. 12, 2004, effective Sept. 13, 2004]

§ 41.12 Citation of authority.

(a) Citations to authority must include:

(1) *For any United States Supreme Court decision,* a United States Reports citation.

(2) *For any decision other than a United States Supreme Court decision,* parallel citation to both the West Reporter System and to the United States Patents Quarterly whenever the case is published in both. Other parallel citations are discouraged.

(3) *Pinpoint citations* whenever a specific holding or portion of an authority is invoked.

(b) Non-binding authority should be used sparingly. If the authority is not an authority of the Office and is not reproduced in one of the reporters listed in paragraph (a) of this section, a copy of the authority should be filed with the first paper in which it is cited.

[Added, 69 FR 49959, Aug. 12, 2004, effective Sept. 13, 2004]

§ 41.20 Fees.

(a) *Petition fee.* The fee for filing a petition under this part is: $400.00

(b) *Appeal fees.* (1) For filing a notice of appeal from the examiner to the Board:

By a small entity (§ 1.27(a) of this title) $270.00

By other than a small entity $540.00

(2) In addition to the fee for filing a notice of appeal, for filing a brief in support of an appeal:

By a small entity (§ 1.27(a) of this title) $270.00

By other than a small entity $540.00

(3) For filing a request for an oral hearing before the Board in an appeal under 35 U.S.C. 134:

By a small entity (§ 1.27(a) .. $540.00

By other than a small entity ... $1,080.00

[Added, 69 FR 49959, Aug. 12, 2004, effective Sept. 13, 2004; paras. (b)(1) through (b)(3) revised, 69 FR 52604, Aug. 27, 2004, effective Oct. 1, 2004; para. (b)(3) corrected, 69 FR 55505, Sept. 15, 2004, effective Oct. 1, 2004; para. (a) revised, 69 FR 56481, Sept. 21, 2004, effective Nov. 22, 2004; para. (b) revised, 70 FR 3880, Jan. 27, 2005, effective Dec. 8, 2004; paras. (b)(1) through (b)(3) revised, 72 FR 46899, Aug. 22, 2007, effective Sept. 30, 2007; para. (b) revised, 73 FR 47534, Aug. 14, 2008, effective Oct. 2, 2008]

Subpart B — *Ex Parte* Appeals

§ 41.30   Definitions.

In addition to the definitions in § 41.2, the following definitions apply to proceedings under this subpart unless otherwise clear from the context:

Applicant means either the applicant in a national application for a patent or the applicant in an application for reissue of a patent.

Owner means the owner of the patent undergoing ex parte reexamination under § 1.510 of this title.

Proceeding means either a national application for a patent, an application for reissue of a patent, or an *ex parte* reexamination proceeding. Appeal to the Board in an *inter partes* reexamination proceeding is controlled by subpart C of this part.

[Added, 69 FR 49959, Aug. 12, 2004, effective Sept. 13, 2004]

§ 41.31   Appeal to Board.

(a)   *Who may appeal and how to file an appeal.* (1) Every applicant, any of whose claims has been twice rejected, may appeal from the decision of the examiner to the Board by filing a notice of appeal accompanied by the fee set forth in § 41.20(b)(1) within the time period provided under § 1.134 of this title for reply.

(2)   Every owner of a patent under *ex parte* reexamination filed under § 1.510 of this title before November 29, 1999, any of whose claims has been twice rejected, may appeal from the decision of the examiner to the Board by filing a notice of appeal accompanied by the fee set forth in § 41.20(b)(1) within the time period provided under § 1.134 of this title for reply.

(3)   Every owner of a patent under *ex parte* reexamination filed under § 1.510 of this title on or after November 29, 1999, any of whose claims has been finally (§ 1.113 of this title) rejected, may appeal from the decision of the examiner to the Board by filing a notice of appeal accompanied by the fee set forth in § 41.20(b)(1) within the time period provided under § 1.134 of this title for reply.

(b)   The signature requirement of § 1.33 of this title does not apply to a notice of appeal filed under this section.

(c)   An appeal, when taken, must be taken from the rejection of all claims under rejection which the applicant or owner proposes to contest. Questions relating to matters not affecting the merits of the invention may be required to be settled before an appeal can be considered.

(d)   The time periods set forth in paragraphs (a)(1) through (a)(3) of this section are extendable under the provisions of § 1.136 of this title for patent applications and § 1.550(c) of this title for *ex parte* reexamination proceedings.

[Added, 69 FR 49959, Aug. 12, 2004, effective Sept. 13, 2004]

§ 41.33   Amendments and affidavits or other evidence after appeal.

(a)   Amendments filed after the date of filing an appeal pursuant to § 41.31(a)(1) through (a)(3) and prior to the date a brief is filed pursuant to § 41.37 may be admitted as provided in § 1.116 of this title.

(b)   Amendments filed on or after the date of filing a brief pursuant to § 41.37 may be admitted:

(1)   To cancel claims, where such cancellation does not affect the scope of any other pending claim in the proceeding, or

(2)   To rewrite dependent claims into independent form.

(c)   All other amendments filed after the date of filing an appeal pursuant to § 41.31(a)(1) through (a)(3) will not be admitted except as permitted by §§ 41.39(b)(1), 41.50(a)(2)(i), 41.50(b)(1) and 41.50(c).

(d)(1) An affidavit or other evidence filed after the date of filing an appeal pursuant to § 41.31(a)(1) through (a)(3) and prior to the date of filing a brief pursuant to § 41.37 may be admitted if the examiner determines that the affidavit or other evidence overcomes all rejections under appeal and that a showing of good and sufficient reasons why the affidavit or other evidence is necessary and was not earlier presented has been made.

(2)   All other affidavits or other evidence filed after the date of filing an appeal pursuant to § 41.31(a)(1) through (a)(3) will not be admitted except as permitted by §§ 41.39(b)(1), 41.50(a)(2)(i) and 41.50(b)(1).

[Added, 69 FR 49959, Aug. 12, 2004, effective Sept. 13, 2004]

§ 41.35 Jurisdiction over appeal.

(a) Jurisdiction over the proceeding passes to the Board upon transmittal of the file, including all briefs and examiner's answers, to the Board.

(b) If, after receipt and review of the proceeding, the Board determines that the file is not complete or is not in compliance with the requirements of this subpart, the Board may relinquish jurisdiction to the examiner or take other appropriate action to permit completion of the file.

(c) Prior to the entry of a decision on the appeal by the Board, the Director may sua sponte order the proceeding remanded to the examiner.

[Added, 69 FR 49959, Aug. 12, 2004, effective Sept. 13, 2004]

§ 41.37 Appeal brief.

(a)(1)Appellant must file a brief under this section within two months from the date of filing the notice of appeal under § 41.31.

(2) The brief must be accompanied by the fee set forth in § 41.20(b)(2)

(b) On failure to file the brief, accompanied by the requisite fee, within the period specified in paragraph (a) of this section, the appeal will stand dismissed.

(c)(1)The brief shall contain the following items under appropriate headings and in the order indicated in paragraphs (c)(1)(i) through (c)(1)(x) of this section, except that a brief filed by an appellant who is not represented by a registered practitioner need only substantially comply with paragraphs (c)(1)(i) through (c)(1)(iv) and (c)(1)(vii) through (c)(1)(x) of this section:

(i) *Real party in interest.* A statement identifying by name the real party in interest.

(ii) *Related appeals and interferences.* A statement identifying by application, patent, appeal or interference number all other prior and pending appeals, interferences or judicial proceedings known to appellant, the appellant's legal representative, or assignee which may be related to, directly affect or be directly affected by or have a bearing on the Board's decision in the pending appeal. Copies of any decisions rendered by a court or the Board in any proceeding identified under this paragraph must be included in an appendix as required by paragraph (c)(1)(x) of this section.

(iii) *Status of claims.* A statement of the status of all the claims in the proceeding (*e.g.*, rejected, allowed or confirmed, withdrawn, objected to, canceled) and an identification of those claims that are being appealed.

(iv) *Status of amendments.* A statement of the status of any amendment filed subsequent to final rejection.

(v) *Summary of claimed subject matter.* A concise explanation of the subject matter defined in each of the independent claims involved in the appeal, which shall refer to the specification by page and line number, and to the drawing, if any, by reference characters. For each independent claim involved in the appeal and for each dependent claim argued separately under the provisions of paragraph (c)(1)(vii) of this section, every means plus function and step plus function as permitted by 35 U.S.C. 112, sixth paragraph, must be identified and the structure, material, or acts described in the specification as corresponding to each claimed function must be set forth with reference to the specification by page and line number, and to the drawing, if any, by reference characters.

(vi) *Grounds of rejection to be reviewed on appeal.* A concise statement of each ground of rejection presented for review.

(vii) *Argument.* The contentions of appellant with respect to each ground of rejection presented for review in paragraph (c)(1)(vi) of this section, and the basis therefor, with citations of the statutes, regulations, authorities, and parts of the record relied on. Any arguments or authorities not included in the brief or a reply brief filed pursuant to § 41.41 will be refused consideration by the Board, unless good cause is shown. Each ground of rejection must be treated under a separate heading. For each ground of rejection applying to two or more claims, the claims may be argued separately or as a group. When multiple claims subject to the same ground of rejection are argued as a group by appellant, the Board may select a single claim from the group of claims that are argued together to decide the appeal with respect to the group of claims as to the ground of rejection on the basis of the selected claim alone. Notwithstanding any other provision of this paragraph, the failure of appellant to separately argue claims which appellant has grouped together shall constitute a waiver of any argument that the Board must consider the patentability of any grouped claim separately. Any claim argued separately should be placed under a subheading identifying the claim by number. Claims argued as a group should be placed under a subheading identifying the claims by number. A statement which merely points out what a claim recites will not be considered an argument for separate patentability of the claim.

    (viii)   *Claims appendix*. An appendix containing a copy of the claims involved in the appeal.

    (ix)   *Evidence appendix*. An appendix containing copies of any evidence submitted pursuant to §§ 1.130, 1.131, or 1.132 of this title or of any other evidence entered by the examiner and relied upon by appellant in the appeal, along with a statement setting forth where in the record that evidence was entered in the record by the examiner. Reference to unentered evidence is not permitted in the brief. See § 41.33 for treatment of evidence submitted after appeal. This appendix may also include copies of the evidence relied upon by the examiner as to grounds of rejection to be reviewed on appeal.

    (x)   *Related proceedings appendix*. An appendix containing copies of decisions rendered by a court or the Board in any proceeding identified pursuant to paragraph (c)(1)(ii) of this section.

    (2)   A brief shall not include any new or non-admitted amendment, or any new or non-admitted affidavit or other evidence. See § 1.116 of this title for amendments, affidavits or other evidence filed after final action but before or on the same date of filing an appeal and § 41.33 for amendments, affidavits or other evidence filed after the date of filing the appeal.

    (d)   If a brief is filed which does not comply with all the requirements of paragraph (c) of this section, appellant will be notified of the reasons for non-compliance and given a time period within which to file an amended brief. If appellant does not file an amended brief within the set time period, or files an amended brief which does not overcome all the reasons for non-compliance stated in the notification, the appeal will stand dismissed.

    (e)   The time periods set forth in this section are extendable under the provisions of § 1.136 of this title for patent applications and § 1.550(c) of this title for *ex parte* reexamination proceedings.

[Added, 69 FR 49959, Aug. 12, 2004, effective Sept. 13, 2004]

§ 41.39   Examiner's answer.

    (a)(1)The primary examiner may, within such time as may be directed by the Director, furnish a written answer to the appeal brief including such explanation of the invention claimed and of the references relied upon and grounds of rejection as may be necessary, supplying a copy to appellant. If the primary examiner determines that the appeal does not comply with the provisions of §§ 41.31 and 41.37 or does not relate to an appealable action, the primary examiner shall make such determination of record.

    (2)   An examiner's answer may include a new ground of rejection.

    (b)   If an examiner's answer contains a rejection designated as a new ground of rejection, appellant must within two months from the date of the examiner's answer exercise one of the following two options to avoid sua sponte dismissal of the appeal as to the claims subject to the new ground of rejection:

    (1)   *Reopen prosecution*. Request that prosecution be reopened before the primary examiner by filing a reply under § 1.111 of this title with or without amendment or submission of affidavits (§§ 1.130, 1.131 or 1.132 of this title) or other evidence. Any amendment or submission of affidavits or other evidence must be relevant to the new ground of rejection. A request that complies with this paragraph will be entered and the application or the patent under *ex parte* reexamination will be reconsidered by the examiner under the provisions of § 1.112 of this title. Any request that prosecution be reopened under this paragraph will be treated as a request to withdraw the appeal.

    (2)   *Maintain appeal*. Request that the appeal be maintained by filing a reply brief as set forth in § 41.41. Such a reply brief must address each new ground of rejection as set forth in § 41.37(c)(1)(vii) and should follow the other requirements of a brief as set forth in § 41.37(c). A reply brief may not be accompanied by any amendment, affidavit (§§ 1.130, 1.131 or 1.132 of this title) or other evidence. If a reply brief filed pursuant to this section is accompanied by any amendment, affidavit or other evidence, it shall be treated as a request that prosecution be reopened before the primary examiner under paragraph (b)(1) of this section.

    (c)   Extensions of time under § 1.136 (a) of this title for patent applications are not applicable to the time period set forth in this section. See § 1.136 (b) of this title for extensions of time to reply for patent applications and § 1.550 (c) of this title for extensions of time to reply for *ex parte* reexamination proceedings.

[Added, 69 FR 49959, Aug. 12, 2004, effective Sept. 13, 2004]

§ 41.41   Reply brief.

(a)(1)Appellant may file a reply brief to an examiner's answer within two months from the date of the examiner's answer.

(2)   A reply brief shall not include any new or non-admitted amendment, or any new or non-admitted affidavit or other evidence. See § 1.116 of this title for amendments, affidavits or other evidence filed after final action but before or on the same date of filing an appeal and § 41.33 for amendments, affidavits or other evidence filed after the date of filing the appeal.

(b)   A reply brief that is not in compliance with paragraph (a) of this section will not be considered. Appellant will be notified if a reply brief is not in compliance with paragraph (a) of this section.

(c)   Extensions of time under § 1.136 (a) of this title for patent applications are not applicable to the time period set forth in this section. See § 1.136 (b) of this title for extensions of time to reply for patent applications and § 1.550 (c) of this title for extensions of time to reply for ex parte reexamination proceedings.

[Added, 69 FR 49959, Aug. 12, 2004, effective Sept. 13, 2004]

§ 41.43   Examiner's response to reply brief.

(a)(1)After receipt of a reply brief in compliance with § 41.41, the primary examiner must acknowledge receipt and entry of the reply brief. In addition, the primary examiner may withdraw the final rejection and reopen prosecution or may furnish a supplemental examiner's answer responding to any new issue raised in the reply brief.

(2)   A supplemental examiner's answer responding to a reply brief may not include a new ground of rejection.

(b)   If a supplemental examiner's answer is furnished by the examiner, appellant may file another reply brief under § 41.41 to any supplemental examiner's answer within two months from the date of the supplemental examiner's answer.

(c)   Extensions of time under § 1.136(a) of this title for patent applications are not applicable to the time period set forth in this section. See § 1.136(b) of this title for extensions of time to reply for patent applications and § 1.550(c) of this title for extensions of time to reply for *ex parte* reexamination proceedings.

[Added, 69 FR 49959, Aug. 12, 2004, effective Sept. 13, 2004]

§ 41.47   Oral hearing.

(a)   An oral hearing should be requested only in those circumstances in which appellant considers such a hearing necessary or desirable for a proper presentation of the appeal. An appeal decided on the briefs without an oral hearing will receive the same consideration by the Board as appeals decided after an oral hearing.

(b)   If appellant desires an oral hearing, appellant must file, as a separate paper captioned "REQUEST FOR ORAL HEARING," a written request for such hearing accompanied by the fee set forth in § 41.20(b)(3) within two months from the date of the examiner's answer or supplemental examiner's answer.

(c)   If no request and fee for oral hearing have been timely filed by appellant as required by paragraph (b) of this section, the appeal will be assigned for consideration and decision on the briefs without an oral hearing.

(d)   If appellant has complied with all the requirements of paragraph (b) of this section, a date for the oral hearing will be set, and due notice thereof given to appellant. If an oral hearing is held, an oral argument may be presented by, or on behalf of, the primary examiner if considered desirable by either the primary examiner or the Board. A hearing will be held as stated in the notice, and oral argument will ordinarily be limited to twenty minutes for appellant and fifteen minutes for the primary examiner unless otherwise ordered.

(e)(1)Appellant will argue first and may reserve time for rebuttal. At the oral hearing, appellant may only rely on evidence that has been previously entered and considered by the primary examiner and present argument that has been relied upon in the brief or reply brief except as permitted by paragraph (e)(2) of this section. The primary examiner may only rely on argument and evidence relied upon in an answer or a supplemental answer except as permitted by paragraph (e)(2) of this section.

(2)   Upon a showing of good cause, appellant and/or the primary examiner may rely on a new argument based upon a recent relevant decision of either the Board or a Federal Court.

(f)   Notwithstanding the submission of a request for oral hearing complying with this rule, if the Board decides that a hearing is not necessary, the Board will so notify appellant.

(g)   Extensions of time under § 1.136(a) of this title for patent applications are not applicable to the time periods set forth in this section. See § 1.136(b) of this title for extensions of time to reply for patent applications and § 1.550(c) of this title for extensions of time to reply for *ex parte* reexamination proceedings.

[Added, 69 FR 49959, Aug. 12, 2004, effective Sept. 13, 2004]

§ 41.50 Decisions and other actions by the Board.

(a)(1)The Board, in its decision, may affirm or reverse the decision of the examiner in whole or in part on the grounds and on the claims specified by the examiner. The affirmance of the rejection of a claim on any of the grounds specified constitutes a general affirmance of the decision of the examiner on that claim, except as to any ground specifically reversed. The Board may also remand an application to the examiner.

(2)   If a supplemental examiner's answer is written in response to a remand by the Board for further consideration of a rejection pursuant to paragraph (a)(1) of this section, the appellant must within two months from the date of the supplemental examiner's answer exercise one of the following two options to avoid sua sponte dismissal of the appeal as to the claims subject to the rejection for which the Board has remanded the proceeding:

(i)   *Reopen prosecution.* Request that prosecution be reopened before the examiner by filing a reply under § 1.111 of this title with or without amendment or submission of affidavits (§§ 1.130, 1.131 or 1.132 of this title) or other evidence. Any

amendment or submission of affidavits or other evidence must be relevant to the issues set forth in the remand or raised in the supplemental examiner's answer. A request that complies with this paragraph will be entered and the application or the patent under *ex parte* reexamination will be reconsidered by the examiner under the provisions of § 1.112 of this title. Any request that prosecution be reopened under this paragraph will be treated as a request to withdraw the appeal.

(ii)   *Maintain appeal.* Request that the appeal be maintained by filing a reply brief as provided in § 41.41. If such a reply brief is accompanied by any amendment, affidavit or other evidence, it shall be treated as a request that prosecution be reopened before the examiner under paragraph (a)(2)(i) of this section.

(b)   Should the Board have knowledge of any grounds not involved in the appeal for rejecting any pending claim, it may include in its opinion a statement to that effect with its reasons for so holding, which statement constitutes a new ground of rejection of the claim. A new ground of rejection pursuant to this paragraph shall not be considered final for judicial review. When the Board makes a new ground of rejection, the appellant, within two months from the date of the decision, must exercise one of the following two options with respect to the new ground of rejection to avoid termination of the appeal as to the rejected claims:

(1)   *Reopen prosecution.* Submit an appropriate amendment of the claims so rejected or new evidence relating to the claims so rejected, or both, and have the matter reconsidered by the examiner, in which event the proceeding will be remanded to the examiner. The new ground of rejection is binding upon the examiner unless an amendment or new evidence not previously of record is made which, in the opinion of the examiner, overcomes the new ground of rejection stated in the decision. Should the examiner reject the claims, appellant may again appeal to the Board pursuant to this subpart.

(2)   *Request rehearing.* Request that the proceeding be reheard under § 41.52 by the Board upon the same record. The request for rehearing must address any new ground of rejection and state with particularity the points believed to have been misapprehended or overlooked in entering the new ground

of rejection and also state all other grounds upon which rehearing is sought.

(c) The opinion of the Board may include an explicit statement of how a claim on appeal may be amended to overcome a specific rejection. When the opinion of the Board includes such a statement, appellant has the right to amend in conformity therewith. An amendment in conformity with such statement will overcome the specific rejection. An examiner may reject a claim so-amended, provided that the rejection constitutes a new ground of rejection.

(d) The Board may order appellant to additionally brief any matter that the Board considers to be of assistance in reaching a reasoned decision on the pending appeal. Appellant will be given a non-extendable time period within which to respond to such an order. Failure to timely comply with the order may result in the sua sponte dismissal of the appeal.

(e) Whenever a decision of the Board includes a remand, that decision shall not be considered final for judicial review. When appropriate, upon conclusion of proceedings on remand before the examiner, the Board may enter an order otherwise making its decision final for judicial review.

(f) Extensions of time under § 1.136(a) of this title for patent applications are not applicable to the time periods set forth in this section. See § 1.136(b) of this title for extensions of time to reply for patent applications and § 1.550(c) of this title for extensions of time to reply for *ex parte* reexamination proceedings.

[Added, 69 FR 49959, Aug. 12, 2004, effective Sept. 13, 2004]

§ 41.52 Rehearing.

(a)(1) Appellant may file a single request for rehearing within two months of the date of the original decision of the Board. No request for rehearing from a decision on rehearing will be permitted, unless the rehearing decision so modified the original decision as to become, in effect, a new decision, and the Board states that a second request for rehearing would be permitted. The request for rehearing must state with particularity the points believed to have been misapprehended or overlooked by the Board. Arguments not raised in the briefs before the Board and evidence not previously relied upon in the brief and any reply brief(s) are not permitted in the request for rehearing except as permitted by paragraphs (a)(2) and (a)(3) of this section. When a request for rehearing is made, the Board shall render a decision on the request for rehearing. The decision on the request for rehearing is deemed to incorporate the earlier opinion reflecting its decision for appeal, except for those portions specifically withdrawn on rehearing, and is final for the purpose of judicial review, except when noted otherwise in the decision on rehearing.

(2) Upon a showing of good cause, appellant may present a new argument based upon a recent relevant decision of either the Board or a Federal Court.

(3) New arguments responding to a new ground of rejection made pursuant to § 41.50(b) are permitted.

(b) Extensions of time under § 1.136(a) of this title for patent applications are not applicable to the time period set forth in this section. See § 1.136(b) of this title for extensions of time to reply for patent applications and § 1.550(c) of this title for extensions of time to reply for *ex parte* reexamination proceedings.

[Added, 69 FR 49959, Aug. 12, 2004, effective Sept. 13, 2004]

§ 41.54 Action following decision.

After decision by the Board, the proceeding will be returned to the examiner, subject to appellant's right of appeal or other review, for such further action by appellant or by the examiner, as the condition of the proceeding may require, to carry into effect the decision.

[Added, 69 FR 49959, Aug. 12, 2004, effective Sept. 13, 2004]

Subpart C — *Inter Partes* Appeals

§ 41.60 Definitions.

In addition to the definitions in § 41.2, the following definitions apply to proceedings under this subpart unless otherwise clear from the context:

Appellant means any party, whether the owner or a requester, filing a notice of appeal or cross appeal under § 41.61. If more than one party appeals or cross appeals, each appealing or cross appealing party is an appellant with respect to the claims to which his or her appeal or cross appeal is directed.

Filing means filing with a certificate indicating service of the document under § 1.903 of this title.

Owner means the owner of the patent undergoing *inter partes* reexamination under § 1.915 of this title.

Proceeding means an *inter partes* reexamination proceeding. Appeal to the Board in an *ex parte* reexamination proceeding is controlled by subpart B of this part. An *inter partes* reexamination proceeding is not a contested case subject to subpart D.

Requester means each party, other than the owner, who requested that the patent undergo *inter partes* reexamination under § 1.915 of this title.

Respondent means any requester responding under § 41.68 to the appellant's brief of the owner, or the owner responding under § 41.68 to the appellant's brief of any requester. No requester may be a respondent to the appellant brief of any other requester.

[Added, 69 FR 49959, Aug. 12, 2004, effective Sept. 13, 2004]

§ 41.61 Notice of appeal and cross appeal to Board.

(a)(1)Upon the issuance of a Right of Appeal Notice under § 1.953 of this title, the owner may appeal to the Board with respect to the final rejection of any claim of the patent by filing a notice of appeal within the time provided in the Right of Appeal Notice and paying the fee set forth in § 41.20(b)(1).

(2) Upon the issuance of a Right of Appeal Notice under § 1.953 of this title, the requester may appeal to the Board with respect to any final decision favorable to the patentability, including any final determination not to make a proposed rejection, of any original, proposed amended, or new claim of the patent by filing a notice of appeal within the time provided in the Right of Appeal Notice and paying the fee set forth in § 41.20(b)(1).

(b)(1)Within fourteen days of service of a requester's notice of appeal under paragraph (a)(2) of this section and upon payment of the fee set forth in § 41.20(b)(1), an owner who has not filed a notice of appeal may file a notice of cross appeal with respect to the final rejection of any claim of the patent.

(2) Within fourteen days of service of an owner's notice of appeal under paragraph (a)(1) of this section and upon payment of the fee set forth in §

41.20 (b)(1), a requester who has not filed a notice of appeal may file a notice of cross appeal with respect to any final decision favorable to the patentability, including any final determination not to make a proposed rejection, of any original, proposed amended, or new claim of the patent.

(c) The notice of appeal or cross appeal in the proceeding must identify the appealed claim(s) and must be signed by the owner, the requester, or a duly authorized attorney or agent.

(d) An appeal or cross appeal, when taken, must be taken from all the rejections of the claims in a Right of Appeal Notice which the patent owner proposes to contest or from all the determinations favorable to patentability, including any final determination not to make a proposed rejection, in a Right of Appeal Notice which a requester proposes to contest. Questions relating to matters not affecting the merits of the invention may be required to be settled before an appeal is decided.

(e) The time periods for filing a notice of appeal or cross appeal may not be extended.

(f) If a notice of appeal or cross appeal is timely filed but does not comply with any requirement of this section, appellant will be notified of the reasons for non-compliance and given a non-extendable time period within which to file an amended notice of appeal or cross appeal. If the appellant does not then file an amended notice of appeal or cross appeal within the set time period, or files a notice which does not overcome all the reasons for non-compliance stated in the notification of the reasons for non-compliance, that appellant's appeal or cross appeal will stand dismissed.

[Added, 69 FR 49959, Aug. 12, 2004, effective Sept. 13, 2004]

§ 41.63 Amendments and affidavits or other evidence after appeal.

(a) Amendments filed after the date of filing an appeal pursuant to § 41.61 canceling claims may be admitted where such cancellation does not affect the scope of any other pending claim in the proceeding.

(b) All other amendments filed after the date of filing an appeal pursuant to § 41.61 will not be admitted except as permitted by § 41.77(b)(1).

(c) Affidavits or other evidence filed after the date of filing an appeal pursuant to § 41.61 will not be admitted except as permitted by reopening prosecution under § 41.77(b)(1).

[Added, 69 FR 49959, Aug. 12, 2004, effective Sept. 13, 2004]

§ 41.64 Jurisdiction over appeal in *inter partes* reexamination.

(a) Jurisdiction over the proceeding passes to the Board upon transmittal of the file, including all briefs and examiner's answers, to the Board.

(b) If, after receipt and review of the proceeding, the Board determines that the file is not complete or is not in compliance with the requirements of this subpart, the Board may relinquish jurisdiction to the examiner or take other appropriate action to permit completion of the file.

(c) Prior to the entry of a decision on the appeal by the Board, the Director may sua sponte order the proceeding remanded to the examiner.

[Added, 69 FR 49959, Aug. 12, 2004, effective Sept. 13, 2004]

§ 41.66 Time for filing briefs.

(a) An appellant's brief must be filed no later than two months from the latest filing date of the last-filed notice of appeal or cross appeal or, if any party to the proceeding is entitled to file an appeal or cross appeal but fails to timely do so, no later than two months from the expiration of the time for filing (by the last party entitled to do so) such notice of appeal or cross appeal. The time for filing an appellant's brief or an amended appellant's brief may not be extended.

(b) Once an appellant's brief has been properly filed, any brief must be filed by respondent within one month from the date of service of the appellant's brief. The time for filing a respondent's brief or an amended respondent's brief may not be extended.

(c) The examiner will consider both the appellant's and respondent's briefs and may prepare an examiner's answer under § 41.69.

(d) Any appellant may file a rebuttal brief under § 41.71 within one month of the date of the examiner's answer. The time for filing a rebuttal brief or an amended rebuttal brief may not be extended.

(e) No further submission will be considered and any such submission will be treated in accordance with § 1.939 of this title.

[Added, 69 FR 49959, Aug. 12, 2004, effective Sept. 13, 2004]

§ 41.67 Appellant's brief.

(a)(1) Appellant(s) may once, within time limits for filing set forth in § 41.66, file a brief and serve the brief on all other parties to the proceeding in accordance with § 1.903 of this title.

(2) The brief must be signed by the appellant, or the appellant's duly authorized attorney or agent and must be accompanied by the requisite fee set forth in § 41.20(b)(2).

(b) An appellant's appeal shall stand dismissed upon failure of that appellant to file an appellant's brief, accompanied by the requisite fee, within the time allowed under § 41.66(a).

(c)(1) The appellant's brief shall contain the following items under appropriate headings and in the order indicated in paragraphs (c)(1)(i) through (c)(1)(xi) of this section.

(i) *Real party in interest.* A statement identifying by name the real party in interest.

(ii) *Related appeals and interferences.* A statement identifying by application, patent, appeal or interference number all other prior and pending appeals, interferences or judicial proceedings known to appellant, the appellant's legal representative, or assignee which may be related to, directly affect or be directly affected by or have a bearing on the Board's decision in the pending appeal. Copies of any decisions rendered by a court or the Board in any proceeding identified under this paragraph must be included in an appendix as required by paragraph (c)(1)(xi) of this section.

(iii) *Status of claims.* A statement of the status of all the claims in the proceeding (e.g., rejected, allowed or confirmed, withdrawn, objected to, canceled). If the appellant is the owner, the appellant must also identify the rejected claims whose rejection is being appealed. If the appellant is a requester, the appellant must identify the claims that the examiner has made a determination favorable to patentability, which determination is being appealed.

(iv) *Status of amendments.* A statement of the status of any amendment filed subsequent to the close of prosecution.

(v) *Summary of claimed subject matter.* A concise explanation of the subject matter defined in each of the independent claims involved in the appeal, which shall refer to the specification by column and line number, and to the drawing(s), if any, by reference characters. For each independent claim involved in the appeal and for each dependent claim argued separately under the provisions of paragraph (c)(1)(vii) of this section, every means plus function and step plus function as permitted by 35 U.S.C. 112, sixth paragraph, must be identified and the structure, material, or acts described in the specification as corresponding to each claimed function must be set forth with reference to the specification by page and line number, and to the drawing, if any, by reference characters.

(vi)   *Issues to be reviewed on appeal.* A concise statement of each issue presented for review. No new ground of rejection can be proposed by a third party requester appellant, unless such ground was withdrawn by the examiner during the prosecution of the proceeding, and the third party requester has not yet had an opportunity to propose it as a third party requester proposed ground of rejection.

(vii)   *Argument.* The contentions of appellant with respect to each issue presented for review in paragraph (c)(1)(vi) of this section, and the basis therefor, with citations of the statutes, regulations, authorities, and parts of the record relied on. Any arguments or authorities not included in the brief permitted under this section or §§ 41.68 and 41.71 will be refused consideration by the Board, unless good cause is shown. Each issue must be treated under a separate heading. If the appellant is the patent owner, for each ground of rejection in the Right of Appeal Notice which appellant contests and which applies to two or more claims, the claims may be argued separately or as a group. When multiple claims subject to the same ground of rejection are argued as a group by appellant, the Board may select a single claim from the group of claims that are argued together to decide the appeal with respect to the group of claims as to the ground of rejection on the basis of the selected claim alone. Notwithstanding any other provision of this paragraph, the failure of appellant to separately argue claims which appellant has grouped together shall constitute a waiver of any argument that the Board must consider the patentability of any grouped claim separately. Any claim argued separately should be placed under a subheading identifying the claim by number. Claims argued as a group should be placed under a subheading identifying the claims by number. A statement which merely points out what a claim recites will not be considered an argument for separate patentability of the claim.

(viii)   *Claims appendix.* An appendix containing a copy of the claims to be reviewed on appeal.

(ix)   *Evidence appendix.* An appendix containing copies of any evidence submitted pursuant to §§ 1.130, 1.131, or 1.132 of this title or of any other evidence entered by the examiner and relied upon by appellant in the appeal, along with a statement setting forth where in the record that evidence was entered in the record by the examiner. Reference to unentered evidence is not permitted in the brief. See § 41.63 for treatment of evidence submitted after appeal. This appendix may also include copies of the evidence relied upon by the examiner in any ground of rejection to be reviewed on appeal.

(x)   *Related proceedings appendix.* An appendix containing copies of decisions rendered by a court or the Board in any proceeding identified pursuant to paragraph (c)(1)(ii) of this section.

(xi)   *Certificate of service.* A certification that a copy of the brief has been served in its entirety on all other parties to the reexamination proceeding. The names and addresses of the parties served must be indicated.

(2)   A brief shall not include any new or non-admitted amendment, or any new or non-admitted affidavit or other evidence. See § 1.116 of this title for amendments, affidavits or other evidence filed after final action but before or on the same date of filing an appeal and § 41.63 for amendments, affidavits or other evidence after the date of filing the appeal.

(d)   If a brief is filed which does not comply with all the requirements of paragraph (a) and paragraph (c) of this section, appellant will be notified of the reasons for non-compliance and given a non-extendable time period within which to file an amended brief. If appellant does not file an amended brief within the set time period, or files an amended brief which does not overcome all the reasons for non-compliance stated in the notification, that appellant's appeal will stand dismissed.

[Added, 69 FR 49959, Aug. 12, 2004, effective Sept. 13, 2004]

§ 41.68 Respondent's brief.

(a)(1)Respondent(s) in an appeal may once, within the time limit for filing set forth in § 41.66, file a respondent brief and serve the brief on all parties in accordance with § 1.903 of this title.

(2) The brief must be signed by the party, or the party's duly authorized attorney or agent, and must be accompanied by the requisite fee set forth in § 41.20(b)(2).

(3) The respondent brief shall be limited to issues raised in the appellant brief to which the respondent brief is directed.

(4) A requester's respondent brief may not address any brief of any other requester.

(b)(1)The respondent brief shall contain the following items under appropriate headings and in the order here indicated, and may include an appendix containing only those portions of the record on which reliance has been made.

(i) *Real Party in Interest.* A statement identifying by name the real party in interest.

(ii) *Related Appeals and Interferences.* A statement identifying by application, patent, appeal or interference number all other prior and pending appeals, interferences or judicial proceedings known to respondent, the respondent's legal representative, or assignee which may be related to, directly affect or be directly affected by or have a bearing on the Board's decision in the pending appeal. Copies of any decisions rendered by a court or the Board in any proceeding identified under this paragraph must be included in an appendix as required by paragraph (b)(1)(ix) of this section.

(iii) *Status of claims.* A statement accepting or disputing appellant's statement of the status of claims. If appellant's statement of the status of claims is disputed, the errors in appellant's statement must be specified with particularity.

(iv) *Status of amendments.* A statement accepting or disputing appellant's statement of the status of amendments. If appellant's statement of the status of amendments is disputed, the errors in appellant's statement must be specified with particularity.

(v) *Summary of claimed subject matter.* A statement accepting or disputing appellant's summary of the subject matter defined in each of the independent claims involved in the appeal. If appellant's summary of the subject matter is disputed, the errors in appellant's summary must be specified.

(vi) *Issues to be reviewed on appeal.* A statement accepting or disputing appellant's statement of the issues presented for review. If appellant's statement of the issues presented for review is disputed, the errors in appellant's statement must be specified. A counter statement of the issues for review may be made. No new ground of rejection can be proposed by a requester respondent.

(vii) *Argument.* A statement accepting or disputing the contentions of appellant with each of the issues presented by the appellant for review. If a contention of the appellant is disputed, the errors in appellant's argument must be specified, stating the basis therefor, with citations of the statutes, regulations, authorities, and parts of the record relied on. Each issue must be treated under a separate heading. An argument may be made with each of the issues stated in the counter statement of the issues, with each counter-stated issue being treated under a separate heading.

(viii) *Evidence appendix.* An appendix containing copies of any evidence submitted pursuant to §§ 1.130, 1.131, or 1.132 of this title or of any other evidence entered by the examiner and relied upon by respondent in the appeal, along with a statement setting forth where in the record that evidence was entered in the record by the examiner. Reference to unentered evidence is not permitted in the respondent's brief. See § 41.63 for treatment of evidence submitted after appeal.

(ix) *Related proceedings appendix.* An appendix containing copies of decisions rendered by a court or the Board in any proceeding identified pursuant to paragraph (b)(1)(ii) of this section.

(x) *Certificate of service.* A certification that a copy of the respondent brief has been served in its entirety on all other parties to the reexamination proceeding. The names and addresses of the parties served must be indicated.

(2) A respondent brief shall not include any new or non-admitted amendment, or any new or non-admitted affidavit or other evidence. See § 1.116 of this title for amendments, affidavits or other evidence filed after final action but before or on the same date of filing an appeal and § 41.63 for amendments, affi-

davits or other evidence filed after the date of filing the appeal.

(c) If a respondent brief is filed which does not comply with all the requirements of paragraph (a) and paragraph (b) of this section, respondent will be notified of the reasons for non-compliance and given a non-extendable time period within which to file an amended brief. If respondent does not file an amended respondent brief within the set time period, or files an amended respondent brief which does not overcome all the reasons for non-compliance stated in the notification, the respondent brief and any amended respondent brief by that respondent will not be considered.

[Added, 69 FR 49959, Aug. 12, 2004, effective Sept. 13, 2004]

§ 41.69   Examiner's answer.

(a) The primary examiner may, within such time as directed by the Director, furnish a written answer to the owner's and/or requester's appellant brief or respondent brief including, as may be necessary, such explanation of the invention claimed and of the references relied upon, the grounds of rejection, and the reasons for patentability, including grounds for not adopting any proposed rejection. A copy of the answer shall be supplied to the owner and all requesters. If the primary examiner determines that the appeal does not comply with the provisions of §§ 41.61, 41.66, 41.67 and 41.68 or does not relate to an appealable action, the primary examiner shall make such determination of record.

(b) An examiner's answer may not include a new ground of rejection.

(c) An examiner's answer may not include a new determination not to make a proposed rejection of a claim.

(d) Any new ground of rejection, or any new determination not to make a proposed rejection, must be made in an Office action reopening prosecution.

[Added, 69 FR 49959, Aug. 12, 2004, effective Sept. 13, 2004]

§ 41.71   Rebuttal brief.

(a) Within one month of the examiner's answer, any appellant may once file a rebuttal brief.

(b)(1) The rebuttal brief of the owner may be directed to the examiner's answer and/or any respondent brief.

(2) The rebuttal brief of the owner shall not include any new or non-admitted amendment, or an affidavit or other evidence. See § 1.116 of this title for amendments, affidavits or other evidence filed after final action but before or on the same date of filing an appeal and § 41.63 for amendments, affidavits or other evidence filed after the date of filing the appeal.

(c)(1) The rebuttal brief of any requester may be directed to the examiner's answer and/or the respondent brief of the owner.

(2) The rebuttal brief of a requester may not be directed to the respondent brief of any other requester.

(3) No new ground of rejection can be proposed by a requester.

(4) The rebuttal brief of a requester shall not include any new or non-admitted affidavit or other evidence. See § 1.116(d) of this title for affidavits or other evidence filed after final action but before or on the same date of filing an appeal and § 41.63(c) for affidavits or other evidence filed after the date of filing the appeal.

(d) The rebuttal brief must include a certification that a copy of the rebuttal brief has been served in its entirety on all other parties to the proceeding. The names and addresses of the parties served must be indicated.

(e) If a rebuttal brief is timely filed under paragraph (a) of this section but does not comply with all the requirements of paragraphs (a) through (d) of this section, appellant will be notified of the reasons for non-compliance and provided with a non-extendable period of one month within which to file an amended rebuttal brief. If the appellant does not file an amended rebuttal brief during the one-month period, or files an amended rebuttal brief which does not overcome all the reasons for non-compliance stated in the notification, that appellant's rebuttal brief and any amended rebuttal brief by that appellant will not be considered.

[Added, 69 FR 4995 9, Aug. 12, 2004, effective Sept. 13, 2004]

§ 41.73 Oral hearing.

(a) An oral hearing should be requested only in those circumstances in which an appellant or a respondent considers such a hearing necessary or desirable for a proper presentation of the appeal. An appeal decided on the briefs without an oral hearing will receive the same consideration by the Board as an appeal decided after an oral hearing.

(b) If an appellant or a respondent desires an oral hearing, he or she must file, as a separate paper captioned "REQUEST FOR ORAL HEARING," a written request for such hearing accompanied by the fee set forth in § 41.20(b)(3) within two months after the date of the examiner's answer. The time for requesting an oral hearing may not be extended. The request must include a certification that a copy of the request has been served in its entirety on all other parties to the proceeding. The names and addresses of the parties served must be indicated.

(c) If no request and fee for oral hearing have been timely filed by appellant or respondent as required by paragraph (b) of this section, the appeal will be assigned for consideration and decision on the briefs without an oral hearing.

(d) If appellant or respondent has complied with all the requirements of paragraph (b) of this section, a hearing date will be set, and notice given to the owner and all requesters. If an oral hearing is held, an oral argument may be presented by, or on behalf of, the primary examiner if considered desirable by either the primary examiner or the Board. The notice shall set a non-extendable period within which all requests for oral hearing shall be submitted by any other party to the appeal desiring to participate in the oral hearing. A hearing will be held as stated in the notice, and oral argument will be limited to thirty minutes for each appellant or respondent who has requested an oral hearing, and twenty minutes for the primary examiner unless otherwise ordered. No appellant or respondent will be permitted to participate in an oral hearing unless he or she has requested an oral hearing and submitted the fee set forth in § 41.20(b)(3).

(e)(1)At the oral hearing, each appellant and respondent may only rely on evidence that has been previously entered and considered by the primary examiner and present argument that has been relied upon in the briefs except as permitted by paragraph (e)(2) of this section. The primary examiner may only rely on argument and evidence relied upon in an answer except as permitted by paragraph (e)(2) of this section. The Board will determine the order of the arguments presented at the oral hearing.

(2) Upon a showing of good cause, appellant, respondent and/or the primary examiner may rely on a new argument based upon a recent relevant decision of either the Board or a Federal Court.

(f) Notwithstanding the submission of a request for oral hearing complying with this rule, if the Board decides that a hearing is not necessary, the Board will so notify the owner and all requesters.

[Added, 69 FR 4 9959, Aug. 12, 2004, effective Sept. 13, 2004]

§ 41.77 Decisions and other actions by the Board.

(a) The Board of Patent Appeals and Interferences, in its decision, may affirm or reverse each decision of the examiner on all issues raised on each appealed claim, or remand the reexamination proceeding to the examiner for further consideration. The reversal of the examiner's determination not to make a rejection proposed by the third party requester constitutes a decision adverse to the patentability of the claims which are subject to that proposed rejection which will be set forth in the decision of the Board of Patent Appeals and Interferences as a new ground of rejection under paragraph (b) of this section. The affirmance of the rejection of a claim on any of the grounds specified constitutes a general affirmance of the decision of the examiner on that claim, except as to any ground specifically reversed.

(b) Should the Board reverse the examiner's determination not to make a rejection proposed by a requester, the Board shall set forth in the opinion in support of its decision a new ground of rejection; or should the Board have knowledge of any grounds not raised in the appeal for rejecting any pending claim, it may include in its opinion a statement to that effect with its reasons for so holding, which statement shall constitute a new ground of rejection of the claim. Any decision which includes a new ground of rejection pursuant to this paragraph shall not be considered final for judicial review. When the Board makes a new ground of rejection, the owner, within one month from the date of the decision, must exercise one of the following two options with respect to the new ground of rejection to avoid termination of the appeal proceeding as to the rejected claim:

(1) *Reopen prosecution.* The owner may file a response requesting reopening of prosecution before the examiner. Such a response must be either an amendment of the claims so rejected or new evidence relating to the claims so rejected, or both.

(2) *Request rehearing.* The owner may request that the proceeding be reheard under § 41.79 by the Board upon the same record. The request for rehearing must address any new ground of rejection and state with particularity the points believed to have been misapprehended or overlooked in entering the new ground of rejection and also state all other grounds upon which rehearing is sought.

(c) Where the owner has filed a response requesting reopening of prosecution under paragraph (b)(1) of this section, any requester, within one month of the date of service of the owner's response, may once file comments on the response. Such written comments must be limited to the issues raised by the Board's opinion reflecting its decision and the owner's response. Any requester that had not previously filed an appeal or cross appeal and is seeking under this subsection to file comments or a reply to the comments is subject to the appeal and brief fees under § 41.20 (b)(1) and (2), respectively, which must accompany the comments or reply.

(d) Following any response by the owner under paragraph (b)(1) of this section and any written comments from a requester under paragraph (c) of this section, the proceeding will be remanded to the examiner. The statement of the Board shall be binding upon the examiner unless an amendment or new evidence not previously of record is made which, in the opinion of the examiner, overcomes the new ground of rejection stated in the decision. The examiner will consider any owner response under paragraph (b)(1) of this section and any written comments by a requester under paragraph (c) of this section and issue a determination that the rejection is maintained or has been overcome.

(e) Within one month of the examiner's determination pursuant to paragraph (d) of this section, the owner or any requester may once submit comments in response to the examiner's determination. Within one month of the date of service of comments in response to the examiner's determination, the owner and any

requesters may file a reply to the comments. No requester reply may address the comments of any other requester reply. Any requester that had not previously filed an appeal or cross appeal and is seeking under this subsection to file comments or a reply to the comments is subject to the appeal and brief fees under § 41.20 (b)(1) and (2), respectively, which must accompany the comments or reply.

(f) After submission of any comments and any reply pursuant to paragraph (e) of this section, or after time has expired, the proceeding will be returned to the Board which shall reconsider the matter and issue a new decision. The new decision is deemed to incorporate the earlier decision, except for those portions specifically withdrawn.

(g) The time period set forth in paragraph (b) of this section is subject to the extension of time provisions of § 1.956 of this title when the owner is responding under paragraph (b)(1) of this section. The time period set forth in paragraph (b) of this section may not be extended when the owner is responding under paragraph (b)(2) of this section. The time periods set forth in paragraphs (c) and (e) of this section may not be extended.

[Added, 69 FR 49959, Aug. 12, 2004, effective Sept. 13, 2004]

§ 41.79 Rehearing.

(a) Parties to the appeal may file a request for rehearing of the decision within one month of the date of:

(1) The original decision of the Board under § 41.77(a),

(2) The original § 41.77(b) decision under the provisions of § 41.77(b)(2),

(3) The expiration of the time for the owner to take action under § 41.77(b)(2), or

(4) The new decision of the Board under § 41.77(f).

(b)(1)The request for rehearing must state with particularity the points believed to have been misapprehended or overlooked in rendering the Board's opinion reflecting its decision. Arguments not raised in the briefs before the Board and evidence not previously relied upon in the briefs are not permitted in the request for rehearing except as permitted by paragraphs (b)(2) and (b)(3) of this section.

(2) Upon a showing of good cause, appellant and/or respondent may present a new argument based upon a recent relevant decision of either the Board or a Federal Court.

(3) New arguments responding to a new ground of rejection made pursuant to § 41.77(b) are permitted.

(c) Within one month of the date of service of any request for rehearing under paragraph (a) of this section, or any further request for rehearing under paragraph (d) of this section, the owner and all requesters may once file comments in opposition to the request for rehearing or the further request for rehearing. The comments in opposition must be limited to the issues raised in the request for rehearing or the further request for rehearing.

(d) If a party to an appeal files a request for rehearing under paragraph (a) of this section, or a further request for rehearing under this section, the Board shall render a decision on the request for rehearing. The decision on the request for rehearing is deemed to incorporate the earlier opinion reflecting its decision for appeal, except for those portions specifically withdrawn on rehearing and is final for the purpose of judicial review, except when noted otherwise in the decision on rehearing. If the Board opinion reflecting its decision on rehearing becomes, in effect, a new decision, and the Board so indicates, then any party to the appeal may, within one month of the new decision, file a further request for rehearing of the new decision under this subsection. Such further request for rehearing must comply with paragraph (b) of this section.

(e) The times for requesting rehearing under paragraph (a) of this section, for requesting further rehearing under paragraph (c) of this section, and for submitting comments under paragraph (b) of this section may not be extended.

[Added, 69 FR 49959, Aug. 12, 2004, effective Sept. 13, 2004]

§ 41.81 Action following decision.

The parties to an appeal to the Board may not appeal to the U.S. Court of Appeals for the Federal Circuit under § 1.983 of this title until all parties' rights to request rehearing have been exhausted, at which time the decision of the Board is final and appealable by any party to the appeal to the Board.

[Added, 69 FR 49959, Aug. 12, 2004, effective Sept. 13, 2004]

Subpart D — Contested Cases

§ 41.100 Definitions.

In addition to the definitions in § 41.2, the following definitions apply to proceedings under this subpart:

Business day means a day other than a Saturday, Sunday, or Federal holiday within the District of Columbia.

Involved means the Board has declared the patent application, patent, or claim so described to be a subject of the contested case.

[Added, 69 FR 49959, Aug. 12, 2004, effective Sept. 13, 2004]

§ 41.101 Notice of proceeding.

(a) Notice of a contested case will be sent to every party to the proceeding. The entry of the notice initiates the proceeding.

(b) When the Board is unable to provide actual notice of a contested case on a party through the correspondence address of record for the party, the Board may authorize other modes of notice, including:

(1) Sending notice to another address associated with the party, or

(2) Publishing the notice in the Official Gazette of the United States Patent and Trademark Office.

[Added, 69 FR 49959, Aug. 12, 2004, effective Sept. 13, 2004]

§ 41.102 Completion of examination.

Before a contested case is initiated, except as the Board may otherwise authorize, for each involved application and patent:

(a) Examination or reexamination must be completed, and

(b) There must be at least one claim that:

(1) Is patentable but for a judgment in the contested case, and

(2) Would be involved in the contested case.

[Added, 69 FR 49959, Aug. 12, 2004, effective Sept. 13, 2004]

§ 41.103 Jurisdiction over involved files.

The Board acquires jurisdiction over any involved file when the Board initiates a contested case. Other proceedings for the involved file within the Office are suspended except as the Board may order.

[Added, 69 FR 49959, Aug. 12, 2004, effective Sept. 13, 2004]

§ 41.104 Conduct of contested cases.

(a) The Board may determine a proper course of conduct in a proceeding for any situation not specifically covered by this part and may enter non-final orders to administer the proceeding.

(b) An administrative patent judge may waive or suspend in a proceeding the application of any rule in this subpart, subject to such conditions as the administrative patent judge may impose.

(c) Times set in this subpart are defaults. In the event of a conflict between a time set by rule and a time set by order, the time set by order is controlling. Action due on a day other than a business day may be completed on the next business day unless the Board expressly states otherwise.

[Added, 69 FR 49959, Aug. 12, 2004, effective Sept. 13, 2004]

§ 41.106 Filing and service.

(a) *General format requirements.* (1) The paper used for filings must be durable and white. A party must choose to file on either A4-sized paper or 8½ inch x 11 inch paper except in the case of exhibits that require a larger size in order to preserve details of the original. A party may not switch between paper sizes in a single proceeding. Only one side of the paper may be used.

(2) In papers, including affidavits, created for the proceeding:

(i) Markings must be in black ink or must otherwise provide an equivalently permanent, dark, high-contrast image on the paper. The quality of printing must be equivalent to the quality produced by a laser printer. Either a proportional or monospaced font may be used, but the proportional font must be 12-point or larger and a monospaced font must not contain more than 4 characters per centimeter (10 charac-

ters per inch). Case names must be underlined or italicized.

(ii) Double spacing must be used except in headings, tables of contents, tables of authorities, indices, signature blocks, and certificates of service. Block quotations may be single-spaced and must be indented. Margins must be at least 2.5 centimeters (1 inch) on all sides.

(b) *Papers other than exhibits*—(1) *Cover sheet.* (i) The cover sheet must include the caption the Board specifies for the proceeding, a header indicating the party and contact information for the party, and a title indicating the sequence and subject of the paper. For example, "JONES MOTION 2, For benefit of an earlier application".

(ii) If the Board specifies a color other than white for the cover sheet, the cover sheet must be that color.

(2) Papers must have two 0.5 cm (¼ inch) holes with centers 1 cm (½ inch) from the top of the page and 7 cm (2¾ inch) apart, centered horizontally on the page.

(3) *Incorporation by reference; combined papers.* Arguments must not be incorporated by reference from one paper into another paper. Combined motions, oppositions, replies, or other combined papers are not permitted.

(4) *Exhibits.* Additional requirements for exhibits appear in § 41.154(c).

(c) *Working copy.* Every paper filed must be accompanied by a working copy marked "APJ Copy".

(d) *Specific filing forms.* (1) *Filing by mail.* A paper filed using the EXPRESS MAIL® service of the United States Postal Service will be deemed to be filed as of "date-in" on the EXPRESS MAIL® mailing label; otherwise, mail will be deemed to be filed as of the stamped date of receipt at the Board.

(2) *Other modes of filing.* The Board may authorize other modes of filing, including electronic filing and hand filing, and may set conditions for the use of such other modes.

(e) *Service.* (1) Papers filed with the Board, if not previously served, must be served simultaneously on every opposing party except as the Board expressly directs.

(2) If a party is represented by counsel, service must be on counsel.

(3) Service must be by EXPRESS MAIL® or by means at least as fast and reliable as EXPRESS MAIL®. Electronic service is not permitted without Board authorization.

(4) The date of service does not count in computing the time for responding.

(f) *Certificate of service.* (1) Papers other than exhibits must include a certificate of service as a separate page at the end of each paper that must be served on an opposing party.

(2) Exhibits must be accompanied by a certificate of service, but a single certificate may accompany any group of exhibits submitted together.

(3) A certificate of service must state:

(i) The date and manner of service,

(ii) The name and address of every person served, and

(iii) For exhibits filed as a group, the name and number of each exhibit served.

(4) A certificate made by a person other than a registered patent practitioner must be in the form of an affidavit.

[Added, 69 FR 49959, Aug. 12, 2004, effective Sept. 13, 2004]

§ 41.108 Lead counsel.

(a) A party may be represented by counsel. The Board may require a party to appoint a lead counsel. If counsel is not of record in a party's involved application or patent, then a power of attorney for that counsel for the party's involved application or patent must be filed with the notice required in paragraph (b) of this section.

(b) Within 14 days of the initiation of each contested case, each party must file a separate notice identifying its counsel, if any, and providing contact information for each counsel identified or, if the party has no counsel, then for the party. Contact information must, at a minimum, include:

(1) A mailing address;

(2) An address for courier delivery when the mailing address is not available for such delivery (for example, when the mailing address is a Post Office box);

(3) A telephone number;

(4) A facsimile number; and

(5) An electronic mail address.

(c) A party must promptly notify the Board of any change in the contact information required in paragraph (b) of this section.

[Added, 69 FR 49959, Aug. 12, 2004, effective Sept. 13, 2004]

§ 41.109 Access to and copies of Office records.

(a) *Request for access or copies.* Any request from a party for access to or copies of Office records directly related to a contested case must be filed with the Board. The request must precisely identify the records and in the case of copies include the appropriate fee set under § 1.19(b) of this title.

(b) *Authorization of access and copies.* Access and copies will ordinarily only be authorized for the following records:

(1) The application file for an involved patent;

(2) An involved application; and

(3) An application for which a party has been accorded benefit under subpart E of this part.

(c) *Missing or incomplete copies.* If a party does not receive a complete copy of a record within 21 days of the authorization, the party must promptly notify the Board.

[Added, 69 FR 49959, Aug. 12, 2004, effective Sept. 13, 2004]

§ 41.110 Filing claim information.

(a) *Clean copy of claims.* Within 14 days of the initiation of the proceeding, each party must file a clean copy of its involved claims and, if a biotechnology material sequence is a limitation, a clean copy of the sequence.

(b) *Annotated copy of claims.* Within 28 days of the initiation of the proceeding, each party must:

(1) For each involved claim having a limitation that is illustrated in a drawing or biotechnology material sequence, file an annotated copy of the claim indicating in bold face between braces ({}) where each limitation is shown in the drawing or sequence.

(2) For each involved claim that contains a means-plus-function or step-plus-function limitation in the form permitted under 35 U.S.C. 112(6), file an annotated copy of the claim indicating in bold face between braces ({}) the specific portions of the speci-

fication that describe the structure, material, or acts corresponding to each claimed function.

(c)   Any motion to add or amend a claim must include:

(1)   A clean copy of the claim,

(2)   A claim chart showing where the disclosure of the patent or application provides written description of the subject matter of the claim, and

(3)   Where applicable, a copy of the claims annotated according to paragraph (b) of this section.

[Added, 69 FR 49959, Aug. 12, 2004, effective Sept. 13, 2004]

§ 41.120 Notice of basis for relief.

(a)   The Board may require a party to provide a notice stating the relief it requests and the basis for its entitlement to relief. The Board may provide for the notice to be maintained in confidence for a limited time.

(b)   *Effect.* If a notice under paragraph (a) of this section is required, a party will be limited to filing substantive motions consistent with the notice. Ambiguities in the notice will be construed against the party. A notice is not evidence except as an admission by a party-opponent.

(c)   *Correction.* A party may move to correct its notice. The motion should be filed promptly after the party becomes aware of the basis for the correction. A correction filed after the time set for filing notices will only be entered if entry would serve the interests of justice.

[Added, 69 FR 49959, Aug. 12, 2004, effective Sept. 13, 2004]

§ 41.121 Motions.

(a)   *Types of motions—*(1) *Substantive motions.* Consistent with the notice of requested relief, if any, and to the extent the Board authorizes, a party may file a motion:

(i)   To redefine the scope of the contested case,

(ii)   To change benefit accorded for the contested subject matter, or

(iii)   For judgment in the contested case.

(2)   *Responsive motions.* The Board may authorize a party to file a motion to amend or add a claim, to change inventorship, or otherwise to cure a defect raised in a notice of requested relief or in a substantive motion.

(3)   *Miscellaneous motions.* Any request for relief other than a substantive or responsive motion must be filed as a miscellaneous motion.

(b)   *Burden of proof.* The party filing the motion has the burden of proof to establish that it is entitled to the requested relief.

(c)   *Content of motions; oppositions and replies.* (1) Each motion must be filed as a separate paper and must include:

(i)   A statement of the precise relief requested,

(ii)   A statement of material facts (see paragraph (d) of this section), and

(iii)   A full statement of the reasons for the relief requested, including a detailed explanation of the significance of the evidence and the governing law, rules, and precedent.

(2)   *Compliance with rules.* Where a rule in part 1 of this title ordinarily governs the relief sought, the motion must make any showings required under that rule in addition to any showings required in this part.

(3)   The Board may order additional showings or explanations as a condition for filing a motion.

(d)   *Statement of material facts.* (1) Each material fact shall be set forth as a separate numbered sentence with specific citations to the portions of the record that support the fact.

(2)   The Board may require that the statement of material facts be submitted as a separate paper.

(e)   *Claim charts.* Claim charts must be used in support of any paper requiring the comparison of a claim to something else, such as another claim, prior art, or a specification. Claim charts must accompany the paper as an appendix. Claim charts are not a substitute for appropriate argument and explanation in the paper.

(f)   The Board may order briefing on any issue that could be raised by motion.

[Added, 69 FR 49959, Aug. 12, 2004, effective Sept. 13, 2004]

§ 41.122 Oppositions and replies.

(a)   Oppositions and replies must comply with the content requirements for motions and must include a statement identifying material facts in dispute. Any material fact not specifically denied shall be considered admitted.

(b) All arguments for the relief requested in a motion must be made in the motion. A reply may only respond to arguments raised in the corresponding opposition.

[Added, 69 FR 49959, Aug. 12, 2004, effective Sept. 13, 2004]

§ 41.123 Default filing times.

(a) A *motion*, other than a miscellaneous motion, may only be filed according to a schedule the Board sets. The default times for acting are:

(1) An *opposition* is due 30 days after service of the motion.

(2) A *reply* is due 30 days after service of the opposition.

(3) A *responsive motion* is due 30 days after the service of the motion.

(b) *Miscellaneous motions.* (1) If no time for filing a specific miscellaneous motion is provided in this part or in a Board order:

(i) The opposing party must be consulted prior to filing the miscellaneous motion, and

(ii) If an opposing party plans to oppose the miscellaneous motion, the movant may not file the motion without Board authorization. Such authorization should ordinarily be obtained through a telephone conference including the Board and every other party to the proceeding. Delay in seeking relief may justify a denial of the motion.

(2) An opposition may not be filed without authorization. The default times for acting are:

(i) An *opposition* to a miscellaneous motion is due five business days after service of the motion.

(ii) A *reply* to a miscellaneous motion opposition is due three business days after service of the opposition.

(c) *Exhibits.* Each exhibit must be filed and served with the first paper in which it is cited except as the Board may otherwise order.

[Added, 69 FR 49959, Aug. 12, 2004, effective Sept. 13, 2004]

§ 41.124 Oral argument.

(a) *Request for oral argument.* A party may request an oral argument on an issue raised in a paper within five business days of the filing of the paper. The request must be filed as a separate paper and must specify the issues to be considered.

(b) *Copies for panel.* If an oral argument is set for a panel, the movant on any issue to be argued must provide three working copies of the motion, the opposition, and the reply. Each party is responsible for providing three working copies of its exhibits relating to the motion.

(c) *Length of argument.* If a request for oral argument is granted, each party will have a total of 20 minutes to present its arguments, including any time for rebuttal.

(d) *Demonstrative exhibits* must be served at least five business days before the oral argument and filed no later than the time of the oral argument.

(e) *Transcription.* The Board encourages the use of a transcription service at oral arguments but, if such a service is to be used, the Board must be notified in advance to ensure adequate facilities are available and a transcript must be filed with the Board promptly after the oral argument.

[Added, 69 FR 49959, Aug. 12, 2004, effective Sept. 13, 2004]

§ 41.125 Decision on motions.

(a) *Order of consideration.* The Board may take up motions for decisions in any order, may grant, deny, or dismiss any motion, and may take such other action appropriate to secure the just, speedy, and inexpensive determination of the proceeding. A decision on a motion may include deferral of action on an issue until a later point in the proceeding.

(b) *Interlocutory decisions.* A decision on motions without a judgment is not final for the purposes of judicial review. A panel decision on an issue will govern further proceedings in the contested case.

(c) *Rehearing*—(1) Time for request. A request for rehearing of a decision on a motion must be filed within fourteen days of the decision.

(2) *No tolling.* The filing of a request for rehearing does not toll times for taking action.

(3) *Burden on rehearing.* The burden of showing a decision should be modified lies with the party attacking the decision. The request must specifically identify:

(i) All matters the party believes to have been misapprehended or overlooked, and

(ii) The place where the matter was previously addressed in a motion, opposition, or reply.

(4) *Opposition; reply.* Neither an opposition nor a reply to a request for rehearing may be filed without Board authorization.

(5) *Panel rehearing.* If a decision is not a panel decision, the party requesting rehearing may request that a panel rehear the decision. A panel rehearing a procedural decision will review the decision for an abuse of discretion.

[Added, 69 FR 49959, Aug. 12, 2004, effective Sept. 13, 2004]

§ 41.126 Arbitration.

(a) Parties to a contested case may resort to binding arbitration to determine any issue in a contested case. The Office is not a party to the arbitration. The Board is not bound and may independently determine questions of patentability, jurisdiction, and Office practice.

(b) The Board will not authorize arbitration unless:

(1) It is to be conducted according to Title 9 of the United States Code.

(2) The parties notify the Board in writing of their intention to arbitrate.

(3) The agreement to arbitrate:

(i) Is in writing,

(ii) Specifies the issues to be arbitrated,

(iii) Names the arbitrator, or provides a date not more than 30 days after the execution of the agreement for the selection of the arbitrator, and

(iv) Provides that the arbitrator's award shall be binding on the parties and that judgment thereon can be entered by the Board.

(4) A copy of the agreement is filed within 20 days after its execution.

(5) The arbitration is completed within the time the Board sets.

(c) The parties are solely responsible for the selection of the arbitrator and the conduct of proceedings before the arbitrator.

(d) Issues not disposed of by the arbitration will be resolved in accordance with the procedures established in this subpart.

(e) The Board will not consider the arbitration award unless it:

(1) Is binding on the parties,

(2) Is in writing,

(3) States in a clear and definite manner each issue arbitrated and the disposition of each issue, and

(4) Is filed within 20 days of the date of the award.

(f) Once the award is filed, the parties to the award may not take actions inconsistent with the award. If the award is dispositive of the contested subject matter for a party, the Board may enter judgment as to that party.

[Added, 69 FR 49959, Aug. 12, 2004, effective Sept. 13, 2004]

§ 41.127 Judgment.

(a) *Effect within Office—*(1) *Estoppel.* A judgment disposes of all issues that were, or by motion could have properly been, raised and decided. A losing party who could have properly moved for relief on an issue, but did not so move, may not take action in the Office after the judgment that is inconsistent with that party's failure to move, except that a losing party shall not be estopped with respect to any contested subject matter for which that party was awarded a favorable judgment.

(2) *Final disposal of claim.* Adverse judgment against a claim is a final action of the Office requiring no further action by the Office to dispose of the claim permanently.

(b) *Request for adverse judgment.* A party may at any time in the proceeding request judgment against itself. Actions construed to be a request for adverse judgment include:

(1) Abandonment of an involved application such that the party no longer has an application or patent involved in the proceeding,

(2) Cancellation or disclaiming of a claim such that the party no longer has a claim involved in the proceeding,

(3) Concession of priority or unpatentability of the contested subject matter, and

(4) Abandonment of the contest.

(c) *Recommendation.* The judgment may include a recommendation for further action by the examiner or by the Director. If the Board recommends rejection of a claim of an involved application, the examiner must enter and maintain the recommended rejection unless an amendment or showing of facts not previously of record is filed which, in the opinion of the examiner, overcomes the recommended rejection.

(d) *Rehearing.* A party dissatisfied with the judgment may file a request for rehearing within 30 days of the entry of the judgment The request must specifically identify all matters the party believes to have been misapprehended or overlooked, and the place where the matter was previously addressed in a motion, opposition or reply.

[Added, 69 FR 49959, Aug. 12, 2004, effective Sept. 13, 2004; para. (d) revised, 69 FR 58260, Sept. 30, 2004, effective Sept. 30, 2004]

§ 41.128 Sanctions.

(a) The Board may impose a sanction against a party for misconduct, including:

(1) Failure to comply with an applicable rule or order in the proceeding;

(2) Advancing a misleading or frivolous request for relief or argument; or

(3) Engaging in dilatory tactics.

(b) Sanctions include entry of:

(1) An order holding certain facts to have been established in the proceeding;

(2) An order expunging, or precluding a party from filing, a paper;

(3) An order precluding a party from presenting or contesting a particular issue;

(4) An order precluding a party from requesting, obtaining, or opposing discovery;

(5) An order excluding evidence;

(6) An order awarding compensatory expenses, including attorney fees;

(7) An order requiring terminal disclaimer of patent term; or

(8) Judgment in the contested case.

[Added, 69 FR 49959, Aug. 12, 2004, effective Sept. 13, 2004]

§ 41.150 Discovery.

(a) *Limited discovery.* A party is not entitled to discovery except as authorized in this subpart. The parties may agree to discovery among themselves at any time.

(b) *Automatic discovery.* (1) Within 21 days of a request by an opposing party, a party must:

(i) Serve a legible copy of every requested patent, patent application, literature reference, and test standard mentioned in the specification of the party's involved patent or application, or application upon which the party will rely for benefit, and, if the requested material is in a language other than English, a translation, if available, and

(ii) File with the Board a notice (without copies of the requested materials) of service of the requested materials.

(2) Unless previously served, or the Board orders otherwise, any exhibit cited in a motion or in testimony must be served with the citing motion or testimony.

(c) *Additional discovery.* (1) A party may request additional discovery. The requesting party must show that such additional discovery is in the interests of justice. The Board may specify conditions for such additional discovery.

(2) When appropriate, a party may obtain production of documents and things during cross examination of an opponent's witness or during testimony authorized under § 41.156.

[Added, 69 FR 49959, Aug. 12, 2004, effective Sept. 13, 2004]

§ 41.151 Admissibility.

Evidence that is not taken, sought, or filed in accordance with this subpart shall not be admissible.

[Added, 69 FR 49959, Aug. 12, 2004, effective Sept. 13, 2004]

§ 41.152 Applicability of the Federal Rules of Evidence.

(a) *Generally.* Except as otherwise provided in this subpart, the Federal Rules of Evidence shall apply to contested cases.

(b) *Exclusions.* Those portions of the Federal Rules of Evidence relating to criminal proceedings, juries, and other matters not relevant to proceedings under this subpart shall not apply.

(c) *Modifications in terminology*. Unless otherwise clear from context, the following terms of the Federal Rules of Evidence shall be construed as indicated:

Appellate court means United States Court of Appeals for the Federal Circuit or a United States district court when judicial review is under 35 U.S.C. 146.

Civil action, civil proceeding, action, and *trial* mean contested case.

Courts of the United States, U.S. Magistrate, court, trial court, and *trier of fact* mean Board.

Hearing means:

(i) In Federal Rule of Evidence 703, the time when the expert testifies.

(ii) In Federal Rule of Evidence 804(a)(5), the time for taking testimony.

Judge means the Board.

Judicial notice means official notice.

Trial or hearing means, in Federal Rule of Evidence 807, the time for taking testimony.

(d) The Board, in determining foreign law, may consider any relevant material or source, including testimony, whether or not submitted by a party or admissible under the Federal Rules of Evidence.

[Added, 69 FR 49959, Aug. 12, 2004, effective Sept. 13, 2004]

§ 41.153 Records of the Office.

Certification is not necessary as a condition to admissibility when the evidence to be submitted is a record of the Office to which all parties have access.

[Added, 69 FR 49959, Aug. 12, 2004, effective Sept. 13, 2004]

§ 41.154 Form of evidence.

(a) Evidence consists of affidavits, transcripts of depositions, documents, and things. All evidence must be submitted in the form of an exhibit.

(b) *Translation required.* When a party relies on a document or is required to produce a document in a language other than English, a translation of the document into English and an affidavit attesting to the accuracy of the translation must be filed with the document.

(c)(1) Each exhibit must have an exhibit label with a unique number in a range assigned by the Board, the names of the parties, and the proceeding number in the following format:

JONES EXHIBIT 2001

Jones v. Smith

Contested Case 104,999

(2) When the exhibit is a paper:

(i) Each page must be uniquely numbered in sequence, and

(ii) The exhibit label must be affixed to the lower right corner of the first page of the exhibit without obscuring information on the first page or, if obscuring is unavoidable, affixed to a duplicate first page.

(d) *Exhibit list.* Each party must maintain an exhibit list with the exhibit number and a brief description of each exhibit. If the exhibit is not filed, the exhibit list should note that fact. The Board may require the filing of a current exhibit list prior to acting on a motion.

[Added, 69 FR 49959, Aug. 12, 2004, effective Sept. 13, 2004; para. (c)(1) revised, 69 FR 58260, Sept. 30, 2004, effective Sept. 30, 2004]

§ 41.155 Objection; motion to exclude; motion in limine.

(a) *Deposition.* Objections to deposition evidence must be made during the deposition. Evidence to cure the objection must be provided during the deposition unless the parties to the deposition stipulate otherwise on the deposition record.

(b) *Other than deposition.* For evidence other than deposition evidence:

(1) *Objection.* Any objection must be served within five business days of service of evidence, other than deposition evidence, to which the objection is directed.

(2) *Supplemental evidence.* The party relying on evidence for which an objection is timely served may respond to the objection by serving supplemental evidence within ten business days of service of the objection.

[Added, 69 FR 49959, Aug. 12, 2004, effective Sept. 13, 2004; para. (b) revised, 69 FR 58260, Sept. 30, 2004, effective Sept. 30, 2004]

§ 41.156 Compelling testimony and production.

(a) *Authorization required.* A party seeking to compel testimony or production of documents or things must file a miscellaneous motion for authorization. The miscellaneous motion must describe the general relevance of the testimony, document, or thing and must:

(1) In the case of testimony, identify the witness by name or title, and

(2) In the case of a document or thing, the general nature of the document or thing.

(b) *Outside the United States.* For testimony or production sought outside the United States, the motion must also:

(1) *In the case of testimony.* (i) Identify the foreign country and explain why the party believes the witness can be compelled to testify in the foreign country, including a description of the procedures that will be used to compel the testimony in the foreign country and an estimate of the time it is expected to take to obtain the testimony; and

(ii) Demonstrate that the party has made reasonable efforts to secure the agreement of the witness to testify in the United States but has been unsuccessful in obtaining the agreement, even though the party has offered to pay the expenses of the witness to travel to and testify in the United States.

(2) *In the case of production of a document or thing.* (i) Identify the foreign country and explain why the party believes production of the document or thing can be compelled in the foreign country, including a description of the procedures that will be used to compel production of the document or thing in the foreign country and an estimate of the time it is expected to take to obtain production of the document or thing; and

(ii) Demonstrate that the party has made reasonable efforts to obtain the agreement of the individual or entity having possession, custody, or control of the document to produce the document or thing in the United States but has been unsuccessful in obtaining that agreement, even though the party has offered to pay the expenses of producing the document or thing in the United States.

[Added, 69 FR 49959, Aug. 12, 2004, effective Sept. 13, 2004]

§ 41.157 Taking testimony.

(a) *Form.* Direct testimony must be submitted in the form of an affidavit except when the testimony is compelled under 35 U.S.C. 24, in which case it may be in the form of a deposition transcript.

(b) *Time and location.* (1) *Uncompelled direct testimony* may be taken at any time; otherwise, testimony may only be taken during such time period as the Board may authorize.

(2) *Other testimony.* (i) Except as the Board otherwise orders, authorized testimony may be taken at any reasonable time and location within the United States before any disinterested official authorized to administer oaths at that location.

(ii) Testimony outside the United States may only be taken as the Board specifically directs.

(c) *Notice of deposition.* (1) Prior to the taking of testimony, all parties to the proceeding must agree on the time and place for taking testimony. If the parties cannot agree, the party seeking the testimony must initiate a conference with the Board to set a time and place.

(2) Cross-examination should ordinarily take place after any supplemental evidence relating to the direct testimony has been filed and more than a week before the filing date for any paper in which the cross-examination testimony is expected to be used. A party requesting cross-examination testimony of more than one witness may choose the order in which the witnesses are to be cross-examined.

(3) In the case of direct testimony, at least three business days prior to the conference in paragraph (c)(1) of this section, the party seeking the direct testimony must serve:

(i) A list and copy of each document under the party's control and on which the party intends to rely, and

(ii) A list of, and proffer of reasonable access to, any thing other than a document under the party's control and on which the party intends to rely.

(4) Notice of the deposition must be filed at least two business days before a deposition. The notice limits the scope of the testimony and must list:

(i) The time and place of the deposition,

(ii) The name and address of the witness,

(iii) A list of the exhibits to be relied upon during the deposition, and

(iv)   A general description of the scope and nature of the testimony to be elicited.

(5)   *Motion to quash.* Objection to a defect in the notice is waived unless a miscellaneous motion to quash is promptly filed.

(d)   *Deposition in a foreign language.* If an interpreter will be used during the deposition, the party calling the witness must initiate a conference with the Board at least five business days before the deposition.

(e)   *Manner of taking testimony.* (1) Each witness before giving a deposition shall be duly sworn according to law by the officer before whom the deposition is to be taken. The officer must be authorized to take testimony under 35 U.S.C. 23.

(2)   The testimony shall be taken in answer to interrogatories with any questions and answers recorded in their regular order by the officer, or by some other disinterested person in the presence of the officer, unless the presence of the officer is waived on the record by agreement of all parties.

(3)   Any exhibits relied upon must be numbered according to the numbering scheme assigned for the contested case and must, if not previously served, be served at the deposition.

(4)   All objections made at the time of the deposition to the qualifications of the officer taking the deposition, the manner of taking it, the evidence presented, the conduct of any party, and any other objection to the proceeding shall be noted on the record by the officer. Evidence objected to shall be taken subject to a ruling on the objection.

(5)   When the testimony has been transcribed, the witness shall read and sign (in the form of an affidavit) a transcript of the deposition unless:

(i)   The parties otherwise agree in writing,

(ii)   The parties waive reading and signature by the witness on the record at the deposition, or

(iii)   The witness refuses to read or sign the transcript of the deposition.

(6)   The officer shall prepare a certified transcript by attaching to the transcript of the deposition a certificate in the form of an affidavit signed and sealed by the officer. Unless the parties waive any of the following requirements, in which case the certificate shall so state, the certificate must state:

(i)   The witness was duly sworn by the officer before commencement of testimony by the witness;

(ii)   The transcript is a true record of the testimony given by the witness;

(iii)   The name of the person who recorded the testimony and, if the officer did not record it, whether the testimony was recorded in the presence of the officer;

(iv)   The presence or absence of any opponent;

(v)   The place where the deposition was taken and the day and hour when the deposition began and ended;

(vi)   The officer has no disqualifying interest, personal or financial, in a party; and

(vii)   If a witness refuses to read or sign the transcript, the circumstances under which the witness refused.

(7)   The officer must promptly provide a copy of the transcript to all parties. The proponent of the testimony must file the original as an exhibit.

(8)   Any objection to the content, form, or manner of taking the deposition, including the qualifications of the officer, is waived unless made on the record during the deposition and preserved in a timely filed miscellaneous motion to exclude.

(f)   *Costs.* Except as the Board may order or the parties may agree in writing, the proponent of the testimony shall bear all costs associated with the testimony, including the reasonable costs associated with making the witness available for the cross-examination.

[Added, 69 FR 49959, Aug. 12, 2004, effective Sept. 13, 2004]

§ 41.158   Expert testimony; tests and data.

(a)   Expert testimony that does not disclose the underlying facts or data on which the opinion is based is entitled to little or no weight. Testimony on United States patent law will not be admitted.

(b)   If a party relies on a technical test or data from such a test, the party must provide an affidavit explaining:

(1)   Why the test or data is being used,

(2)   How the test was performed and the data was generated,

(3)   How the data is used to determine a value,

(4)   How the test is regarded in the relevant art, and

(5)   Any other information necessary for the Board to evaluate the test and data.

[Added, 69 FR 49959, Aug. 12, 2004, effective Sept. 13, 2004]

Subpart E — Patent Interferences

§ 41.200 Procedure; pendency.

(a)   A patent interference is a contested case subject to the procedures set forth in subpart D of this part.

(b)   [Reserved]

(c)   Patent interferences shall be administered such that pendency before the Board is normally no more than two years.

[Added, 69 FR 49959, Aug. 12, 2004, effective Sept. 13, 2004; para. (b) removed and reserved, 75 FR 19958, Apr. 15, 2010, effective Apr. 15, 2010]

§ 41.201 Definitions.

In addition to the definitions in §§ 41.2 and 41.100, the following definitions apply to proceedings under this subpart:

Accord benefit means Board recognition that a patent application provides a proper constructive reduction to practice under 35 U.S.C. 102(g)(1).

Constructive reduction to practice means a described and enabled anticipation under 35 U.S.C. 102(g)(1) in a patent application of the subject matter of a count. *Earliest constructive reduction to practice* means the first constructive reduction to practice that has been continuously disclosed through a chain of patent applications including in the involved application or patent. For the chain to be continuous, each subsequent application must have been co-pending under 35 U.S.C. 120 or 121 or timely filed under 35 U.S.C. 119 or 365(a).

Count means the Board's description of the interfering subject matter that sets the scope of admissible proofs on priority. Where there is more than one count, each count must describe a patentably distinct invention.

Involved claim means, for the purposes of 35 U.S.C.135(a), a claim that has been designated as corresponding to the count.

Senior party means the party entitled to the presumption under § 41.207(a)(1) that it is the prior inventor. Any other party is a *junior party*.

Threshold issue means an issue that, if resolved in favor of the movant, would deprive the opponent of standing in the interference. Threshold issues may include:

(1)   No interference-in-fact, and

(2)   In the case of an involved application claim first made after the publication of the movant's application or issuance of the movant's patent:

(i)   Repose under 35 U.S.C. 135(b) in view of the movant's patent or published application, or

(ii)   Unpatentability for lack of written description under 35 U.S.C. 112(1) of an involved application claim where the applicant suggested, or could have suggested, an interference under § 41.202(a).

[Added, 69 FR 49959, Aug. 12, 2004, effective Sept. 13, 2004]

§ 41.202 Suggesting an interference.

(a)   *Applicant.* An applicant, including a reissue applicant, may suggest an interference with another application or a patent. The suggestion must:

(1)   Provide sufficient information to identify the application or patent with which the applicant seeks an interference,

(2)   Identify all claims the applicant believes interfere, propose one or more counts, and show how the claims correspond to one or more counts,

(3)   For each count, provide a claim chart comparing at least one claim of each party corresponding to the count and show why the claims interfere within the meaning of § 41.203(a),

(4)   Explain in detail why the applicant will prevail on priority,

(5)   If a claim has been added or amended to provoke an interference, provide a claim chart showing the written description for each claim in the applicant's specification, and

(6)   For each constructive reduction to practice for which the applicant wishes to be accorded benefit, provide a chart showing where the disclosure provides a constructive reduction to practice within the scope of the interfering subject matter.

(b)   *Patentee.* A patentee cannot suggest an interference under this section but may, to the extent permitted under § 1.99 and § 1.291 of this title, alert the examiner of an application claiming interfering subject matter to the possibility of an interference.

(c)   *Examiner.* An examiner may require an applicant to add a claim to provoke an interference. Failure to satisfy the requirement within a period (not less than one month) the examiner sets will operate as a concession of priority for the subject matter of the claim. If the interference would be with a patent, the applicant must also comply with paragraphs (a)(2) through (a)(6) of this section. The claim the examiner proposes to have added must, apart from the question of priority under 35 U.S.C. 102 (g):

(1)   Be patentable to the applicant, and

(2)   Be drawn to patentable subject matter claimed by another applicant or patentee.

(d)   *Requirement to show priority under 35 U.S.C. 102(g).*(1) When an applicant has an earliest constructive reduction to practice that is later than the apparent earliest constructive reduction to practice for a patent or published application claiming interfering subject matter, the applicant must show why it would prevail on priority.

(2)   If an applicant fails to show priority under paragraph (d)(1) of this section, an administrative patent judge may nevertheless declare an interference to place the applicant under an order to show cause why judgment should not be entered against the applicant on priority. New evidence in support of priority will not be admitted except on a showing of good cause. The Board may authorize the filing of motions to redefine the interfering subject matter or to change the benefit accorded to the parties.

(e)   *Sufficiency of showing.* (1) A showing of priority under this section is not sufficient unless it would, if unrebutted, support a determination of priority in favor of the party making the showing.

(2)   When testimony or production necessary to show priority is not available without authorization under § 41.150(c) or § 41.156(a), the showing shall include:

(i)   Any necessary interrogatory, request for admission, request for production, or deposition request, and

(ii)   A detailed proffer of what the response to the interrogatory or request would be expected to be and an explanation of the relevance of the response to the question of priority.

[Added, 69 FR 49959, Aug. 12, 2004, effective Sept. 13, 2004]

§ 41.203 Declaration.

(a)   *Interfering subject matter.* An interference exists if the subject matter of a claim of one party would, if prior art, have anticipated or rendered obvious the subject matter of a claim of the opposing party and vice versa.

(b)   *Notice of declaration.* An administrative patent judge declares the patent interference on behalf of the Director. A notice declaring an interference identifies:

(1)   The interfering subject matter;

(2)   The involved applications, patents, and claims;

(3)   The accorded benefit for each count; and

(4)   The claims corresponding to each count.

(c)   *Redeclaration.* An administrative patent judge may redeclare a patent interference on behalf of the Director to change the declaration made under paragraph (b) of this section.

(d)   A party may suggest the addition of a patent or application to the interference or the declaration of an additional interference. The suggestion should make the showings required under § 41.202(a) of this part.

[Added, 69 FR 49959, Aug. 12, 2004, effective Sept. 13, 2004]

§ 41.204 Notice of basis for relief.

(a)   *Priority statement.* (1) A party may not submit evidence of its priority in addition to its accorded benefit unless it files a statement setting forth all bases on which the party intends to establish its entitlement to judgment on priority.

(2) The priority statement must:

(i) State the date and location of the party's earliest corroborated conception,

(ii) State the date and location of the party's earliest corroborated actual reduction to practice,

(iii) State the earliest corroborated date on which the party's diligence began, and

(iv) Provide a copy of the earliest document upon which the party will rely to show conception.

(3) If a junior party fails to file a priority statement overcoming a senior party's accorded benefit, judgment shall be entered against the junior party absent a showing of good cause.

(b) *Other substantive motions.* The Board may require a party to list the motions it intends to file, including sufficient detail to place the Board and the opponent on notice of the precise relief sought.

(c) *Filing and service.* The Board will set the times for filing and serving statements required under this section.

[Added, 69 FR 49959, Aug. 12, 2004, effective Sept. 13, 2004]

§ 41.205 Settlement agreements.

(a) *Constructive notice; time for filing.* Pursuant to 35 U.S.C. 135(c), an agreement or understanding, including collateral agreements referred to therein, made in connection with or in contemplation of the termination of an interference must be filed prior to the termination of the interference between the parties to the agreement. After a final decision is entered by the Board, an interference is considered terminated when no appeal (35 U.S.C. 141) or other review (35 U.S.C. 146) has been or can be taken or had. If an appeal to the U.S. Court of Appeals for the Federal Circuit (under 35 U.S.C. 141) or a civil action (under 35 U.S.C. 146) has been filed the interference is considered terminated when the appeal or civil action is terminated. A civil action is terminated when the time to appeal the judgment expires. An appeal to the U.S. Court of Appeals for the Federal Circuit, whether from a decision of the Board or a judgment in a civil action, is terminated when the mandate is issued by the Court.

(b) *Untimely filing.* The Chief Administrative Patent Judge may permit the filing of an agreement under paragraph (a) of this section up to six months after termination upon petition and a showing of good cause for the failure to file prior to termination.

(c) *Request to keep separate.* Any party to an agreement under paragraph (a) of this section may request that the agreement be kept separate from the interference file. The request must be filed with or promptly after the agreement is filed.

(d) *Access to agreement.* Any person, other than a representative of a Government agency, may have access to an agreement kept separate under paragraph (c) of this section only upon petition and on a showing of good cause. The agreement will be available to Government agencies on written request.

[Added, 69 FR 49959, Aug. 12, 2004, effective Sept. 13, 2004]

§ 41.206 Common interests in the invention.

An administrative patent judge may decline to declare, or if already declared the Board may issue judgment in, an interference between an application and another application or patent that are commonly owned.

[Added, 69 FR 49959, Aug. 12, 2004, effective Sept. 13, 2004]

§ 41.207 Presumptions.

(a) *Priority*—(1) *Order of invention.* Parties are presumed to have invented interfering subject matter in the order of the dates of their accorded benefit for each count. If two parties are accorded the benefit of the same earliest date of constructive reduction to practice, then neither party is entitled to a presumption of priority with respect to the other such party.

(2) *Evidentiary standard.* Priority may be proved by a preponderance of the evidence except a party must prove priority by clear and convincing evidence if the date of its earliest constructive reduction to practice is after the issue date of an involved patent or the publication date under 35 U.S.C. 122(b) of an involved application or patent.

(b) *Claim correspondence.* (1) For the purposes of determining priority and derivation, all claims of a party corresponding to the count are presumed to stand or fall together. To challenge this presumption, a party must file a timely substantive motion to have a corresponding claim designated as not corresponding to the count. No presumption based on claim correspondence regarding the grouping of claims exists for other grounds of unpatentability.

(2) A claim corresponds to a count if the subject matter of the count, treated as prior art to the claim, would have anticipated or rendered obvious the subject matter of the claim.

(c) *Cross-applicability of prior art.* When a motion for judgment of unpatentability against an opponent's claim on the basis of prior art is granted, each of the movant's claims corresponding to the same count as the opponent's claim will be presumed to be unpatentable in view of the same prior art unless the movant in its motion rebuts this presumption.

[Added, 69 FR 49959, Aug. 12, 2004, effective Sept. 13, 2004]

§ 41.208 Content of substantive and responsive motions.

The general requirements for motions in contested cases are stated at § 41.121(c).

(a) In an interference, substantive motions must:

(1) Raise a threshold issue,

(2) Seek to change the scope of the definition of the interfering subject matter or the correspondence of claims to the count,

(3) Seek to change the benefit accorded for the count, or

(4) Seek judgment on derivation or on priority.

(b) To be sufficient, a motion must provide a showing, supported with appropriate evidence, such that, if unrebutted, it would justify the relief sought. The burden of proof is on the movant.

(c) *Showing patentability.* (1) A party moving to add or amend a claim must show the claim is patentable.

(2) A party moving to add or amend a count must show the count is patentable over prior art.

[Added, 69 FR 49959, Aug. 12, 2004, effective Sept. 13, 2004]

SUBCHAPTER B – ADMINISTRATION

PART 102 — DISCLOSURE OF GOVERNMENT INFORMATION

Subpart A - Freedom of Information Act

Sec.
102.1 General.
102.2 Public reference facilities.
102.3 Records under FOIA.
102.4 Requirements for making requests.
102.5 Responsibility for responding to requests.
102.6 Time limits and expedited processing.
102.7 Responses to requests.
102.9 Business Information.
102.10 Appeals from initial determinations or untimely delays.
102.11 Fees.

Subpart B - Privacy Act

102.21 Purpose and scope.
102.22 Definitions.
102.23 Procedures for making inquiries.
102.24 Procedures for making requests for records.
102.25 Disclosure of requested records to individuals.
102.26 Special procedures: Medical records.
102.27 Procedures for making requests for correction or amendment.
102.28 Review of requests for correction or amendment.
102.29 Appeal of initial adverse determination on correction or amendment.
102.30 Disclosure of record to person other than the individual to whom it pertains.
102.31 Fees.
102.32 Penalties.
102.33 General exemptions.
102.34 Specific exemptions.

Appendix to Part 102— Systems of Records Noticed by Other Federal Agencies and Applicable to USPTO Records, and Applicability of this Part Thereto

Subpart A — Freedom of Information Act

§ 102.1 General.

(a)   The information in this part is furnished for the guidance of the public and in compliance with the requirements of the Freedom of Information Act (FOIA), as amended (5 U.S.C. 552). This part sets forth the procedures the United States Patent and Trademark Office (USPTO) follows to make publicly available the materials and indices specified in 5 U.S.C. 552(a)(2) and records requested under 5 U.S.C. 552(a)(3). Information routinely provided to the public as part of a regular USPTO activity (for example, press releases issued by the Office of Public Affairs) may be provided to the public without following this part. USPTO's policy is to make discretionary disclosures of records or information exempt from disclosure under FOIA whenever disclosure would not foreseeably harm an interest protected by a FOIA exemption, but this policy does not create any right enforceable in court.

(b)   As used in this subpart, *FOIA Officer* means the USPTO employee designated to administer FOIA for USPTO. To ensure prompt processing of a request, correspondence should be addressed to the FOIA Officer, United States Patent and Trademark Office, P.O. Box 1450, Alexandria, Virginia 22313-1450, or delivered by hand to 10B20, Madison Building East, 600 Dulany Street, Alexandria, Virginia.

[Added, 65 FR 52916, Aug. 31, 2000, effective Oct. 2, 2000; para. (b) revised, 68 FR 14332, Mar. 25, 2003, effective May 1, 2003; para. (b) revised, 70 FR 10488, Mar. 4, 2005, effective Mar. 4, 2005]

§ 102.2 Public reference facilities.

(a)   USPTO maintains a public reference facility that contains the records FOIA requires to be made regularly available for public inspection and copying; furnishes information and otherwise assists the public concerning USPTO operations under FOIA; and receives and processes requests for records under FOIA. The FOIA Officer is responsible for determining which of USPTO's records are required to be made available for public inspection and copying, and for making those records available in USPTO's reference and records inspection facility. The FOIA Officer shall maintain and make available for public inspection and copying a current subject-matter index of USPTO's public inspection facility records. Each index shall be updated regularly, at least quarterly, with respect to newly included records. In accordance with 5 U.S.C. 552(a)(2), USPTO has determined that it is unnecessary and impracticable to publish quarterly, or more frequently, and distribute copies of the index and supplements thereto. The public reference facility is located in the Public Search Room, Madison Building East, First Floor, 600 Dulany Street, Alexandria, Virginia.

(b)   The FOIA Officer shall also make public inspection facility records created by USPTO on or after November 1, 1996, available electronically through USPTO's World Wide Web site (http://www.uspto.gov). Information available at the site shall include:

(1)   The FOIA Officer's index of the public inspection facility records, which indicates which records are available electronically; and

(2)   The general index referred to in paragraph (c)(3) of this section.

(c)   USPTO maintains and makes available for public inspection and copying:

(1)   A current index providing identifying information for the public as to any matter that is issued, adopted, or promulgated after July 4, 1967, and that is retained as a record and is required to be made available or published. Copies of the index are available upon request after payment of the direct cost of duplication;

(2)   Copies of records that have been released and that the FOIA Officer determines, because of their subject matter, have become or are likely to become the subject of subsequent requests for substantially the same records;

(3)   A general index of the records described in paragraph (c)(2) of this section;

(4)   Final opinions and orders, including concurring and dissenting opinions made in the adjudication of cases;

(5)   Those statements of policy and interpretations that have been adopted by USPTO and are not published in the *Federal Register*; and

(6)   Administrative staff manuals and instructions to staff that affect a member of the public.

[Added, 65 FR 52916, Aug. 31, 2000, effective Oct. 2, 2000; para. (a) revised, 75 FR 36294, June 25, 2010, effective June 25, 2010]

§ 102.3 Records under FOIA.

(a) Records under FOIA include all Government records, regardless of format, medium or physical characteristics, and include electronic records and information, audiotapes, videotapes, and photographs.

(b) There is no obligation to create, compile, or obtain from outside USPTO a record to satisfy a FOIA request. With regard to electronic data, the issue of whether records are created or merely extracted from an existing database is not always apparent. When responding to FOIA requests for electronic data where creation of a record or programming becomes an issue, USPTO shall undertake reasonable efforts to search for the information in electronic format.

(c) USPTO officials may, upon request, create and provide new information pursuant to user fee statutes, such as the first paragraph of 15 U.S.C. 1525, or in accordance with authority otherwise provided by law. This is outside the scope of FOIA.

(d) The FOIA Officer shall preserve all correspondence pertaining to the requests received under this subpart, as well as copies of all requested records, until disposition or destruction is authorized by Title 44 of the United States Code or a National Archives and Records Administration's General Records Schedule. The FOIA Officer shall not dispose of records while they are the subject of a pending request, appeal, or lawsuit under FOIA.

[Added, 65 FR 52916, Aug. 31, 2000, effective Oct. 2, 2000]

§ 102.4 Requirements for making requests.

(a) A request for USPTO records that are not customarily made available to the public as part of USPTO's regular informational services must be in writing, and shall be processed under FOIA, regardless of whether FOIA is mentioned in the request. Requests should be sent to the USPTO FOIA Officer, United States Patent and Trademark Office, P.O. Box 1450, Alexandria, Virginia 22313-1450 (records FOIA requires to be made regularly available for public inspection and copying are addressed in § 102.2(c)). For the quickest handling, the request letter and envelope should be marked "Freedom of Information Act Request." For requests for records about oneself, § 102.24 contains additional requirements. For requests for records about another individual, either a written authorization signed by that individual permitting disclosure of those records to the requester or proof that individual is deceased (for example, a copy of a death certificate or an obituary) facilitates processing the request.

(b) The records requested must be described in enough detail to enable USPTO personnel to locate them with a reasonable amount of effort. Whenever possible, a request should include specific information about each record sought, such as the date, title or name, author, recipient, and subject matter of the record, and the name and location of the office where the record is located. Also, if records about a court case are sought, the title of the case, the court in which the case was filed, and the nature of the case should be included. If known, any file designations or descriptions for the requested records should be included. In general, the more specifically the request describes the records sought, the greater the likelihood that USPTO will locate those records. If the FOIA Officer determines that a request does not reasonably describe records, the FOIA Officer will inform the requester what additional information is needed or why the request is otherwise insufficient. The FOIA Officer also may give the requester an opportunity to discuss the request so that it may be modified to meet the requirements of this section.

[Added, 65 FR 52916, Aug. 31, 2000, effective Oct. 2, 2000; para. (a) revised, 68 FR 14332, Mar. 25, 2003, effective May 1, 2003]

§ 102.5 Responsibility for responding to requests.

(a) *In general*. Except as stated in paragraph (b) of this section, the USPTO will process FOIA requests directed to USPTO. In determining records responsive to a request, the FOIA Officer shall include only those records within USPTO's possession and control as of the date the FOIA Officer receives the request.

(b) *Consultations and referrals*. If the FOIA Officer receives a request for a record in USPTO's possession in which another Federal agency subject to FOIA has the primary interest, the FOIA Officer shall refer the record to that agency for direct response to the requester. The FOIA Officer shall consult with another Federal agency before responding to a requester if the FOIA Officer receives a request for a record in which another Federal agency subject to

FOIA has a significant interest, but not the primary interest; or another Federal agency not subject to FOIA has the primary interest or a significant interest. Ordinarily, the agency that originated a record will be presumed to have the primary interest in it.

(c) *Notice of referral.* Whenever a FOIA Officer refers a document to another Federal agency for direct response to the requester, the FOIA Officer will ordinarily notify the requester in writing of the referral and inform the requester of the name of the agency to which the document was referred.

(d) *Timing of responses to consultations and referrals.* All consultations and referrals shall be handled according to the date the FOIA request was received by the first Federal agency.

(e) *Agreements regarding consultations and referrals.* The FOIA Officer may make agreements with other Federal agencies to eliminate the need for consultations or referrals for particular types of records.

[Added, 65 FR 52916, Aug. 31, 2000, effective Oct. 2, 2000]

§ 102.6 Time limits and expedited processing.

(a) *In general.* The FOIA Officer ordinarily shall respond to requests according to their order of receipt.

(b) *Initial response and appeal.* Subject to paragraph (c)(1) of this section, an initial response shall be made within 20 working days (*i.e.,* excluding Saturdays, Sundays, and legal public holidays) of the receipt of a request for a record under this part by the proper FOIA Officer identified in accordance with § 102.5(a), and an appeal shall be decided within 20 working days of its receipt by the Office of the General Counsel.

(c) *Unusual circumstances.*

(1) In unusual circumstances as specified in paragraph (c)(2) of this section, the FOIA Officer may extend the time limits in paragraph (b) of this section by notifying the requester in writing as soon as practicable of the unusual circumstances and of the date by which processing of the request is expected to be completed. Extensions of time for the initial determination and extensions on appeal may not exceed a total of ten working days, unless the requester agrees to a longer extension, or the FOIA Officer provides the requester with an opportunity either to limit the scope of the request so that it may be processed within the applicable time limit, or to arrange an alternative time frame for processing the request or a modified request.

(2) As used in this section, *unusual circumstances*, means, but only to the extent reasonably necessary to properly process the particular request:

(i) The need to search for and collect the requested records from field facilities or other establishments separate from the office processing the request;

(ii) The need to search for, collect, and appropriately examine a voluminous amount of separate and distinct records that are the subject of a single request; or

(iii) The need for consultation, which shall be conducted with all practicable speed, with another Federal agency having a substantial interest in the determination of the request.

(3) Unusual circumstances do not include a delay that results from a predictable workload of requests, unless USPTO demonstrates reasonable progress in reducing its backlog of pending requests. Refusal to reasonably modify the scope of a request or arrange an alternate time frame may affect a requester's ability to obtain judicial review.

(4) If the FOIA Officer reasonably believes that multiple requests submitted by a requester, or by a group of requesters acting in concert, constitute a single request that would otherwise involve unusual circumstances, and the requests involve clearly related matters, the FOIA Officer may aggregate them. Multiple requests involving unrelated matters will not be aggregated.

(d) *Multitrack processing.*

(1) The FOIA Officer may use two or more processing tracks by distinguishing between simple and more complex requests based on the number of pages involved, or some other measure of the amount of work and/or time needed to process the request, and whether the request qualifies for expedited processing as described in paragraph (e) of this section.

(2) The FOIA Officer may provide requesters in a slower track with an opportunity to limit the scope of their requests in order to qualify for faster processing. The FOIA Officer may contact the requester by telephone or by letter, whichever is most efficient in each case.

(e)   *Expedited processing.*

(1)   Requests and appeals shall be taken out of order and given expedited treatment whenever it is determined they involve:

(i)   Circumstances in which the lack of expedited treatment could reasonably be expected to pose an imminent threat to the life or physical safety of an individual;

(ii)   The loss of substantial due process rights;

(iii)   A matter of widespread and exceptional media interest in which there exist questions about the Government's integrity that affect public confidence; or

(iv)   An urgency to inform the public about an actual or alleged Federal Government activity, if made by a person primarily engaged in disseminating information.

(2)   A request for expedited processing may be made at the time of the initial request for records or at any later time. For a prompt determination, a request for expedited processing should be sent to the FOIA Officer.

(3)   A requester who seeks expedited processing must submit a statement, certified to be true and correct to the best of that person's knowledge and belief, explaining in detail the basis for requesting expedited processing. For example, a requester within the category described in paragraph (e)(1)(iv) of this section, if not a full-time member of the news media, must establish that he or she is a person whose main professional activity or occupation is information dissemination, though it need not be his or her sole occupation. A requester within the category described in paragraph (e)(1)(iv) of this section must also establish a particular urgency to inform the public about the Government activity involved in the request, beyond the public's right to know about Government activity generally. The formality of certification may be waived as a matter of administrative discretion.

(4)   Within ten calendar days of receipt of a request for expedited processing, the FOIA Officer will decide whether to grant it and shall notify the requester of the decision. If a request for expedited treatment is granted, the request shall be given priority and processed as soon as practicable. If a request for expedited processing is denied, any appeal of that decision shall be acted on expeditiously.

[Added, 65 FR 52916, Aug. 31, 2000, effective Oct. 2, 2000]

§ 102.7   Responses to requests.

(a)   *Grants of requests.* If the FOIA Officer makes a determination to grant a request in whole or in part, the FOIA Officer will notify the requester in writing. The FOIA Officer will inform the requester in the notice of any fee charged under § 102.11 and disclose records to the requester promptly upon payment of any applicable fee. Records disclosed in part shall be marked or annotated to show each applicable FOIA exemption and the amount of information deleted, unless doing so would harm an interest protected by an applicable exemption. The location of the information deleted shall also be indicated on the record, if feasible.

(b)   *Adverse determinations of requests.* If the FOIA Officer makes an adverse determination regarding a request, the FOIA Officer will notify the requester of that determination in writing. An adverse determination is a denial of a request in any respect, namely: A determination to withhold any requested record in whole or in part; a determination that a requested record does not exist or cannot be located; a determination that a record is not readily reproducible in the form or format sought by the requester; a determination that what has been requested is not a record subject to FOIA (except that a determination under § 102.11(j) that records are to be made available under a fee statute other than FOIA is not an adverse determination); a determination against the requester on any disputed fee matter, including a denial of a request for a fee waiver; or a denial of a request for expedited treatment. Each denial letter shall be signed by the FOIA Officer and shall include:

(1)   The name and title or position of the denying official;

(2)   A brief statement of the reason(s) for the denial, including applicable FOIA exemption(s);

(3)   An estimate of the volume of records or information withheld, in number of pages or some other reasonable form of estimation. This estimate need not be provided if the volume is otherwise indicated through deletions on records disclosed in part, or if providing an estimate would harm an interest protected by an applicable FOIA exemption; and

(4) A statement that the denial may be appealed, and a list of the requirements for filing an appeal under § 102.10(b).

[Added, 65 FR 52916, Aug. 31, 2000, effective Oct. 2, 2000]

§ 102.9 Business Information.

(a) *In general.* Business information obtained by USPTO from a submitter will be disclosed under FOIA only under this section.

(b) *Definitions.* For the purposes of this section:

(1) *Business information* means commercial or financial information, obtained by USPTO from a submitter, which may be protected from disclosure under FOIA exemption 4 (5 U.S.C. 552(b)(4)).

(2) *Submitter* means any person or entity outside the Federal Government from whom USPTO obtains business information, directly or indirectly. The term includes corporations; state, local and tribal governments; and foreign governments.

(c) *Designation of business information.* A submitter of business information should designate by appropriate markings, either at the time of submission or at a reasonable time thereafter, any portions of its submission that it considers to be protected from disclosure under FOIA exemption 4. These designations will expire ten years after the date of the submission unless the submitter requests, and provides justification for, a longer designation period.

(d) *Notice to submitters.* The FOIA Officer shall provide a submitter with prompt written notice of a FOIA request or administrative appeal that seeks its business information whenever required under paragraph (e) of this section, except as provided in paragraph (h) of this section, in order to give the submitter an opportunity under paragraph (f) of this section to object to disclosure of any specified portion of that information. Such written notice shall be sent via certified mail, return receipt requested, or similar means. The notice shall either describe the business information requested or include copies of the requested records containing the information. When notification of a large number of submitters is required, notification may be made by posting or publishing the notice in a place reasonably likely to accomplish notification.

(e) *When notice is required.* Notice shall be given to the submitter whenever:

(1) The information has been designated in good faith by the submitter as protected from disclosure under FOIA exemption 4; or

(2) The FOIA Officer has reason to believe that the information may be protected from disclosure under FOIA exemption 4.

(f) *Opportunity to object to disclosure.* The FOIA Officer shall allow a submitter seven working days (*i.e.,* excluding Saturdays, Sundays, and legal public holidays) from the date of receipt of the written notice described in paragraph (d) of this section to provide the FOIA Officer with a detailed statement of any objection to disclosure. The statement must specify all grounds for withholding any portion of the information under any exemption of FOIA and, in the case of exemption 4, it must show why the information is a trade secret or commercial or financial information that is privileged or confidential. If a submitter fails to respond to the notice within the time specified, the submitter will be considered to have no objection to disclosure of the information. Information a submitter provides under this paragraph may itself be subject to disclosure under FOIA.

(g) *Notice of intent to disclose.* The FOIA Officer shall consider a submitter's objections and specific grounds under FOIA for nondisclosure in deciding whether to disclose business information. If the FOIA Officer decides to disclose business information over the objection of a submitter, the FOIA Officer shall give the submitter written notice via certified mail, return receipt requested, or similar means, which shall include:

(1) A statement of reason(s) why the submitter's objections to disclosure were not sustained;

(2) A description of the business information to be disclosed; and

(3) A statement that the FOIA Officer intends to disclose the information seven working days from the date the submitter receives the notice.

(h) *Exceptions to notice requirements.* The notice requirements of paragraphs (d) and (g) of this section shall not apply if:

(1) The FOIA Officer determines that the information should not be disclosed;

(2) The information has been lawfully published or has been officially made available to the public;

(3) Disclosure of the information is required by statute (other than FOIA) or by a regulation issued in accordance with Executive Order 12600; or

(4) The designation made by the submitter under paragraph (c) of this section appears obviously frivolous, in which case the FOIA Officer shall provide the submitter written notice of any final decision to disclose the information seven working days from the date the submitter receives the notice.

(i) *Notice of FOIA lawsuit.* Whenever a requester files a lawsuit seeking to compel the disclosure of business information, the FOIA Officer shall promptly notify the submitter.

(j) *Corresponding notice to requesters.* Whenever a FOIA Officer provides a submitter with notice and an opportunity to object to disclosure under paragraph (d) of this section, the FOIA Officer shall also notify the requester(s). Whenever a submitter files a lawsuit seeking to prevent the disclosure of business information, the FOIA Officer shall notify the requester(s).

[Added, 65 FR 52916, Aug. 31, 2000, effective Oct. 2, 2000]

§ 102.10 Appeals from initial determinations or untimely delays.

(a) If a request for records is initially denied in whole or in part, or has not been timely determined, or if a requester receives an adverse initial determination regarding any other matter under this subpart (as described in § 102.7(b)), the requester may file a written appeal, which must be received by the Office of General Counsel within thirty calendar days of the date of the written denial or, if there has been no determination, may be submitted anytime after the due date, including the last extension under § 102.6(c), of the determination.

(b) Appeals shall be decided by a Deputy General Counsel. Appeals should be addressed to the General Counsel, United States Patent and Trademark Office, PO Box 1450, Alexandria, Virginia 22313-1450. Both the letter and the appeal envelope should be clearly marked "Freedom of Information Appeal". The appeal must include a copy of the original request and the initial denial, if any, and may include a statement of the reasons why the records requested should be made available and why the initial denial, if any,

was in error. No opportunity for personal appearance, oral argument or hearing on appeal is provided.

(c) If an appeal is granted, the person making the appeal shall be immediately notified and copies of the releasable documents shall be made available promptly thereafter upon receipt of appropriate fees determined in accordance with § 102.11.

(d) If no determination of an appeal has been sent to the requester within the twenty-working-day period specified in § 102.6(b) or the last extension thereof, the requester is deemed to have exhausted his administrative remedies with respect to the request, giving rise to a right of judicial review under 5 U.S.C. 552(a)(6)(C). If the person making a request initiates a civil action against USPTO based on the provision in this paragraph, the administrative appeal process may continue.

(e) A determination on appeal shall be in writing and, when it denies records in whole or in part, the letter to the requester shall include:

(1) A brief explanation of the basis for the denial, including a list of applicable FOIA exemptions and a description of how the exemptions apply;

(2) A statement that the decision is final;

(3) Notification that judicial review of the denial is available in the United States district court for the district in which the requester resides or has its principal place of business, the United States District Court for the Eastern District of Virginia, or the District of Columbia; and

(4) The name and title or position of the official responsible for denying the appeal.

[Added, 65 FR 52916, Aug. 31, 2000, effective Oct. 2, 2000; para. (b) revised, 68 FR 14332, Mar. 25, 2003, effective May 1, 2003]

§ 102.11 Fees.

(a) *In general.* USPTO shall charge for processing requests under FOIA in accordance with paragraph (c) of this section, except when fees are limited under paragraph (d) of this section or when a waiver or reduction of fees is granted under paragraph (k) of this section. USPTO shall collect all applicable fees before sending copies of requested records to a requester. Requesters must pay fees by check or money order made payable to the Treasury of the United States.

(b) *Definitions*. For purposes of this section:

(1) *Commercial use request* means a request from or on behalf of a person who seeks information for a use or purpose that furthers his or her commercial, trade, or profit interests, which can include furthering those interests through litigation. The FOIA Officer shall determine, whenever reasonably possible, the use to which a requester will put the requested records. When it appears that the requester will put the records to a commercial use, either because of the nature of the request itself or because the FOIA Officer has reasonable cause to doubt a requester's stated use, the FOIA Officer shall provide the requester a reasonable opportunity to submit further clarification.

(2) *Direct costs* means those expenses USPTO incurs in searching for and duplicating (and, in the case of commercial use requests, reviewing) records to respond to a FOIA request. Direct costs include, for example, the labor costs of the employee performing the work (the basic rate of pay for the employee, plus 16 percent of that rate to cover benefits). Not included in direct costs are overhead expenses such as the costs of space and heating or lighting of the facility in which the records are kept.

(3) *Duplication* means the making of a copy of a record, or of the information contained in it, necessary to respond to a FOIA request. Copies may take the form of paper, microform, audiovisual materials, or electronic records (for example, magnetic tape or disk), among others. The FOIA Officer shall honor a requester's specified preference of form or format of disclosure if the record is readily reproducible with reasonable efforts in the requested form or format.

(4) *Educational institution* means a preschool, a public or private elementary or secondary school, an institution of undergraduate higher education, an institution of graduate higher education, an institution of professional education, or an institution of vocational education, that operates a program of scholarly research. To be in this category, a requester must show that the request is authorized by and is made under the auspices of a qualifying institution, and that the records are sought to further scholarly research rather than for a commercial use.

(5) *Noncommercial scientific institution* means an institution that is not operated on a "commercial" basis, as that term is defined in paragraph (b)(1) of this section, and that is operated solely for the purpose of conducting scientific research, the results of which are not intended to promote any particular product or industry. To be in this category, a requester must show that the request is authorized by and is made under the auspices of a qualifying institution and that the records are sought to further scientific research rather than for a commercial use.

(6) *Representative of the news media, or news media requester* means any person actively gathering news for an entity that is organized and operated to publish or broadcast news to the public. The term "news" means information that is about current events or that would be of current interest to the public. Examples of news media entities include television or radio stations broadcasting to the public at large and publishers of periodicals (but only if they can qualify as disseminators of "news") that make their products available for purchase or subscription by the general public. For "freelance" journalists to be regarded as working for a news organization, they must demonstrate a solid basis for expecting publication through that organization. A publication contract would be the clearest proof, but the FOIA Officer shall also look to the past publication record of a requester in making this determination. To be in this category, a requester must not be seeking the requested records for a commercial use. However, a request for records supporting the news-dissemination function of the requester shall not be considered to be for a commercial use.

(7) *Review* means the examination of a record located in response to a request in order to determine whether any portion of it is exempt from disclosure. It also includes processing any record for disclosure—for example, doing all that is necessary to redact it and prepare it for disclosure. Review costs are recoverable even if a record ultimately is not disclosed. Review time does not include time spent resolving general legal or policy issues regarding the application of exemptions.

(8) *Search* means the process of looking for and retrieving records or information responsive to a request. It includes page-by-page or line-by-line identification of information within records and also includes reasonable efforts to locate and retrieve information from records maintained in electronic form or format. The FOIA Officer shall ensure that

searches are done in the most efficient and least expensive manner reasonably possible.

(c)   *Fees.* In responding to FOIA requests, the FOIA Officer shall charge the fees summarized in chart form in paragraphs (c)(1) and (c)(2) of this section and explained in paragraphs (c)(3) through (c)(5) of this section, unless a waiver or reduction of fees has been granted under paragraph (k) of this section.

(1)   The four categories and chargeable fees are:

Category	Chargeable fees
(i) Commercial Use Requesters	Search, Review, and Duplication.
(ii) Educational and Non-commercial Scientific Institution Requesters	Duplication (excluding the cost of the first 100 pages).
(iii) Representatives of the News Media	Duplication (excluding the cost of the first 100 pages).
(iv) All Other Requesters	Search and Duplication (excluding the cost of the first 2 hours of search and 100 pages).

(2)   *Uniform fee schedule.*

Service	Rate
(i) Manual search	Actual salary rate of employee involved, plus 16 percent of salary rate.
(ii) Computerized search	Actual direct cost, including operator time.
(iii) Duplication of records: (A) Paper copy reproduction (B) Other reproduction (*e.g.*, computer disk or print-out, microfilm, micro-fiche, or microform)	$.15 per page Actual direct cost, including operator time

Service	Rate
(iv) Review of records (includes preparation for release, *i.e.* excising)	Actual salary rate of employee conducting review, plus 16 percent of salary rate.

(3)   *Search.*

(i)   Search fees shall be charged for all requests—other than requests made by educational institutions, noncommercial scientific institutions, or representatives of the news media—subject to the limitations of paragraph (d) of this section. The FOIA Officer will charge for time spent searching even if no responsive records are located or if located records are entirely exempt from disclosure. Search fees shall be the direct costs of conducting the search by the involved employees

(ii)   For computer searches of records, requesters will be charged the direct costs of conducting the search, although certain requesters (as provided in paragraph (d)(1) of this section) will be charged no search fee and certain other requesters (as provided in paragraph (d)(3) of this section) are entitled to the cost equivalent of two hours of manual search time without charge. These direct costs include the costs, attributable to the search, of operating a central processing unit and operator/programmer salary.

(4)   *Duplication.* Duplication fees will be charged to all requesters, subject to the limitations of paragraph (d) of this section. For a paper photocopy of a record (no more than one copy of which need be supplied), the fee shall be $.15 cents per page. For copies produced by computer, such as tapes or print-outs, the FOIA Officer shall charge the direct costs, including operator time, of producing the copy. For other forms of duplication, the FOIA Officer will charge the direct costs of that duplication.

(5)   *Review.* Review fees shall be charged to requesters who make a commercial use request. Review fees shall be charged only for the initial record review—the review done when the FOIA Officer determines whether an exemption applies to a particular record at the initial request level. No charge will be made for review at the administrative appeal level for an exemption already applied. However, records withheld under an exemption that is subse-

quently determined not to apply may be reviewed again to determine whether any other exemption not previously considered applies, and the costs of that review are chargeable. Review fees shall be the direct costs of conducting the review by the involved employees.

(d) *Limitations on charging fees.*

(1) No search fee will be charged for requests by educational institutions, noncommercial scientific institutions, or representatives of the news media.

(2) No search fee or review fee will be charged for a quarter-hour period unless more than half of that period is required for search or review.

(3) Except for requesters seeking records for a commercial use, the FOIA Officer will provide without charge:

(i) The first 100 pages of duplication (or the cost equivalent); and

(ii) The first two hours of search (or the cost equivalent).

(4) Whenever a total fee calculated under paragraph (c) of this section is $20.00 or less for any request, no fee will be charged.

(5) The provisions of paragraphs (d) (3) and (4) of this section work together. This means that for requesters other than those seeking records for a commercial use, no fee will be charged unless the cost of the search in excess of two hours plus the cost of duplication in excess of 100 pages totals more than $20.00.

(e) *Notice of anticipated fees over $20.00.* When the FOIA Officer determines or estimates that the fees to be charged under this section will be more than $20.00, the FOIA Officer shall notify the requester of the actual or estimated fees, unless the requester has indicated a willingness to pay fees as high as those anticipated. If only a portion of the fee can be estimated readily, the FOIA Officer shall advise the requester that the estimated fee may be only a portion of the total fee. If the FOIA Officer has notified a requester that actual or estimated fees are more than $20.00, the FOIA Officer shall not consider the request received or process it further until the requester agrees to pay the anticipated total fee. Any such agreement should be in writing. A notice under this paragraph shall offer the requester an opportunity to discuss the matter with USPTO personnel in order to reformulate the request to meet the requester's needs at a lower cost.

(f) *Charges for other services.* Apart from the other provisions of this section, the FOIA Officer shall ordinarily charge the direct cost of special services. Such special services could include certifying that records are true copies or sending records by other than ordinary mail.

(g) *Charging interest.* The FOIA Officer shall charge interest on any unpaid bill starting on the 31st calendar day following the date of billing the requester. Interest charges shall be assessed at the rate provided in 31 U.S.C. 3717 and accrue from the date of the billing until payment is received by the FOIA Officer. The FOIA Officer shall follow the provisions of the Debt Collection Improvement Act of 1996 (Pub. L. 104-134), as amended, and its administrative procedures, including the use of consumer reporting agencies, collection agencies, and offset.

(h) *Aggregating requests.* If a FOIA Officer reasonably believes that a requester or a group of requesters acting together is attempting to divide a request into a series of requests for the purpose of avoiding fees, the FOIA Officer may aggregate those requests and charge accordingly. The FOIA Officer may presume that multiple requests of this type made within a 30-calendar-day period have been made in order to avoid fees. If requests are separated by a longer period, the FOIA Officer shall aggregate them only if a solid basis exists for determining that aggregation is warranted under all the circumstances involved. Multiple requests involving unrelated matters shall not be aggregated.

(i) *Advance payments.*

(1) For requests other than those described in paragraphs (i)(2) and (3) of this section, the FOIA Officer shall not require the requester to make an advance payment: a payment made before work is begun or continued on a request. Payment owed for work already completed (*i.e.,* a payment before copies are sent to a requester) is not an advance payment.

(2) If the FOIA Officer determines or estimates that a total fee to be charged under this section will be more than $250.00, the requester must pay the entire anticipated fee before beginning to process the request, unless the FOIA Officer receives a satisfactory assurance of full payment from a requester who has a history of prompt payment.

(3) If a requester has previously failed to pay a properly charged FOIA fee to USPTO or another responsible Federal agency within 30 calendar days of the date of billing, the FOIA Officer shall require the requester to pay the full amount due, plus any applicable interest, and to make an advance payment of the full amount of any anticipated fee, before the FOIA Officer begins to process a new request or continues to process a pending request from that requester.

(4) In cases in which the FOIA Officer requires payment under paragraphs (i)(2) or (3) of this section, the request shall not be considered received and further work will not be done on it until the required payment is received.

(5) Upon the completion of processing of a request, when a specific fee is determined to be payable and appropriate notice has been given to the requester, the FOIA Officer shall make records available to the requester only upon receipt of full payment of the fee.

(j) *Other statutes specifically providing for fees.* The fee schedule of this section does not apply to fees charged under any statute (except for FOIA) that specifically requires USPTO or another responsible Federal agency to set and collect fees for particular types of records. If records responsive to requests are maintained for distribution by agencies operating such statutorily based fee schedule programs, the FOIA Officer shall inform requesters of how to obtain records from those sources.

(k) *Requirements for waiver or reduction of fees.*

(1) Records responsive to a request will be furnished without charge or at a charge reduced below that established under paragraph (c) of this section if the FOIA Officer determines, based on all available information, that the requester has demonstrated that:

(i) Disclosure of the requested information is in the public interest because it is likely to contribute significantly to public understanding of the operations or activities of the Government; and

(ii) Disclosure of the information is not primarily in the commercial interest of the requester.

(2) To determine whether the first fee waiver requirement is met, the FOIA Officer shall consider the following factors:

(i) *The subject of the request*: whether the subject of the requested records concerns the operations or activities of the Government. The subject of the requested records must concern identifiable operations or activities of the Federal Government, with a connection that is direct and clear, not remote or attenuated.

(ii) *The informative value of the information to be disclosed:* whether the disclosure is "likely to contribute" to an understanding of Government operations or activities. The disclosable portions of the requested records must be meaningfully informative about Government operations or activities in order to be "likely to contribute" to an increased public understanding of those operations or activities. The disclosure of information that already is in the public domain, in either a duplicative or a substantially identical form, would not be likely to contribute to such understanding.

(iii) *The contribution to an understanding of the subject by the public likely to result from disclosure:* whether disclosure of the requested information will contribute to the understanding of a reasonably broad audience of persons interested in the subject, as opposed to the individual understanding of the requester. A requester's expertise in the subject area and ability and intention to effectively convey information to the public shall be considered. It shall be presumed that a representative of the news media satisfies this consideration. It shall be presumed that a requester who merely provides information to media sources does not satisfy this consideration.

(iv) *The significance of the contribution to public understanding:* whether the disclosure is likely to contribute "significantly" to public understanding of Government operations or activities. The public's understanding of the subject in question prior to the disclosure must be significantly enhanced by the disclosure.

(3) To determine whether the second fee waiver requirement is met, the FOIA Officer shall consider the following factors:

(i) *The existence and magnitude of a commercial interest*: whether the requester has a commercial interest that would be furthered by the requested disclosure. The FOIA Officer shall consider any commercial interest of the requester (with reference to the definition of "commercial use request" in paragraph (b)(1) of this section), or of any person on whose behalf the requester may be acting, that would be furthered by the requested disclosure. Requesters shall be given an opportunity to provide explanatory information regarding this consideration.

(ii) *The primary interest in disclosure:* whether any identified commercial interest of the requester is sufficiently large, in comparison with the public interest in disclosure, that disclosure is "primarily in the commercial interest of the requester." A fee waiver or reduction is justified if the public interest standard (paragraph (k)(1)(i) of this section) is satisfied and the public interest is greater than any identified commercial interest in disclosure. The FOIA Officer ordinarily shall presume that if a news media requester has satisfied the public interest standard, the public interest is the primary interest served by disclosure to that requester. Disclosure to data brokers or others who merely compile and market Government information for direct economic return shall not be presumed to primarily serve the public interest.

(4) If only some of the records to be released satisfy the requirements for a fee waiver, a waiver shall be granted for those records.

(5) Requests for the waiver or reduction of fees should address the factors listed in paragraphs (k)(2) and (3) of this section, insofar as they apply to each request.

[Added, 65 FR 52916, Aug. 31, 2000, effective Oct. 2, 2000]

Subpart B — Privacy Act

§ 102.21 Purpose and scope.

(a) The purpose of this subpart is to establish policies and procedures for implementing the Privacy Act of 1974, as amended (5 U.S.C. 552a) (the Act). The main objectives are to facilitate full exercise of rights conferred on individuals under the Act and to ensure the protection of privacy as to individuals on whom USPTO maintains records in systems of records under the Act. USPTO accepts the responsibility to act promptly and in accordance with the Act upon receipt of any inquiry, request or appeal from a citizen of the United States or an alien lawfully admitted for permanent residence into the United States, regardless of the age of the individual. Further, USPTO accepts the obligations to maintain only such information on individuals as is relevant and neces-

sary to the performance of its lawful functions, to maintain that information with such accuracy, relevancy, timeliness, and completeness as is reasonably necessary to assure fairness in determinations made by USPTO about the individual, to obtain information from the individual to the extent practicable, and to take every reasonable step to protect that information from unwarranted disclosure. USPTO will maintain no record describing how an individual exercises rights guaranteed by the First Amendment unless expressly authorized by statute or by the individual about whom the record is maintained or unless pertinent to and within the scope of an authorized law enforcement activity. An individual's name and address will not be sold or rented by USPTO unless such action is specifically authorized by law; however, this provision shall not be construed to require the withholding of names and addresses otherwise permitted to be made public.

(b) This subpart is administered by the Privacy Officer of USPTO.

(c) Matters outside the scope of this subpart include the following:

(1) Requests for records which do not pertain to the individual making the request, or to the individual about whom the request is made if the requester is the parent or guardian of the individual;

(2) Requests involving information pertaining to an individual which is in a record or file but not within the scope of a system of records notice published in the *Federal Register*;

(3) Requests to correct a record where a grievance procedure is available to the individual either by regulation or by provision in a collective bargaining agreement with USPTO, and the individual has initiated, or has expressed in writing the intention of initiating, such grievance procedure. An individual selecting the grievance procedure waives the use of the procedures in this subpart to correct or amend a record; and,

(4) Requests for employee-employer services and counseling which were routinely granted prior to enactment of the Act, including, but not limited to, test calculations of retirement benefits, explanations of health and life insurance programs, and explanations of tax withholding options.

(d) Any request for records which pertains to the individual making the request, or to the individual about whom the request is made if the requester is the parent or guardian of the individual, shall be processed under the Act and this subpart and under the Freedom of Information Act and USPTO's implementing regulations at Subpart A of this part, regardless whether the Act or the Freedom of Information Act is mentioned in the request.

[Added, 65 FR 52916, Aug. 31, 2000, effective Oct. 2, 2000]

§ 102.22 Definitions.

(a)　All terms used in this subpart which are defined in 5 U.S.C. 552a shall have the same meaning herein.

(b)　As used in this subpart:

(1)　*Act* means the "Privacy Act of 1974, as amended (5 U.S.C. 552a)".

(2)　*Appeal* means a request by an individual to review and reverse an initial denial of a request by that individual for correction or amendment.

(3)　*USPTO* means the United States Patent and Trademark Office.

(4)　*Inquiry* means either a request for general information regarding the Act and this subpart or a request by an individual (or that individual's parent or guardian) that USPTO determine whether it has any record in a system of records which pertains to that individual.

(5)　*Person* means any human being and also shall include but not be limited to, corporations, associations, partnerships, trustees, receivers, personal representatives, and public or private organizations.

(6)　*Privacy Officer* means a USPTO employee designated to administer this subpart.

(7)　*Request for access* means a request by an individual or an individual's parent or guardian to see a record which is in a particular system of records and which pertains to that individual.

(8)　*Request for correction or amendment* means the request by an individual or an individual's parent or guardian that USPTO change (either by correction, amendment, addition or deletion) a particular record in a system of records which pertains to that individual.

[Added, 65 FR 52916, Aug. 31, 2000, effective Oct. 2, 2000]

§ 102.23 Procedures for making inquiries.

(a)　Any individual, regardless of age, who is a citizen of the United States or an alien lawfully admitted for permanent residence into the United States may submit an inquiry to USPTO. The inquiry should be made either in person at 10B20, Madison Building East, 600 Dulany Street, Alexandria, Virginia, or by mail addressed to the Privacy Officer, United States Patent and Trademark Office, P.O. Box 1450, Alexandria, Virginia 22313-1450, or to the official identified in the notification procedures paragraph of the systems of records notice published in the *Federal Register*. If an individual believes USPTO maintains a record pertaining to that individual but does not know which system of records might contain such a record, the USPTO Privacy Officer will provide assistance in person or by mail.

(b)　Inquiries submitted by mail should include the words "PRIVACY ACT INQUIRY" in capital letters at the top of the letter and on the face of the envelope. If the inquiry is for general information regarding the Act and this subpart, no particular information is required. USPTO reserves the right to require compliance with the identification procedures appearing at § 102.24(d) where circumstances warrant. If the inquiry is a request that USPTO determine whether it has, in a given system of records, a record which pertains to the individual, the following information should be submitted:

(1)　Name of individual whose record is sought;

(2)　Individual whose record is sought is either a U.S. citizen or an alien lawfully admitted for permanent residence;

(3)　Identifying data that will help locate the record (for example, maiden name, occupational license number, period or place of employment, etc.);

(4)　Record sought, by description and by record system name, if known;

(5)　Action requested (that is, sending information on how to exercise rights under the Act; determining whether requested record exists; gaining access to requested record; or obtaining copy of requested record);

(6)　Copy of court guardianship order or minor's birth certificate, as provided in § 102.24(f)(3), but only if requester is guardian or parent of individual whose record is sought;

(7) Requester's name (printed), signature, address, and telephone number (optional);

(8) Date; and,

(9) Certification of request by notary or other official, but only if

(i) Request is for notification that requested record exists, for access to requested record or for copy of requested record;

(ii) Record is not available to any person under 5 U.S.C. 552; and

(iii) Requester does not appear before an employee of USPTO for verification of identity.

(c) Any inquiry which is not addressed as specified in paragraph (a) of this section or which is not marked as specified in paragraph (b) of this section will be so addressed and marked by USPTO personnel and forwarded immediately to the Privacy Officer. An inquiry which is not properly addressed by the individual will not be deemed to have been "received" for purposes of measuring the time period for response until actual receipt by the Privacy Officer. In each instance when an inquiry so forwarded is received, the Privacy Officer shall notify the individual that his or her inquiry was improperly addressed and the date the inquiry was received at the proper address.

(d)(1)Each inquiry received shall be acted upon promptly by the Privacy Officer. Every effort will be made to respond within ten working days (*i.e.,* excluding Saturdays, Sundays and legal public holidays) of the date of receipt. If a response cannot be made within ten working days, the Privacy Officer shall send an acknowledgment during that period providing information on the status of the inquiry and asking for such further information as may be necessary to process the inquiry. The first correspondence sent by the Privacy Officer to the requester shall contain USPTO's control number assigned to the request, as well as a note that the requester should use that number in all future contacts in order to facilitate processing. USPTO shall use that control number in all subsequent correspondence.

(2) If the Privacy Officer fails to send an acknowledgment within ten working days, as provided above, the requester may ask the General Counsel to take corrective action. No failure of the Privacy Officer to send an acknowledgment shall confer administrative finality for purposes of judicial review.

(e) An individual shall not be required to state a reason or otherwise justify his or her inquiry.

(f) Special note should be taken of the fact that certain agencies are responsible for publishing notices of systems of records having Government-wide application to other agencies, including USPTO. The agencies known to be publishing these general notices and the types of records covered therein appear in an appendix to this part. The provisions of this section, and particularly paragraph (a) of this section, should be followed in making inquiries with respect to such records. Such records in USPTO are subject to the provisions of this part to the extent indicated in the appendix to this part. The exemptions, if any, determined by an agency publishing a general notice shall be invoked and applied by USPTO after consultation, as necessary, with that other agency.

[Added, 65 FR 52916, Aug. 31, 2000, effective Oct. 2, 2000; para. (a) revised, 68 FR 14332, Mar. 25, 2003, effective May 1, 2003; para. (a) revised, 70 FR 10488, Mar. 4, 2005, effective Mar. 4, 2005]

§ 102.24 Procedures for making requests for records.

(a) Any individual, regardless of age, who is a citizen of the United States or an alien lawfully admitted for permanent residence into the United States may submit a request for access to records to USPTO. The request should be made either in person at 10B20, Madison Building East, 600 Dulany Street, Alexandria, Virginia, or by mail addressed to the Privacy Officer, United States Patent and Trademark Office, P.O. Box 1450, Alexandria, Virginia 22313-1450.

(b) Requests submitted by mail should include the words "PRIVACY ACT REQUEST" in capital letters at the top of the letter and on the face of the envelope. Any request which is not addressed as specified in paragraph (a) of this section or which is not marked as specified in this paragraph will be so addressed and marked by USPTO personnel and forwarded immediately to the Privacy Officer. A request which is not properly addressed by the individual will not be deemed to have been "received" for purposes of measuring time periods for response until actual receipt by the Privacy Officer. In each instance when a request so forwarded is received, the Privacy Officer shall notify the individual that his or her request was improperly addressed and the date when the request was received at the proper address.

(c)   If the request follows an inquiry under § 102.23 in connection with which the individual's identity was established by USPTO, the individual need only indicate the record to which access is sought, provide the USPTO control number assigned to the request, and sign and date the request. If the request is not preceded by an inquiry under § 102.23, the procedures of this section should be followed.

(d)   The requirements for identification of individuals seeking access to records are as follows:

(1)   *In person.* Each individual making a request in person shall be required to present satisfactory proof of identity. The means of proof, in the order of preference and priority, are:

(i)   A document bearing the individual's photograph (for example, driver's license, passport or military or civilian identification card);

(ii)   A document, preferably issued for participation in a federally sponsored program, bearing the individual's signature (for example, unemployment insurance book, employer's identification card, national credit card, and professional, craft or union membership card); and

(iii)   A document bearing neither the photograph nor the signature of the individual, preferably issued for participation in a federally sponsored program (for example, Medicaid card). In the event the individual can provide no suitable documentation of identity, USPTO will require a signed statement asserting the individual's identity and stipulating that the individual understands the penalty provision of 5 U.S.C. 552a(i)(3) recited in § 102.32(a). In order to avoid any unwarranted disclosure of an individual's records, USPTO reserves the right to determine the adequacy of proof of identity offered by any individual, particularly when the request involves a sensitive record.

(2)   *Not in person.* If the individual making a request does not appear in person before the Privacy Officer or other employee authorized to determine identity, a certification of a notary public or equivalent officer empowered to administer oaths must accompany the request under the circumstances prescribed in § 102.23(b)(9). The certification in or attached to the letter must be substantially in accordance with the following text:

City of _____

County of _____ :ss

(Name of individual), who affixed (his) (her) signature below in my presence, came before me, a (title), in and for the aforesaid County and State, this _____ day of _____, 20__, and established (his) (her) identity to my satisfaction.

My commission expires _____.

(Signature)

(3)   *Parents of minors and legal guardians.* An individual acting as the parent of a minor or the legal guardian of the individual to whom a record pertains shall establish his or her personal identity in the same manner prescribed in either paragraph (d)(1) or (d)(2) of this section. In addition, such other individual shall establish his or her identity in the representative capacity of parent or legal guardian. In the case of the parent of a minor, the proof of identity shall be a certified or authenticated copy of the minor's birth certificate. In the case of a legal guardian of an individual who has been declared incompetent due to physical or mental incapacity or age by a court of competent jurisdiction, the proof of identity shall be a certified or authenticated copy of the court's order. For purposes of the Act, a parent or legal guardian may represent only a living individual, not a decedent. A parent or legal guardian may be accompanied during personal access to a record by another individual, provided the provisions of § 102.25(f) are satisfied.

(e)   When the provisions of this subpart are alleged to impede an individual in exercising his or her right to access, USPTO will consider, from an individual making a request, alternative suggestions regarding proof of identity and access to records.

(f)   An individual shall not be required to state a reason or otherwise justify his or her request for access to a record.

[Added, 65 FR 52916, Aug. 31, 2000, effective Oct. 2, 2000; para. (a) revised, 68 FR 14332, Mar. 25, 2003, effective May 1, 2003; para. (a) revised, 70 FR 10488, Mar. 4, 2005, effective Mar. 4, 2005]

§ 102.25 Disclosure of requested records to individuals.

(a)(1)   The Privacy Officer shall act promptly upon each request. Every effort will be made to respond within ten working days (*i.e.,* excluding Saturdays, Sundays, and legal public holidays) of the date of receipt. If a response cannot be made within ten working days due to unusual circumstances, the Privacy Officer shall send an acknowledgment during that period providing information on the status of the request and asking for any further information that may be necessary to process the request. "Unusual circumstances" shall include circumstances in which

(i) A search for and collection of requested records from inactive storage, field facilities or other establishments is required;

(ii) A voluminous amount of data is involved;

(iii) Information on other individuals must be separated or expunged from the particular record; or

(iv) Consultations with other agencies having a substantial interest in the determination of the request are necessary.

(2) If the Privacy Officer fails to send an acknowledgment within ten working days, as provided above in paragraph (a) of this section, the requester may ask the General Counsel to take corrective action. No failure of the Privacy Officer to send an acknowledgment shall confer administrative finality for purposes of judicial review.

(b) *Grant of access—*

(1) *Notification.* An individual shall be granted access to a record pertaining to him or her, except where the provisions of paragraph (g)(1) of this section apply. The Privacy Officer will notify the individual of a determination to grant access, and provide the following information:

(i) The methods of access, as set forth in paragraph (b)(2) of this section;

(ii) The place at which the record may be inspected;

(iii) The earliest date on which the record may be inspected and the period of time that the records will remain available for inspection. In no event shall the earliest date be later than thirty calendar days from the date of notification;

(iv) The estimated date by which a copy of the record could be mailed and the estimate of fees pursuant to § 102.31. In no event shall the estimated date be later than thirty calendar days from the date of notification;

(v) The fact that the individual, if he or she wishes, may be accompanied by another individual during personal access, subject to the procedures set forth in paragraph (f) of this section; and,

(vi) Any additional requirements needed to grant access to a specific record.

(2) *Methods of access.* The following methods of access to records by an individual may be available depending on the circumstances of a given situation:

(i) Inspection in person may be had in a location specified by the Privacy Officer during business hours;

(ii) Transfer of records to a Federal facility more convenient to the individual may be arranged, but only if the Privacy Officer determines that a suitable facility is available, that the individual's access can be properly supervised at that facility, and that transmittal of the records to that facility will not unduly interfere with operations of USPTO or involve unreasonable costs, in terms of both money and manpower; and

(iii) Copies may be mailed at the request of the individual, subject to payment of the fees prescribed in § 102.31. USPTO, on its own initiative, may elect to provide a copy by mail, in which case no fee will be charged the individual.

(c) Access to medical records is governed by the provisions of § 102.26.

(d) USPTO will supply such other information and assistance at the time of access as to make the record intelligible to the individual.

(e) USPTO reserves the right to limit access to copies and abstracts of original records, rather than the original records. This election would be appropriate, for example, when the record is in an automated data media such as tape or diskette, when the record contains information on other individuals, and when deletion of information is permissible under exemptions (for example, 5 U.S.C. 552a(k)(2)). In no event shall original records of USPTO be made available to the individual except under the immediate supervision of the Privacy Officer or the Privacy Officer's designee.

(f) Any individual who requests access to a record pertaining to that individual may be accompanied by another individual of his or her choice. "Accompanied" includes discussion of the record in the presence of the other individual. The individual to whom the record pertains shall authorize the presence of the other individual in writing. The authorization shall include the name of the other individual, a specific description of the record to which access is sought, the USPTO control number assigned to the request, the date, and the signature of the individual to whom the record pertains. The other individual shall sign the authorization in the presence of the Privacy Officer. An individual shall not be required to state a reason or otherwise justify his or her decision to be accompanied by another individual during personal access to a record.

(g)   *Initial denial of access—*

(1)   *Grounds.* Access by an individual to a record which pertains to that individual will be denied only upon a determination by the Privacy Officer that:

(i)   The record is exempt under § 102.33 or § 102.34, or exempt by determination of another agency publishing notice of the system of records, as described in § 102.23(f);

(ii)   The record is information compiled in reasonable anticipation of a civil action or proceeding;

(iii)   The provisions of § 102.26 pertaining to medical records temporarily have been invoked; or

(iv)   The individual has unreasonably failed to comply with the procedural requirements of this part.

(2)   *Notification.* The Privacy Officer shall give notice of denial of access to records to the individual in writing and shall include the following information:

(i)   The Privacy Officer's name and title or position;

(ii)   The date of the denial;

(iii)   The reasons for the denial, including citation to the appropriate section of the Act and this part;

(iv)   The individual's opportunities, if any, for further administrative consideration, including the identity and address of the responsible official. If no further administrative consideration within USPTO is available, the notice shall state that the denial is administratively final; and

(v)   If stated to be administratively final within USPTO, the individual's right to judicial review provided under 5 U.S.C. 552a(g)(1), as limited by 5 U.S.C. 552a(g)(5).

(3)   *Administrative review.* When an initial denial of a request is issued by the Privacy Officer, the individual's opportunities for further consideration shall be as follows:

(i)   As to denial under paragraph (g)(1)(i) of this section, two opportunities for further consideration are available in the alternative:

(A)   If the individual contests the application of the exemption to the records, review procedures in § 102.25(g)(3)(ii) shall apply; or

(B)   If the individual challenges the exemption itself, the procedure is a petition for the issuance, amendment, or repeal of a rule under 5 U.S.C. 553(e). If the exemption was determined by USPTO, such petition shall be filed with the General Counsel. If the exemption was determined by another agency (as described in § 102.23(f)), USPTO will provide the individual with the name and address of the other agency and any relief sought by the individual shall be that provided by the regulations of the other agency. Within USPTO, no such denial is administratively final until such a petition has been filed by the individual and disposed of on the merits by the General Counsel.

(ii)   As to denial under paragraphs (g)(1)(ii) of this section, (g)(1)(iv) of this section or (to the limited extent provided in paragraph (g)(3)(i)(A) of this section) paragraph (g)(1)(i) of this section, the individual may file for review with the General Counsel, as indicated in the Privacy Officer's initial denial notification. The procedures appearing in § 102.28 shall be followed by both the individual and USPTO to the maximum extent practicable.

(iii)   As to denial under paragraph (g)(1)(iii) of this section, no further administrative consideration within USPTO is available because the denial is not administratively final until expiration of the time period indicated in § 102.26(a).

(h)   If a request is partially granted and partially denied, the Privacy Officer shall follow the appropriate procedures of this section as to the records within the grant and the records within the denial.

[Added, 65 FR 52916, Aug. 31, 2000, effective Oct. 2, 2000]

§ 102.26 Special procedures: Medical records.

(a)   No response to any request for access to medical records by an individual will be issued by the Privacy Officer for a period of seven working days (*i.e.,* excluding Saturdays, Sundays, and legal public holidays) from the date of receipt.

(b) USPTO has published as a routine use, for all systems of records containing medical records, consultations with an individual's physician or psychologist if, in the sole judgment of USPTO, disclosure could have an adverse effect upon the individual. The mandatory waiting period set forth in paragraph (a) of this section will permit exercise of this routine use in appropriate cases. USPTO will pay no cost of any such consultation.

(c) In every case of a request by an individual for access to medical records, the Privacy Officer shall:

(1) Inform the individual of the waiting period prescribed in paragraph (a) of this section;

(2) Obtain the name and address of the individual's physician and/or psychologist, if the individual consents to give them;

(3) Obtain specific, written consent for USPTO to consult the individual's physician and/or psychologist in the event that USPTO believes such consultation is advisable, if the individual consents to give such authorization;

(4) Obtain specific, written consent for USPTO to provide the medical records to the individual's physician or psychologist in the event that USPTO believes access to the record by the individual is best effected under the guidance of the individual's physician or psychologist, if the individual consents to give such authorization; and

(5) Forward the individual's medical record to USPTO's medical expert for review and a determination on whether consultation with or transmittal of the medical records to the individual's physician or psychologist is warranted. If the consultation with or transmittal of such records to the individual's physician or psychologist is determined to be warranted, USPTO's medical expert shall so consult or transmit. Whether or not such a consultation or transmittal occurs, USPTO's medical officer shall provide instruction to the Privacy Officer regarding the conditions of access by the individual to his or her medical records.

(d) If an individual refuses in writing to give the names and consents set forth in paragraphs (c)(2) through (c)(4) of this section and USPTO has determined that disclosure could have an adverse effect

upon the individual, USPTO shall give the individual access to said records by means of a copy, provided without cost to the requester, sent registered mail return receipt requested.

[Added, 65 FR 52916, Aug. 31, 2000, effective Oct. 2, 2000]

§ 102.27 Procedures for making requests for correction or amendment.

(a) Any individual, regardless of age, who is a citizen of the United States or an alien lawfully admitted for permanent residence into the United States may submit a request for correction or amendment to USPTO. The request should be made either in person or by mail addressed to the Privacy Officer who processed the individual's request for access to the record, and to whom is delegated authority to make initial determinations on requests for correction or amendment. The office of the Privacy Officer is open to the public between the hours of 9 a.m. and 4 p.m., Monday through Friday (excluding legal public holidays).

(b) Requests submitted by mail should include the words "PRIVACY ACT REQUEST" in capital letters at the top of the letter and on the face of the envelope. Any request which is not addressed as specified in paragraph (a) of this section or which is not marked as specified in this paragraph will be so addressed and marked by USPTO personnel and forwarded immediately to the Privacy Officer. A request which is not properly addressed by the individual will not be deemed to have been "received" for purposes of measuring the time period for response until actual receipt by the Privacy Officer. In each instance when a request so forwarded is received, the Privacy Officer shall notify the individual that his or her request was improperly addressed and the date the request was received at the proper address.

(c) Since the request, in all cases, will follow a request for access under § 102.25, the individual's identity will be established by his or her signature on the request and use of the USPTO control number assigned to the request.

(d) A request for correction or amendment should include the following:

(1) Specific identification of the record sought to be corrected or amended (for example,

description, title, date, paragraph, sentence, line and words);

(2) The specific wording to be deleted, if any;

(3) The specific wording to be inserted or added, if any, and the exact place at which to be inserted or added; and

(4) A statement of the basis for the requested correction or amendment, with all available supporting documents and materials which substantiate the statement. The statement should identify the criterion of the Act being invoked, that is, whether the information in the record is unnecessary, inaccurate, irrelevant, untimely or incomplete.

[Added, 65 FR 52916, Aug. 31, 2000, effective Oct. 2, 2000]

§ 102.28 Review of requests for correction or amendment.

(a)(1)(i) Not later than ten working days (*i.e.*, excluding Saturdays, Sundays and legal public holidays) after receipt of a request to correct or amend a record, the Privacy Officer shall send an acknowledgment providing an estimate of time within which action will be taken on the request and asking for such further information as may be necessary to process the request. The estimate of time may take into account unusual circumstances as described in § 102.25(a). No acknowledgment will be sent if the request can be reviewed, processed, and the individual notified of the results of review (either compliance or denial) within the ten working days. Requests filed in person will be acknowledged in writing at the time submitted.

(ii) If the Privacy Officer fails to send the acknowledgment within ten working days, as provided in paragraph (a)(1)(i) of this section, the requester may ask the General Counsel to take corrective action. No failure of the Privacy Officer to send an acknowledgment shall confer administrative finality for purposes of judicial review.

(2) Promptly after acknowledging receipt of a request, or after receiving such further information as might have been requested, or after arriving at a decision within the ten working days, the Privacy Officer shall either:

(i) Make the requested correction or amendment and advise the individual in writing of such action, providing either a copy of the corrected or amended record or a statement as to the means whereby the correction or amendment was effected in cases where a copy cannot be provided (for example, erasure of information from a record maintained only in magnetically recorded computer files); or

(ii) Inform the individual in writing that his or her request is denied and provide the following information:

(A) The Privacy Officer's name and title or position;

(B) The date of the denial;

(C) The reasons for the denial, including citation to the appropriate sections of the Act and this subpart; and

(D) The procedures for appeal of the denial as set forth in § 102.29, including the address of the General Counsel.

(3) The term *promptly* in this section means within thirty working days (*i.e.*, excluding Saturdays, Sundays, and legal public holidays). If the Privacy Officer cannot make the determination within thirty working days, the individual will be advised in writing of the reason therefor and of the estimated date by which the determination will be made.

(b) Whenever an individual's record is corrected or amended pursuant to a request by that individual, the Privacy Officer shall be responsible for notifying all persons and agencies to which the corrected or amended portion of the record had been disclosed prior to its correction or amendment, if an accounting of such disclosure required by the Act was made. The notification shall require a recipient agency maintaining the record to acknowledge receipt of the notification, to correct or amend the record, and to apprise any agency or person to which it had disclosed the record of the substance of the correction or amendment.

(c) The following criteria will be considered by the Privacy Officer in reviewing a request for correction or amendment:

(1) The sufficiency of the evidence submitted by the individual;

(2) The factual accuracy of the information;

(3) The relevance and necessity of the information in terms of purpose for which it was collected;

(4) The timeliness and currency of the information in light of the purpose for which it was collected;

(5) The completeness of the information in terms of the purpose for which it was collected;

(6) The degree of risk that denial of the request could unfairly result in determinations adverse to the individual;

(7) The character of the record sought to be corrected or amended; and

(8) The propriety and feasibility of complying with the specific means of correction or amendment requested by the individual.

(d) USPTO will not undertake to gather evidence for the individual, but does reserve the right to verify the evidence which the individual submits.

(e) Correction or amendment of a record requested by an individual will be denied only upon a determination by the Privacy Officer that:

(1) The individual has failed to establish, by a preponderance of the evidence, the propriety of the correction or amendment in light of the criteria set forth in paragraph (c) of this section;

(2) The record sought to be corrected or amended is part of the official record in a terminated judicial, quasi-judicial, or quasi-legislative proceeding to which the individual was a party or participant;

(3) The information in the record sought to be corrected or amended, or the record sought to be corrected or amended, is the subject of a pending judicial, quasi-judicial, or quasi-legislative proceeding to which the individual is a party or participant;

(4) The correction or amendment would violate a duly enacted statute or promulgated regulation; or

(5) The individual has unreasonably failed to comply with the procedural requirements of this part.

(f) If a request is partially granted and partially denied, the Privacy Officer shall follow the appropriate procedures of this section as to the records within the grant and the records within the denial.

[Added, 65 FR 52916, Aug. 31, 2000, effective Oct. 2, 2000]

§ 102.29 Appeal of initial adverse determination on correction or amendment.

(a) When a request for correction or amendment has been denied initially under § 102.28, the individual may submit a written appeal within thirty working days (*i.e.*, excluding Saturdays, Sundays and legal public holidays) after the date of the initial denial. When an appeal is submitted by mail, the postmark is conclusive as to timeliness.

(b) An appeal should be addressed to the General Counsel, United States Patent and Trademark Office, PO Box 1450, Alexandria, Virginia 22313-1450. An appeal should include the words "PRIVACY APPEAL" in capital letters at the top of the letter and on the face of the envelope. An appeal not addressed and marked as provided herein will be so marked by USPTO personnel when it is so identified and will be forwarded immediately to the General Counsel. An appeal which is not properly addressed by the individual will not be deemed to have been "received" for purposes of measuring the time periods in this section until actual receipt by the General Counsel. In each instance when an appeal so forwarded is received, the General Counsel shall notify the individual that his or her appeal was improperly addressed and the date when the appeal was received at the proper address.

(c) The individual's appeal shall include a statement of the reasons why the initial denial is believed to be in error and USPTO's control number assigned to the request. The appeal shall be signed by the individual. The record which the individual requests be corrected or amended and all correspondence between the Privacy Officer and the requester will be furnished by the Privacy Officer who issued the initial denial. Although the foregoing normally will comprise the entire record on appeal, the General Counsel may seek additional information necessary to assure that the final determination is fair and equitable and, in such instances, disclose the additional information to the individual to the greatest extent possible, and provide an opportunity for comment thereon.

(d) No personal appearance or hearing on appeal will be allowed.

(e) The General Counsel shall act upon the appeal and issue a final determination in writing not later than thirty working days (*i.e.*, excluding Saturdays, Sundays and legal public holidays) from the date on which the appeal is received, except that the General Counsel may extend the thirty days upon deciding that a fair and equitable review cannot be made within that period, but only if the individual is advised in writing of the reason for the extension and the estimated date by which a final determination will issue. The estimated date should not be later than the sixtieth working day after receipt of the appeal unless unusual circumstances, as described in § 102.25(a), are met.

(f) If the appeal is determined in favor of the individual, the final determination shall include the specific corrections or amendments to be made and a copy thereof shall be transmitted promptly both to the individual and to the Privacy Officer who issued the initial denial. Upon receipt of such final determination, the Privacy Officer promptly shall take the actions set forth in § 102.28(a)(2)(i) and (b).

(g) If the appeal is denied, the final determination shall be transmitted promptly to the individual and state the reasons for the denial. The notice of final determination also shall inform the individual of the following:

(1) The right of the individual under the Act to file a concise statement of reasons for disagreeing with the final determination. The statement ordinarily should not exceed one page and USPTO reserves the right to reject a statement of excessive length. Such a statement shall be filed with the General Counsel. It should provide the USPTO control number assigned to the request, indicate the date of the final determination and be signed by the individual. The General Counsel shall acknowledge receipt of such statement and inform the individual of the date on which it was received.

(2) The facts that any such disagreement statement filed by the individual will be noted in the disputed record, that the purposes and uses to which the statement will be put are those applicable to the record in which it is noted, and that a copy of the statement will be provided to persons and agencies to which the record is disclosed subsequent to the date of receipt of such statement;

(3) The fact that USPTO will append to any such disagreement statement filed by the individual, a copy of the final determination or summary thereof which also will be provided to persons and agencies to which the disagreement statement is disclosed; and,

(4) The right of the individual to judicial review of the final determination under 5 U.S.C. 552a(g)(1)(A), as limited by 5 U.S.C. 552a(g)(5).

(h) In making the final determination, the General Counsel shall employ the criteria set forth in § 102.28(c) and shall deny an appeal only on the grounds set forth in § 102.28(e).

(i) If an appeal is partially granted and partially denied, the General Counsel shall follow the appropriate procedures of this section as to the records within the grant and the records within the denial.

(j) Although a copy of the final determination or a summary thereof will be treated as part of the individual's record for purposes of disclosure in instances where the individual has filed a disagreement statement, it will not be subject to correction or amendment by the individual.

(k) The provisions of paragraphs (g)(1) through (g)(3) of this section satisfy the requirements of 5 U.S.C. 552a(e)(3).

[Added, 65 FR 52916, Aug. 31, 2000, effective Oct. 2, 2000; para. (b) revised, 68 FR 14332, Mar. 25, 2003, effective May 1, 2003]

§ 102.30 Disclosure of record to person other than the individual to whom it pertains.

(a) USPTO may disclose a record pertaining to an individual to a person other than the individual to whom it pertains only in the following instances:

(1) Upon written request by the individual, including authorization under § 102.25(f);

(2) With the prior written consent of the individual;

(3) To a parent or legal guardian under 5 U.S.C. 552a(h);

(4) When required by the Act and not covered explicitly by the provisions of 5 U.S.C. 552a(b); and

(5) When permitted under 5 U.S.C. 552a(b)(1) through (12), which read as follows:[1]

---

[1] 5 U.S.C. 552a(b)(4) has no application within USPTO.

(i) To those officers and employees of the agency which maintains the record who have a need for the record in the performance of their duties;

(ii) Required under 5 U.S.C. 552;

(iii) For a routine use as defined in 5 U.S.C. 552a(a)(7) and described under 5 U.S.C. 552a(e)(4)(D);

(iv) To the Bureau of the Census for purposes of planning or carrying out a census or survey or related activity pursuant to the provisions of Title 13;

(v) To a recipient who has provided the agency with advance adequate written assurance that the record will be used solely as a statistical research or reporting record, and the record is to be transferred in a form that is not individually identifiable;

(vi) To the National Archives and Records Administration as a record which has sufficient historical or other value to warrant its continued preservation by the United States Government, or for evaluation by the Archivist of the United States or the designee of the Archivist to determine whether the record has such value;

(vii) To another agency or to an instrumentality of any governmental jurisdiction within or under the control of the United States for a civil or criminal law enforcement activity if the activity is authorized by law, and if the head of the agency or instrumentality has made a written request to the agency which maintains the record specifying the particular portion desired and the law enforcement activity for which the record is sought;

(viii) To a person pursuant to a showing of compelling circumstances affecting the health or safety of an individual if upon such disclosure notification is transmitted to the last known address of such individual;

(ix) To either House of Congress, or, to the extent of matter within its jurisdiction, any committee or subcommittee thereof, any joint committee of Congress or subcommittee of any such joint committee;

(x) To the Comptroller General, or any of his authorized representatives, in the course of the performance of the duties of the General Accounting Office;

(xi) Pursuant to the order of a court of competent jurisdiction; or

(xii) To a consumer reporting agency in accordance with section 3711(e) of Title 31.

(b) The situations referred to in paragraph (a)(4) of this section include the following:

(1) 5 U.S.C. 552a(c)(4) requires dissemination of a corrected or amended record or notation of a disagreement statement by USPTO in certain circumstances;

(2) 5 U.S.C. 552a(d) requires disclosure of records to the individual to whom they pertain, upon request; and

(3) 5 U.S.C. 552a(g) authorizes civil action by an individual and requires disclosure by USPTO to the court.

(c) The Privacy Officer shall make an accounting of each disclosure by him of any record contained in a system of records in accordance with 5 U.S.C. 552a(c) (1) and (2). Except for a disclosure made under 5 U.S.C. 552a(b)(7), the Privacy Officer shall make such accounting available to any individual, insofar as it pertains to that individual, on request submitted in accordance with § 102.24. The Privacy Officer shall make reasonable efforts to notify any individual when any record in a system of records is disclosed to any person under compulsory legal process, promptly upon being informed that such process has become a matter of public record.

[Added, 65 FR 52916, Aug. 31, 2000, effective Oct. 2, 2000]

§ 102.31 Fees.

The only fees to be charged to or collected from an individual under the provisions of this part are for duplication of records at the request of the individual. The Privacy Officer shall charge fees for duplication of records under the Act in the same way in which they charge duplication fees under § 102.11, except as provided in this section.

(a) No fees shall be charged or collected for the following: Search for and retrieval of the records; review of the records; copying at the initiative of USPTO without a request from the individual; transportation of records and personnel; and first-class postage.

(b) It is the policy of USPTO to provide an individual with one copy of each record corrected or amended pursuant to his or her request without charge as evidence of the correction or amendment.

(c) As required by the United States Office of Personnel Management in its published regulations implementing the Act, USPTO will charge no fee for a single copy of a personnel record covered by that agency's Government-wide published notice of systems of records.

[Added, 65 FR 52916, Aug. 31, 2000, effective Oct. 2, 2000]

§ 102.32 Penalties.

(a)　The Act provides, in pertinent part:

Any person who knowingly and willfully requests or obtains any record concerning an individual from an agency under false pretenses shall be guilty of a misdemeanor and fined not more than $5,000. (5 U.S.C. 552a(i)(3)).

(b)　A person who falsely or fraudulently attempts to obtain records under the Act also may be subject to prosecution under such other criminal statutes as 18 U.S.C. 494, 495 and 1001.

[Added, 65 FR 52916, Aug. 31, 2000, effective Oct. 2, 2000]

§ 102.33 General exemptions.

(a)　Individuals may not have access to records maintained by USPTO but which were provided by another agency which has determined by regulation that such information is subject to general exemption under 5 U.S.C. 552a(j). If such exempt records are within a request for access, USPTO will advise the individual of their existence and of the name and address of the source agency. For any further information concerning the record and the exemption, the individual must contact that source agency.

(b)　The general exemption determined to be necessary and proper with respect to systems of records maintained by USPTO, including the parts of each system to be exempted, the provisions of the Act from which they are exempted, and the justification for the exemption, is as follows: *Investigative Records—Contract and Grant Frauds and Employee Criminal Misconduct—COMMERCE/DEPT.—12.* Pursuant to 5 U.S.C. 552a(j)(2), these records are hereby determined to be exempt from all provisions of the Act, except 5 U.S.C. 552a (b), (c) (1) and (2), (e)(4) (A) through (F), (e) (6), (7), (9), (10), and (11), and (i). These exemptions are necessary to ensure the proper functions of the law enforcement activity, to protect confidential sources of information, to fulfill promises of confidentiality, to prevent interference

with law enforcement proceedings, to avoid the disclosure of investigative techniques, to avoid the endangering of law enforcement personnel, to avoid premature disclosure of the knowledge of criminal activity and the evidentiary bases of possible enforcement actions, and to maintain the integrity of the law enforcement process.

[Added, 65 FR 52916, Aug. 31, 2000, effective Oct. 2, 2000]

§ 102.34 Specific exemptions.

(a)(1)　Some systems of records under the Act which are maintained by USPTO contain, from time-to-time, material subject to the exemption appearing at 5 U.S.C. 552a(k)(1), relating to national defense and foreign policy materials. The systems of records published in the *Federal Register* by USPTO which are within this exemption are: COMMERCE/PAT-TM-6, COMMERCE/PAT-TM-7, COMMERCE/PAT-TM-8, COMMERCE/PAT-TM-9.

(2)　USPTO hereby asserts a claim to exemption of such materials wherever they might appear in such systems of records, or any systems of records, at present or in the future. The materials would be exempt from 5 U.S.C. 552a (c)(3), (d), (e)(1), (e)(4) (G), (H), and (I), and (f) to protect materials required by Executive order to be kept secret in the interest of the national defense and foreign policy.

(b)　The specific exemptions determined to be necessary and proper with respect to systems of records maintained by USPTO, including the parts of each system to be exempted, the provisions of the Act from which they are exempted, and the justification for the exemption, are as follows:

(1)(i)　Exempt under 5 U.S.C. 552a(k)(2). The systems of records exempt (some only conditionally), the sections of the Act from which exempted, and the reasons therefor are as follows:

(A)　Investigative Records—Contract and Grant Frauds and Employee Criminal Misconduct—COMMERCE/DEPT—12, but only on condition that the general exemption claimed in § 102.33(b)(3) is held to be invalid;

(B)　Investigative Records—Persons Within the Investigative Jurisdiction of USPTO—COMMERCE/DEPT-13;

(C)　Litigation, Claims and Administrative Proceeding Records—COMMERCE/DEPT-14;

(D) Attorneys and Agents Registered to Practice Before the Office—COMMERCE/PAT-TM-1;

(E) Complaints, Investigations and Disciplinary Proceedings Relating to Registered Patent Attorneys and Agents—COMMERCE/PAT-TM-2; and

(F) Non-Registered Persons Rendering Assistance to Patent Applicants—COMMERCE/PAT-TM-5.

(ii) The foregoing are exempted from 5 U.S.C. 552a (c)(3), (d), (e)(1), (e)(4)(G), (H), and (I), and (f). The reasons for asserting the exemption are to prevent subjects of investigation from frustrating the investigatory process, to insure the proper functioning and integrity of law enforcement activities, to prevent disclosure of investigative techniques, to maintain the ability to obtain necessary information, to fulfill commitments made to sources to protect their identities and the confidentiality of information and to avoid endangering these sources and law enforcement personnel. Special note is taken of the fact that the proviso clause in this exemption imports due process and procedural protections for the individual. The existence and general character of the information exempted will be made known to the individual to whom it pertains.

(2)(i) Exempt under 5 U.S.C. 552a(k)(5). The systems of records exempt (some only conditionally), the sections of the act from which exempted, and the reasons therefor are as follows:

(A) Investigative Records—Contract and Grant Frauds and Employee Criminal Misconduct—COMMERCE/DEPT-12, but only on condition that the general exemption claimed in § 102.33(b)(3) is held to be invalid;

(B) Investigative Records—Persons Within the Investigative Jurisdiction of USPTO—COMMERCE/DEPT-13; and

(C) Litigation, Claims, and Administrative Proceeding Records—COMMERCE/DEPT-14.

(ii) The foregoing are exempted from 5 U.S.C. 552a (c)(3), (d), (e)(1), (e)(4)(G), (H), and (I), and (f). The reasons for asserting the exemption are to maintain the ability to obtain candid and necessary information, to fulfill commitments made to sources to protect the confidentiality of information, to avoid endangering these sources and, ultimately, to facilitate

proper selection or continuance of the best applicants or persons for a given position or contract. Special note is made of the limitation on the extent to which this exemption may be asserted. The existence and general character of the information exempted will be made known to the individual to whom it pertains.

(c) At the present time, USPTO claims no exemption under 5 U.S.C. 552a(k)(3), (4), (6) and (7).

[Added, 65 FR 52916, Aug. 31, 2000, effective Oct. 2, 2000]

Appendix to Part 102 - Systems of Records Noticed by Other Federal Agencies[1] and Applicable to USPTO Records and Applicability of this Part Thereto

Category of records	Other federal agency
Federal Personnel Records	Office of Personnel Management.[2]
Federal Employee Compensation Act Program	Department of Labor.[3]
Equal Employment Opportunity Appeal Complaints	Equal Employment Opportunity Commission.[4]
Formal Complaints/Appeals of Adverse Personnel Actions	Merit Systems Protection Board.[5]

[1] Other than systems of records noticed by the Department of Commerce. Where the system of records applies only to USPTO, these regulations apply. Where the system of records applies generally to components of the Department of Commerce, the regulations of that department attach at the point of any denial for access or for correction or amendment.

[2] The provisions of this part do not apply to these records covered by notices of systems of records published by the Office of Personnel Management for all agencies. The regulations of OPM alone apply.

[3] The provisions of this part apply only initially to these records covered by notices of systems of records published by the U.S. Department of Labor for all agencies. The regulations of that department attach at the point of any denial for access or for correction or amendment.

Category of records	Other federal agency
[4] The provisions of this part do not apply to these records covered by notices of systems of records published by the Equal Employment Opportunity Commission for all agencies. The regulations of the Commission alone apply.	
[5] The provisions of this part do not apply to these records covered by notices of systems of records published by the Merit Systems Protection Board for all agencies. The regulations of the Board alone apply.	

[Added, 65 FR 52916, Aug. 31, 2000, effective Oct. 2, 2000]

PART 104 — LEGAL PROCESSES

Subpart A — General Provisions

Sec.

104.1   Definitions.

104.2   Address for mail and service; telephone number.

104.3   Waiver of rules.

104.4   Relationship of this Part to the Federal Rules of Civil and Criminal Procedure.

Subpart B — Service of Process

104.11   Scope and purpose.

104.12   Acceptance of service of process.

Subpart C — Employee Testimony and Production of Documents in Legal Proceedings

104.21   Scope and purpose.

104.22 Demand for testimony or production of documents.

104.23 Expert or opinion testimony.

104.24 Demands or requests in legal proceedings for records protected by confidentiality statutes.

Subpart D — Employee Indemnification

104.31 Scope.

104.32 Procedure for requesting indemnification.

Subpart E — Tort Claims

104.41 Procedure for filing claims.

104.42 Finality of settlement or denial of claims.

Subpart A — General Provisions

§ 104.1   Definitions.

Demand means a request, order, or subpoena for testimony or documents for use in a legal proceeding.

Director means the Under Secretary of Commerce for Intellectual Property and Director of the United States Patent and Trademark Office (*see* § 1.9(j)).

Document means any record, paper, and other property held by the Office, including without limitation, official letters, telegrams, memoranda, reports, studies, calendar and diary entries, maps, graphs, pamphlets, notes, charts, tabulations, analyses, statistical or informational accumulations, any kind of summaries of meetings and conversations, film impressions, magnetic tapes, and sound or mechanical reproductions.

Employee means any current or former officer or employee of the Office.

Legal proceeding means any pretrial, trial, and posttrial stages of existing or reasonably anticipated judicial or administrative actions, hearings, investigations, or similar proceedings before courts, commissions, boards or other tribunals, foreign or domestic. This phrase includes all phases of discovery as well as responses to formal or informal requests by attorneys or others involved in legal proceedings.

Office means the United States Patent and Trademark Office, including any operating unit in the United States Patent and Trademark Office, and its predecessors, the Patent Office and the Patent and Trademark Office.

Official business means the authorized business of the Office.

General Counsel means the General Counsel of the Office.

Testimony means a statement in any form, including personal appearances before a court or other legal tribunal, interviews, depositions, telephonic, televised, or videotaped statements or any responses given during discovery or similar proceedings, which response would involve more than the production of documents, including a declaration under 35 U.S.C. 25 or 28 U.S.C. 1746.

United States means the Federal Government, its departments and agencies, individuals acting on behalf of the Federal Government, and parties to the extent they are represented by the United States.

[Added, 66 FR 47387, Sept. 12, 2001, effective Sept. 12, 2001; second sentence revised, 68 FR 14332, Mar. 25, 2003, effective May 1, 2003]

§ 104.2 Address for mail and service; telephone number.

(a)   Mail under this part should be addressed to the Office of the General Counsel, United States Patent and Trademark Office, P.O. Box 1450, Alexandria, Virginia 22313-1450.

(b)   Service by hand should be made during business hours to the Office of the General Counsel, 10B20, Madison Building East, 600 Dulany Street, Alexandria, Virginia.

(c)   The Office of the General Counsel may be reached by telephone at 571–272–7000 during business hours.

[Added, 66 FR 47387, Sept. 12, 2001, effective Sept. 12, 2001; paras. (b) and (c) revised, 70 FR 10488, Mar. 4, 2005, effective Mar. 4, 2005; para. (a) revised, 75 FR 36294, June 25, 2010, effective June 25, 2010]

§ 104.3 Waiver of rules.

In extraordinary situations, when the interest of justice requires, the General Counsel may waive or suspend the rules of this part, *sua sponte* or on petition of an interested party to the Director, subject to such requirements as the General Counsel may impose. Any such petition must be accompanied by a petition fee of $130.00.

[Added, 66 FR 47387, Sept. 12, 2001, effective Sept. 12, 2001; revised, 69 FR 56481, Sept. 21, 2004, effective Oct. 21, 2004]

§ 104.4 Relationship of this Part to the Federal Rules of Civil or Criminal Procedure.

Nothing in this part waives or limits any requirement under the Federal Rules of Civil or Criminal Procedure.

[Added, 66 FR 47387, Sept. 12, 2001, effective Sept. 12, 2001]

Subpart B — Service of Process

§ 104.11 Scope and purpose.

(a)   This subpart sets forth the procedures to be followed when a summons and complaint is served on the Office or on the Director or an employee in his or her official capacity.

(b)   This subpart is intended, and should be construed, to ensure the efficient administration of the Office and not to impede any legal proceeding.

(c)   This subpart does not apply to subpoenas, the procedures for which are set out in subpart C.

(d)   This subpart does not apply to service of process made on an employee personally on matters not related to official business of the Office or to the official responsibilities of the employee.

[Added, 66 FR 47387, Sept. 12, 2001, effective Sept. 12, 2001]

§ 104.12 Acceptance of service of process.

(a)   Any summons and complaint to be served in person or by registered or certified mail or as otherwise authorized by law on the Office, on the Director, or on an employee in his or her official capacity, shall be served as indicated in § 104.2.

(b)   Any employee of the Office served with a summons and complaint shall immediately notify, and shall deliver the summons and complaint to, the Office of the General Counsel.

(c)   Any employee receiving a summons and complaint shall note on the summons and complaint the date, hour, and place of service and whether service was by hand or by mail.

(d)   When a legal proceeding is brought to hold an employee personally liable in connection with an action taken in the conduct of official business, rather than liable in an official capacity, the employee by law is to be served personally with process. *See Fed. R. Civ. P.* 4(e). An employee sued personally for an action taken in the conduct of official business shall immediately notify and deliver a copy of the summons and complaint to the General Counsel.

(e)   An employee sued personally in connection with official business may be represented by the

Department of Justice at its discretion (28 CFR 50.15 and 50.16).

(f)   The Office will only accept service of process for an employee in the employee's official capacity.

[Added, 66 FR 47387, Sept. 12, 2001, effective Sept. 12, 2001]

Subpart C — Employee Testimony and Production of Documents in Legal Proceedings

§ 104.21 Scope and purpose.

(a)   This subpart sets forth the policies and procedures of the Office regarding the testimony of employees as witnesses in legal proceedings and the production or disclosure of information contained in Office documents for use in legal proceedings pursuant to a demand.

(b)   *Exceptions.* This subpart does not apply to any legal proceeding in which:

(1)   An employee is to testify regarding facts or events that are unrelated to official business; or

(2)   A former employee is to testify as an expert in connection with a particular matter in which the former employee did not participate personally while at the Office.

[Added, 66 FR 47387, Sept. 12, 2001, effective Sept. 12, 2001]

§ 104.22 Demand for testimony or production of documents.

(a)   Whenever a demand for testimony or for the production of documents is made upon an employee, the employee shall immediately notify the Office of the General Counsel at the telephone number or addresses in §104.2 and make arrangements to send the subpoena to the General Counsel promptly.

(b)   An employee may not give testimony, produce documents, or answer inquiries from a person not employed by the Office regarding testimony or documents subject to a demand or a potential demand under the provisions of this subpart without the approval of the General Counsel. The General Counsel may authorize the provision of certified copies not

otherwise available under Part 1 of this title subject to payment of applicable fees under §1.19.

(c)(1)   *Demand for testimony or documents.* A demand for the testimony of an employee under this subpart shall be addressed to the General Counsel as indicated in § 104.2.

(2)   *Subpoenas.* A subpoena for employee testimony or for a document shall be served in accordance with the Federal Rules of Civil or Criminal Procedure or applicable state procedure, and a copy of the subpoena shall be sent to the General Counsel as indicated in § 104.2.

(3)   *Affidavits.* Except when the United States is a party, every demand shall be accompanied by an affidavit or declaration under 28 U.S.C. 1746 or 35 U.S.C. 25(b) setting forth the title of the legal proceeding, the forum, the requesting party's interest in the legal proceeding, the reason for the demand, a showing that the desired testimony or document is not reasonably available from any other source, and, if testimony is requested, the intended use of the testimony, a general summary of the desired testimony, and a showing that no document could be provided and used in lieu of testimony.

(d)   Failure of the attorney to cooperate in good faith to enable the General Counsel to make an informed determination under this subpart may serve as a basis for a determination not to comply with the demand.

(e)   A determination under this subpart to comply or not to comply with a demand is not a waiver or an assertion of any other ground for noncompliance, including privilege, lack of relevance, or technical deficiency.

(f)   *Noncompliance.* If the General Counsel makes a determination not to comply, he or she will seek Department of Justice representation for the employee and will attempt to have the subpoena modified or quashed. If Department of Justice representation cannot be arranged, the employee should appear at the time and place set forth in the subpoena. In such a case, the employee should produce a copy of these rules and state that the General Counsel has advised the employee not to provide the requested testimony nor to produce the requested document. If a legal tribunal rules that the demand in the subpoena must be complied with, the employee shall respectfully decline to comply with the demand, citing *United States ex rel. Touhy* v. *Ragen,* 340 U.S. 462 (1951).

[Added, 66 FR 47387, Sept. 12, 2001, effective Sept. 12, 2001]

§ 104.23 Expert or opinion testimony.

(a)(1) If the General Counsel authorizes an employee to give testimony in a legal proceeding not involving the United States, the testimony, if otherwise proper, shall be limited to facts within the personal knowledge of the employee. Employees, with or without compensation, shall not provide expert testimony in any legal proceedings regarding Office information, subjects, or activities except on behalf of the United States or a party represented by the United States Department of Justice.

(2) The General Counsel may authorize an employee to appear and give the expert or opinion testimony upon the requester showing, pursuant to §104.3 of this part, that exceptional circumstances warrant such testimony and that the anticipated testimony will not be adverse to the interest of the Office or the United States.

(b)(1) If, while testifying in any legal proceeding, an employee is asked for expert or opinion testimony regarding Office information, subjects, or activities, which testimony has not been approved in advance in writing in accordance with the regulations in this subpart, the witness shall:

(i) Respectfully decline to answer on the grounds that such expert or opinion testimony is forbidden by this subpart;

(ii) Request an opportunity to consult with the General Counsel before giving such testimony; and

(iii) Explain that upon such consultation, approval for such testimony may be provided.

(2) If the tribunal conducting the proceeding then orders the employee to provide expert or opinion testimony regarding Office information, subjects, or activities without the opportunity to consult with the General Counsel, the employee shall respectfully refuse to provide such testimony, citing *United States ex rel. Touhy* v. *Ragen,* 340 U.S. 462 (1951).

(c) If an employee is unaware of the regulations in this subpart and provides expert or opinion testimony regarding Office information, subjects, or activities in a legal proceeding without the aforementioned consultation, the employee shall, as soon after testifying as possible, inform the General Counsel that such testimony was given and provide a written summary of the expert or opinion testimony provided.

(d) *Proceeding where the United States is a party.* In a proceeding in which the United States is a party or is representing a party, an employee may not testify as an expert or opinion witness for any party other than the United States.

[Added, 66 FR 47387, Sept. 12, 2001, effective Sept. 12, 2001]

§ 104.24 Demands or requests in legal proceedings for records protected by confidentiality statutes.

Demands in legal proceedings for the production of records, or for the testimony of employees regarding information protected by the confidentiality provisions of the Patent Act (35 U.S.C. 122), the Privacy Act (5 U.S.C. 552a), the Trade Secrets Act (18 U.S.C. 1905), or any other confidentiality statute, must satisfy the requirements for disclosure set forth in those statutes and associated rules before the records may be provided or testimony given.

[Added, 66 FR 47387, Sept. 12, 2001, effective Sept. 12, 2001]

Subpart D — Employee Indemnification

§ 104.31 Scope.

The procedure in this subpart shall be followed if a civil action or proceeding is brought, in any court, against an employee (including the employee's estate) for personal injury, loss of property, or death, resulting from the employee's activities while acting within the scope of the employee's office or employment. When the employee is incapacitated or deceased, actions required of an employee should be performed by the employee's executor, administrator, or comparable legal representative.

[Added, 66 FR 47387, Sept. 12, 2001, effective Sept. 12, 2001]

§ 104.32 Procedure for requesting indemnification.

(a)   After being served with process or pleadings in such an action or proceeding, the employee shall within five (5) calendar days of receipt, deliver to the General Counsel all such process and pleadings or an attested true copy thereof, together with a fully detailed report of the circumstances of the incident giving rise to the court action or proceeding.

(b)(1) An employee may request indemnification to satisfy a verdict, judgment, or award entered against that employee only if the employee has timely satisfied the requirements of paragraph (a) of this section.

(2)   No request for indemnification will be considered unless the employee has submitted a written request through the employee's supervisory chain to the General Counsel with:

(i)   Appropriate documentation, including copies of the verdict, judgment, appeal bond, award, or settlement proposal;

(ii)   The employee's explanation of how the employee was acting within the scope of the employee's employment; and;

(iii)   The employee's statement of whether the employee has insurance or any other source of indemnification.

[Added, 66 FR 47387, Sept. 12, 2001, effective Sept. 12, 2001]

Subpart E — Tort Claims

§ 104.41 Procedure for filing claims.

Administrative claims against the Office filed pursuant to the administrative claims provision of the Federal Tort Claims Act (28 U.S.C. 2672) and the corresponding Department of Justice regulations (28 CFR Part 14) shall be filed with the General Counsel as indicated in §104.2.

[Added, 66 FR 47387, Sept. 12, 2001, effective Sept. 12, 2001]

§ 104.42 Finality of settlement or denial of claims.

Only a decision of the Director or the General Counsel regarding settlement or denial of any claim under this subpart may be considered final for the purpose of judicial review.

[Added, 66 FR 47387, Sept. 12, 2001, effective Sept. 12, 2001]

SUBCHAPTER C – PROTECTION OF FOREIGN MASK WORKS

PART 150 — REQUESTS FOR PRESIDENTIAL PROCLAMATIONS PURSUANT TO 17 U.S.C. 902(a)(2)

Sec.

150.1   Definitions.
150.2   Initiation of evaluation.
150.3   Submission of requests.
150.4   Evaluation.
150.5   Duration of proclamation.
150.6   Mailing address.

§ 150.1   Definitions.

(a)   *Director* means the Under Secretary of Commerce for Intellectual Property and Director of the United States Patent and Trademark Office (*see* § 1.9(j)).

(b)   *Foreign government* means the duly-constituted executive of a foreign nation, or an international or regional intergovernmental organization which has been empowered by its member states to request issuance of Presidential proclamations on their behalf under this part.

(c)   *Interim order* means an order issued by the Secretary of Commerce under 17 U.S.C. 914.

(d)   *Mask work* means a series of related images, however fixed or encoded —

(1)   Having or representing the predetermined, three-dimensional pattern of metallic, insulating, or semiconductor material present or removed from the layers of a semiconductor chip product; and

(2)   In which series the relation of the images to one another is that each image has the pattern of the surface of one form of the semiconductor chip product.

(e)   *Presidential proclamation* means an action by the President extending to foreign nationals, domiciliaries and sovereign authorities the privilege of applying for registrations for mask works pursuant to 17 U.S.C. 902.

(f) *Request* means a request by a foreign government for the issuance of a Presidential proclamation.

(g) *Proceeding* means a proceeding to issue an interim order extending protection to foreign nationals, domiciliaries and sovereign authorities under 17 U.S.C. Chapter 9.

(h) *Secretary* means the Secretary of Commerce.

[Added, 53 FR 24447, June 29, 1988, effective August 1, 1988; para. (a) revised, 68 FR 14332, Mar. 25, 2003, effective May 1, 2003]

§ 150.2   Initiation of evaluation.

(a) The Director independently or as directed by the Secretary, may initiate an evaluation of the propriety of recommending the issuance, revision, suspension or revocation of a section 902 proclamation.

(b) The Director shall initiate an evaluation of the propriety of recommending the issuance of a section 902 proclamation upon receipt of a request from a foreign government.

[Added, 53 FR 24447, June 29, 1988, effective August 1, 1988; revised, 68 FR 14332, Mar. 25, 2003, effective May 1, 2003]

§ 150.3   Submission of requests.

(a) Requests for the issuance of a section 902 proclamation shall be submitted by foreign governments for review by the Director.

(b) Requests for issuance of a proclamation shall include:

(1) A copy of the foreign law or legal rulings that provide protection for U.S. mask works which provide a basis for the request.

(2) A copy of any regulations or administrative orders implementing the protection.

(3) A copy of any laws, regulations, or administrative orders establishing or regulating the registration (if any) of mask works.

(4) Any other relevant laws, regulations, or administrative orders.

(5) All copies of laws, legal rulings, regulations, or administrative orders submitted must be in unedited, full-text form, and if possible, must be reproduced from the original document.

(6) All material submitted must be in the original language, and if not in English, must be accompanied by a certified English translation.

[Added, 53 FR 24447, June 29, 1988, effective August 1, 1988; para. (a) revised, 68 FR 14332, Mar. 25, 2003, effective May 1, 2003]

§ 150.4   Evaluation.

(a) Upon submission of a request by a foreign government for the issuance of a section 902 proclamation, if an interim order under section 914 has not been issued, the Director may initiate a section 914 proceeding if additional information is required.

(b) If an interim order under section 914 has been issued, the information obtained during the section 914 proceeding will be used in evaluating the request for a section 902 proclamation.

(c) After the Director receives the request of a foreign government for a section 902 proclamation, or after a determination is made by the Director to initiate independently an evaluation pursuant to § 150.2(a) of this part, a notice will be published in the *Federal Register* to request relevant and material comments on the adequacy and effectiveness of the protection afforded U.S. mask works under the system of law described in the notice. Comments should include detailed explanations of any alleged deficiencies in the foreign law or any alleged deficiencies in its implementation. If the alleged deficiencies include problems in administration such as registration, the respondent should include as specifically as possible full detailed explanations, including dates for and the nature of any alleged problems. Comments shall be submitted to the Director within sixty (60) days of the publication of the *Federal Register* notice.

(d) The Director shall notify the Register of Copyrights and the Committee on the Judiciary of the Senate and the House of Representatives of the initiation of an evaluation under these regulations.

(e) If the written comments submitted by any party present relevant and material reasons why a proclamation should not issue, the Director will:

(1) Contact the party raising the issue for verification and any needed additional information;

(2)　Contact the requesting foreign government to determine if the issues raised by the party can be resolved; and,

(i)　If the issues are resolved, continue with the evaluation; or,

(ii)　If the issues cannot be resolved on this basis, hold a public hearing to gather additional information.

(f)　The comments, the section 902 request, information obtained from a section 914 proceeding, if any, and information obtained in a hearing held pursuant to paragraph (e)(ii) of this section, if any, will be evaluated by the Director.

(g)　The Director will forward the information to the Secretary, together with an evaluation and a draft recommendation.

(h)　The Secretary will forward a recommendation regarding the issuance of a section 902 proclamation to the President.

[Added, 53 FR 24448, June 29, 1988, effective August 1, 1988; paras. (a) & (c)-(f) revised, 68 FR 14332, Mar. 25, 2003, effective May 1, 2003]

§ 150.5　Duration of proclamation.

(a)　The recommendation for the issuance of a proclamation may include terms and conditions regarding the duration of the proclamation.

(b)　Requests for the revision, suspension or revocation of a proclamation may be submitted by any interested party. Requests for revision, suspension or revocation of a proclamation will be considered in substantially the same manner as requests for the issuance of a section 902 proclamation.

[Added 53 FR 24448, June 29, 1988, effective August 1, 1988]

§ 150.6　Mailing address.

Requests and all correspondence pursuant to these guidelines shall be addressed to: Mail Stop Congressional Relations, Director of the United States Patent and Trademark Office, P.O. Box 1450, Alexandria, Virginia 22313-1450.

[Added 53 FR 24448, June 29, 1988, effective Aug. 1, 1988; revised, 68 FR 14332, Mar. 25, 2003, effective May 1, 2003; revised, 70 FR 10488, Mar. 4, 2005, effective Mar. 4, 2005]

CPSIA information can be obtained at www.ICGtesting.com
Printed in the USA
LVOW091817161012

303106LV00004B/4/P

9 781468 168891